2018 release

Adobe® Photoshop® CC

The Professional Portfolio

AGAINST THE CLOCK
mastering graphic technology

Managing Editor: Ellenn Behoriam
Cover & Interior Design: Erika Kendra

Cover image by Nigel Tadyanehondo on Unsplash.com.

10 9 8 7 6 5 4 3

Print ISBN: 978-1-946396-03-7
Ebook ISBN: 978-1-946396-04-4

AGAINST THE CLOCK
mastering graphic technology

4710 28th Street North, Saint Petersburg, FL 33714
800-256-4ATC • www.againsttheclock.com

Acknowledgements

About Against The Clock

Against The Clock, long recognized as one of the nation's leaders in courseware development, has been publishing high-quality educational materials for the graphic and computer arts industries since 1990. The company has developed a solid and widely-respected approach to teaching people how to effectively use graphics applications, while maintaining a disciplined approach to real-world problems.

Having developed the *Against The Clock* and the *Essentials for Design* series with Prentice Hall/Pearson Education, ATC drew from years of professional experience and instructor feedback to develop *The Professional Portfolio Series*, focusing on the Adobe Creative Suite. These books feature step-by-step explanations, detailed foundational information, and advice and tips from professionals that offer practical solutions to technical issues.

About the Author

Erika Kendra holds a BA in History and a BA in English Literature from the University of Pittsburgh. She began her career in the graphic communications industry as an editor at Graphic Arts Technical Foundation before moving to Los Angeles in 2000.

Erika is the author or co-author of more than thirty books about Adobe graphic design software. She has also written several books about graphic design concepts such as color reproduction and preflighting, and dozens of articles for industry online and print journals. Working with Against The Clock for more than fifteen years, Erika was a key partner in developing *The Professional Portfolio Series* of software training books.

Contributing Editors and Artists

A big thank you to the people whose comments and expertise contributed to the success of these books:

- **Dan Cristensen,** technical editor
- **Debbie Davidson,** technical editor
- **Jose Moncada,** technical editor
- **Roger Morrissey,** technical editor
- **Susan Chiellini,** copy editor

Images used in the projects throughout this book are in the public domain unless otherwise noted. Individual artists' credit follow:

Project 1:
Sunrise.jpg photo by Stefan Kunze on Unsplash.com.
Lightning.jpg photo by David Mourn on Unsplash.com
Tornado.jpg photo by Jean Beaufort on Publicdomainpictures.net

Project 2:
amg.jpg photo by Mike on Pexels.com
inset1.jpg photo by Kyle Murfin on Unsplash.com
inset2.jpg photo by Jake Weirick on Pexels.com
inset3.jpg photo by Sergiusz Rydosz on Publicdomainpictures.net
tires.jpg photo by Imthaz Ahamed on Pexels.com

Project 3:
Museum images in this project are courtesy of the Getty's Open Content Program: getty.edu/about/whatwedo/opencontentfaq.html
HDR image exposures by Charlie Essers.

Project 4:
Images used in this project are copyright Against The Clock, Inc.
Roshambo.jpg photo by Charlie Essers.

Project 5:
Photos used in this composition are by skeeze on Pixabay.com

Project 6:
Images used in this project are copyright Against The Clock, Inc.
Images in the supplied banner ad are photos by Jesse Darland and Dark Rider on Unsplash.com

Project 8:
Images used in this project are copyright Against The Clock, Inc.

Walk-Through

Car Magazine Cover

project 2

Your client publishes a monthly magazine for car enthusiasts. Your agency has been hired to take over the magazine design; you have been tasked with designing the cover for the next issue.

This project incorporates the following skills:
- ❑ Resizing and resampling supplied images
- ❑ Creating complex vector paths and shape layers
- ❑ Compositing images as Smart Objects
- ❑ Applying non-destructive styles, effects, and filters
- ❑ Developing a custom artistic background

Project Goals

Each project begins with a clear description of the overall concepts that are explained in the project; these goals closely match the different "stages" of the project workflow.

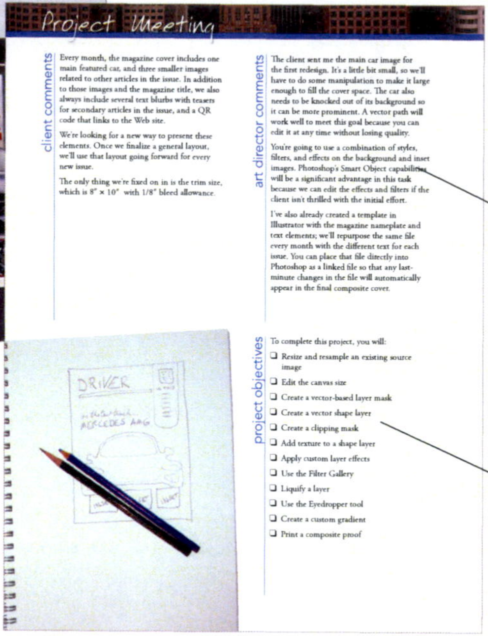

Project Meeting

client comments

Every month, the magazine cover includes one main featured car, and three smaller images related to other articles in the issue. In addition to those images and the magazine title, we also always include several text blurbs with teasers for secondary articles in the issue, and a QR code that links to the Web site.

We're looking for a new way to present these elements. Once we finalize a general layout, we'll use that layout going forward for every new issue.

The only thing we're fixed on in is the trim size, which is 8" × 10" with 1/8" bleed allowance.

art director comments

The client sent me the main car image for the first redesign. It's a little bit small, so we'll have to do some manipulation to make it large enough to fill the cover space. The car also needs to be knocked out of its background so it can be more prominent. A vector path will work well to meet this goal because you can edit it at any time without losing quality.

You're going to use a combination of styles, filters, and effects on the background and inset images. Photoshop's Smart Object capabilities will be a significant advantage in this task because we can edit the effects and filters if the client isn't thrilled with the initial effort.

I've also already created a template in Illustrator with the magazine nameplate and text elements; we'll repurpose the same file every month with the different text for each issue. You can place that file directly into Photoshop as a linked file so that any last-minute changes in the file will automatically appear in the final composite cover.

project objectives

To complete this project, you will:
- ❑ Resize and resample an existing source image
- ❑ Edit the canvas size
- ❑ Create a vector-based layer mask
- ❑ Create a vector shape layer
- ❑ Create a clipping mask
- ❑ Add texture to a shape layer
- ❑ Apply custom layer effects
- ❑ Use the Filter Gallery
- ❑ Liquify a layer
- ❑ Use the Eyedropper tool
- ❑ Create a custom gradient
- ❑ Print a composite proof

The Project Meeting

Each project includes the client's initial comments, which provide valuable information about the job. The Project Art Director, a vital part of any design workflow, also provides fundamental advice and production requirements.

Project Objectives

Each Project Meeting includes a summary of the specific skills required to complete the project.

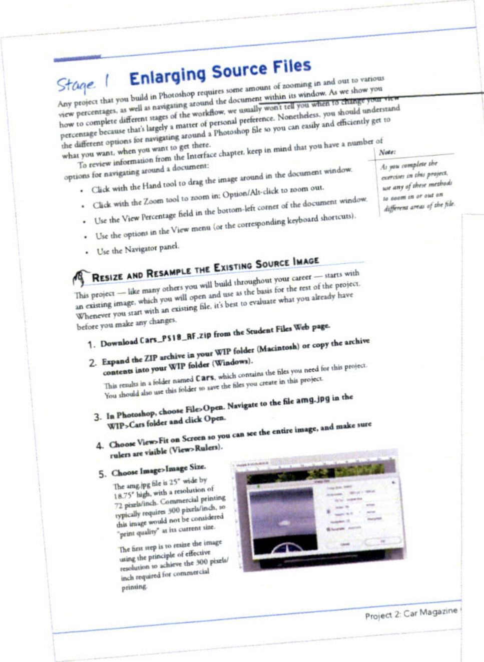

Stage 1 Enlarging Source Files

Any project that you build in Photoshop requires some amount of zooming in and out to various view percentages, as well as navigating around the document within its window. As we show you how to complete different stages of the workflow, we usually won't tell you when to change your view percentage because that's largely a matter of personal preference. Nonetheless, you should understand the different options for navigating around a Photoshop file so you can easily and efficiently get to what you want, when you want to get there.

To review information from the Interface chapter, keep in mind that you have a number of options for navigating around a document:
- Click with the Hand tool to drag the image around in the document window.
- Click with the Zoom tool to zoom in; Option/Alt-click to zoom out.
- Use the View Percentage field in the bottom-left corner of the document window.
- Use the options in the View menu (or the corresponding keyboard shortcuts).
- Use the Navigator panel.

Note: As you complete the exercises in this project, use any of these methods to zoom in or out on different areas of the file.

Resize and Resample the Existing Source Image

This project — like many others you will build throughout your career — starts with an existing image, which you will open and use as the basis for the rest of the project. Whenever you start with an existing file, it's best to evaluate what you already have before you make any changes.

1. Download Cars_PS18_RF.zip from the Student Files Web page.
2. Expand the ZIP archive in your WIP folder (Macintosh) or copy the archive contents into your WIP folder (Windows).
   This results in a folder named Cars, which contains the files you need for this project. You should also use this folder to save the files you create in this project.
3. In Photoshop, choose File>Open. Navigate to the file amg.jpg in the WIP>Cars folder and click Open.
4. Choose View>Fit on Screen so you can see the entire image, and make sure rulers are visible (View>Rulers).
5. Choose Image>Image Size.
   The amg.jpg file is 25" wide by 18.75" high, with a resolution of 72 pixels/inch. Commercial printing typically requires 300 pixels/inch, so this image would not be considered "print quality" at its current size.
   The first step is to resize the image using the principle of effective resolution to achieve the 300 pixels/inch required for commercial printing.

Project 2: Car Magazine

Real-World Workflow

Projects are broken into logical lessons or "stages" of the workflow. Brief introductions at the beginning of each stage provide vital foundational material required to complete the task.

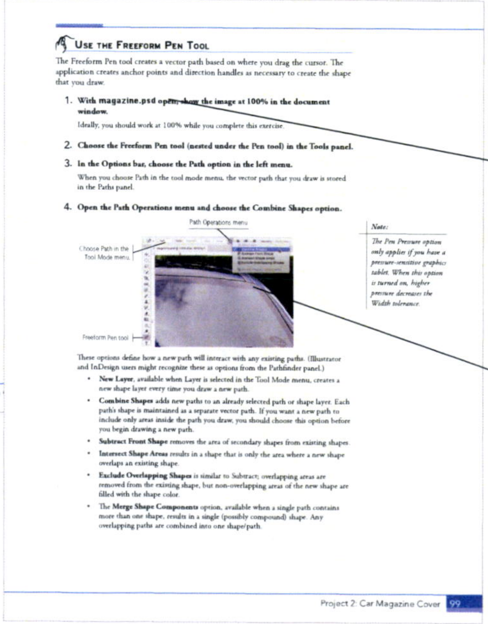

Use the Freeform Pen Tool

The Freeform Pen tool creates a vector path based on where you drag the cursor. The application creates anchor points and direction handles as necessary to create the shape that you draw.

1. With magazine.psd open, show the image at 100% in the document window.
   Ideally, you should work at 100% while you complete this exercise.
2. Choose the Freeform Pen tool (nested under the Pen tool) in the Tools panel.
3. In the Options bar, choose the Path option in the tool mode menu.
   When you choose Path in the tool mode menu, the vector path that you draw is stored in the Paths panel.
4. Open the Path Operations menu and choose the Combine Shapes option.

Note: The Pen Pressure option only applies if you have a pressure-sensitive graphics tablet. When this option is turned on, higher pressure decreases the Width tolerance.

These options define how a new path will interact with any existing paths. (Illustrator and InDesign users might recognize these as options from the Pathfinder panel.)
- New Layer, available when Layer is selected in the Tool Mode menu, creates a new shape layer every time you draw a new path.
- Combine Shapes adds new paths to an already selected path or shape layer. Each path's shape is maintained as a separate vector path. If you want a new path to include only areas inside the path you draw, you should choose this option before you begin drawing a new path.
- Subtract Front Shape removes the area of secondary shapes from existing shapes.
- Intersect Shape Areas results in a shape that is only the area where a new shape overlaps an existing shape.
- Exclude Overlapping Shapes is similar to Subtract; overlapping areas are removed from the existing shape, but non-overlapping areas of the new shape are filled with the shape color.
- The Merge Shape Components option, available when a single path contains more than one shape, results in a single (possibly compound) shape. Any overlapping paths are combined into one shape/path.

Project 2: Car Magazine Cover 99

Step-By-Step Exercises

Every stage of the workflow is broken into multiple hands-on, step-by-step exercises.

Visual Explanations

Wherever possible, screen shots are annotated so students can quickly identify important information.

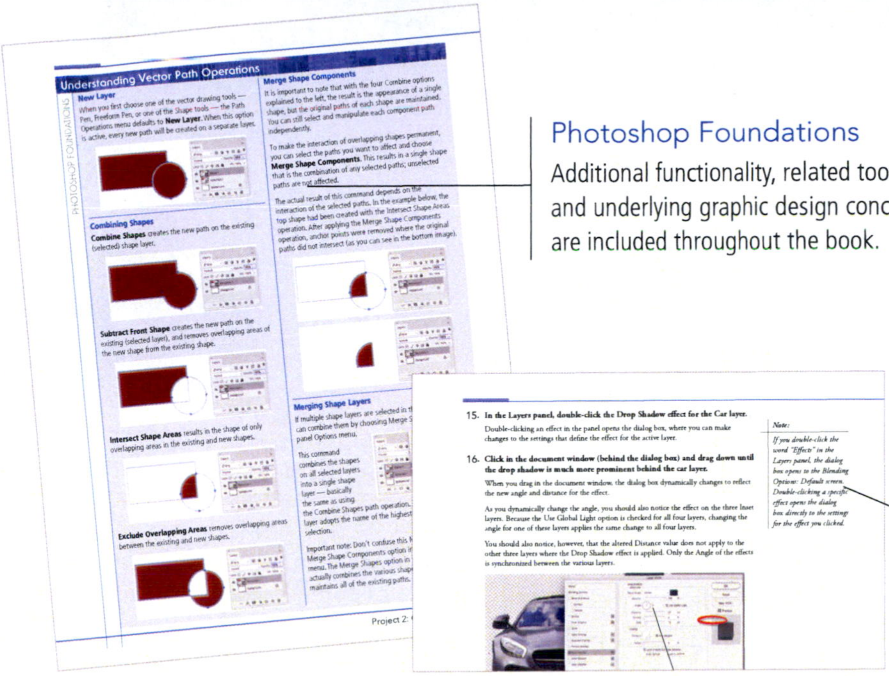

Photoshop Foundations

Additional functionality, related tools, and underlying graphic design concepts are included throughout the book.

Advice and Warnings

Where appropriate, sidebars provide shortcuts, warnings, or tips about the topic at hand.

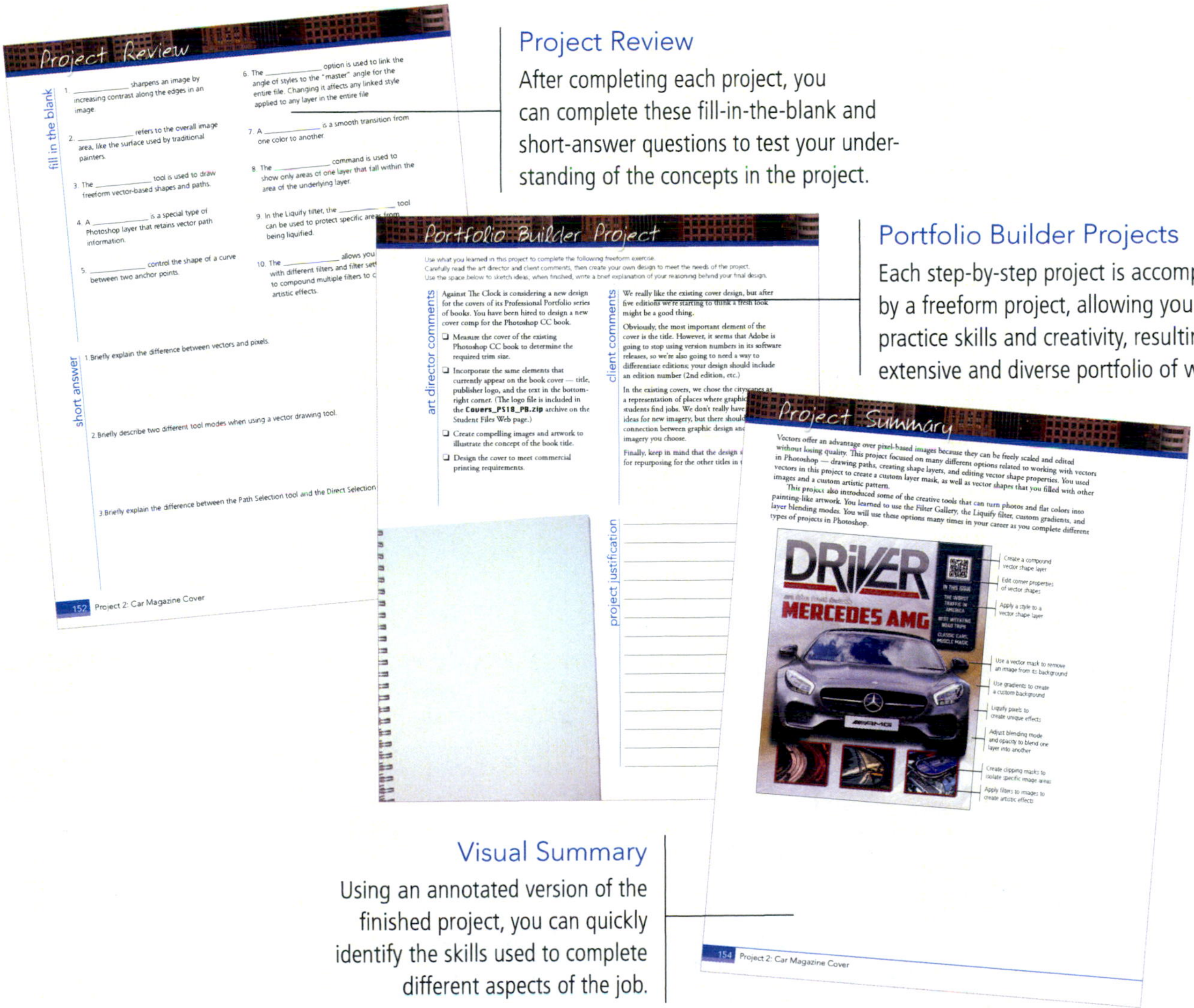

Project Review

After completing each project, you can complete these fill-in-the-blank and short-answer questions to test your understanding of the concepts in the project.

Portfolio Builder Projects

Each step-by-step project is accompanied by a freeform project, allowing you to practice skills and creativity, resulting in an extensive and diverse portfolio of work.

Visual Summary

Using an annotated version of the finished project, you can quickly identify the skills used to complete different aspects of the job.

Projects at a Glance

Against The Clock's *The Professional Portfolio Series* teaches graphic design software tools and techniques entirely within the framework of real-world projects; we introduce and explain skills where they would naturally fall into a real project workflow.

The project-based approach in *The Professional Portfolio Series* allows you to get in-depth with the software beginning in Project 1 — you don't have to read several chapters of introductory material before you can start creating finished artwork.

Our approach also prevents "topic tedium" — in other words, we don't require you to read pages and pages of information about text (for example); instead, we explain text tools and options as part of a larger project (in this case, as part of a postcard series).

Clear, easy-to-read, step-by-step instructions walk you through every phase of each job, from creating a new file to saving the finished piece. Wherever logical, we also offer practical advice and tips about underlying concepts and graphic design practices that will benefit students as they enter the job market.

The projects in this book reflect a range of different types of Photoshop jobs, from creating a magazine ad to correcting menu images to building a web page. When you finish the eight projects in this book (and the accompanying Portfolio Builder exercises), you will have a substantial body of work that should impress any potential employer.

The eight Photoshop projects are described briefly here; more detail is provided in the full table of contents (beginning on Page viii).

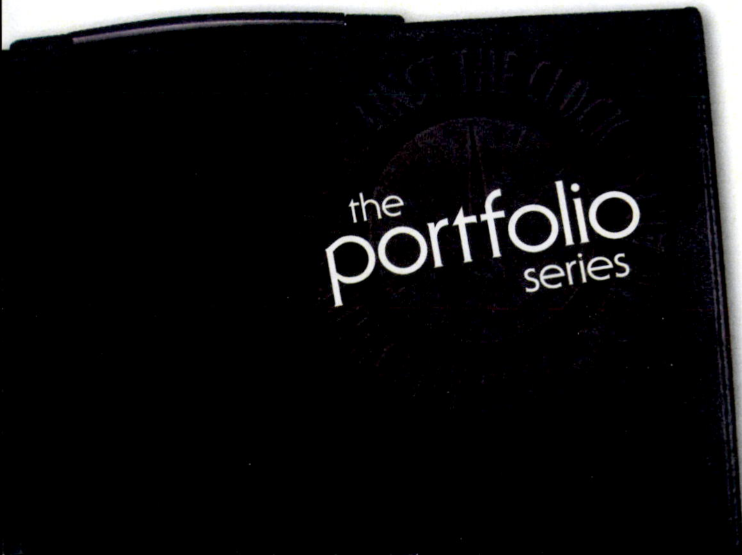

project 1

Music CD Artwork

- ❑ Compositing Images and Artwork
- ❑ Managing Layers
- ❑ Creating Complex Selections
- ❑ Saving Files for Multiple Media

project 2

Car Magazine Cover

- ❑ Enlarging Source Files
- ❑ Working with Vector Tools
- ❑ Applying Styles and Filters

project 3

Museum Image Correction

- ❑ Retouching Damaged Images
- ❑ Correcting Lighting Problems
- ❑ Correcting Color Problems
- ❑ Preparing Images for Print
- ❑ Working with HDR Images

project 4

City Promotion Cards

- ❑ Creating New Files
- ❑ Manipulating Pixels
- ❑ Working with Type
- ❑ Creating Style with Layers
- ❑ Working in 3D

project 7

House Painting

- ❑ Filling Solid Areas
- ❑ Painting with Brushes
- ❑ Working with Patterns
- ❑ Painting Nature

project 5

Calendar Cover

- ❑ Managing Missing Fonts
- ❑ Creating Custom Vector Shapes
- ❑ Creating a Complex Mask
- ❑ Working with Spot Channels

project 8

Photographer's Web Page

- ❑ Automating Repetitive Tasks
- ❑ Editing Layers for Visual Effect
- ❑ Generating Web-Ready Assets

project 6

Advertising Samples

- ❑ Cleaning and Adjusting Images
- ❑ Working in Perspective
- ❑ Working with Lighting

Our goal in this book is to familiarize you with the majority of the Photoshop tool set, so you can be more productive and more marketable in your career as a graphic designer.

It is important to keep in mind that Photoshop is an extremely versatile and powerful application. The sheer volume of available tools, panels, and features can seem intimidating when you first look at the software interface. Most of these tools, however, are fairly simple to use with a bit of background information and a little practice.

Wherever necessary, we explain the underlying concepts and terms that are required for understanding the software. We're confident that these projects provide the practice you need to be able to create sophisticated artwork by the end of the very first project.

Contents

Project 7
House Painting 363

Project 8
Photographer's Web Page 419

Getting Started

Prerequisites

To use *The Professional Portfolio Series,* you should know how to use your mouse to point and click, as well as how to drag items around the screen. You should be able to resize and arrange windows on your desktop to maximize your available space. You should know how to access drop-down menus, and understand how check boxes and radio buttons work. It also doesn't hurt to have a good understanding of how your operating system (OS) organizes files and folders, and how to navigate your way around them. If you're familiar with these fundamental skills, then you know all that's necessary to use the Portfolio Series.

Resource Files

All the files you need to complete the projects in this book — except, of course, the Photoshop application files — are on the Student Files web page at againsttheclock.com. See the inside back cover of this book for access information.

Each archive (ZIP) file is named according to the related project (e.g., **Music_PS18_RF.zip**). At the beginning of each project, you must download the archive for that project and expand it to access the resource files that you need to complete the exercises. Detailed instructions for this process are included in the Interface chapter.

Files required for the related Portfolio Builder exercises at the end of each project are also available on the Student Files page; these archives are also named by project (e.g., **Airborne_PS18_PB.zip**).

ATC Fonts

You must download and install the ATC fonts from the Student Files web page to ensure that your exercises and projects work as described in the book. You should replace older (pre-2013) ATC fonts with the ones on the Student Files web page.

Software Versions

This book was written and tested using the initial 2018 release of Adobe Photoshop CC software (version 19.0), released in October 2017. You can find the specific version number in the Splash Screen that appears while your application is launching.

Because Adobe has announced periodic upgrades rather than releasing new full versions, some features and functionality might have changed since publication. Please check the Errata section of the Against The Clock website for any significant issues that might have arisen from these periodic upgrades.

System Requirements

The Professional Portfolio Series was designed to work on both Macintosh or Windows computers; where differences exist from one platform to another, we include specific instructions relative to each platform. One issue that remains different from Macintosh to Windows is the use of different modifier keys (Control, Shift, etc.) to accomplish the same task. When we present key commands, we always follow the same Macintosh/Windows format — Macintosh keys are listed first, then a slash, followed by the Windows key commands.

The Photoshop CC User Interface

Adobe Photoshop is the industry-standard application for working with pixels — both manipulating existing ones and creating new ones. Many Photoshop experts specialize in certain types of work. Photo retouching, artistic painting, image compositing, and color correction are only a few types of work you can create with Photoshop. Our goal in this book is to teach you how to use the available tools to succeed with different types of jobs that you might encounter in your professional career.

Although not intended as a layout-design application, you can use Photoshop to combine type, graphics, and images into a finished design; many people create advertisements, book covers, and other projects entirely in Photoshop. Others argue that Photoshop should never be used for layout design; Adobe InDesign is the preferred page-layout application. We do not advocate doing *all* or even *most* layout composite work in Photoshop, but because many people use the application to create composite designs, we feel the projects in this book portray a realistic workflow.

The simple exercises in this introduction are designed to let you explore the Photoshop user interface. Whether you are new to the application or upgrading from a previous version, we highly recommend following these steps to click around and become familiar with the basic workspace.

Explore the Photoshop Interface

The first time you launch Photoshop, you will see the default user interface (UI) settings as defined by Adobe. When you relaunch after you or another user has quit, the workspace defaults to the last-used settings — including open panels and the position of those panels on your screen. We designed the following exercises so you can explore different ways of controlling panels in the Photoshop user interface.

1. **Create a new empty folder named WIP (Work in Progress) on any writable disk (where you plan to save your work).**

2. **Download the InterfacePS_PS18_RF.zip archive from the Student Files web page.**

3. **Macintosh users: Place the ZIP archive in your WIP folder, then double-click the file icon to expand it.**

   Windows users: Double-click the ZIP archive file to open it. Click the folder inside the archive and drag it into your primary WIP folder.

   The resulting **InterfacePS** folder contains all the files you need to complete the exercises in this introduction.

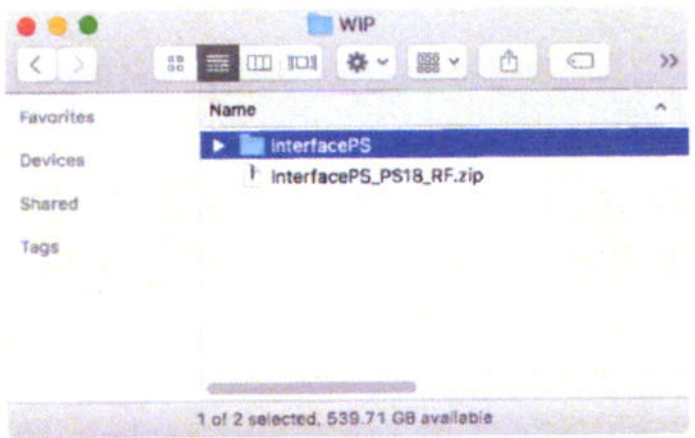

Macintosh: Double-click the archive file icon to expand it.

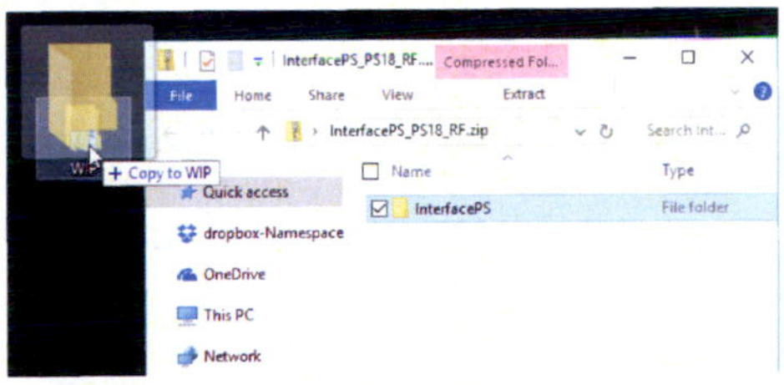

Windows: Open the archive file, then drag the InterfacePS folder from the archive to your WIP folder.

4. **Macintosh users: While pressing Command-Option-Shift, launch Photoshop. Click Yes when asked if you want to delete Settings files.**

   Windows users: Launch Photoshop, and then immediately press Control-Alt-Shift. Click Yes when asked if you want to delete the Settings files.

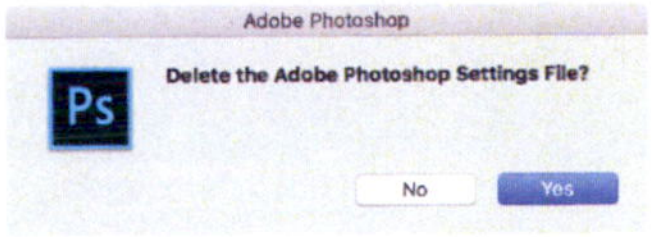

5. **Macintosh users: Open the Window menu and make sure the Application Frame option is toggled on.**

This option should be checked.

Many menu commands and options in Photoshop are **toggles**, which means they are either on or off; when an option is already checked, that option is toggled on (visible or active). You can toggle an active option off by choosing the checked menu command, or toggle an inactive option on by choosing the unchecked menu command.

6. **Review the options in the Start screen.**

The default user interface shows a stored "Start" workspace. No panels are visible in this workspace. Instead, you have one-click access to a list of recently opened files (if any); buttons to create a new file or open an existing one; and links to additional functionality provided by the Adobe Creative Cloud suite.

This workspace appears by default whenever Photoshop is running but no actual file is open. As soon as you open or create a file, the interface reverts to show the last-used workspace arrangement.

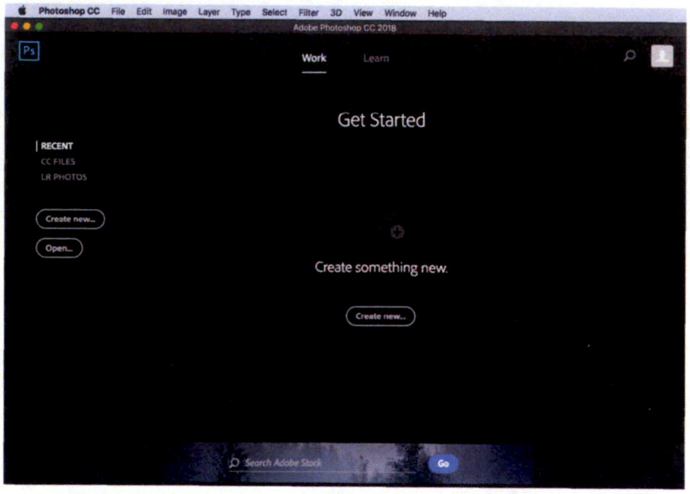

Understanding the Application Frame

PHOTOSHOP FOUNDATIONS

On Windows, each running application is contained within its own frame; all elements of the application — including the Menu bar, panels, tools, and open documents — are contained within the Application frame.

Adobe also offers the Application frame to Macintosh users as an option for controlling the workspace. When the Application frame is active, the entire workspace exists in a self-contained area that can be moved around the screen.

All elements of the workspace (excluding the Menu bar) move when you move the Application frame.

The Application frame is active by default, but you can toggle it off by choosing Window>Application Frame. If the menu option is checked, the Application frame is active; if the menu option is not checked, it is inactive. (On Windows, the Application Frame menu command is not available; you can't turn off the Application Frame on the Windows OS.)

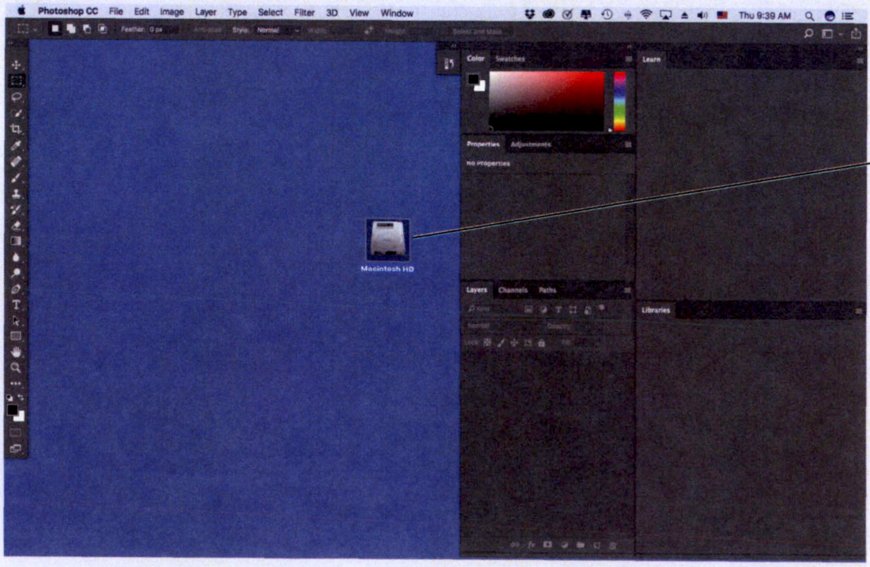

When the Application frame is not active, the desktop is visible behind the workspace elements.

7. **Choose Window>Workspace>Essentials (Default).**

The software includes a number of built-in saved workspaces, which provide one-click access to a defined group of panels, that are designed to meet common workflows.

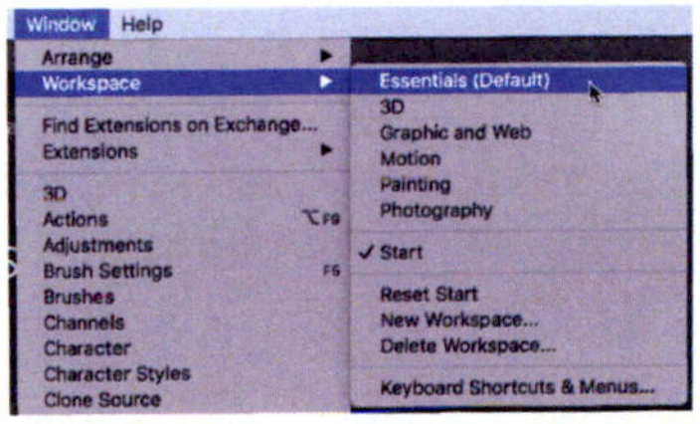

8. **Choose Window>Workspace>Reset Essentials.**

This step might or might not do anything, depending on what was done in Photoshop before you started this project. If you or someone else changed anything and then quit the application, those changes are remembered when Photoshop is relaunched. You are resetting the user interface in this step so that what you see will match our screen shots.

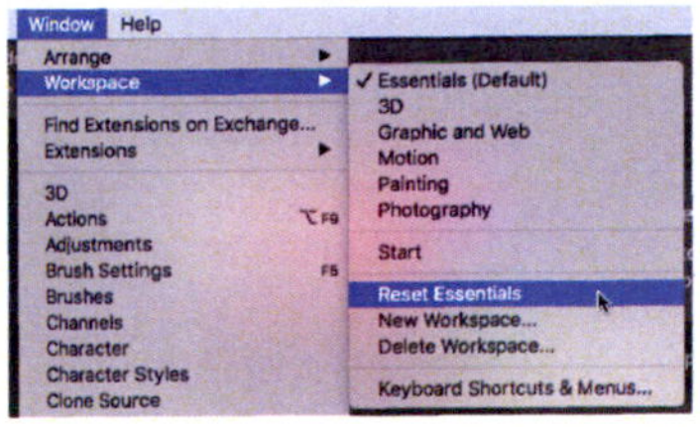

9. **Macintosh users: Choose Photoshop>Preferences>Interface.**
Windows users: Choose Edit>Preferences>Interface.

Remember that on Macintosh systems, the Preferences dialog box is accessed in the Photoshop menu; Windows users access the Preferences dialog box in the Edit menu.

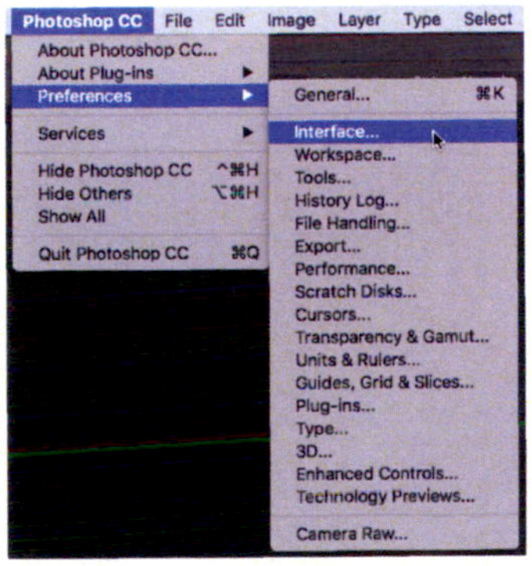

Macintosh

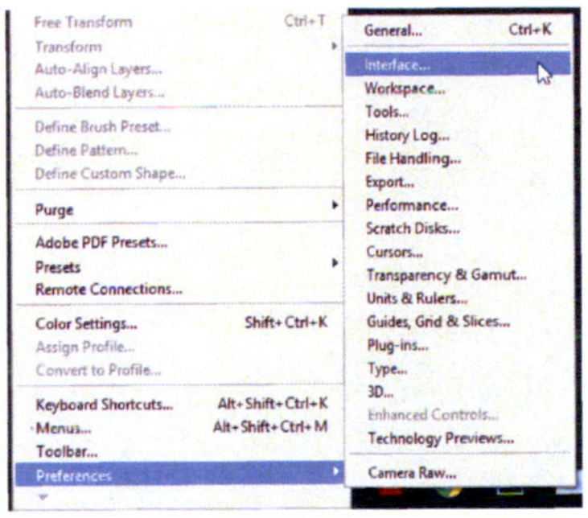

Windows

Note:

As you work your way through this book, you will learn not only what you can do with these different collections of Preferences, but also ***why*** *and* ***when*** *you might want to adjust them.*

10. **In the Color Theme section, choose any option that you prefer.**

Preferences customize the way many of the program's tools and options function. When you open the Preferences dialog box, the active pane is the one you choose in the Preferences submenu. Once open, however, you can access any of the categories by clicking a different option in the left pane.

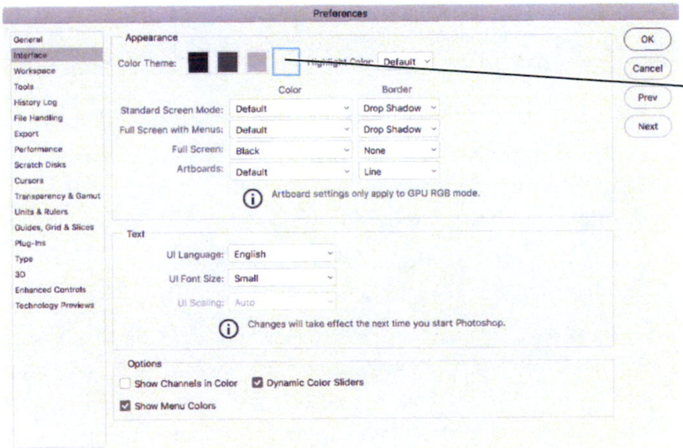

Use these options to lighten or darken the user interface.

You might have already noticed the rather dark appearance of the panels and interface background. Photoshop CC uses the medium-dark "theme" as the default. (We used the Light option throughout this book because text in the interface elements is easier to read in printed screen captures.)

11. **Click OK to close the Preferences dialog box.**

12. **Continue to the next exercise.**

Explore the Arrangement of Photoshop Panels

As you gain familiarity with Photoshop, you will develop personal artistic and working styles. You will also find that different types of jobs often require different but specific sets of tools. Adobe recognizes this wide range of needs and preferences among users; Photoshop includes a number of options for arranging and managing the numerous panels so you can customize and personalize the workspace to suit your specific needs.

We designed the following exercise to give you an opportunity to explore different ways of controlling Photoshop panels. Because workspace preferences are largely a matter of personal taste, the projects in this book instruct you to use certain tools and panels, but where you place those elements within the interface is up to you.

1. **With Photoshop open, review the options in the user interface.**

   The default Essentials workspace includes the Tools panel on the left side of the screen, the Options bar at the top of the screen, and a set of panels attached to the right side of the screen. (The area where the panels are stored is called the **panel dock**.)

Macintosh

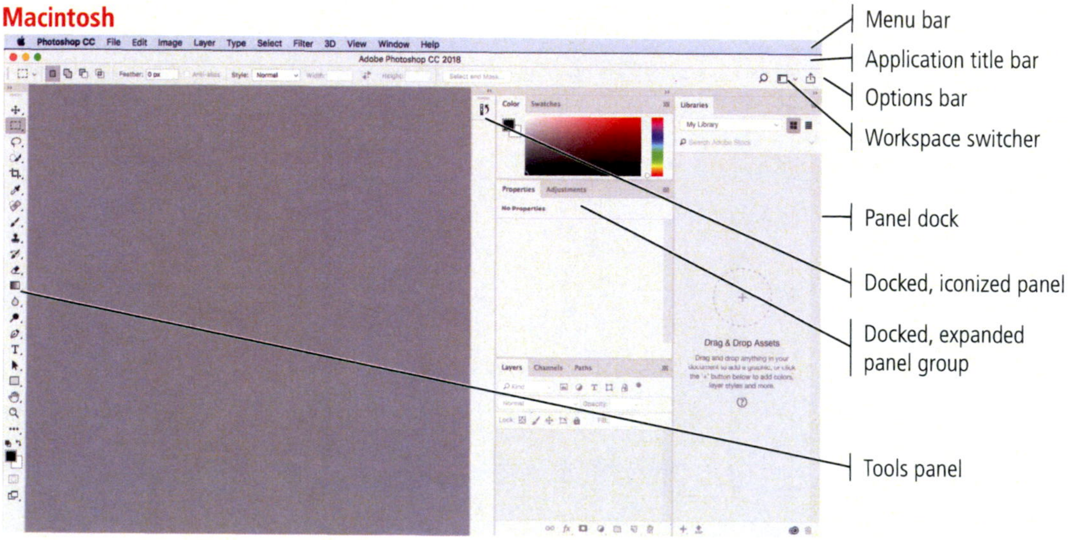

Windows

The Macintosh and Windows workspaces are virtually identical, with a few primary exceptions:

- On Macintosh, the application's title bar appears below the Menu bar; the Close, Minimize, and Restore buttons appear on the left side of the title bar, and the Menu bar is not part of the Application frame.
- On Windows, the Close, Minimize, and Restore buttons appear at the right end of the Menu bar, which is part of the overall Application frame.
- Macintosh users have two extra menus (consistent with the Macintosh OS structure). The Apple menu provides access to system-specific commands. The Photoshop menu follows the Macintosh system-standard format for all applications; this menu controls basic application operations such as About, Hide, Preferences, and Quit.

2. **If you see the Libraries panel expanded on the right side of the screen, click the Libraries panel tab and drag until a blue highlight surrounds the Properties/Adjustments panel group.**

Depending on your screen resolution, the default Essentials workspaces are slightly different from one machine to another. This step make the workspaces on most computers match more closely, so the following steps and explanations will make sense to users on either OS.

If you see different panels in different locations, we still encourage you to follow the steps as written. Your final workspace arrangement might be slightly different than what you see in our screen captures, but the overall processes still work.

> *Note:*
>
> *If you do not see the Libraries panel in its own column in the default Essentials workspace, then your Properties panel is docked and iconized below the History panel in the left dock column.*
>
> *We cannot explain the discrepancy, but it has no significant effect on the steps on this exercise.*

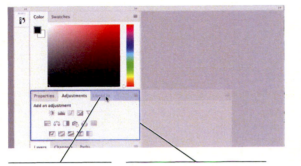

Click a panel tab and drag to move the panel to another location.

The blue highlight shows where the panel will be placed if you release the mouse button.

When you release the mouse button, the Libraries panel becomes part of a Properties/ Adjustment panel group.

3. **Control/right-click the title bar above the left column of docked panel icons. Choose Auto-Collapse Iconic Panels in the contextual menu to toggle on that option.**

As we explained in the Getting Started section, when commands are different for the Macintosh and Windows operating systems, we include the different commands in the Macintosh/Windows format. In this case, Macintosh users who do not have right-click mouse capability can press the Control key and click to access the contextual menu. You do not have to press Control *and* right-click to access the menus.

(If you're using a Macintosh and don't have a mouse with right-click capability, we highly recommend that you purchase one.)

Control/right-clicking a dock title bar opens the dock contextual menu, where you can change the default panel behavior. If you toggle on the Auto-Collapse Iconic Panels option — which is inactive by default — a panel will collapse as soon as you click away from it. (The Auto-Collapse Iconic Panels option is also available in the User Interface pane of the Preferences dialog box, which you can open directly from the dock contextual menu.)

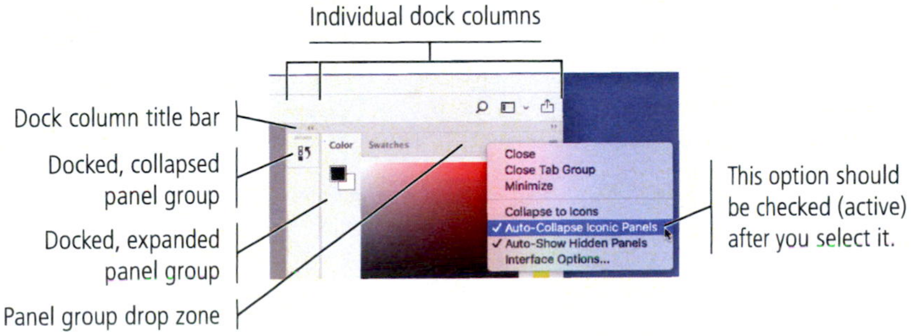

4. **In the left column of the panel dock, hover your mouse cursor over the top button until you see the name of the related panel ("History") in a tool tip.**

5. **Click the History button to expand that panel.**

The expanded panel is still referred to as a **panel group** even though the History panel is the only panel in the group.

Tool tips identify collapsed panels when you hover your mouse cursor over the icon.

Clicking a panel button expands that panel to the left of the button.

Click here to manually collapse the panel back into the dock.

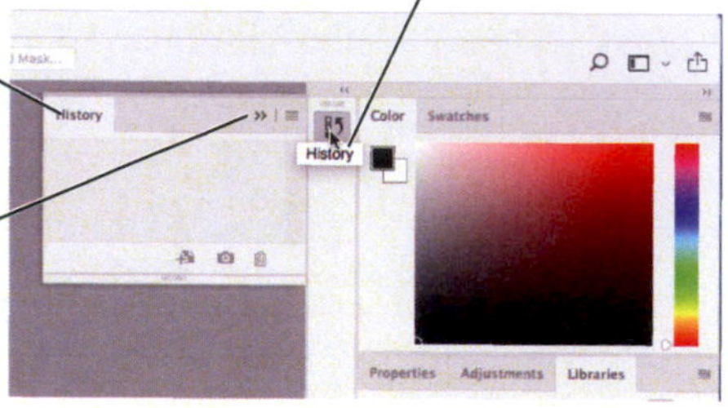

Note:

*Collapsed panels are referred to as **iconized** or **iconic**.*

Note:

When you expand an iconized panel that is part of a group, the entire group expands; the button you clicked is the active panel in the expanded group.

6. **Click away from the expanded panel, anywhere in the workspace.**

Because the Auto-Collapse Iconic Panels option is toggled on (from Step 1), the History panel collapses as soon as you click away from the panel.

7. **Click the History panel button to re-expand the panel. Control/right-click the expanded panel tab and choose Close from the contextual menu.**

The panel group's contextual menu is the only way to close a docked panel. You can choose Close to close only the active panel, or close an entire panel group by choosing Close Tab Group from the contextual menu.

Control/right-click a panel tab or icon to access that panel group's contextual menu.

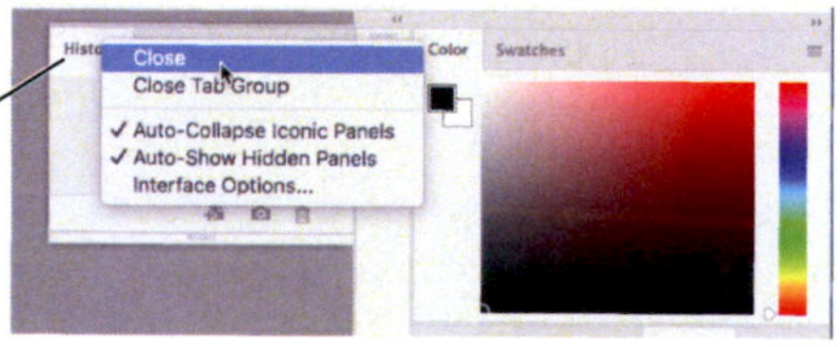

Closing all panels in a column effectively removes that column from the dock.

8. **In the remaining dock column, Control/right-click the drop zone of the Libraries/Adjustments/Properties panel group and choose Close Tab Group from the contextual menu.**

When you close a docked group, other panel groups in the same column expand to fill the available space.

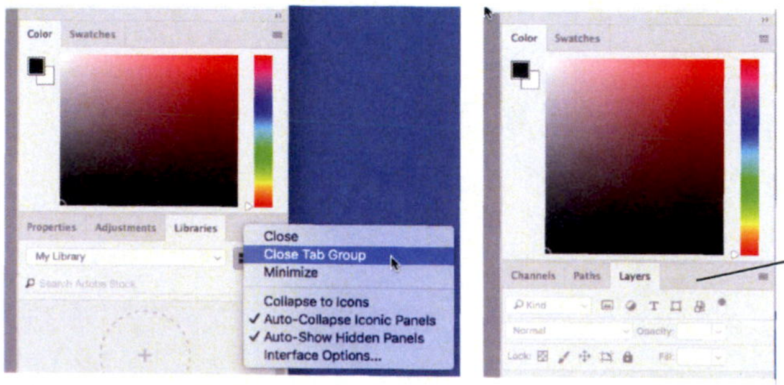

The remaining groups in the dock column expand to fill the available space.

Note:

All panels can be toggled on and off using the Window menu.

If you choose a panel that is open but iconized, the panel expands to the left of its icon.

If you choose a panel that is open in an expanded group, that panel comes to the front of the group.

If you choose a panel that isn't currently open, it opens in the same position as when it was last closed.

9. **Click the Layers panel tab and drag left, away from the panel dock.**

A panel that is not docked is called a **floating panel**. You can iconize floating panels (or panel groups) by double-clicking the title bar of the floating panel group.

Macintosh | Windows

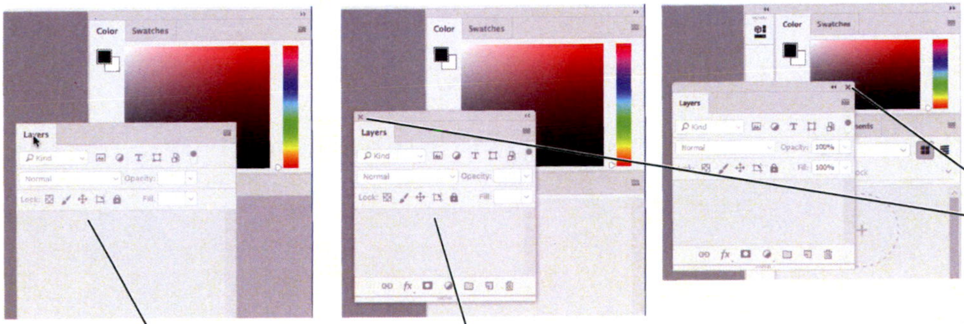

Floating panel Close button

Click the panel tab and drag to move the panel.

When you release the mouse button, the panel floats freely in the workspace.

Note:

Many screen shots in this book show floating panels so we can focus on the most important issue in a particular image. In our production workflow, we make heavy use of docked and iconized panels, and we take full advantage of saved custom workspaces.

10. **Click the Layers panel tab (in the floating panel group). Drag between the two existing docked panel groups until a blue line appears, then release the mouse button.**

To move a single panel to a new location, click the panel tab and drag. To move an entire panel group, click the panel group drop zone and drag. If you are moving panels to another position in the dock, the blue highlight indicates where the panel (group) will be placed when you release the mouse button.

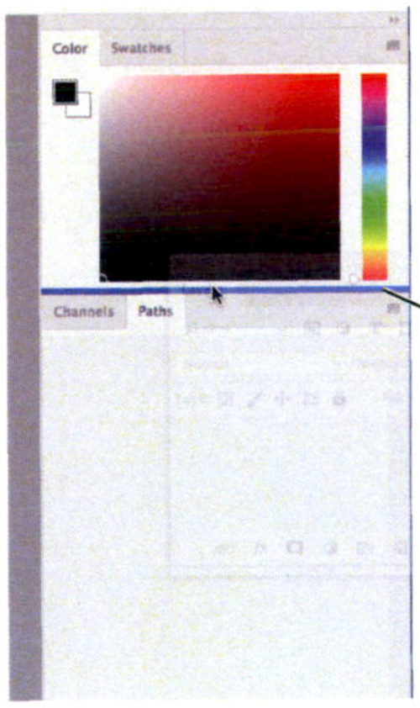

The blue highlight shows where the panel will be placed if you release the mouse button.

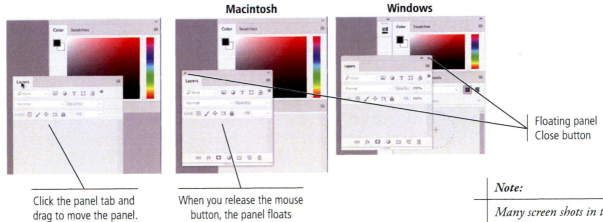

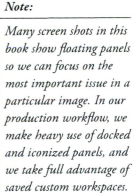

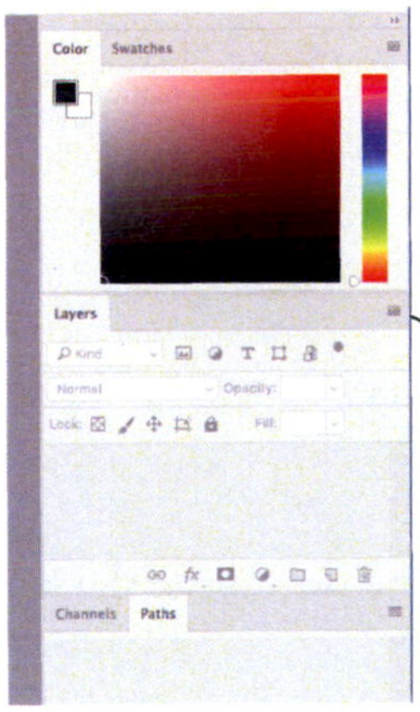

When you release the mouse button, the Layers panel becomes part of a separate panel group.

To add a panel to an existing group, drag the panel to the target group's drop zone. A blue highlight will surround the group where the moved panel will be added.

11. **Control/right-click the drop zone behind the Colors/Swatches panel group, and choose Minimize from the contextual menu.**

When a group is minimized, only the panel tabs are visible. Clicking a tab in a collapsed panel group expands that group and makes the selected panel active.

You can also double-click a panel tab to minimize the panel group.

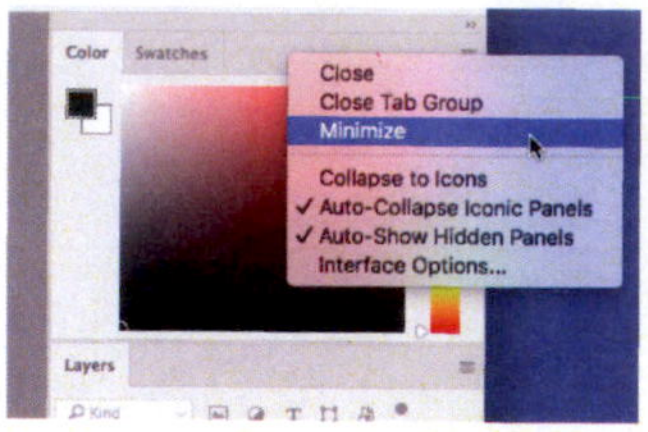

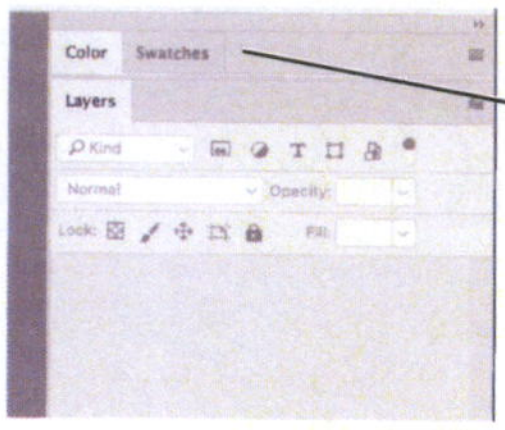

Minimizing a panel group collapses it to show only the panel tabs.

12. **Move the cursor over the line between the Layers and Channels/Paths panel groups. When the cursor becomes a double-headed arrow, click and drag up or down until the Layers panel occupies approximately half of the available dock column space.**

You can drag the bottom edge of a docked panel group to vertically expand or shrink the panel; other panels in the same column expand or contract to fit the available space.

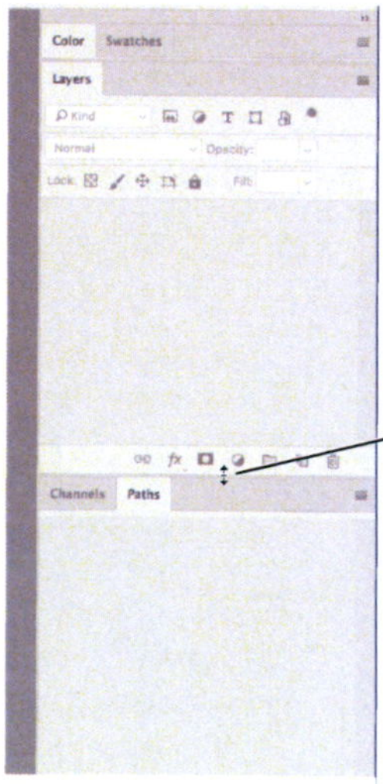

When the cursor becomes a double-headed arrow, click and drag the line between panel groups to change the height of a panel.

Note:

To create a new dock column, drag a panel or panel group until a pop-out "drawer" outlines the edge where the new column will be added.

Each column, technically considered a separate dock, can be expanded or collapsed independently of other columns.

13. **Double-click the title bar above the column of docked panels to collapse those panels to icons.**

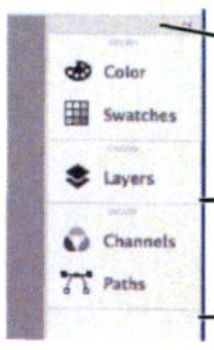

Double-clicking the dock title bar collapses an expanded column (or vice versa).

Buttons that are grouped together in the dock represent a panel group.

Note:

Dragging the left edge of a dock column changes the width of all panels in that dock column. This works for both iconized and expanded columns.

14. **Move the cursor over the left edge of the dock column. When the cursor becomes a double-headed arrow, click and drag right.**

If you only see the icons, you can also drag the dock edge to the left to reveal the panel names. This can be particularly useful until you are more familiar with the application and the icons used to symbolize the different panels.

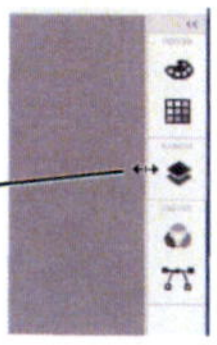

Click here and drag right to hide the panel names.

15. On the left side of the workspace, double-click the Tools panel title bar.

The Tools panel can't be expanded, but it can be displayed as either one or two columns; double-clicking the Tools panel title bar toggles between the two modes.

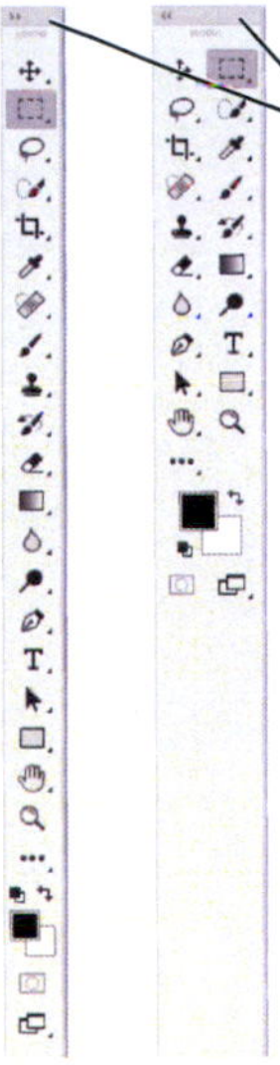

Double-click the Tools panel title bar to toggle between the one-column and two-column layouts.

The one- or two-column format is a purely personal choice. The one-column layout takes up less horizontal space on the screen, which can be useful if you have a small monitor. The two-column format fits in a smaller vertical space, which can be especially useful if you have a widescreen monitor.

The Tools panel can also be floated by clicking its title bar and dragging away from the edge of the screen. To re-dock the floating Tools panel, simply click the title bar and drag back to the left edge of the screen; when the blue line highlights the edge of the workspace, releasing the mouse button puts the Tools panel back into the dock.

> ***Note:***
>
> *Throughout this book, our screen shots show the Tools panel in the one-column format. Feel free to work with the panel in two columns if you prefer.*

16. Continue to the next exercise.

Customizing the Photoshop Tools Panel

Near the bottom of the Tools panel, the Edit Toolbar (•••) provides access to a dialog box where you can customize the options that appear in the Tools panel. If you click and hold on this button, you can choose the option to Edit Toolbar in the pop-up menu.

In the Customize Toolbar dialog box, you can select and move individual tools or entire groups of tools into the Extra Tools window. Any tools in that window are moved from their regular position in the default Tools panel to a single position, nested under the Edit Toolbar option.

You can toggle the buttons in the bottom-left corner of the dialog box to show or hide several options in the Tools panel. From left to right:

- Edit Toolbar
- Default Foreground and Background Colors
- Edit in Quick Mask Mode
- Change Screen Mode

If you choose to hide the Edit Toolbar option, any tools in the Extra Tools list are simply hidden; you will not be able to access them unless you customize the Tools panel again. (In this case, you can accomplish this task by choosing Edit>Toolbar.)

Clicking the Restore Defaults button in the Customize Toolbar dialog box resets all tools and options in the panel to their original default positions and visibility.

Click and drag tools from the Toolbar list to the Extra Tools list.

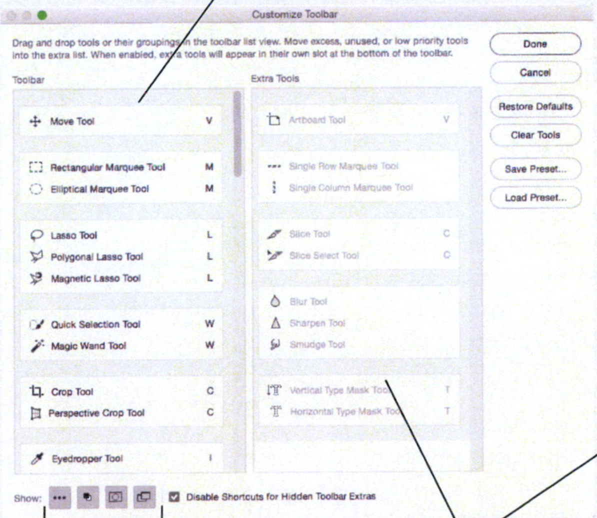

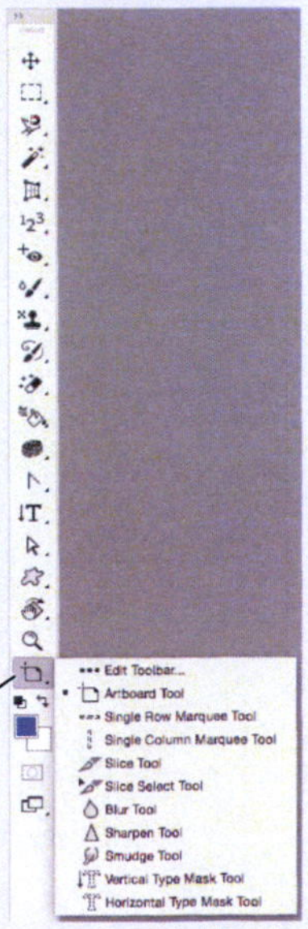

Toggle these buttons to show and hide extra options at the bottom of the Tools panel.

Tools in this window are moved to a single group at the bottom of the Tools panel, nested below the Edit Toolbar option.

Accessing Photoshop Tools

In the Tools panel, tools with a small mark in the lower-right corner have **nested tools**.

This arrow means the tool has other nested tools.

Rich tool tip

If you hover your mouse over a tool, a rich **tool tip** shows the name of the tool, the associated keyboard shortcut (if any), a small animation related to that tool, and a link to video tutorials related to the specific tools.

(You can disable overall tool tips or rich tool tips in the Tools pane of the Preferences dialog box. If you disable only rich tool tips, you would see the only tool name and keyboard shortcut when you hover over a tool.)

You can access nested tools by clicking the primary tool and holding down the mouse button, or by Control/right-clicking the primary tool to open the menu of nested options.

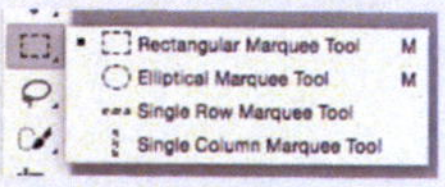

If a tool has a defined shortcut, pressing that key activates the associated tool. Most nested tools have the same shortcut as the default tool. By default, you have to press Shift plus the shortcut key to access the nested variations. You can change this behavior in the Tools pane of the Preferences dialog box by unchecking the Use Shift Key for Tool Switch option; when unchecked, you can simply press the shortcut key multiple times to cycle through variations.

Finally, if you press and hold a tool's keyboard shortcut, you can temporarily call the appropriate tool (called **spring-loaded keys**); after releasing the shortcut key, you return to the tool you were using previously. For example, you might use this technique to switch temporarily from the Brush tool to the Eraser tool while painting.

The following chart offers a quick reference of nested tools, as well as the shortcut for each tool (if any). Nested tools are shown indented.

- Move tool (V)
  - Artboard tool (V)
- Rectangular Marquee tool (M)
  - Elliptical Marquee tool (M)
  - Single Row Marquee tool
  - Single Column Marquee tool
- Lasso tool (L)
  - Polygonal Lasso tool (L)
  - Magnetic Lasso tool (L)
- Quick Selection tool (W)
  - Magic Wand tool (W)
- Crop tool (C)
  - Perspective Crop tool (C)
  - Slice tool (C)
  - Slice Select tool (C)
- Eyedropper tool (I)
  - 3D Material Eyedropper tool (I)
  - Color Sampler tool (I)
  - Ruler tool (I)
  - Note tool (I)
  - Count tool (I)
- Spot Healing Brush tool (J)
  - Healing Brush tool (J)
  - Patch tool (J)
  - Content Aware Move tool (J)
  - Red Eye tool (J)
- Brush tool (B)
  - Pencil tool (B)
  - Color Replacement tool (B)
  - Mixer Brush tool (B)
- Clone Stamp tool (S)
  - Pattern Stamp tool (S)
- History Brush tool (Y)
  - Art History Brush tool (Y)
- Eraser tool (E)
  - Background Eraser tool (E)
  - Magic Eraser tool (E)
- Gradient tool (G)
  - Paint Bucket tool (G)
  - 3D Material Drop tool (G)
- Blur tool
  - Sharpen tool
  - Smudge tool
- Dodge tool (O)
  - Burn tool (O)
  - Sponge tool (O)
- Pen tool (P)
  - Freeform Pen tool (P)
  - Curvature Pen tool (P)
  - Add Anchor Point tool
  - Delete Anchor Point tool
  - Convert Point tool
- Horizontal Type tool (T)
  - Vertical Type tool (T)
  - Horizontal Type Mask tool (T)
  - Vertical Type Mask tool (T)
- Path Selection tool (A)
  - Direct Selection tool (A)
- Rectangle tool (U)
  - Rounded Rectangle tool (U)
  - Ellipse tool (U)
  - Polygon tool (U)
  - Line tool (U)
  - Custom Shape tool (U)
- Hand tool (H)
  - Rotate View tool (R)
- Zoom tool (Z)

Create a Saved Workspace

You have extensive control over the appearance of your Photoshop workspace — you can choose what panels are visible, where they appear, and even the size of individual panels or panel groups. Over time you will develop personal preferences — the Layers panel always appears at the top, for example — based on your work habits and project needs. Rather than re-establishing every workspace element each time you return to Photoshop, you can save your custom workspace settings so they can be recalled with a single click.

> *Note:*
>
> *Because workspace preferences are largely a matter of personal taste, the projects in this book instruct you regarding which panels to use, but not where to place those elements within the interface.*

1. **Choose Window>Workspace>New Workspace.**

   Saved workspaces can be accessed in the Window>Workspace submenu as well as the Workspace switcher on the Options bar.

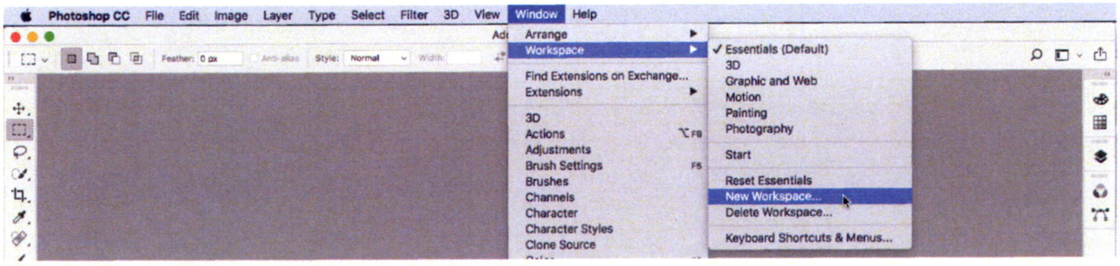

2. **In the New Workspace dialog box, type Portfolio and then click Save.**

   You didn't define custom keyboard shortcuts, menus, or toolbars, so those options are not relevant in this exercise.

> *Note:*
>
> *If a menu option is grayed out, it is not available for the active selection.*

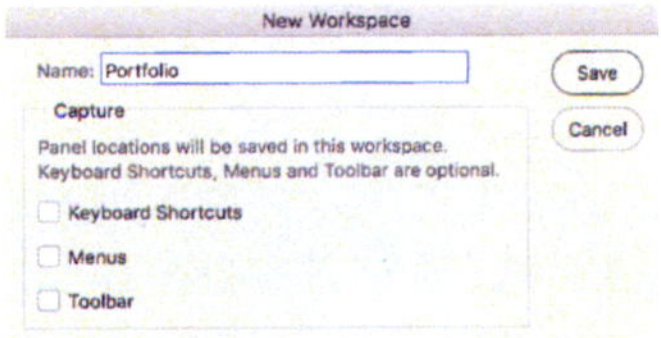

3. **Open the Window menu and choose Workspace>Essentials (Default).**

> *Note:*
>
> *The Delete Workspace option opens a dialog box where you can choose a specific user-defined workspace to delete. You can't delete the default workspaces that come with the application.*

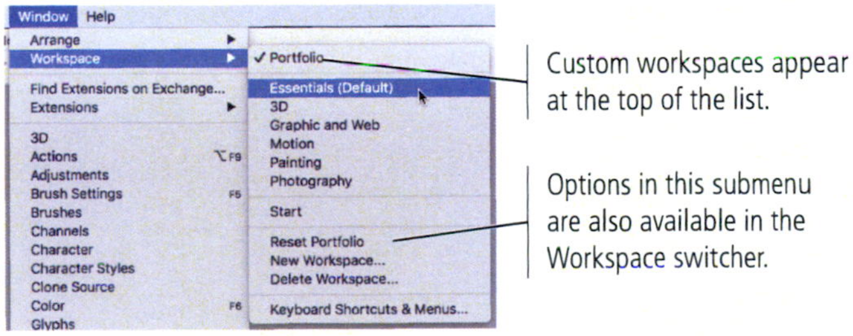

   Calling a saved workspace restores the last-used state of the workspace. You made a number of changes since calling the Essentials workspace at the beginning of the previous exercise, so calling the Essentials workspace restores the last state of that workspace — in essence, nothing changes from the saved Portfolio workspace.

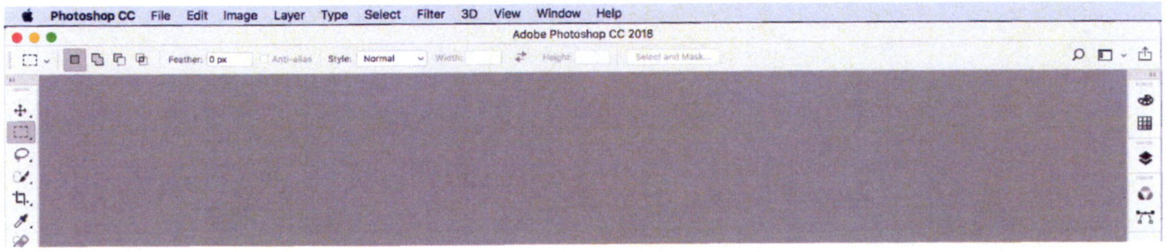

4. **Open the Workspace switcher and choose Reset Essentials (or choose Window>Workspace>Reset Essentials).**

Remember, saved workspaces remember the last-used state; calling a workspace again restores the panels exactly as they were the last time you used that workspace. For example, if you close a panel that is part of a saved workspace, the closed panel will not be reopened the next time you call the same workspace. To restore the saved state of the workspace, including opening closed panels or repositioning moved ones, you have to use the Reset option.

Note:

If you change anything and quit the application, those changes are remembered even when Photoshop is relaunched.

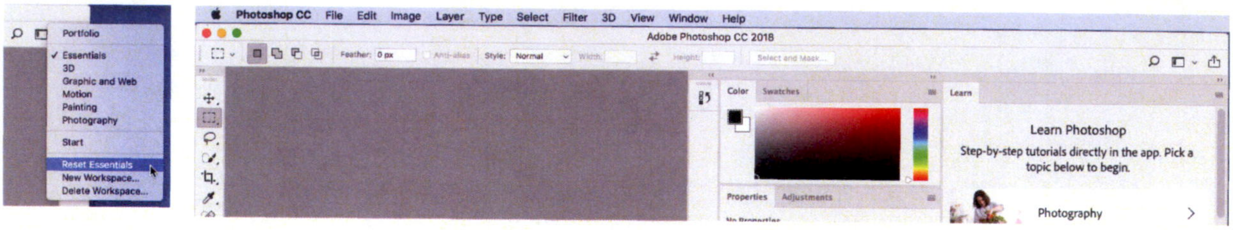

5. **Using the Window>Workspace menu or the Workspace switcher, call the saved Portfolio workspace.**

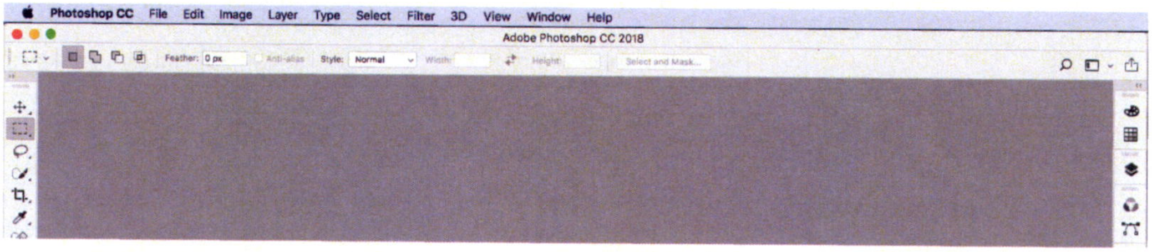

6. **Continue to the next exercise.**

Customizing Keyboard Shortcuts and Menus

PHOTOSHOP FOUNDATIONS

People use Photoshop for many different reasons; some use only a limited set of tools to complete specific projects. Photoshop allows you to define the available menu options and the keyboard shortcuts that are associated with menu commands, panel menus, and tools.

At the bottom of the Edit menu, two options (Keyboard Shortcuts and Menus) open different tabs of the same dialog box. (If you don't see the Keyboard Shortcuts or Menus options in the Edit menu, choose Show all Menu Items to reveal the hidden commands.) Once you have defined custom menus or shortcuts, you can save your choices as a set so you can access the same custom choices again without having to redo the work.

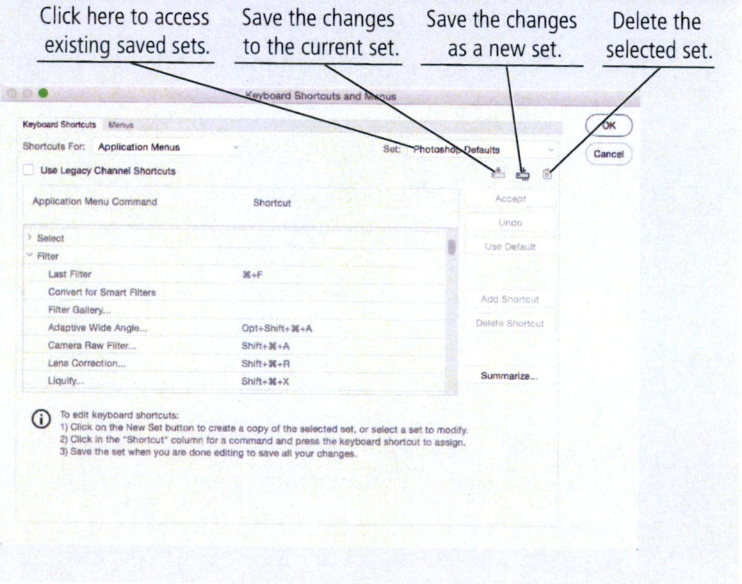

Explore the Photoshop Document Views

There is much more to using Photoshop than arranging the workspacc. What you do with those panels — and even which panels you need — depends on the type of work you are doing in a particular file. In this exercise, you open a Photoshop file and explore interface elements that will be important as you begin creating digital artwork.

1. **In Photoshop, choose File>Open. If you see a warning message about insufficient vRAM, click OK.**

   The 3D features in Photoshop CC require a graphics card with at least 512 MB of video RAM (vRAM). The first time you try to create a new file or open an existing one, you will see a warning message if your hardware is not sufficient to run those features.

> *Note:*
>
> *If you see this message, you will not be able to complete Project 4: City Promotion Cards or Project 8: Photographer's Web Page.*

2. **Navigate to your WIP>InterfacePS folder and select hubble.jpg in the list of available files. Press Shift, and then click supernova.jpg.**

   The Open dialog box is a system-standard navigation dialog. This is one area of significant difference between Macintosh and Windows users.

   On both operating systems, this step selects all files including and between the two you click. Pressing Shift allows you to select multiple consecutive files in the list. You can also press Command/Control and click to select multiple non-consecutive files.

> *Note:*
>
> *Press Command/Control-O to access the Open dialog box.*

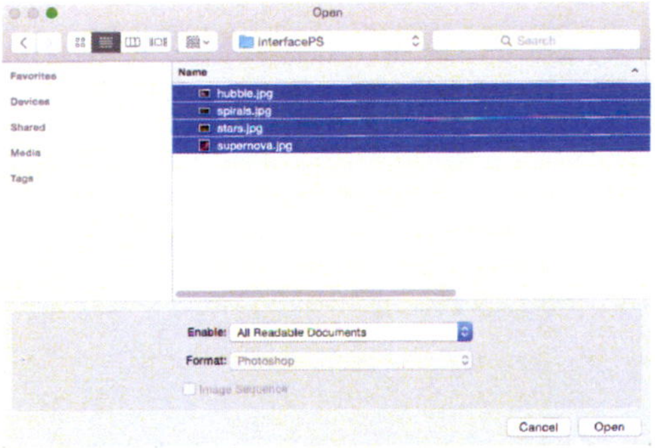

Macintosh

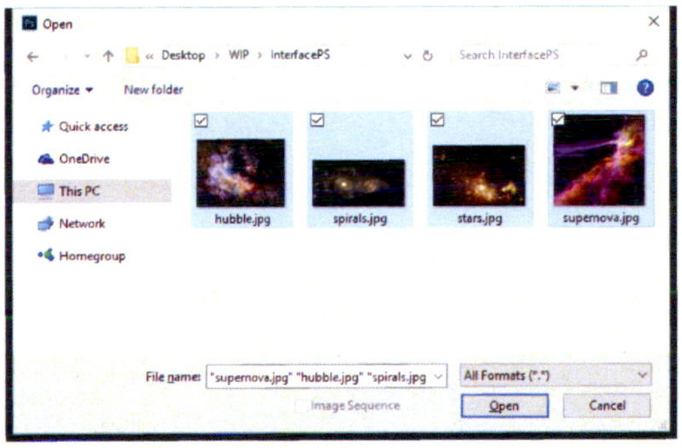

Windows

3. **Click Open.**

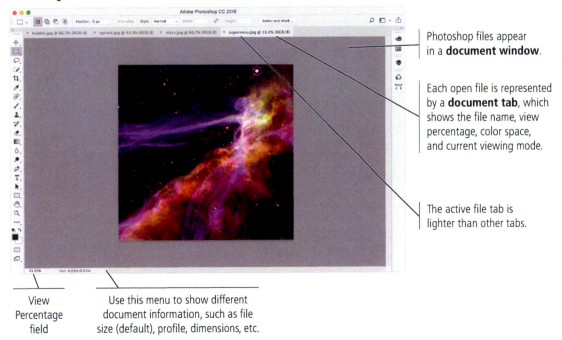

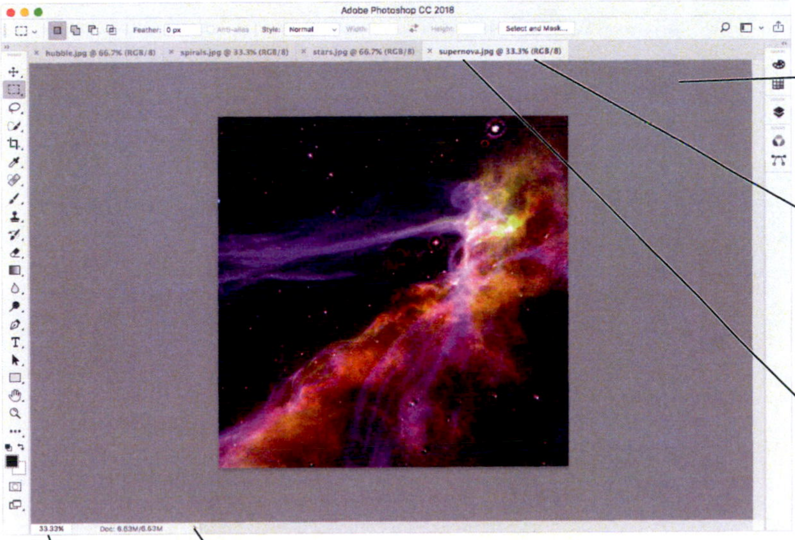

Photoshop files appear in a **document window**.
Each open file is represented by a **document tab**, which shows the file name, view percentage, color space, and current viewing mode.
The active file tab is lighter than other tabs.
View Percentage field
Use this menu to show different document information, such as file size (default), profile, dimensions, etc.

4. **Click the spirals.jpg tab to make that document active.**

5. **Highlight the current value in the View Percentage field (in the bottom-left corner of the document window). Type 45, then press Return/Enter.**

   Different people prefer larger or smaller view percentages, depending on a number of factors (eyesight, monitor size, and so on). As you complete the projects in this book, you will see our screen shots zoom in or out as necessary to show you the most relevant part of a particular file. In most cases we do not tell you what specific view percentage to use for a particular exercise, unless it is specifically required for the work being done.

Note:

Macintosh users: If you turn off the Application frame, opening multiple files creates a document window that has a separate title bar showing the name of the active file.

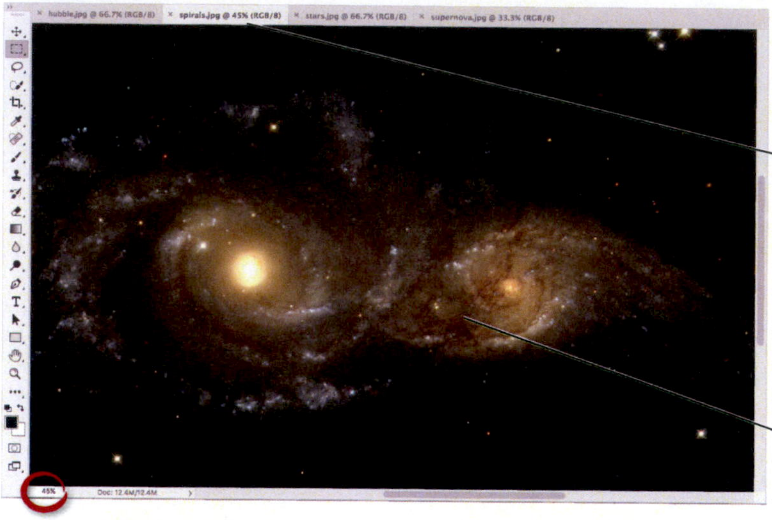

Click the tab to activate a specific file in the document window.
Changing the view percentage of the file does not affect the size of the document window.

6. **Choose View>100%.**

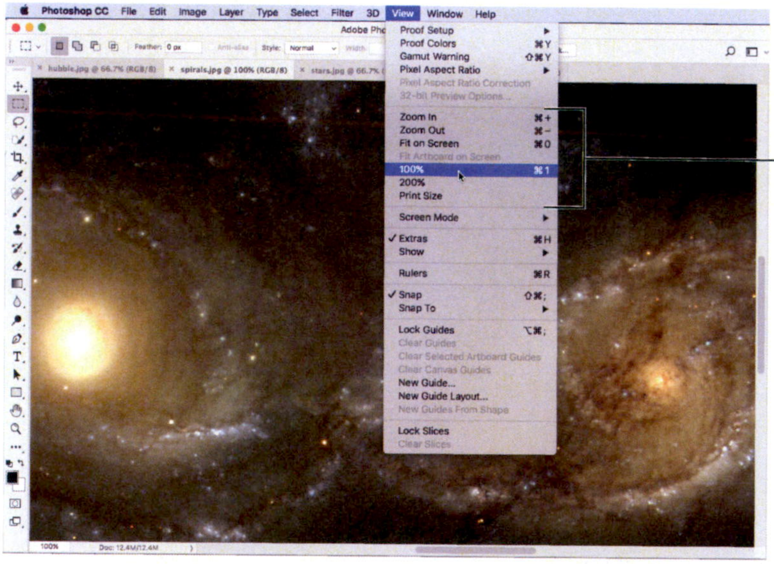

7. **Click the Hand tool (near the bottom of the Tools panel). Click in the document window, hold down the mouse button, and drag around.**

The Hand tool is a very easy and convenient option for changing the area of an image that is currently visible in the document window.

(If the Scroll All Windows option is checked in the Options bar, dragging in one window affects the visible area of all open files.)

Hand tool cursor

Note:

You can press the Spacebar to access the Hand tool when another tool (other than the Type tool) is active.

8. **Click the Zoom tool in the Tools panel. Press Option/Alt, and then click anywhere in the document window.**

One final reminder: we list differing commands in the Macintosh/Windows format. On Macintosh, you need to press the Option key; on Windows, press the Alt key. (We will not repeat this explanation every time different commands are required for the different operating systems.)

Clicking with the Zoom tool enlarges the view percentage in specific, predefined percentage steps. Pressing Option/Alt while clicking with the Zoom tool reduces the view percentage in the reverse sequence of the same percentages.

Note:

You can zoom a document between approximately 0.098% and 3200%. We say approximately because the actual smallest size is dependent on the original image size; you can zoom out far enough to "show" the image as a single tiny square, regardless of what percentage of the image that represents.

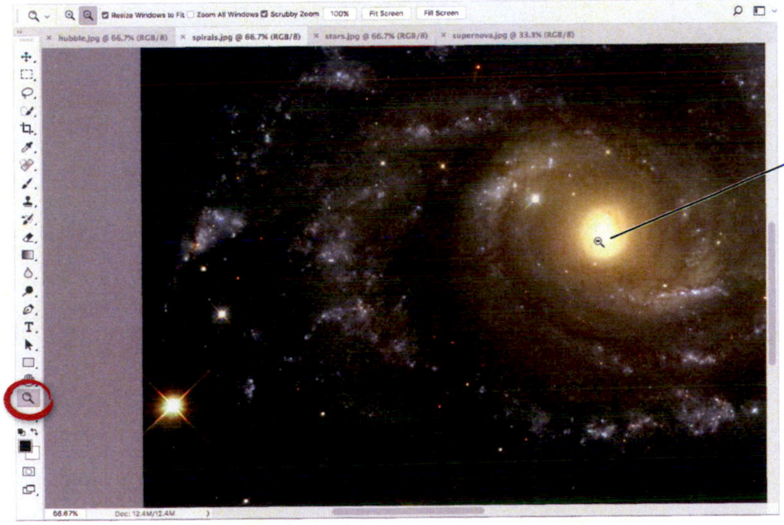
When the Zoom tool is active, pressing Option/Alt changes the cursor to the Zoom Out icon.

Note:

Dragging with the Zoom tool enlarges the selected area to fill the document window.

9. **In the Options bar, click the Fit Screen button.**

The Options bar appears by default at the top of the workspace below the Menu bar. It is context sensitive, which means it provides different options depending on which tool is active. When the Zoom tool is active:

- If Resize Windows to Fit is checked, zooming in a floating window affects the size of the actual document window.
- If Zoom All Windows is checked, zooming in one window affects the view percentage of all open files.
- Scrubby Zoom enables dynamic image zooming depending on the direction you drag in the document window.
- The 100% button changes the view percentage to 100%.
- The Fit Screen option changes the image view to whatever percentage is necessary to show the entire image in the document window. (This has the same effect as choosing Window>Fit on Screen.)
- The Fill Screen button changes the image view to whatever percentage is necessary to fill the available space in the document window.

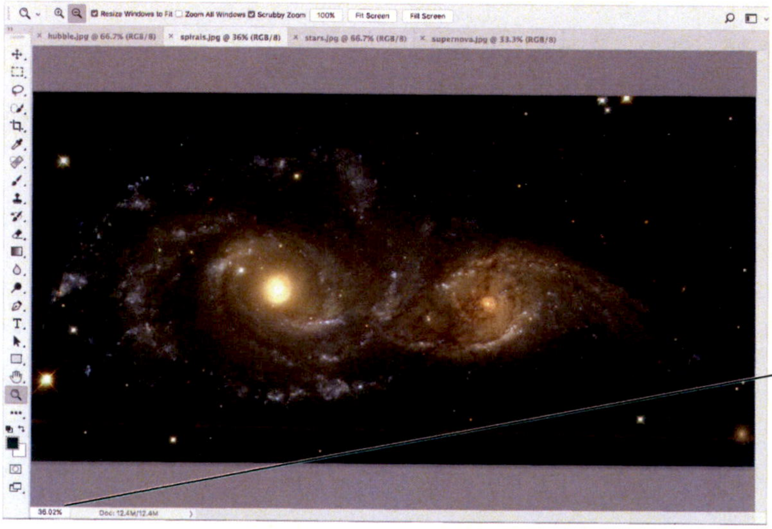

The Fit Screen command automatically calculates view percentage based on the size of the document window.

Note:

You can toggle the Options bar on or off by choosing Window>Options.

Note:

If you check the Enable Narrow Options Bar option in the Workspace pane of the Preferences dialog box, many options in the Options bar will appear as small icons that you can click to toggle on and off. This saves horizontal space on narrow monitors.

10. **In the Tools panel, choose the Rotate View tool (nested under the Hand tool). Click in the document window and drag right to turn the document clockwise.**

The Rotate View tool turns an image without permanently altering the orientation of the file; the actual image data remains unchanged. This tool allows you to more easily work on objects or elements that are not oriented horizontally (for example, working with text that appears on an angle in the final image).

In the Options bar, you can type a specific angle in the Rotation Angle field or click the rotation proxy icon to dynamically rotate the view. At any time, you can click the Reset View button to restore the original rotation (0°) of the image. If Rotate All Windows is checked, dragging in one window affects the view angle of all open files.

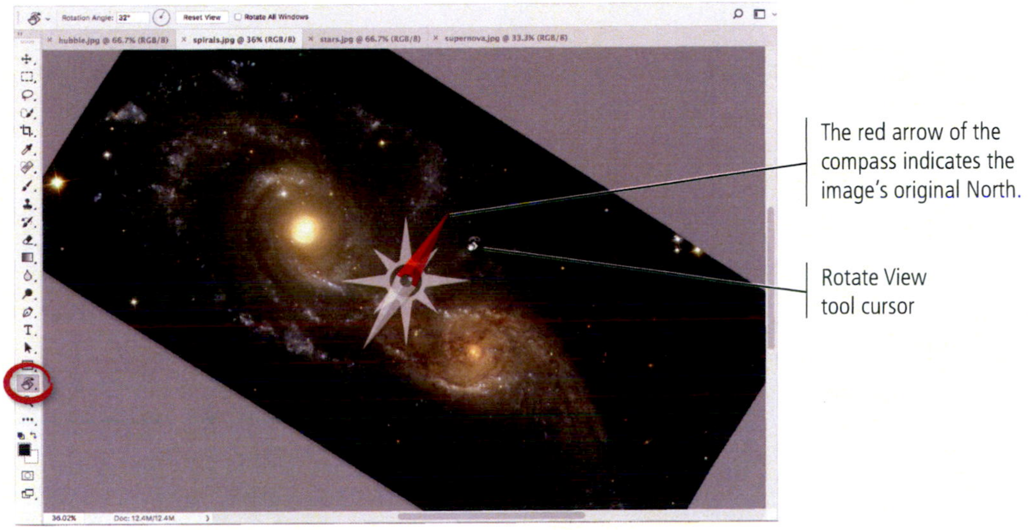

The red arrow of the compass indicates the image's original North.
Rotate View tool cursor

If you are unable to rotate the image view, your graphics processor does not support OpenGL — a hardware/software combination that makes it possible to work with complex graphics operations. If your computer does not support OpenGL, you will not be able to use a number of Photoshop features (including the Rotate View tool).

11. **In the Options bar, click the Reset View button.**

As we said, the Rotate View tool is **non-destructive** (i.e., it does not permanently affect the pixels in the image). You can easily use the tool's options to define a specific view angle or to restore an image to its original orientation.

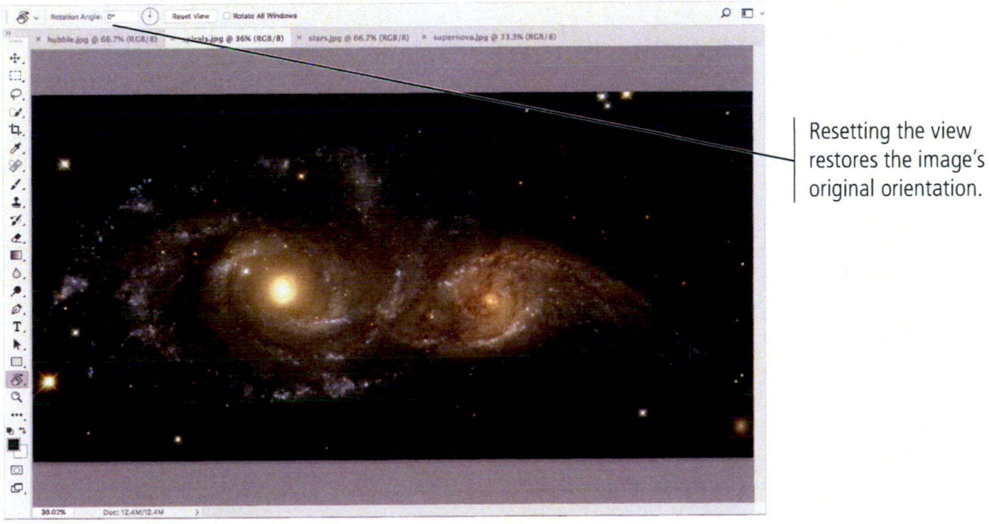

Resetting the view restores the image's original orientation.

12. **Continue to the next exercise.**

Summing Up the Photoshop View Options

Most Photoshop projects require some amount of zooming in and out to various view percentages, as well as navigating around the document within its window. As we show you how to complete different stages of the workflow, we usually won't tell you when to change your view percentage because that's largely a matter of personal preference. However, you should understand the different options for navigating around a Photoshop file so you can easily and efficiently get to what you want, when you want to get there.

View Percentage Field

You can type a specific percentage in the View Percentage field in the bottom-left corner of the document window.

View Menu

The View menu also provides options for changing the view percentage, including the associated keyboard shortcuts. (The Zoom In and Zoom Out options step through the same predefined view percentages that the Zoom tool uses.)

Zoom In	Command/Control-plus (+)
Zoom Out	Command/Control-minus (-)
Fit On Screen	Command/Control-0 (zero)
Actual Pixels (100%)	Command/Control-1

Zoom Tool

You can click with the **Zoom tool** to increase the view percentage in specific, predefined intervals. Pressing Option/Alt with the Zoom tool allows you to zoom out in the same predefined percentages. If you drag a marquee with the Zoom tool, you can zoom into a specific location; the area surrounded by the marquee fills the available space in the document window.

When the Zoom tool is active, you can also activate the Scrubby Zoom option in the Options bar. This allows you to click and drag left to reduce the view percentage, or drag right to increase the view percentage; in this case, the tool does not follow predefined stepped percentages.

Hand Tool

Whatever your view percentage, you can use the **Hand tool** to drag the file around in the document window. The Hand tool changes only what is visible in the window; it has no effect on the actual pixels in the image.

Mouse Scroll Wheel

If your mouse has a scroll wheel, rolling the scroll wheel up or down moves the image up or down within the document window. If you press Command/Control and scroll the wheel, you can move the image left (scroll up) or right (scroll down) within the document window. You can also press Option/Alt and scroll the wheel up to zoom in or scroll the wheel down to zoom out.

(In the General pane of the Preferences dialog box, the Zoom with Scroll Wheel option is unchecked by default. If you check this option, scrolling up or down with no modifier key zooms in or out and does not move the image within the document window.)

Navigator Panel

The **Navigator panel** is another method of adjusting how close your viewpoint is and what part of the page you're currently viewing (if you're zoomed in close enough so you can see only a portion of the page). The Navigator panel shows a thumbnail of the active file; a red rectangle represents exactly how much of the document shows in the document window.

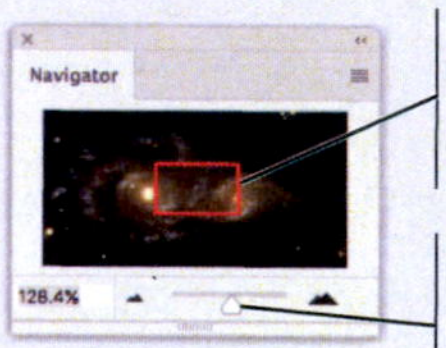

Drag the red rectangle to change the visible portion of the file.

Use the slider and field at the bottom of the panel to change the view percentage.

Explore the Arrangement of Multiple Documents

You will often need to work with more than one Photoshop file at once. Photoshop incorporates a number of options for arranging multiple documents. We designed the following simple exercise so you can explore these options.

1. **With all four files from the WIP>InterfacePS folder open, click the hubble.jpg document tab to make that the active file.**

2. **Choose Window>Arrange>Float in Window.**

   You can also separate all open files by choosing Window>Arrange>Float All In Windows.

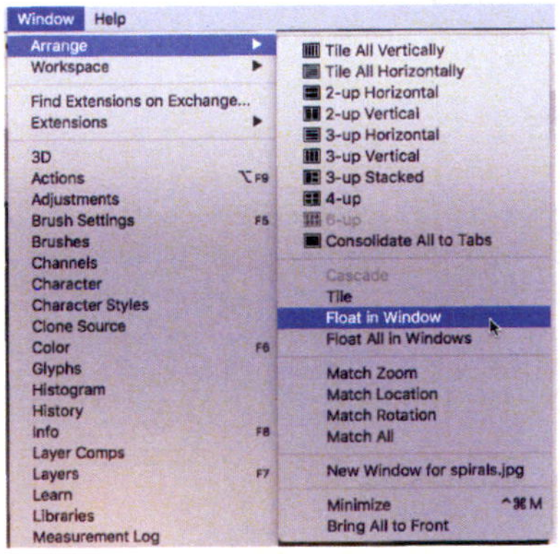

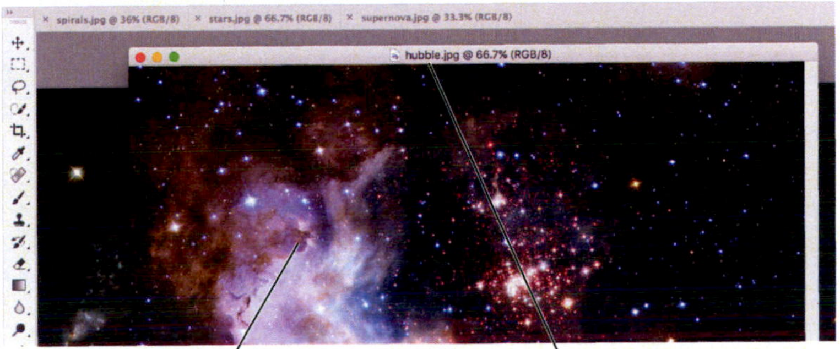

Floating a document separates the file into its own document window.

The title bar of the separate document window shows the same information that was in the document tab.

3. **Choose Window>Arrange>4-up.**

   The defined arrangements provide a number of options for tiling multiple open files within the available workspace. These arrangements manage all open files, including those in floating windows.

   The options' icons suggest the result of each command. The active file remains active; this is indicated by the brighter text in the active document's tab.

Note:

All open files are listed at the bottom of the Window menu.

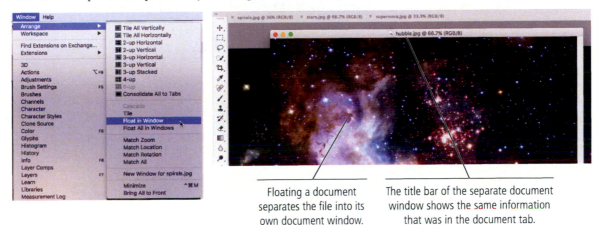

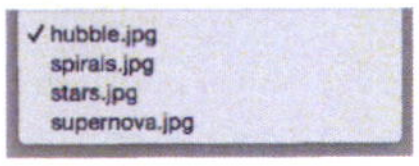

Note:

If more files are open than what a specific arrangement indicates, the extra files will be consolidated as tabs into the window with the active file.

4. **Choose Window>Arrange>Consolidate All to Tabs.**

   This command restores all documents — floating or not— into a single tabbed document window.

5. **At the bottom of the Tools panel, click the Change Screen Mode button.**

   Photoshop has three different **screen modes**, which change the way the document window displays on the screen. The default mode, which you saw when you opened these three files, is called Standard Screen mode.

Note:

Press F to cycle through the different screen modes.

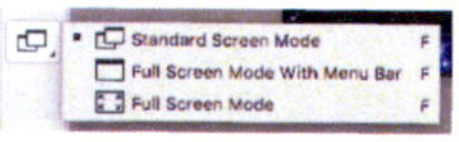

6. **Choose Full Screen Mode with Menu Bar from the Change Screen Mode menu.**

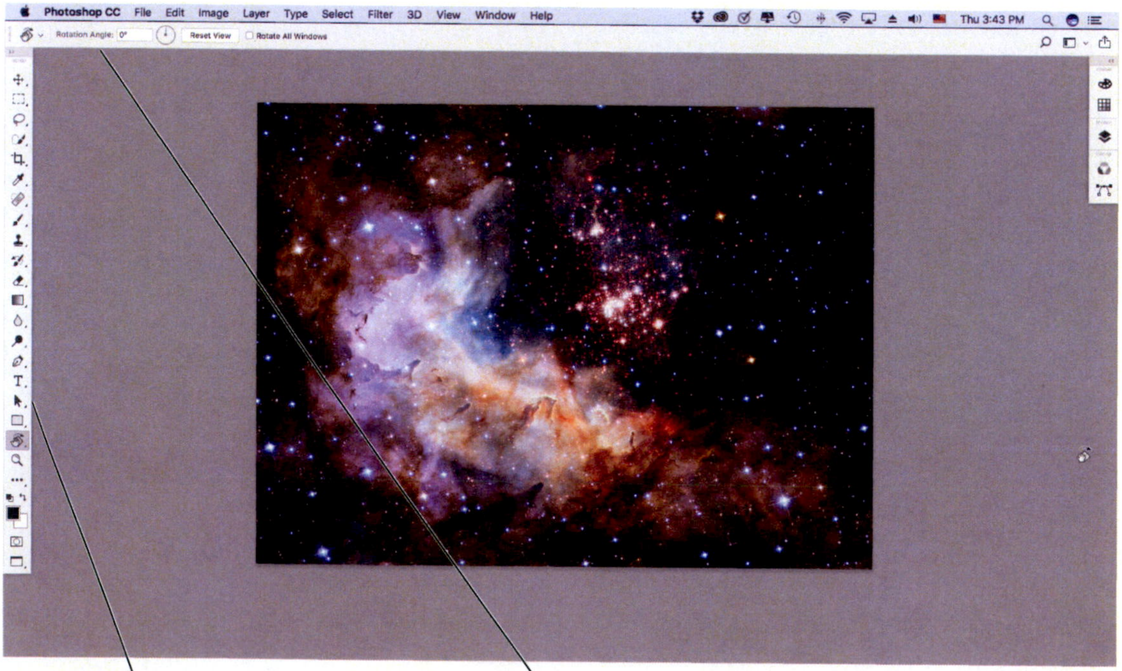

In Full Screen Mode with Menu Bar, the document window fills the entire workspace.

Document tabs are hidden behind the Menu bar.

7. **Click the Change Screen Mode button in the Tools panel and choose Full Screen Mode. Read the resulting warning dialog box, and then click Full Screen.**

In Full Screen Mode, the Menu bar, title bar, and all panels are hidden.

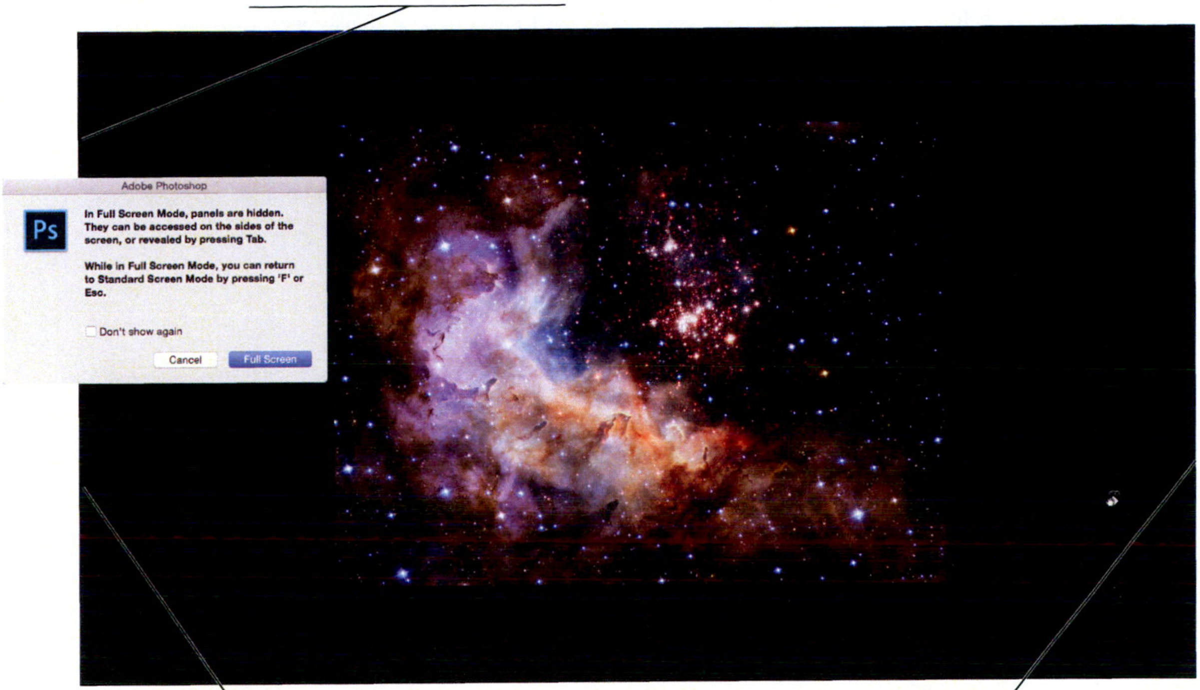

Move your mouse cursor to the left edge of the screen to temporarily show the Tools panel.

Move your mouse cursor to the right edge of the screen to temporarily show docked panels.

8. **Press the Escape key to return to Standard Screen mode.**

9. **Click the Close button on the hubble.jpg tab.**

10. **Macintosh: Click the Close button in the top-left corner of the Application frame.**

    Closing the Macintosh Application frame closes all open files, but does *not* quit the application.

    Windows: Click the Close button on each document tab to close the files.

    Clicking the Close button on the Windows Menu bar closes all open files *and* quits the application. To close open files *without* quitting, you have to manually close each file.

Closing the Application frame closes all open files.

Macintosh

Windows

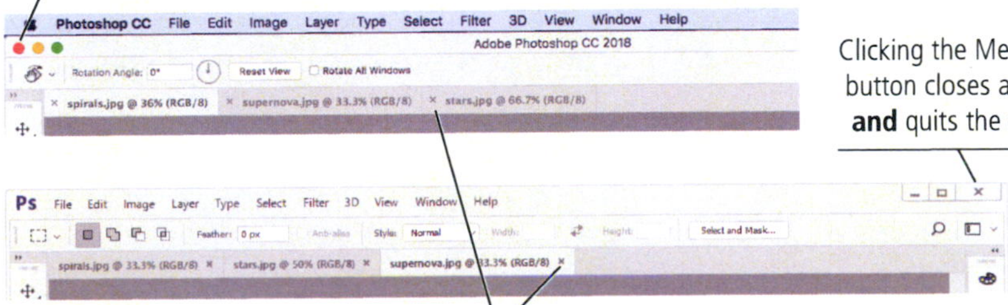

Clicking the Menu bar Close button closes all open files, **and** quits the application.

Click the Close buttons on each document tab to close individual files.

project 1

Music CD Artwork

You have been hired to create the artwork for a local band's new CD release. The final artwork will be used for an album sleeve, in CD cases, on digital music libraries, as well as in advertisements in a variety of printed media (newspapers, magazines, and so on).

This project incorporates the following skills:

- ❑ Creating a single composite ad from multiple supplied images
- ❑ Compositing multiple photographs, using various techniques to select the focal object in each image
- ❑ Incorporating vector graphics as rasterized layers and Smart Object layers
- ❑ Moving and transforming layer content in relation to the page and to each other
- ❑ Managing individual layout elements using layers and layer groups
- ❑ Saving multiple versions of a file to meet different output requirements

Project Meeting

client comments

Our new CD, Storm Front Conspiracy, kind of tells a story across the 11 tracks — the husband goes away on military service, the wife waits for him, he comes home but doesn't remember her, she looks for answers to his amnesia.

Our band is a combination of rock, country, and alternative/punk. We want the artwork for the new CD to be dramatic, to reflect both our personalities and the story we are telling.

We're actually releasing this first as a limited-edition album on vinyl; the sleeve for that version is 10″ square. We also need files for a standard-size printed CD insert, and for digital libraries like iTunes.

art director comments

The band loved the initial concept sketch I submitted last week, so we're ready to start building the files. In addition to the band's logo, I've gathered the photographs I want to use. I also already created a title treatment in Photoshop, so I'll send you that file as well.

The special edition LP will be 10″ square, but you need to incorporate 1/8″ bleed allowance and 1/4″ safe margin since the cover sleeve will be printed.

The 10″ file should be large enough for most print advertising applications, so we can just use the same file for those projects.

A standard CD insert is 4.75″ square; that version needs to incorporate 1/8″ bleeds as well, but it only needs 1/8″ safe margin according to our printer.

For digital media formats, we'll go with the current standards for iTunes music cover art. They require artwork to be at least 3000 × 3000 pixels, delivered as high-quality JPEG or PNG files. That format should be sufficient for most other online catalogs.

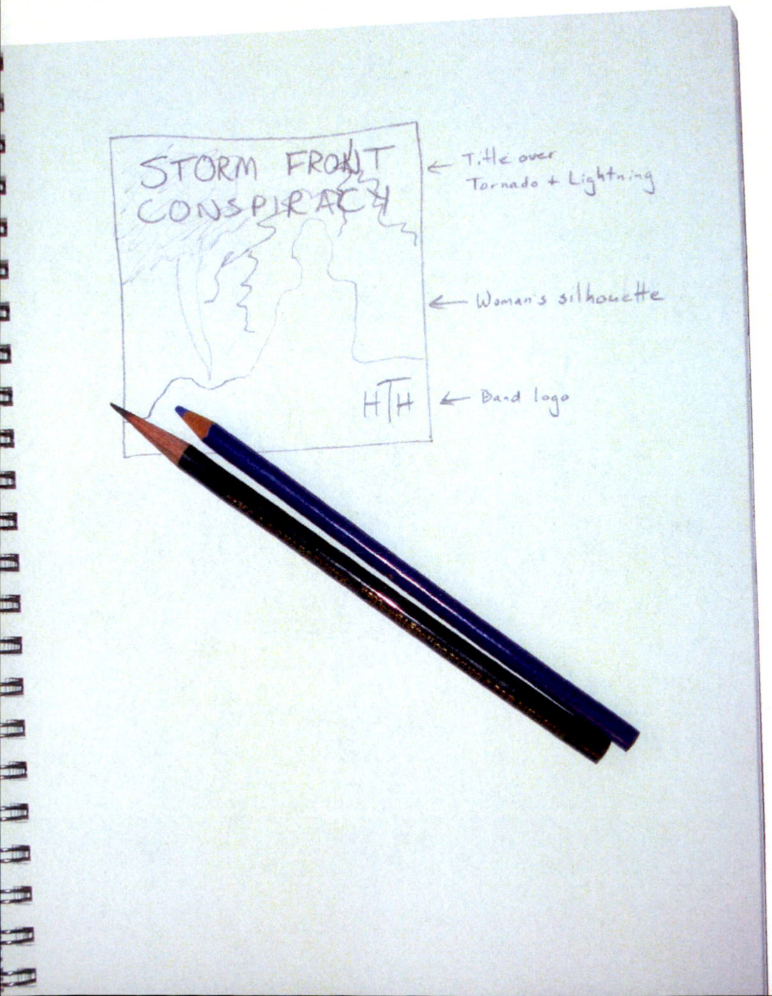

project objectives

To complete this project, you will:

- ❑ Resize a raster image to change resolution
- ❑ Composite multiple images into a single background file
- ❑ Incorporate both raster and vector elements into the same design
- ❑ Transform and arrange individual layers to create a cohesive design
- ❑ Create layer groups to easily manage related layer content
- ❑ Use selection techniques to isolate images from their backgrounds
- ❑ Save two different types of TIFF files for different ad requirements

Stage 1 Compositing Images and Artwork

Technically speaking, **compositing** is the process of combining any two or more objects (images, text, illustrations, etc.) into an overall design. When we talk about compositing in Photoshop, we're typically referring to the process of combining multiple images into a single cohesive image. Image compositing might be as simple as placing two images into different areas of a background file; or it could be as complex as placing a person into a group photo, carefully clipping out the individual's background, and adjusting the shadows to match the lighting in the group.

The ad you're building in this project requires compositing four digital photographs. You will also incorporate title treatment and logo files that were created in Adobe Illustrator by other members of your creative team. The various elements that make up the ad are fairly representative of the type of work you can (and probably will) create in Photoshop.

Types of Images

There are two primary types of digital artwork: vector graphics and raster images.

Vector graphics are composed of mathematical descriptions of a series of lines and shapes. Vector graphics are **resolution independent**; they can be freely enlarged or reduced, and they are automatically output at the resolution of the output device. The shapes that you create in Adobe InDesign, or in drawing applications such as Adobe Illustrator, are vector graphics.

Raster images, such as photographs, are made up of a grid of independent pixels (rasters or bits) in rows and columns (called a **bitmap**). Raster files are **resolution dependent** — their resolution is fixed, determined when you scan, photograph, or otherwise create the file. You can typically reduce raster images, but you cannot enlarge them without losing image quality.

Line art is actually a type of raster image that is made up entirely of 100% solid areas; the pixels in a line-art image have only two options: they can be all black or all white. Examples of line art are UPC bar codes or pen-and-ink drawings.

Screen Ruling

The file that you will be building in this project is intended to be placed in print magazines, so you have to build the new file with the appropriate settings for commercial printing. When reproducing a photograph on a printing press, the image must be converted into a set of printable dots that fool the eye into believing it sees continuous tones. Prior to image-editing software, pictures that were being prepared for printing on a press were photographed through a screen to create a grid of halftone dots. The result of this conversion is a halftone image; the dots used to simulate continuous tone are called **halftone dots**. Light tones in a photograph are represented as small halftone dots; dark tones become large halftone dots.

> *Note:*
>
> *Despite their origins in pre-digital print workflows, these terms persist in the digital environment.*

The screens used to create the halftone images had a finite number of available dots in a horizontal or vertical inch. That number was the **screen ruling**, or **lines per inch (lpi)** of the halftone. A screen ruling of 133 lpi means that in a square inch there are 133 × 133 (17,689) possible locations for a halftone dot. If the screen ruling is decreased, there are fewer total halftone dots, producing a grainier image; if the screen ruling is increased, there are more halftone dots, producing a clearer image.

Line screen is a finite number based on a combination of the intended output device and paper. You can't randomly select a line screen. Ask your printer what line screen will be used before you begin creating your images. If you can't find out ahead of time, or if you're unsure, follow these general guidelines:

- Newspaper or newsprint: 85–100 lpi
- Magazine or general commercial printing: 133–150 lpi
- Premium-quality-paper jobs (such as art books or annual reports): 150–175 lpi; some specialty jobs might use 200 lpi or more

Image Resolution

When a printer creates halftone dots, it calculates the average value of a group of pixels in the raster image and generates a spot of appropriate size. A raster image's resolution — measured in **pixels per inch (ppi)** — determines the quantity of pixel data the printer can read. Regardless of their source — camera, scanner, or files created in Photoshop — images need to have sufficient resolution so the output device can generate enough halftone dots to create the appearance of continuous tone. In the images above, the same raster image is reproduced at 72 ppi (left) and 300 ppi (right); notice the obvious degradation in quality in the 72-ppi version.

Ideally, the printer will have four pixels for each halftone dot created. In the image to the right, each white square represents a pixel. The highlighted area shows the pixel information used to generate a halftone dot. If an image only has 72 pixels per inch, the output device has to generate four halftone dots per pixel, resulting in poor printed quality.

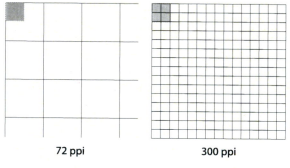

72 ppi

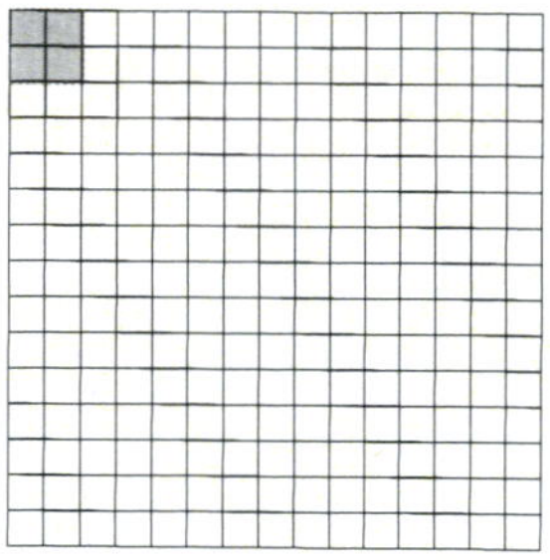

300 ppi

The relationship between pixels and halftone dots defines the rule of resolution for raster-based images — the resolution of a raster image (ppi) should be two times the screen ruling (lpi) that will be used for printing.

For line art, the general rule is to scan the image at the same resolution as the output device. Many laser printers and digital presses image at 600–1200 dots per inch (dpi); imagesetters used to make printing plates for a commercial press typically output at much higher resolution, possibly 2400 dpi or more.

Open and Resize an Image

Every raster image has a defined, specific resolution that is established when the image is created. If you scan an image to be 3″ high by 3″ wide at 150 ppi, that image has 450 pixels in each vertical column and 450 pixels in each horizontal row. Simply resizing the image stretches or compresses those pixels into a different physical space, but does not add or remove pixel information. If you resize the 3″ × 3″ image to 6″ × 6″ (200% of the original), the 450 pixels in each column or row are forced to extend across 6″ instead of 3″, causing a marked loss of quality.

The **effective resolution** of an image is the resolution calculated after any scaling is taken into account. This number is equally important as the original image resolution — and perhaps more so. The effective resolution can be calculated with a fairly simple equation:

Original resolution ÷ (% magnification ÷ 100) = Effective resolution

If a 300-ppi image is magnified 150%, the effective resolution is:

300 ppi ÷ 1.5 = 200 ppi

In other words, the more you enlarge a raster image, the lower its effective resolution becomes. In general, you can make an image 10% or 15% larger without significant adverse effects; the more you enlarge an image, however, the worse the results. Even Photoshop, which offers very sophisticated formulas (called "algorithms") for sizing images, cannot guarantee perfect results.

Effective resolution can be a very important consideration when working with client-supplied images, especially those that come from consumer-level digital cameras. Many of those devices capture images with a specific number of pixels rather than a number of pixels per inch (ppi). In this exercise, you will explore the effective resolution of an image to see if it can be used for a full-page printed magazine ad.

1. **Download `Music_PS18_RF.zip` from the Student Files web page.**

2. **Expand the ZIP archive in your WIP folder (Macintosh) or copy the archive contents into your WIP folder (Windows).**

   This results in a folder named **Music**, which contains all of the files you need for this project. You should also use this folder to save the files you create in this project.

   If necessary, refer to Page 1 of the Interface chapter for specific information on expanding or accessing the required resource files.

3. **Choose File>Open and navigate to your WIP>Music folder. Select `Sunrise.jpg` and click Open.**

4. **If the rulers are not visible on the top and left edges, choose View>Rulers (or press Command/Control-R).**

   As you can see in the rulers, this image has a very large physical size.

Rulers display values in the default units of measurement.

5. **Choose Image>Image Size.**

   The Image Size dialog box shows the number of pixels in the image, as well as the image dimensions and current resolution. You can change any value in this dialog box, but you should understand what those changes mean before you do so.

   As you can see, this image is approximately 69″ wide and 46″ high, but it was captured at 72 pixels/inch. For most commercial printing, you need at least 300 ppi. You can use the principle of effective resolution to change the file to a high enough resolution for printing.

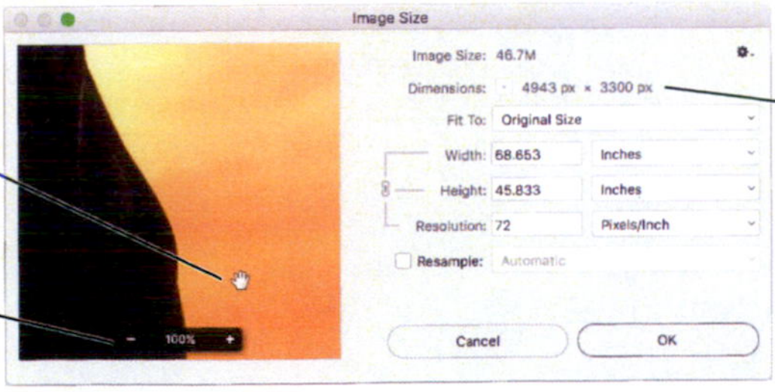

Click and drag in the preview window to show a different area.

Use this widget to change the preview percentage.

The actual number of pixels in the image is the most important information.

Note:

We are intentionally overlooking issues of color space for the sake of this project. You will learn about color spaces and color management in Project 3: Museum Image Correction.

Note:

You can change the default unit of measurement in the Units & Rulers pane of the Preferences dialog box. Double-clicking either ruler opens the appropriate pane of the Preferences dialog box.

Note:

Press Command-Option-I/Control-Alt-I to open the Image Size dialog box.

6. **Check the Resample option at the bottom of the dialog box (if necessary).**

The options in this dialog box remember the last-used choices. The Resample option might already be checked in your dialog box.

Resampling means maintaining the existing resolution in the new image dimensions; in other words, you are either adding or deleting pixels to the existing image. When this option is turned on, you can change the dimensions of an image without affecting the resolution, or you can change the resolution of an image (useful for removing excess resolution or **downsampling**) without affecting the image size.

Note:

When the Resample option is checked, you can use the attached menu to tell Photoshop how to generate extra pixel data when increasing the image size, or which pixels to discard when reducing the image size. Each option also includes a parenthetical notation about when it is best used (enlargement, smooth gradients, etc.).

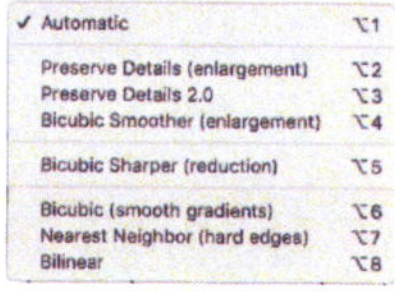

7. **Change the Resolution field to 300 pixels/inch.**

When you change the resolution with resampling turned on, you do not change the file's physical size. To achieve 300-ppi resolution at the new size, Photoshop needs to add a huge number of pixels to the image. You can see at the top of the dialog box that this change would increase the total number of pixels from 4943 × 3300 to 20596 × 13750.

You can also see that changing the resolution of an image without affecting its physical dimensions would have a significant impact on the file size. Changing the resolution to 300 ppi at the current size would increase the file size to over 810 megabytes.

When Resample is checked, changing the Resolution value adds or removes pixels.

Higher resolution means larger file sizes, which translates to longer processing time for printing or longer download time over the Internet. When you scale an image to a smaller size, simply resizing can produce files with far greater effective resolution than you need. Resampling allows you to reduce physical size without increasing the resolution, resulting in a smaller file size.

The caveat is that once you discard (delete) pixels, they are gone. If you later try to re-enlarge the smaller image, you will not achieve the same quality as the original (before it was reduced). You should save reduced images as copies instead of overwriting the originals.

8. **Press Option/Alt and click the Reset button to restore the original image dimensions in the dialog box.**

In many Photoshop dialog boxes, pressing the Option/Alt key changes the Cancel button to Reset. You can click the Reset button to restore the original values that existed when you opened the dialog box.

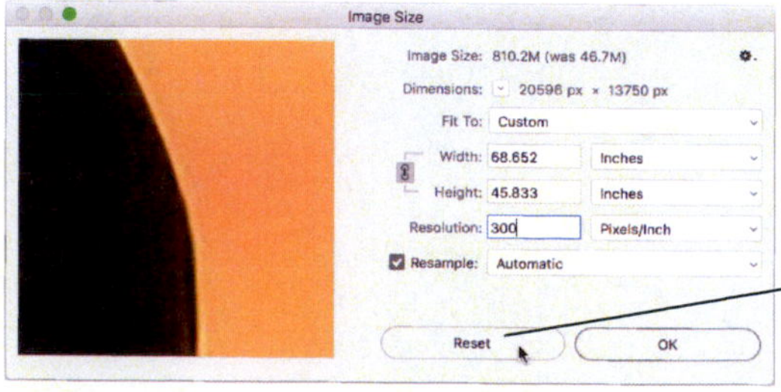

Pressing Option/Alt changes the Cancel button to Reset.

9. **Uncheck the Resample option at the bottom of the dialog box.**

10. **Change the Resolution field to 300 pixels/inch.**

Resizing *without* resampling basically means distributing the same number of pixels over a different amount of physical space. When you resize an image without resampling, you do not change the number of pixels in the image. (In fact, those fields in the dialog box become simple text; the fields are unavailable and you cannot change the number of pixels in the image.)

You can see how changing one of the linked fields (Resolution) directly affects the other linked fields (Width and Height). By resizing the image to be 300 ppi — enough for commercial print quality — you now have an image that is approximately 16.5″ × 11″.

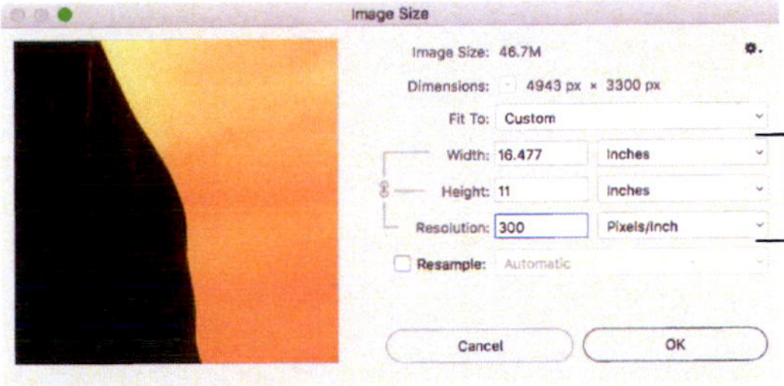

When the Resample option is unchecked, these three fields are all linked.

Note:

Although many magazines are printed at 133 lpi, some are printed at 150 lpi. By setting the resolution to 300, your file will work for any magazine that prints at 133 or 150 lpi.

11. **Click OK to apply the change and return to the document window.**

The rulers change to reflect the new dimensions of the file.

Because you did not resample the image, the screen display does not change.

12. **Choose File>Save As. If necessary, navigate to your WIP>Music folder as the target location. Change the file name (in the Save As/File Name field) to cd-artwork.**

Since this is a basic image file with only one layer (so far), most of the other options in the Save As dialog box are grayed out (not available).

13. **Choose Photoshop in the Format/Save As Type menu and then click Save.**

You can save a Photoshop file in a number of different formats, all of which have specific capabilities, limitations, and purposes. While you are still working on a file, it's best to keep it as a native Photoshop (PSD) file. When you choose a different format, the correct extension is automatically added to the file name.

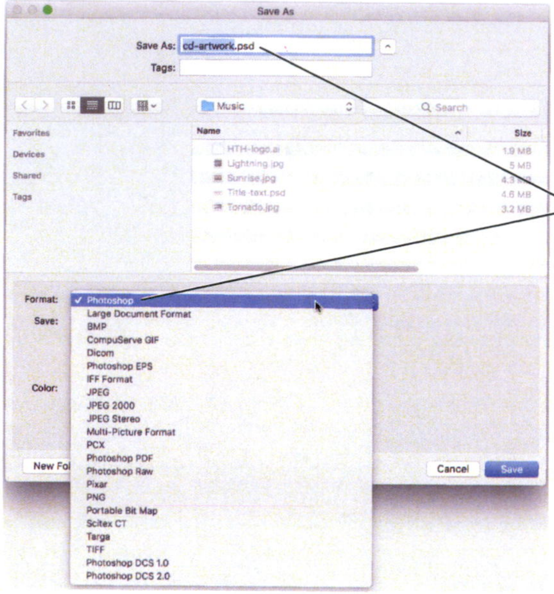

Files saved in the native Photoshop format display a ".psd" extension.

> ***Note:***
>
> *Also called "native", the PSD format is the most flexible format to use while building files in Photoshop.*

14. **Continue to the next exercise.**

Crop the Canvas and Place Ruler Guides

The final step in preparing the workspace is defining the live area of the page. **Trim size** is the actual size of a page once it has been cut out of the press sheet. According to your client, the final required has a trim size of 10″ × 10″.

Any elements that print right to the edge of a page (called **bleeding**) must actually extend beyond the defined trim size. The **bleed allowance** is the amount of extra space that should be included for these bleed objects; most applications require at least 1/8″ bleed allowance on any bleed edge.

Because of inherent variation in the mechanical printing and trimming processes, most printing projects also define a safe or **live area**; all important design elements — especially text — should stay within this live area. The live area for this project is 9.5″ × 9.5″ (leaving a 0.25″ safe margin on each edge of the artwork).

> ***Note:***
>
> *You should familiarize yourself with the most common fraction-to-decimal equivalents:*
>
> *1/8 = 0.125*
>
> *1/4 = 0.25*
>
> *3/8 = 0.375*
>
> *1/2 = 0.5*
>
> *5/8 = 0.625*
>
> *3/4 = 0.75*
>
> *7/8 = 0.875*

1. **With `cd-artwork.psd` open, choose the Crop tool in the Tools panel.**

When you choose the Crop tool, a crop marquee appears around the edges of the image. The marquee has eight handles, which you can drag to change the size of the crop area.

Crop tool

Marquee handles allow you to resize the crop area before finalizing the crop.

Understanding File Saving Preferences

You can control a number of options related to saving files in the File Handling pane of the Preferences dialog box.

Image Previews. You can use this menu to always or never include image thumbnails in the saved file. If you choose Ask When Saving in this menu, the Save As dialog box includes an option to include the preview/thumbnail.

On Macintosh, you have an additional option to include a thumbnail in the saved file. If checked, the image thumbnail appears in dialog boxes instead of the Photoshop file icon.

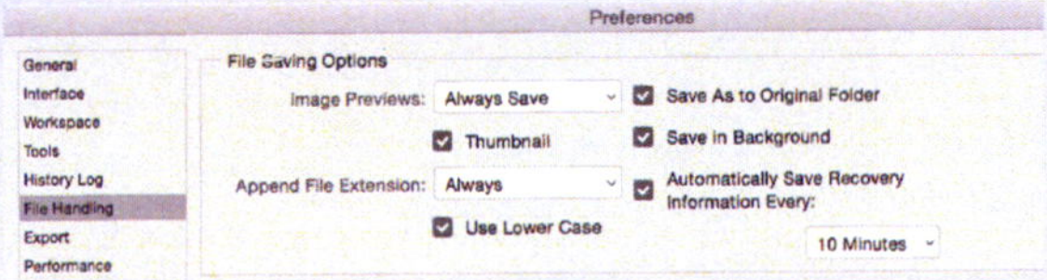

Macintosh

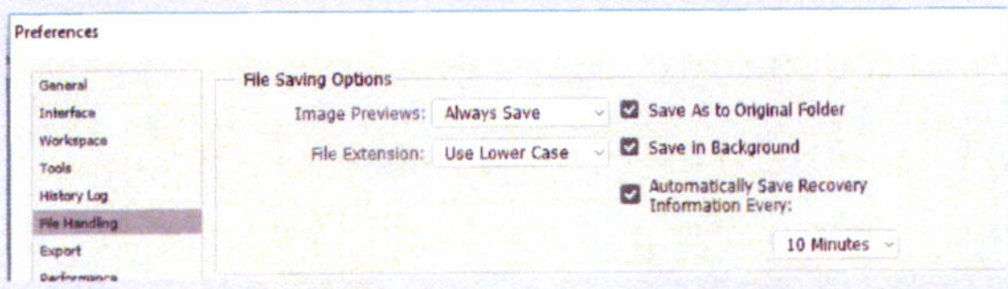

Windows

Append File Extension. On Macintosh, you can use this menu to always or never include the file extension in the saved file. If the Ask When Saving option is selected in this menu, the Save As dialog box includes options to append the file extension (in lower case or not).

On Windows, file extensions are always added to saved files; this preference menu has only two options: Use Upper Case and Use Lower Case.

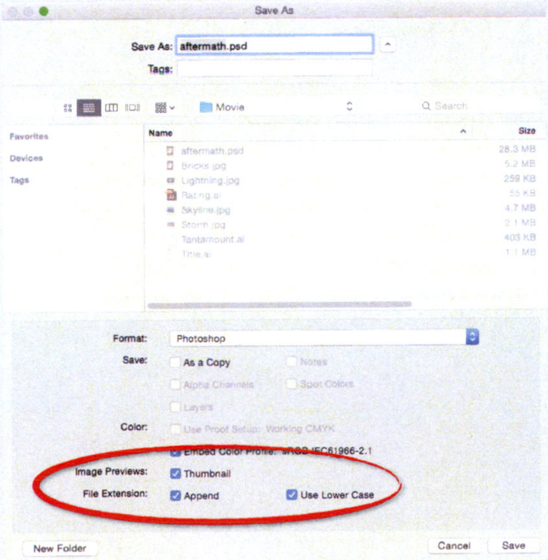

Save As to Original Folder. When this option is checked, choosing File>Save As automatically defaults to the location where the original file is located.

Save in Background. The Save process occurs by default in the background; in other words, you can continue working even while a file is being saved. Especially when you work with large files, this can be a significant time saver because you don't have to sit and wait the several minutes it might take to save a very large file. (The only thing you can't do while a file is being saved is use the Save As command; if you try, you will see a warning advising you to wait until the background save is complete.)

When a file is being saved in the background, the completed percentage appears in the document tab.

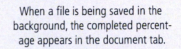

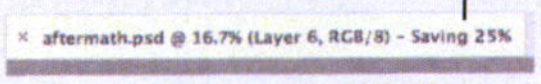

Automatically Save Recovery Information Every... When checked, this option means that your work is saved in a temporary file, every 10 minutes by default; if something happens — such as a power outage — you will be able to restore your work back to the last auto-saved version. In other words, the most you will lose is 10 minutes' work!

2. **In the Options bar, make sure the Delete Cropped Pixels option is checked.**

   When this option is checked, areas outside the cropped areas are permanently removed from all layers in the file. If this option is not checked, cropped pixels remain in the file, but exist outside the edges of the file canvas; the Background layer, if one exists, is converted to a regular layer (you'll learn more about Background layers later in this project).

   This is an important distinction — by maintaining cropped pixels, you can later transform or reposition layers to reveal different parts of the layer within the newly cropped canvas size.

Note:

You can press the Escape key to cancel the crop marquee and return to the uncropped image.

Note:

You can rotate a crop marquee by placing the cursor slightly away from a corner handle.

3. **Click the right-center handle of the crop marquee and drag left until the cursor feedback shows W: 10.250 in.**

   When you drag certain elements in the document window, live cursor feedback (also called "heads-up display") shows information about the transformation. When dragging a side crop marquee handle, for example, the feedback shows the new width of the area.

   You might need to zoom into at least 33.3% or 66.67% view percentage to achieve the exact dimensions needed for this project.

Use the cursor feedback to find the appropriate measurement.

Click and drag the marquee handle to resize the marquee area.

4. **Repeat Step 3 with the top-center handle until feedback shows the area of H: 10.250 in.**

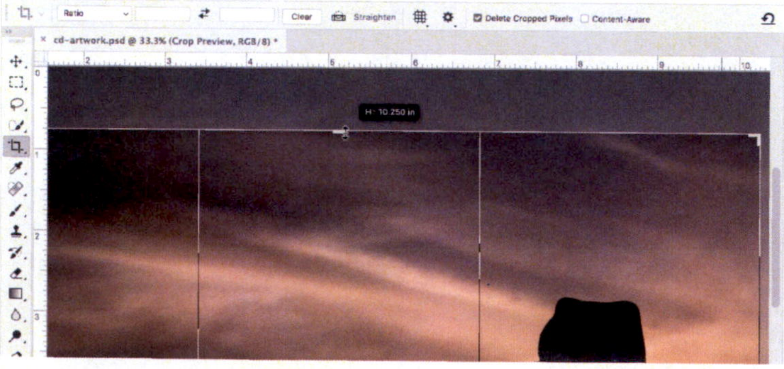

Note:

It might be helpful to toggle off the Snap feature (View>Snap), which causes certain file elements to act as magnets when you move a marquee or drag a selection.

   Remember, the defined trim size for this ad is 10″ × 10″. Anything that runs to the page edge has to incorporate a 0.125″ bleed allowance, so the actual canvas size must be large enough to accommodate the bleed allowance on all edges:

   [Width] 10″ + 0.125″ + 0.125″ = 10.25″

   [Height] 10-″ + 0.125″ + 0.125″ = 10.25″

5. **Zoom out until you can see the entire canvas in the document window.**

6. **Click inside the crop area and drag to reposition the image so that the woman's silhouette is on the left side of the crop area (use the following image as a guide).**

   When you change the size of the marquee, the area outside the marquee is "shielded" by a darkened overlay so you can get an idea of what will remain after you finalize the crop.

   You can drag the image inside the crop area to change the portion that will remain in the cropped image. By default, the crop area remains centered in the document window; instead, the image moves behind the crop area.

Note:

You can also use the Arrow keys on your keyboard to "nudge" the image in a specific direction.

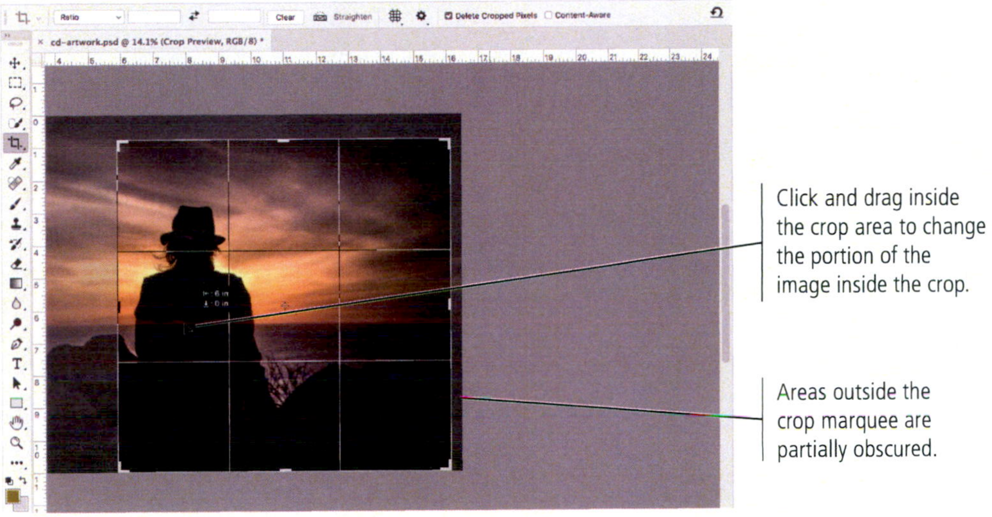

7. **Press Return/Enter to finalize the crop.**

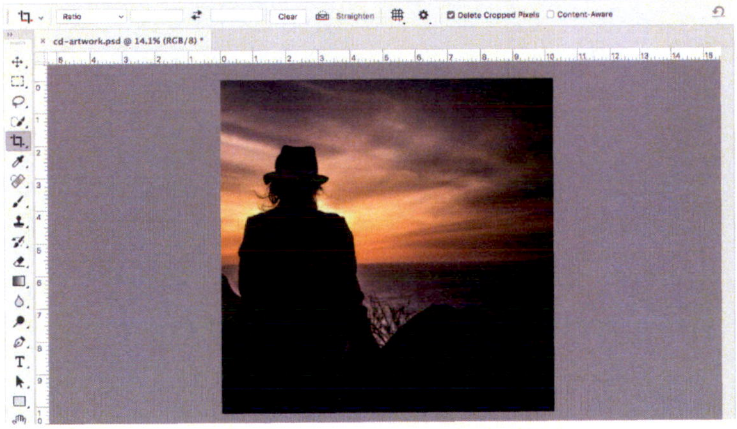

Note:

The X coordinate refers to an object's horizontal position and Y refers to the vertical position.

8. **Choose View>New Guide Layout.**

This dialog box makes it very easy to define a page grid using non-printing guides. The dialog box defaults to add 8 columns with a 20-pixel (0.067 in) gutter. In the document window, you can see the guides (blue lines) that will be created based on the active settings in the New Guide Layout dialog box.

9. **Uncheck the Columns option and check the Margin option. Type `0.125` in each of the available margin fields.**

You can use the Margin fields to place guides at specific distances from each edge of the canvas. You don't need to type the unit of measurement because the default unit for this file is already inches. Photoshop automatically assumes the value you type is in the default unit of measurement.

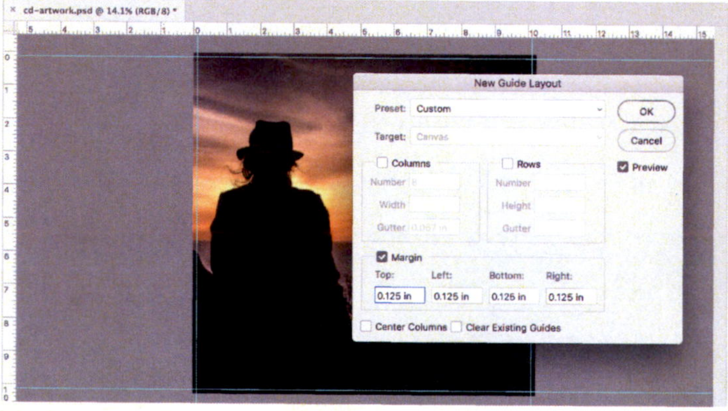

10. **Click OK to return to the document and add the required margin guides.**

At this point you should have four guides – two vertical and two horizontal, each 1/8″ from the file edges. These mark the trim size of your final 10″ × 10″ file.

11. **Choose View>100%.**

It helps to zoom in to a higher view percentage if you want to precisely place guides. To complete the following steps accurately, we found it necessary to use at least 100% view.

12. **In the top-left corner of the document window, click the zero-point crosshairs and drag to the top-left intersection of the guides.**

You can reposition the zero point to the top-left corner of the bleed allowance by double-clicking the zero-point crosshairs.

Zero-point crosshairs
Drag to here to change the 0/0 point of the rulers.
This new zero point will be the origin for measurments.

13. **Choose the Move tool, and then open the Info panel (Window>Info).**

As we explained in the Interface chapter, the panels you see depend on what was done the last time you (or someone else) used the Photoshop application. Because workspace arrangement is such a personal preference, we tell you what panels you need to use, but we don't tell you where to put them.

Remember, for this file, the live area should be 0.25" inset from the trim edge. In the next few steps you will add guides to identify that live area.

14. **Click the horizontal page ruler at the top of the page and drag down to create a guide positioned at the 1/4" (0.25") mark.**

If you watch the vertical ruler, you can see a marker indicating the position of the cursor. In addition to the live cursor feedback, the Info panel also shows the precise numeric position of the guide you are dragging.

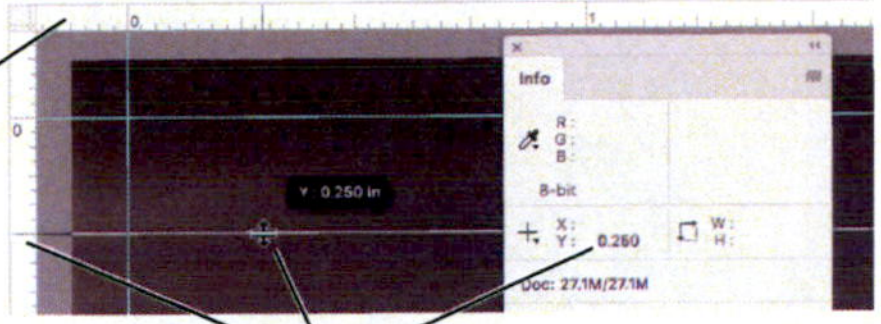

Click and drag from the horizontal ruler to add a horizontal guide.

Watch the ruler, cursor feedback, or Info panel to see the location of the guide you're dragging.

15. **Click the vertical ruler at the left and drag right to place a guide at the 0.25" mark.**

Watch the marker on the horizontal ruler to judge the guide's position.

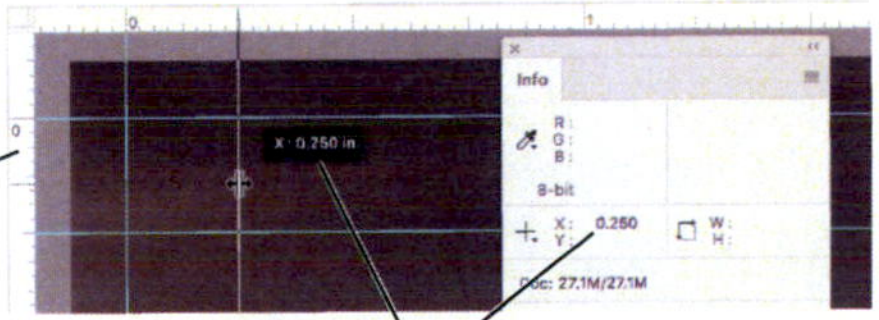

Drag from the vertical ruler to add a vertical guide.

The cursor feedback and Info panel show the exact X location of the guide you're dragging.

16. **Double-click the intersection of the two rulers.**

This resets the file's zero point to the original position (the top-left corner of the canvas).

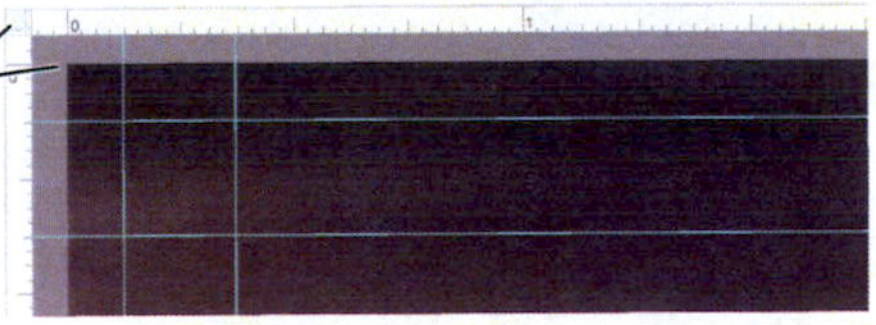

Double-click the ruler intersection to reset the original zero point.

17. **Zoom out so you can see the entire canvas in the document window.**

Note:

Use the Move tool to reposition placed guides. Remove individual guides by dragging them back onto the ruler.

If you try to reposition a guide and can't, choose View>Lock Guides. If this option is checked, guides are locked; you can't move them until you toggle this option off.

Note:

Press Option/Alt and click a guide to change it from vertical to horizontal (or vice versa). The guide rotates around the point where you click, which can be useful if you need to find a corner based on the position of an existing guide.

Note:

You can press Command/Control-; to toggle the visibility of page guides.

18. **Choose View>New Guide. In the resulting dialog box, choose the Horizontal option and type 9.875 in the field and click OK.**

This dialog box always measures the position of guides from the canvas's top-left corner, regardless of the zero point as reflected in the rulers.

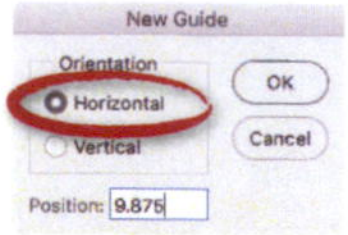

19. **Choose View>New Guide again. Choose the Vertical option and type 9.875 in the field. Click OK.**

20. **Click the View menu and make sure a checkmark appears to the left of Lock Guides. If no checkmark is there, choose Lock Guides to toggle on that option.**

After you carefully position specific guides, it's a good idea to lock them so you don't accidentally move or delete them later. If you need to move a guide at any point, simply choose View>Lock Guides to toggle off the option temporarily.

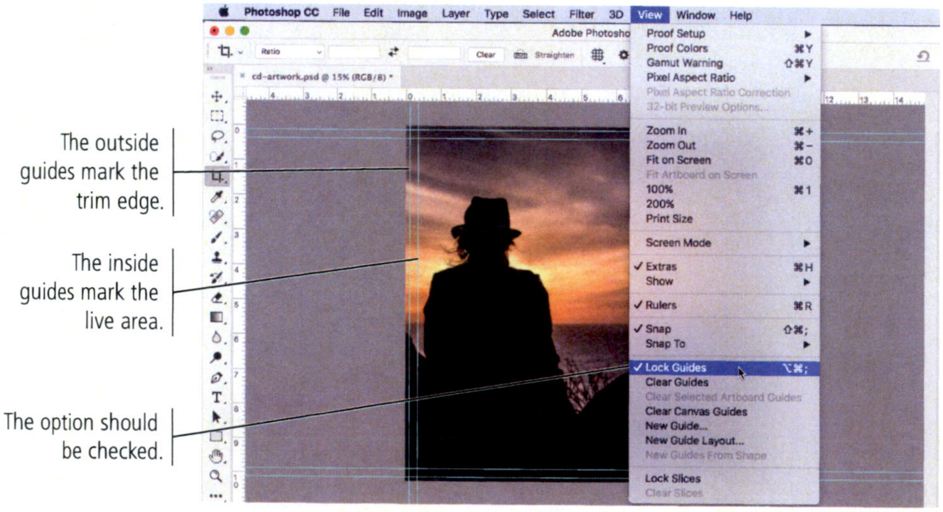

21. **Save the file and continue to the next exercise.**

Because you have already saved this working file with a new name, you can simply choose File>Save, or press Command/Control-S to save without opening a dialog box. If you want to change the file name, you can always choose File>Save As.

The Crop Tools in Depth

When the Crop tool is selected, the Options bar can be used to define a number of settings related to the cropped area.

The left menu includes a number of common aspect ratio presets. If you choose one of these, the crop marquee is constrained to the selected aspect ratio. It's important to note that these presets define only the aspect ratio of the crop, not the actual size.

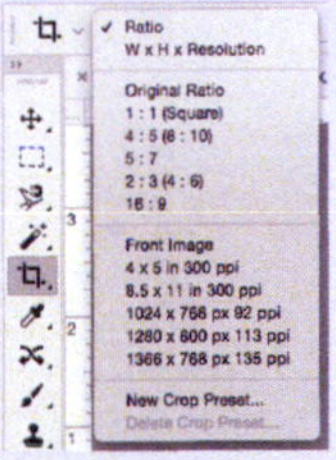

You can also choose the **W x H x Resolution** option to define custom settings for the result of a crop. For example, if you define the width and height of a crop area as 9″ × 9″ at 300 ppi, when you click and drag to draw, the crop area will be restricted to the same proportions defined in the Width and Height fields (in this example, 1:1).

When you finalize the crop, the resulting image will be resized to be 9″ × 9″, regardless of the actual size of the crop marquee. This presents a problem if you remember the principles of resolution.

Enlarging a 3″ × 3″ area (for example) to 9″ × 9″ means the application needs to create enough pixels to fill in the 6 extra inches — at 300 ppi, Photoshop needs to create ("interpolate") more than 1800 pixels per linear inch. Although Photoshop can enlarge images with reasonable success, such a significant amount of new data will not result in the best possible quality. As a general rule, you should avoid enlarging raster images by such a large percentage.

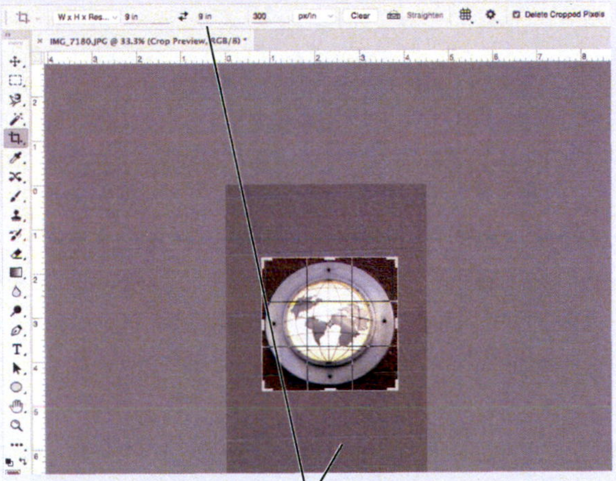

The crop area is constrained to the aspect ratio of the defined width and height.

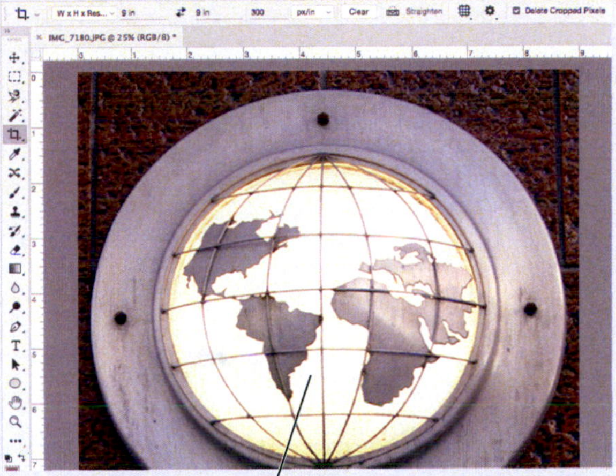

The resulting cropped image is the actual size defined in the Crop Image Size & Resolution dialog box.

You can use the **Set Overlay Options** menu (⊞) to show a variety of overlays within the crop area; these follow basic design principles, such as the Rule of Thirds and the Golden Spiral.

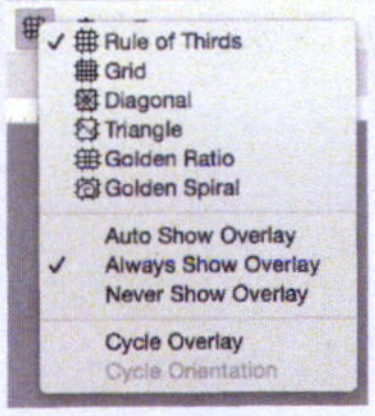

You can also use the commands in this menu to turn the overlay on or off. If you choose Auto Show Overlay, the selected overlay only appears when you drag the marquee handles or click inside the marquee area to move the image inside the crop area.

You can also click the **Set Additional Crop Options** button (⚙) to access a variety of crop-related choices.

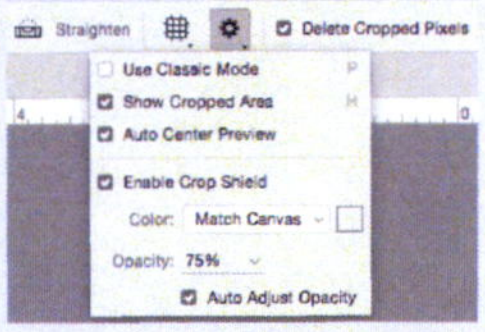

- If you check the **Use Classic Mode** option, the crop marquee reverts to the same appearance and behavior as in previous versions of Photoshop.
- When **Show Cropped Area** is checked, the area outside the crop marquee remains visible in the document window until you finalize the crop.
- When **Auto Center Preview** is checked, the crop area will always be centered in the document window; the image dynamically moves in the document window as you resize the crop area.
- When **Enable Crop Shield** is checked, areas outside the crop marquee are partially obscured by a semi-transparent solid color. You can use the related options to change the color and opacity of the shielded area.

The Crop Tools in Depth (continued)

When the Crop tool is selected, you can click the **Straighten** button in the Options bar and then draw a line in the image to define what should be a straight line in the resulting image. The image behind the crop marquee rotates to show what will remain in the cropped canvas; the line you drew is adjusted to be perfectly horizontal or vertical.

Click the Straighten button, then draw a line representing what you want to be "straight" in the cropped image.

The image is rotated behind the crop marquee to be "straight" based on the line you drew.

You can draw a crop area larger than the existing canvas to effectively enlarge the canvas. Using the default settings, the new areas outside the original canvas size become transparent on regular layers, or are filled with the defined background color on the locked Background layer.

If you check the **Content-Aware** option in the Options bar, Photoshop generates new pixels based on the existing image, filling the new pixels with content that better matches the previous image edges.

Drag the crop area handles larger than the existing image to enlarge the canvas.

New areas on the Background layer are filled with the defined background color.

New areas on the Background layer are filled with content generated to better match the existing image pixels.

The **Perspective Crop tool** (nested under the Crop tool) can be used to draw a non-rectangular crop area. To define the area you want to keep, simply click to place the four corners of the area, then drag the corners in any direction as necessary. When you finalize the crop, the image inside the crop area is straightened to a front-on viewing angle. You should use this option with care, however, because it can badly distort an image.

In the following example, we used apparent lines in the photograph to draw the perspective crop marquee.
After finalizing the crop, the building appears to be straight rather than the original viewing angle at which it was photographed. (Be careful using this tool, however, as it can result in obvious distortion.)

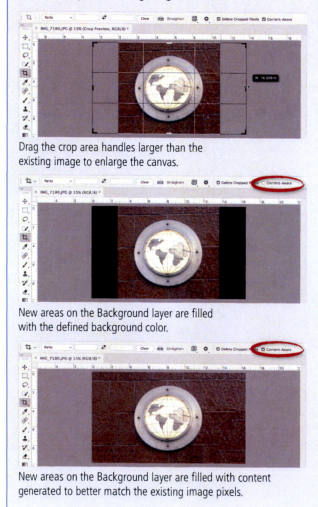

Copy and Paste Selected Pixels

Like many processes in Photoshop — especially one as common as compositing multiple images into a single file — there are many different possible methods for compositing multiple images into a single file. In this exercise, you will use the most basic selection tool — the Rectangle Marquee tool.

Note:

When you created the background file for this project, you created a raster image that contains pixels. Digital photographs and scans are also pixel-based, which is why you use Photoshop to edit and manipulate those types of files.

1. **With `cd-artwork.psd` open, choose View>Fit on Screen to show the entire image centered in the document window.**

2. **Open the file `Tornado.jpg` from your WIP>Music folder.**

   If you see a profile mismatch warning when opening the files for this project, choose the option to use the embedded profile. Color management will be explained in Project 3: Museum Image Correction.

3. **With Tornado.jpg the active file in the document window, open the Image Size dialog box (Image>Image Size).**

   This image is only 150 ppi, but it has a physical size much larger than the defined size for the CD artwork. As with the original image, the principle of effective resolution might make this image usable in the composite ad.

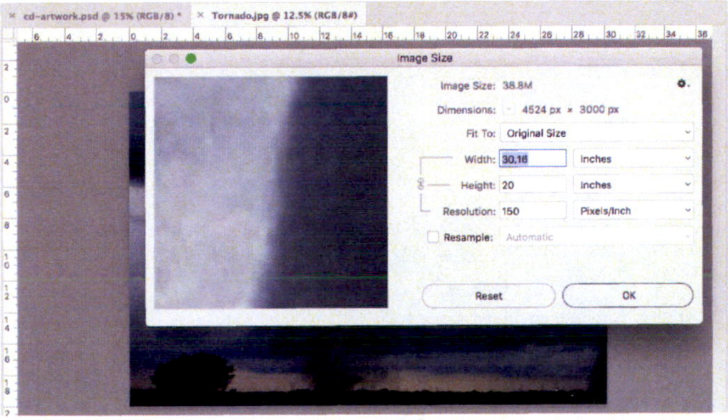

Note:

You can press Command-Option-I/Control-Alt-I to open the Image Size dialog box.

4. **Click Cancel to close the Image Size dialog box.**

5. **Choose the Rectangular Marquee tool in the Tools panel and review the options in the Options bar.**

   By default, dragging with a marquee tool creates a new selection. You can use the buttons on the left end of the Options bar to define what happens if you draw more than one marquee.

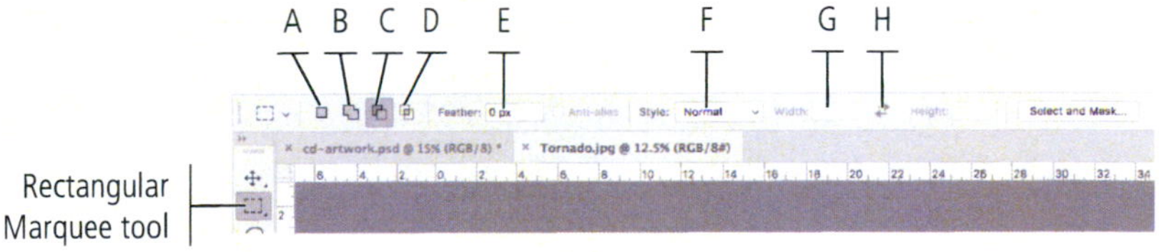

   A. New Selection creates a new selection each time you create a new marquee.
   B. Add to Selection adds the area of a new marquee to the existing selected area.
   C. Subtract from Selection removes the area of a new marquee from the existing selection.
   D. Intersect with Selection results in a selection only where a new marquee overlaps an existing selection.
   E. Feather (soften) the edges of a selection by a specified number of pixels.
   F. Choose a normal selection, a fixed-ratio selection, or a fixed-size selection.
   G. When Fixed Ratio or Fixed Size is selected, enter the size of the selection in the Width and Height fields.
   H. Click this button to reverse the Width and Height fields.

6. **Choose the New Selection option in the Options bar. Click outside of the top-left corner, drag down past the bottom edge of the image, and drag right to create a selection area that is approximately 20.5″ wide.**

   You can't select an area larger than the current canvas, so the top, left, and bottom edges of the selection snap to the canvas edges. The live cursor feedback, as well as the mark on the horizontal ruler, help to determine the selection area's width.

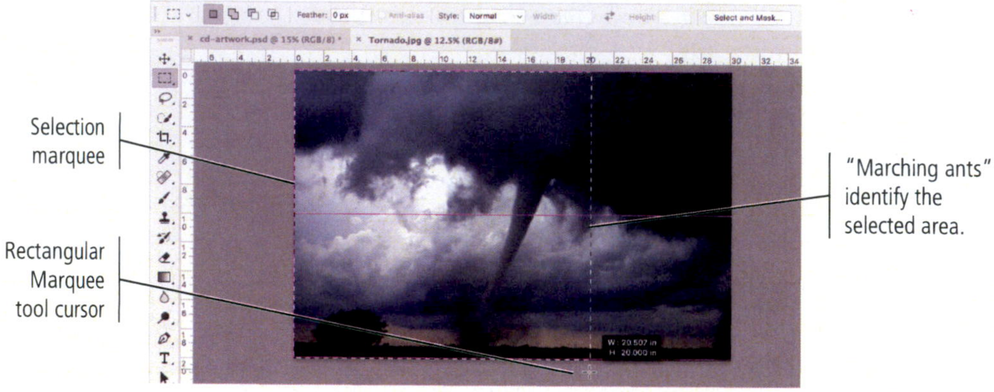

> *Note:*
>
> *Press Shift while dragging a new marquee to constrain the selection to a square (using the Rectangular Marquee tool) or circle (using the Elliptical Marquee tool).*

7. **In the Options bar, choose the Subtract from Selection option.**

8. **Click outside the top-left corner of the image, drag down and right to create a selection area that is wider than the original selection area and approximately 2″ high.**

> *Note:*
>
> *Command/Control-clicking a layer thumbnail results in a selection around the contents of that layer.*

Subtract from Selection is active.
The cursor shows a minus sign because you are subtracting from the existing selection.
Click here...
...and drag to here.

   When you release the mouse button, the area you drew in this step is removed from the original selection area:

> *Note:*
>
> *When the New Selection option is active, you can move a selection marquee by clicking inside the selected area with the Marquee tool and dragging to the desired area of the image.*
>
> *The live cursor feedback shows how far you have moved the area. The pink horizontal lines that appear as you drag are smart guides, which help you to reposition objects (including selection marquees) relative to other objects or to the canvas.*

9. **Choose Edit>Copy.**

The standard Cut, Copy, and Paste options are available in Photoshop, just as they are in most applications. Whatever you have selected will be copied to the Clipboard, and whatever is in the Clipboard will be pasted.

10. **Click the Close button on the Tornado.jpg document tab to close that file.**

11. **With the cd-artwork.psd file active, choose Edit>Paste.**

The copied selection is pasted in the center of the document window. If you remember from the Image Size dialog box, the tornado image was approximately 30″ × 20″ at 150 ppi. Photoshop cannot maintain multiple resolutions in a single file. When you paste the copied content into the cd-artwork file, it adopts the resolution of the target file (in this case, 300 ppi). The concept of effective resolution transforms the selected area (20.5″ × 18″) of the tornado image to approximately 10.25″ × 9″ at 300 ppi.

12. **Open the Layers panel (Window>Layers).**

The original cd-artwork.psd file had only one layer — Background. When you copy or drag content from one file into another, it is automatically placed on a new layer with the default name "Layer *n*", where "n" is a sequential number.

The document tab shows the name of the active layer.

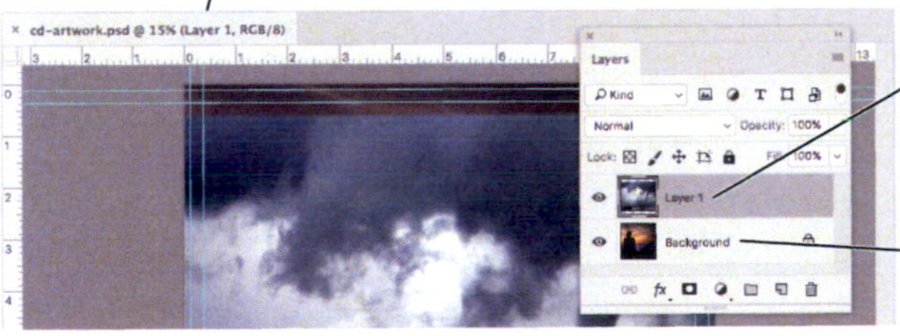

A new layer (Layer 1) is added to contain the contents that you pasted from the Tornado.jpg file.

The Background layer contains the original Sunrise.jpg file content.

13. **Choose File>Save, and read the resulting message.**

Because this is the first time you have saved the file after adding new layers, you should see the Photoshop Format Options dialog box with the Maximize Compatibility check box already activated. It's a good idea to leave this check box selected so that your files will be compatible with other Adobe applications and other versions of Photoshop.

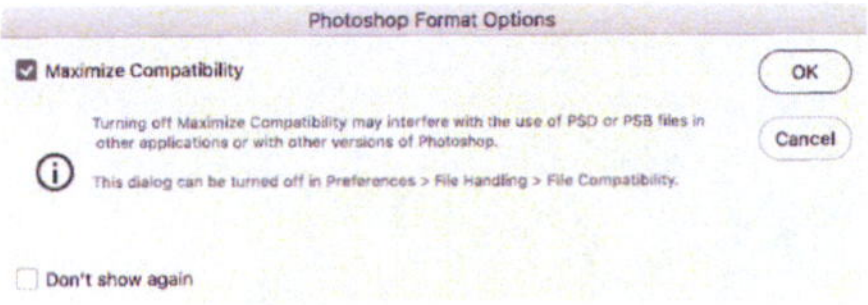

14. **Make sure the Maximize Compatibility check box is selected and click OK, then continue to the next exercise.**

Note:

If you want to move a marquee, make sure the Marquee tool is still selected. If the Move tool is active, clicking inside the marquee and dragging will actually move the contents within the selection area.

Note:

When creating a new selection with a marquee tool, pressing Option/Alt places the center of the selection marquee at the point where you click; when you drag out, the marquee is created around that point.

Note:

When the New Selection option is active, press Shift to add to the current selection or press Option/Alt to subtract from the current selection.

Note:

If you don't see this warning, check the File Handling pane of the Preferences dialog box. You can set the Maximize PSD and PSB File Compatibility menu to Always, Never, or Ask.

Create a Feathered Selection

The Marquee tool you used in the previous exercise created a basic rectangular selection. The basic Lasso tool works like a pencil, following the path where you drag the mouse; you will use that method in this exercise.

1. **With `cd-artwork.psd` open, open `Lightning.jpg` from your WIP>Music folder.**

2. **Choose the Lasso tool in the Tools panel. In the Control panel, choose the New Selection option.**

   Most options in the Control panel are the same for the Lasso tool as they are for the Marquee tools.

3. **Click at the top edge of the canvas, just to the left of the lightning bolt. Hold down the mouse button and drag around the general lightning shape in the image. Keep the following points in mind as you drag:**

   - **Avoid dragging past the bottom edge of the canvas.**
   - **Drag past the right image edge and up to the top of the image.**

     When you drag past the image edge, the marquee follows the image edge instead of the actual cursor position.

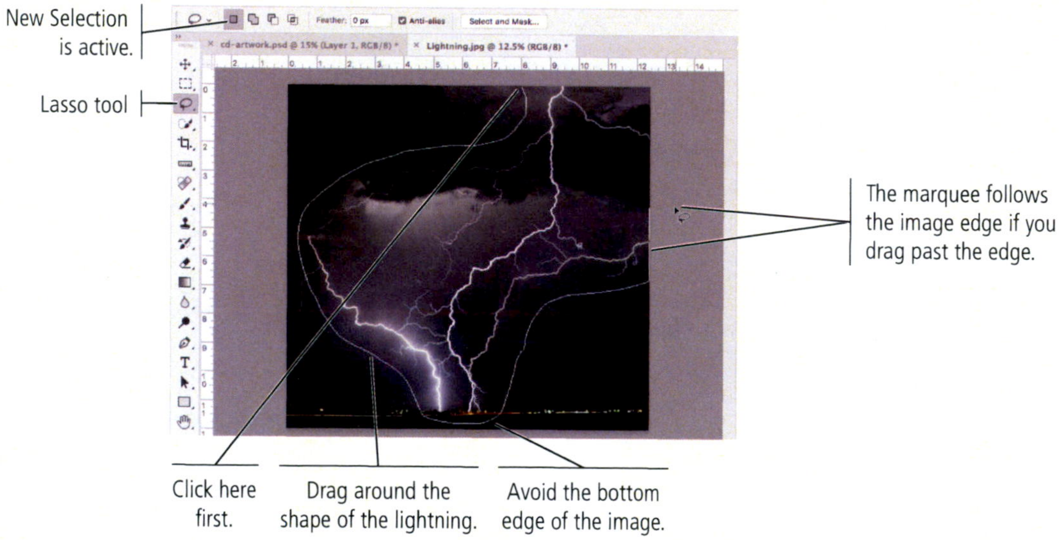

4. **Release the mouse button.**

   When you release the mouse button, the software automatically connects the first point you clicked with the last location of the mouse cursor with a straight line.

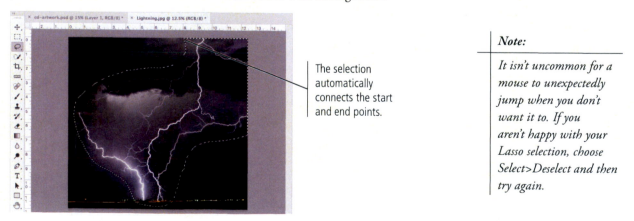

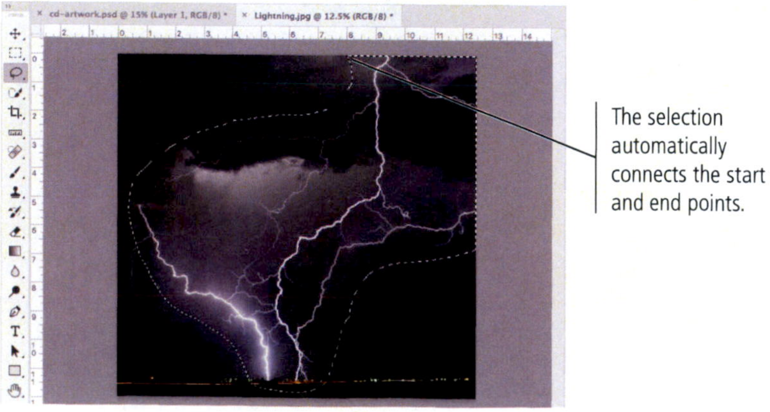

The selection automatically connects the start and end points.

Note:

It isn't uncommon for a mouse to unexpectedly jump when you don't want it to. If you aren't happy with your Lasso selection, choose Select>Deselect and then try again.

5. **With the marching ants active, choose Select>Modify>Feather.**

Photoshop offers a number of options for modifying an exiting selection marquee. In the Select>Modify menu:

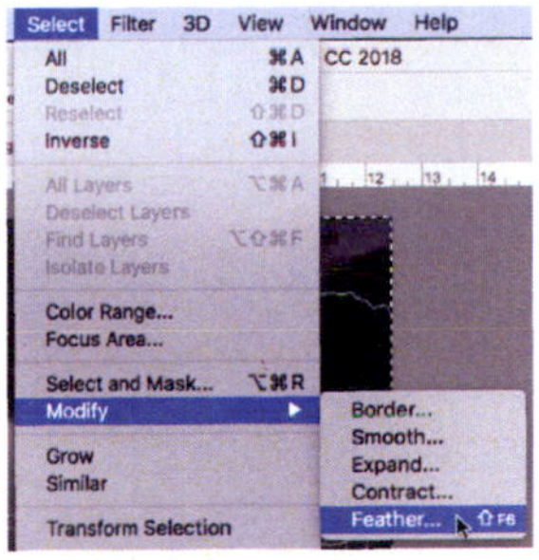

- **Border** creates a selection of a defined number of pixels around the edge of the active marquee.
- **Smooth** helps to clean up stray pixels at the edge of a selection. Within a defined radius from the selection edge, pixels with less than half of the surrounding pixels are excluded from the selection.
- **Expand** and **Contract** enlarge and shrink a selection (respectively) by a defined number of pixels.
- **Feather** creates a blended edge to the active selection area.
- **Select>Grow** expands the selection to include all adjacent pixels that fall within the tolerance defined for the Magic Wand tool.
- **Select>Similar** expands the selection to include all pixels throughout the image that fall within the tolerance range, even if they are not adjacent to the active selection.
- **Select>Transform Selection** shows bounding box handles around the selection marquee, which you can use to transform the selection as you would transform layer content.

6. **In the resulting dialog box, type `100` in the Feather Radius field. Make sure Apply Effect at Canvas Bounds is not checked, then click OK.**

Feathering means to soften the edge of a selection so the image blends into the background instead of showing a sharp line around the edge. The Feather Radius defines the distance from solid to transparent.

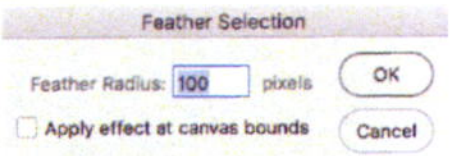

If the Apply Effect... checkbox is active, the feathering will be applied at the top and right edges of the canvas, where you dragged past the image edge while making the selection. You want these edges to remain hard, so the option should remain unchecked.

7. **Click the Edit in Quick Mask button at the bottom of the Tools panel to toggle into Quick Mask mode.**

Marching ants do not show degrees of transparency. Quick Mask mode creates a temporary red overlay (called an Alpha channel) that shows the feathered selection. By default, the overlay is semi-transparent, which allows you to see the underlying image.

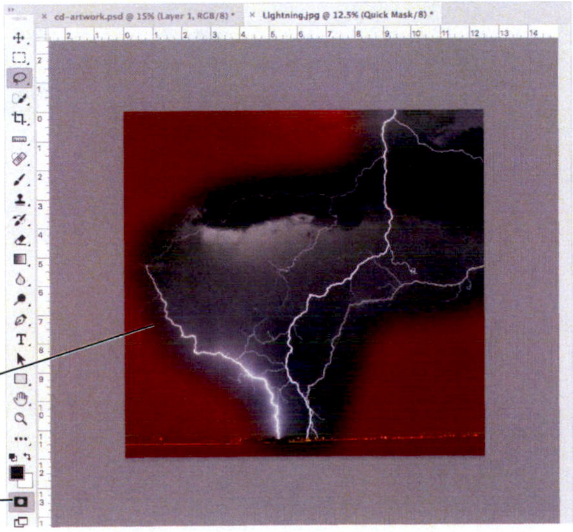

The semi-transparent overlay shows the smooth transition that was created by feathering the selection.

Edit in Quick Mask button

Note:

*You could also create a feathered selection by typing in the Feather field of the Options bar **before** drawing the selection marquee.*

Keep in mind, however, that if you draw a feathered selection (using the tool option setting), you can't undo the feather without also undoing the selection area.

8. **Click the Edit in Standard Mode button at the bottom of the Tools panel to toggle off the Quick Mask.**

   When Quick Mask mode is active, the Edit in Quick Mask mode toggles to become the Edit in Standard Mode button.

9. **Choose Edit>Copy to copy the active selection.**

10. **Click the Close button on the Lightning.jpg document tab to close that file. Click Don't Save when asked.**

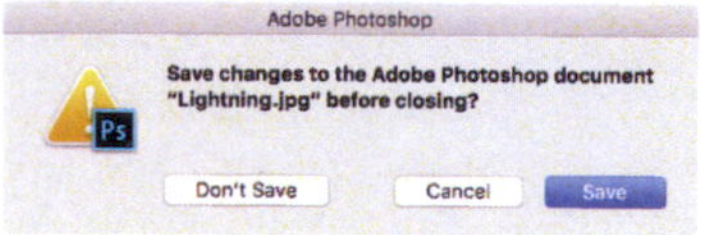

11. **With cd-artwork.psd active, choose Edit>Paste.**

    The feathered selection is pasted into the file as a new layer.

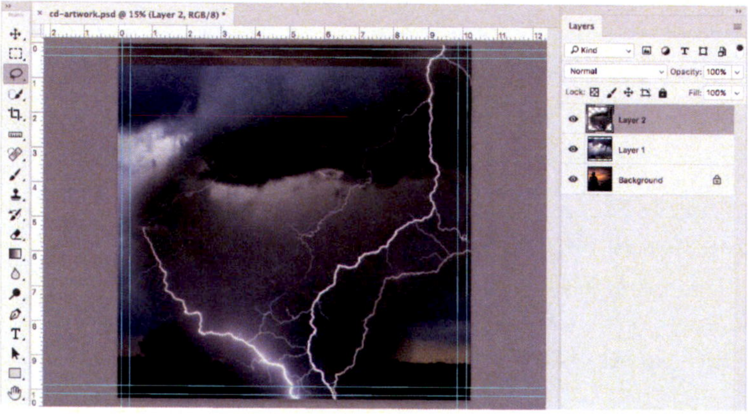

12. **Continue to the next exercise.**

Understanding the Lasso Tool Variations

PHOTOSHOP FOUNDATIONS

The **Polygonal Lasso tool** creates selections with straight lines, anchoring a line each time you click the mouse. To close a selection area, you must click the first point in the selection.

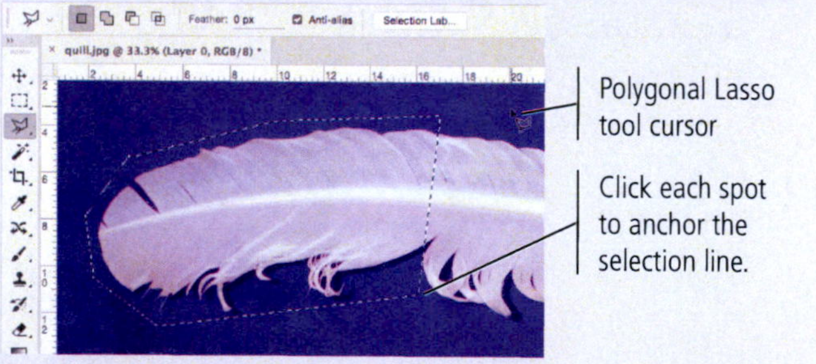

The **Magnetic Lasso tool** snaps to high-contrast edges; you can use the Options bar to control the way Photoshop detects edges of an image.

- **Width** is the distance away from the edge the cursor can be and still detect edges; if you set this higher, you can move the cursor farther from edges.
- **Contrast** is how different the foreground can be from the background and still be detected; if there is a sharp distinction between the foreground and background, you can set this value higher.
- **Frequency** is the number of points that will be created to make the selection; setting this number higher creates finer selections, while setting it lower creates smoother edges.

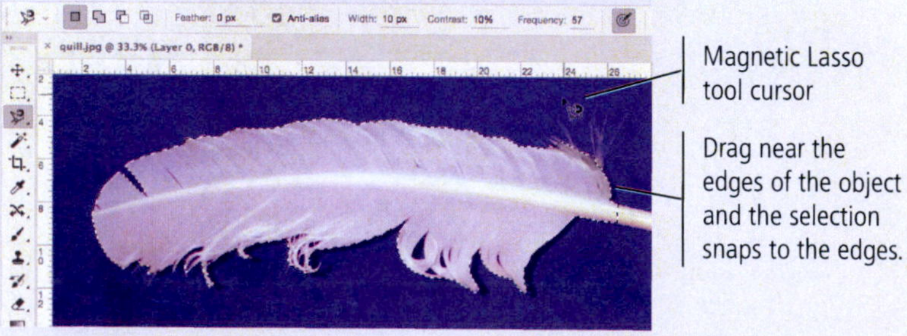

Rasterize a Vector File

Logos and title treatments — such as the ones you will use in this project — are commonly created as vector graphics. Although Photoshop is typically a pixel-based application, you can also open and work with vector graphics created in illustration programs like Adobe Illustrator.

1. **With cd-artwork.psd open, choose File>Open. Select HHT-logo.ai (in your WIP>Music folder) and then click Open.**

   This is an Adobe Illustrator file of the band's logo. The Format menu defaults to Photoshop PDF because Illustrator uses PDF as its underlying file structure.

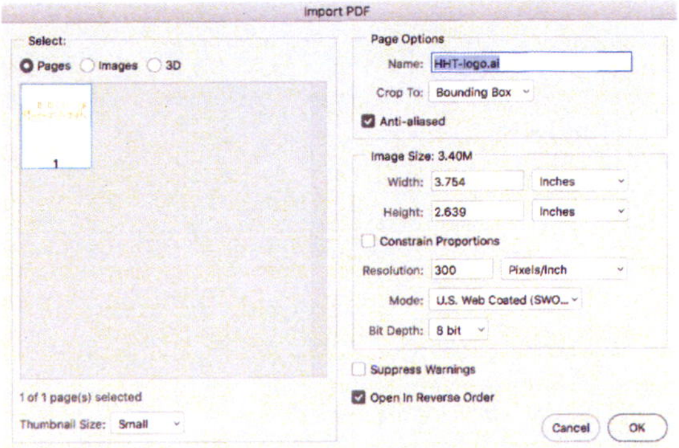

   When you open a vector file (Illustrator, EPS, or PDF) in Photoshop, it is rasterized (converted to a raster graphic). The resulting Import PDF dialog box allows you to determine exactly what and how to rasterize the file.

   The Crop To options determine the outside dimensions of the opened file. Depending on how the file was created, some of these values might be the same as others:

   - **Bounding Box** is the outermost edges of the artwork in the file.
   - **Media Box** is the size of the paper as defined in the file.
   - **Crop Box** is the size of the page/artboard including printer's marks.
   - **Bleed Box** is the trim size plus any defined bleed allowance.
   - **Trim Box** is the trim size as defined in the file.
   - **Art Box** is the area of the page as defined in the file.

   The Image Size fields default to the settings of the bounding box you select. You can change the size, resolution, color mode, and bit depth by entering new values. You can check the Constrain Proportions option to keep the height and width proportional to the original dimensions.

Note:

If you're opening a multi-page PDF or an Illustrator file with more than one artboard, the preview window on the left side of the dialog box shows thumbnails of each "page" in the file. You can click a specific thumbnail to select anything other than Page 1. (Press Shift and click to select multiple consecutive pages, or press Command/Control and click to select multiple non-consecutive pages.)

2. **Make sure Bounding Box is selected in the Crop To field, and the Resolution field is set to 300 pixels/inch.**

3. **Click OK.**

   The logo file opens in Photoshop. The checkered area behind the text indicates that the background is transparent. If you look at the Layers panel, you will see that Layer 1 isn't locked; because it's transparent, it is not considered a background layer.

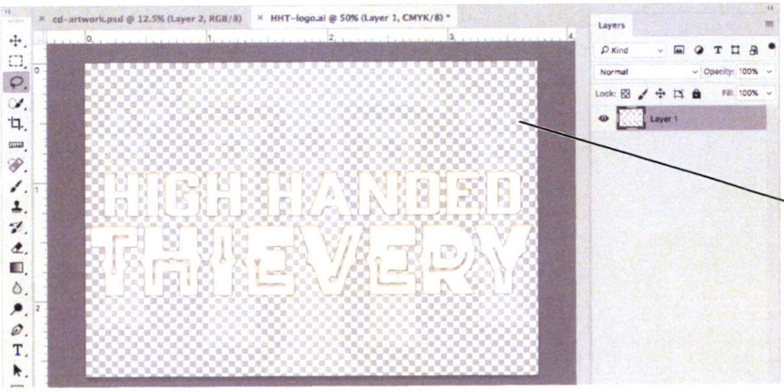

The gray-and-white checked pattern identifies areas of transparency in the layer content.

4. **Open the Window>Arrange menu and choose 2-up Vertical to show both open files at one time.**

   As you saw in the Interface chapter, these options are useful for arranging and viewing multiple open files within your workspace.

5. **Choose the Move tool in the Tools panel.**

6. **Click in the HHT-logo.ai image window and drag into the cd-artwork.psd image window, then release the mouse button.**

   Basic compositing can be as simple as dragging a selection from one file to another. If no active selection appears in the source document, this action moves the entire active layer from the source document.

Move tool

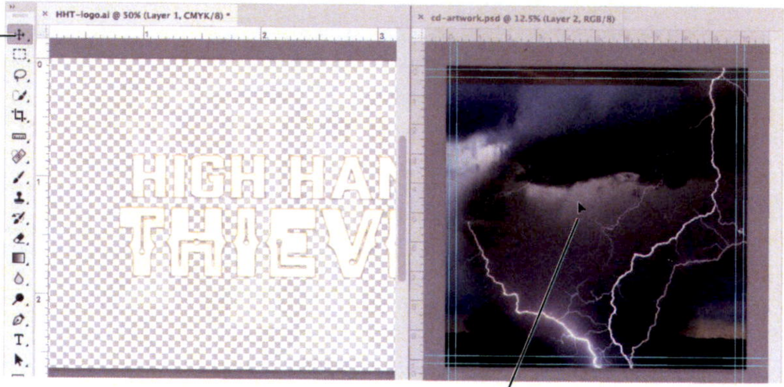

This cursor shows that you are dragging a layer. In this case, you're dragging it into another document window.

> *Note:*
>
> *On Windows, the cursor shows a plus sign to indicate that you are adding the image as a new layer in the document to which you dragged.*

7. **Click the Close button on the HHT-logo document tab to close that file. Click Don't Save when asked.**

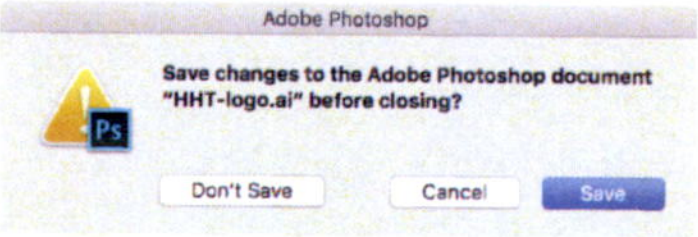

   After closing the logo file, the cd-artwork.psd document window expands to fill the available space.

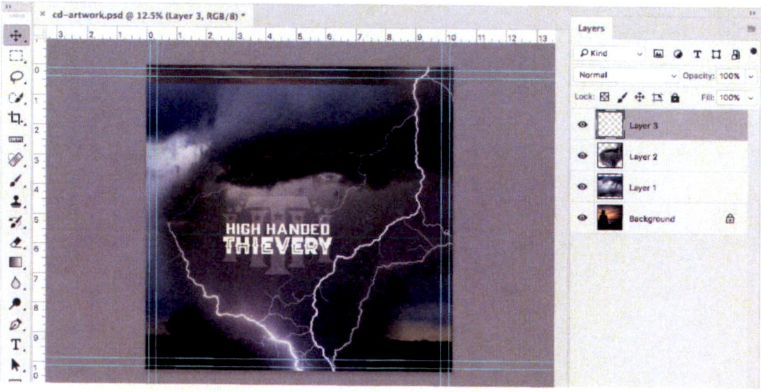

8. **Save cd-artwork.psd and continue to the next exercise.**

Place Files as Smart Object Layers

As you have seen in the last few exercises, copying layer content from one file to another results in new regular layers for the pasted content. Photoshop also supports Smart Object layers, in which you place one file into another instead of pasting layer content. Smart Objects provide a number of advantages over regular layers, which you will explore later in this project. In this exercise, you will create a Smart Object layer for the remaining image element.

> ***Note:***
>
> *Smart Objects provide extremely tight integration between Adobe Photoshop and Adobe Illustrator. You can take advantage of the sophisticated vector-editing features in Adobe Illustrator, and then place those files into Photoshop without losing the ability to edit the vector information.*

1. **With `cd-artwork.psd` open, choose File>Place Embedded.**

   Two options in the File menu — Place Embedded and Place Linked — give you the option to embed the placed file data into the active file, or to place smart objects as links to the original placed file. (See Page 48 for more about placing linked files.)

2. **Choose the `Title-text.psd` file (in your WIP>Music folder) and click Place.**

   The placed file appears with bounding box handles and crossed diagonal lines. The placement isn't final until you press Return/Enter; if you press the Escape key, the file will not be placed.

   In the Options bar, you can see that the placed image has been scaled to approximately 70% to fit into the document where it is being placed.

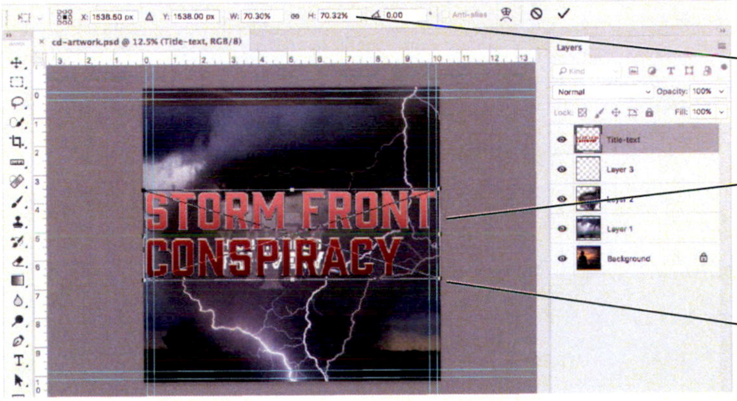

STORM FRONT
CONSPIRACY
The Options bar shows that the placed image has been scaled to fit into the active canvas.
The placed image is centered in the document window.
Crossed diagonal lines and bounding box handles indicate that the placement is not yet final.

3. **Press Return/Enter to finalize the placement.**

   After you finalize the placement, the bounding box handles and crossed diagonal lines disappear. In the Layers panel, the placed file has its own layer (just as the copied layers do). This layer, however, is automatically named, based on the name of the placed file.

   The layer's thumbnail indicates that this layer is a **Smart Object**. Because you placed this file using the embedded option, it is not dynamically linked to the original file. Instead, Photoshop maintains the original file data within the Smart Object layer. The advantages of this technique will become clear in the next stage of this project.

> ***Note:***
>
> *If you check **Skip Transform when Placing** in the General pane of the Preferences dialog box, you will not see the diagonal lines and transform handles when you first place a Smart Object layer.*

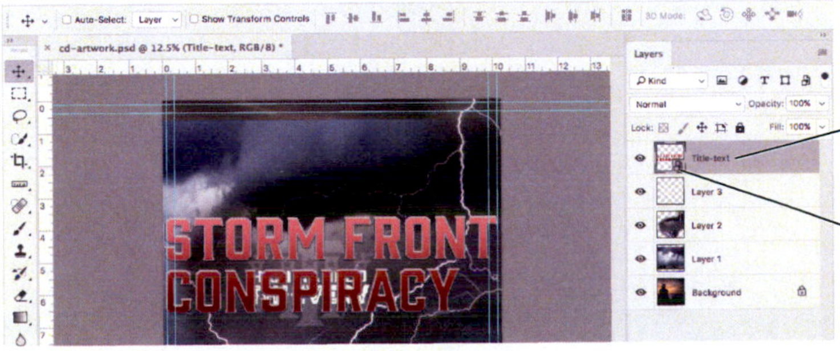

STORM FRONT
CONSPIRACY
The layer adopts the name of the placed file.
This icon identifies an embedded Smart Object layer.

4. **Save the file and continue to the next stage of the project.**

Working with Embedded and Linked Smart Objects

In the previous exercise you used the Place Embedded option to create Smart Object layers that contain the placed file data. Using that method the embedded file data becomes a part of the parent file.

If you double-click the thumbnail icon of an embedded Smart Object, the embedded file opens in an application that can edit the stored data — AI files open in Illustrator; PSD, TIFF, and JPEG files open in Photoshop.

When you first open a Smart Object file, the application provides advice for working with Smart Objects:

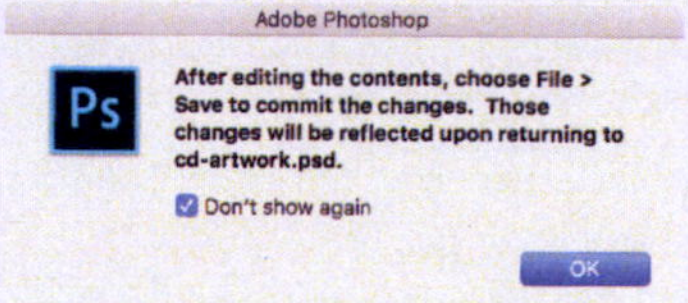

After you make necessary changes, you can save the file and close it, then return to Photoshop (if necessary). Your changes in the Smart Object file will automatically reflect in the parent file where the Smart Object layer is placed.

Important note: Do not use the Save As option when editing Smart Object layers. The changes will not reflect in the parent file if you save changes with a different file name.

If you choose the Place Linked option in the File menu, Smart Object layer stores a link to the original file data rather than embedding that data inside the parent file.

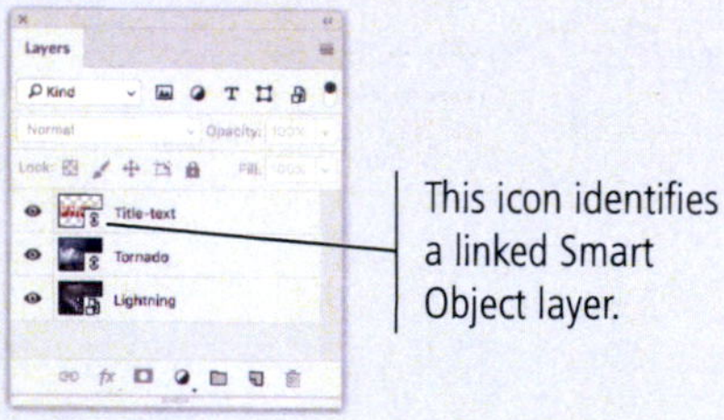

This provides an opportunity for maintaining consistency because you only need to change one instance of a file to reflect those changes anywhere the file is placed.

Say you place a logo created in Illustrator into a Photoshop file. The same logo is also placed as a link in a number of InDesign documents. If you open the logo in Illustrator and change the main color (for example), then save the changes in the original logo file, the new color automatically reflects in any file — whether InDesign or Photoshop — that is linked to the edited logo.

If you use the Place Embedded option in Photoshop, the Smart Object layer is not linked to the original, edited logo file; you would have to open the embedded Smart Object and make the same color change a second time.

Linked files also have potential disadvantages. As we mentioned previously, double-clicking a Smart Object layer thumbnail opens the linked or embedded file in an application that can edit the relevant data. If you are working with *linked* Smart Object layers, any changes you make affect the original file data. This means your changes appear not only in the parent Photoshop file where it is linked, but also any other file that links to the same data.

For a file to output properly, linked Smart Object layers must be present and up to date at the time of output.

If the linked file has been modified while the parent file is open, the changes automatically reflect in the parent file when you return to that document. If the parent file is not open in Photoshop when the linked file is edited, you will see a Modified icon for the linked Smart Object layer.

If the linked file is deleted or moved to another location after it has been placed, the parent file will show a Missing icon for the linked Smart Object layer.

If a linked Smart Object has been moved while the parent file is not open, you will see a warning dialog box when you open the parent Photoshop file. You can use that dialog box to locate the missing link, or close it and use the options in the Layers panel to correct the problem.

Control/right-clicking a linked Smart Object layer name opens a contextual menu with options to update modified content and resolve broken links.

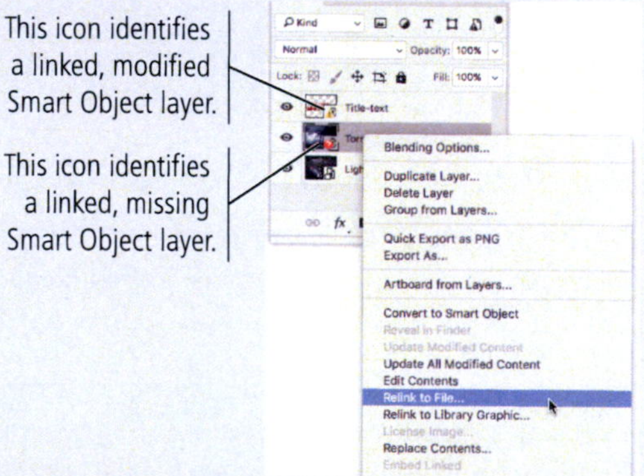

To avoid potential problems with missing linked files, you can use the File>Package command to create a job folder. The parent file is copied to a new folder, along with a Links subfolder containing any files that are placed as linked Smart Object layers.

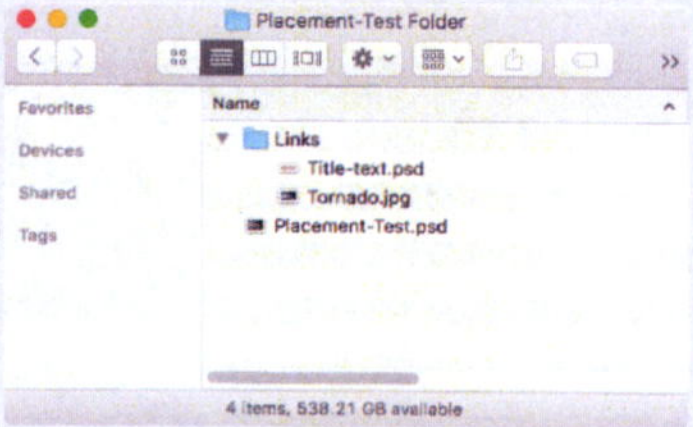

Working with CC Libraries

If you have an individual-user subscription to the Adobe Creative Cloud, you have access to CC Library functionality, which allows you to easily share assets across various Adobe CC applications. This technology makes it very easy to maintain consistency across a design campaign — for example, using the same color swatches for all pieces, whether created in Illustrator, InDesign, or Photoshop.

In Photoshop, you can create new libraries from scratch (using the menu at the top of the Libraries panel), or use the "Auto-Vacuum" feature to create a library based on an existing file's contents.

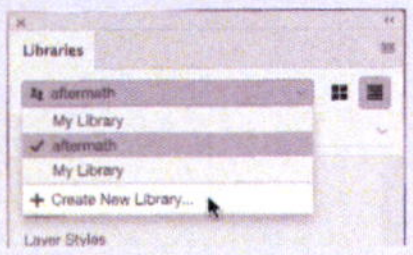

Once you create a library, it is stored in your Creative Cloud account so you can access the same assets in other Adobe applications. You can add new assets to the active library using the buttons at the bottom of the Libraries panel.

A Library list
B Show Items as Icons
C Show Items in a List
D Add Content menu
E New Library from Document
F Libraries Sync Status
G Delete

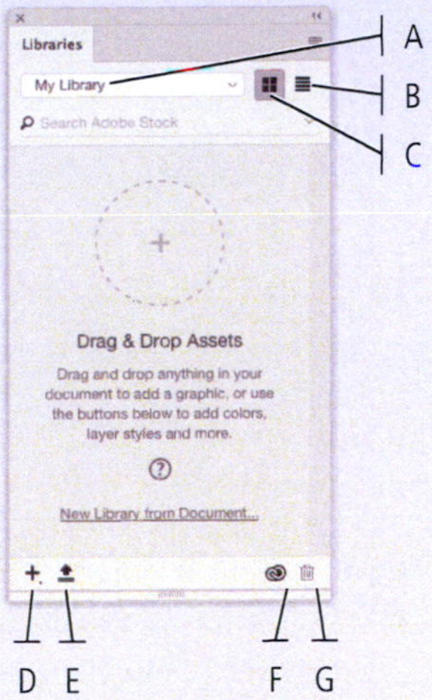

Creating Library Items

You can add new items to a library using the Add Content menu at the bottom of the Libraries panel.

Add Graphic adds the content on the active layer as an object ("graphic") in the library.

- If you add a Smart Object layer, the layer becomes linked to the new library item instead of to the original file that created the Smart Object layer.
- If you add a regular layer, it is not dynamically linked to the new library item.

Add Character Style creates a type style in the library based on the active type layer. If more than one set of character formatting options is applied within the type layer, only the formatting options in the first character of the layer are stored in the library item.

Add Layer Style creates an item in the library that includes all layer styles applied to the active layer when you click.

Add Foreground Color stores the active foreground color as a color swatch in the library.

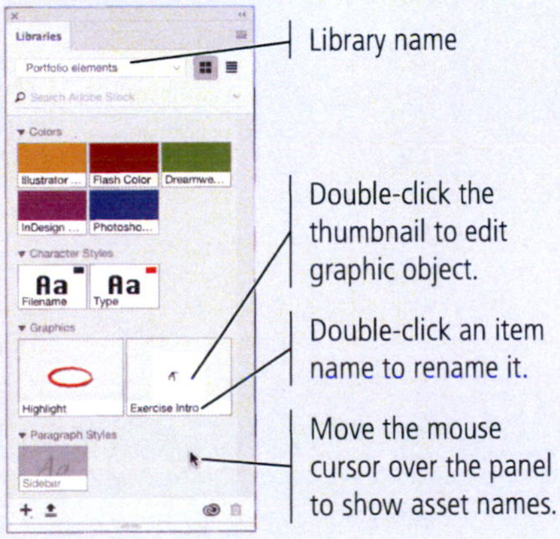

Understanding Auto-Vacuum

When you open a file with more than a flat background layer, you will see a dialog box asking if you want to create a new library from the document you are opening. If you click Cancel, no library is created. However, you can always initiate the Auto-Vacuum function using the Library from Document button at the bottom of the Libraries panel, or the Create New Library from Document item in the panel's Options menu.

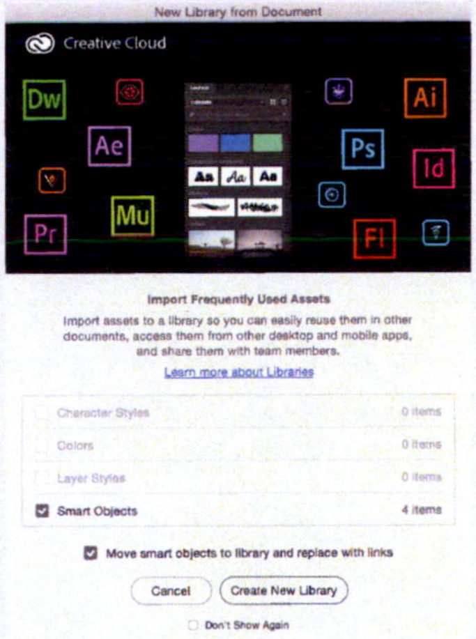

If you use the Auto-Vacuum feature, the new library automatically adopts the name of the file from which the library is created. Any character styles, defined color swatches, applied layer styles, and smart object layers are added to the new library by default.

Working with CC Libraries (continued)

Working with Library Items

Clicking a color swatch in the library changes the active foreground color in Photoshop.

Clicking a layer style in the library applies the stored layer styles to the active layer (in the Layers panel).

Clicking a character style applies the defined formatting options to all text on the active type layer. (You cannot apply a library character style to only certain characters on a type layer.)

To place a graphic from a library, simply drag it from the Libraries panel onto the Photoshop canvas. This creates a linked Smart Object layer, in this case linked to the Library item instead of to an external file on your desktop.

Linked Smart Object layers in Photoshop are identified by a special icon in the Layers panel.

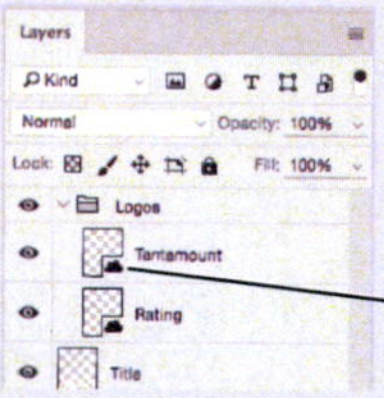

This icon identifies a Smart Object layer that is linked to a library item.

By default, objects placed from a library are linked to the library file. Any changes you make to the library item will reflect in all placed instances.

Say you change the color of text in a logo. Any instance of that logo that has been placed from the library — in any Adobe CC application — will automatically reflect the new type color as long as the library link is active.

If you press Option/Alt when you drag an object from the panel, you create a non-linked regular layer with the content from the object you dragged onto the canvas. In this case, there is no dynamic link to the library.

Sharing and Collaboration

Libraries also offer a powerful opportunity to communicate assets with other users.

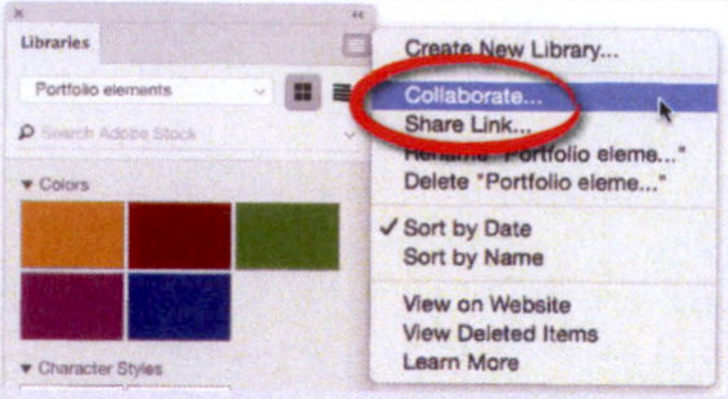

- If you invite others to collaborate, authorized users can edit assets in the library.
- If you share a link to a library, invited users can view a library's contents but not edit those assets.

The options in the Libraries panel submenu navigate to your online Adobe CC account page, and automatically ask you to invite specific users (for collaborating) or create a public link (for sharing).

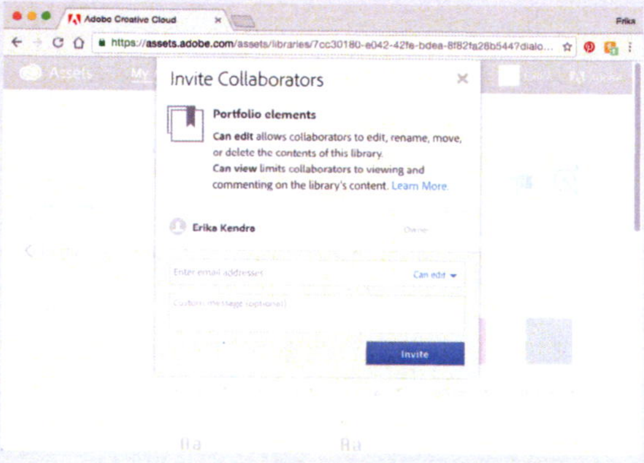

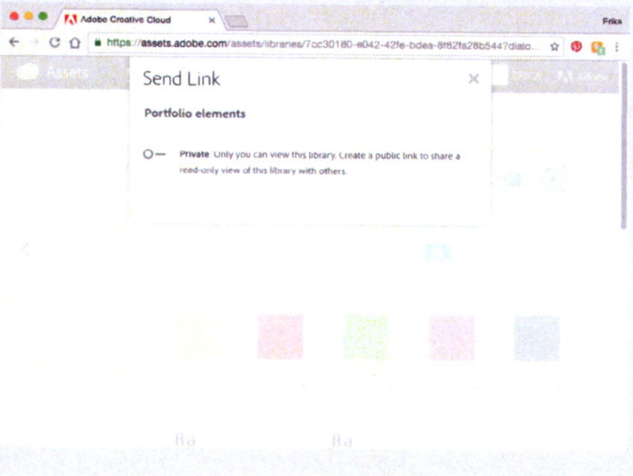

Stage 2 Managing Layers

When you composite images into a cohesive design, you almost certainly need to manipulate and transform some of the layers to make all of the pieces work together. Photoshop includes a number of options for managing layers: naming layers for easier recognition, creating layer groups so multiple layers can be manipulated at once, moving layers around on the canvas, transforming layers both destructively and non-destructively, controlling individual layer visibility, and arranging the top-to-bottom stacking order of layers to determine exactly what is visible. You will use all of these options in this stage of the project.

Name Layers and Layer Groups

It's always a good idea to name your layers because it makes managing the file much easier — especially when you work with files that include dozens of layers. Even with only four unnamed layers in this file (counting the Background layer), it would be tedious to have to toggle each layer on to find the one you want.

1. **With `cd-artwork.psd` open, review the Layers panel.**
2. **Option/Alt-click the eye icon for Layer 1 to hide all other layers.**

   Toggling layer visibility is an easy way to see only what you want to see at any given stage in a project.

   Clicking the Eye icon for a specific layer hides that layer; clicking the empty space where the Eye icon should be shows the hidden layer. To show or hide a series of consecutive layers, click the visibility icon (or empty space) for the first layer you want to affect, hold down the mouse button, and drag down to the last layer you want to show or hide.

3. **Double-click the Layer 1 layer name, and then type `Tornado`. Press Return/Enter to finalize the new layer name.**

   You can rename any layer by simply double-clicking the name and typing.

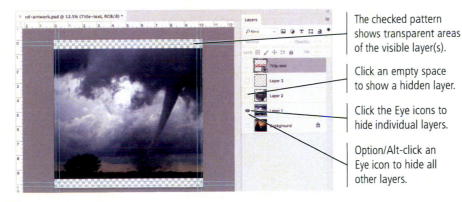

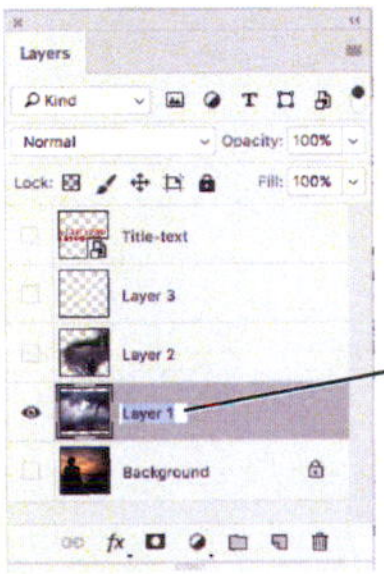

Double-click the layer name to access it.

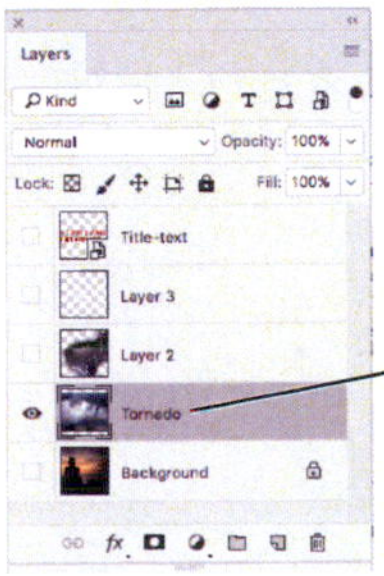

Press Return/Enter after typing to finalize the new name.

4. **Click the Eye icon to hide the renamed Tornado layer, and then click the empty space to the left of Layer 2 to show only that layer.**

5. **Double-click the Layer 2 name, then type `Lightning`. Press Return/Enter to finalize the new layer name.**

6. **Repeat Steps 4–5 to rename Layer 3 as `Logo`.**

7. **Click the spaces on the left side of the Layers panel (where the Eye icons were) to show all hidden layers.**

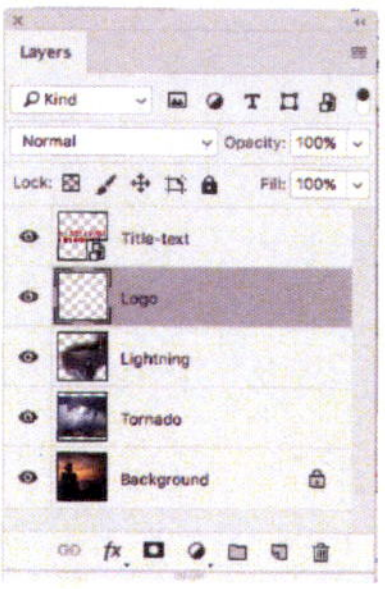

8. **In the Layers panel, click the Title-text layer to select it.**

9. **Press Shift and click the Logo layer to select that layer as well.**

   Press Shift and click to select consecutive layers in the Layers panel. Press Command/Control and click to select non-consecutive layers in the Layers panel.

10. **With the two layers selected, click the Create a New Group button at the bottom of the panel.**

    This button creates a group that automatically contains the selected layers. The new group is automatically named "Group N" (N is simply a sequential number); of course, you can rename a layer group just as easily as you can rename a layer. You can also choose New Group from Layers in the panel Options menu.

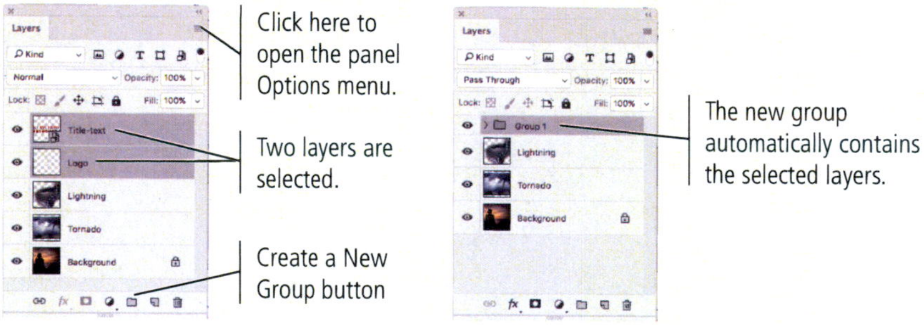

Click here to open the panel Options menu.
Two layers are selected.
Create a New Group button
The new group automatically contains the selected layers.

    To create a new empty layer group, make sure nothing is selected in the Layers panel before clicking the Create a New Group button. Alternatively, choose New Group in the panel Options menu; this option results in an empty layer group even if layers are currently selected.

> ***Note:***
> *Deselect all layers by clicking in the empty area at the bottom of the Layers panel.*

11. **Double-click the Group 1 name in the Layers panel to highlight it, then type `Logotypes`. Press Return/Enter to finalize the new layer group name.**

    As with any other layer, you should name groups based on what they contain so you can easily identify them later.

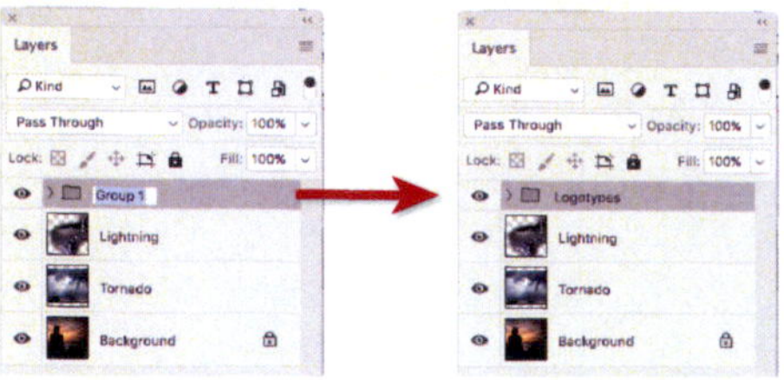

> ***Note:***
> *You can create up to ten levels of nested layer groups, or groups inside of other groups.*

12. **Click the arrow to the left of the Logotypes group name to expand the layer group.**

    You have to expand the layer group to be able to access and edit individual layers in the group. If you select the entire layer group, you can move all layers within the group at the same time. Layers in the group maintain their position relative to one another.

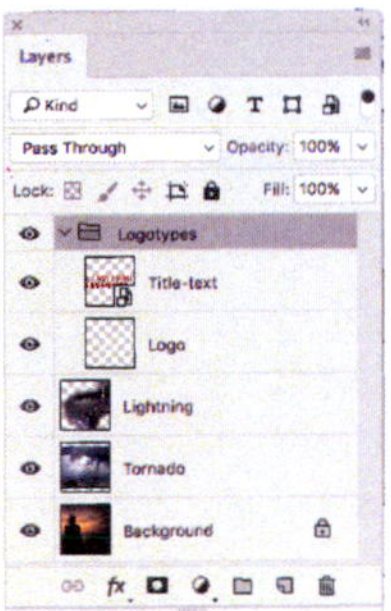

> *Note:*
>
> *You can click the Eye icon for a layer folder to hide the entire layer group (and all layers inside the folder).*

13. **Save the file and continue to the next exercise.**

Move and Transform a Smart Object Layer

Photoshop makes scaling, rotating, and other transformations fairly easy to implement, but it is important to realize the potential impact of your transformations.

1. **With `cd-artwork.psd` open, click the Title-text layer (in the Logotypes folder) in the Layers panel to select only that layer.**

2. **Choose the Move tool in the Tools panel.**

    As the name suggests, the Move tool is used to move a selection around on the canvas. You can select a specific area, and then click and drag to move only the selection on the active layer. If there is no active selection area, you can click and drag to move the contents of the entire active layer.

3. **In the Options bar, make sure the Auto-Select option is not checked.**

    When Auto-Select is checked, you can click in the image window and drag to move the contents of the layer containing the pixels where you click; you do not need to first select the layer in the Layers panel before moving the layer content. This is very useful in some cases, but not so much in others — for example, when the contents of multiple layers are stacked on top of each other (as is the case in your file as it exists now).

4. **Click in the image window and drag until the Logo layer content snaps to the top and left live-area guides.**

    If you toggled off the Snap feature when you used the Crop tool, you should turn it back on now by choosing View>Snap.

Uncheck this option.

Move tool

Select the layer you want to move, then click and drag in the document window to move the layer content.

Understanding Smart Guides

As you dragged the layer in the previous exercise, you might have noticed a series of pink lines appearing in different locations. These lines are a function of Smart Guides, which make it easier to align layer content to other layers or to the overall canvas.

Smart Guides are active by default, but you can toggle them on and off in the View>Show submenu.

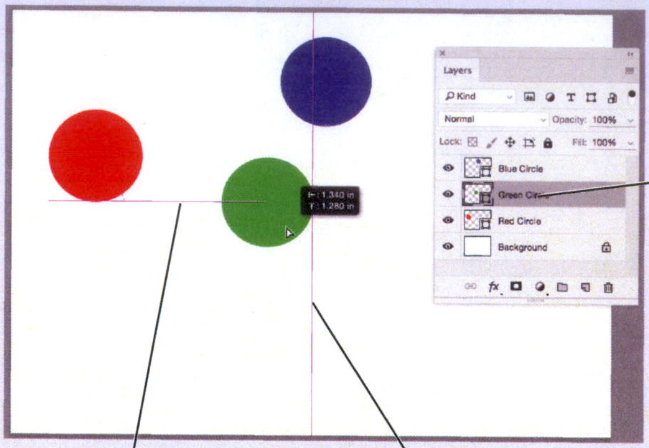

We dragged the Green Circle layer with the Move tool.

Smart Guides identify the center and edges of content on other layers.

Smart Guides identify the center and edges of the overall canvas.

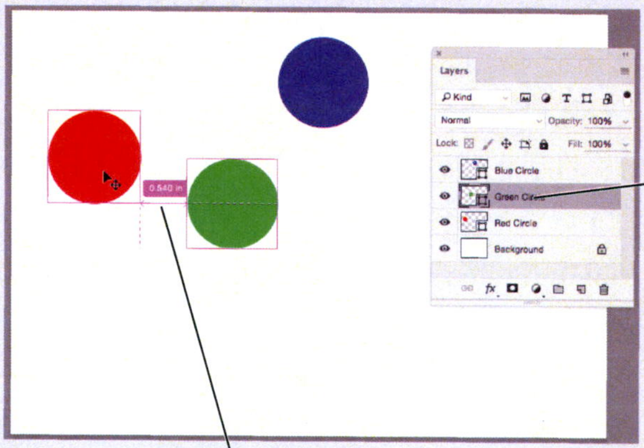

The Green Circle layer is selected.

Press Command/Control and hover over an object to find the distance between it and the selected layer.

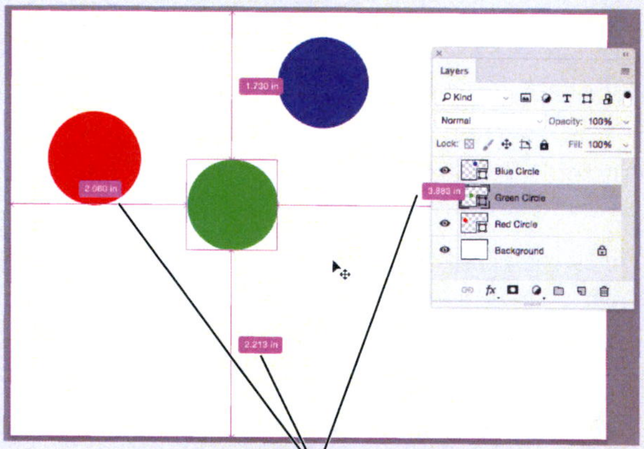

Press Command/Control and hover over the canvas find the distance between the selected layer content and the canvas edges.

5. **With the Title-text layer still active, choose Edit>Free Transform.**

When you use the transform options, bounding box handles surround the selection in the document window. The Options bar gives you a number of options for controlling the transformations numerically:

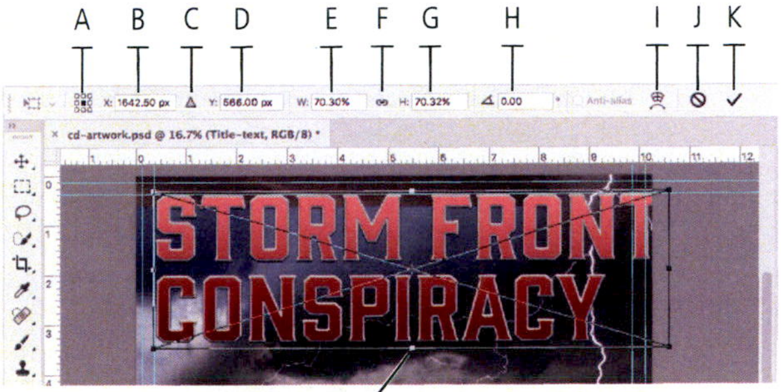

Bounding box handles surround the content that is being transformed.

- **A Reference Point Location.** This point determines the point around which transformations are made. It always defaults to the center point.
- **B Set Horizontal Position of Reference Point.** This is the X position of the reference point for the content being transformed. If the center reference point is selected, for example, this is the X position of the center point of the active content.
- **C Use Relative Positioning for Reference Point.** If this option is active, the Set Horizontal Position and Set Vertical Position fields default to 0; changing these values moves the reference point by the value you type. For example, typing "–25" in the Set Horizontal Position field moves the active content 25 pixels to the left.
- **D Set Vertical Position of Reference Point.** This is the Y position of the reference point for the content being transformed.
- **E Set Horizontal Scale.** Use this field to change the horizontal scale percentage of the transformed content.
- **F Maintain Aspect Ratio.** When active, the horizontal scale and vertical scale fields are locked to have the same value.
- **G Set Vertical Scale.** Use this field to change the vertical scale percentage of the transformed content.
- **H Rotate.** Use this field to rotate the transformed content by a specific angle.
- **I Switch Between Free Transform and Warp Modes.** If available, click this button to apply a built-in warp to the active selection.
- **J Cancel Transform.** Click this button (or press the Esc key) to exit Free Transform mode without applying any transformation.
- **K Commit Transform.** Click this button (or press Return/Enter) to finalize the transformation that you applied while in Free Transform mode.

6. **Press Shift, click the bottom-right bounding box handle, and then drag up and left until the title treatment fits inside the live area guides on both sides of the canvas.**

The selection (in this case, the entire Title-text layer) dynamically changes as you scale the layer. Pressing Shift while you drag a handle constrains the image proportions as you resize it. When you release the mouse button, the handles remain in place until you finalize ("commit") the transformation.

While you're manually transforming a layer or selection, the Options bar shows the specifics. You can also type into these fields to apply specific numeric transformations.

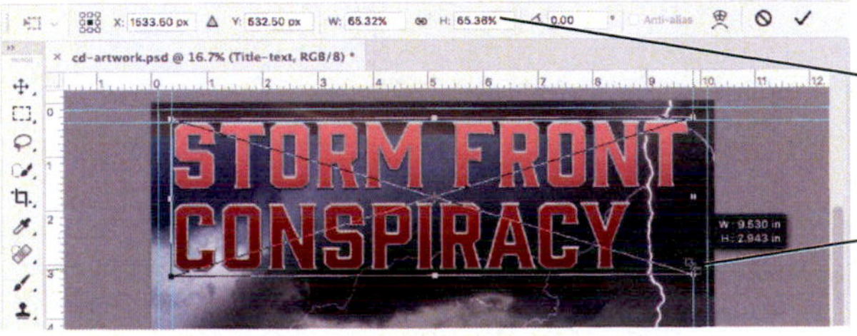

Manual transformations in the document window reflect in the Options bar fields.

Shift-click and drag a handle to scale the content proportionally.

7. **Press Return/Enter to finalize the transformation.**

   After finalizing the transformation, the bounding-box handles disappear.

8. **With the Title-text layer still active, press Command/Control-T to enter Free Transform mode again and look at the Options bar.**

   Because the rating layer is a Smart Object layer, the W and H fields still show the scaling percentage based on the original.

STORM FRONT
CONSPIRACY

9. **In the Options bar, click the Maintain Aspect Ratio button to activate that option.**

   It is not uncommon for a placed image to have slightly different height and width percentages when it is placed. Activating the Maintain Aspect Ratio option forces the X and Y percentage fields to the same value. The change will be slight, but it's a good idea to check this issue so that you maintain the integrity of the placed artwork.

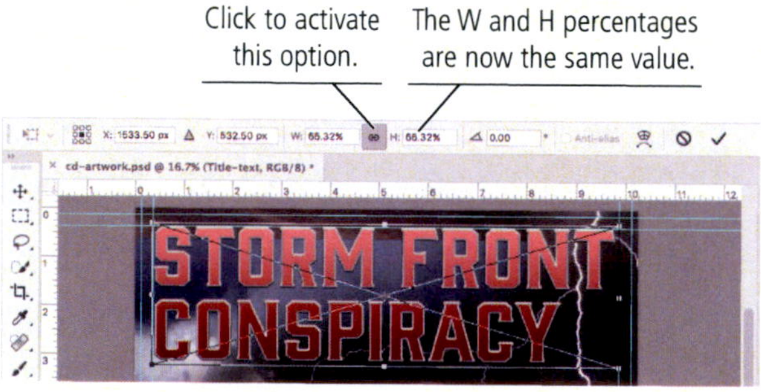
Click to activate this option.
The W and H percentages are now the same value.
STORM FRONT
CONSPIRACY

10. **In the Options bar, change the W field to 65%.**

    Because Maintain Aspect Ratio is active, the value in the H field also changes.

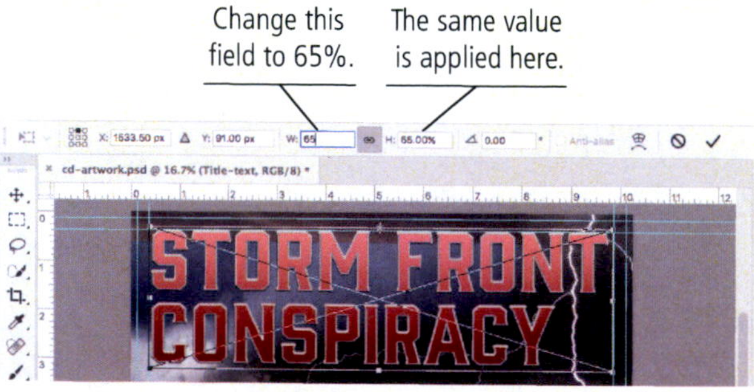
Change this field to 65%.
The same value is applied here.
STORM FRONT
CONSPIRACY

11. **Click the Commit Transform button on the Options bar (or press Return/Enter) to finalize the transformation.**

    If you press Return/Enter, you have to press it two times to finalize the transformation. The first time you press it, you apply the change to the active field; the second time, you finalize the transformation and exit Free Transform mode.

12. **Save the file and continue to the next exercise.**

Move and Transform Regular Layers

Smart Object layers enable non-destructive transformations, which means those transformations can be changed or undone without affecting the quality of the layer content. Transforming a regular layer, on the other hand, is destructive and permanent.

1. **With `cd-artwork.psd` open, hide all but the Tornado layer. Click the Tornado layer in the Layers panel to select it.**

2. **Using the Move tool, drag the layer content up so there is no transparent area at the top of the canvas.**

> *Note:*
>
> *When the Move tool is active, you can move the selected object or layer 1 pixel by pressing the Arrow keys. Pressing Shift with any of the Arrow keys moves the selected object/layer by 10 pixels.*

3. **Choose Edit>Transform>Flip Horizontal.**

   The Transform submenu commands affect only the selected layer.

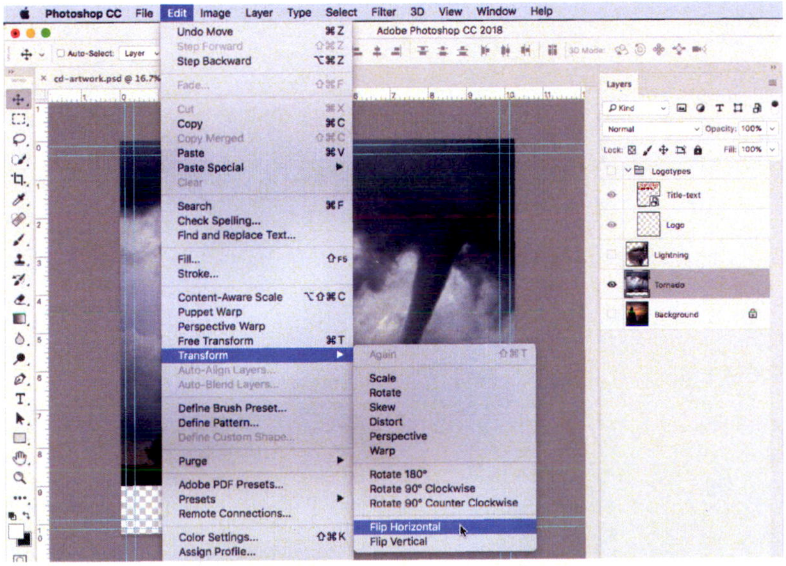

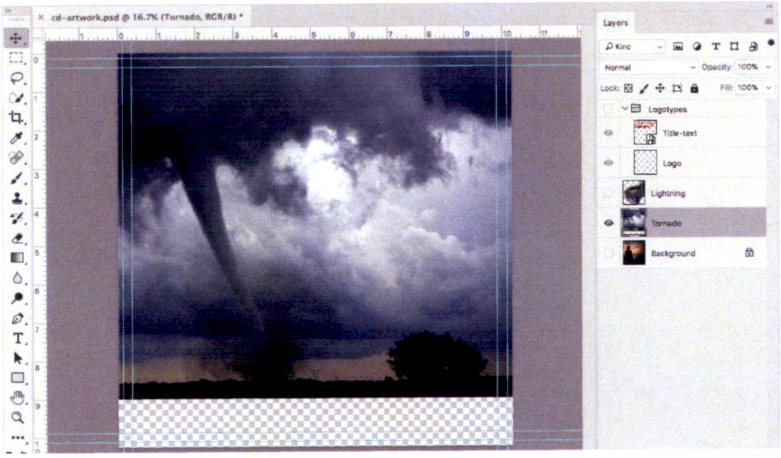

> *Note:*
>
> *You can also use the Edit>Transform submenu to apply specific transformations to a layer or selection.*

4. **Show and select the Lightning layer, then press Command/Control-T to enter Free Transform mode.**

   Some handles might not be visible within the boundaries of the document window. If necessary, zoom out so you can see all eight handles of the layer content.

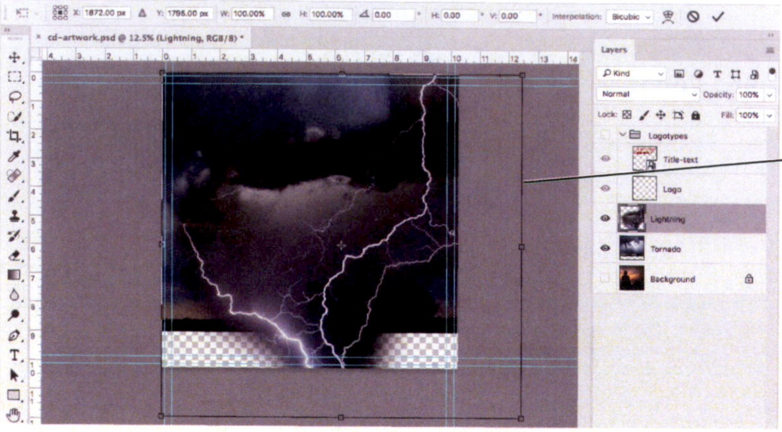

The edge of the bounding box shows that some parts of the layer do not fit within the current file dimensions.

5. **Click inside the bounding-box area and drag until the layer content snaps to the top and right canvas edges.**

7. **On the left side of the Options bar, choose the top-right reference point.**

6. **Click the Maintain Aspect Ratio button to make that option active.**

8. **Place the cursor over the W field label to access the scrubby slider for that field.**

   When you see the scrubby slider cursor, you can drag right to increase or drag left to decrease the value in the related field.

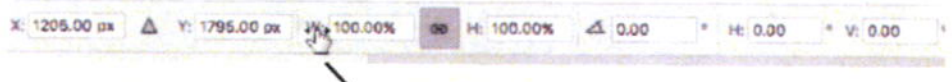

9. **Click and drag left until the W field shows approximately 75%.**

   Because you selected the top-right reference point, the top-right corner of the layer remains in place when you scale the selection. The bottom-left corner moves based on the scaling you define.

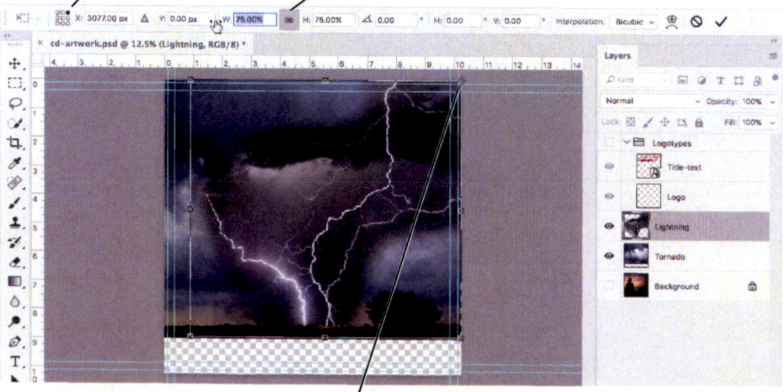

10. **Press Return/Enter to finalize the transformation.**

11. **With the Lightning layer still active, press Command/Control-T to re-enter Free Transform mode.**

    Once you commit the transformation on a regular layer, the transformation is final. Looking at the Options bar now, you can see that it shows the layer at 100% instead of the 75% from Step 7.

    If you transform a Smart Object layer, the scale percentage is maintained even after you finalize the change — unlike scaling a regular layer, where the layer re-calibrates so the new size is considered 100% once you finalize the scaling.

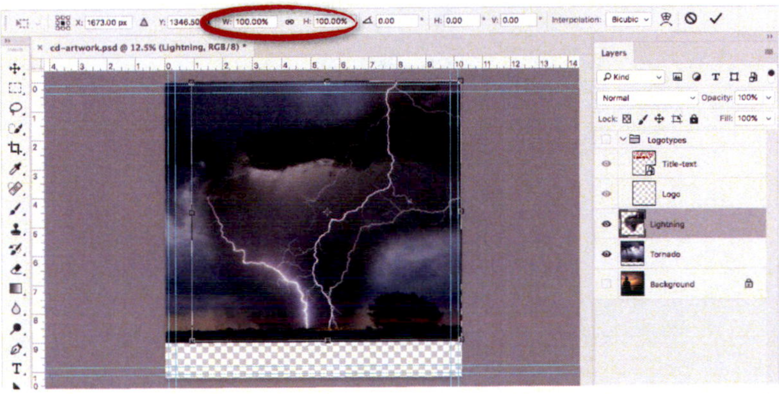

12. **Press Esc to exit Free Transform mode without changing anything.**

13. **Save the file and continue to the next exercise.**

Transform the Background Layer

Your file currently has a number of layers, most of which were created by pasting or placing external files into the original file. Because every photograph and scan (and some images that you create from scratch in Photoshop) begins with a default locked Background layer, it is important to understand the special characteristics of that layer:

- You can't apply layer transformations, styles, or masks to the Background layer.
- You can't move the contents of the Background layer around in the document.
- If you delete pixels from the Background layer, you must determine the color that will be used in place of the deleted pixels.
- The Background layer cannot include transparent pixels, which are necessary for underlying layers to be visible.
- The Background layer is always the bottom layer in the stacking order; you can't add or move layers lower than the Background layer.

In the final composite file for this project, you need to flip the woman's silhouette from left to right, and remove the sunset from the image background. For either of these options to work properly, you need to convert the default Background layer to a regular layer.

Note:

If you crop an image that includes a Background layer, the Background layer is automatically converted to a regular layer if the Delete Cropped Pixels option is not checked.

1. **With cd-artwork.psd open, show only the Background layer.**

2. **Click the Background layer to select it and then choose Edit>Transform.**

   The Transform submenu commands are not available for the locked Background layer.

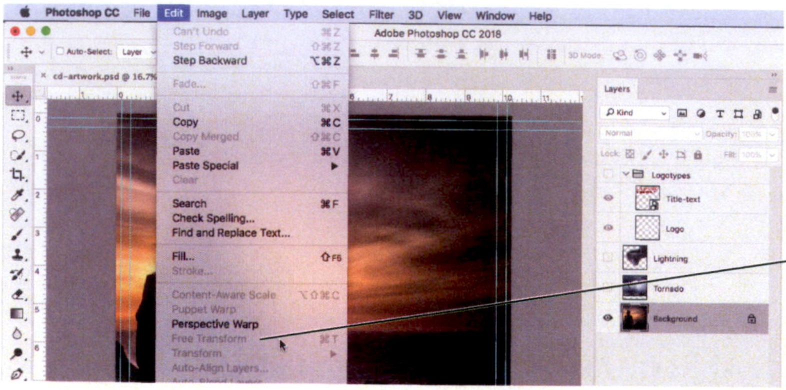

Many commands are not available because the Background layer is locked.

3. **With the Background layer still selected, choose Image>Image Rotation> Flip Canvas Horizontal.**

   To affect the locked background layer, you have to flip the actual canvas.

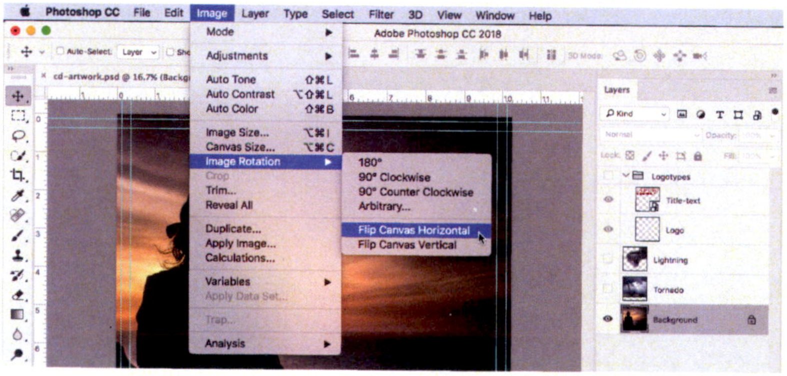

Note:

Although the Background layer exists by default in many files, it is not a required component.

4. **Show the Logotypes layer group.**

   Because you flipped the canvas, the Title-text and Logo layers are also flipped left-to-right. Rotating or flipping the entire canvas affects all layers in the file; this is obviously not what you want to do.

Because you flipped the canvas, the logos are now backward.

Showing the layer group shows all layers in that group.

5. **Choose Edit>Undo Flip Canvas Horizontal.**

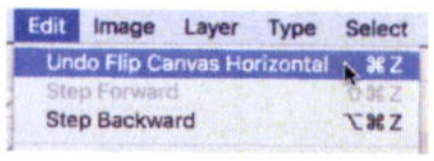

   The Undo command affects the last action you performed; the actual command changes to reflect the action that will be undone. Showing or hiding a layer is not considered an "action," so the Undo command simply un-flips the canvas. The Logotypes group is again hidden, as it was when you flipped the canvas in Step 3.

6. **In the Layers panel, click the Lock icon on the Background layer.**

   Clicking the Lock icon unlocks the layer and immediately converts the previous Background layer to a regular layer named "Layer 0."

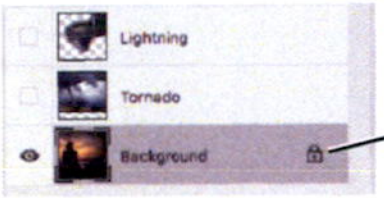

Click the lock icon to unlock the Background layer.

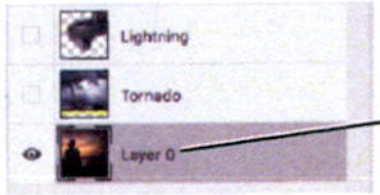

The layer is automatically converted to a regular layer named Layer 0.

7. **Double-click the Layer 0 layer name to highlight it, then type Sunrise to rename the layer. Press Return/Enter to finalize the new layer name.**

8. **With the Sunrise layer selected in the panel, choose Edit>Transform>Flip Horizontal.**

   Because the layer is no longer locked, you can now access and apply the transform commands that affect only the selected layer.

9. **Show the Logos layer group again.**

   Because you flipped only the selected layer, the Title-text and Logo layers are not flipped; they appear in the correct position and orientation.

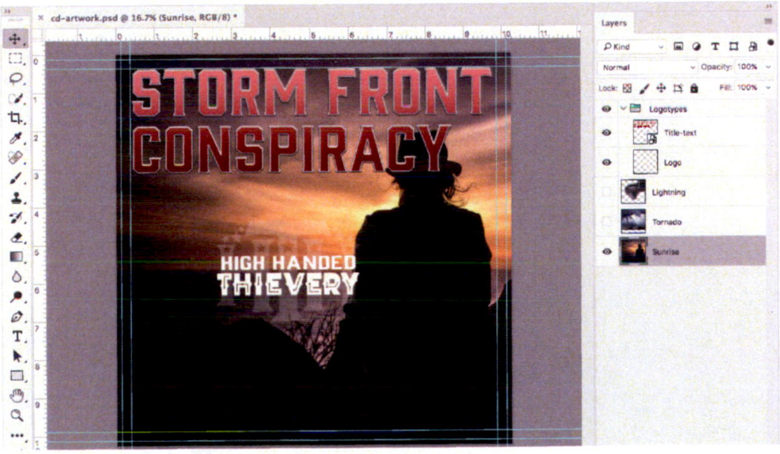

10. **Choose the Logo layer in the Layers panel.**

11. **Using the Move tool, move the Logo layer content until it snaps to the bottom and right live area guides.**

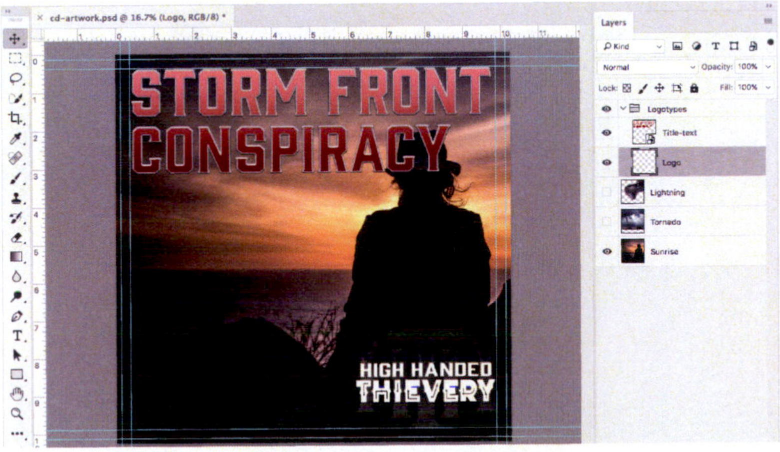

12. **Save the file and continue to the next stage of the project.**

Navigating the History

The Undo command (Edit>Undo or Command/Control-Z) only steps back to the last action completed; after you use the Undo command, it toggles to Redo. You can also use the Step Backward command (Edit>Step Backward or Command-Option-Z/Control-Alt-Z) to move back in the history one step at a time, or use the History panel (Window>History) to navigate back to earlier stages.

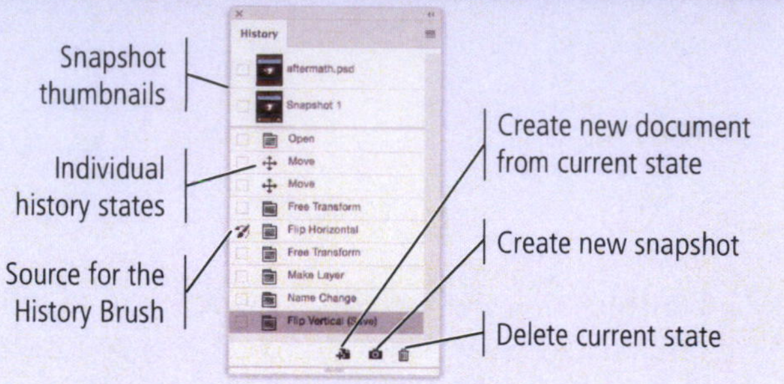

Every action you take is recorded as a state in the History panel. You can click any state to return to that particular point in the document progression. You can also delete specific states or create a new document from a particular state using the buttons at the bottom of the panel.

By default, the History panel stores the last 50 states; older states are automatically deleted. You can change that setting in the Performance pane of the Preferences dialog box. Keep in mind, however, that storing a larger number of states will increase the memory that is required to work with a specific file.

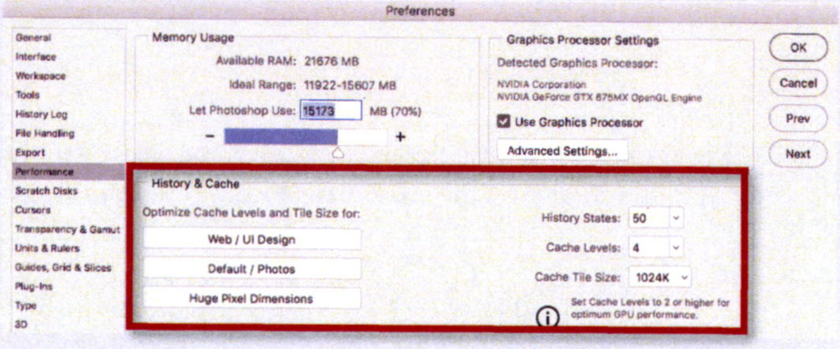

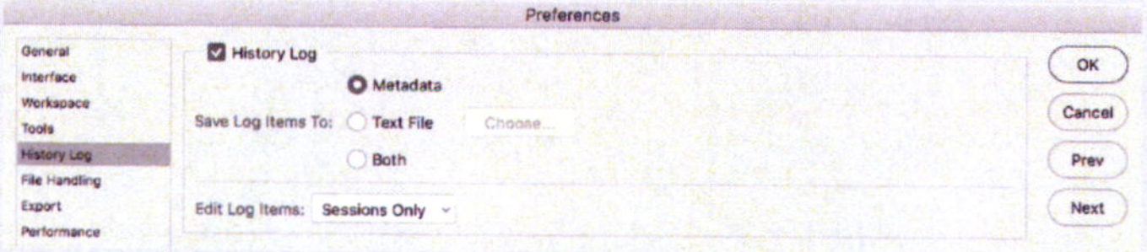

Keep the following in mind when using the History panel:

- The default snapshot is the image state when it was first opened.
- The oldest state is at the top of the list; the most recent state appears at the bottom.
- You can save any particular state as a snapshot to prevent it from being deleted when that state is no longer within the number of states that can be stored.
- The history is only stored while the file is open; when you close a file, the history and snapshots are not saved.
- When you select a specific state, the states below it are dimmed so you can see which changes will be discarded if you go back to a particular history state.
- Selecting a state and then changing the image eliminates all states that come after it.
- Deleting a state deletes that state and those after it. If you choose Allow Non-Linear History in the History Options dialog box (accessed in the History panel Options menu), deleting a state deletes only that state.

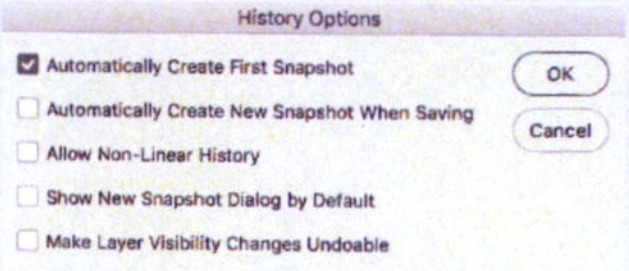

If you need to keep a record of a file's history even after you close the file, you can activate the History Log option in the History Log pane of the Preferences dialog box. When this option is checked, you can save the history log as metadata, in a text file, or both. You can also determine the level of detail that will be recorded in the history log.

- Sessions Only records each time you launch or quit and each time you open and close individual files.
- Concise adds the text that appears in the History panel to the Sessions information.
- Detailed gives you a complete history of all changes made to files.

Stage 3 Creating Complex Selections

In an earlier lesson you learned how to use the Rectangular Marquee and Lasso tools to draw basic selections. Photoshop includes a number of other options for making selections based on the color content of an image. The method you use will vary depending on the actual content of your image, as well as what you hope to accomplish.

The **Magic Wand tool** is an easy way to select large areas of solid color.

- The first four options in the Options bar are the same as those for the Marquee tools (New Selection, Add to Selection, Subtract from Selection, and Intersect with Selection).
- **Tolerance** is the degree of variation between the color you click and the colors Photoshop will select; higher tolerance values select a larger range based on the color you click.
- The **Anti-alias** check box allows edges to blend more smoothly into the background, preventing a jagged, stair-stepped appearance. (Anti-aliasing is the process of blending shades of pixels to create the illusion of sharp lines.)

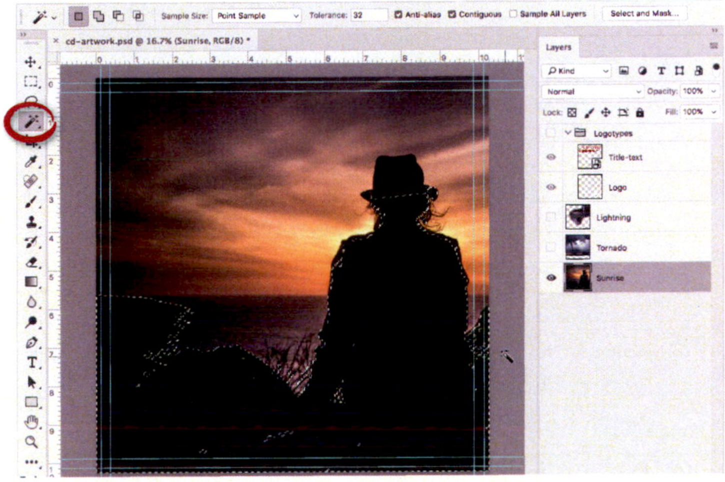

Clicking with the Magic Wand tool creates a selection of pixels within the tolerance of the pixel where you click.

- When **Contiguous** is selected, the tool only selects adjacent areas of the color; unchecking this option allows you to select all pixels within the color tolerance, even if some pixels are non-contiguous (for example, inside the shape of the letter Q).
- By default, selections relate to the active layer only. You can check **Sample All Layers** to make a selection of all layers in the file.
- The **Select and Mask** button opens a special interface where you can use a number of tools to fine-tune the selection edge.

The **Quick Selection tool** essentially allows you to "paint" a selection. As you drag, the selection expands and automatically finds the edges in the image.

- In the Options panel, you can use the options to create a new selection, add to, or subtract from the current selection.
- Open the Brush Options to change the brush size, so that your selection includes a smaller or wider range of color.
- **Auto-Enhance** allows the software to refine the edges of the selection based on internal algorithms. (Although many "auto" features in the software are very useful starting points, never rely entirely on this type of automatic result.)

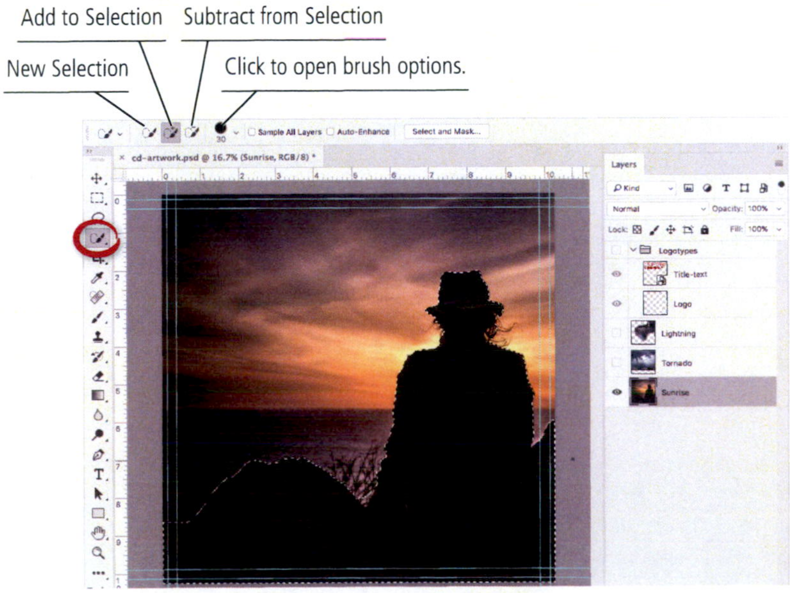

The **Select>Color Range** menu command opens a dialog box that you can use to select areas of an image based on sampled colors.

- On the right side of the dialog box, the Eyedropper tool is selected by default. You can click a color in the image, either in the document window or in the dialog box preview window, to select define the color range you want to select (called **sampling**). You can then use the Add to Sample and Subtract from Sample eyedroppers to refine your selection.

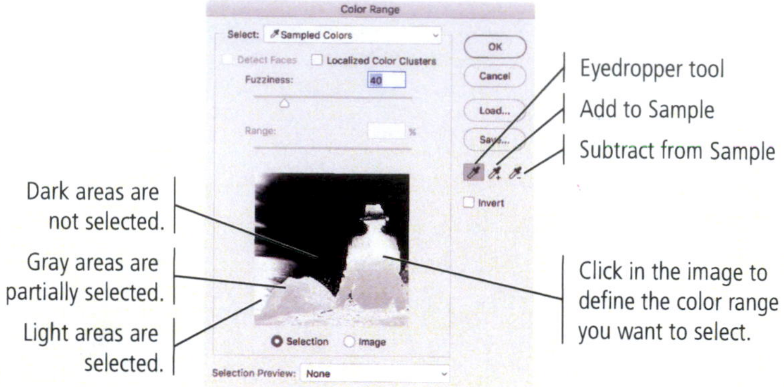

- The **Select** menu at the top of the dialog box includes several presets for isolating specific ranges of primary colors (Reds, Yellows, Greens, Cyans, Blues, or Magentas), or specific ranges of color (highlights, midtones, or shadows).
- If you select the Skin Tones preset, you can then activate the **Detect Faces** option at the top of the dialog box. By adjusting the Fuzziness slider, you can use this dialog box to make reasonably good selections of people's skin. (Again, remember that no automatic option is a perfect substitute when subjective decision-making is required. Other tones in an image might be similar enough to a "skin tone" that unwanted areas will be included in the selection.)
- The **Localized Color Clusters** option can be used to select specific areas of a selected color. When this option is checked, the Range slider defines how far away (in physical distance) a color can be located from the point you click and still be included in the selection.
- **Fuzziness** is similar to the Tolerance setting for the Magic Wand tool. Changing the Fuzziness value expands (higher numbers) or contracts (lower numbers) the selection. Be careful, though, since higher fuzziness values can eliminate fine lines and detail.
- The Selection Preview menu determines how the selection appears in the document window:
  - **None** shows the normal image in the document window.
  - **Grayscale** shows the entire image in shades of gray; selected areas are solid white and unselected areas are solid black.
  - **Black Matte** shows unselected areas in solid black; selected areas appear in color.
  - **White Matte** shows unselected areas in solid white; selected areas appear in color.
  - **Quick Mask** adds a partially transparent overlay to unselected areas.
- You can check the **Invert** box to return a selection that is the opposite of the color range you select. This is useful if you want to isolate (select) the background instead of the actual areas you selected in the dialog box.

Create and Refine a Color-Based Selection

Many images have both hard and soft edges, and/or very fine detail that needs to be isolated from its background (think of a model's blowing hair overlapping the title on the cover of a magazine). In this exercise, you are going to use two techniques to isolate the woman's silhouette (and the ground where she is sitting) in the Sunrise image layer.

1. **With `cd-artwork.psd` open, hide all but the Sunrise layer. Click the Sunrise layer to make it active.**

2. **Choose the Quick Selection tool in the Tools panel.**

3. **In the Options bar, make sure the Sample All Layers option is not checked.**

   You only want to select an area based on the Sunrise layer content, so you do not want to make a selection based on the content of other layers in the file.

4. **Click near the bottom-left corner of the image, then drag right and up into the woman's head.**

   The resulting selection marquee shows that the software does a good job of isolating the obvious foreground elements of the image (the ground and the woman's silhouette). If you look closely, however, areas of fine detail — the woman's hair and the grass in front of her — are not included. You will need to use a different method to refine the selection edge and add the areas of detail.

5. **Click the Select and Mask button in the Options bar.**

The Select and Mask workspace is a specialized workspace that contains only the tools you need to refine a complex selection.

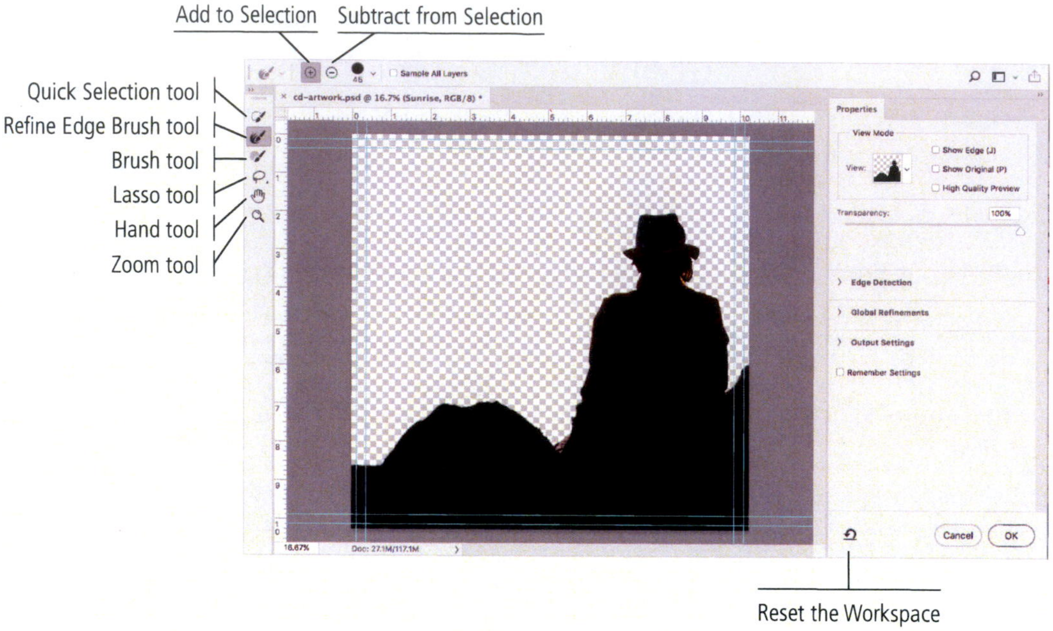

6. **In the Properties panel, open the View menu and make sure Onion Skin is selected.**

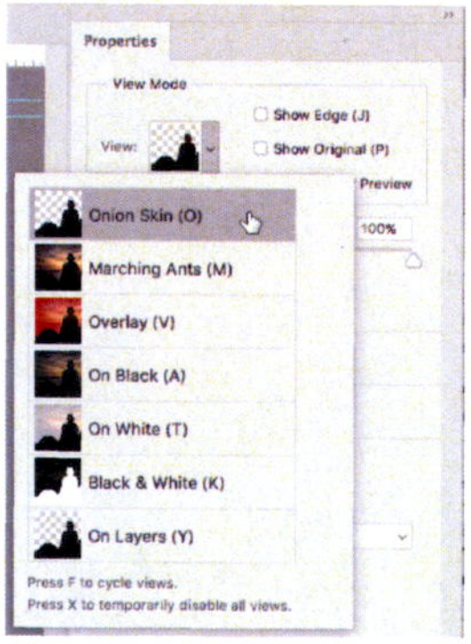

The different types of preview change the way your image appears while you refine the edges within the workspace.

- **Onion Skin**, the default, shows unselected (masked) areas as semi-transparent, based on the value in the Transparency slider. You can make the masked areas more or less transparent by increasing or decreasing (respectively) the Transparency value.
- **Marching Ants** shows the basic standard selection.
- **Overlay** shows the unselected areas with a Quick Mask overlay.
- **On Black** shows the selection in color against a black background.
- **On White** shows the selection in color against a white background.
- **Black & White** shows the selected area in white and the unselected area in black.
- **On Layers** shows only the selected area; unselected areas are hidden so that underlying layers are visible in masked areas in the preview.

7. **In the Properties panel, set the Transparency slider to 50%.**

Using the 50% transparency setting, masked pixels are partially visible, so that you can see the areas you want to add to the selection.

8. **Zoom into the woman's head in the image, then choose the Refine Edge Brush tool.**

   This tool has edge detection capabilities, which means you can simply "paint" over areas to identify edges of very small areas of detail.

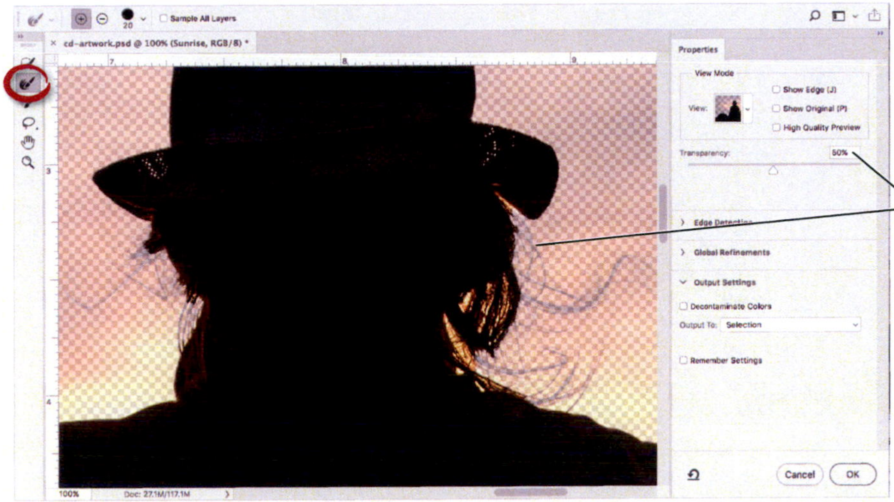

Reducing the onion skin transparency allows you to see the unselected areas of the image layer.

9. **Click and drag over the wispy areas of the woman's hair.**

   You might not see much of a difference as you drag, but when you release the mouse button you should see some of the thin details appear solid (selected) instead of transparent (not selected).

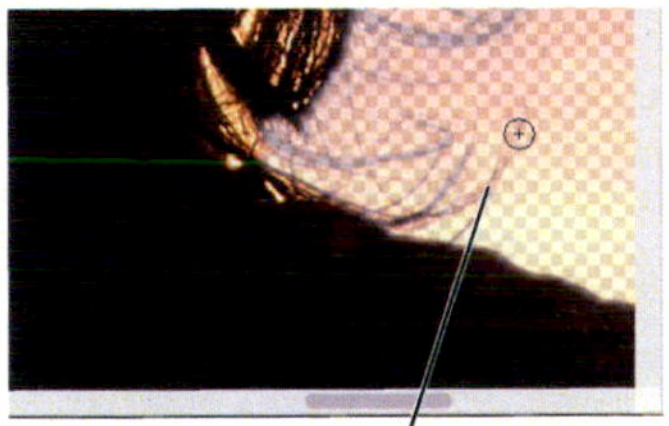

Paint over the detail areas that are currently unselected.

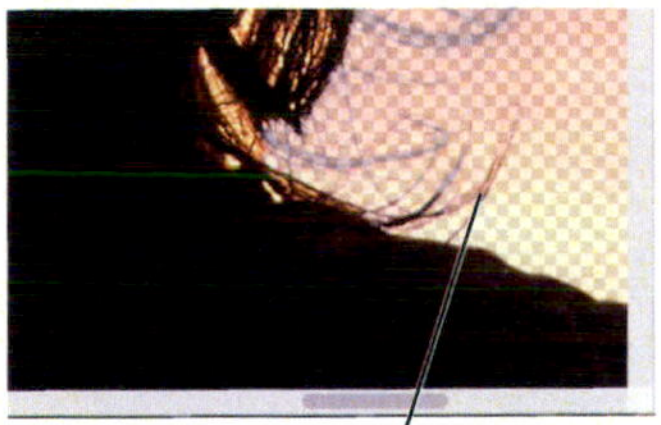

Details appear solid (selected) after you paint over them and release the mouse button.

Note:

You can use the Zoom and Hand tools, as well as their associated shortcuts, to change the image preview in the Select and Mask workspace.

10. **Continue to drag over the details on both sides of the woman's head until you are satisfied with the results.**

    You don't need to be precise when you drag over the details, although dragging approximately over the details generally does produce better results.

Original Selection

Refined Selection

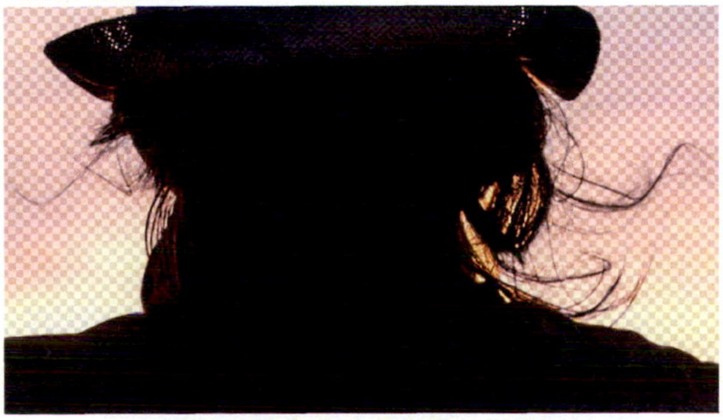

11. **Repeat this process to add the grass (near the woman's arm) to the selection.**

It might be helpful in this area to reduce the onion skin transparency, so that you can better see the details in this portion of the image.

Original Selection

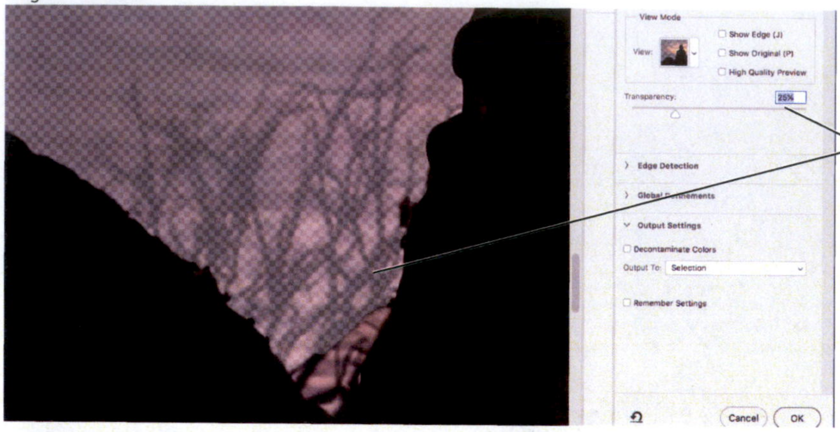

Reducing the transparency allows you to better see the unselected details in this area.

Refined Selection

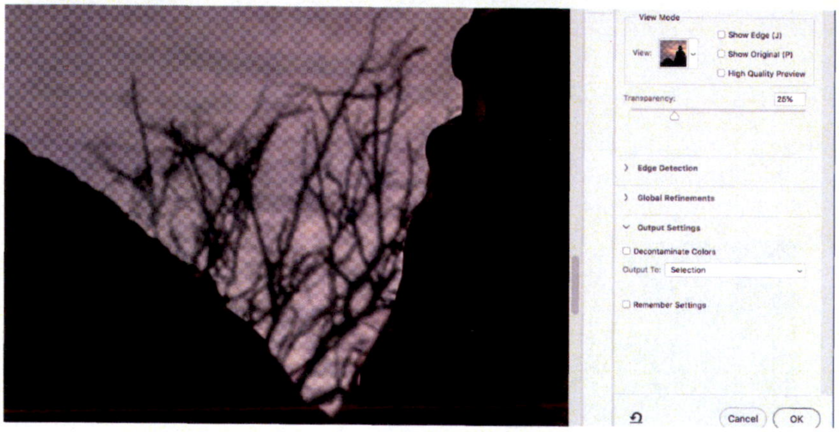

12. **Expand the Edge Detection and Global Refinements sections of the Properties panel and review the options.**

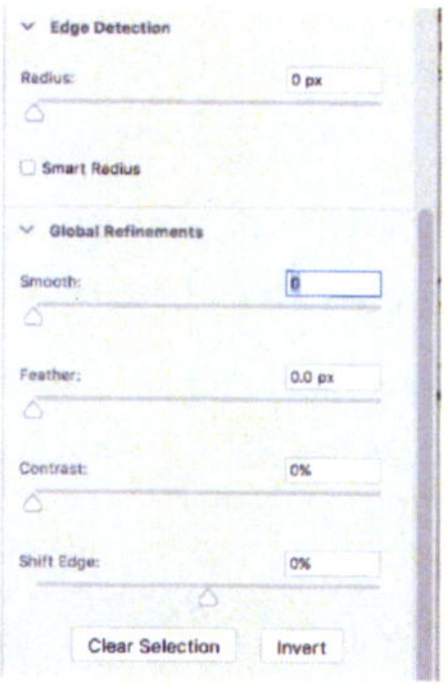

- **Radius** is the number of pixels around the edge that are affected. Higher radius values result in softer edges and lower values result in sharper edges.
- **Smart Radius** automatically adjusts the radius for hard and soft edges found in the border region. You should turn off this option if your selection area has all hard edges or all soft edges, or if you prefer to manually control the Radius.
- **Smooth** reduces the number of points that make up your selection and, as the name suggests, makes a smoother edge. You can set smoothness from 0 (very detailed selection) to 100 (very smooth selection).
- **Feather** softens the selection edge, resulting in a transition that does not have a hard edge (in other words, blends into the background). You can feather the selection up to 250 pixels.
- **Contrast** is the degree of variation allowed in the selection edge. Higher Contrast values (up to 100%) mean sharper selection edges.
- **Shift Edge** shrinks or grows the selection edge by the defined percentage (from –100% to 100%).
- **Invert** reverses the mask; selected areas become unselected and vice versa.

13. **Experiment with the various adjustments until you're satisfied with the selection edge.**

We increased the Smooth value to 10 to reduce jagged effects at the selection edge.

14. **Expand the Output Settings in the Properties panel and choose the Layer Mask option in the Output To menu.**

This menu can be used to create a new layer or file (with or without a mask) from the selection. You want to mask the existing layer, so you are using the Layer Mask option.

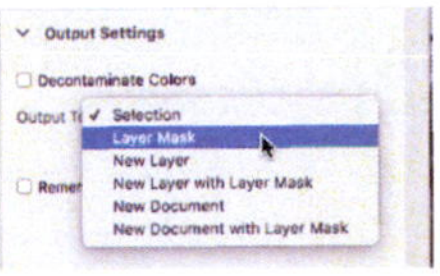

Note:

***Decontaminate Colors** can be checked to remove a certain percentage of color from the edge of a selection.*

15. **Click OK to accept your refined selection.**

When you pasted the feathered selection from the original Lightning.jpg file, you pasted only the pixels inside the selection area; unselected pixels from the original image are not a part of the composite file.

Rather than simply excluding or deleting pixels, a **layer mask** simply hides unwanted pixels. The mask you just created is a raster-based pixel mask; unselected (masked) areas are hidden but not deleted, so you can later edit the mask to change the visible part of the image. This is a non-destructive way to hide certain elements of a layer without permanently deleting pixels; you can edit or disable the layer mask at any time.

Note:

A layer mask is basically an Alpha channel that is connected to a specific layer.

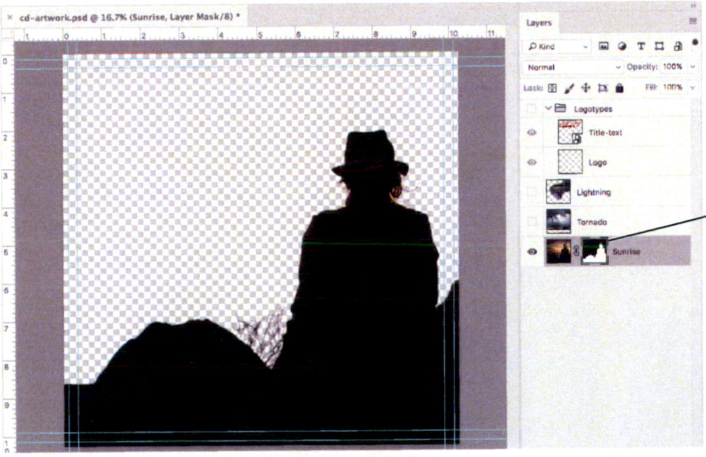

The resulting layer mask hides areas that were not selected.

16. **Control/right-click the mask thumbnail and choose Disable Layer Mask from the contextual menu.**

When you disable the mask, the background pixels are again visible. This is one of the advantages of using masks — the background pixels are not permanently removed, they are simply hidden.

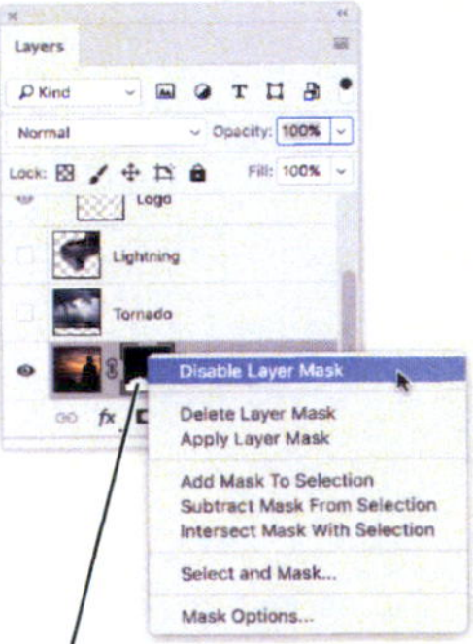

Click the thumbnail to open the mask's contextual menu.

When the mask is disabled, the masked pixels are visible.

A red X indicates that the mask is disabled.

17. **Control/right-click the mask thumbnail and choose Apply Layer Mask from the contextual menu.**

This option applies the mask to the attached layer, permanently removing the masked pixels from the layer.

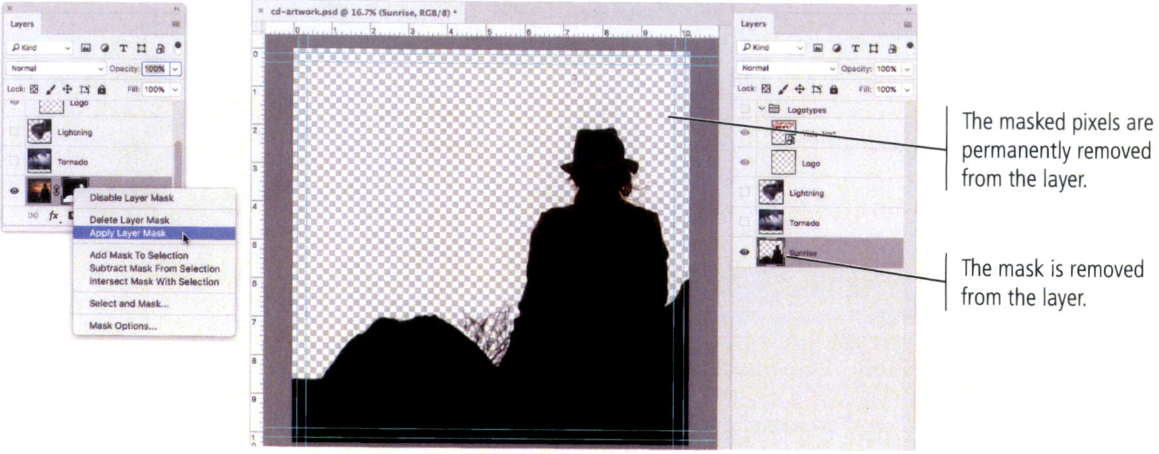

18. **Choose Edit>Undo Apply Layer Mask to restore the layer mask.**

As you saw in the previous step, applying a mask permanently removes the masked pixels. This essentially defeats the purpose of a mask, so you are restoring it in this step.

19. **Control/right-click the mask thumbnail and choose Enable Layer Mask from the contextual menu.**

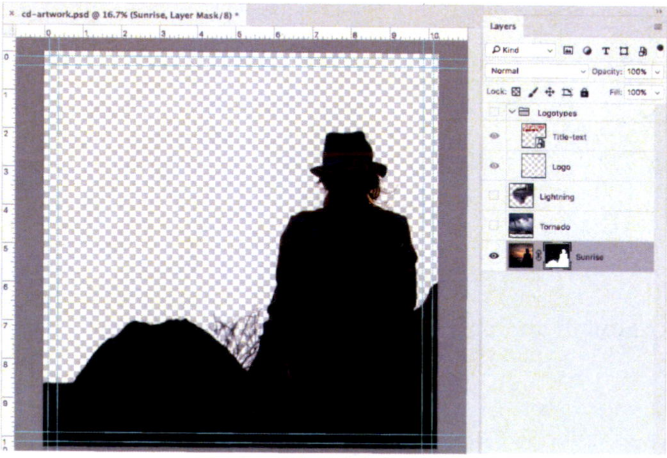

20. **Save the file and continue to the next exercise.**

Understanding Channels

You need a bit of background about channels to understand what's happening in the Quick Mask you will use in the next exercise. (You will use channels extensively in later projects.)

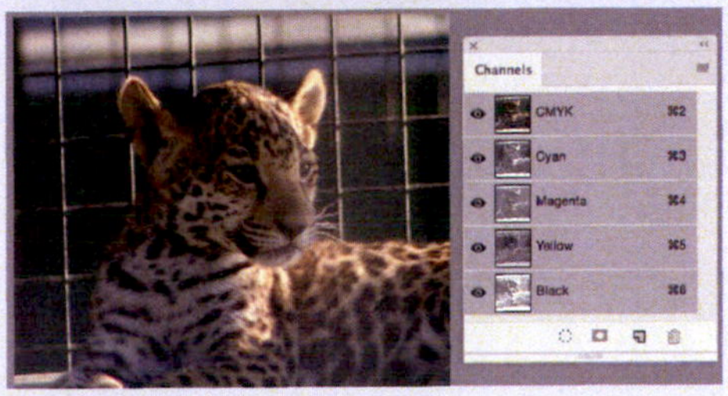

Every image has one channel for each component color. Each channel contains the information for the amount of that component color in any given pixel. An RGB image has three channels: Red, Green, and Blue (above right). A CMYK image has four channels: Cyan, Magenta, Yellow, and Black (below right).

In RGB images, the three additive primaries can have a value of 0 (none of that color) to 255 (full intensity of that color). Combining a value of 255 for each primary results in white; a value of 0 for each primary results in black.

In CMYK images, the three subtractive primaries plus black are combined in percentages from 0 (none of that color) to 100 (full intensity of that color) to create the range of printable colors. Channels in a CMYK image represent the printing plates or separations required to output the job.

Understanding Alpha Channels

An Alpha channel is a special type of channel in which the value determines the degree of transparency of a pixel. In other words, a 50% value in the Alpha channel means that area of the image will be 50% transparent.

When working in Quick Mask mode, a temporary Quick Mask channel stores the degree of transparency based on the current selection. A semi-transparent red overlay shows areas being masked (i.e., the areas that are not included in the current selection).

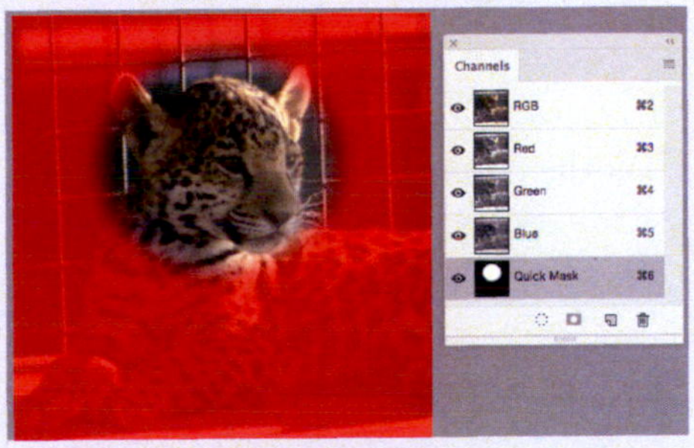

Quick Masks are useful when you need to work with a temporary selection, or if you are still defining the exact selection area. As long as you stay in Quick Mask mode, the temporary Alpha channel remains in the Channels panel (listed as "Quick Mask"). If you return to Standard mode, the Quick Mask disappears from the window and the panel.

You can save a Quick Mask channel as a permanent Alpha channel by dragging the Quick Mask channel onto the New Channel button at the bottom of the Channels panel. This adds a channel named "Quick Mask copy," which becomes a permanent part of the file even if you exit Quick Mask mode. You can then double-click the Alpha channel name in the panel to rename it, as we did in the following image (naming the channel "Baby Face").

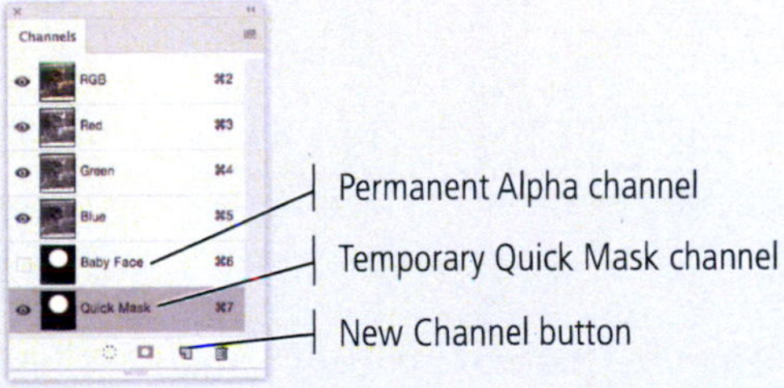

You can change the appearance of an Alpha channel mask by double-clicking a channel thumbnail in the Channels panel. In the top half of the resulting dialog box, you can change the overlay to show selected areas instead of the default masked areas.

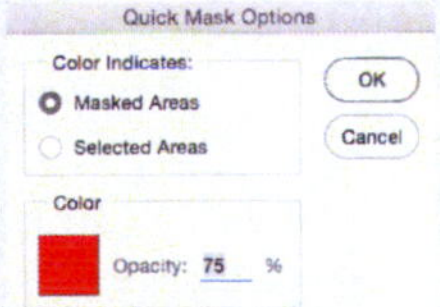

Clicking the Color swatch opens a Color Picker, where you can change the color of the Quick Mask overlay. You can also use the Opacity field to change the transparency of the overlay (the default is 50%). Keep in mind that these settings only affect the appearance of the mask in Photoshop; the density of the selection is not affected by changing the overlay opacity.

Edit a Layer Mask

If you look closely, the bottom-left corner of the masked image layer includes some of the background water because the dark colors are very close to the dark colors in the foreground rock. In this exercise, you will use built-in painting tools to manually edit the mask and remove the remaining water from the visible layer pixels.

1. **With `cd-artwork.psd` open, zoom in to the bottom-left corner of the image.**

   It might be difficult to see, but if you look carefully you can see that part of the visible area is water instead of foreground rocks. (We outlined the area in red for the sake of illustration.)

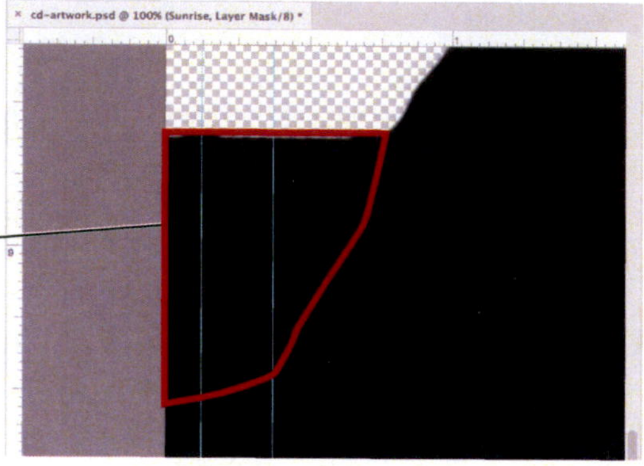

Some of this area
is actually water. It
should be masked out.

2. **In the Layers panel, click the Sunrise layer mask thumbnail to select it.**

These corner icons
indicate that the
base layer is selected.
Clicking the layer mask
thumbnail selects the
mask so you can edit it.

3. **Open the Channels panel (Window>Channels), then click the empty space on the left side of the panel to make the Sunrise Mask channel visible.**

   Layer masks are not visible by default; you have to turn them on in the Channels panel to see them. This isn't strictly necessary, since you can paint a mask without seeing it, but it is easier (at least when you're first learning) to be able to see what you're painting. By painting on a layer mask, you're not really "painting" anything; instead, you're actually "painting" the visibility of the associated layer.

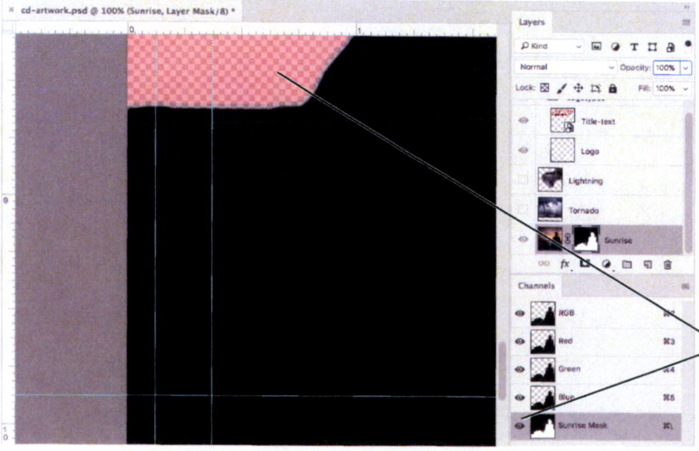

Making the mask
channel visible allows
you to see the red
overlay in the image.

4. **In the Channels panel, double-click the Sunrise Mask channel thumbnail. Change the Opacity value to 100% in the Layer Mask Display Options dialog box, then click OK.**

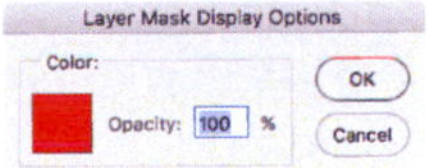

Remember, this change only affects the transparency of the mask, not the degree of transparency applied to the layer. By setting the mask opacity to 100%, you know that anything solid red will be hidden and anything with no red will be visible.

5. **Choose the Brush tool in the Tools panel.**

6. **Click the Default Foreground and Background Colors button at the bottom of the Tools panel.**

If you look at the layer mask thumbnail for the layer, you can see it's just a black-and-white shape. White areas of the thumbnail show which parts of the layer are visible in the main document; the black parts of the mask hide the associated areas of the layer. This is an important distinction: painting with black on a layer mask hides those areas; painting with white on a layer mask reveals those areas.

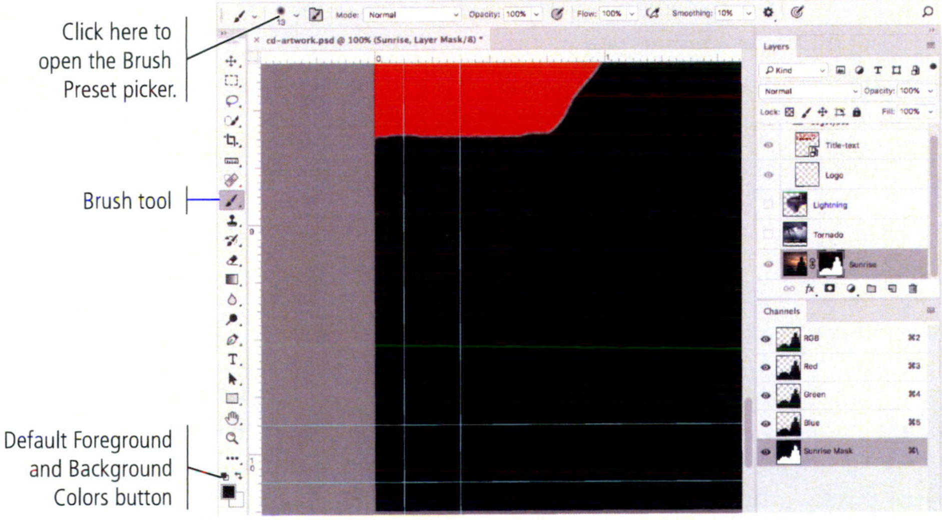

7. **In the Options bar, open the Brush Preset picker to access the tool options.**

This panel shows the different brushes that are included with Photoshop. The default brush set includes a number of specific-diameter hard- and soft-edge brushes, as well as some artistic options. A number below a brush icon shows the size of the brush; if you click a specific brush in the panel, the same number displays in the Size field.

8. **In the top half of the Brush Preset picker, change the Size value to 50 px and change the Hardness value to 100%.**

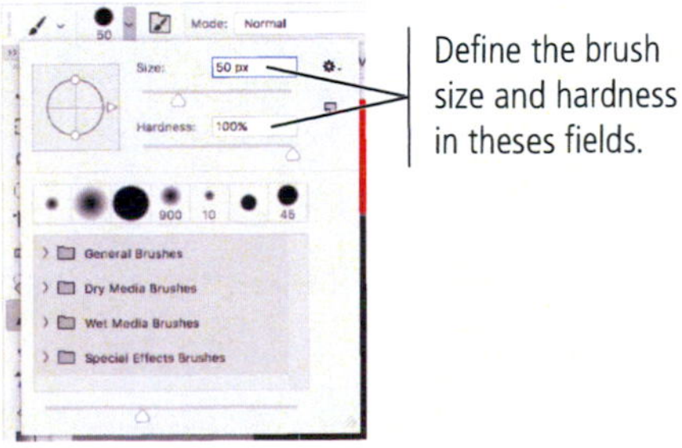

Define the brush size and hardness in theses fields.

Note:

You will use brushes extensively in Project 7: House Painting; for now, you only need to know how to select a brush and how to paint with it.

9. **Press Return/Enter to dismiss the Brush Preset picker.**

10. **With the Brush tool active and Black as the active foreground color, click and drag over the area that you want to add to the mask.**

The Brush tool paints with whatever is defined as the foreground color, which is black in this case. Remember: When painting on a mask, black adds to the mask and hides pixels on the masked layer.

> *Note:*
>
> *Even though you're painting with black, the stroke appears as red because that's the defined mask color.*

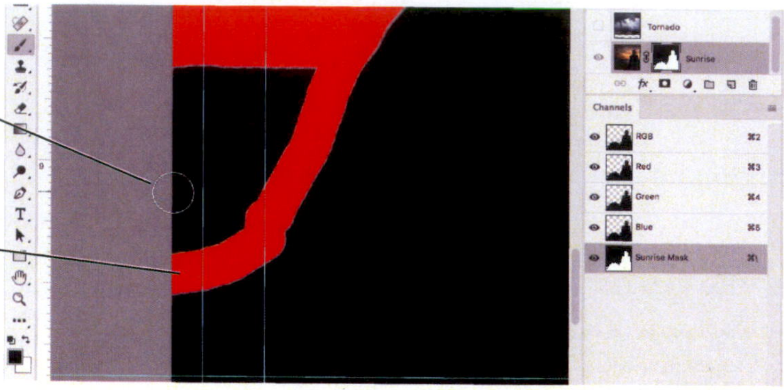
The Brush tool cursor reflects the size of the brush.
Paint with black to remove pixels from the image (add to the mask).

11. **Continue to paint on the mask channel until you are satisfied with your mask. Keep the following points in mind as you paint:**

- You can use the bracket keys to enlarge (]) or reduce ([) the brush size.
- Painting on a mask with white removes from the mask area, revealing the masked layer's pixels.
- Click the Switch Foreground and Background Colors button near the bottom of the Tools panel.
- You can press X to switch the current foreground and background colors. This is very useful to remember when you are painting on a mask, because you can reset the default (black and white) colors and switch them as necessary depending on what you want to accomplish.
- You can also use the Eraser tool on a mask. Be careful, though, because erasing an area of the mask when the foreground color is white has the same effect as painting with the background color.

Paint the mask with white to reveal areas.
Switch Foreground and Background Colors button

12. **Save the file and continue to the next exercise.**

Edit Layer Mask Properties

The most important thing to understand in this series of exercises is that layer masks are non-destructive. You can change the mask to change the visible area of the layer, temporarily hide the mask to show the entire layer, or even delete the mask entirely if you decide you don't want or need it. You can also edit a number of mask properties to further refine the mask and its effect on the masked layer contents.

1. **With cd-artwork.psd open, double-click the Sunrise Mask channel icon in the Channels panel.**

2. **Change the Opacity field to 50%, then click OK.**

   Remember, the Layer Mask Display Options setting only affects the mask's visibility in the document window. This does *not* affect the degree to which the mask affects pixels on the masked layer.

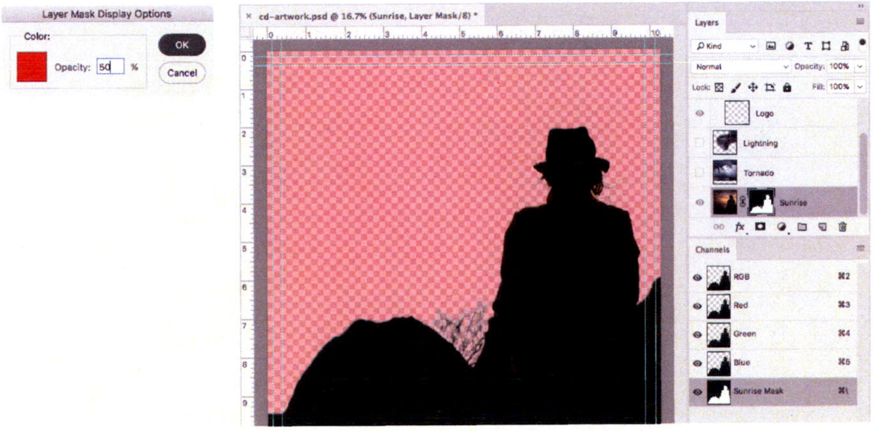

3. **In the Channels panel, click the eye icon for the Sunrise Mask channel.**

   Even when the actual mask channel is not visible, the mask remains in tact on the layer.

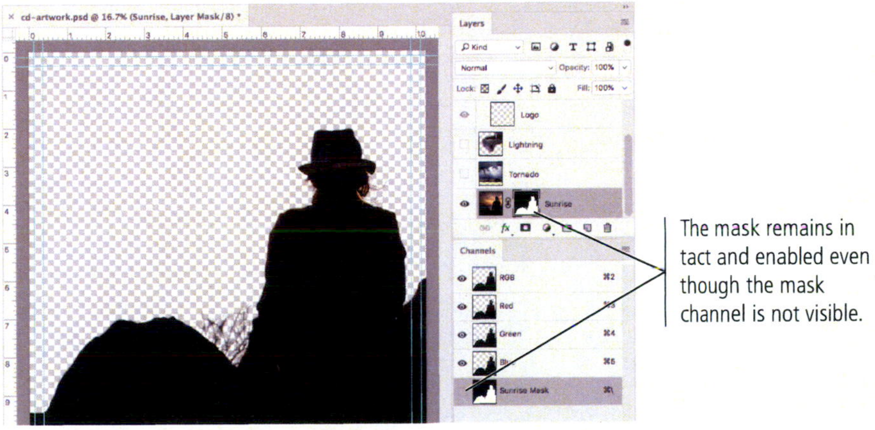

The mask remains in tact and enabled even though the mask channel is not visible.

4. **With the layer mask still selected in the Layers panel, open the Properties panel (Window>Properties).**

   Like the Options bar, the Properties panel is contextual. Different options are available in the panel depending on what is selected in the Layers panel. When a layer mask is selected, you can manipulate a variety of properties related to the selected mask.

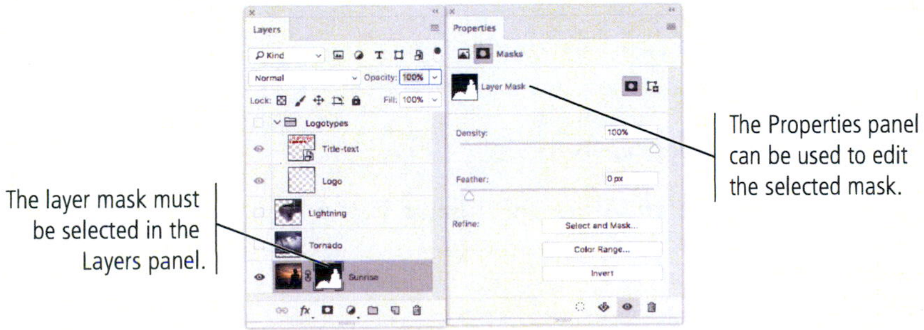

The layer mask must be selected in the Layers panel.
The Properties panel can be used to edit the selected mask.

   The Density slider changes the opacity of the overall mask. If you reduce the density to 80%, for example, underlying layers will be 20% visible through the mask. (Don't confuse this with the opacity of an alpha channel, which only affects the appearance of the mask on screen.)

> **Note:**
>
> *The Select and Mask button opens the Select and Mask workspace. The Color Range button opens the [Select] Color Range dialog box.*

5. **In the Properties panel, change the Feather value to 25 px.**

   If you feather a selection and then make a layer mask from that selection, the feathering becomes a permanent part of the mask. The Properties panel allows you to adjust the feathering of a hard-edge mask, and then later change or even remove the feathering if necessary, without painting on the mask.

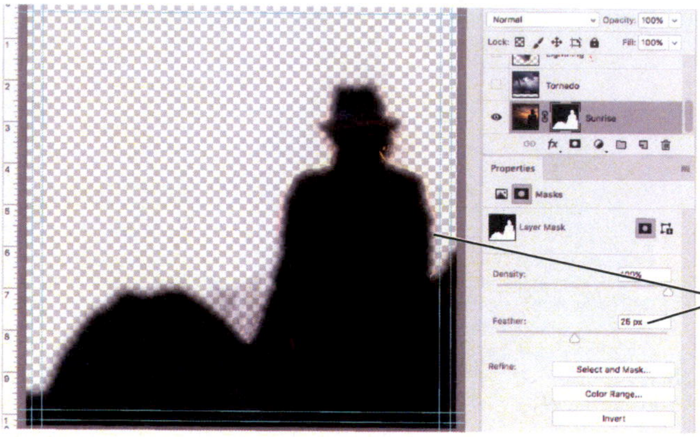

Use the Properties panel to feather the mask edge non-destructively.

6. **Change the Feather value to 1 px.**

   This small feathering value will help to remove (or at least minimize) any remaining background artifacts around the edges of your mask.

7. **Save the file and continue to the next exercise.**

Arrange Layer Position and Stacking Order

The ad is almost final, but a few pieces are still not quite in position. You already know you can use the Move tool to move the contents of a layer around on the canvas. You can also move a layer to any position in the stacking order (the top-to-bottom position of a layer) by simply dragging it to a new position in the Layers panel.

1. **With `cd-artwork.psd` open, make all layers visible.**

2. **Click the Sunrise layer in the Layers panel and drag up. When a heavy bar appears above the Lightning layer, release the mouse button.**

The heavy line indicates where the layer will be positioned when you release the mouse button.

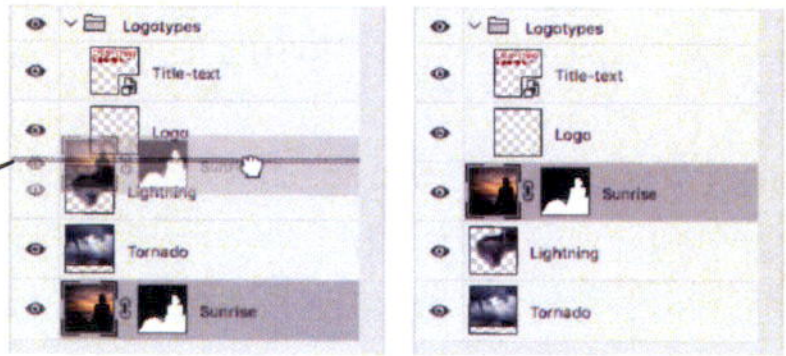

Note:

Be careful when dragging layers near a layer group: If the border appears around a layer group, releasing the mouse button would place the dragged layer inside of the group.

After you restack the layers, you can see that a small blank space appears in the bottom-right corner. (Yours might be slightly different depending on how you painted the mask in the previous exercise.)

This transparent area needs to be filled for the overall composition to be complete.

> *Note:*
>
> *Press Command/ Control-[(left bracket) to move a layer down in the stacking order.*
>
> *Press Command/ Control-] (right bracket) to move a layer up in the stacking order.*

3. **In the Layers panel, select the Tornado layer as the active one.**
4. **Press Command/Control-T to enter Free Transform mode.**
5. **Press Shift, then drag the bottom-right corner until the transparent area in the bottom-left corner is filled.**

   Keep in mind that you are now enlarging a raster-image layer, which can cause loss of image detail. Because this is a very small increase in size, and because the layer is the background image behind several other elements, you can make this enlargement without ruining the integrity of the composition.

Shift-drag the bottom-right corner to enlarge the active layer until this area is filled.

6. **Press Return/Enter to finalize the transformation.**
7. **Select the Lightning layer in Layers panel, then change the layer opacity to 35%.**

   Layer opacity is the degree to which you can see underlying layers through the layer you are editing. Because you made the lightning only 35% opaque, the underlying tornado image is strongly visible the lightning.

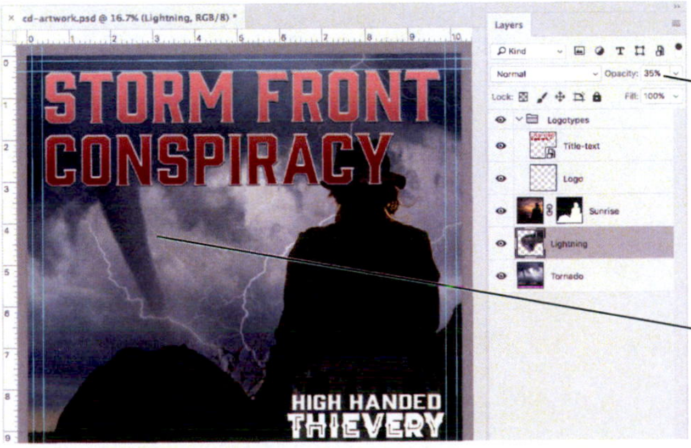

Type in this field to change the active layer's opacity.

The underlying Tornado layer is now visible through the Lightning layer.

8. **Save the file and then continue to the final stage of the project.**

Filtering Layers

When you work with complex files, you might find yourself with dozens — or even hundreds — of layers. Descriptive names can help you navigate through the layers, but you still have to scroll through the panel to find what you need.

Layer filtering, available at the top of the Layers panel, allows you to narrow down the panel to only layers that meet certain criteria — making it much easier to locate a specific layer.

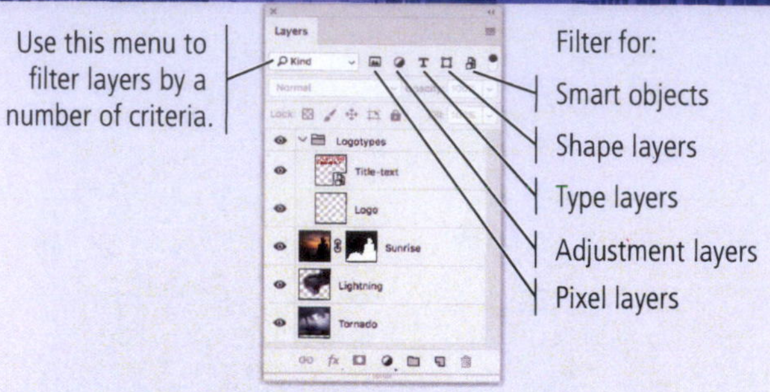

Use this menu to filter layers by a number of criteria.

Pixel layers

When **Kind** is selected in the menu, you can use the associated buttons to show only certain types of layers (adjustment layers, smart objects, etc.).

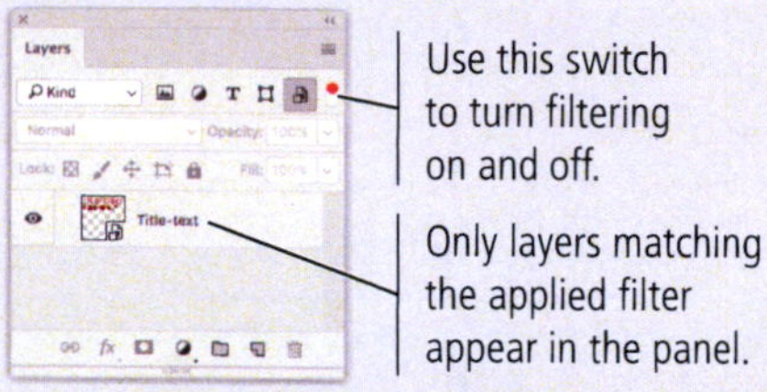

Use this switch to turn filtering on and off.
Only layers matching the applied filter appear in the panel.

When **Name** is selected, you can type in the attached field to find layers with names that include the text you enter in the field. The defined text string does not need to be at the beginning of the layer name; for example, typing "r" would return both Sunrise and Tornado layers in the file for this project.

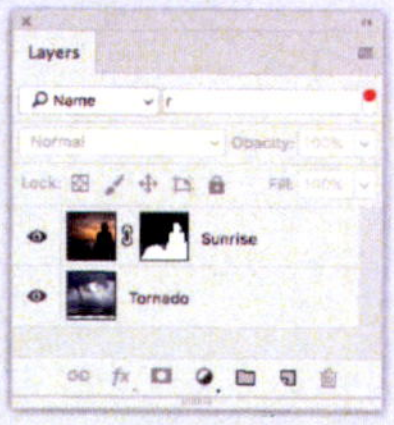

When **Effect** is selected, you can use the secondary menu to find only layers with a specified effect (applied using the Layer>Layer Style submenu).

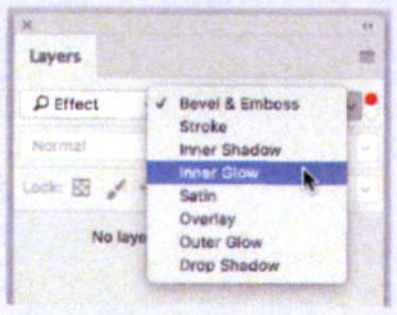

When **Attribute** is selected, you can choose from a number of layer attributes — visible, linked, clipped, masked, etc.

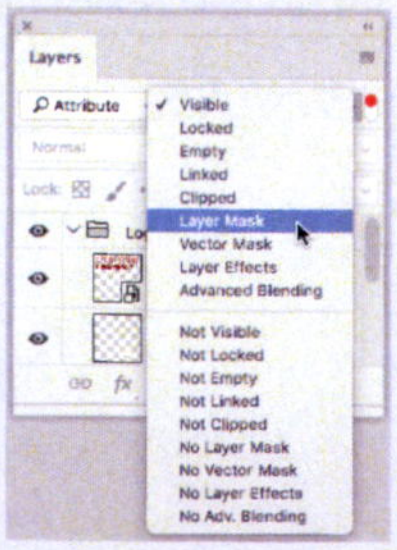

When **Color** is selected, you can choose any of the built-in colors from the secondary menu. (These colors, which appear around the layer's visibility icon, can be assigned to individual layers in each layer's contextual menu.)

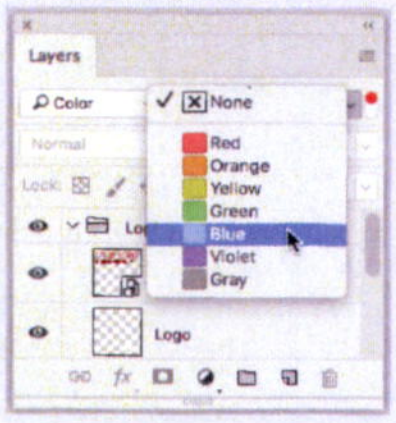

When **Mode** is selected, you can use the secondary menu to find only layers to which a certain blending mode has been assigned.

When **Smart Object** is selected, you can use the buttons at the top of the panel to find linked layers, layers with modified source data, layers with missing source data, or embedded layers. These buttons are non-exclusive, which means you can select more than one option at a time (for example, all layers with missing and modified source data).

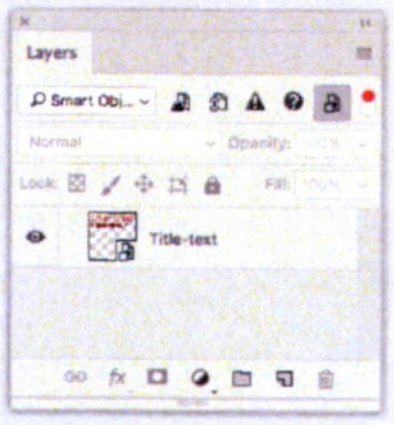

The **Selected** option shows a subset of layers that exist in Isolation mode. To create a subset, select one or more layers in the Layers panel and then choose Select>Isolate Layers. The Layers panel automatically shows a subset of only the selected layers, and Selected appears in the Filter By menu.

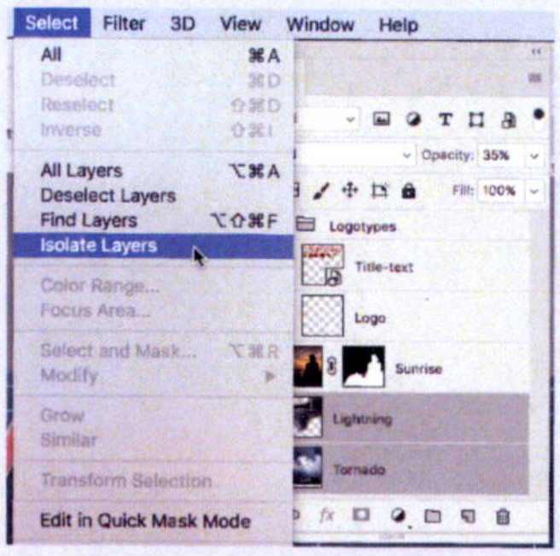

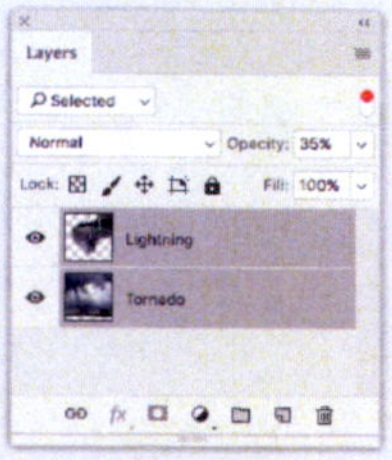

Stage 4 Saving Files for Multiple Media

Many Photoshop projects require saving the completed file in more than one format. Many artists prefer to leave all files in the native PSD format since there is only one file to track. Others prefer to send only flattened TIFF files of their artwork because the individual elements can't be changed. Ultimately, the formats you use will depend on where and how the file is being placed.

Many Photoshop projects are pieces of a larger composition; the overall project defines the format you need. The ad you just created, for example, will be placed in magazine layouts, which will be built in a page-layout application such as Adobe InDesign. Although the current versions of industry-standard page-layout applications can support native layered PSD files, older versions can't import those native files. As the Photoshop artist, you have to save your work in a format that is compatible with the process being used by the magazine designer.

As you know, the artwork you created will be used in a variety of ways. You need to save three different versions of the artwork to meet those requirements.

Photoshop can save files in a number of common formats, including:

- **Photoshop**, with the extension PSD, is the native format.
- **JPEG** is a lossy compressed file format that does not support transparency.
- **Photoshop PDF** can contain all required font and image information in a single file, which can be compressed to reduce file size.
- **PNG** is a raster-based format that supports both continuous-tone color and transparency. It is more commonly used in digital publishing (specifically, web design), and does not support CMYK color required for commercial printing.
- **TIFF** is a raster-based image format that supports layers, alpha channels, and file compression.

Save a Flattened TIFF File

The TIFF format is commonly used for print applications. Although the format can include layers, many designers prefer to send flattened files for output to avoid any potential problems that might be caused by older output devices (which is still an issue, since many service providers do not update very expensive output equipment until it becomes absolutely necessary).

In this exercise you will save the finished artwork as a flattened TIFF file that can be used for the album cover sleeve, as well as for most print advertising requirements.

1. **With cd-artwork.psd open, choose File>Save As.**

   The CD artwork is complete in the native Photoshop file. In the next few exercises you are going to make changes that you don't want to become a permanent part of the file. Saving it now, if you haven't already, means the finished artwork file won't be compromised in the following exercises.

2. **If necessary, navigate to your WIP>Music folder as the target location.**

   The Save As dialog box defaults to the last-used location. If you continued the entire way through this project without stopping, you won't have to navigate.

3. **In the Save As/File Name field, type -album at the end of the current file name (before the .psd extension).**

4. **Click the Format/Save As Type menu and choose TIFF.**

5. **In the bottom half of the dialog box, uncheck the Layers option.**

Because this file contains layers, the Layers option is checked by default.

The As a Copy box is now selected by default. A warning shows that the file must be saved as a copy when the Layers option is unchecked. (This is basically a failsafe built into Photoshop that prevents you from overwriting your layered file with a flattened version.)

If your file contained alpha channels, annotations, or spot colors, those check boxes would also be available.

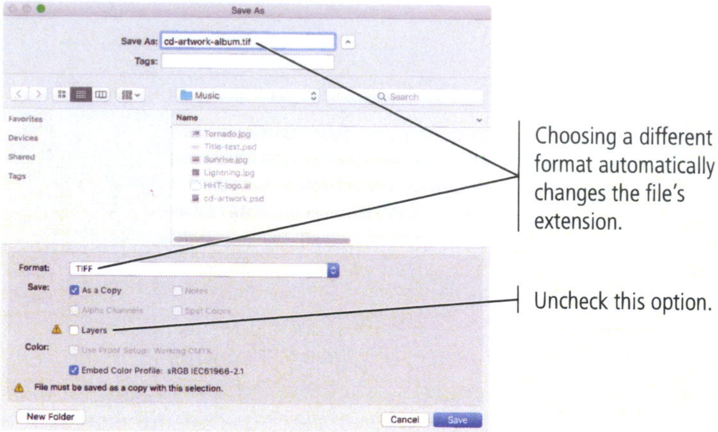

6. **Leave the remaining options at their default values and click Save.**

7. **In the resulting TIFF Options dialog box, make sure the None image compression option is selected.**

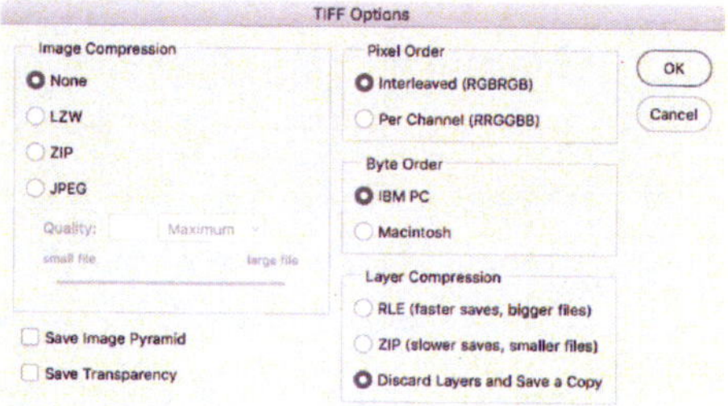

TIFF files can be compressed (made smaller) using three methods:

- **None** (as the name implies) applies no compression to the file. This option is safe if file size is not an issue, but digital file transmission often requires files to be smaller than a full-page, multi-layered Photoshop file.
- **LZW** (Lempel-Ziv-Welch) compression is **lossless**, which means all file data is maintained in the compressed file.
- **ZIP** compression is also lossless, but is not supported by all desktop-publishing software (especially older versions).
- **JPEG** is a **lossy** compression scheme, which means some data will be thrown away to reduce the file size. If you choose JPEG compression, the Quality options determine how much data can be discarded. Maximum quality means less data is thrown out and the file is larger. Minimum quality discards the most data and results in a smaller file size.

8. **Leave the Pixel Order radio button at the default value, and choose the Byte Order option for your operating system.**

Pixel Order determines how channel data is encoded. The Interleaved (RGBRGB) option is the default; Per Channel (RRGGBB) is called "planar" order.

Byte Order determines which platform can use the file, although this is somewhat deceptive. On older versions of most desktop-publishing software, Macintosh systems can read the PC byte order but Windows couldn't read the Macintosh byte order — which is why even the Macintosh system defaults to the IBM PC option. This option is becoming obsolete because most newer software can read either byte order.

Save Image Pyramid creates a tiered file with multiple resolution versions; this isn't widely used or supported by other applications, so you can typically leave it unchecked.

If your file contains transparency, the **Save Transparency** check box will be available. If you don't choose this option, transparent areas will be white in the saved file.

Note:

Some experts argue that choosing the order for your system can improve print quality, especially on desktop output devices.

9. **In the Layer Compression area, make sure the Discard option is selected.**

These three options explain — right in the dialog box — what they do.

10. **Click OK to save the file, then continue to the next exercise.**

Reduce the Physical File Size

The CD insert artwork needs to be approximately half the size of the album artwork. Reducing the file's physical size is an easy process, although you need to check the positioning of various elements to make sure they meet the output requirements. In this exercise you will reduce the file's physical size, then make necessary layer adjustments to meet the needs of the CD insert.

1. **With `cd-artwork.psd` open in Photoshop, choose Image>Image Size.**

2. **Make sure the Resample option is checked.**

   You are resizing this image, which means you are changing the physical dimensions (and the actual number of pixels in the file). If Resample was not checked, you would simply be redistributing the same number of pixels across a different physical space.

3. **With Inches selected in the Width and Height Units menus, type 5 in the Width field.**

   The CD insert is 4.75″ square, but it requires 1/8″ bleeds on all four sides:

   4.75″ + 0.125″ + 0.125″ = 5″

   Because the width and height are constrained by default, changing one value applies a proportional change to the other value.

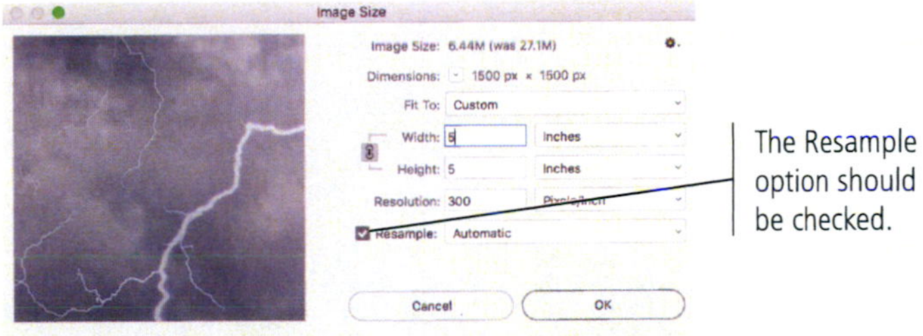

4. **Click OK to change the file size.**

5. **Zoom in to the top-left corner and review the position of the guides.**

   Reducing the file size affects all elements of the file, including guides. As you can see, the position of the various guides is reduced by approximately half (for example, the bleed guides are near the 1/16″ mark instead of the 1/8″ mark).

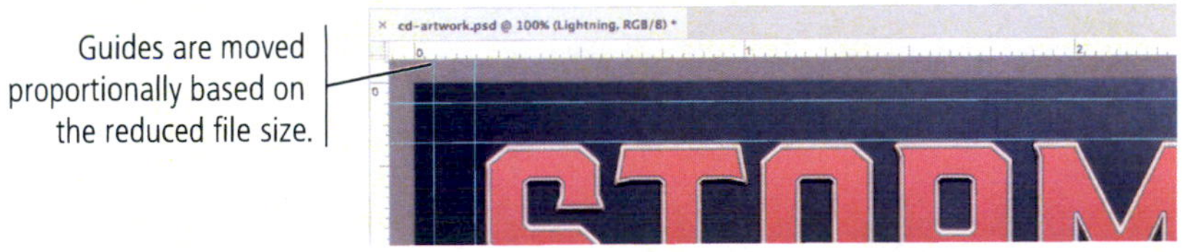

Guides are moved proportionally based on the reduced file size.

6. **Choose View>Clear Guides.**

   Rather than manually dragging each guide on the page, you are going to simply replace them with new ones. This command removes all existing guides from the canvas.

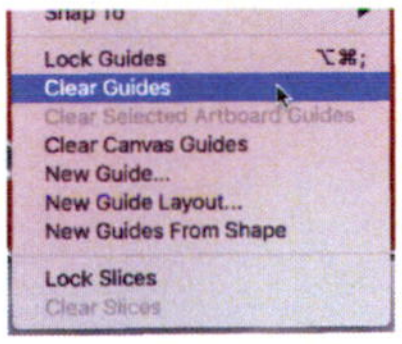

7. **Choose View>New Guide Layout.**

8. **With the Margin option checked, change all four fields to `0.125 in`. Click OK to add the new guides.**

   This set of guides defines the trim size of the CD insert, marking a 1/8″ bleed allowance on all four edges of the file.

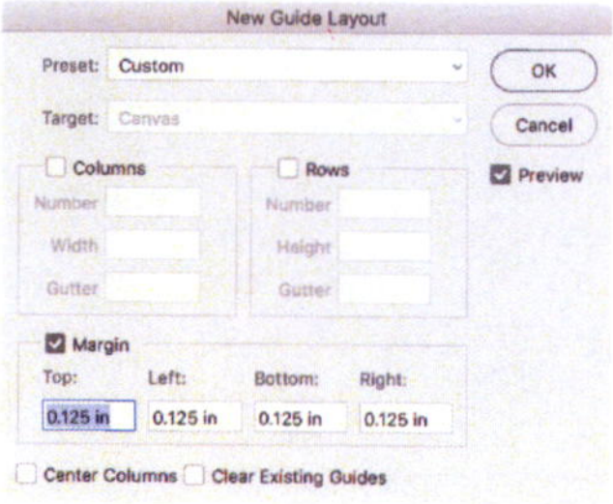

9. **Choose View>New Guide Layout again.**

10. **With the Margin option checked, change all four fields to `0.25 in`. Click OK to add the new guides.**

    This second set of guides define the live area for the CD insert, marking the required 1/8″ safe margin. Although they are 1/4″ from the canvas edge, they are 1/8″ from the guides that define the trim size.

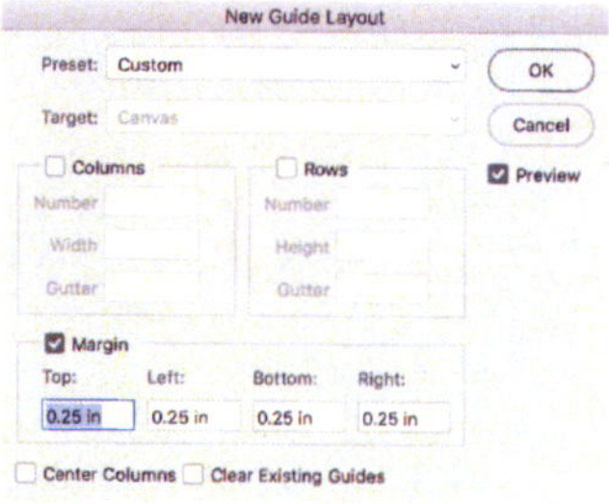

11. **Zoom out so you can see the entire top of the artwork.**

12. **Choose the Move tool in the Tools panel. In the Options bar, make sure the Auto-Select option is checked and Layer is selected in the attached menu.**

    When active, clicking in the document window automatically selects the layer containing the layers where you click.

    Because Layer is selected in the menu, only the relevant layer will move even if it is part of a layer group. If you want all layers in a group containing the selected layer to move, you can choose Group in the menu.

13. **Click any of the letters in the album title and drag until the layer snaps to the top and left margin guides.**

> ***Note:***
>
> *If Auto-Select is active and Layer is selected in the menu, only the relevant layer will move even if it is part of a layer group. If you want all layers in a group containing the selected layer to move, you can choose Group in the menu.*

14. **Press Command/Control-T to enter Free Transform mode. Press Shift, then click and drag the bottom-right bounding box handle until the title fits inside the margin guides in the reduced file.**

Shift-drag the bottom-left handle to fit the title into the live area.

15. **Press Return/Enter to finalize the transformation.**

16. **With the Move tool still active, click any pixel in the logo and drag until it snaps to the bottom and right margin guides.**

Because the Auto-Select option is active, you don't need to first select the target layer in the Layers panel to move the content.

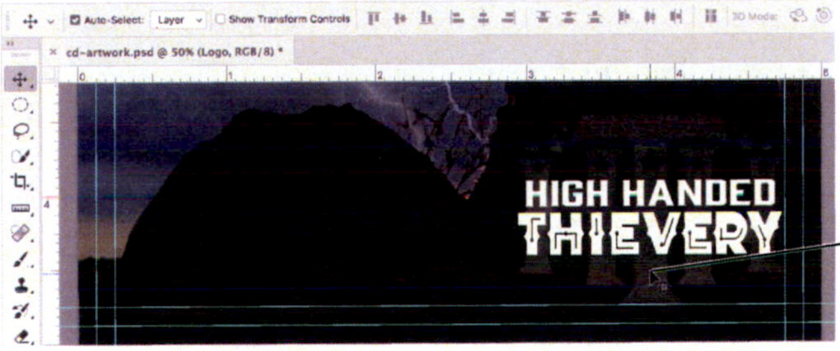

Click any pixel in the logo artwork and drag to move the layer content.

17. **Choose File>Save As. Using the same method as in the previous exercise, save this file as a flat TIFF file named cd-artwork-insert.tif. Click OK to accept the default TIFF options.**

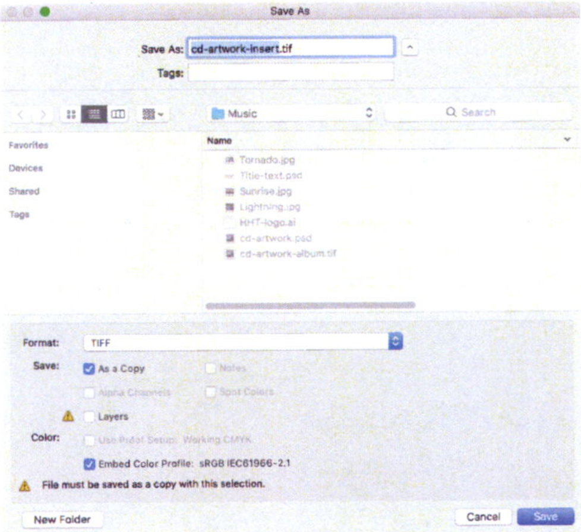

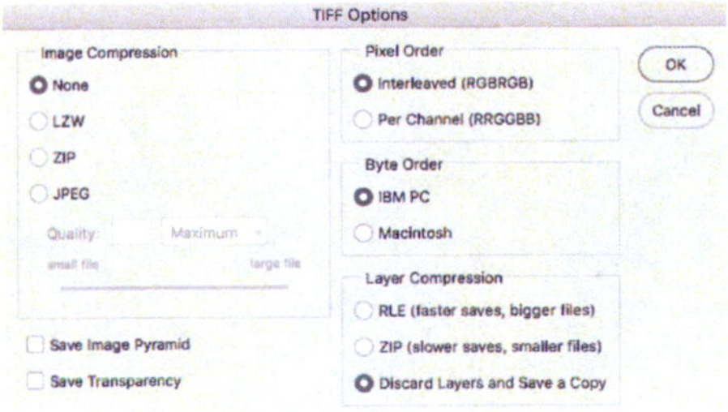

18. **With `cd-artwork.psd` still active, choose File>Revert.**

This command restores the file to the last-saved version. Because you saved the completed artwork at the beginning of this stage, the command restores the artwork to its original 10.25″ file size.

Because enlarging a raster image to such a degree (more than 200% to go from 5″ to 10.25″) would almost certainly cause image degradation, you are restoring the larger version instead of saving the smaller one.

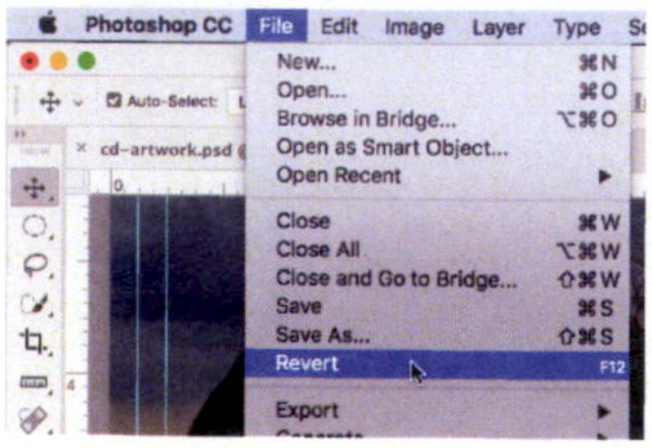

19. **Continue to the next exercise.**

Save a JPEG File for Digital Media

The final file required for this project is a 3000 x 3000 pixel, high-quality JPEG file.

1. **With `cd-artwork.psd` open and restored to its last-saved state, choose Image>Image Size.**

2. **Choose Pixels in the Width menu.**

3. **With the Resample option checked, change the Width field to `3000`.**

Again, you are defining the actual number of pixels to include in the file. If the resample was not checked, changing the width or height would only change the distribution of pixels instead of changing the actual number of pixels in the file.

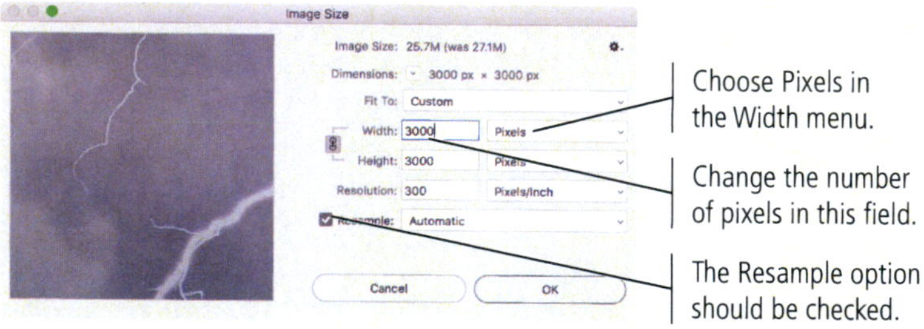

4. **Click OK to finalize the new size.**

This file is not being printed, so you don't need to worry about the bleed and margin areas. Because the size reduction is slight in this case, no further adjustment is required before saving the JPEG file for digital music libraries.

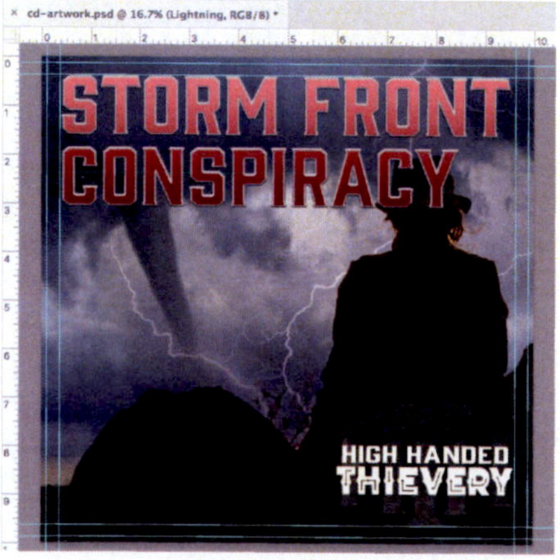

5. **Choose File>Save As.**

6. **Choose JPEG in the Format/Save As Type menu, then change the file name to cd-artwork-digital.jpg.**

   The JPEG format does not support layers, alpha channels, or spot colors, so those options are unavailable in the bottom of the dialog box.

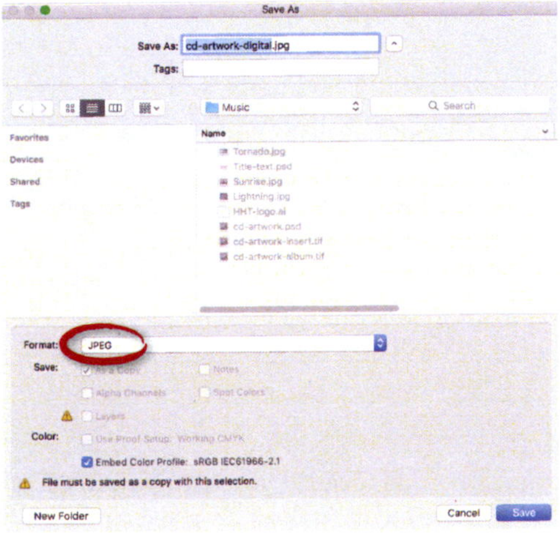

7. **Click Save.**

8. **In the resulting JPEG Options dialog box, choose High in the Image Options Quality menu.**

   This menu determines how much compression will be used in the resulting file:

   - Higher values mean less compression, better quality, and larger file size.
   - Lower values mean more compression, lower quality, and smaller file size.

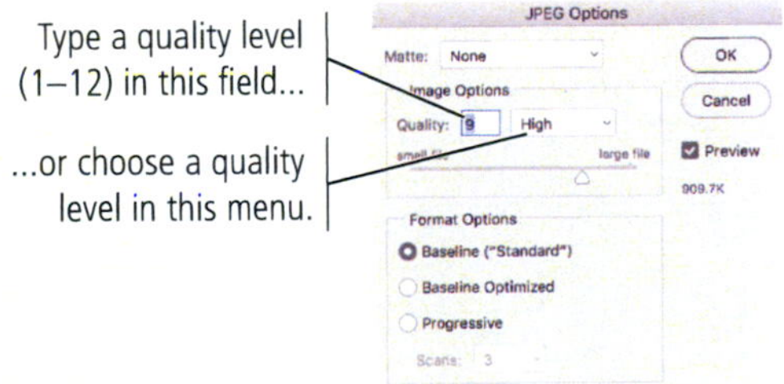

9. **Click OK to save the JPEG file.**

10. **Close the cd-artwork.psd file without saving.**

Project Review

fill in the blank

1. _______________ is likely to cause degradation of a raster image when it's reproduced on a printing press.

2. A _______________ is a linked file that you placed into another Photoshop document.

3. The _______________ is context sensitive, providing access to different functions depending on what tool is active.

4. The _______________ is the final size of a printed page.

5. The _______________ tool is used to draw irregular-shaped selection marquees.

6. The _______________ tool is used to select areas of similar color by clicking and dragging in the image window.

7. The _______________ tool can be used to drag layer contents to another position within the image, or into another open document.

8. When selecting color ranges, the _______________ value determines how much of the current color range falls into the selection.

9. A _______________ can be used to non-destructively hide certain areas of a layer.

10. _______________ is a lossy compression method that is best used when large file size might be a problem.

short answer

1. Briefly describe the difference between raster images and vector graphics.

2. Briefly explain three separate methods for isolating an image from its background.

3. Briefly explain the concept of a layer mask.

Portfolio Builder Project

Use what you learned in this project to complete the following freeform exercise.
Carefully read the art director and client comments, then create your design to meet the needs of the project.
Use the space below to sketch ideas; when finished, write a brief explanation of the reasoning behind your design.

art director comments

Your client's friend liked your work on the new CD artwork. She would like to hire you again to create the ad concept and final files for a new movie that they're releasing early next year.

To complete this project, you should:

- ❑ Download the **Airborne_PS18_PB.zip** archive from the Student Files web page to access the client-supplied title artwork and rating placeholder file.
- ❑ Find appropriate background and foreground images for the movie theme (see the client's comments at right).
- ❑ Incorporate the title artwork, logos, and rating placeholder that the client provided.
- ❑ Composite the different elements into a single completed file; save both a layered version and a flattened version.

client comments

The movie is titled *Above and Beyond*. Although the story is fictionalized, it will focus on the men who led the first U.S. Airborne unit (the 501st), which suffered more than 2,000 casualties in the European theater of World War II.

We don't have any other images in mind, but the final ad should reflect the time period (the 1940s) of the movie. The 501st Parachute Infantry Battalion was trained to parachute into battle, so you should probably incorporate some kind of parachute image.

This movie is a joint venture between Sun and Tantamount, so both logos need to be included in the new ad. It isn't rated yet, so please use the "This Movie Is Not Yet Rated" artwork as a placeholder.

Create this ad big enough to fit on an 8.5″ × 11″ page, but keep the live area an inch inside the trim so the ad can be used in different-sized magazines.

project justification

Project Summary

Making selections is one of the most basic, and most important, skills that you will learn in Photoshop. Selections are so important that Photoshop dedicates an entire menu to the process.

As you created the movie ad in this project, you used a number of skills and techniques that you will apply in many (if not all) projects you build in Photoshop. You learned a number of ways to make both simple and complex selections — and you will learn additional methods in later projects. You also learned how to work with multiple layers, which will be an important part of virtually every Photoshop project you create, both in this book and throughout your career.

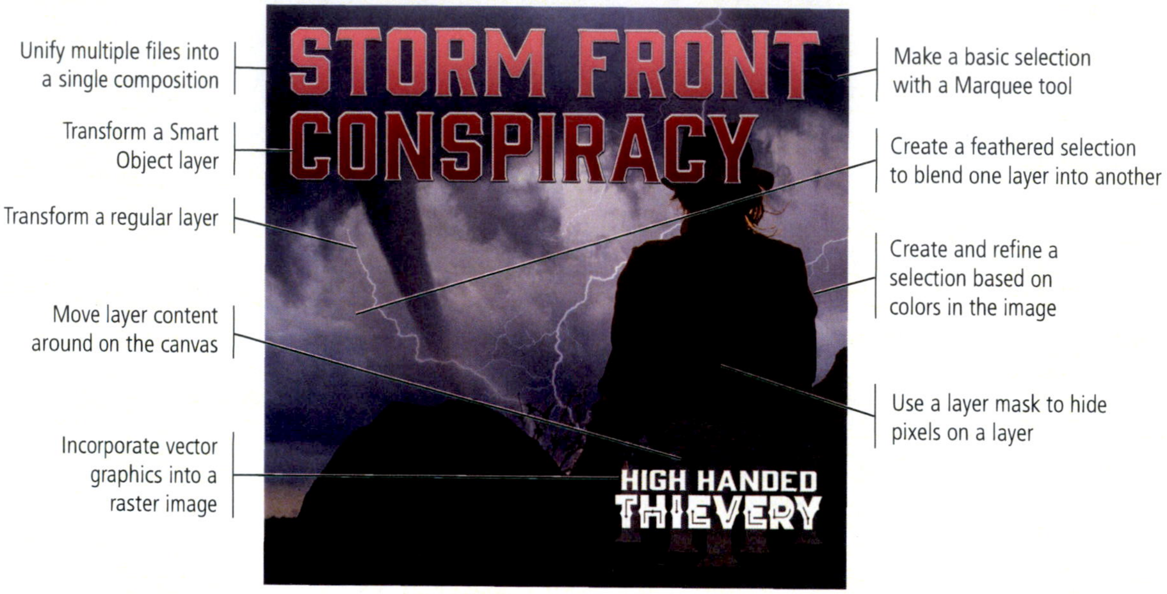

Unify multiple files into a single composition
Transform a Smart Object layer
Transform a regular layer
Move layer content around on the canvas
Incorporate vector graphics into a raster image
STORM FRONT
CONSPIRACY
HIGH HANDED
THIEVERY
Make a basic selection with a Marquee tool
Create a feathered selection to blend one layer into another
Create and refine a selection based on colors in the image
Use a layer mask to hide pixels on a layer

project 2

Car Magazine Cover

Your client publishes a monthly magazine for car enthusiasts. Your agency has been hired to take over the magazine design; you have been tasked with designing the cover for the next issue.

This project incorporates the following skills:

- ❏ Resizing and resampling supplied images
- ❏ Creating complex vector paths and shape layers
- ❏ Compositing images as Smart Objects
- ❏ Applying non-destructive styles, effects, and filters
- ❏ Developing a custom artistic background

Project Meeting

client comments

Every month, the magazine cover includes one main featured car, and three smaller images related to other articles in the issue. In addition to those images and the magazine title, we also always include several text blurbs with teasers for secondary articles in the issue, and a QR code that links to the website.

We're looking for a new way to present these elements. Once we finalize a general layout, we'll use that layout going forward for every new issue.

The only thing we're fixed on is the trim size, which is 8″ × 10″ with 1/8″ bleed allowance.

art director comments

The client sent me the main car image for the first redesign. It's a little bit small, so we'll have to do some manipulation to make it large enough to fill the cover space. The car also needs to be knocked out of its background so it can be more prominent. A vector path will work well to meet this goal because you can edit it at any time without losing quality.

You're going to use a combination of styles, filters, and effects on the background and inset images. Photoshop's Smart Object capabilities will be a significant advantage in this task because we can edit the effects and filters if the client isn't thrilled with the initial effort.

I've also already created a template in Illustrator with the magazine nameplate and text elements; we'll repurpose the same file every month with the different text for each issue. You can place that file directly into Photoshop as a linked file so that any last-minute changes in the file will automatically appear in the final composite cover.

project objectives

To complete this project, you will:

- ❑ Resize and resample an existing source image
- ❑ Edit the canvas size
- ❑ Create a vector-based layer mask
- ❑ Create a vector shape layer
- ❑ Create a clipping mask
- ❑ Add texture to a shape layer
- ❑ Apply custom layer effects
- ❑ Use the Filter Gallery
- ❑ Liquify a layer
- ❑ Use the Eyedropper tool
- ❑ Create a custom gradient
- ❑ Print a composite proof

Stage 1 Enlarging Source Files

Any project that you build in Photoshop requires some amount of zooming in and out to various view percentages, as well as navigating around the document within its window. As we show you how to complete different stages of the workflow, we usually won't tell you when to change your view percentage because that's largely a matter of personal preference. Nonetheless, you should understand the different options for navigating around a Photoshop file so you can easily and efficiently get to what you want, when you want to get there.

To review information from the Interface chapter, keep in mind that you have a number of options for navigating around a document:

- Click with the Hand tool to drag the image around in the document window.
- Click with the Zoom tool to zoom in; Option/Alt-click to zoom out.
- Use the View Percentage field in the bottom-left corner of the document window.
- Use the options in the View menu (or the corresponding keyboard shortcuts).
- Use the Navigator panel.

Note:

As you complete the exercises in this project, use any of these methods to zoom in or out on different areas of the file.

Resize and Resample the Existing Source Image

This project — like many others you will build throughout your career — starts with an existing image, which you will open and use as the basis for the rest of the project. Whenever you start with an existing file, it's best to evaluate what you already have before you make any changes.

1. **Download Cars_PS18_RF.zip from the Student Files web page.**
2. **Expand the ZIP archive in your WIP folder (Macintosh) or copy the archive contents into your WIP folder (Windows).**

   This results in a folder named **Cars**, which contains the files you need for this project. You should also use this folder to save the files you create in this project.

3. **In Photoshop, choose File>Open. Navigate to the file amg.jpg in the WIP>Cars folder and click Open.**
4. **Choose View>Fit on Screen so you can see the entire image, and make sure rulers are visible (View>Rulers).**
5. **Choose Image>Image Size.**

   The amg.jpg file is 25″ wide by 18.75″ high, with a resolution of 72 pixels/inch. Commercial printing typically requires 300 pixels/inch, so this image would not be considered "print quality" at its current size.

   The first step is to resize the image using the principle of effective resolution to achieve the 300 pixels/inch required for commercial printing.

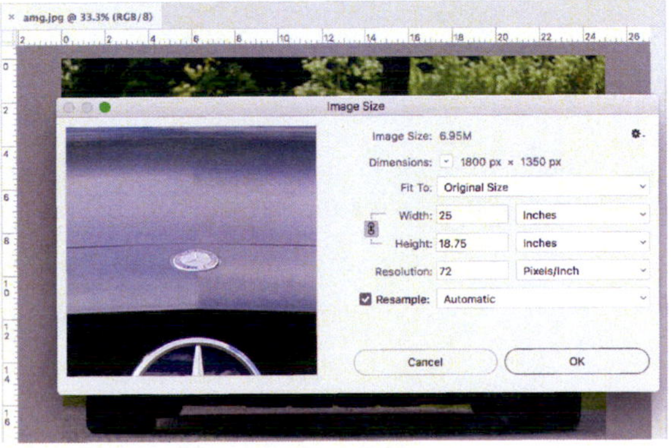

6. **At the bottom of the dialog box, uncheck the Resample option and change the Resolution field to `300`.**

   Remember: When resampling is not active, the image retains the same number of pixels when you change the size or resolution fields. The image's physical size is now smaller since you compressed 300 pixels into an inch instead of the original 72 ppi.

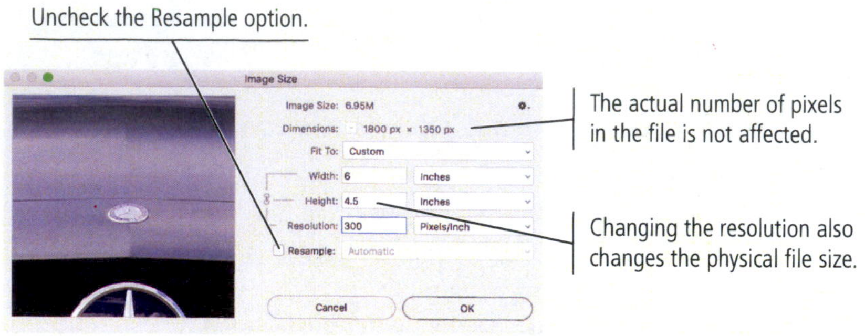

7. **Click OK to resize the source image.**

   As you can see, the image view in the document window does not change because the image still has the same number of pixels. The rulers at the left and top edges of the document window show the new measurements that are associated with the resized image.

Rulers show the new dimensions of the image.
The image preview does not change because it has the same number of pixels.

8. **Choose Image>Image Size again.**

   Because you already defined the appropriate resolution for this image, you now need to make the image large enough to meet the overall job requirements.

   Resampling adds or removes pixels to create the size you define, without affecting the defined resolution.

9. **Click in the Preview window and drag until the logo on the car's grill is visible.**

   Areas of greater detail are the most prone to distortion when you enlarge an image. The Image Size preview area allows you to review the results before finalizing the process.

10. **At the bottom of the dialog box, check the Resample option.**

When the Resample option is checked, you can change the actual number of pixels in the image without affecting its resolution.

11. **Open the Resample menu and choose Preserve Details (enlargement).**

Although you should try to capture images at the size you will need them, this is not always possible when working with client-supplied images. The Preserve Details option significantly improves the results of artificially enlarging an existing image.

12. **Make sure the Constrain option is active.**

13. **With the units menus set to Inches, change the Width field to 8.25.**

The overall project requires a finished image that is 8.25″ wide by 10.25″ high. If you enlarged the picture to match the required height, it would be too wide for the entire car to fit into the composition. Instead, you are enlarging the image to match the required width; you will later adjust the canvas to suit the project's height requirement.

As you can see, increasing the image's physical size with resampling adds more pixels to the image. This also significantly increases the file weight (its size in bytes).

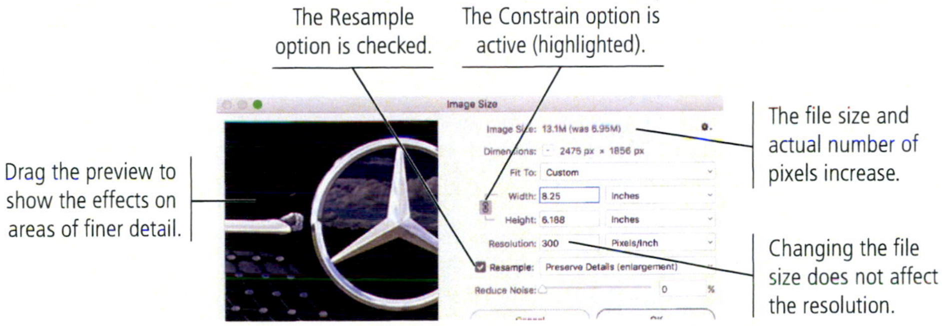
The Resample option is checked.
The Constrain option is active (highlighted).
Drag the preview to show the effects on areas of finer detail.
The file size and actual number of pixels increase.
Changing the file size does not affect the resolution.
Areas of flat color are prone to artifacts when enlarging an image.
Image Size
Width: 8.25
Height: 6.188
Resolution: 300
Resample: Preserve Details (enlargement)
Reduce Noise:

14. **Drag in the Preview window to show an area with flat areas of color near a high-contrast edge.**

Artificially enlarging an image often results in small pixels of varying color, especially in areas of solid color and near high-contrast edges. When you choose the Preserve Details option, you can use the Reduce Noise slider to help reduce those artifacts.

15. **Change the Reduce Noise slider to 20%.**

The Preview window shows the results that will be achieved when you finalize the resampling.

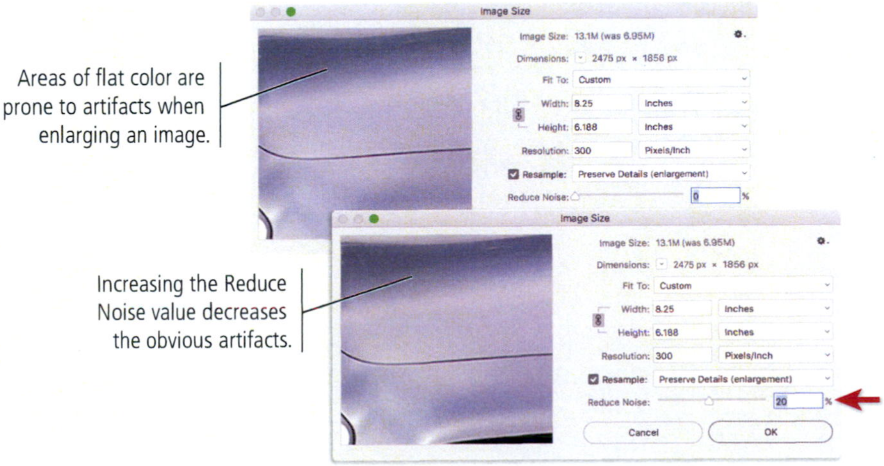

16. **Click OK to finalize the resampling.**

Resampling the image (enlarging) adds pixels to the file. The image no longer fits in the document window at the current view percentage.

The image now has more pixels, so less of the image is visible in the document window.

Note:

You're adding a sizeable amount of information to this file, so the resampling process might take a few seconds. Depending on the power and speed of your computer, you might see a progress bar as the image size is remapped.

17. **Choose View>Fit On Screen to show the entire image.**

18. **Choose File>Save As. Save the file as a native Photoshop file named magazine.psd in your WIP>Cars folder.**

19. **Continue to the next exercise.**

Sharpen the Enlarged Image

When you enlarge an image in Photoshop, the application must generate new data. The algorithm underlying the Preserve Details option does a significantly better job of generating new pixels than was available in previous versions, but the pixels are still not original to the image. This can result in a loss of detail, especially near apparent edges or areas of high contrast. Whenever you enlarge an image, **sharpening** can help to restore detail and make the image appear more crisp.

Note:

The Sharpen, Sharpen More, and Sharpen Edges filters apply sharpening with no user control.

1. **With magazine.psd open, choose Filter>Sharpen>Unsharp Mask.**

2. **Make sure the Preview check box is active in the dialog box.**

Unsharp masking sharpens an image by increasing contrast along the edges in an image.

- **Amount** determines how much the contrast in edges will increase; typically, 150–200% creates good results in high-resolution images.
- **Radius** determines how many pixels will be included in the edge comparison; higher radius values result in more pronounced edge effects.
- **Threshold** defines the difference that is required for Photoshop to identify an edge. A threshold of 15 means that colors must be more than 15 levels different.

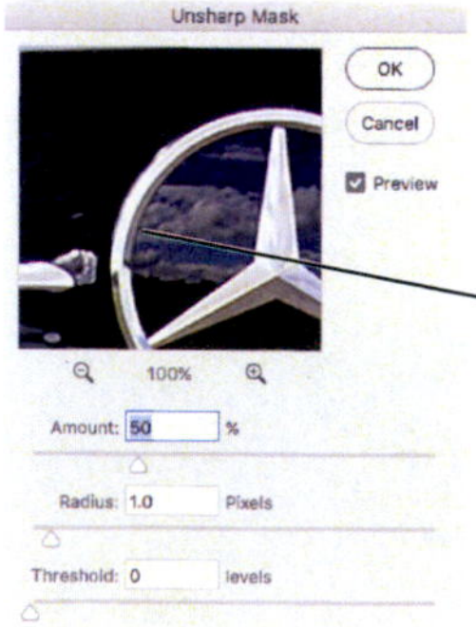

Drag here or click in the document window to change the visible area in the preview window.

3. **Change the Amount to 100%, the Radius to 2.0 pixels, and the Threshold to 3 levels.**

4. **Toggle the Preview option off and on to review the results in the document window.**

Sharpening is most obvious in areas of high contrast.

5. **Click OK to apply the Unsharp Mask filter.**

6. **Save the file and continue to the next exercise.**

Edit the Canvas Size

As you learned in the project meeting, the final artwork for this project needs to be 8.25″ wide by 10.25″ high. You already accomplished the required width when you resampled the source file. In this exercise, you are going to enlarge the canvas to meet the project's height requirement.

1. **With magazine.psd open, make the Layers panel visible.**

   Photos and scans almost always default to exist on the Background layer when you first open them.

2. **Choose Image>Canvas Size.**

   In Photoshop, **canvas** refers to the overall image area — like the surface of a canvas used by traditional artists. It is not directly connected to the content of most layers (except for the Background layer, as you will see shortly).

   You can use this dialog box to change the size of the canvas to specific measurements.

3. Choose the top-center anchor option.

The Anchor area shows the reference point around which the canvas will be enlarged or cropped. Using this option, all new pixels will be added at the bottom of the image.

4. Change the Height field to `10.25` [inches], and choose White in the Canvas Extension Color menu.

This menu defines what color will appear in the new pixels on the Background layer.

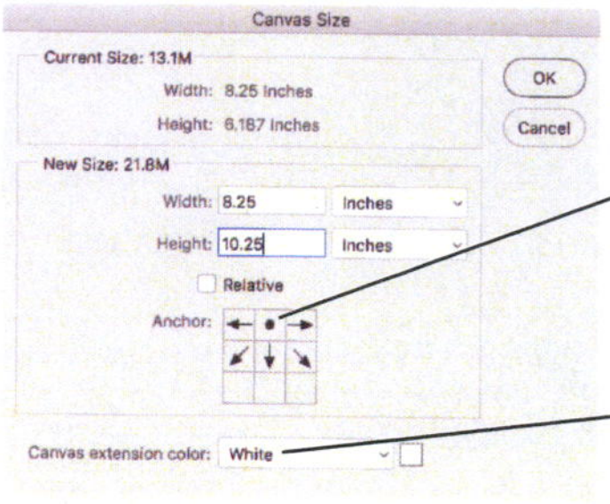
Canvas Size
Current Size: 13.1M
Width: 8.25 Inches
Height: 6.187 Inches
New Size: 21.8M
Width: 8.25
Height: 10.25
Inches
Relative
Anchor:
Canvas extension color: White
OK
Cancel
Anchoring the top edge means new pixels will be added to the bottom of the existing canvas.
Use this menu to define the color of new pixels on the Background layer.

Note:

If you define smaller measurements, you are basically accomplishing the same thing as using the Crop tool.

5. Click OK to apply the change, then choose View>Fit On Screen.

As you can see, new pixels were added to the bottom of the canvas. Because the existing image content exists on the Background layer, and the Background layer cannot contain transparent pixels, the new pixels are filled with white.

magazine.psd @ 26.1% (RGB/8) *
Layers
Background
Because the photo existed on the locked Background layer, new pixels are filled with white.

Note:

If you reduce the canvas size, clicking OK in the Canvas Size dialog box results in a warning that some clipping will occur.

Content on the Background layer that is outside the new canvas size is permanently removed from the layer. Content on other layers is maintained.

6. Choose Edit>Undo Canvas Size.

Press Command/Control-Z to undo the previous action.

Press Command-Option-Z/Control-Alt-Z to step backward one action at a time through the file history.

7. In the Layers panel, click the Lock icon to unlock the Background layer.

8. Double-click the Layer 0 name, type `Car` to rename the layer, then press Return/Enter.

9. **Choose Image>Canvas Size again. Select the top-center Anchor option, then change the Height field to 10.25 [inches].**

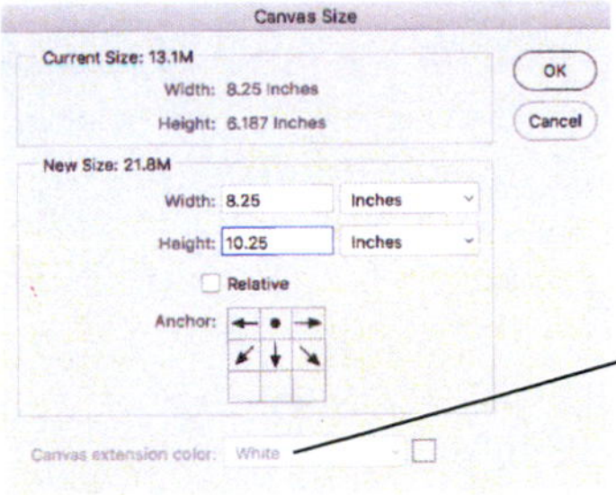

This menu is not available because the file no longer has a locked Background layer.

> *Note:*
>
> *If you check the Relative option, you can change the canvas size by specific amounts. For example, to make the canvas one inch narrower you would type **–1** in the Width field. Photoshop automatically calculates the resulting canvas size based on the selected Anchor position.*

10. **Click OK to apply the change.**

Regular layers support transparency, so the new pixels are not filled with a solid color. The gray-and-white checked pattern identifies transparent areas of the visible layer.

Because regular layers can include transparency, no color appears in the area of the new pixels.

11. **Save the file. With Maximize Compatibility checked, click OK in the Photoshop Format Options dialog box.**

Because you converted the Background layer to a regular image layer, you see the dialog box that asks if you want to maximize compatibility the first time you save the file.

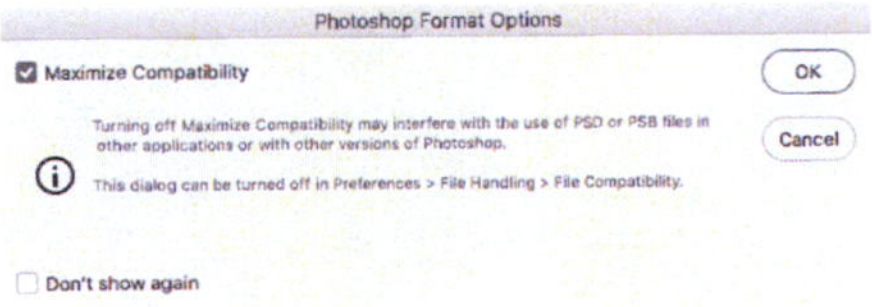

12. **Continue to the next stage of the project.**

Stage 2 Working with Vector Tools

Vector paths, also called Bézier curves, are defined mathematically based on the position of anchor points and the length and angle of direction handles that are connected to those anchor points. Unlike the pixels in a raster image, vector paths do not have a defined resolution until they are output. Because of this, vector paths can be edited at any time without any loss of quality.

Photoshop includes a number of tools for creating vector paths:

> ***Note:***
>
> *The Type tool is also technically a vector-based tool because digital type uses vectors to define the character shapes.*

- The **Pen tool** places individual anchor points each time you click; line segments connect each point. If you click and drag, you create a point with direction handles, which precisely control the shape of the connecting segments.
- The **Freeform Pen tool** draws vector paths wherever you drag, just as you would draw with a pencil on paper.
- The **Rectangle** and **Ellipse tools** create shapes that you would expect based on the tool names. If you press Shift while you click and drag, you create a shape with equal height and width (a square or circle, respectively).
- The **Polygon tool** creates a shape with any number of sides. Clicking once opens a dialog box where you can define the number of sides.

  If you check the Smooth Corners option, each anchor point has direction handles that make the corners rounded instead of sharp.

  If you choose the Star option, the Indent Sides By value determines where the inner points of the star appear relative to the overall shape diameter.

  You can also check the Smooth Indents option to create smooth curves on the inside points of the shape (instead of corner points).

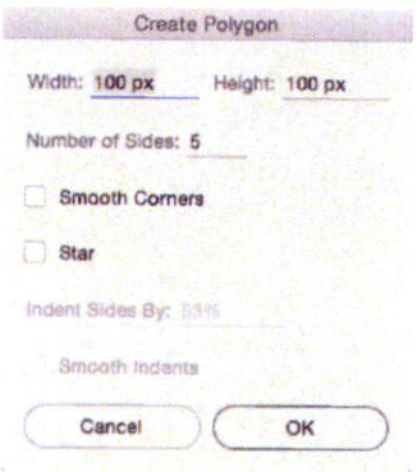

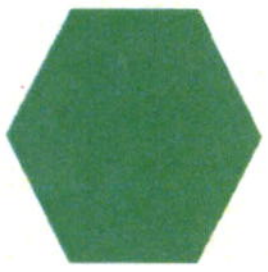

Polygon created with all options unchecked

Polygon created with the Star option checked

Polygon (star) created with the Smooth Corners option checked

Polygon (star) created with the Smooth Corners and Smooth Indents options checked

- The **Line tool** creates open straight lines with two points, one at each end. When first created, the points have no direction handles and the connecting segment is a straight line.
- The **Custom Shape tool** creates vector-based shapes from built-in or external libraries. (You will use this tool in Project 5: Calendar Cover.)

When you use the vector drawing tools, you have the option to create a new shape, path, or pixels.

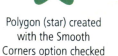

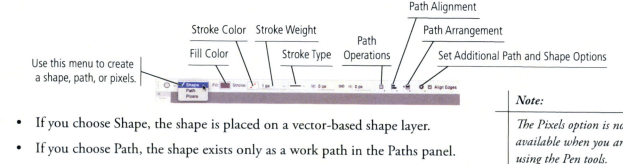

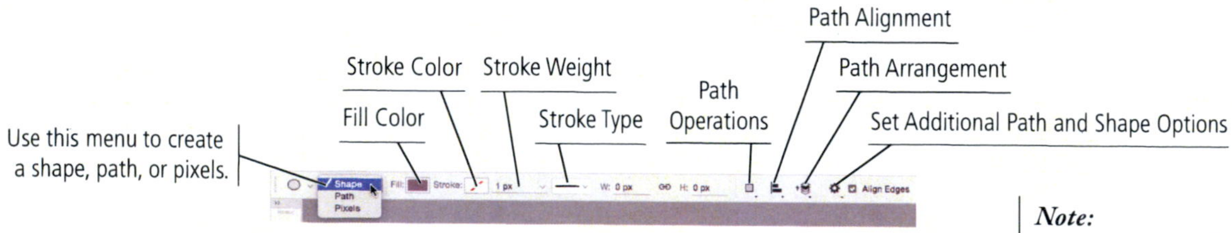

> ***Note:***
>
> *The Pixels option is not available when you are using the Pen tools.*

- If you choose Shape, the shape is placed on a vector-based shape layer.
- If you choose Path, the shape exists only as a work path in the Paths panel.
- If you choose Pixels, the resulting shape is created as pixels on the previously selected layer. No vector path is created.

Use the Freeform Pen Tool

The Freeform Pen tool creates a vector path based on where you drag the cursor. The application creates anchor points and direction handles as necessary to create the shape that you draw.

1. **With magazine.psd open, show the image at 100% in the document window.**

   Ideally, you should work at 100% while you complete this exercise.

2. **Choose the Freeform Pen tool (nested under the Pen tool) in the Tools panel.**

3. **In the Options bar, choose the Path option in the left menu.**

   When you choose Path in the tool mode menu, the vector path that you draw is stored in the Paths panel.

4. **Open the Path Operations menu and choose the Combine Shapes option.**

These options define how a new path will interact with any existing paths. (Illustrator and InDesign users might recognize these as options from the Pathfinder panel.)

- **New Layer**, available when Layer is selected in the Tool Mode menu, creates a new shape layer every time you draw a new path.
- **Combine Shapes** adds new paths to an already selected path or shape layer. Each path's shape is maintained as a separate vector path. If you want a new path to include only areas inside the path you draw, you should choose this option before you begin drawing a new path.
- **Subtract Front Shape** removes the area of secondary shapes from existing shapes.
- **Intersect Shape Areas** results in a shape that is only the area where a new shape overlaps an existing shape.
- **Exclude Overlapping Shapes** is similar to Subtract; overlapping areas are removed from the existing shape, but non-overlapping areas of the new shape are filled with the shape color.
- The **Merge Shape Components** option, available when a single path contains more than one shape, results in a single (possibly compound) shape. Any overlapping paths are combined into one shape/path.

Note:

The Pen Pressure option only applies if you have a pressure-sensitive graphics tablet. When this option is turned on, higher pressure decreases the Width tolerance.

5. **Check the Magnetic option in the Options bar, then click the Set Additional Path and Shape Options button.**

   When you draw with the Pen tool, the default path appears in the document window as a thin, medium blue line. You can use the Thickness and Color options to change the appearance of the path. (The settings here do not affect the actual stroke color and width of a path; they refer only to the appearance of paths in the document window.)

   Curve Fit determines how closely the curves will match the path that you drag with the mouse cursor. When the Magnetic option is active, you can also define settings that control how the magnetic function behaves:

   Width determines how far from an edge you have to drag (1–256 pixels) for Photoshop to still find the edge.

   Contrast determines how much variation (1–100%) must exist between pixels for Photoshop to define an edge.

   Frequency determines the rate at which Photoshop places anchor points. Higher values (up to 100) create anchor points faster than lower values (down to 0).

6. **Define the following settings in the pop-up menu, then press Return/Enter to apply your settings:**

Thickness:	**2 pt**
Color:	**Light Red**
Curve Fit:	**2 px**
Width:	**15 px**
Contrast:	**10%**
Frequency:	**25**

Open this menu.
Check this option.

Note:

The default path color is very similar to the colors in the image you're working with; you are changing it to a thicker red path so it will be easier to see as you work through this project.

7. **Click at the corner where the left side mirror meets the car to place the first anchor point. Drag up and around the car shape.**

   You don't have to hold down the mouse button when you draw with the Freeform Pen tool in Magnetic mode.

   As you drag, the magnetic function creates anchor points to define a vector path around obvious edges where you drag.

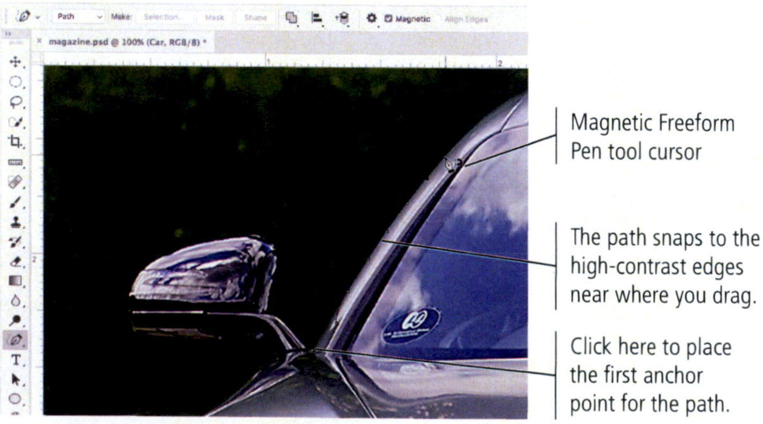

Magnetic Freeform Pen tool cursor
The path snaps to the high-contrast edges near where you drag.
Click here to place the first anchor point for the path.

Note:

When you draw by holding down a button (mouse button or the button on a graphics tablet/pen) it is not uncommon for the line to "jump" where you don't want it to jump. If this happens, press Esc to remove your selection or path and start drawing again.

8. **Continue dragging around the car shape to create the initial outline.**

   Skip the tires for now, and don't worry if the path is not perfect as you outline the car shape. You will fine-tune the path in the next few exercises.

9. **If you can't see the entire car in the document window, press the Spacebar to temporarily access the Hand tool and move the image so you can see the edges that you need to follow.**

   The Spacebar temporarily switches to the Hand tool, so you can drag the image in the window even while working on another task. When you release the Spacebar, you return to the previously selected tool, so you can continue drawing the path of the car's shape.

   If you drag past the edge of the document window, Photoshop automatically scrolls the visible area of the image. Manually repositioning with the Hand tool gives you better control over exactly what you see.

Press the Spacebar to temporarily access the Hand tool.

10. **When you reach an obvious corner in the car's outline, click to place a specific anchor point.**

    Although Photoshop automatically creates anchor points based on the defined magnetic behavior, you can also click to place anchor points in specific locations.

Click to manually place an anchor point at apparent corners.

11. **Continue outlining the car shape. When you get back to your original starting point, click to create a closed path.**

    When the tool cursor is over the original starting point, a hollow circle in the icon indicates that clicking will close the path.

The hollow circle indicates that clicking will close the path.

Note:

Some users report processor-related issues when temporarily switching to the Hand tool while drawing with the Freeform Pen tool in Magnetic mode.

If you experience performance problems, try zooming out and in with the keyboard commands instead of dragging with the Hand tool.

12. Open the Layers and Paths panels.

As you can see, no layer has been added. The path you drew is stored in the Paths panel as the Work Path, which is a temporary path that exists only until you create another path.

No layer is added to the file.
The path you drew is stored as the Work Path.
Some parts of the car are not included inside the path.

13. With the Work Path selected in the Paths panel, open the panel Options menu and choose Save Path.

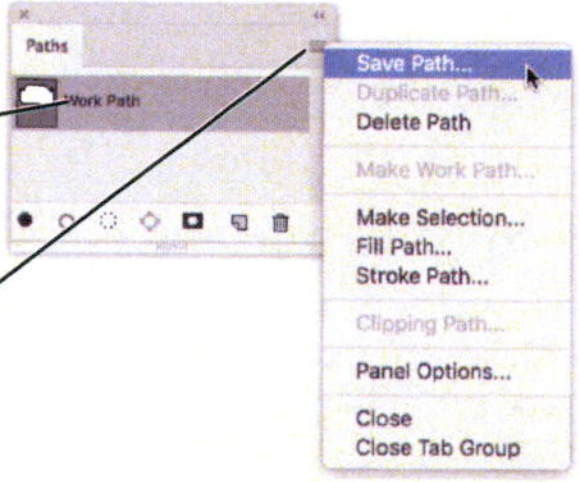
The highlight indicates that the path is selected.
Click here to open the panel Options menu.

More about Working with the Paths Panel

PHOTOSHOP FOUNDATIONS

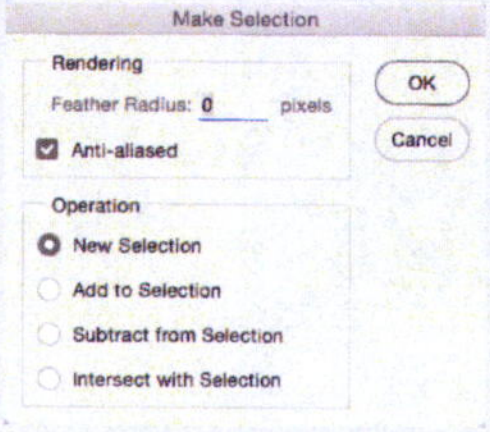

In the Paths panel options menu, you can choose **Make Selection** to make a marching-ants selection based on the path shape. You can use the resulting dialog box to define the details of the selection.

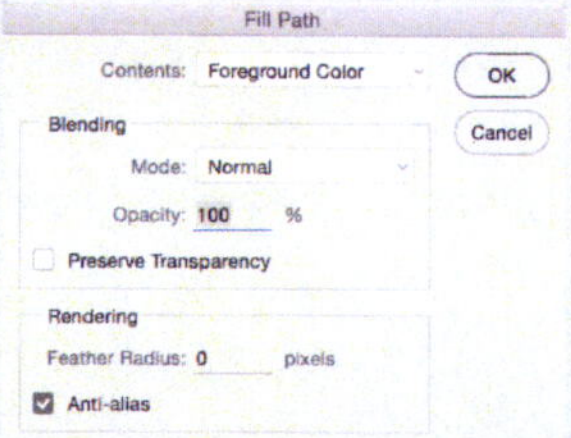

If you choose **Fill Path** in the Options menu, you can use the resulting dialog box to determine how the fill will be created. You can choose a color or pattern, blending mode and opacity, and whether to feather the edge of the fill so it blends smoothly into underlying layers.

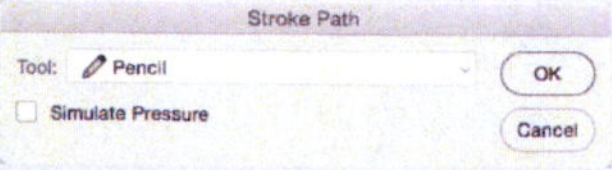

If you choose the **Stroke Path** option, you must also choose which tool will create the stroke; the applied stroke will have the last-used settings for the selected tool. In other words, you have to define the tool options (brush size, hardness, etc.) that you want before using this option.

The Fill Path and Stroke Path options add the resulting pixels to the currently active layer — an important distinction from the Shape Layer option, which automatically creates a new layer when you begin drawing the vector path. It is also important to remember that although the path remains a vector path, color that is applied to the fill or stroke of the path is raster or pixel-based; it does not have the same scalability as a vector shape layer.

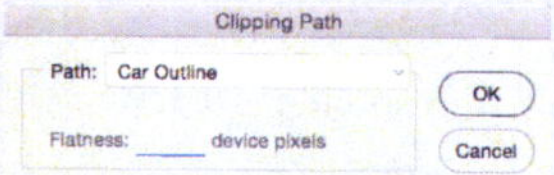

If you choose the **Clipping Path** option, the selected path will become a clipping path, which is essentially a vector mask that defines the visible area of an image if the file is placed into a page-layout application such as Adobe InDesign. (The white area in the path thumbnail defines what areas will be visible in the image.)

Buttons across the bottom of the Paths panel provide quick access to many of the features explained here. They are, from left:

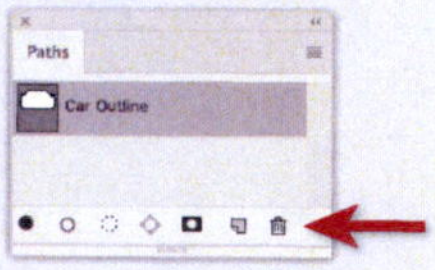

- Fill Path with Foreground Color
- Stroke Path with Brush
- Load Path as a Selection
- Make Work Path from Selection
- Add Layer Mask
- Create New Path
- Delete Path

14. Type Car Outline in the resulting dialog box, then click OK.

After you save the path, the new name appears instead of "Work Path;" this path will remain in the file even if you create a different temporary Work Path.

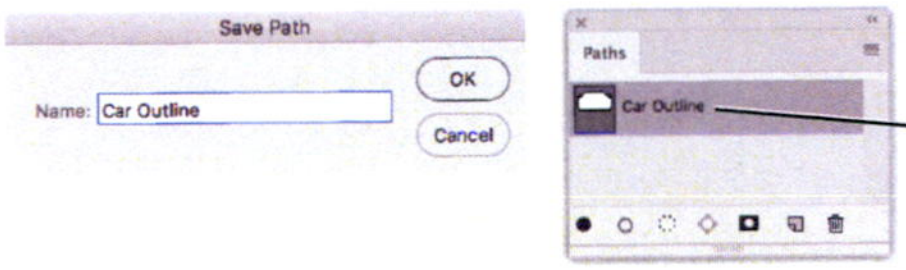

The saved path is permanent.

Understanding Anchor Points and Handles

An **anchor point** marks the end of a line **segment**, and the point **handles** determine the shape of that segment. That's the basic definition of a vector, but there is a bit more to it than that. (The Photoshop Help files refer to handles as direction lines, and distinguishes different types of points. Our aim here is to explain the overall concept of vector paths, so we use the generic industry-standard terms. For more information on Adobe's terminology, refer to the Photoshop Help files.)

Each segment in a path has two anchor points, and can have two associated handles.

You can create corner points by simply clicking with the Pen tool instead of clicking and dragging. Corner points do not have their own handles; the connected segments are controlled by the handles of the other associated points.

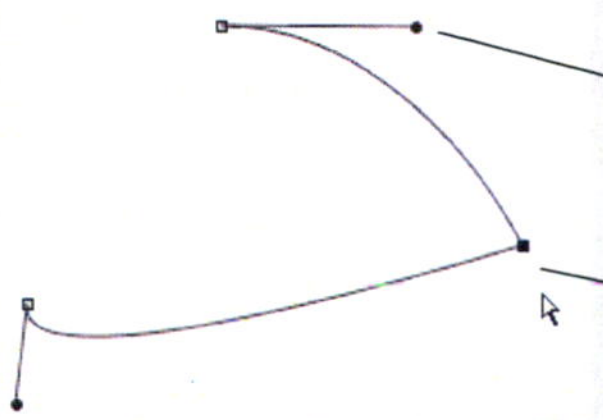

Handle of other connected point controls the segment shape.

Corner point has no handles.

In the following image, we first clicked to create Point A and dragged (without releasing the mouse button) to create Handle A1. We then clicked and dragged to create Point B and Handle B1; Handle B2 was automatically created as a reflection of B1 (Point B is a **symmetrical point**).

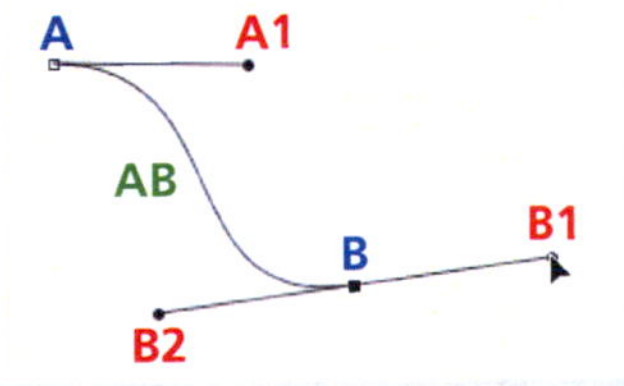

This image shows the result of dragging Handle B1 to the left instead of to the right when we created the initial curve. Notice the difference in the curve here, compared to the curve above. When you drag a handle, the connecting segment arcs away from the direction you drag.

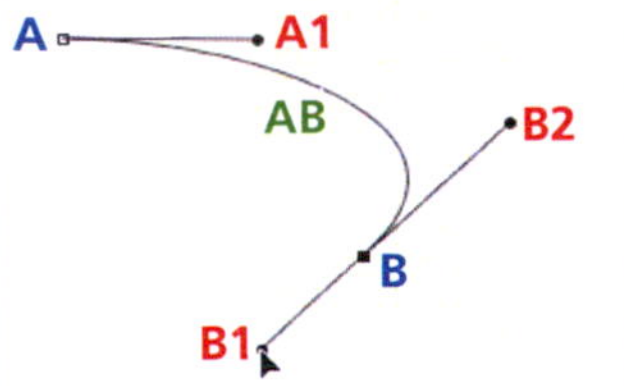

It's important to understand that every line segment is connected to two handles. In this example, Handle A1 and Handle B2 determine the shape of Segment AB. Dragging either handle affects the shape of the connected segment.

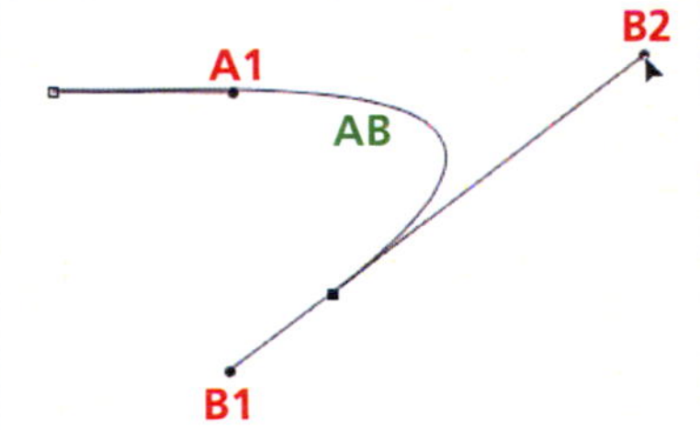

When you use the Pen tool, clicking and dragging a point creates a symmetrical (smooth) point; both handles start out at equal length, directly opposite one another. Changing the angle of one handle of a symmetrical point also changes the opposing handle of that point. In the example here, repositioning Handle B1 also moves Handle B2, which affects the shape of Segment AB. (You can, however, change the length of one handle without affecting the length of the other handle.)

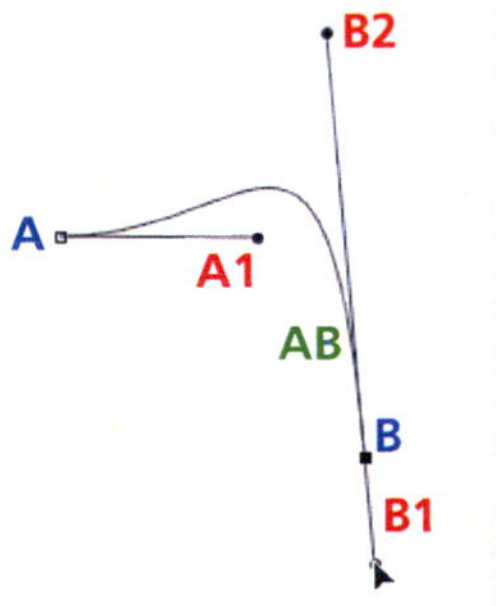

15. **Click the bottom area of the Paths panel to deselect the path.**

    When the path is not selected, you can't see its anchor points and connecting segments in the document window.

16. **Save the file and continue to the next exercise.**

Add to an Existing Path

In the previous exercise, you used the Freeform Pen tool in magnetic mode to draw a rough outline of the car's shape. You intentionally skipped the wheels because the tool's magnetic properties perform better with higher-contrast edges than what is evident where the tires meet the pavement. In this exercise, you will use the Pen tool to add the wheels to the existing path.

1. **With `magazine.psd` open, make sure the view percentage is 100% and position the image so the right wheel is entirely visible.**

2. **Choose the Pen tool (nested under the Freeform Pen tool) in the Tools panel.**

    When you choose a nested tool, it becomes the default option in that position of the Tools panel. To access the original default tool — the Pen tool in this case — you have to click the tool and hold down the mouse button to access the nested tools menu.

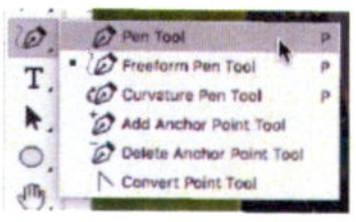

3. **In the Paths panel, click the Car Outline path to make it visible in the document window.**

    You want to add more shapes to the existing path, so the path needs to be selected and visible in the document window.

4. **In the Options bar, choose Path in the Tool Mode menu.**

5. **Click the Path Operations button and choose Combine Shapes (if it is not already selected).**

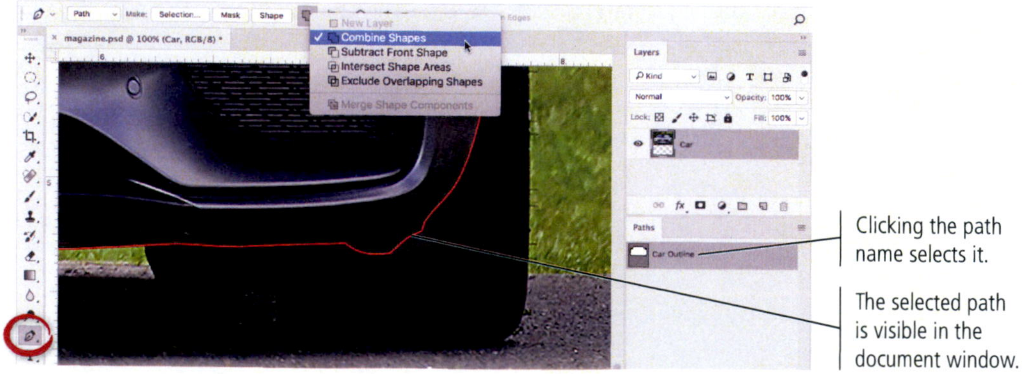

6. **Click the Pen tool in the Tools panel to hide the anchor points of the existing path (if necessary).**

   If the existing path's anchor points are visible, you can use the Pen tool to add anchor points to the existing path. You want to create a second shape in the same path, so you need to turn off the existing path's anchor points.

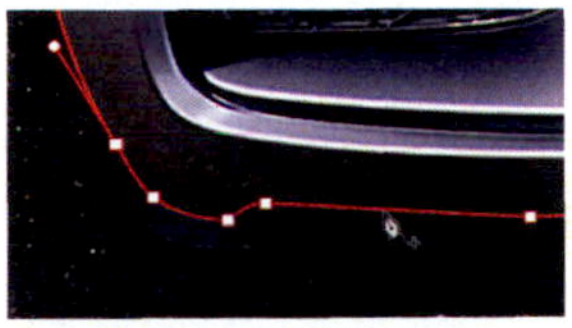

If the existing path's anchor points are visible, clicking would add a new point to the existing path.

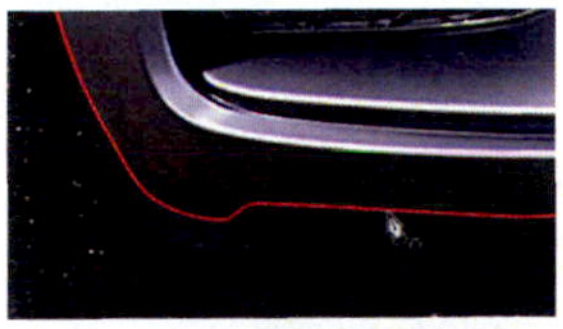

If the existing path's anchor points are not visible, clicking creates a new shape that is part of the same path.

7. **Click with the Pen tool cursor where the rear tire meets the car undercarriage.**

   Clicking once with the Pen tool creates a corner anchor point with no direction handles.

8. **Move the cursor down and right along the tire edge (as shown after Step 9).**

9. **Click to create an anchor point, hold down the mouse button, and drag down and right to create direction handles for the point.**

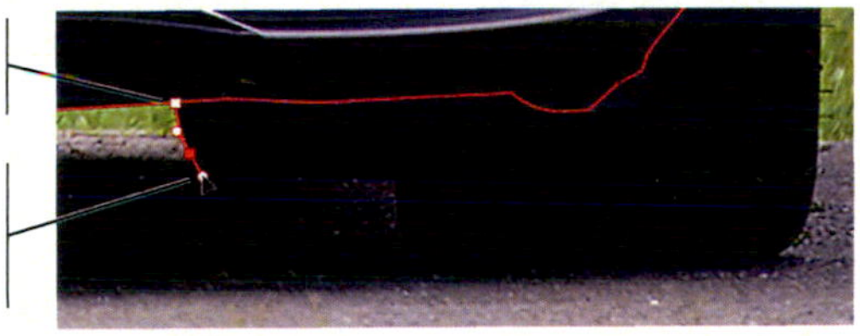
Click here to place the first point.
Click and drag to create a new point with direction handles.

10. **When the shape of the connecting segment between the two points matches the shape of the tire, release the mouse button.**

    When you click and drag with the Pen tool, you create a smooth point with symmetrical direction handles. As you drag, you can see the handles extend equal distances from both sides of the point you just created. The length and angle of the direction handles control the shape of segments that connect two anchor points.

    As long as you hold down the mouse button, you can drag to change the length and angle of the point's handles, which also changes the shape of the connecting segment.

> *Note:*
>
> *Don't worry if the curve isn't quite perfect; you will learn how to edit anchor points and handles in the next exercise.*

11. **Move the cursor to the right, following the bottom edge of the rear tire. Click and drag to create another anchor point with symmetrical direction handles. When the connecting segment matches the shape of the tire, release the mouse button.**

    When you click-drag to create a smooth point, the point is automatically symmetrical. In other words, the handles on each side of the point are the same length.

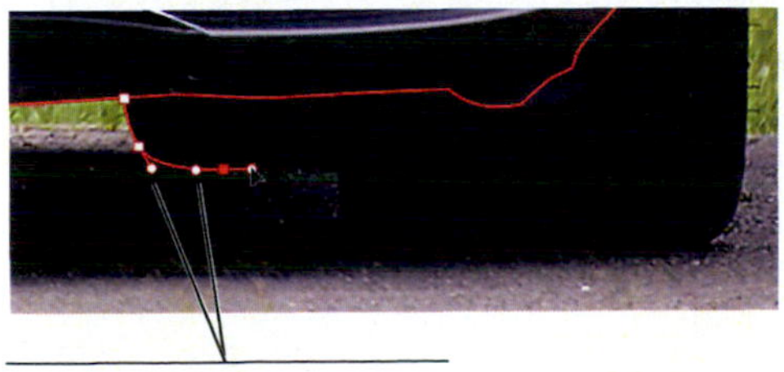

These handles affect the shape of the connecting segment.

12. **Click without dragging where the rear tire meets the front tire.**

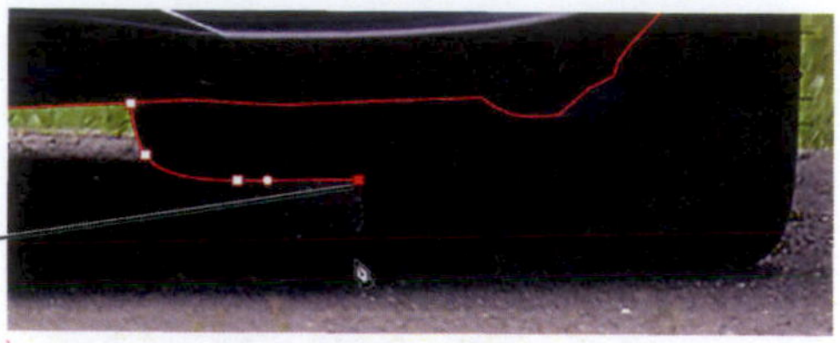

Click without dragging to create a corner point.

13. **Continue adding symmetrical smooth points to the path, placing the final point where the front tire meets the body of the car.**

Add a point where the tire meets the body.

14. **Click and drag to place another smooth point inside the area of the bumper.**

You are intentionally overlapping the new path with the existing one. Later you will combine the multiple separate shapes into a single path.

15. **Move the cursor over the original starting point. When you see a hollow circle in the cursor icon, click to close the path.**

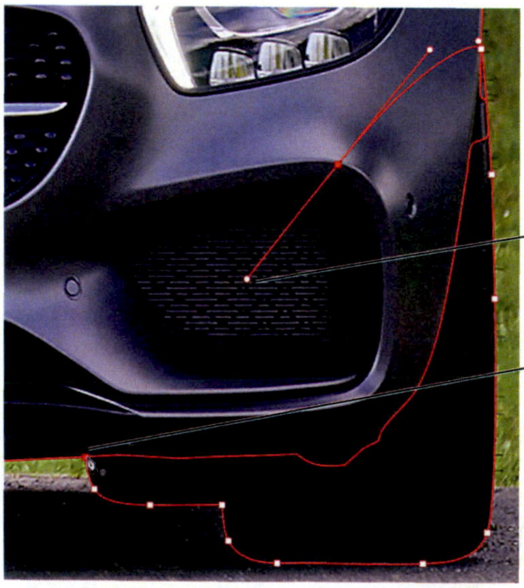

Add a point in the car area so the second path overlaps the first.

Click the original point to close the second shape.

16. **Repeat the process from this exercise to add another path around the left wheels.**

Remember, clicking without dragging creates a corner point, which does not have direction handles.

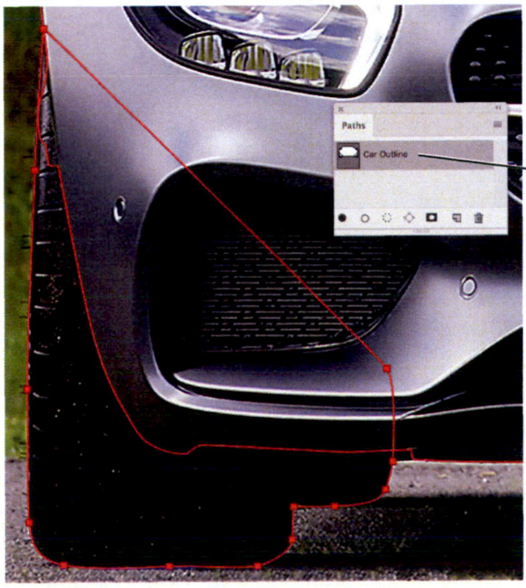

The Car Outline path is still selected.

17. **Change your view percentage so you can see the entire car in the document window.**

18. **With the Car Outline path selected in the Paths panel, make sure the Pen tool is still active.**

19. **Open the Path Operations menu in the Options bar and choose Merge Shape Components.**

The three original paths are combined into a single shape. Photoshop adds anchor points where necessary and removes overlapping segments from the original paths.

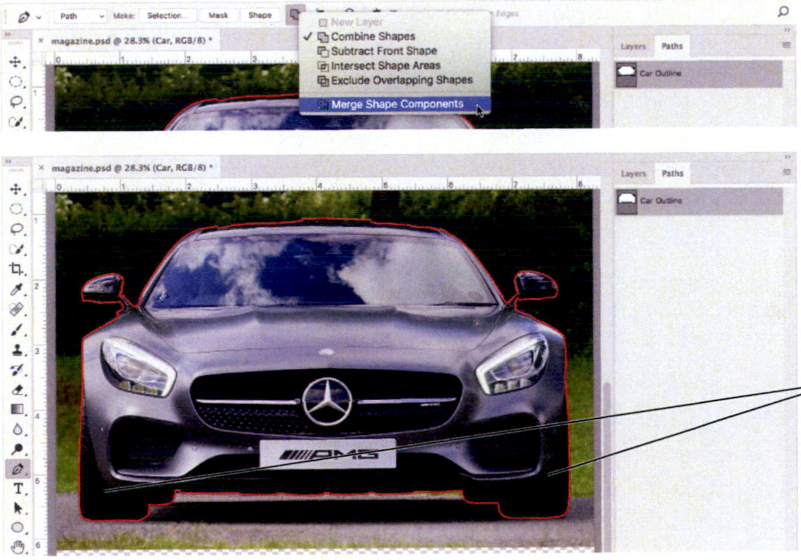

After merging shapes, the three separate paths are combined into a single path that is the outermost path of each component.

20. **Save the file and continue to the next exercise.**

Edit Vector Paths

You probably noticed that the path you created in the previous exercises is not a perfect outline of the car. The Freeform Pen tool can be a very good starting point for creating odd-shaped paths, but you will almost always need to edit and fine-tune the resulting paths to accurately reflect the path you want. Fortunately, Photoshop offers a number of options for editing vector paths.

You can use the **Path Selection tool** ( ) to select an entire path, or use the **Direct Selection tool** ( ) to select a specific anchor point or segment.

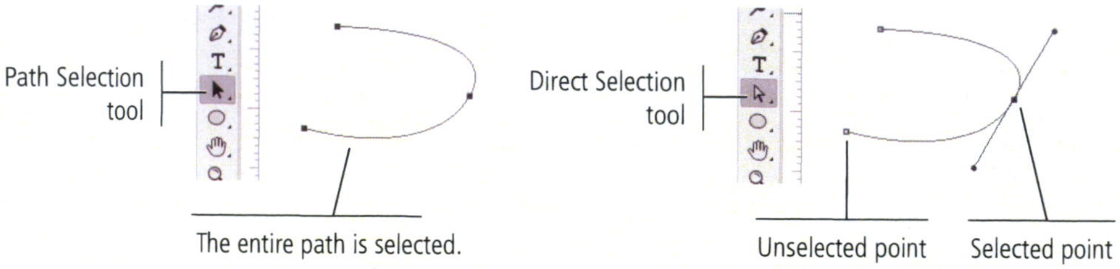

You can use the **Add Anchor Point tool** ( ) to add a new anchor point to an existing path. Photoshop automatically creates handles for the new point and adjusts handles for existing points to maintain the existing path shape.

Note:

When the Pen tool is active, placing the cursor over an existing selected path automatically shows the Add Anchor Point tool cursor.

You can use the **Delete Anchor Point tool** ( ) to remove an existing point from a path. Photoshop removes the selected point and adjusts the handles of remaining points to try to maintain the original path shape.

Note:

When the Pen tool is active, placing the cursor over an existing point on a selected path automatically shows the Delete Anchor Point tool cursor.

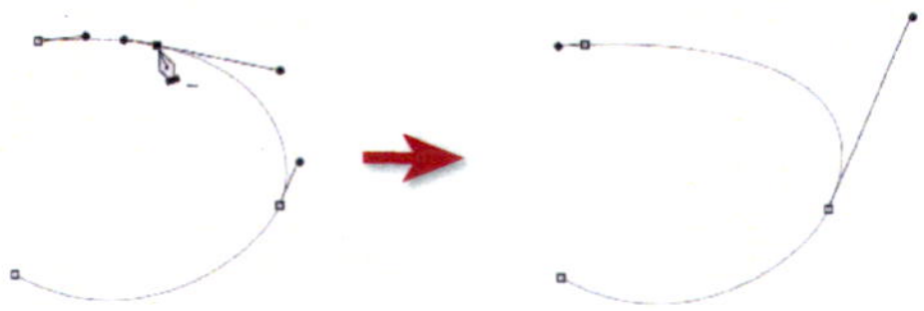

Clicking a smooth point with the **Convert Point tool** ( ) converts that point to a corner point by removing its handles (below left). Clicking and dragging from a corner point with this tool converts it to a smooth, symmetrical point (below right).

Note:

When the Pen tool is active, you can press Option/Alt to temporarily access the Convert Point tool cursor.

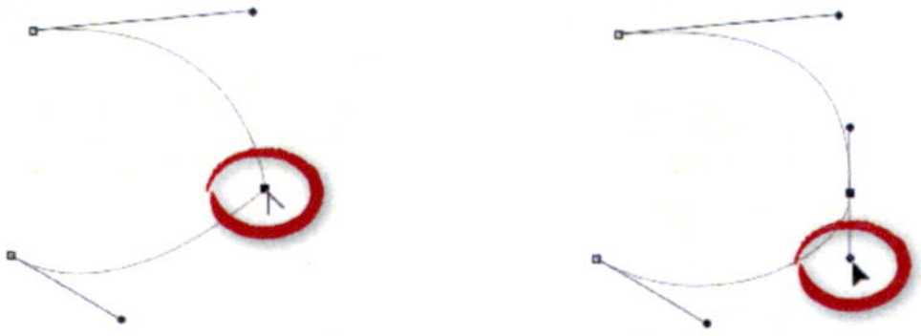

You can add a handle to only one side of a corner point by Option/Alt-clicking a point with the Convert Point tool and dragging (below left). You can also click a handle with the Convert Point tool and drag to move only one handle of the point, resulting in a corner point with asymmetrical handles (below right).

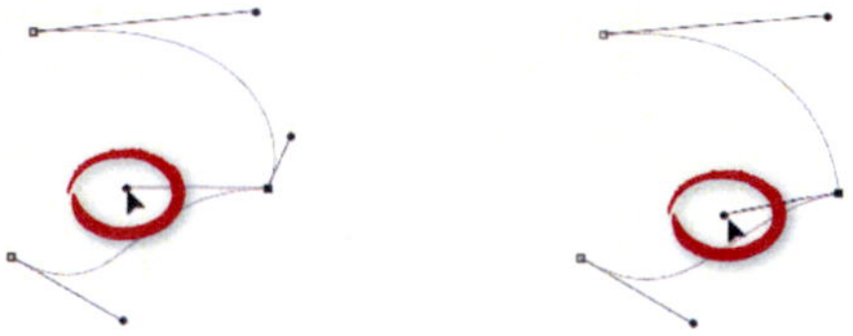

1. **With magazine.psd open, set your view percentage to at least 100%.**

2. **Drag around the image to review the Car Outline path.**

   Although your results might differ from our screen shots, the path almost certainly does not accurately outline the car. You must use what you learned on Page 103 and 108 to edit the path to exactly match the car's shape.

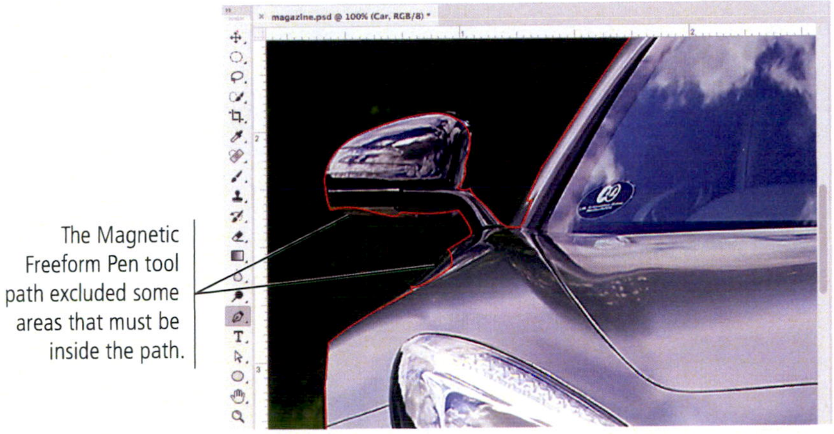

The Magnetic Freeform Pen tool path excluded some areas that must be inside the path.

3. **Use the following information to fine-tune your Car Outline path.**

   This is one place where we can't give you specific instructions because everyone's path will be a bit different. Keep the following points in mind as you refine your shape:

   - Use the Direct Selection tool to select and edit specific segments or points on the path. You can move points to a new position by dragging (or using the Arrow keys), or move their handles to change segment shapes.
   - Use the Add Anchor Point tool to add a point to the path.
   - Use the Delete Anchor Point tool to remove a point from the path.
   - Use the Convert Point tool to change a corner point to a smooth point, and vice versa.

4. **Save the file and continue to the next exercise.**

Drawing with the Curvature Pen Tool

PHOTOSHOP FOUNDATIONS

The Curvature Pen tool, nested under the regular Pen tool, can be used to create and edit complex paths without manually manipulating anchor points.

Using the Curvature Pen tool, begin by clicking to place points in a new path. As you drag after creating the first two points, the software shows a rubber-band preview of the path that will be created by clicking again.

If you don't see the rubber-band behavior, open the Set Additional Pen and Path Options menu in the Options bar and make sure Rubber Band is checked.

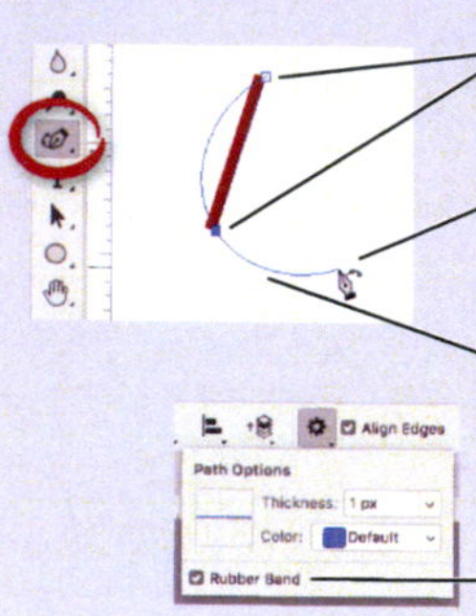

Click to place the first two points.

Move the mouse cursor to another location...

...and rubber-band behavior previews the curve that would be created by clicking again.

Make sure Rubber Band is checked.

As long as the Curvature Pen tool is active, you do not need to change tools to edit the path:

- Option/Alt-click click to create a corner point.
- Click anywhere along an existing path to add a new anchor point.
- Double-click any point to toggle it between a smooth and corner point.
- Click a point to select it.
- Drag a selected point to move it.
- Press Delete to remove the selected point; the existing curve is maintained.
- Press the Esc key to stop drawing the current shape.

Create a Vector-Based Layer Mask

Now that your car outline shape is nearly complete, you are going to use the path to create a vector-based layer mask, which will remove the car from the surrounding background. The edges of a vector mask are defined by a vector path, which means they cannot have degrees of transparency. To edit the mask edge, you have to edit the vector path.

1. **With `magazine.psd` open, set your view percentage so you can see the entire car in the document window.**

2. **Select the Car Outline path in the Paths panel and select the Car layer in the Layers panel.**

3. **Choose Layer>Vector Mask>Current Path.**

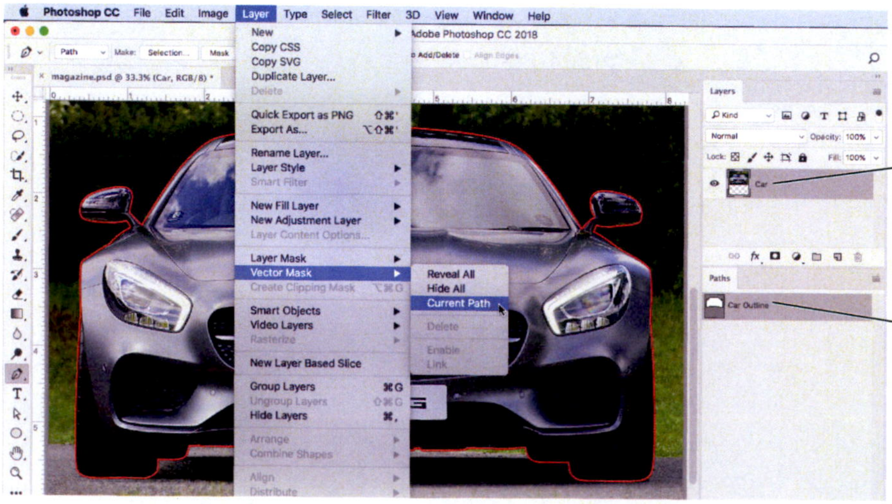

The layer you want to mask is selected.

The path you want to use as the mask is selected.

As you can see, a new path is added to the Paths panel. The name "Car Vector Mask" identifies this path as a vector mask for the layer named Car. This temporary path only appears in the panel when the masked layer is selected.

Nothing is added to the Channels panel because channels are raster-based; they do not store vector-based path information.

The mask thumbnail is added to the masked layer.
The mask path is visible in the Paths panel when the masked layer is selected.
No alpha channel is added to the file.

4. **Click the empty area at the bottom of the Layers panel to deselect the layer.**

When the masked layer is not selected, the mask path does not appear in the Paths panel. This is an important distinction — if you want to edit the mask path, you have to make sure the correct path is selected first. Editing the original Car Outline path will have no effect on the mask path.

When the masked layer is not selected, the mask path does not appear in the Paths panel.

5. **Save the file and continue to the next exercise.**

Create a Vector Shape Layer

A shape layer is a special type of Photoshop layer that retains vector path information. The vector shape functions as a mask, revealing the defined fill color for the shape. Any vector paths can have defined stroke properties (color, width, and type/style), and can be edited using the same tools that you used to edit the paths in the previous exercises.

In this exercise, you will build a compound vector shape that will provide a background for the magazine's "In This Issue" text.

1. **With magazine.psd open, hide the Car layer.**

2. **In the Tools panel, choose the Rounded Rectangle tool (nested under the Rectangle tool).**

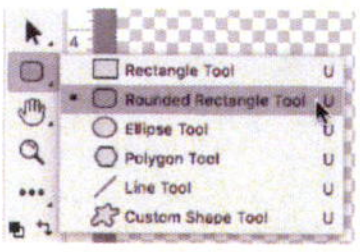

Note:

If a tool is missing from its default spotin the Tools panel, check in the Edit Toolbar menu at the bottom of the Tools panel. You can also reset the Essentials workspace to show all tools in their default locations.

3. **In the Options bar, choose Shape in the Tool Mode menu.**

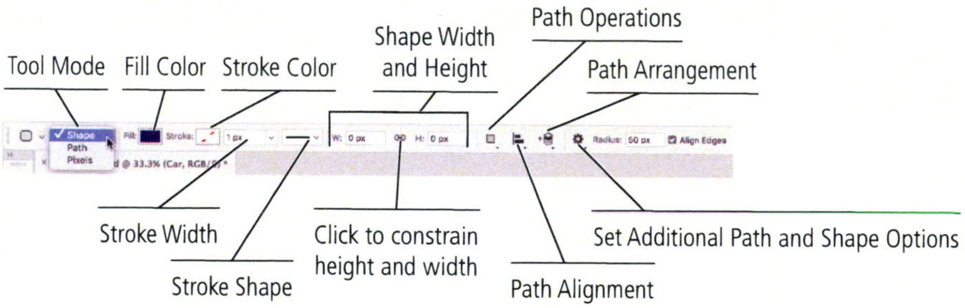

4. **Click the Fill color swatch to open the pop-up Swatches panel. Click the CMYK Blue swatch to select it as the fill color.**

   You can define separate fill and stroke colors of a vector shape layer, just as you might do for an object you create in Adobe Illustrator or InDesign. Clicking the Fill or Stroke color swatch opens a pop-up panel, where you can select a specific swatch to use as the attribute's color. Four buttons at the top of the panel change the attribute to (from left) None, Solid, a Gradient, or a Pattern. You can also click the Color Picker button to define any color that is not already in the Swatches panel.

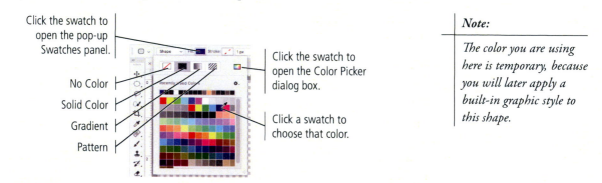

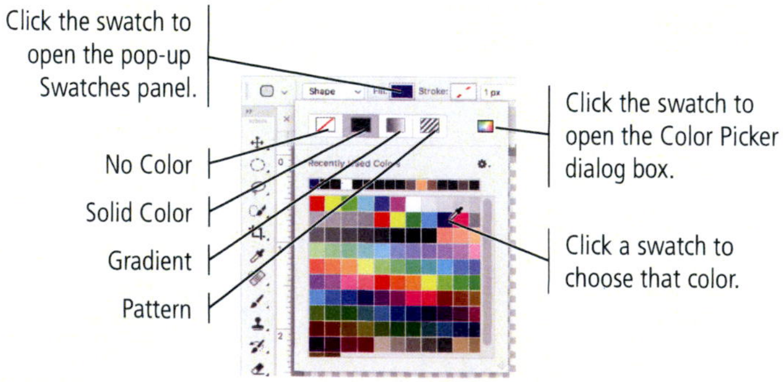

Note:

The color you are using here is temporary, because you will later apply a built-in graphic style to this shape.

5. **Click the Stroke swatch and choose No Color in the pop-up Swatches panel.**

6. **Change the Radius field to `50 px`.**

A rounded-corner rectangle is simply a rectangle with the corners cut at a specific distance from the end (the corner radius). The two sides are connected with one-fourth of a circle, which has a radius equal to the amount of the rounding.

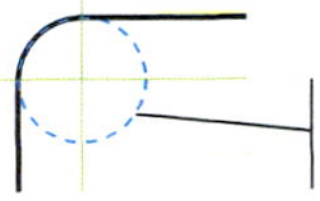
This imaginary circle
has a 50-px radius.

7. **Click in the top-right area of the canvas, then drag down and right to create the new shape.**

When you release the mouse button, the shape you drew fills with the defined Fill color. Because you chose None as the Stroke color, the shape you drew has no applied stroke. The red color you see around the shape is the color you defined earlier as the path color when you drew the car path.

When you use the Shape option in the Tool Mode menu, the resulting vector shape exists by default on its own layer.

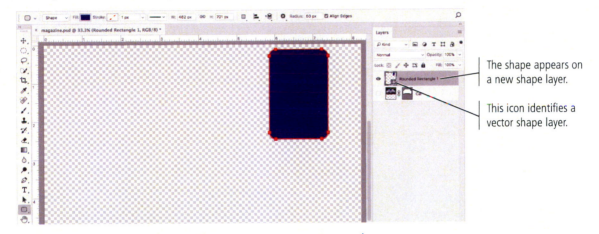

The shape appears on a new shape layer.
This icon identifies a vector shape layer.

8. **Click the empty space at the bottom of the Layers panel to deselect the Rounded Rectangle layer.**

When you deselect the layer, you can see the actual shape without the heavy red vector path. You can now see that the shape you created has no defined stroke color.

The shape layer is not selected.
The red path is no longer visible.

9. **Click the Rounded Rectangle 1 layer to select it again.**

When the shape layer is selected, you can again see the vector path that makes up the shape.

10. **Make sure the rulers are visible (View>Rulers), then review the information in the Properties panel.**

This panel automatically appears when you create a new shape with one of the vector shape tools. It shows the dimensions and position of the resulting shape, as well as other properties that were not available in the Options bar before you created the shape.

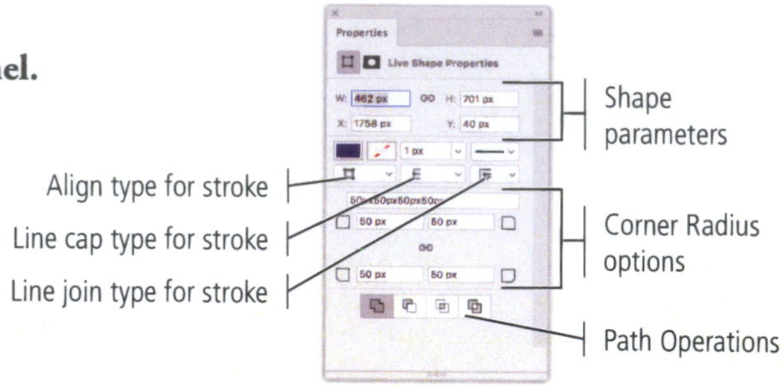

11. **Highlight the current W field and type `500`. Press Tab to highlight the H field, then type `1230`. Press Return/Enter to apply the change.**

The W and H fields define the object's physical dimensions.

The Properties panel defaults to use pixels for shape layers, regardless of the default units for the active file. You can, however, type values in other units of measurement as long as you include the appropriate unit in the value you type (for example, "2 in" or "4 cm").

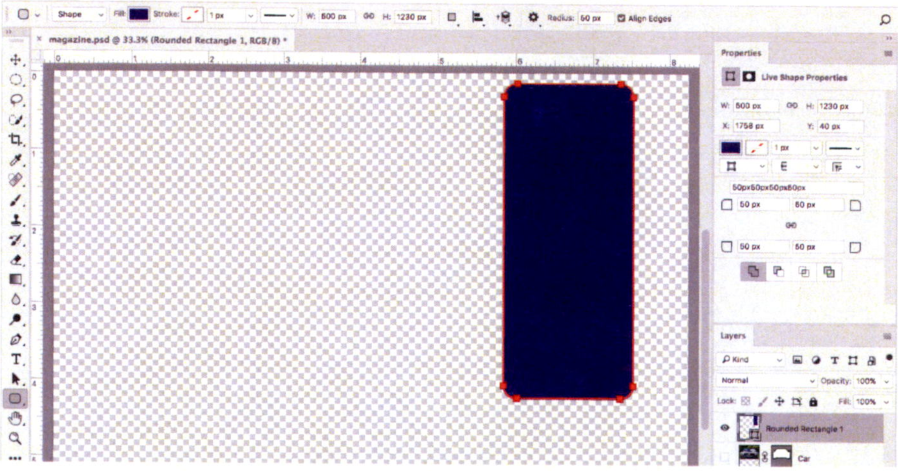

> **Note:**
>
> *Because you are creating a vector shape, you can edit its properties at any time without losing quality or pixel integrity (as would happen for pixel-based raster data).*

12. **Place the Mouse cursor over the X field until you see the scrubby slider cursor. Click and drag right or left until the X field shows 1865 px (the shape is approximately 3/8″ from the right edge of the canvas).**

The X and Y fields in the Properties panel define the object's position based on its top-left corner; unlike transforming objects in the Options panel, you cannot select a difference reference point around which to anchor the transformation.

Scrubby sliders, available in most Photoshop panels, offer a dynamic way to change field values. You can click the field name and drag left to decrease the value or drag right to increase the value.

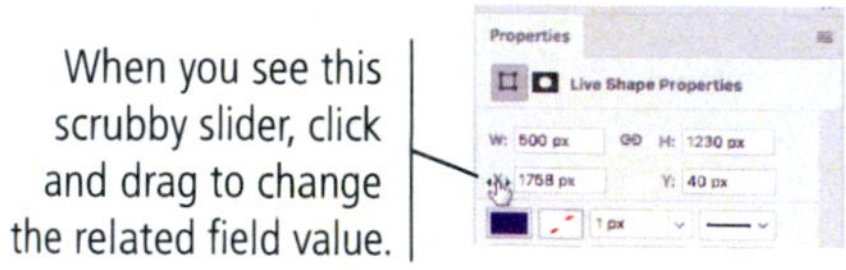

When you see this scrubby slider, click and drag to change the related field value.

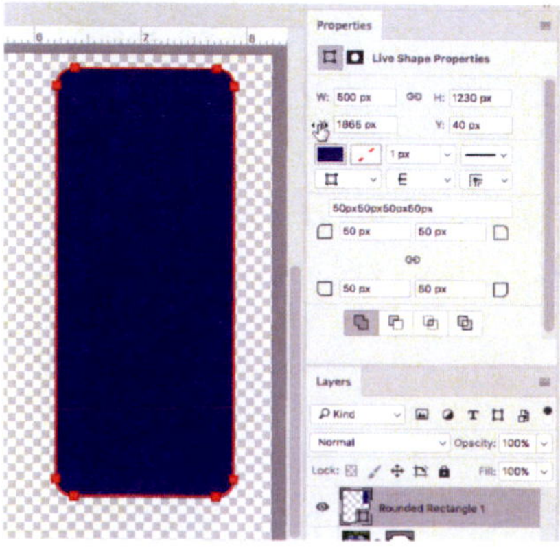

13. **Using either the scrubby slider or the field, change the Y position to 0.**

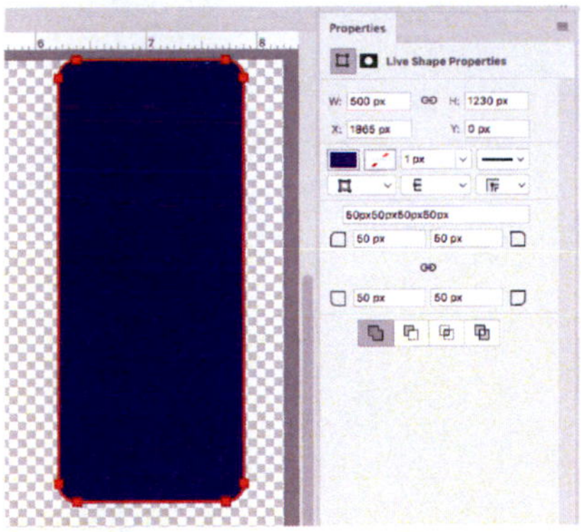

14. **Click the Rounded Rectangle tool in the Tools panel to deselect the existing vector shape and hide the path's anchor handles.**

Although the actual vector path is deselected, the shape layer is still selected in the Layers panel.

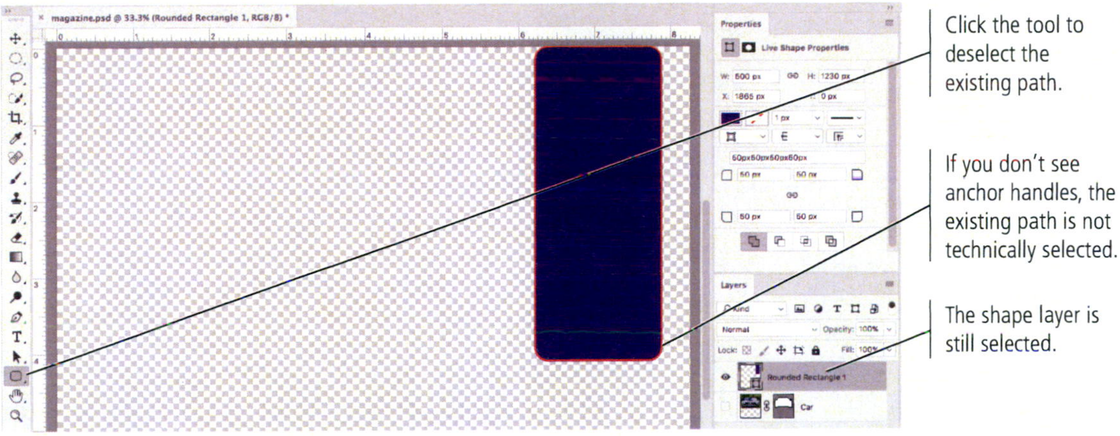
Click the tool to deselect the existing path.
If you don't see anchor handles, the existing path is not technically selected.
The shape layer is still selected.

15. **In the Options bar, open the Path Operations menu and choose Subtract Front Shape.**

If no shape layer is currently selected, the Path Operations menu defaults to New Layer. As long as a shape layer is selected and one of the shape layer tools is active, the menu retains the last-used option. You can continue subtracting (for example) as many new shapes as you like until you switch to a different tool — say, the Direct Selection tool to modify a specific anchor point.

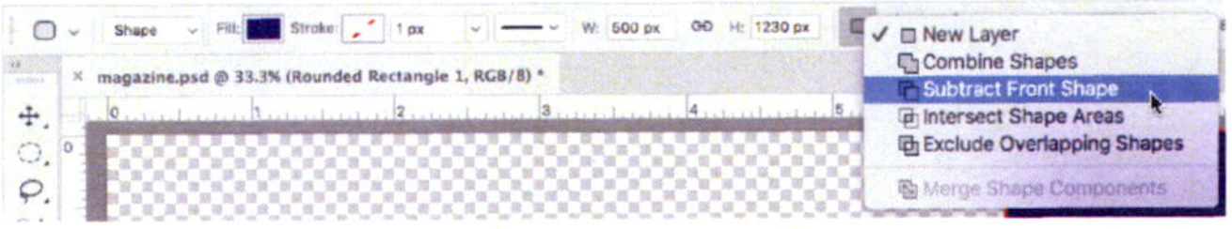

Note:

The Path Operations menu retains the last-used selection as long as the same tool remains active. If you switch to a different tool, the path operation reverts back to the New Layer option.

More About Vector Shape Options

Stroke Types

When a vector drawing tool is active, you can use the Stroke Type menu in the Options bar to choose a preset stroke style (solid, dashed, or dotted).

- The Align menu changes the stroke's alignment relative to the path. The icons in the menu suggest the result.
- The Caps menu determines how the stroke aligns to the ends of the path.
- The Corners menu defines the way the stroke appears at corners on the path.

If you click the More Options button, you can define a custom dash pattern.

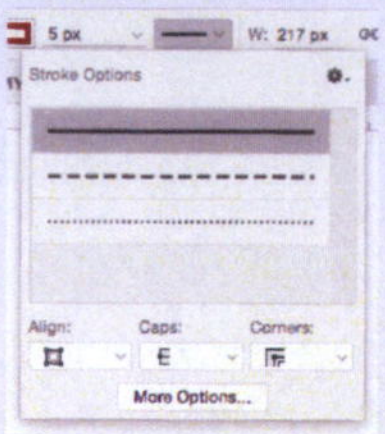

Align

- Align stroke to inside of path
- Align stroke to center of path
- Align stroke to outside of path

Caps

- No end cap
- Rounded end cap
- Square end cap

Corners

- Miter join
- Rounded join
- Beveled join

Path Alignment

You can use the **Path Alignment** to align or distribute multiple shapes on the same layer. For these options to work properly, you must use the Path Selection tool to select the paths you want to align, then choose an option from the menu. When Align to Canvas is selected, you can align one or more paths in relation to the overall canvas.

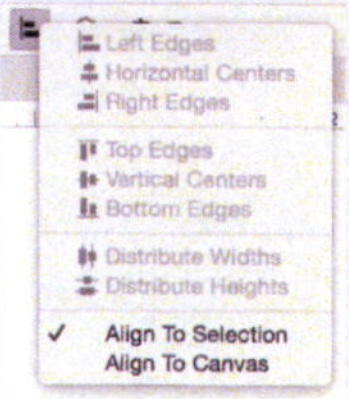

Geometry Options

Pen Tool

For the Pen tool, you can check the Rubber Band option in the Geometry Options menu to show a preview of the path curve as you move the cursor.

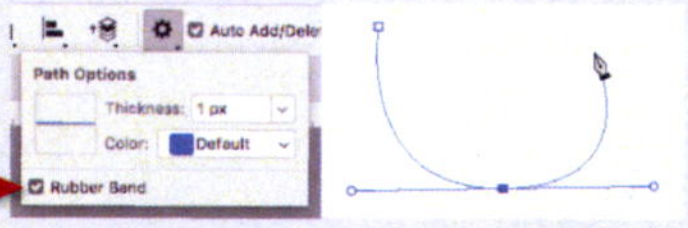

The Rubber Band option shows a preview of the curve that will be created when you click.

Rectangle, Rounded Rectangle, and Ellipse Tools

When **Unconstrained** is selected, you can simply click and drag to create a rectangle of any size.

If you choose the **Square** option (or Circle for the Ellipse tool), the shape you draw will be constrained to equal width and height (1:1 aspect ratio).

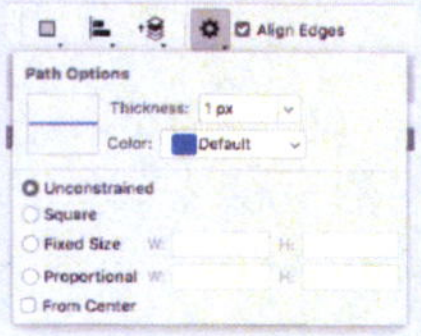

Rectangle/Rounded Rectangle tool

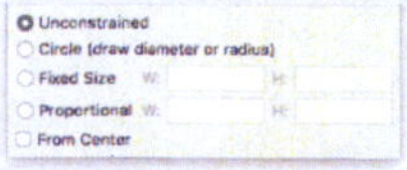

Ellipse tool

You can use the **Fixed Size** option to create a shape at a specific width and height. When you click in the canvas, you see a preview of the shape that will be created; you can drag around to determine where the shape will be placed when you release the mouse button.

You can also use the **Proportional** option to define the aspect ratio of the shape you will create. When you click and drag, the shape is constrained to the proportions you define.

If you choose the **From Center** option, the center of the shape you create will be placed where you first click.

Polygon Tool

Geometry options for this tool are the same as those that are available when you click the tool to define the shape you want to create (see Page 98).

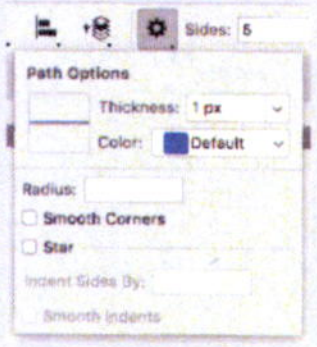

Line Tool

When you draw with the Line tool, you can use the Geometry Options menu to add arrowheads to the start and/or end of the line. The Width and Length fields define those attributes of the arrowheads as a percentage of the line weight; the Concavity field defines the arrowheads' inset as a percentage of its length.

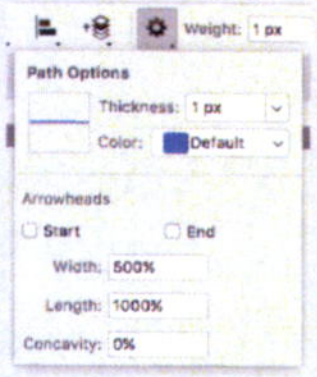

Custom Shape Tool

The Custom Shape tool makes it easy to create custom vector shapes from one of several defined libraries. You can open the Shape panel in the Options bar to access the built-in libraries of shapes. (You will use this tool in Project 5: Calendar Cover.)

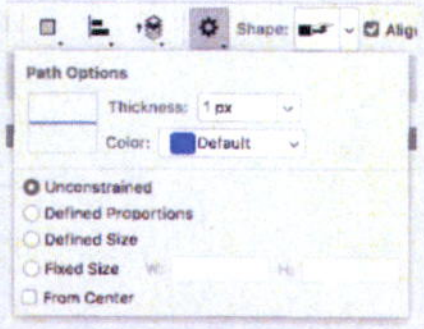

Geometry options for the Custom Shape tool are the same as for the Rectangle and Ellipse tools.

Understanding Vector Path Operations

New Layer

When you first choose one of the vector drawing tools — Pen, Freeform Pen, or one of the Shape tools — the Path Operations menu defaults to **New Layer**. When this option is active, every new path will be created on a separate layer.

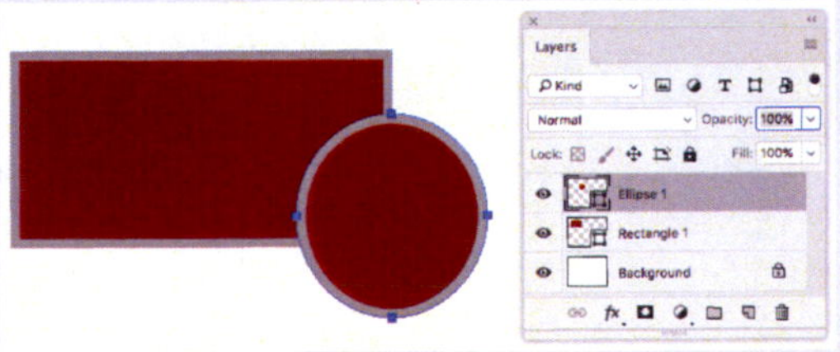

Combining Shapes

Combine Shapes creates the new path on the existing (selected) shape layer.

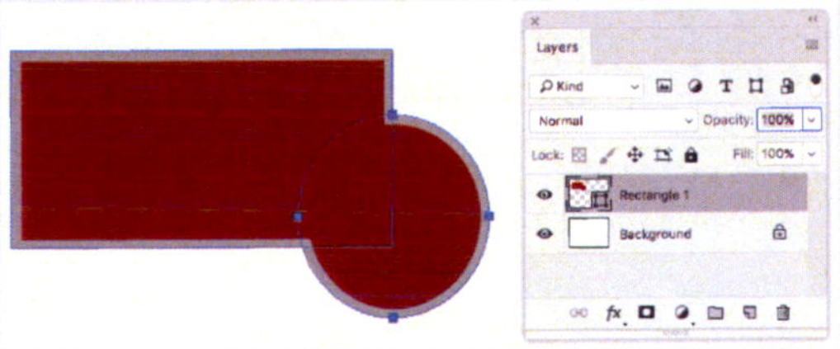

Subtract Front Shape creates the new path on the existing (selected layer), and removes overlapping areas of the new shape from the existing shape.

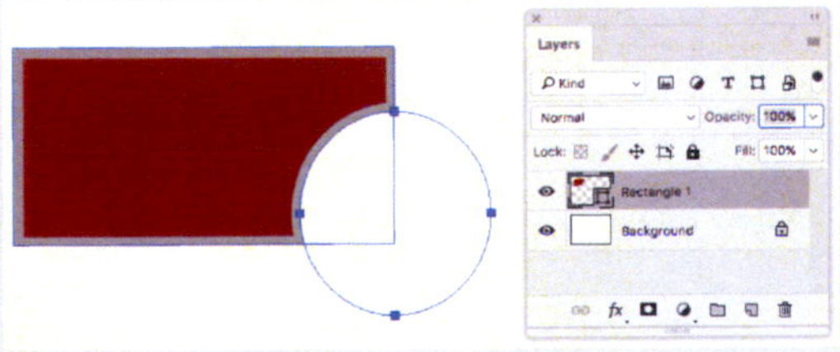

Intersect Shape Areas results in the shape of only overlapping areas in the existing and new shapes.

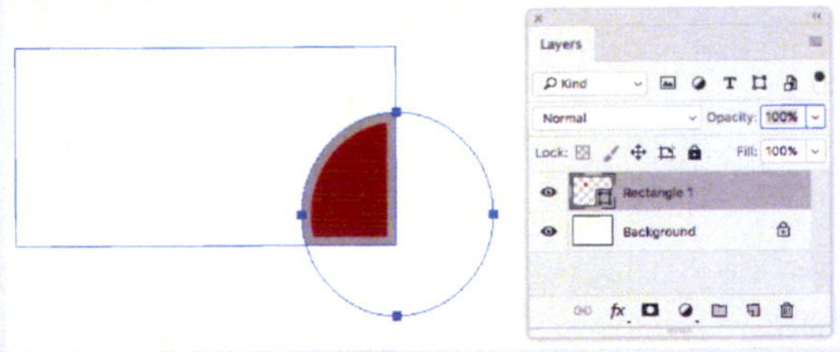

Exclude Overlapping Areas removes overlapping areas between the existing and new shapes.

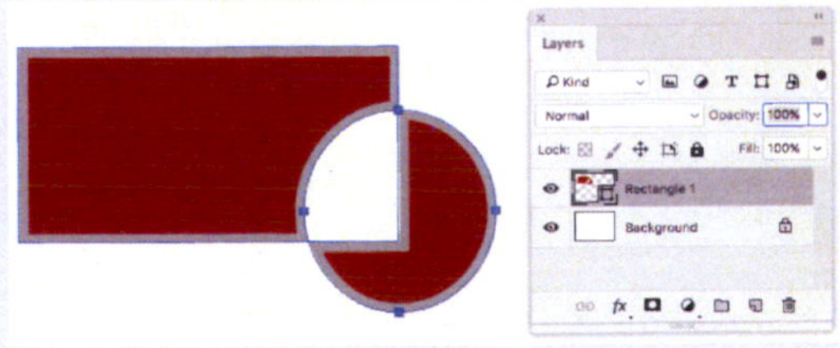

Merge Shape Components

It is important to note that with the four Combine options explained to the left, the result is the appearance of a single shape, but the original paths of each shape are maintained. You can still select and manipulate each component path independently.

To make the interaction of overlapping shapes permanent, you can select the paths you want to affect and choose **Merge Shape Components**. This results in a single shape that is the combination of any selected paths; unselected paths are not affected.

The actual result of this command depends on the interaction of the selected paths. In the example below, the top shape had been created with the Intersect Shape Areas operation. After applying the Merge Shape Components operation, anchor points were removed where the original paths did not intersect (as you can see in the bottom image).

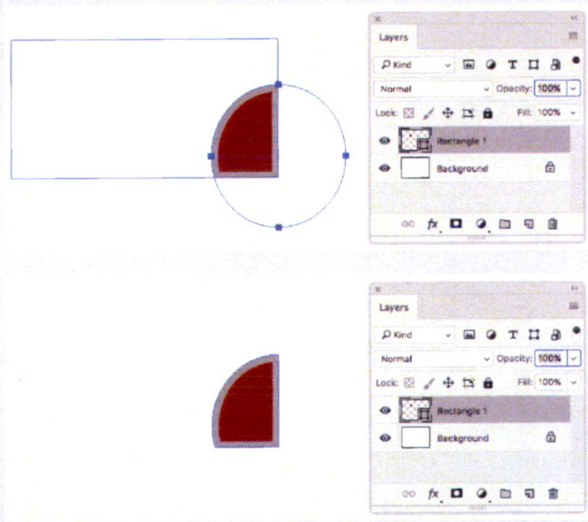

Merging Shape Layers

If multiple shape layers are selected in the Layers panel, you can combine them by choosing Merge Shapes in the Layers panel Options menu.

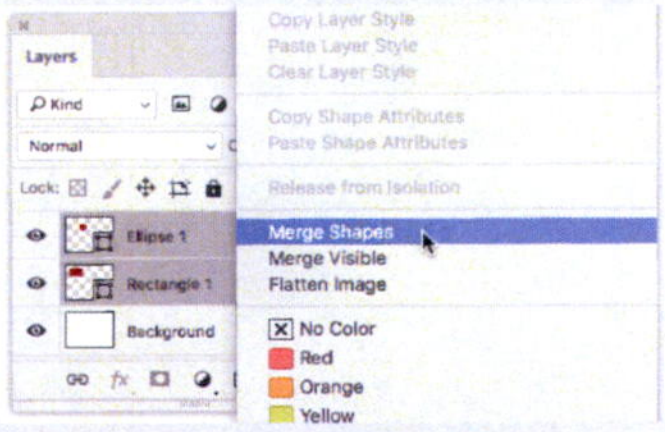

This command combines the shapes on all selected layers into a single shape layer — basically the same as using the Combine Shapes path operation. The new combined layer adopts the name of the highest layer in the previous selection.

Important note: Don't confuse this Merge option with the Merge Shape Components option in the Path Operations menu. The Merge Shapes option in the Layers panel actually combines the various shapes into a single layer, but maintains all of the existing paths.

16. **Click and drag to create another rectangle inside the area of the first.**

Using the Subtract Front Shape option, the second shape removes the overlapping area of underlying shapes, creating a compound path that results in a "window" effect.

Options for the basic Shape tools remember the last-used settings, so the new shape automatically has the 50-px corner radius that you defined for the first shape.

> *Note:*
>
> *A **compound path** is any single shape made up of more than one closed path.*

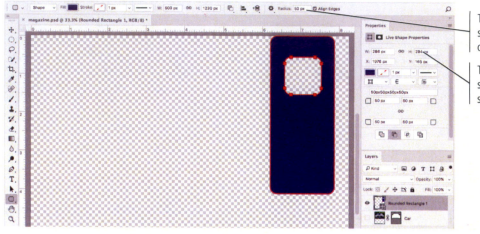

The Options panel shows options for the overall shape layer.
The Properties panel shows options for the selected vector path.

17. **In the Properties panel, change the new shape's parameters to:**

W: 300 px H: 300 px

X: 1965 px Y: 135 px

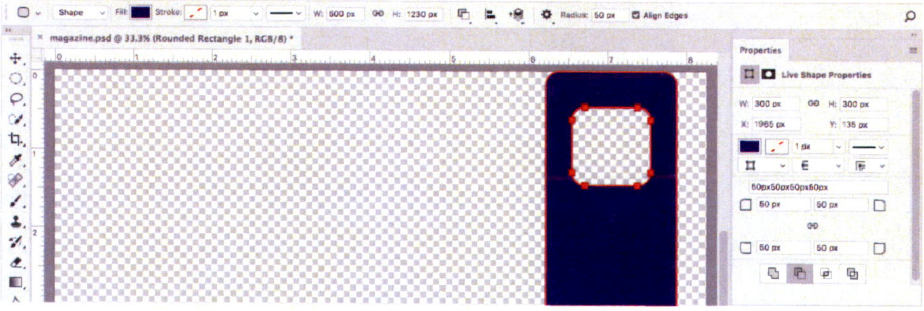

18. **In the lower half of the Properties panel, makes sure the four corner radius fields are linked.**

When the link icon is highlighted (active), changing any one radius value affects the other three corners.

19. **Type 10 in the top-left field, then press Return/Enter to apply your changes.**

When this icon is highlighted, changing one corner radius changes all four corners.
Corners on the unselected path are not affected.

20. **Choose the Path Selection tool in the Tools panel, then click the outer path of the compound shape to select it.**

Each component path of the overall shape is still an independent vector path, which means you can select and edit its properties in the Properties panel at any time.

21. **Unlink the four corner radius fields, then change the top-left and top-right corner radius field to field to `0 px`.**

Although rounded-corner shapes always start with four identical corners, you can use this panel to change each corner radius individually.

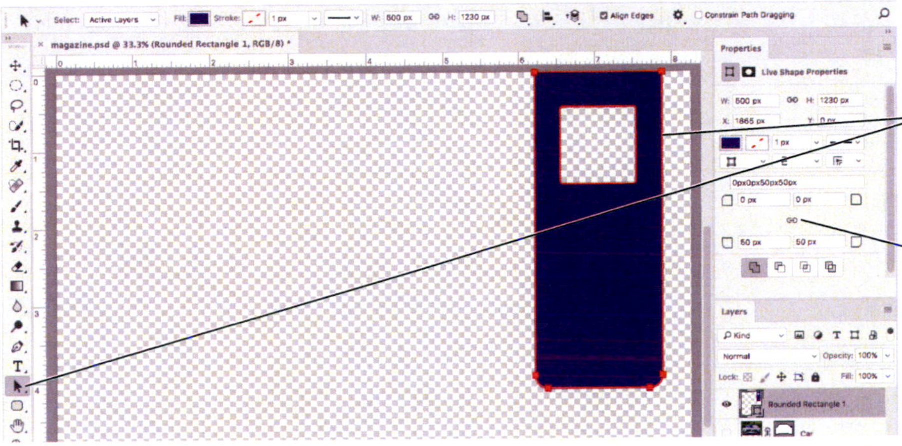

Use the Path Selection tool to select a specific vector path.
When this icon is not highlighted, changing one corner radius has no effect on the other corners.

22. **Save the file and continue to the next exercise.**

Selecting and Modifying Paths

When you draw vector paths, you can use the Path Selection tool to select and move specific paths on a layer.

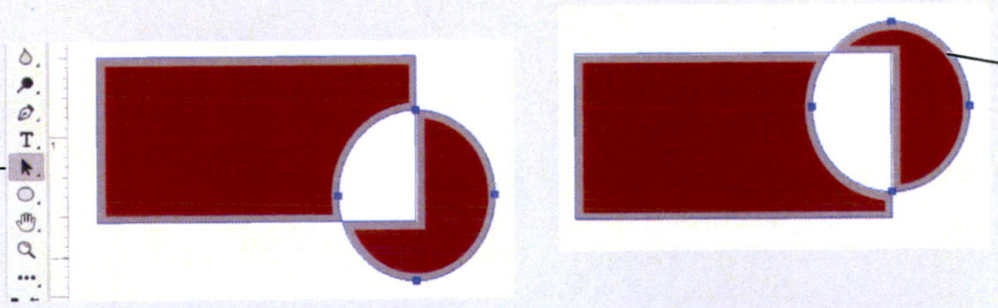

You can also select a specific shape to change the path operation that applies to it (in either the Options or Properties panel). In the example to the right, the rectangle was created first and then the oval was created with the Combine Shapes path operation. We then used the Path Selection tool to select the oval, and chose the Subtract Front Shape operation. Unless you merge the paths into a single shape, you can always select an individual path and change the way it interacts with underlying shapes.

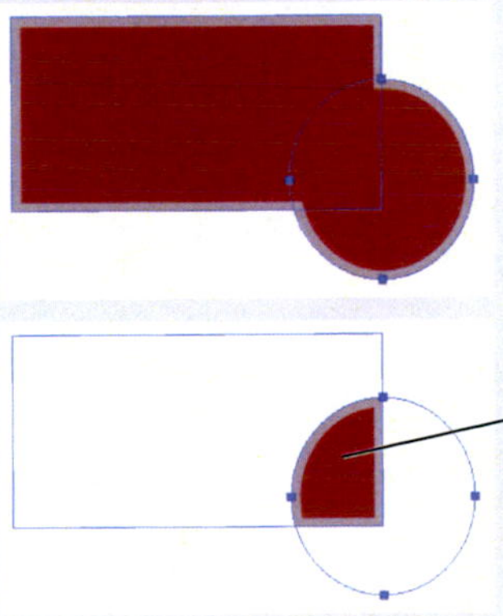

Changing the path operation of the selected path changes the way it interacts with the bottom path.

Because the path operations affect underlying shapes, you should also understand the concept of **stacking order**. When you create multiple shapes on the same shape layer, they exist from bottom to top in the order in which you create them — the first shape is on the bottom, then the next shape, and so on until the last shape created is at the top of the stack. You can use the **Path Arrangement** menu to control the stacking order of selected paths on the same shape layer.

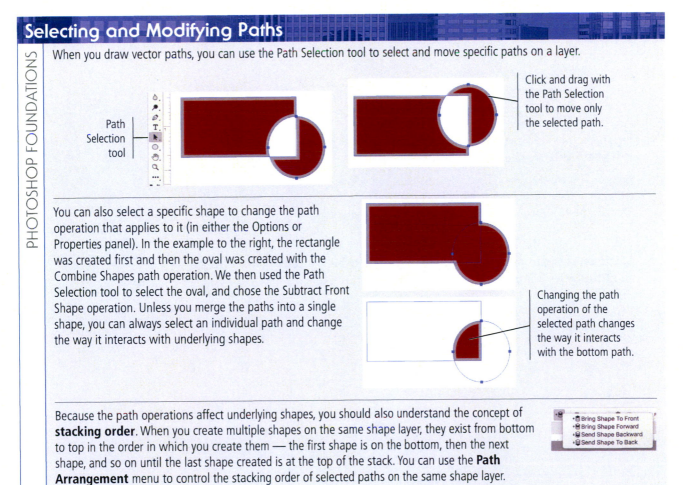

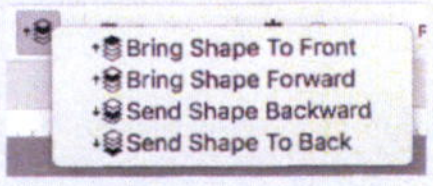

Clone and Align Layers

If you need more than one version of the same layer, you can create a copy by choosing Duplicate Layer in the layer's contextual menu. This command results in a copy of the original layer in the exact same position as the original.

You can also use the Move tool to **clone** a layer, which results in a duplicate copy of the original layer, in the position where you drag to make the clone. In this exercise, you will use cloning to create three rectangle shape layers across the bottom of the canvas. You will then distribute those shape layers evenly across the canvas.

Note:

These shapes will be used to hold additional inset photos to enhance the visual interest of the overall composition.

1. **With `magazine.psd` open, click the empty area at the bottom of the layers panel to deselect the existing shape layer.**

   If you don't first deselect the shape layer, your stroke color changes in the next few steps would affect the existing shape.

2. **Choose the Rectangle tool (nested under the Rounded Rectangle tool if you continued directly from the previous exercise). In the Options bar, define the following settings:**

   Fill Color: White

   Stroke Color: Dark Red

   Stroke Width: 15 px

3. **Open the Path Operations menu and review the options.**

   The Path Operations menu defaults to the New Layer option if an existing shape layer is not selected.

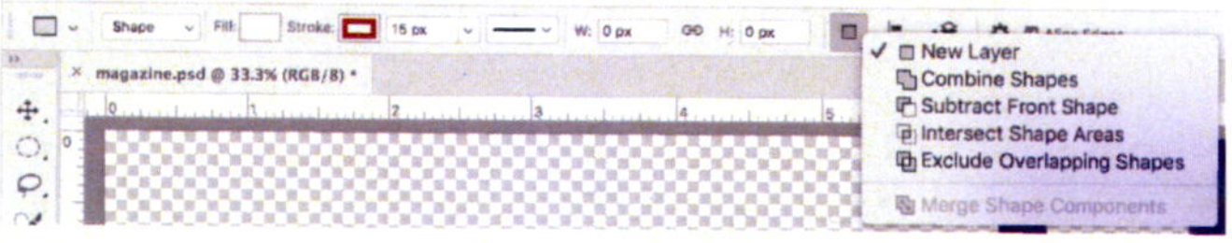

4. **Open the Set Additional Shape and Path Options menu. Define a 1 px thickness and use the Default color.**

   Because you are creating a shape with an actual red stroke, the red path you defined earlier is not a good choice. The thinner Default (blue) option will be far less distracting in this case.

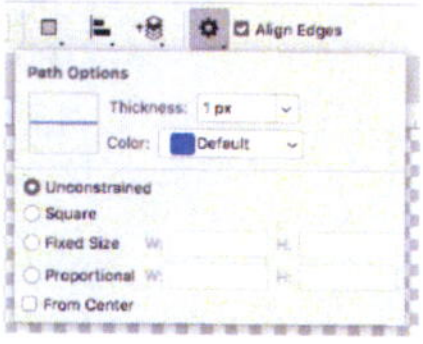

5. **Click and drag to create a rectangle in the lower half of the canvas. Using the Properties panel, define the new shape's parameters as:**

   W: 600 px H: 500 px

   X: 200 px Y: 2430 px

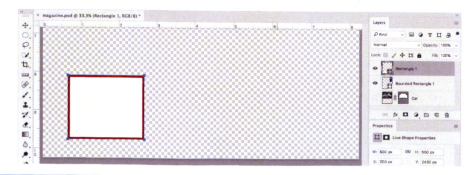

6. **Choose the Move tool in the Tools panel. Press Option/Alt, then click inside the smaller rectangle shape and drag right to clone it.**

   Pressing Option/Alt while dragging a selection clones that selection. Because the shape layer is the active selection, the entire shape layer is cloned. The Smart Guides help you maintain the cloned layer's horizontal alignment to the original. (If you decide to hide Smart Guides, pressing Shift constrains the movement to 45° angles.)

   The new cloned layer appears immediately above the original in the Layers panel, with the name "Rectangle 1 Copy."

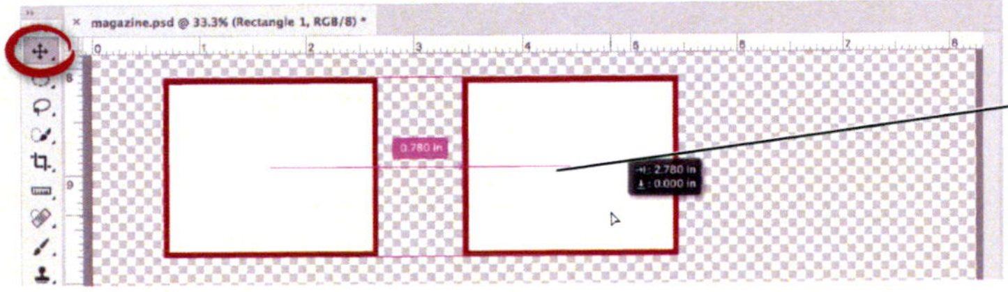

Smart Guides help maintain alignment relative to the original shape layer.

The cloned layer adopts the name of the original, plus the word "copy."

7. **Double-click the name of the Rectangle 1 layer to highlight it. Type Left Inset, then press Return/Enter to change the layer name.**

   Even though you will have only three copies of this shape layer, it could become very confusing later if you don't use meaningful names to differentiate the layers.

8. **Double-click the name of the cloned layer to highlight it. Type Center Inset, then press Return/Enter to change the layer name.**

9. **Repeat Step 6 to create a third shape layer at the bottom of the canvas. Name this new layer Right Inset.**

10. **In the Properties panel, change the X position of the active shape to 1700 px.**

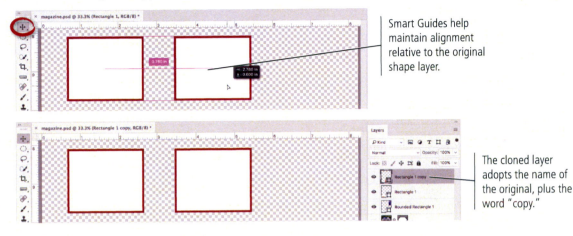

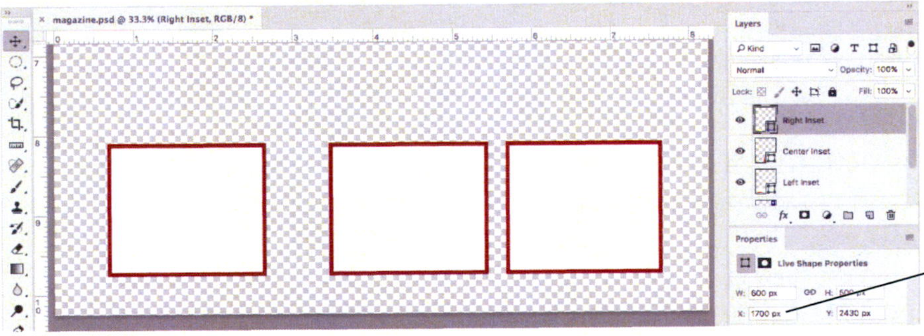

Define the X position of the right shape.

11. **In the Layers panel, Shift-click to select all three Inset shape layers.**

    When multiple layers are selected in the Layers panel, a number of alignment options become available in the Options bar. These are very useful for aligning or distributing the content of multiple layers relative to one another.

12. **With the Move tool active, click the Distribute Horizontal Centers button in the Options bar.**

When the Move tool is active and multiple layers are selected, you can use the Options bar to align the contents of the selected layers relative to one another. The Distribute Horizontal Centers option places an equal amount of space between the center pixel of each selected layer; the positions of layers containing the outermost pixels in the selection are not affected.

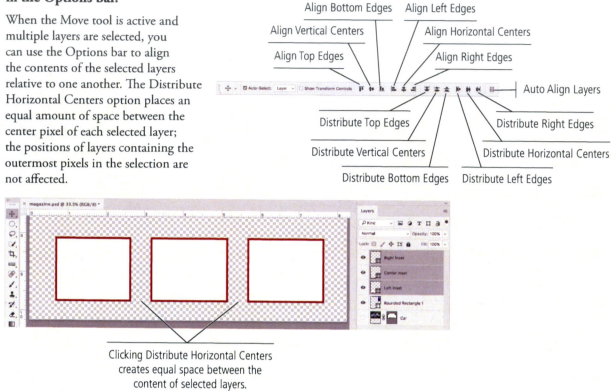

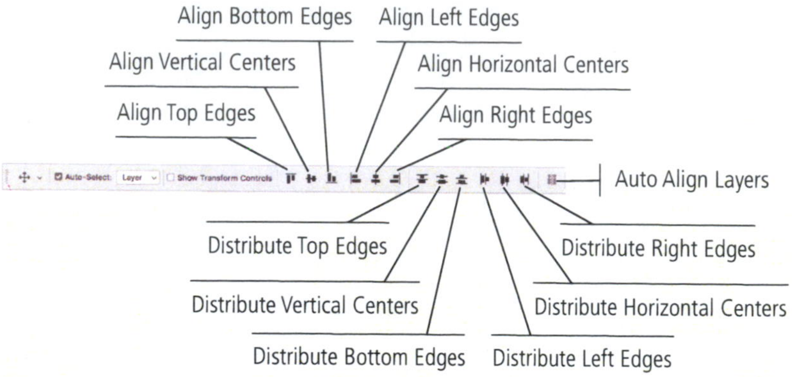

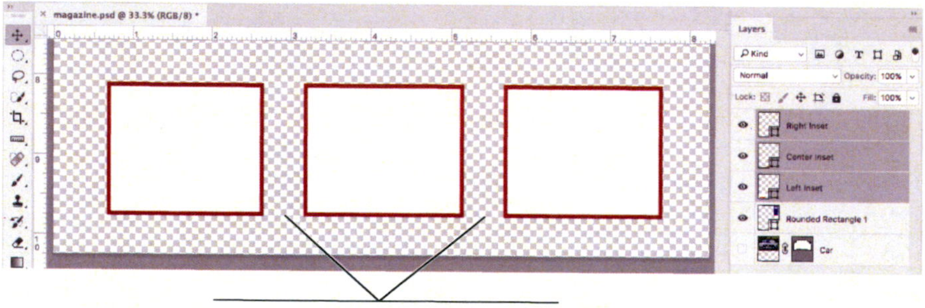

Clicking Distribute Horizontal Centers creates equal space between the content of selected layers.

13. **Save the file and continue to the next exercise.**

Auto-Select Layers

When your files have more than a few layers — a common occurrence — selecting exactly the layer you want can be difficult. As you already learned, the Move tool defaults to affect whatever layer is selected in the Layers panel. Using the Auto-Select option, you can automatically select a specific layer by clicking pixels in the document window rather than manually selecting a layer in the panel first.

1. **With magazine.psd open, choose File>Place Embedded.**

2. **Navigate to inset1.jpg (in your WIP>Cars folder) and click place. When the image appears on the canvas, press Return/Enter to finalize the placement.**

   New Smart Object layers appear immediately above the previously selected layer. In this case, it is at the top of the layer stack.

3. **In the Layers panel, drag inset1 to appear immediately above the Left Inset layer.**

4. **Repeat Steps 1–3 to place inset2.jpg as an embedded file, and position the inset2 layer immediately above the Center Inset layer.**

   Unfortunately, you can only select one file at a time in the Place dialog box.

5. **Repeat Steps 1–3 to place `inset3.jpg` as an embedded file, and position the inset3 layer immediately above the Right Inset layer.**

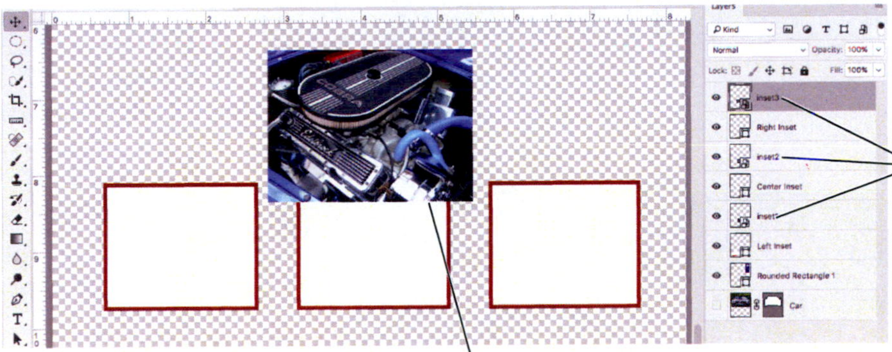

Position each Smart Object layer immediately above the shape layers.

All three Smart Object layers were placed in the center of the document window.

6. **Choose the Move tool in the Tools panel. In the Options bar, check the Auto-Select option.**

7. **Click in the area of the placed images and drag until the inset3 image entirely obscures the bottom-right rectangle shape.**

   When Auto-Select is active, clicking in the canvas automatically selects the layer containing the pixel where you clicked. Because the inset3 image is on top of the other two, clicking in the area of the placed images automatically selects the inset3 layer.

Check the Auto-Select option.

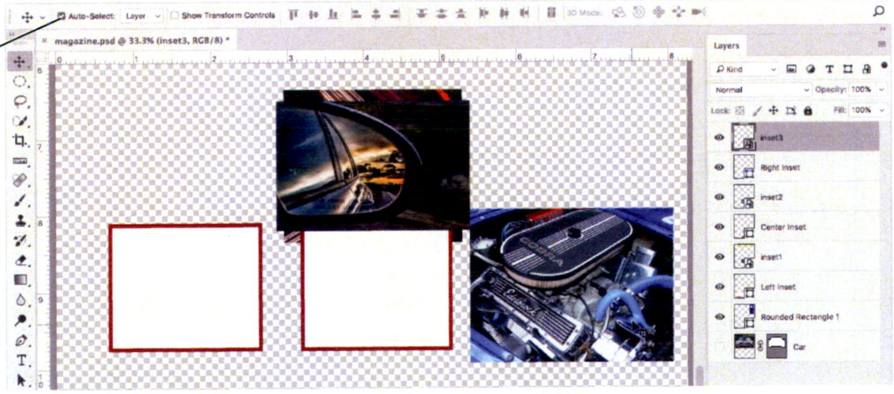

9. **Click again in the original area of the placed images, and drag to move the inset2 image until it entirely obscures the center rectangle.**

   Again, clicking automatically selects the relevant layer. Using the Auto-Select option makes it easier to manage layer contents even when you are not sure which layer contains the pixels you want to affect.

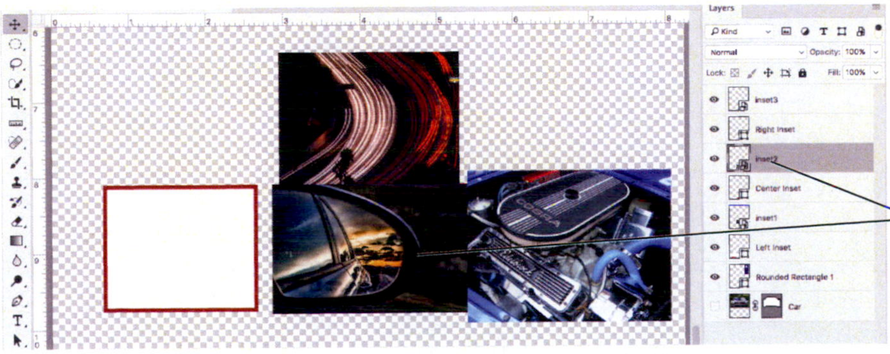

When Auto-Select is checked, clicking automatically selects the layer containing the pixel where you clicked.

10. **Move the inset1 image until it entirely obscures the left rectangle.**

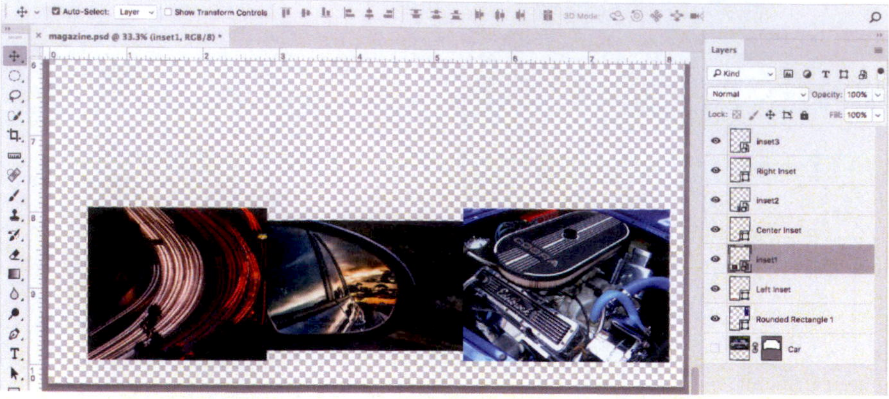

> *Note:*
>
> *Remember, if the Auto-Select option is checked in the Options bar, you can simply click pixels of the layer you want to move without first selecting the layer.*

11. **Save the file and continue to the next exercise.**

Create Clipping Masks

As you can see, the placed images completely hide the underlying layer content. To make the inset images appear only within the area of the underlying shapes, you need to create clipping masks. This task is relatively easy to accomplish.

1. **With magazine.psd open, Control/right-click the inset1 layer to open the layer's contextual menu.**

   Remember, to access the contextual menu for a specific layer, you have to Control/right-click in the area to the right of the layer name.

2. **Choose Create Clipping Mask from the contextual menu.**

   A clipping mask is another way to show only certain areas of a layer; in this case, using the shape of one layer (Left Inset) to show parts of the layer above it (inset1).

   The Layers panel shows that the inset1 layer is clipped by the Left Inset layer.

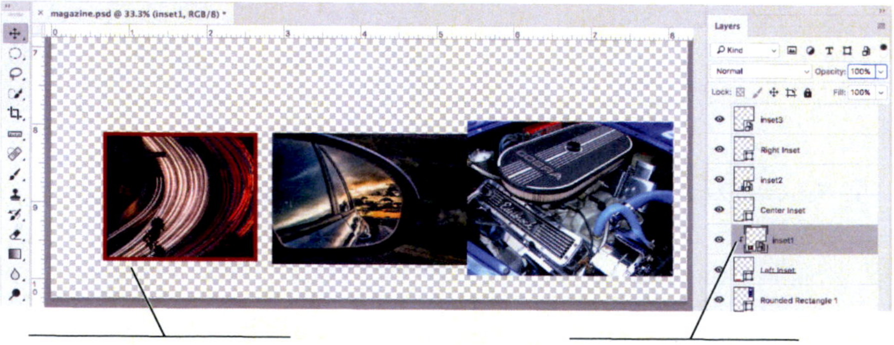

The only visible area is where the image overlaps the shape.

The inset1 layer is indented from and clipped by the Left Inset layer.

3. **If any of the rectangle's white fill area is visible, use the Move tool to reposition the inset1 layer content.**

   Even though a layer is clipped, you can still move it without affecting the position of the clipping layer. Unlike a layer mask, the clipping and clipped layers are not automatically linked.

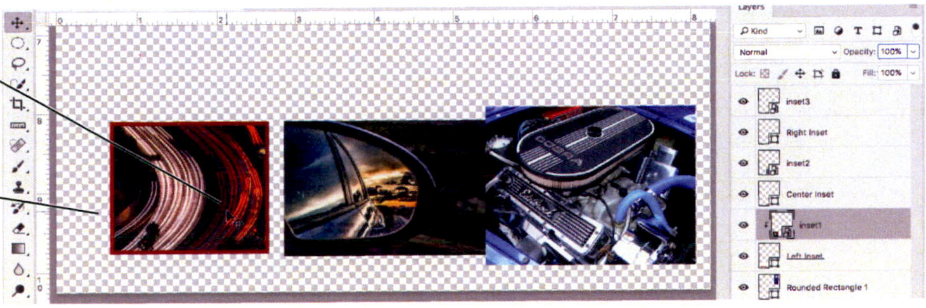

Use the Move tool to reposition the clipped image.
The clipping layer still defines the visible area of the clipped image.

   As with layer masks, clipping masks do not permanently modify the pixels in the layer. You can choose Release Clipping Mask in the clipped layer's contextual menu to undo a clipping mask without altering the affected layers.

4. **Repeat Steps 1–3 to clip the inset2 and inset3 images to their underlying layers.**

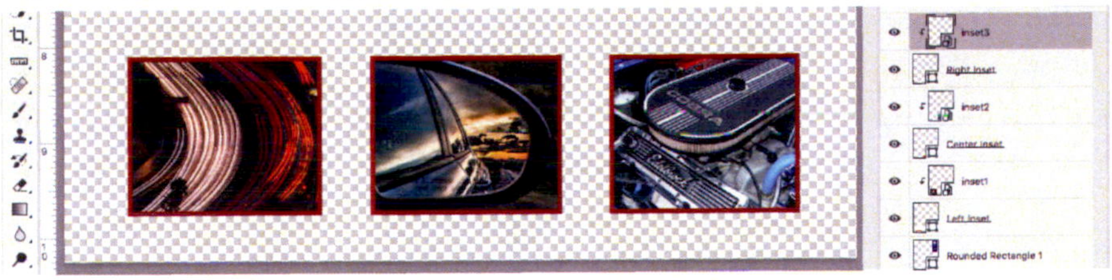

5. **In the Layers panel, show the Car layer and then move it to the top of the layer stack.**

6. **Using the Move tool, position the car so it slightly overlaps the three shape layers at the bottom of the page.**

   Use the following image as a guide.

   If you created a clipping mask for the Car layer, the car would only be visible within the area of the underlying compound shape. To make the car appear to drive out from the cut-out interior shape, you can simply rearrange and move the layers.

7. **Save the file and then continue to the next stage of the project.**

Stage 3 Applying Styles and Filters

Photoshop includes a large number of options for creating artistic effects, including built-in patterns, styles, and filters. You can add texture to the flat fill color of a vector shape layer. You can apply effects such as drop shadows or beveling to add the appearance of depth. You can make images look like pencil sketches, paintings, or any of dozens of other options. You can even compound these filters and styles to create unique effects that would require extreme skill in traditional art techniques such as oil painting. In this stage of the project, you will use a number of these options to enhance your overall composition.

Add Texture to a Shape Layer

Aside from their usefulness as scalable vector paths, shape layers can be filled with solid colors (as the background shape is now), with other images (as the smaller inset shapes are now), or with styles or patterns (which you will add in this exercise).

1. **With magazine.psd open, choose Window>Styles to open the Styles panel.**

   This panel shows the predefined styles that can be applied to a shape layer. The icons give you an idea of what the styles do, but these small squares can be cryptic.

2. **Click the button in the top-right corner of the Styles panel and choose Large List from the Options menu.**

   We prefer the list view because the style names provide a better idea of what the styles do. The Large List option displays a bigger style thumbnail than the Small List view.

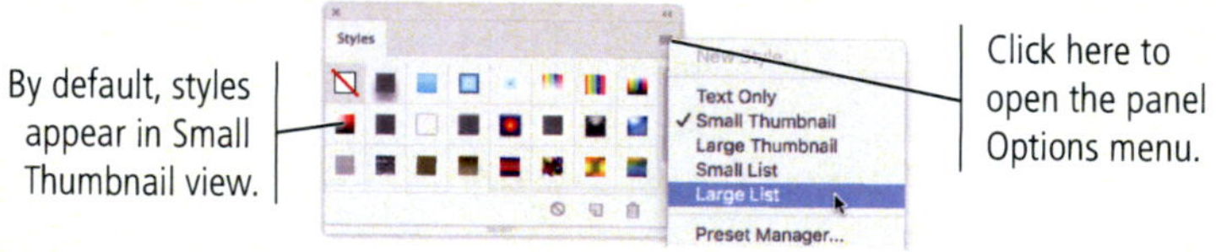

3. **Open the Styles panel Options menu again and choose Web Styles near the bottom of the list.**

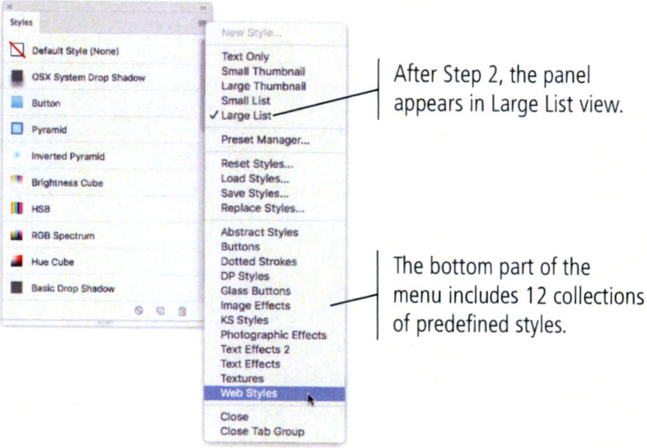

Note:

In the default set, a word in parentheses next to a style name identifies the collection in which that style exists.

4. **Click OK to replace the current set with the Web Styles set.**

When you call a new set of styles, Photoshop asks if you want to replace the current set or append the new set to the existing set(s).

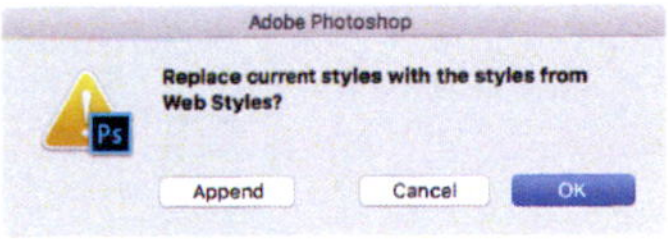

If you select Append, the new styles will be added to the existing ones. This can result in a very long list, which makes it difficult to find what you want. By replacing the current set, you will only see the styles in the texture set. This does not delete the previous styles, it only removes them from the panel; you can recall the previous styles by choosing Reset Styles in the panel Options menu.

5. **Select the Rounded Rectangle 1 shape layer in the Layers panel, then click the Black Anodized Metal style in the Styles panel to apply the style to the shape layer.**

The layers panel shows that a series of effects — the ones that make up the style — has been applied to the layer.

Photoshop styles are non-destructive, which means you can change or delete them without affecting the original layer content. You can temporarily disable all effects by clicking the eye icon to the left of the word "Effects," or disable individual effects by clicking the icon for a specific item in the panel.

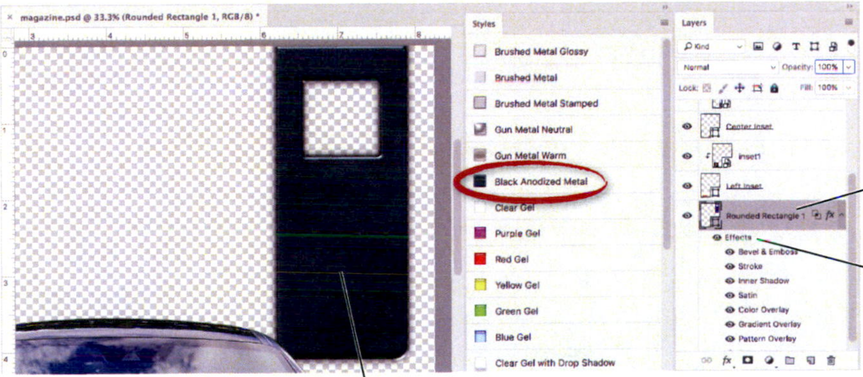

The shape layer is selected.

The Layers panel shows a series of effects that have been applied to the layer.

The selected style fills the shape layer.

6. **In the Layers panel, click the arrow to the right of the fx icon of the Rounded Rectangle 1 layer.**

This collapses the list of applied effects, which helps keep the Layers panel easier to manage.

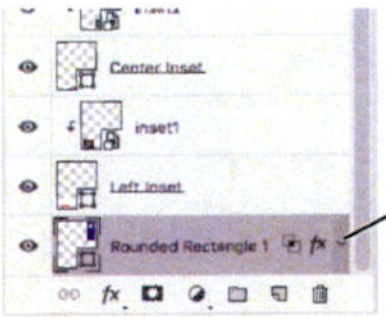

Click here to collapse or expand the list of applied effects.

7. **Save the file and continue to the next exercise.**

Note:

Some users report seeing a message asking if they want to save changes to the current styles before replacing them, even if they did not make changes to the default set. This is a minor bug in the software. If you see this message, click No.

Apply Custom Layer Effects

A style is simply a saved group of effects that can be applied with a single click. You can also create your own styles using the Layer Effects dialog box, which you will do in this exercise.

1. **With `magazine.psd` open, choose the Left Inset layer.**

2. **Choose Layer>Layer Style>Drop Shadow.**

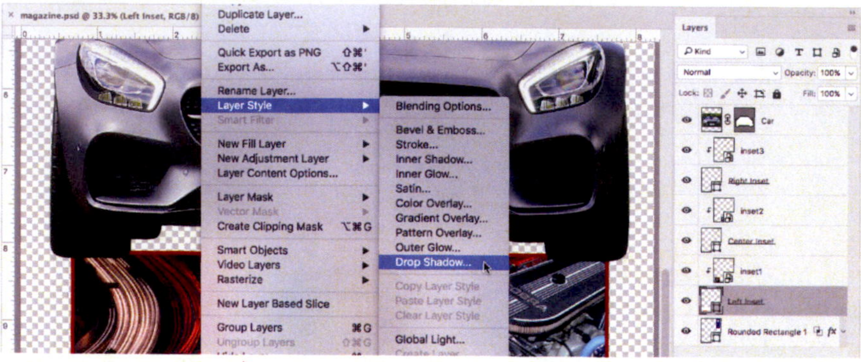

3. **In the resulting dialog box, make sure the Preview option is checked.**

   The Preview option allows you to see the results of your settings while the dialog box is still open.

4. **In the Layer Style dialog box, make sure the Use Global Light option is checked.**

   This option is checked by default, so you should not have to make any change.

   The Angle field defines the position of the effect in relation to the layer. When the Global Light option is checked, changing the style Angle applies the same change to any other layer where an effect is applied using the Use Global Light option.

5. **Make the following changes to the default settings in the dialog box:**

   Opacity: 50%
   Distance: 10 px
   Spread: 5 %
   Size: 10 px

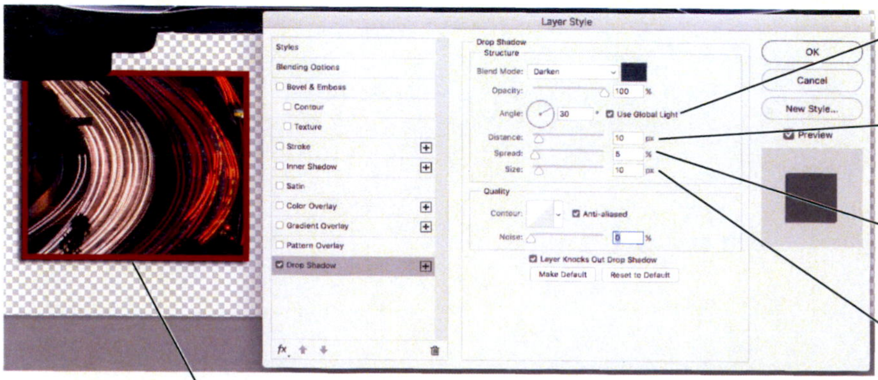

Make sure Use Global Light is checked.

Distance offsets the effect relative to the layer content.

Spread is the percentage the effect expands beyond the layer content.

Size controls the amount of blurring applied to the effect.

When Preview is checked, the drop shadow effect is visible behind the dialog box.

6. **Click the + button to the right of the Drop Shadow layer style.**

   You can apply more than one instance of certain layer styles (those identified with a + to the right of the name). When you click the Plus button, a new instance of the Drop Shadow layer style appears in the list.

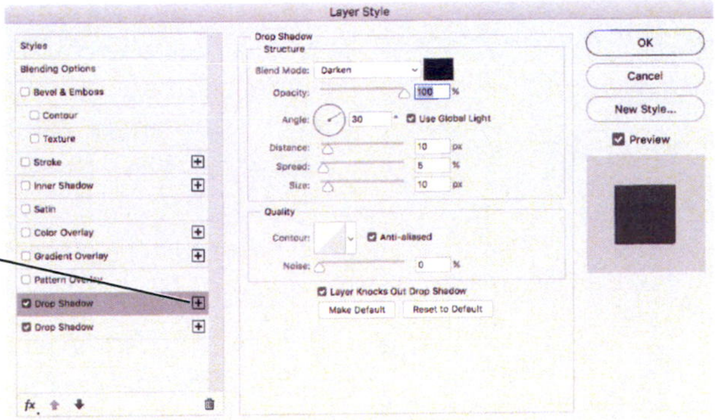

Click the + button to add a second instance of the same layer style.

> ***Note:***
>
> *You can use the buttons at the bottom of the effects list to change the order of applied effects, as well as delete a specific (selected) effect.*
>
> 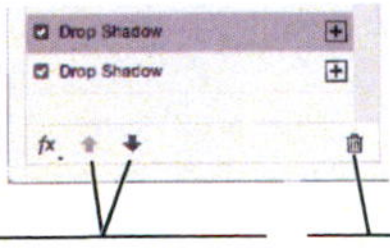
>
> Use these buttons to reorder applied effects.
>
> Delete Effect

7. **With the top Drop Shadow item selected in the list, click the color swatch to the right of the Blend Mode menu.**

8. **When the Color Picker appears, move the mouse cursor over the dark blue color on the car's windshield and click to sample that color. Click OK to close the Color Picker dialog box.**

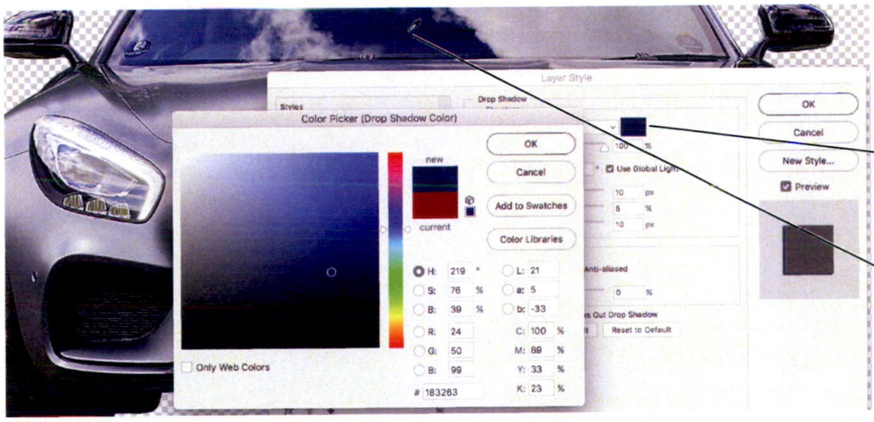

Click the swatch to open the Color Picker for the style.

Click to sample a color that you want to use for the style.

9. **Uncheck the Use Global Light option, then change the Angle field to `-150°`.**

   If you change the angle field while the Use Global Light option is checked, you would change the global angle; that change would apply to any other applied layer style that uses the global light angle. You want to change the angle for only this style instance, so you must uncheck Use Global Light *before* changing the angle field.

10. **Make the following changes to the settings in the dialog box:**

    Opacity: `75%`
    Distance: `20` px
    Spread: `10%`
    Size: `20` px

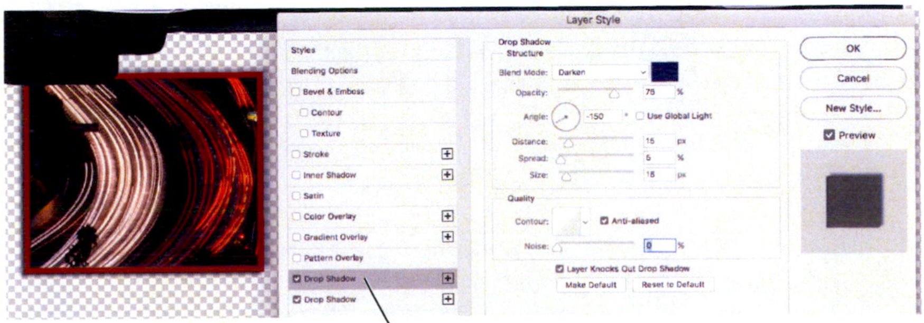

Changes affect only the selected style instance.

Layer Styles in Depth

Photoshop offers ten layer style options, which you can apply individually or in various combinations to create unique flat and dimensional effects for any layer.

Bevel and Emboss

This style has five variations: Outer Bevel, Inner Bevel, Emboss, Pillow Emboss, and Stroke Emboss:

- **Outer Bevel** creates a bevel on the outside edges of the layer contents.
- **Inner Bevel** creates a bevel on the inside edges.
- **Emboss** creates the effect of embossing the layer contents against the underlying layers.
- **Pillow Emboss** creates the effect of stamping the edges of the layer into the underlying layers.
- **Stroke Emboss** applies an embossed effect to a stroke applied to the layer. (The Stroke Emboss effect is not available if you haven't applied a stroke to the layer.)

Any of these styles can be applied as **Smooth** (blurs the edges of the effect), **Chisel Hard** (creates a distinct edge to the effect), or **Chisel Soft** (creates a distinct but slightly blurred edge to the effect).

You can change the **Direction** of the bevel effect. **Up** creates the appearance of the layer coming out of the image; **Down** creates the appearance of something stamped into the image.

The **Size** slider makes the effect smaller or larger, and the **Soften** slider blurs the edges of the effect.

In the Shading area, you can control the light source **Angle** and **Altitude** (think of how shadows differ as the sun moves across the sky). You can also apply a **Gloss Contour** (see the following explanation of Contours). Finally, you can change the Blending Mode, Opacity, and Color settings of both highlights and shadows created in effects.

When a Bevel and Emboss style is applied, you can also apply Contour and Texture effects.

Stroke

The **Stroke** style adds an outline of a specific number of pixels to the layer. The Stroke effect can be added at the outside or inside of the layer edge, or it can be centered over the edge (half the stroke will be inside and half outside the actual layer edge). You can adjust the Blending Mode and Opacity setting of the stroke, and you can also define a specific color, gradient, or pattern to apply as the stroke.

Satin

The Satin options apply interior shading to create a satiny appearance. You can change the Blending Mode, Color, and Opacity settings of the effect, as well as the Angle, Distance, and Size settings.

Drop Shadow and Inner Shadow

Drop Shadow adds a shadow behind the layer; **Inner Shadow** adds a shadow inside the edges of the layer's content. For both types, you can define the blending mode, color, opacity, angle, distance, and size of the shadow.

- **Distance** is the offset of the shadow, or how far away the shadow will be from the original layer.
- **Spread** (for Drop Shadows) is the percentage the shadow expands beyond the original layer.
- **Choke** (for Inner Shadows) is the percentage the shadow shrinks into the original layer.
- **Size** is the blur amount applied to the shadow.

You can also adjust the Contour, Anti-aliasing, and Noise settings in the shadow effect. (See the Contours section later in this discussion for further explanation.)

When checked, the Layer Knocks Out Drop Shadow option removes the drop shadow underneath the original layer area. This is particularly important if you convert a shadow style to a separate layer that you move to a different position, or if the layer is semi-transparent above its shadow.

Global Light. The Use Global Light check box is available for Drop Shadow, Inner Shadow, and Bevel and Emboss styles. When this option is checked, the style is linked to the "master" light source angle for the entire file. Changing the global light affects any linked style applied to any layer in the entire file. You can change the Global Light setting in any of the Layer Style fields, or by choosing Layer>Layer Style>Global Light.

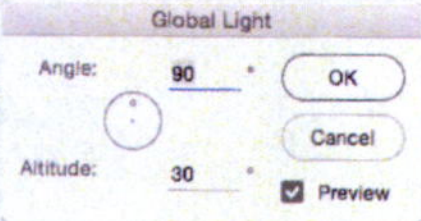

Outer Glow and Inner Glow

Outer Glow and **Inner Glow** styles add glow effects to the outside and inside edges (respectively) of the original layer. For either kind of glow, you can define the Blending Mode, Opacity, and Noise values, as well as whether to use a solid color or a gradient.

- For either kind of glow, you can define the **Technique** as Precise or Softer. **Precise** creates a glow at a specific distance; **Softer** creates a blurred glow and does not preserve detail as well as Precise.
- For Inner Glows, you can also define the **Source** of the glow (Center or Edge). **Center** applies a glow starting from the center of the layer; **Edge** applies the glow starting from the inside edges of the layer.
- The **Spread** and **Choke** sliders affect the percentages of the glow effects.
- The **Size** slider makes the effect smaller or larger.

Layer Styles in Depth (continued)

Contours

Contour options control the shape of the applied styles. Drop Shadow, Inner Shadow, Inner Glow, Outer Glow, Bevel and Emboss, and Satin styles all include Contour options. The default option for all but the Satin style is Linear, which applies a linear effect from solid to 100% transparent.

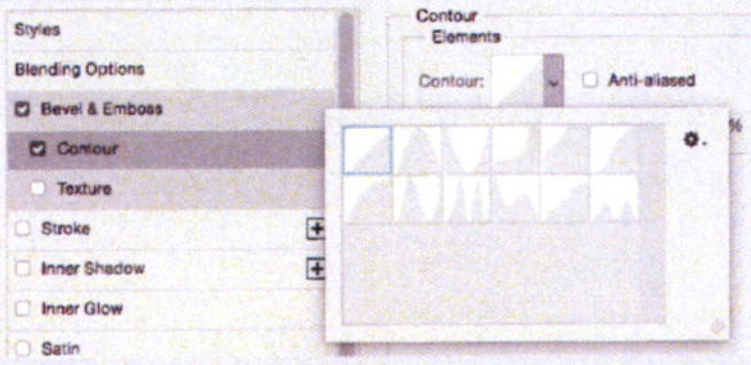

The easiest way to understand the Contour options is through examples. In the following series of images, the same Inner Bevel style was applied in all three examples. In the top image, you can clearly see the size and depth of the bevel. In the center and bottom images, the only difference is the applied contour. If you look carefully at the shape edge, you should be able to see how the applied contour shape maps to the beveled edge in the image.

The Linear contour is applied to the bevel.

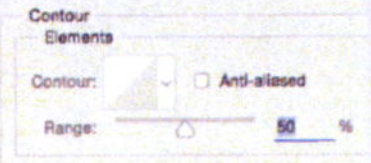

The Gaussian contour is applied to the same bevel.

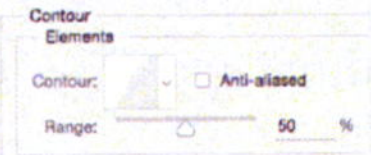

The Cone contour is applied to the same bevel.

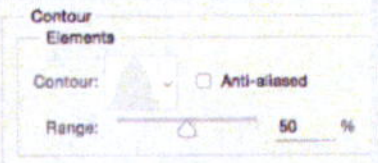

When you apply a contour, the **Range** slider controls which part of the effect is contoured. For Outer Glow or Inner Glow, you can add variation to the contour color and opacity using the **Jitter** slider.

Textures

The Textures options allow you to create texture effects using the built-in patterns.

- The **Scale** slider varies the size of the applied pattern.
- The **Depth** slider varies the apparent depth of the applied pattern.
- The **Invert** option (as the name implies) inverts the applied pattern.
- If you check the **Link with Layer** option, the pattern's position is locked to the layer so you can move the two together. If this option is unchecked, different parts of the pattern are visible if you move the associated layer.
- When you create a texture, you can drag in the image window (behind the Layer Style dialog box) to move the texture. When the Link with Layer option is checked, clicking the **Snap to Origin** button positions the pattern origin at the upper-left corner of the layer. If Link with Layers is unchecked, clicking the Snap to Origin button positions the pattern at the image origin point.

Color Overlay, Gradient Overlay, Pattern Overlay

A **color overlay** is simply a solid color with specific Blending Mode and Opacity value applied. A color overlay can be used to change an entire layer to a solid color (with the Normal blending mode at 100% opacity), or to create unique effects using different Blending Mode and Opacity settings.

A **gradient overlay** is basically the same as a color overlay, except you use a gradient instead of a solid color. You can choose an existing gradient or define a new one, change the Blending Mode and Opacity value of the gradient, apply any of the available gradient styles (Linear, Radial, etc.), and change the Angle and Scale values of the gradient.

A **pattern overlay** is similar to the Texture options for a Bevel and Emboss style. You can choose a specific pattern, change the Blending Mode and Opacity value, and change the applied pattern scale. You can also link the pattern to the layer and snap the pattern to the layer or the file origin.

11. **Click OK to apply the layer style.**

In the Layers panel, the drop shadow styles appear as effects for the Left Inset layer. As with the built-in style you applied in the previous exercise, custom layer styles are non-destructive.

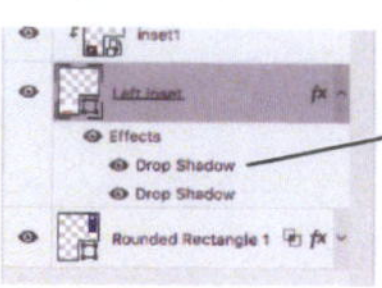

Layer styles are non-destructive; use the Eye icons to turn effects on or off.

12. **Press Option/Alt, then click the word "Effects" in the Layers panel and drag it to the Center Inset layer.**

Just as you cloned a layer in an earlier exercise, pressing Option/Alt allows you to clone effects from one layer to another. This offers an easy way to apply the exact same effects to multiple layers in your file.

The cursor shows you are cloning the applied effects.

The cloned effects now apply to the Center Inset layer.

13. **Repeat Step 12 to add the Drop Shadow effects to the Right Inset layer.**

14. **Press Option/Alt, then click the second (bottom) instance of the Drop Shadow and drag it to the Car layer.**

If you remember, you edited the top instance to use blue as the shadow color. The bottom instance — the one you are cloning here — applies a black shadow at a 30° angle (the global angle).

You can clone an entire set of effects by Option/Alt-dragging the word "Effects" or clone only specific effects by Option/Alt dragging an individual item in the list.

The cursor shows you are cloning only one drop shadow effect.

The single cloned effect now applies to the Car layer.

15. **In the Layers panel, double-click the Drop Shadow effect for the Car layer.**

Double-clicking an effect in the panel opens the dialog box, where you can make changes to the settings that define the effect for the active layer.

16. **Click in the document window (behind the dialog box) and drag down until the drop shadow is much more prominent behind the car layer.**

When you drag in the document window, the dialog box dynamically changes to reflect the new angle and distance for the effect.

As you dynamically change the angle, you should also notice the effect on the three Inset layers. Because the Use Global Light option is checked for all four layers, changing the angle for one of these layers applies the same change to all four layers.

You should also notice, however, that the altered Distance value does not apply to the other three layers where the Drop Shadow effect is applied. Only the Angle of the effects is synchronized between the various layers.

Note:

If you double-click the word "Effects" in the Layers panel, the dialog box opens to the Blending Options: Default screen. Double-clicking a specific effect opens the dialog box directly to the settings for the effect you clicked.

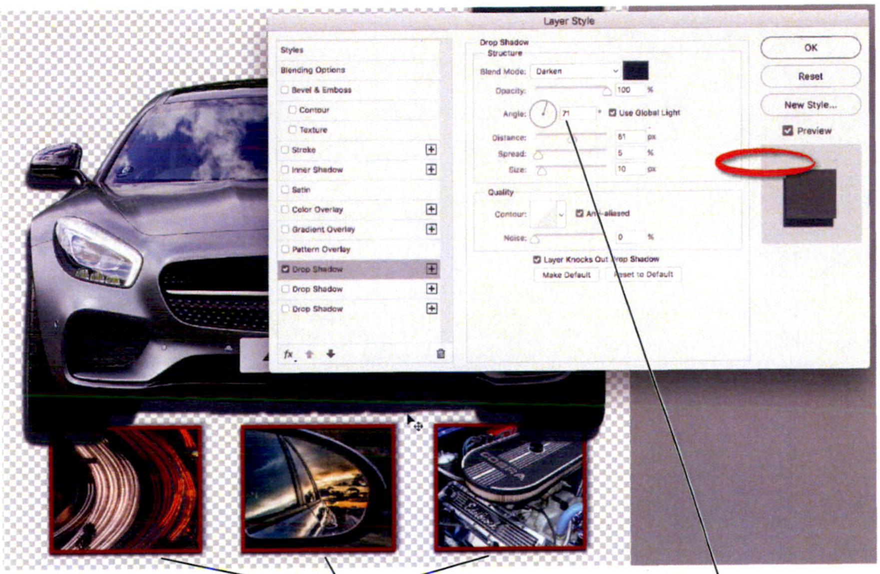

Changing the angle for one effect changes the angle for all effects that use the Global Light option.

Click and drag in the document window to dynamically change the effect settings.

17. **Change the size field to 50 px, then click OK to apply the changed settings.**

18. **In the Layers panel, click the arrow buttons to the right of each fx icon to collapse the effects for all layers.**

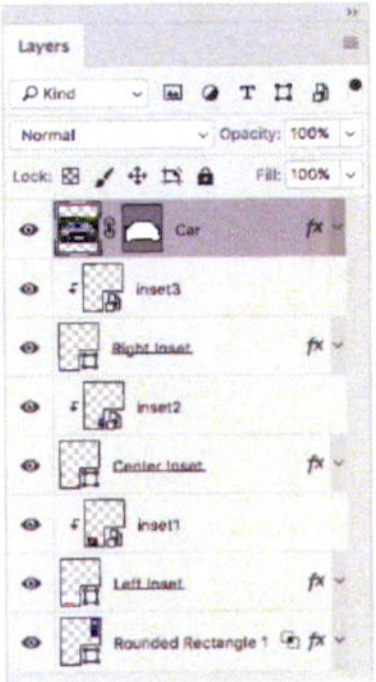

19. **Save the file and continue to the next exercise.**

Use the Filter Gallery

You can apply filters to specific selections, individual layers, or even individual channels depending on what you need to accomplish. If you combine filters with Smart Objects, you can apply nondestructive filters and then change the settings or turn off the filters to experiment with different results.

In addition to the options in the Filter Gallery, a wide range of other filters can be accessed in the various Filter submenus; we encourage you to explore the various settings. Any filter that includes an ellipsis (...) in the menu command opens a secondary dialog box, where you can control the filter's specific settings.

Keep the following points in mind when you use filters:

- Filters can be applied to the entire selected layer or to an active selection.
- Some filters work only on RGB images; if you are in a different color mode, some or all filter options — including the Filter Gallery — will be unavailable.
- All filters can be applied to 8-bit images; available filter options are limited for 16-bit and 32-bit images.

> *Note:*
>
> *Photoshop ships with more than 100 filters divided into 13 categories; some of these are functional while others are purely decorative.*

1. **With magazine.psd open, select the inset3 layer in the Layers panel.**

   Like styles and effects, filters apply to the selected layer, not to the entire file.

2. **Choose Filter>Filter Gallery.**

   If the Filter menu includes the Filter Gallery at the top of the list, the top command applies the last-used filter gallery settings to the selected layer. To open the Filter Gallery dialog box, you have to choose the Filter Gallery command at the third spot in the menu.

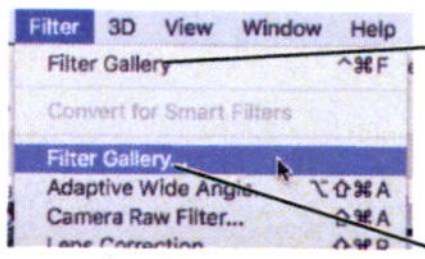

3. **If necessary, adjust the view percentage and position in the dialog box so you can see the inset3 image.**

4. **In the middle pane of the dialog box, expand the Artistic collection of filters and click the Plastic Wrap thumbnail.**

   The left side of the Filter Gallery dialog box shows a preview of the applied filter(s). You can use the menu and field in the bottom-left corner to change the view percentage of the preview.

   In the middle column of the dialog box, the available filters are broken into six categories; inside each folder, thumbnails show a small preview of each filter.

   The top half of the right side of the dialog box shows settings that are specific to the selected filter (from the middle column).

   The bottom half of the right side shows the filters that are applied to the selected layer.

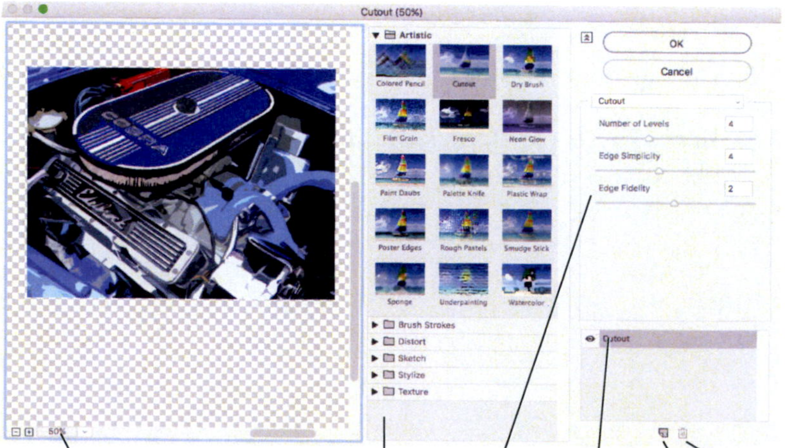

5. **Adjust the filter options until you are satisfied with the result, then click OK to apply the filter.**

   Because the inset3 layer is a Smart Object layer, the filter is applied non-destructively as a Smart Filter. If you apply a filter to a regular layer, it is destructive and cannot be changed or turned off.

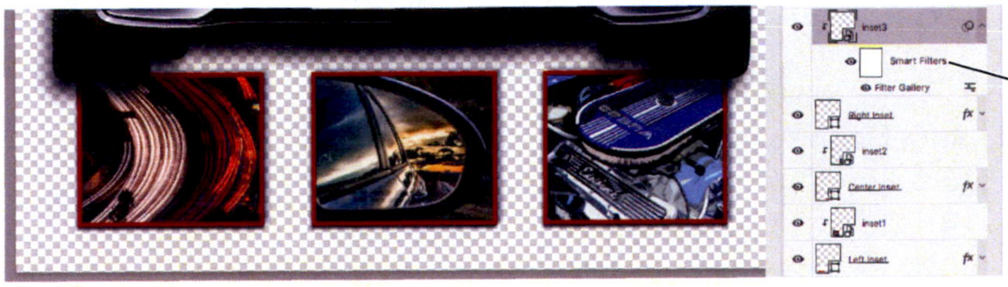

The filter is applied to the Smart Object layer as a Smart Filter.

6. **Press Option/Alt, then click the Filter Gallery listing in the Layers panel and drag it to the inset2 layer.**

   As with layer styles, this method allows you to apply the exact same Smart Filter to multiple layers, without opening any dialog box.

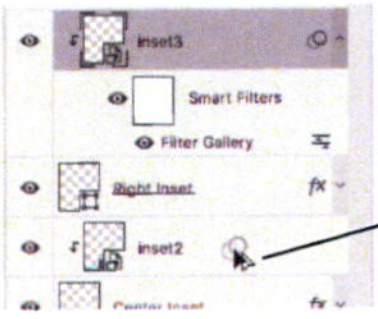

The cursor shows you are cloning the Smart Filter.

> *Note:*
>
> *You can apply more than one filter to a layer by clicking the New Effect Layer button in the bottom-right corner of the Filter Gallery dialog box.*

7. **Repeat Step 6 to apply the Smart Filter to the inset1 layer.**

The Smart Filters have been cloned, but the lists do not automatically expand in the panel.

8. **Collapse the Smart Filters listing for the inset3 layer.**

9. **Save the file and continue to the next exercise.**

Fading Filters

The Fade option (Edit>Fade [Filter]) changes the opacity and blending mode of the last-used filter, painting tool, or color adjustment; you can also fade the effects of the Brush Strokes and Liquify filters. The example here shows the result of fading the Glowing Edges filter (from the Filter Gallery) that was applied to the left image.

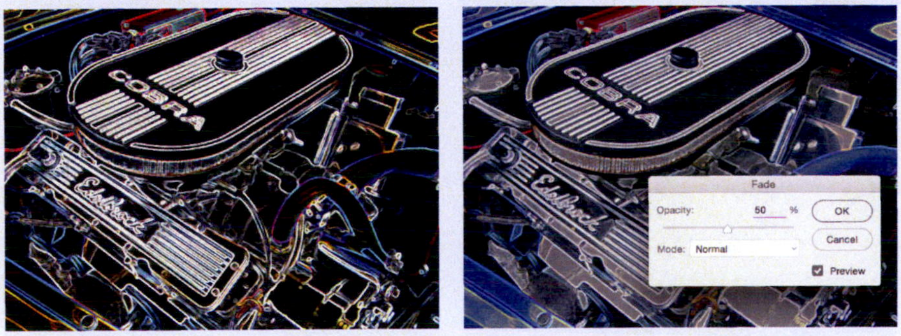

Duplicate a Layer

The next piece of this project is a custom background, which you will create from a provided image. In this exercise, you will use the Duplicate method to move layer content from one file to another.

1. **With magazine.psd open, open the file tires.jpg from your WIP>Cars folder.**

2. **Control/right-click the Background layer in the tires.jpg file and choose Duplicate Layer in the contextual menu.**

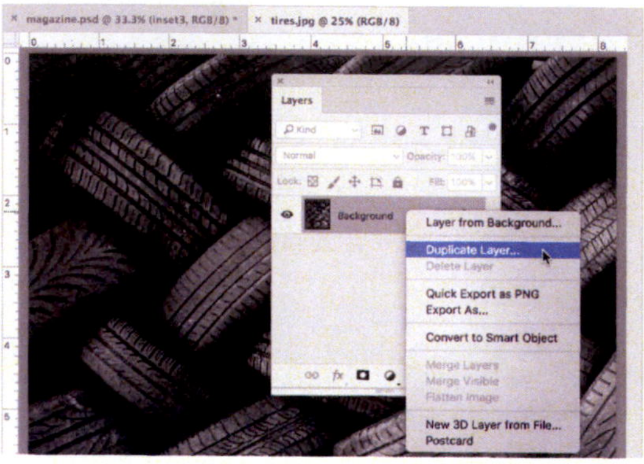

3. **In the resulting dialog box, choose magazine.psd in the Destination Document menu, then click OK.**

   The Duplicate command provides an easy method for copying an entire layer, either in the current file, in any other open file, or into a new file. If you choose the current file as the destination, you can define a new name for the duplicated layer.

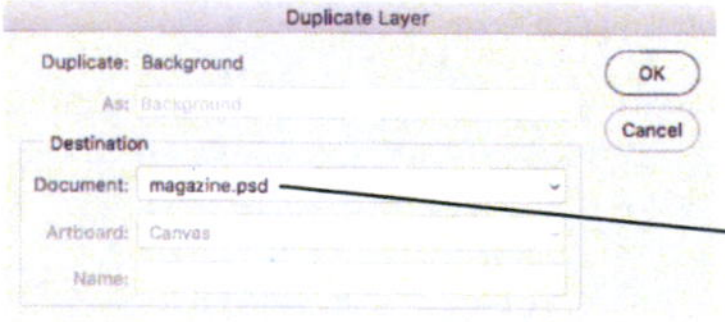

Choose where you want the duplicate layer in this menu.

4. **Close the tires.jpg file and review the current magazine.psd file.**

   The Background layer from the tires file is copied into the magazine file. It is placed immediately above the previously selected layer. Although it is still named "Background" (from the file where it was copied), it is neither locked nor placed at the bottom of the layer stack.

The duplicated layer is placed above the previously selected layer.

5. **Click the Background layer in the Layers panel and drag it to the bottom of the layer stack.**

6. **Double-click the layer name to highlight it. Type Tires as the new layer name, then press Return/Enter to finalize the new name.**

Rename the layer and move it to the bottom of the stack.

7. **Save the file and then continue to the next exercise.**

Liquify a Layer

Rather than just using the image of stacked tires as the background, you are going to create something less patterned and recognizable. In this exercise, you use the Liquify filter to push around layer pixels in a freeform style to create a unique background for the magazine cover.

1. **With magazine.psd open, hide all but the Tires layer.**

   You can Option/Alt-click the eye icon for a layer to hide all other layers.

2. **With the Tires layer selected in the Layers panel, choose Filter>Liquify.**

   The Liquify filter has its own interface and tools. Depending on which tool you select, different options become available in the right side of the dialog box.

3. **In the bottom-left corner of the dialog box, open the View Percentage menu and choose Fit In View.**

   For any of the distortion tools, you have to define a brush size, density (feathering around the edges), and pressure. Some tools also allow you to define the brush rate (how fast distortions are made).

4. **On the right side of the dialog box, check the Pin Edges option.**

   When checked, this option prevents transparent pixels from appearing at the canvas edges.

More about the Liquify Filter

Tools in the Liquify filter distort the brush area when you drag; the distortion is concentrated at the center of the brush area, and the effect intensifies as you hold down the mouse button or repeatedly drag over an area. (The **Hand** and **Zoom tools** have the same function here as in the main Photoshop interface.)

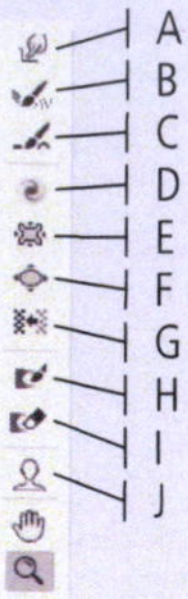

- **A.** The **Forward Warp tool** pushes pixels as you drag.
- **B.** The **Reconstruct tool** restores distorted pixels.
- **C.** The **Smooth tool** helps smooth out jagged edges.
- **D.** The **Twirl Clockwise tool** rotates pixels clockwise as you hold down the mouse button or drag. Press Option/Alt to twirl pixels counterclockwise.
- **E.** The **Pucker tool** moves pixels toward the center of the brush, creating a zoomed-out effect if you simply hold down the mouse button without dragging.
- **F.** The **Bloat tool** moves pixels away from the center of the brush, creating a zoomed-in effect.
- **G.** The **Push Left tool** moves pixels left when you drag up, and right when you drag down. You can also drag clockwise around an object to increase its size, or drag counterclockwise to decrease its size.
- **H.** The **Freeze Mask tool** protects areas where you paint.
- **I.** The **Thaw Mask tool** removes the protection created by the Freeze Mask tool.
- **J.** The **Face tool** reveals on-screen controls for changing the shape of various facial features. For example, you can click and drag to change the shape of the forehead, chin height, jawline, and face width when the overall face shape is selected.

Face-Aware Liquify Options

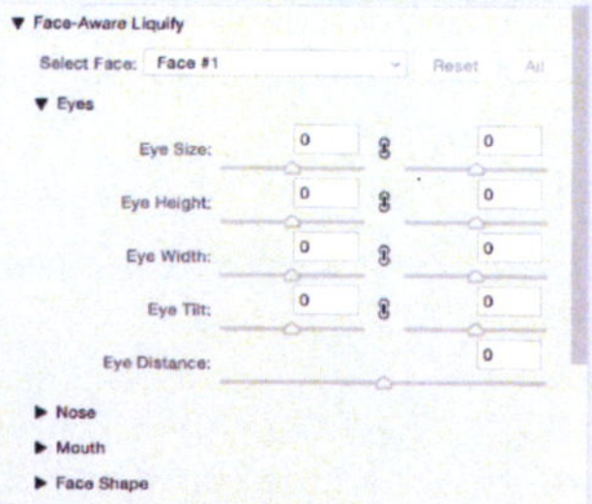

If an image includes faces, the Liquify filter automatically recognizes those and provides options for manipulating the individual eyes, nose, mouth, and overall face shape. You can use the controls on the right side of the dialog box, or use the Face tool to drag on-screen controls in the preview area.

If more than one face exists in the overall image, you can use the Select Face menu to determine which you want to edit using the slider controls.

Mask Options

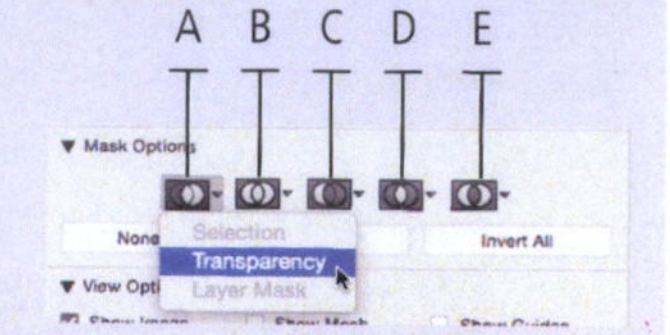

Mask Options allow you to freeze areas in the Liquify preview to protect them from distortion. You can use the Mask options to freeze areas based on existing selections, transparent areas, or layer masks in the original image.

- **A. Replace Selection**
- **B. Add to Selection**
- **C. Subtract from Selection**
- **D. Intersect with Selection**
- **E. Invert Selection**

You can click the **None** button to thaw all masked areas; click the **Mask All** button to mask the entire image; or click the **Invert All** button to reverse the current mask.

Brush Reconstruct Options

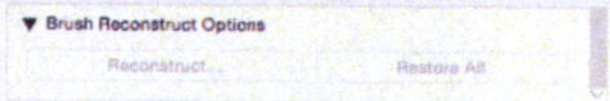

When you manipulate pixels in the Liquify dialog box, you can press Command/Control-Z to undo your last brush stroke in the dialog box. Clicking the **Restore All** button has the same effect as using the Undo keyboard shortcut.

You can also use the **Reconstruct** button to affect the last-applied stroke. Rather than undoing the entire stroke, you can use the resulting Revert Reconstruction dialog box to lessen the effect by a specific percentage.

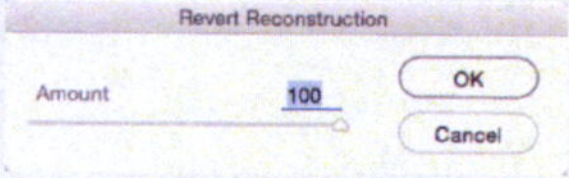

View Options

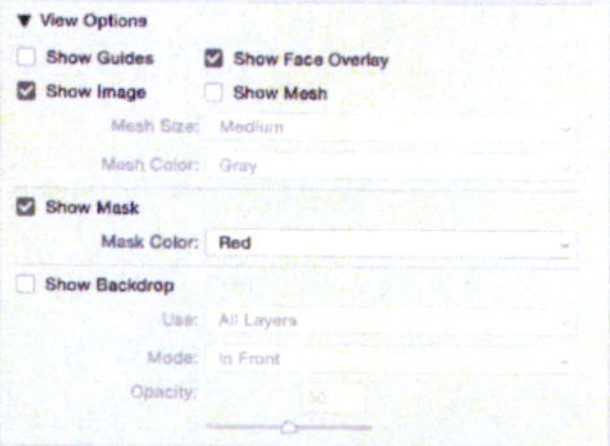

Show Image, active by default, shows the active layer in the filter's preview area. If you check the **Show Mesh** option, the preview also shows a grid that defaults to small, gray lines. You can use the Mesh Size and Mesh Color menus to change the appearance of the grid.

When **Show Mask** is checked, any mask you paint with the Freeze Mask tool appears in the filter's preview area. You can use the Mask Color menu to change the color of the visible mask.

When **Show Backdrop** is checked, you can include other layers in the filter's preview area. The Use menu also lists individual layers in the file so you can show only a certain layer in the preview. You can use the Mode and Opacity menus to change how extra layer(s) appear in the preview.

5. **Click and drag in the preview to warp the tire pattern away from the neat stack in the original image.**

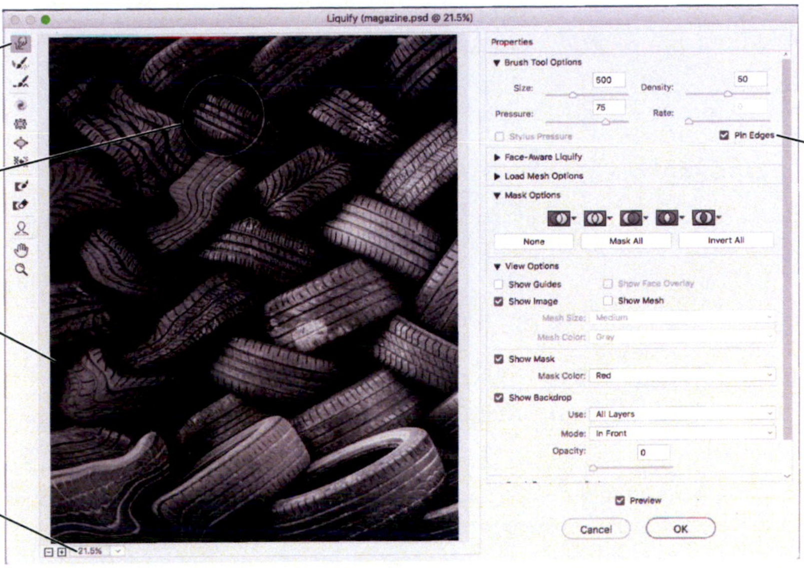

6. **Continue clicking and dragging to push pixels so that all non-masked areas are filled.**

   If necessary, you can press Command/Control-Z to undo your last brush stroke in the Liquify dialog box.

7. **Click OK to return to the image.**

   Depending on the size of the layer you are liquifying, the process might take a while to complete; be patient.

   The Liquify filter is not a smart filter, and cannot be applied to a Smart Object layer; it permanently alters the pixels in the layer where it is applied.

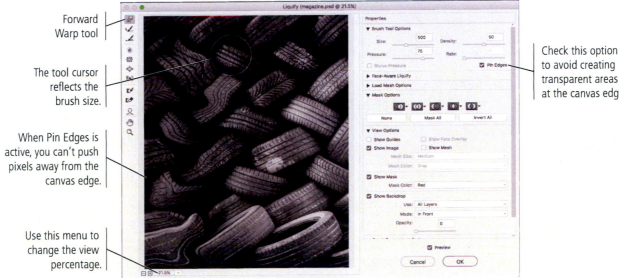

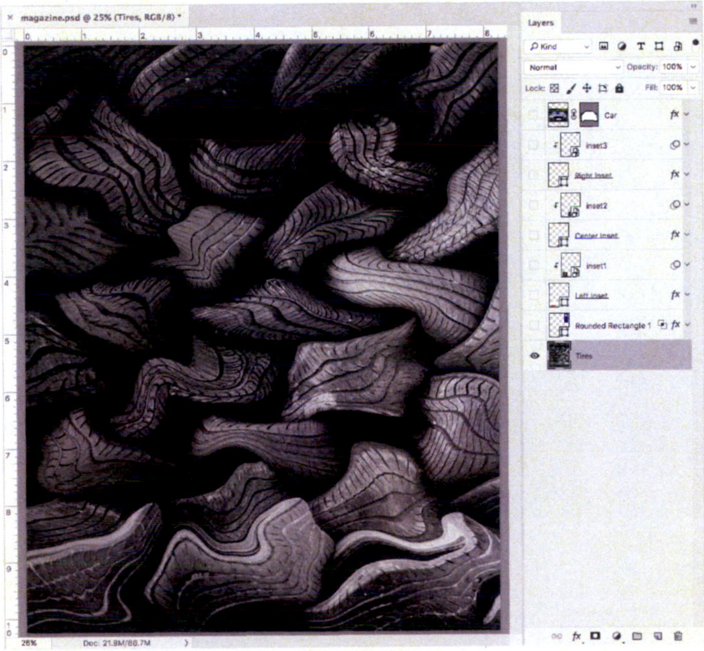

8. **Save the file and continue to the next exercise.**

Use the Eyedropper Tool

In Photoshop, there is almost always more than one way to complete a task. In this exercise, you use the Eyedropper tool to change the Foreground and Background colors by sampling from the original car image. You will then use those colors to create a gradient background for the overall composition.

1. **With `magazine.psd` open, hide all but the Car layer.**

   You can hide multiple layers by clicking and dragging over the eye icons of each layer that you want to hide.

2. **Choose the Eyedropper tool in the Tools panel.**

3. **In the Options bar, choose 5 by 5 Average in the Sample Size menu and choose All Layers in the Sample menu. Make sure the Show Sampling Ring option is checked.**

   The default Eyedropper option — Point Sample — selects the color of the single pixel where you click. Using one of the average values avoids the possibility of sampling an errant artifact color because the tool finds the average color in a range of adjacent pixels.

   By default, the sample will be selected from All [visible] Layers. You can choose Current Layer in the Sample menu to choose a color from only the active layer.

4. **Move the cursor over the light silver color near the left edge of the car (as shown in the following image). Click to change the foreground color.**

   When you click with the Eyedropper tool, the sampling ring appears and shows the previous foreground color on the bottom and the current sample color on the top half.

   If you hold down the mouse button, you can drag around the image to find the color you want. The sampling ring previews what color will be selected if you release the mouse button.

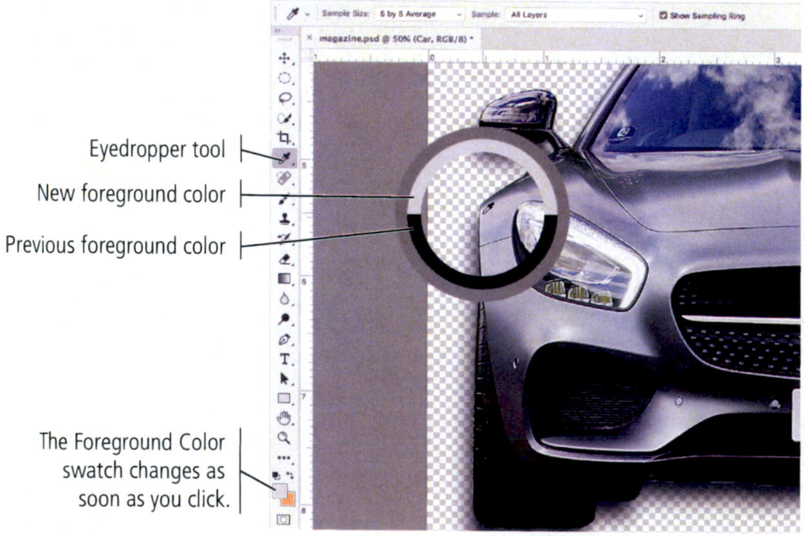

5. **Move the cursor over the yellowish tones in the bottom part of the headlight (as shown in the image below). Option/Alt-click to change the background color.**

   Pressing Option/Alt while you click with the Eyedropper tool changes the Background color. In this case, the sampling ring shows the previous background color on the bottom and the current selection on the top.

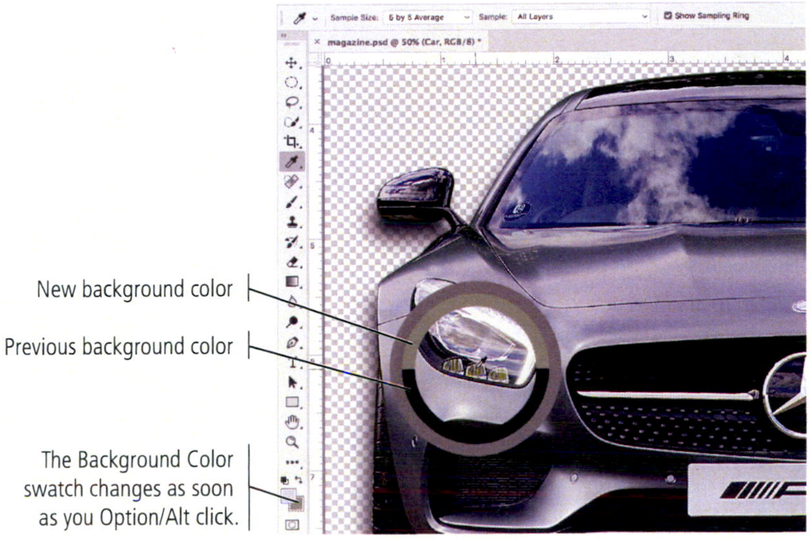

6. **Save the file and continue to the next exercise.**

Create a Custom Gradient

A **gradient** (sometimes called a blend) is a fill that creates a smooth transition from one color to another or across a range of multiple colors. Photoshop can create several different kinds of gradients (linear, radial, etc.) from one color to another, and you can access a number of built-in gradients. You can also create your own custom gradients, which you will do in this exercise.

1. **With magazine.psd open, choose the Gradient tool in the Tools panel.**

2. **In the Options bar, click the arrow to the right of the gradient sample bar to show the Gradient Picker panel.**

   The Gradient Picker panel shows a set of predefined gradients, including black-to-white, foreground-to-transparent, foreground-to-background, and several other common options. You can also access additional gradient libraries in the panel Options menu.

3. **Open the Gradient Picker panel Options menu and choose Small List view.**

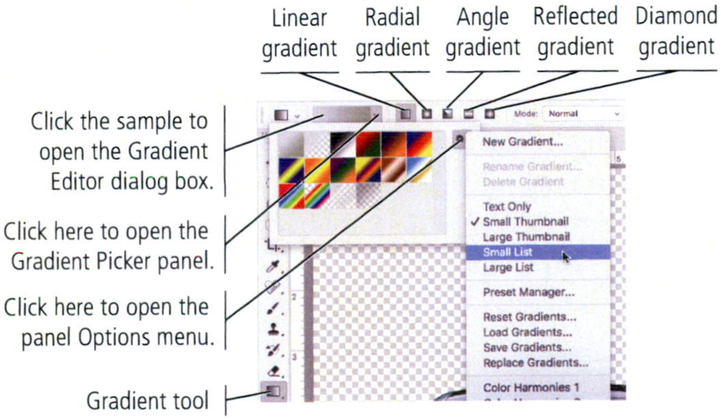

4. **Open the Gradient Picker panel again (if necessary) and choose Foreground to Background from the list of gradients. Press Return/Enter to close the Gradient Picker panel.**

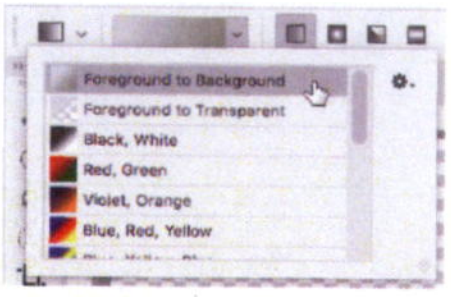

5. **Click the gradient sample in the Options bar to open the Gradient Editor dialog box.**

   You can use this dialog box to edit existing gradients or create new ones.

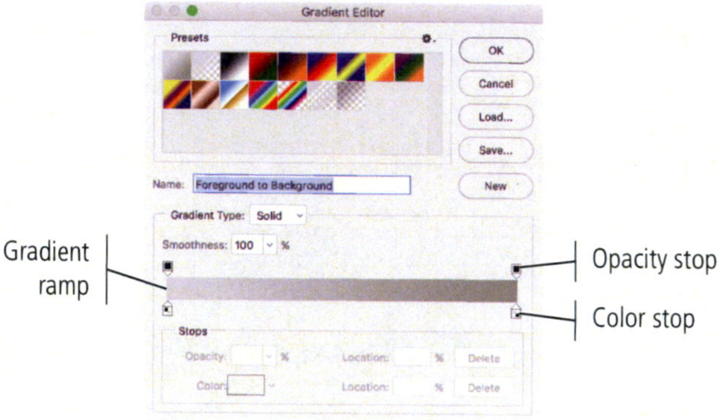

6. **Click the right color stop below the gradient ramp. Drag left until the Location field shows 60%.**

   As soon as you click the color stop, the name changes to Custom because you're defining a custom gradient.

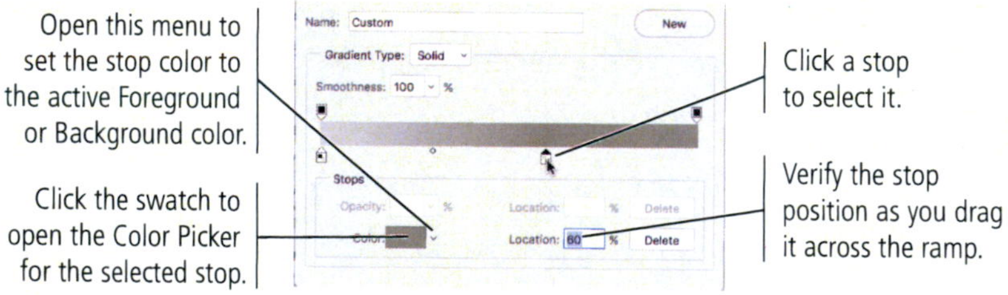

Verify the stop position as you drag it across the ramp.

7. **Double-click the moved stop to open the Color Picker dialog box. Change the stop color to C: 25% M: 40% Y: 80% K: 5%, then click OK.**

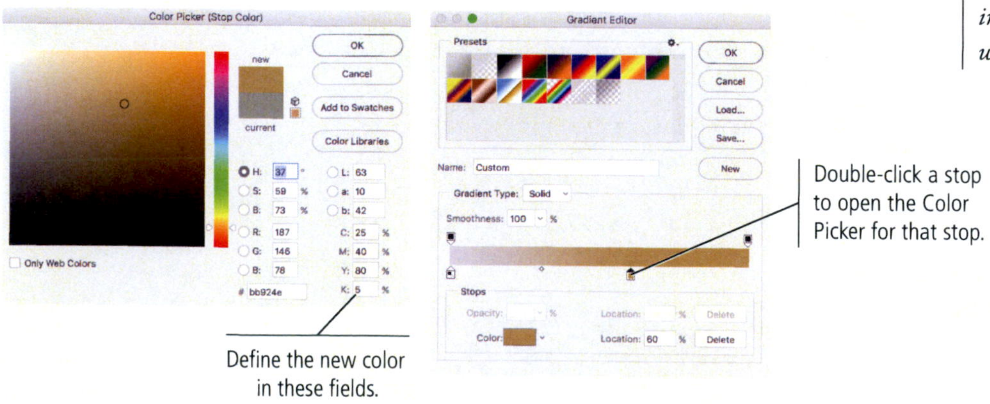

Color Picker (Stop Color)
Gradient Editor
Opacity stop
Define the new color in these fields.
Double-click a stop to open the Color Picker for that stop.

> ***Note:***
>
> *Whenever the Color Picker dialog box is open, you can use the Eyedropper cursor to sample a color from the image in the document window.*

8. **Click the left stop to select it. Drag right until the Location field shows 30%.**

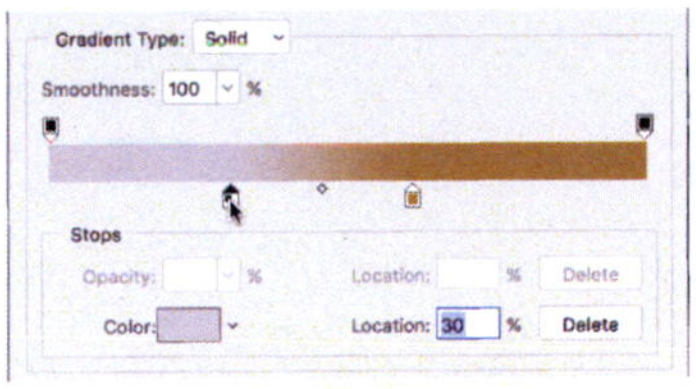

9. **Click the small diamond icon between the first and second stops. Drag right until the Location field shows 70%.**

   This point indicates where the colors of the two surrounding stops are equally mixed. Dragging this point extends the gradient on one side of the point and compresses the gradient on the other side.

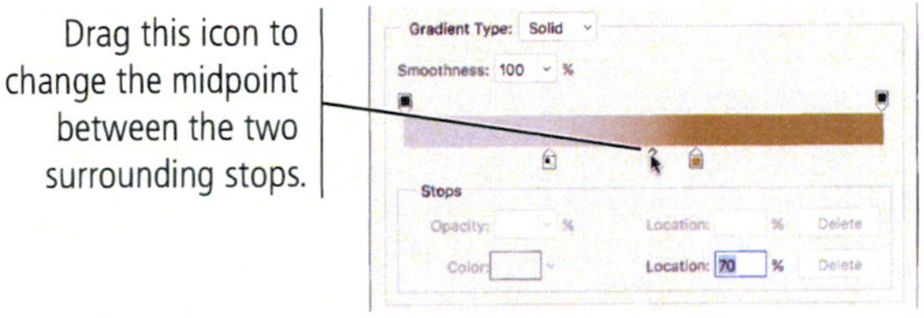

10. **Click below the right side of the ramp. Drag the new stop until the location field shows 80%.**

    Clicking below the ramp adds a new stop to the gradient, using the same color settings as the last-selected stop.

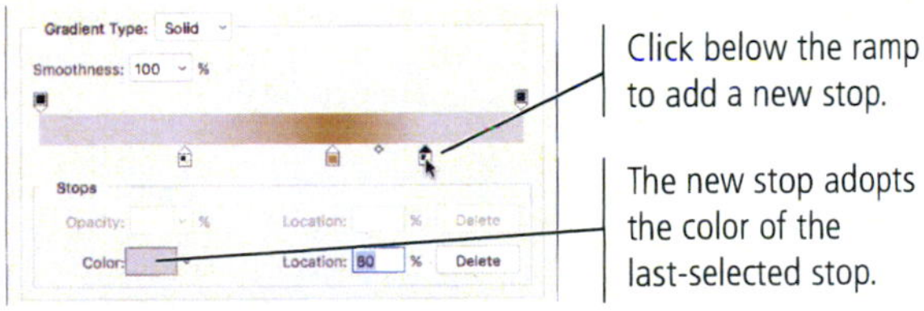

> ***Note:***
>
> *Drag a stop off the gradient ramp to remove it from the gradient.*

11. **Click below the left end of the gradient ramp to add a new stop. Set its location to 0%.**

12. **Double-click the new stop to open the Color Picker dialog box. Change the stop color to white, then click OK.**

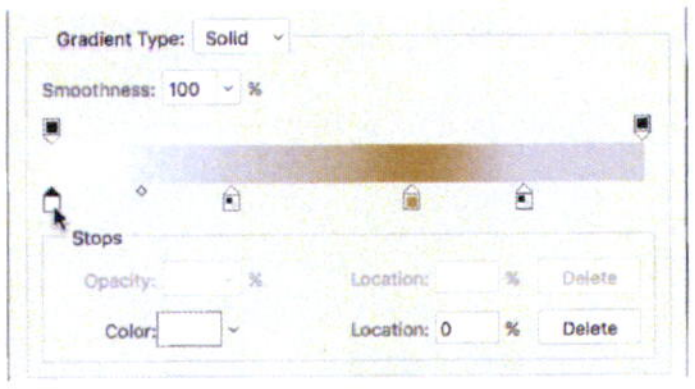

13. **Click the left stop to select it, then click below the right end of the gradient ramp to add another new stop. Set its location to 100%**

    If you didn't click the leftmost stop first, the new stop from this step would have the same color settings as the last-selected stop (from Step 10).

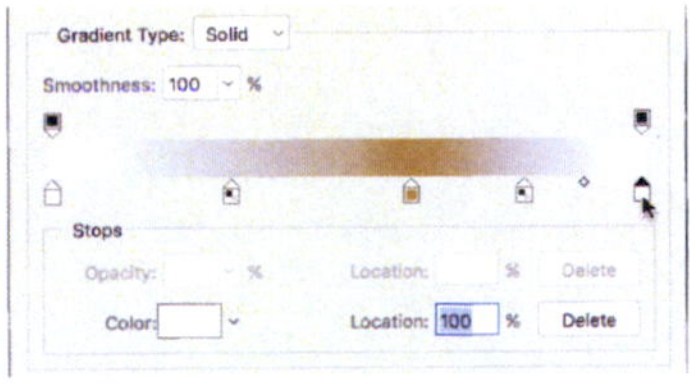

14. **Type Car Background in the Name field and click the New button.**

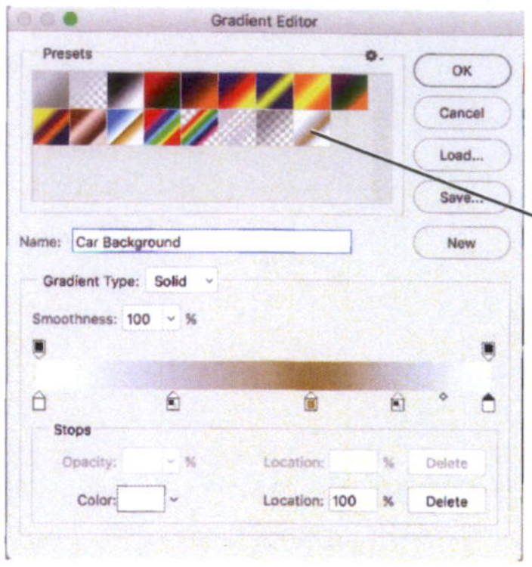

Clicking the New button adds the new swatch to the list of gradient options.

15. **Click OK to close the dialog box.**

16. **Save the file and continue to the next exercise.**

Create a Gradient Fill Layer

Once you define the gradient you want, applying it is fairly easy: add a layer (if necessary), select the type of gradient you want to create, and then click and drag.

1. **With magazine.psd open, make sure the Tires layer is selected.**

2. **Click the Create a New Layer button at the bottom of the Layers panel. Name the new layer Shading.**

   When you add a new layer, it is automatically added directly above the selected layer.

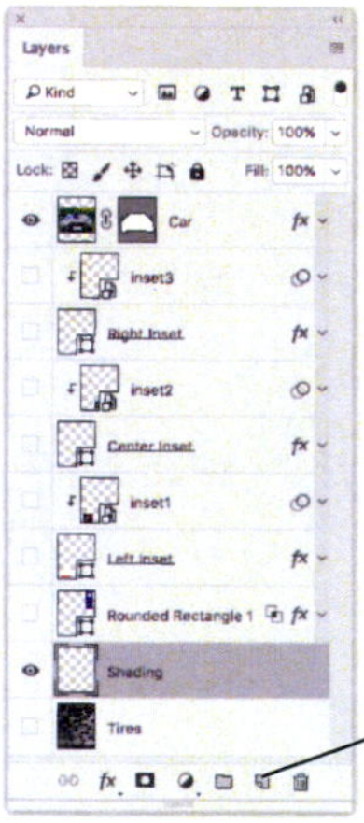

Create a New Layer button

3. **Show all layers, and then click the Shading layer to select it.**

4. **Make sure the Gradient tool is selected. In the Options bar, make sure the Car Background gradient is selected and the Linear Gradient option is active.**

5. **Click in the top edge of the cutout area and drag to the bottom outside edge of the cutout layer (as shown in the following image).**

The Car Background gradient is selected.
The Linear Gradient option is selected.
The Gradient tool is active.
Click here...
...and drag to here.

When you release the mouse button, the layer fills with the gradient. Areas before and after the line drawn with the Gradient tool fill with the start and stop colors of the gradient (in this case, they're both white).

6. **Save the file and continue to the next exercise.**

Adjust Blending Mode and Layer Opacity

The final step to creating your custom background is to blend the gradient you just created into the liquified tires. Photoshop includes a number of options for making this type of adjustment.

1. **With magazine.psd open, select the Shading layer in the Layers panel.**

2. **Open the Blending Mode menu in the Layers panel and choose Overlay.**

   Photoshop provides access to 27 different layer blending modes; the default is Normal, or no blending applied. Using the Overlay mode, colors in the gradient are blended onto the pixels in the underlying Tires layer.

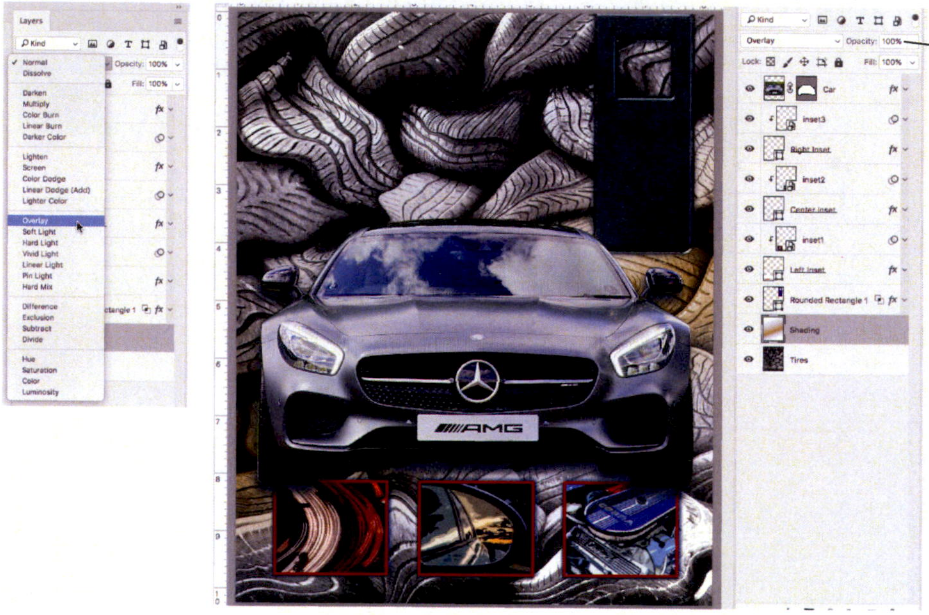

Blending Mode menu

3. **Select the Tires layer in the Layers panel, then change the Opacity field to 10%.**

   Reducing the layer opacity reduces the strength of the layer content so that it is no longer overpowering other elements in the composition. You can now better see the effect created by the blended gradient.

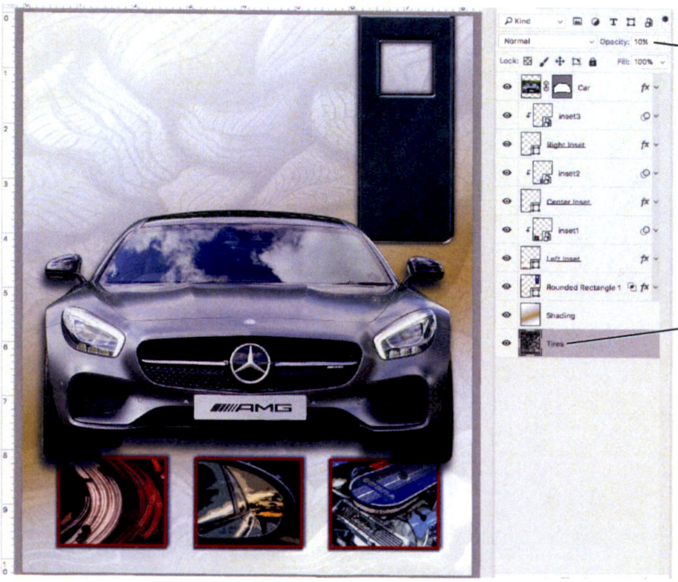

Change the layer opacity in this field.

The selected layer is affected by the change.

4. **Save the file and continue to the next exercise.**

Distinguishing Photoshop Blending Modes

When working with blending modes, think of the top layer as the "blend" layer and the next lowest layer as the "base".

- **Normal** is the default mode (no blending applied).
- **Dissolve** results in a random scattering of pixels of both the blend and base colors.
- **Darken** returns the darker of the blend or base color. Base pixels that are lighter than the blend color are replaced; base pixels that are darker than the blend color remain unchanged.
- **Multiply** multiplies (hence the name) the base color by the blend color, resulting in a darker color. Multiplying any color with black produces black; multiplying any color with white leaves the color unchanged (think of math — any number times 0 equals 0).
- **Color Burn** darkens the base color by increasing the contrast. Blend colors darker than 50% significantly darken the base color by increasing saturation and reducing brightness; blending with white has no effect.
- **Linear Burn** darkens the base color similar to Color Burn; using Linear Burn, the brightness is reduced about twice as much for blend colors in the mid-tone range.
- **Darker Color** compares the channel values of the blend and base colors, resulting in the lower value.
- **Lighten** returns whichever is the lighter color (base or blend). Base pixels that are darker than the blend color are replaced; base pixels that are lighter than the blend color remain unchanged.
- **Screen** is basically the inverse of Multiply, always returning a lighter color. Screening with black has no effect; screening with white produces white.
- **Color Dodge** brightens the base color. Blend colors lighter than 50% significantly increase brightness; blending with black has no effect.
- **Linear Dodge (Add)** is similar to Color Dodge, but creates smoother transitions from areas of high brightness to areas of low brightness.
- **Lighter Color** compares channel values of the blend and base colors, resulting in the higher value.
- **Overlay** multiplies or screens the blend color to preserve the original lightness or darkness of the base.
- **Soft Light** darkens or lightens base colors depending on the blend color. Blend colors lighter than 50% lighten the base color (as if dodged); blend colors darker than 50% darken the base color (as if burned).
- **Hard Light** combines the Multiply and Screen modes. Blend colors darker than 50% are multiplied, and blend colors lighter than 50% are screened.
- **Vivid Light** combines the Color Dodge and Color Burn modes. Blend colors lighter than 50% lighten the base by decreasing contrast; blend colors darker than 50% darken the base by increasing contrast.
- **Linear Light** combines the Linear Dodge and Linear Burn modes. If the blend color is lighter than 50%, the result is lightened by increasing the base brightness. If the blend color is darker than 50%, the result is darkened by decreasing the base brightness.
- **Pin Light** preserves the brightest and darkest areas of the blend color; blend colors in the mid-tone range have little (if any) effect.
- **Hard Mix** pushes all pixels in the resulting blend to either all or nothing. The base and blend values of each pixel in each channel are added together (e.g., R 45 [blend] + R 230 [base] = R 275). Pixels with totals over 255 are shown at 255; pixels with a total lower than 255 are dropped to 0.
- **Difference** inverts base color values according to the brightness value in the blend layer. Lower brightness values in the blend layer have less of an effect on the result; blending with black has no effect.
- **Exclusion** is very similar to Difference, except that mid-tone values in the base color are completely desaturated.
- **Subtract** removes the blend color from the base color.
- **Divide** looks at the color information in each channel and divides the blend color from the base color.
- **Hue** results in a color with the luminance and saturation of the base color and the hue of the blend color.
- **Saturation** results in a color with the luminance and hue of the base color and the saturation of the blend color.
- **Color** results in a color with the luminance of the base color and the hue and saturation of the blend color.
- **Luminosity** results in a color with the hue and saturation of the base color and the luminance of the blend color (basically the opposite of the Color mode).

Finish the Magazine Cover

The final piece required for this job is the nameplate and text treatment, which is created every month from a template in Adobe Illustrator. In this exercise, you will place and position the required file to complete the project.

1. **With magazine.psd open, choose File>Place Linked.**

   You are using the Place Linked option so that any changes in the cover treatment file (a common occurrence in professional design environments) will automatically reflect in your Photoshop file.

2. **Navigate to driver-mag.ai (in your WIP>Cars folder) and click Place.**

3. **Choose Bounding Box in the Crop To menu of the Open as Smart Object dialog box, then click OK.**

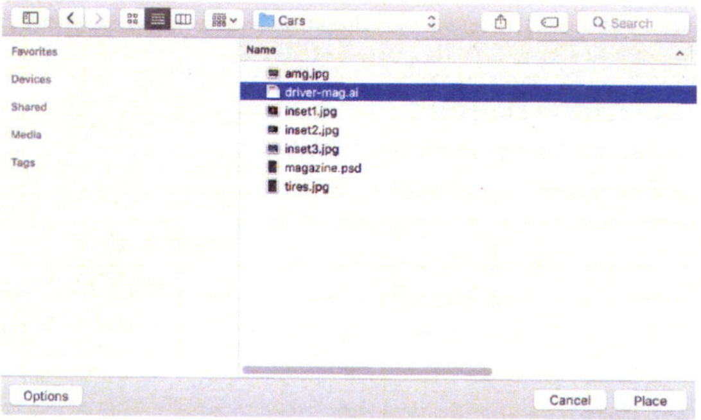

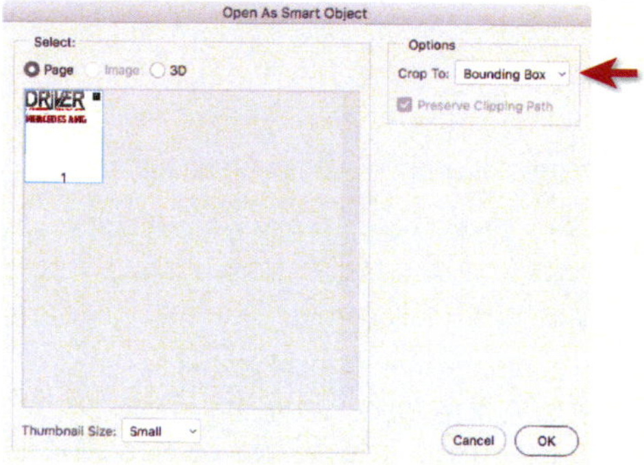

   When you place files in Photoshop, either linked or embedded, they are commonly placed at slightly other than 100%. You should always verify — and correct, if necessary — the scaling of the placed content.

4. **In the Options bar, change the W and H values to 100%, then press Return/Enter to finalize the placement.**

5. **Make sure the driver-mag layer appears at the top of the layer stack.**

6. **Using the Properties panel, change the position of the placed content to X: `0.375 in`, Y: `0.375 in`.**

   The Properties panel only displays two decimal values, so after typing the new position, the fields show only "0.37 in"; this is a minor flaw in the software, but one that is worth noting.

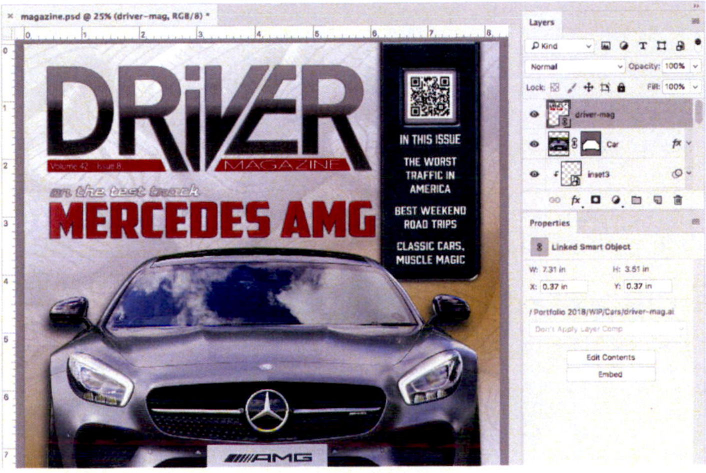

7. **Save the file and then continue to the final exercise.**

Sharing Photoshop Files

PHOTOSHOP FOUNDATIONS

If you are connected to the Internet, you can use the Share an Image button to easily send a JPEG version of your file through a variety of communication media. If you choose Mail in the menu, for example, the image automatically appears in a new mail message in your email client software. If you choose one of the social media outlets, you can create your post directly through a window in the Photoshop interface; you do not need to interact with a browser or separate application to share an image from Photoshop. (Keep in mind that you must have defined accounts in your system preferences for each of the various social media outlets. If an account is not defined, you will be prompted to add one before you can use those options Photoshop.)

Share an Image button

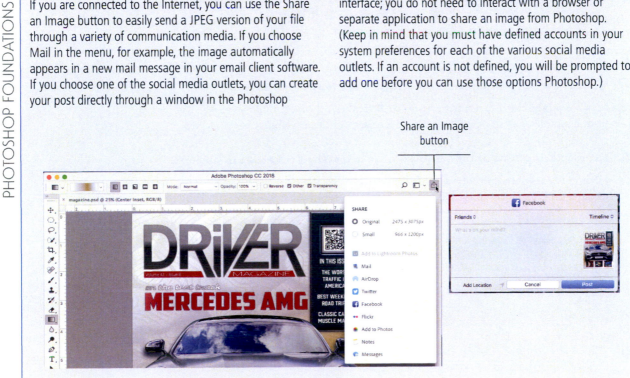

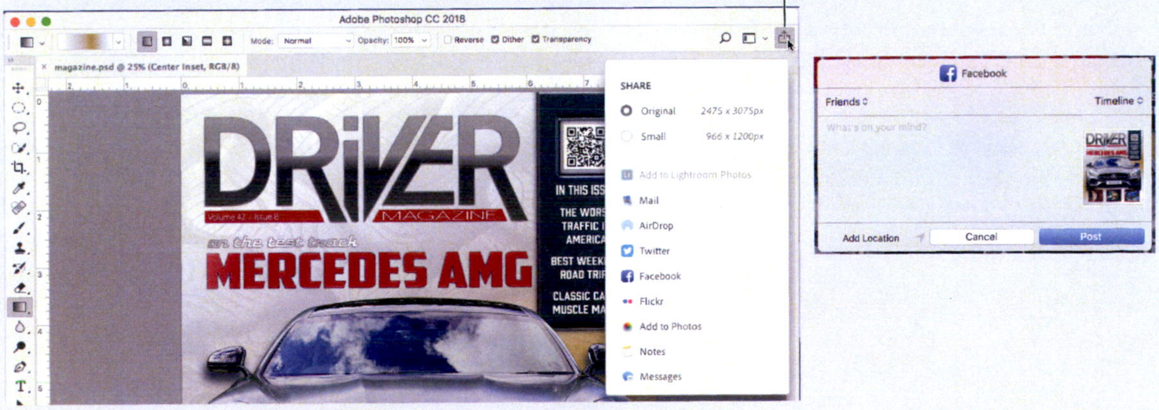

Print a Composite Proof

The last stage of most jobs — after the client has approved the work — is printing a proof. A printed proof is basically the output provider's roadmap of how the final job should look. As more processes move to all-digital workflows, a printed proof is not always required — especially if you're submitting files digitally. But some output providers still require a printed proof, and you might want to print samples of your work at various stages of development.

To output this file at 100%, you need a sheet at least tabloid size (11″ × 17″). If you don't have that option, you can use the Photoshop Print dialog box to fit the job onto letter-size paper. Keep in mind, however, that many of the effects that you created with filters will lose some of their impact when you reduce the file to fit onto a letter-size page.

1. **With `magazine.psd` open, choose File>Print.**

2. **In the Printer menu of the Print dialog box, choose the printer you're using.**

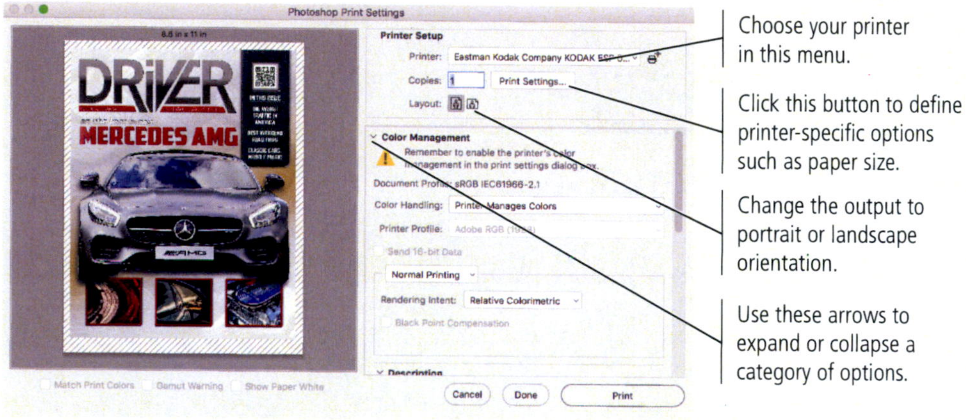

Photoshop Print Settings
Printer Setup
Choose your printer in this menu.
Click this button to define printer-specific options such as paper size.
Change the output to portrait or landscape orientation.
Use these arrows to expand or collapse a category of options.
Cancel
Done
Print

3. **Choose the Portrait layout option (below the number of copies).**

   Ideally, you should always print proofs at 100%. If this is not possible, however, you can print a sample content proof by scaling the page to fit the available paper size.

4. **Review the options in the scrolling pane below the Printer Setup options.**

   Different types of output jobs require different settings. If you are simply printing a desktop proof, you can leave most of these options at their default values.

   As a general rule, proofs should be printed at 100% of the actual file size. If you are printing a file that is larger than the paper size your printer can handle, you can use the Scaled Print Size options to fit the job on the available paper size. Alternatively, you can use the Print Selected Area option to output different portions of the image onto separate sheets, and then manually assemble the multiple sheets into a single page.

5. **Click Print to output the file.**

6. **When the output process is complete, close the file without saving.**

Note:

If you submit a scaled proof with a print job, make sure you note the scale percentage prominently on the proof.

Print Output Options

Use the following as a guide to help you decide which options to include in your output:

Color Management options

(Color management is explained in detail in Project 3: Museum Image Correction.)

- **Color Handling** determines whether color management is applied by the printer or by Photoshop.
- **Printer Profile** defines the known color characteristics of the output device you are using.
- **Normal Printing** simply prints the file to your printer, using no defined output profile for color management.
  - Rendering Intent defines how colors are shifted to fit inside the printer's output capabilities.
  - Black Point Compression adjusts for differences in the black point (the darkest possible black area) between the file and the output device.
- **Hard Proofing** simulates the color output properties of another printer, based on the defined profile in the Proof Setup menu.
  - Simulate Paper Color applies the absolute colorimetric rendering intent to simulate the appearance of color on the actual paper that would be used on the defined output device (for example, newsprint on a web press).
  - Simulate Black Ink simulates the brightness of dark colors as they would appear on the defined output device. If this option is not checked, dark colors are simply printed as dark as possible on the actual printer you are using.

Position and Size Options

- **Position** defines the location of the output on the paper. It is centered by default; you can use the Top and Left fields to position the output at a specific distance from the paper corner. You can also click in the preview area and drag to reposition the image on the paper.
- **Scale** defaults to 100%, creating a full-size print; the **Height** and **Width** fields define the size of the image being printed. If you change the Scale field, the Height and Width fields reflect the proportional size. You can also define a specific size in the Height and Width fields; in this case, the Scale field is adjusted accordingly.
- If you check **Scale to Fit Media**, the image is automatically scaled to fit inside the printable area on the selected paper size.
- **Print Resolution** defines the resolution that will be sent to the output device. Remember the principle of effective resolution; if you print a 300-ppi image at 200%, the printer has only 150 ppi to work with.
- If you check **Print Selected Area**, handles appear in the preview area. You can drag those handles to define the image area that will be output.

Printing Marks

- **Corner Crop Marks** adds crop marks to show the edges of the image (where it should be cut).
- **Center Crop Marks** adds a crop mark at the center of each edge of the image.
- **Registration Marks** adds bulls-eye targets and star targets that are used to align color separations on a printing press. (Calibration bars and star target registration marks require a PostScript printer.)
- **Description** adds description text (from the File>File Info dialog box) outside the trim area in 9-pt Helvetica.
- **Labels** adds the file name above the image.

Functions

- **Emulsion Down** reverses the image on the output. This option is primarily used for output to a filmsetter or imagesetter.
- **Negative** inverts the color values of the entire output. This option is typically used if you are outputting directly to film, which will then be used to image a photo-sensitive printing plate (a slowly disappearing workflow).
- The **Background** option allows you to add a background color that will print outside the image area.
- The **Border** option adds a black border around an image. You can define a specific width (in points) for the border.
- The **Bleed** option moves crop marks inside the image by a specific measurement.

PostScript Options

(If your printer is not PostScript compatible, the PostScript options will not be available.)

- **Calibration Bars** adds swatches of black in 10% increments (starting at 0% and ending at 100%).
- The **Interpolation** option can help reduce the jagged appearance of low-resolution images by automatically resampling up when you print. This option is only available on PostScript Level 2 or 3 printers.
- The **Include Vector Data** option sends vector information in the output stream for a PostScript printer, so the vector data can be output at the highest possible resolution of the output device.

Project Review

fill in the blank

1. _______________ sharpens an image by increasing contrast along the edges in an image.

2. _______________ refers to the overall image area, like the surface used by traditional painters.

3. The _______________ tool is used to draw freeform vector-based shapes and paths.

4. A _______________ is a special type of Photoshop layer that retains vector path information.

5. _______________ control the shape of a curve between two anchor points.

6. The _______________ option is used to link the angle of styles to the "master" angle for the entire file. Changing it affects any linked style applied to any layer in the entire file.

7. A _______________ is a smooth transition from one color to another.

8. The _______________ command is used to show only areas of one layer that fall within the area of the underlying layer.

9. In the Liquify filter, the _______________ tool can be used to protect specific areas from being liquified.

10. The _______________ allows you to experiment with different filters and filter settings, and to compound multiple filters to create unique artistic effects.

short answer

1. Briefly explain the difference between vectors and pixels.

2. Briefly describe two different tool modes when using a vector drawing tool.

3. Briefly explain the difference between the Path Selection tool and the Direct Selection tool.

Portfolio Builder Project

Use what you learned in this project to complete the following freeform exercise.
Carefully read the art director and client comments, then create your own design to meet the needs of the project.
Use the space below to sketch ideas; when finished, write a brief explanation of your reasoning behind your final design.

art director comments

Against The Clock is considering a new design for the covers of its *Professional Portfolio* series of books. You have been hired to design a new cover comp for the Photoshop CC book.

- ❑ Measure the cover of the existing Photoshop CC book to determine the required trim size.
- ❑ Incorporate the same elements that currently appear on the book cover — title, publisher logo, and the text in the bottom-right corner. (The logo file is included in the **Covers_PS18_PB.zip** archive on the Student Files web page.)
- ❑ Create compelling images and artwork to illustrate the concept of the book title.
- ❑ Design the cover to meet commercial printing requirements.

client comments

We really like the existing cover design, but after five editions we're starting to think a fresh look might be a good thing.

Obviously, the most important element of the cover is the title. However, it seems that Adobe is going to stop using version numbers in its software releases, so we're also going to need a way to differentiate editions; your design should include an edition number (2nd edition, etc.)

In the existing covers, we chose the cityscapes as a representation of places where graphic design students find jobs. We don't really have any set ideas for new imagery, but there should be some connection between graphic design and the imagery you choose.

Finally, keep in mind that the design should allow for repurposing for the other titles in the series.

project justification

Project Summary

Vectors offer an advantage over pixel-based images because they can be freely scaled and edited without losing quality. This project focused on many different options related to working with vectors in Photoshop — drawing paths, creating shape layers, and editing vector shape properties. You used vectors in this project to create a custom layer mask, as well as vector shapes that you filled with other images and a custom artistic pattern.

This project also introduced some of the creative tools that can turn photos and flat colors into painting-like artwork. You learned to use the Filter Gallery, the Liquify filter, custom gradients, and layer blending modes. You will use these options many times in your career as you complete different types of projects in Photoshop.

DRiVER
Volume 42 / Issue 8
MAGAZINE
on the test track
MERCEDES AMG
IN THIS ISSUE
THE WORST TRAFFIC IN AMERICA
BEST WEEKEND ROAD TRIPS
CLASSIC CARS, MUSCLE MAGIC
AMG
Create a compound vector shape layer
Edit corner properties of vector shapes
Apply a style to a vector shape layer
Use a vector mask to remove an image from its background
Use gradients to create a custom background
Liquify pixels to create unique effects
Adjust blending mode and opacity to blend one layer into another
Create clipping masks to isolate specific image areas
Apply filters to images to create artistic effects

Project 3

Museum Image Correction

Your client is curator at the local Museum of Art and History. The institution wants to create a printed brochure of images from a recently acquired collection of antiquities. Your job is to adjust the supplied images as necessary to achieve the best possible result when the final brochure is printed.

This project incorporates the following skills:

- ❑ Repairing damaged images
- ❑ Understanding the relationship between tonal range and contrast
- ❑ Correcting image lighting and exposure problems
- ❑ Understanding how gray balance affects overall image color
- ❑ Correcting minor and severe image color problems
- ❑ Preparing corrected images for printing
- ❑ Combining exposures into an HDR image

Project Meeting

client comments

The City Museum of Art and History recently received a large donation from a wealthy patron's estate. We are going to create a printed catalog that will showcase some of the stars in the collection, as well as explain the history behind the various pieces.

We've selected the seven photos that we want to include in the catalog. We want you to make sure they will look as good as possible when printed. You're the expert, so we trust that you know what needs to be done.

We have a photo of one of the family's first American-born descendants, who was responsible for building much of the family's art and antique collection. The picture is a bit grainy and has some damage, though, and we'd like you to clean it up as much as possible.

Finally, we also want to include a picture of the new museum on the back of the catalog, along with contact information, hours, and so on. We are proud of the new space, and we want the photo to be something of a work of art itself.

art director comments

Digital images come from a wide variety of sources: scanned photographs and digital cameras are the two most common, as is the case for the client's images for this project. Some images can be used as is, or at least with only minor correction.

Unfortunately, however, not every project involves a professional photographer. Consumer-level digital cameras and smartphones are common sources of photography that is submitted for professional design work. That means many of those images require a bit of help — and some require a lot.

Even when a professional photographer is involved, not every image comes from a perfectly lit studio. Location shots — where a subject is photographed in a "real-world" setting — can't always be captured perfectly. Those images usually need work as well. Fortunately, Photoshop provides a powerful toolset for solving most image problems, or at least improving the worst of them.

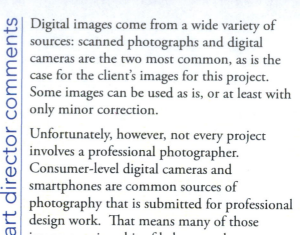

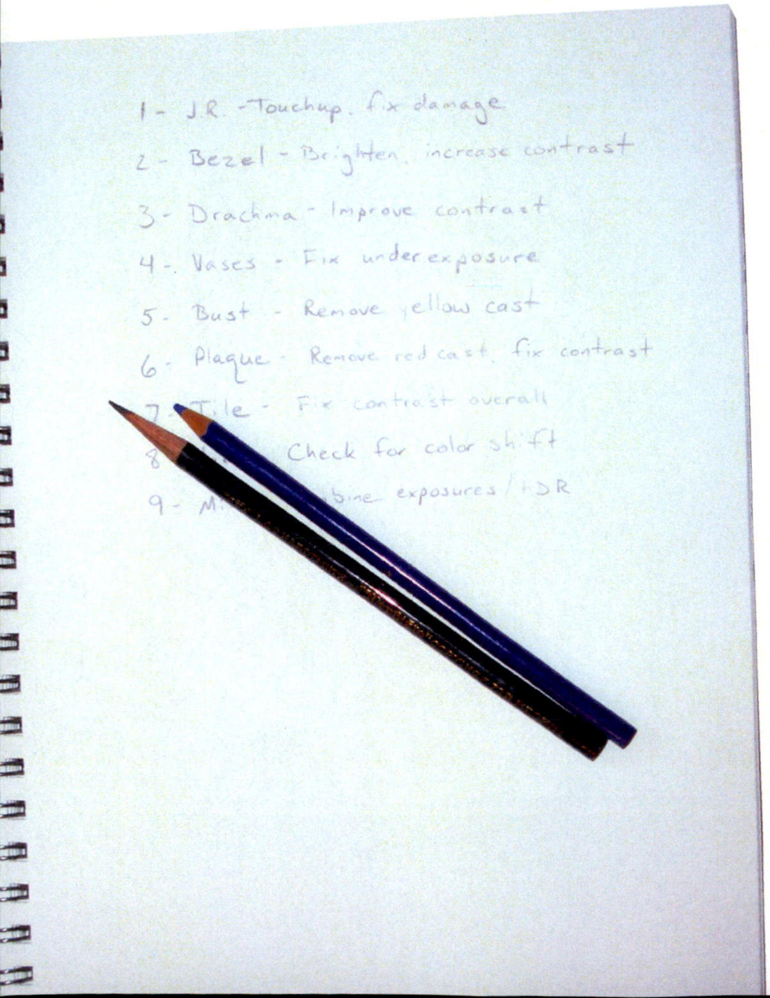

project objectives

To complete this project, you will:

- ❑ Remove grain with blur and sharpen techniques
- ❑ Heal severe scratches
- ❑ Clone out major damage
- ❑ Correct minor problems with the Brightness/Contrast adjustment
- ❑ Correct tonal range with the Levels adjustment
- ❑ Correct lighting problems with the Exposure adjustment
- ❑ Correct overall color problems with the Color Balance adjustment
- ❑ Correct precise color values with the Curves adjustment
- ❑ Correct an RGB image to CMYK gamut limits
- ❑ Embed color profile information in a file
- ❑ Combine multiple exposures with the Merge to HDR Pro utility

Stage 1 Retouching Damaged Images

Image repair is the process of fixing scratches, removing dust, making tears disappear, and generally putting broken or damaged pictures back together again. **Retouching**, on the other hand, is the technique of changing an image by adding something that wasn't there or removing something that was there. Damage can come from a wide range of sources: creases, scratches from any number of abrasive objects, water spots, and tape marks to name just a few. Other image problems such as photographic grain are a natural part of photographs (especially old ones), and dust is common (if not inevitable) whenever photographs are scanned.

There are many different ways to approach image repairs. As you complete the exercises in this stage of the project, you will use several tools to clean up damage in the portrait from the 1940s.

Remove Grain with Blur and Sharpen Techniques

Photographic film is made up of microscopic grains of light-sensitive material. These grains capture the image information, which is eventually processed into a print or transparency. While not usually apparent in a standard photographic print, the grain in a photograph can become pronounced when scanned with a high-resolution scanner. Enlarging an image during scanning further enhances any grain that already exists.

When grain is evident in a digital image, the grain pattern can destroy fine detail and create a mottled appearance in areas of solid color or subtle tone variation. Slower-rated film typically has the smallest and least-evident grain, while faster film can produce significant graininess.

Blurring and Sharpening techniques are the best methods for removing photographic grain. The techniques you use in this exercise work for any image with grain. Older images — such as the one your client wants to use — almost always have obvious grain problems that can be fixed to some degree; antique images can be fixed only just so much. The techniques you learn in this project produce very good results if you need to remove grain from modern scanned images.

1. **Download MOAH_PS18_RF.zip from the Student Files web page.**

2. **Expand the ZIP archive in your WIP folder (Macintosh) or copy the archive contents into your WIP folder (Windows).**

   This results in a folder named **MOAH**, which contains the files you need for this project. You should also use this folder to save the files you create in this project.

3. **Open the file rossi.jpg from your WIP>MOAH folder.**

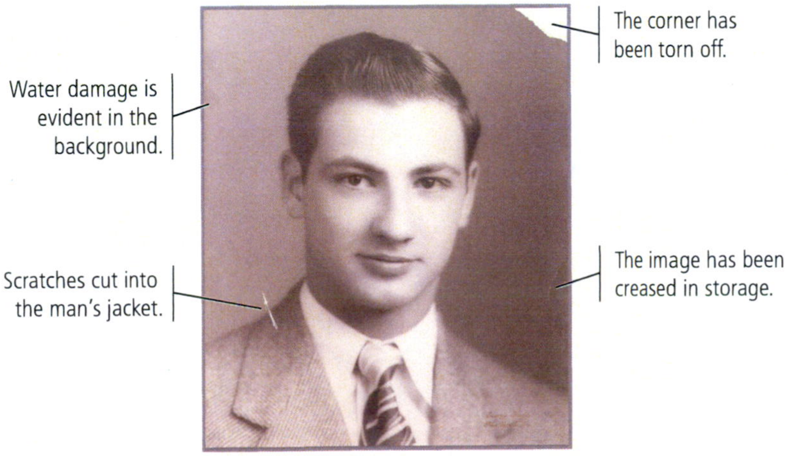

The corner has been torn off.
Water damage is evident in the background.
The image has been creased in storage.
Scratches cut into the man's jacket.

4. **Choose View>100% to show the image at the actual size.**

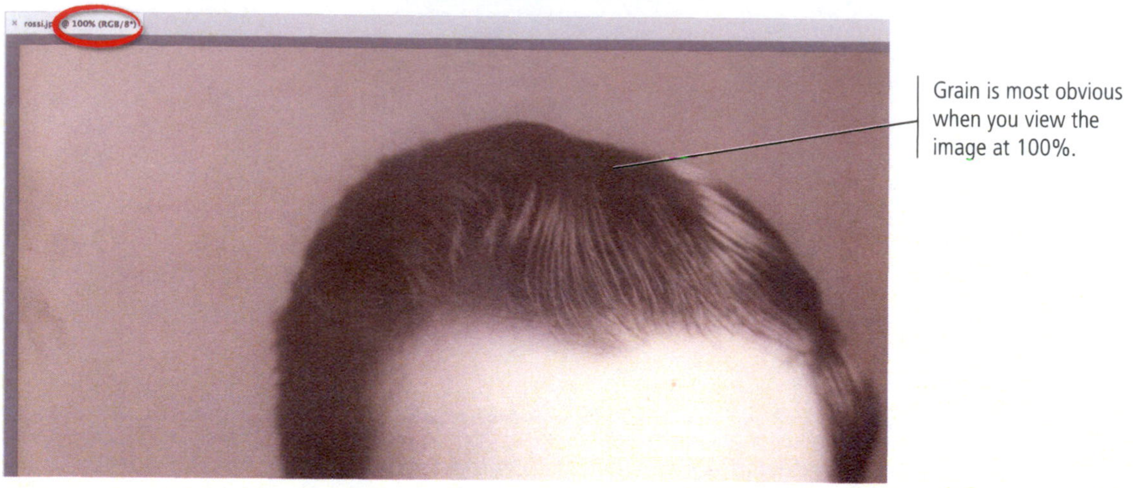
@ 100% (RGB/8*)
Grain is most obvious when you view the image at 100%.

PHOTOSHOP FOUNDATIONS

The Noise Filters

Noise is defined as random pixels that stand out from the surrounding pixels, either hurting the overall appearance of the image (as in the case of visible grains in an old photograph) or helping to prevent printing problems (as in the case of a gradient that extends across a large area). Photoshop includes several filters (Filters>Noise) that can add or remove noise.

The **Add Noise** filter applies random pixels to the image. Uniform distributes color values of noise between 0 and the defined amount. Gaussian distributes color values of noise along a bell-shaped curve. Monochromatic adds random pixels without affecting the colors in the image.

The **Despeckle** filter detects the edges in an image and blurs everything except those edges.

The **Dust & Scratches** filter reduces noise by comparing the contrast of pixels within the defined radius; pixels outside the defined threshold are adjusted.

The **Median** filter reduces noise by blending the brightness of pixels within a selection. The filter compares the brightness of pixels within the defined radius, and replaces pixels that differ too much from surrounding pixels with the median brightness value of the compared pixels.

The **Reduce Noise** filter provides far greater control over different aspects of noise correction. In Basic mode, you can remove luminance noise and color noise in the composite image.

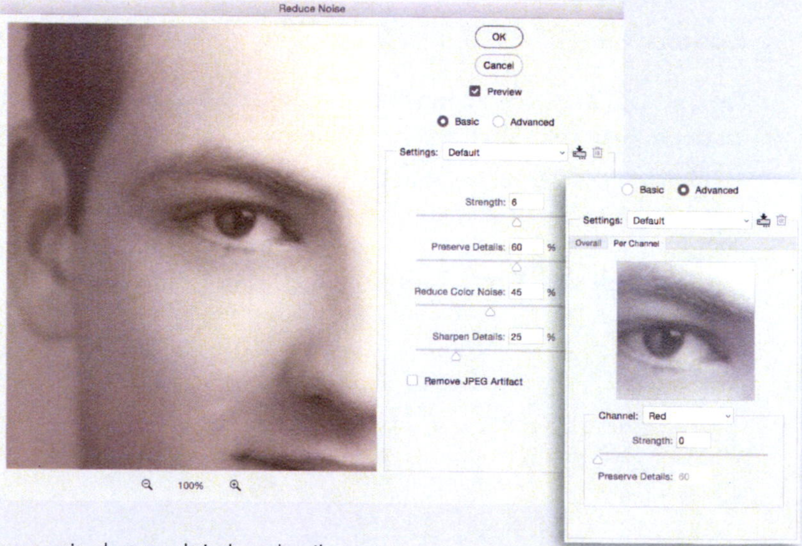

In Advanced mode, you can remove noise from individual color channels. (**Luminance noise**, also called grayscale noise, makes an image appear grainy; **color noise** usually appears as color artifacts in the image.)

- **Strength** controls the amount of luminance noise reduction.
- **Preserve Details** controls how carefully the filter compares the difference in luminance between adjacent pixels. Lower values remove more noise but result in less detail.
- **Reduce Color Noise** removes random color pixels from the image.
- **Sharpen Details** sharpens the image. Because the noise reduction process inherently blurs the image, this option applies the same kind of sharpening that is available in the Photoshop Sharpen filters.
- **Remove JPEG Artifacts** removes artifacts and halos caused by saving an image with a low JPEG quality setting (in other words, using a high lossy compression scheme).

5. **Choose Filter>Blur>Gaussian Blur.**

   All Photoshop blur filters work in essentially the same way: they average the brightness values of contiguous pixels to soften the image.

6. **In the image behind the dialog box, click the area between the man's right eye and eyebrow.**

   When many filter dialog boxes are open, clicking the image (behind the dialog box) changes the visible preview area in the dialog box. You can also click inside the dialog box preview area and drag to change the visible preview area.

7. **Make sure Preview is checked in the dialog box and change the Radius field to 2.0 pixels.**

   The **Radius** field defines (in pixels) the amount of blurring that will be applied. Photoshop uses this value to average the brightness of a pixel with that of surrounding pixels. A small radius value can soften an image and remove most photographic grain.

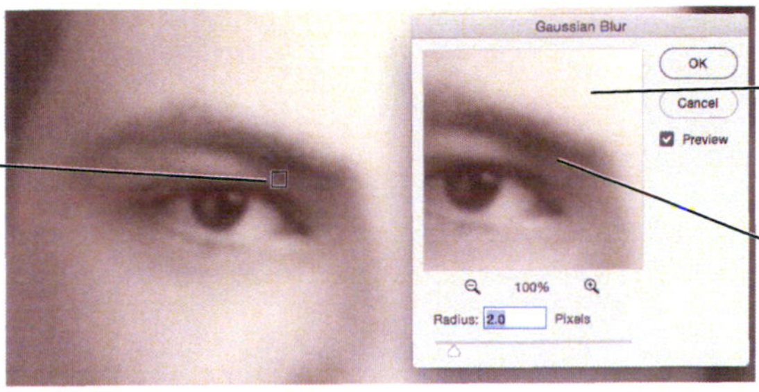

Click the image to change the visible preview area in the dialog box.

A small amount of Gaussian blur removes most of the photographic grain.

Areas of fine detail are also slightly blurred by the Gaussian Blur filter.

8. **Click OK to apply the Gaussian Blur to the image.**

   To remove the photographic grain, you had to blur the entire image; this means that areas of fine detail were also blurred. You can use a second technique — sharpening — to restore some of the lost edge detail.

The Blur Filters

PHOTOSHOP FOUNDATIONS

The Filter>Blur menu includes a number of choices for applying corrective or artistic blurs to an image or selection.

Average finds the average color of an image or selection, and then fills the image or selection with that color to create a smooth appearance.

Blur and **Blur More** smooth transitions by averaging the pixels next to the hard edges of defined lines and shaded areas. When you apply these filters, you have no additional control: Blur is roughly equivalent to a 0.3-pixel radius blur, and Blur More uses approximately a 0.7-pixel radius.

Box Blur averages the color value of neighboring pixels. You can adjust the size of the area used to calculate the average value; a larger radius value results in more blurring.

Gaussian Blur blurs the selection by a specific amount.

Lens Blur adds blur to an image to create the effect of a narrower depth of field so some objects in the image remain in focus, while others areas are blurred.

Motion Blur includes an option for changing the blur angle, as well as a Distance value that defines the number of pixels to blur.

Radial Blur either spins the pixel around the center point of the image, or zooms the pixel around the center point based on the Amount setting. The farther a pixel is from the center point, the more the pixel is blurred. You can drag in the Blur Center window to move the center point of the blur.

Shape Blur uses a specific shape (**kernel**) to create the blur. Radius determines the size of the kernel; the larger the kernel, the greater the blur.

Smart Blur allows you to blur tones closely related in value without affecting edge quality. Threshold determines how closely pixels must be related in tone before being blurred. You can also specify a Quality level, and change the Mode setting. Using Edge Only mode, edges are outlined in white and the image is forced to black. Using Overlay Edges mode, the color image is blurred and edges are outlined in white.

Surface Blur blurs an image while trying to preserve edges. The Radius option specifies the size of the blur in whole numbers. Threshold controls how much the tonal values of neighboring pixels must differ before being blurred.

9. **Choose Filter>Sharpen>Smart Sharpen.**

   The Smart Sharpen filter allows you to sharpen an image based on a specific amount and radius. You can also limit the sharpening that occurs in shadow and highlight areas.

10. **If you don't see the entire dialog box, click the arrow to the left of Shadows/Highlights to show all the available options.**

11. **Make the man's face visible in the dialog box preview area.**

12. **Define the following settings in the dialog box:**

   - **Choose Gaussian Blur in the Remove menu.**

     The **Remove** menu defines the type of blur you want to remove. Because you applied a Gaussian blur to remove the heavy noise, you are now using the Smart Sharpen filter to remove that blur and restore image detail.

     Lens Blur detects edges and detail, and provides finer sharpening of detail and reduced halos. Motion Blur attempts to reduce the effects of blur that is caused by camera movement; you can also define a specific angle of the blur to remove.

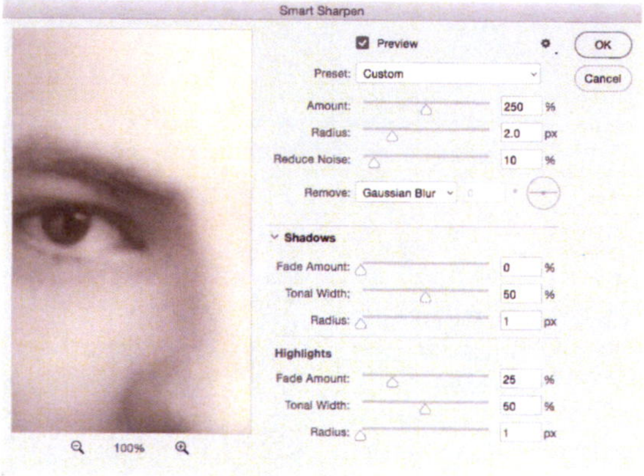

   - **Set the Amount to 250%.**

     Amount defines how much sharpening to apply; a higher amount increases contrast between edge pixels, giving the appearance of greater sharpness. (Be careful, because a too-high amount can result in halos at apparent edges.)

   - **Set the Radius to 2.0 px.**

     Radius defines the number of pixels around edge pixels that will be affected by the sharpening. Higher radius values result in more obvious sharpening.

   - **Set the Reduce Noise slider to 10%.**

     Reduce Noise helps to avoid sharpening any noise that still exists in the image.

   - **In the Highlights section, set the Fade Amount to 25%.**

     In the Shadows and Highlights sections, you can adjust sharpening that will be applied in those areas of the image.

     – **Fade Amount** adjusts the amount of sharpening. By reducing the sharpening in the highlights of this image, you help to further remove the noise that remains in the lighter portions (the faces and background).

     – **Tonal Width** controls the range of tones that will be modified. Smaller values restrict the adjustments to only darker regions for shadows and only lighter regions for highlights.

     – **Radius** defines the size of the area around each pixel used to determine whether a pixel is in the shadows or highlights.

13. **Click OK to apply sharpen the image.**

14. **Choose File>Save As. Save the file as a native Photoshop file named rossi.psd in your WIP>MOAH folder. Continue to the next exercise.**

   Remember, you have to choose File>Save As to save the file with a different name or format.

Understanding the Shake Reduction Filter

As the name suggests, the Shake Reduction filter (Filter>Sharpen>Shake Reduction) was designed to reduce the blur caused by a shaking camera — for example, images that were photographed with a slow shutter speed or without a flash.

Keep in mind that the filter was designed to remove blur caused by a moving camera, not a moving subject. The filter also does not work well on images with specular highlights or noise. Finally, it works best to reduce shake in specific areas of an image, not over an entire image.

When you first open the filter, the image is automatically analyzed. The software determines a "region of interest" and calculates the shape and direction of the blur.

If necessary, you can adjust the automatically defined settings on the right side of the dialog box:

- **Blur Trace Bounds** is the extent of blur size introduced by the camera shake.
- **Source Noise** defines the noise level of the Source image (Auto, Low, Medium, High)
- **Smoothing** reduces high-frequency sharpening noise.
- **Artifact Suppression** reduces larger artifacts that might be enhanced by sharpening.

You can use the Blur Estimation tool to add more than one blur estimation region to the image, or use the Blur Direction tool to manually specify the direction and length of a straight blur.

When Advanced options are expanded, the small icons show previews of the blur shape that was defined for each region.

You can select a specific region in this area to make it active in the larger preview pane. Click the handles on the blur region marquee to resize it, and click the pin in the center of a region to move it.

Using the Detail Loupe

You can use the Detail loupe (pane) to analyze specific areas of the image. You can enlarge the detail preview using the options at the bottom of the pane (.5x, 1x, 2x, 4x).

While the pane is docked, click inside the preview area to change the preview area. You can also undock the Detail pane and drag it over the image to enhance a specific area.

If you click the Enhance at Loupe Location button, the filter creates a new blur estimation region based on what is visible in the Detail pane.

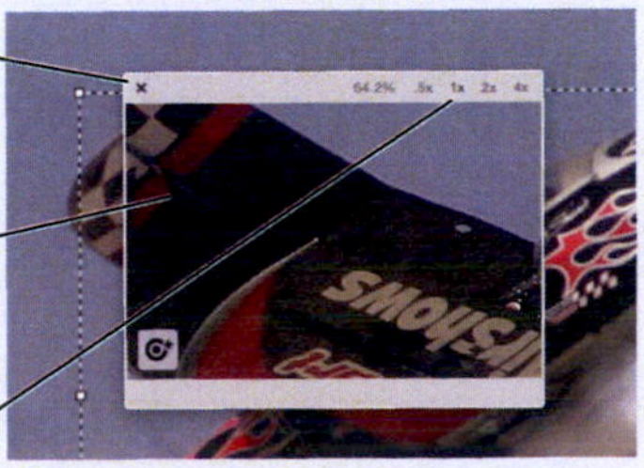

Heal Severe Scratches

The blur and sharpen routine from the previous exercise improved the client's image — the obvious grain is gone. Even though the edges are slightly less sharp than the original scan, they are sharp enough to produce good results when the image is printed. If you're working with images that aren't 70 years old, you will be able to produce far sharper edges using these same techniques.

There are still a number of problems in the image that require intervention. Photoshop includes several tools for changing the pixels in an image — from painting with a brush to nudging selections on a layer to using repair tools specifically designed for adjusting pixels based on other pixels in the image.

The **Spot Healing Brush tool** allows you to remove imperfections by blending surrounding pixels. The **Healing Brush tool** has a similar function, except you can define the source pixels that will be used to heal an area. The **Patch tool** allows you to repair an area with pixels from another area by dragging the selection area.

Note:

Whenever you need to clean up blemishes on images and make other adjustments that require looking at very small areas. It can be very helpful to clean your monitor so you don't mistake on-screen dust and smudges with flaws in the images you are adjusting.

1. **With rossi.psd open, view the image at 100%. Set up the document window so you can see the man's forehead.**

2. **Select the Spot Healing Brush tool in the Tools panel.**

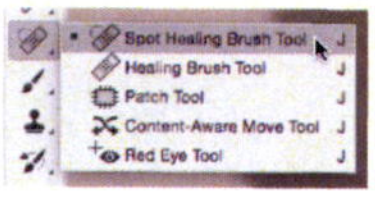

3. **In the Options bar, choose the Proximity Match option. Open the Brush Preset picker and define a 20-pixel brush with 100% hardness.**

Click this button to open the Brush Preset picker, where you can change the brush settings.

Use a 20-pixel hard-edge brush.

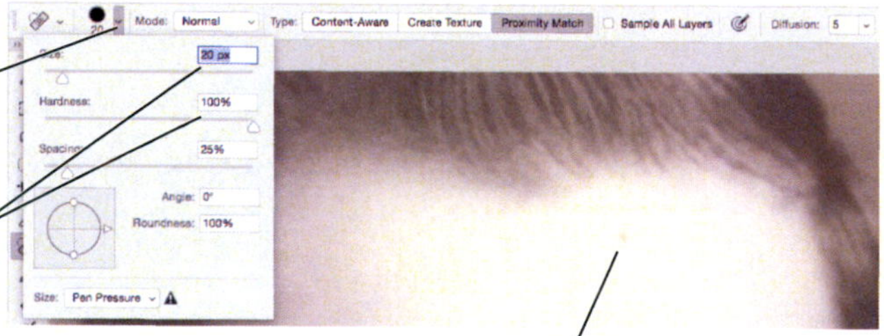

You want to remove this blemish.

Note:

You will work extensively with brushes and brush settings in Project 7: House Painting.

The **Proximity Match** method uses the pixels around the edge of the selection to find an image area to use as a patch for the selected area. The **Create Texture** method uses all the pixels in the selection to create a texture for repairing the area. **Content Aware** mode attempts to match the detail in surrounding areas while healing pixels (this method does not work well for areas with hard edges or sharp contrast). If you select **Sample All Layers**, the tool pulls pixel data from all visible layers.

4. **Place the cursor over the orange spot on the man's forehead. Click immediately over the spot to heal it.**

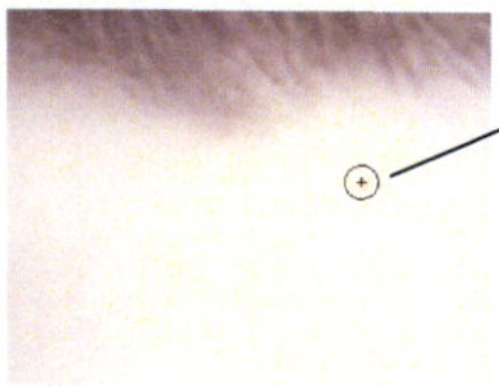

The Spot Healing Brush tool shows the size of the selected brush.

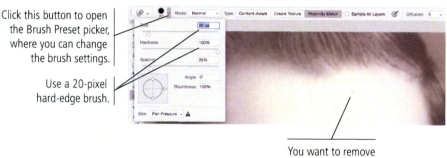

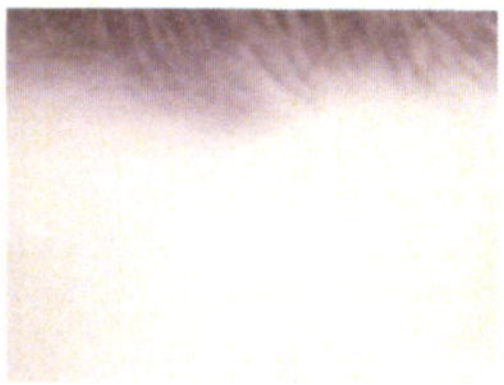

5. **Make the man's chin visible in the document window, then choose the Healing Brush tool (nested under the Spot Healing Brush tool).**

   It might help to zoom in when you want to heal small areas such as this white spot the man's chin. We are working at 200% in the following screen shots.

Healing Brush tool

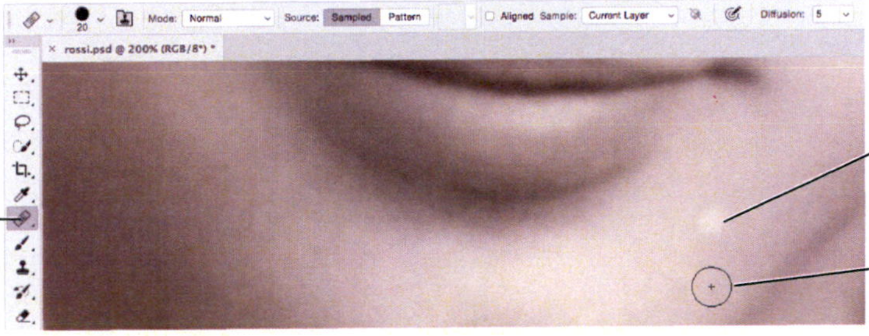

You need to remove this blemish.

The 20-px brush you used earlier is sufficient to remove this spot.

   For the Healing Brush tool, you can define brush settings just as you did for the Spot Healing Brush tool. These options retain the last-used settings until you change them, so the brush size should still be set to 20 px. As the tool cursor shows in the document window, that size is sufficient to cover the white spot on the man's chin.

   The Mode menu determines the blending mode used to heal an area. The default option (Normal) samples the source color and transparency to blend the new pixels smoothly into the area being healed. The Replace mode preserves texture in the healed area when you use a soft-edge brush. Multiple, Screen, Darken, Lighten, Color, and Luminosity modes have the same function as the blending modes for specific layers and brushes.

Note:

You can use the bracket keys to enlarge (]) or reduce ([) the Healing Brush tool brush size.

6. **Place the cursor directly below the spot you want to heal. Press Option/Alt and click to define the healing source.**

   Pressing Option/Alt with the Healing Brush tool changes the cursor icon to a crosshair, which you can click to select the source of the brush (the pixels that will be used to heal the spot where you next click).

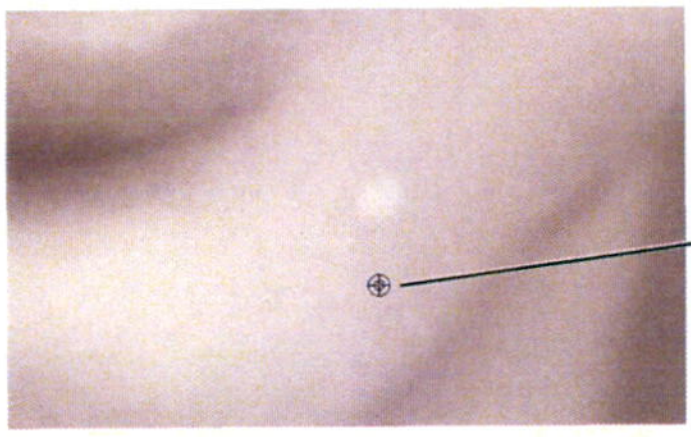

Pressing Option/Alt allows you to define the source pixels that will be used to heal the next spot you click.

7. **Place the cursor over the blemish on the man's chin and click.**

   Unlike the Spot Healing Brush tool, the Healing Brush tool allows you to define the source of the healing. By choosing nearby pixels as the healing source, the blemish on the man's chin disappears, and that spot blends nicely into the surrounding pixels.

   The Healing Brush tool blends colors from the source pixels (which you defined in Step 6) with colors in the area where you click. You can also change the source from Sampled (the pixels you defined by Option/Alt-clicking) to Pattern, which uses pixels from a defined pattern to heal the area — a good choice for creating artistic effects, rather than healing blemishes in a photo.

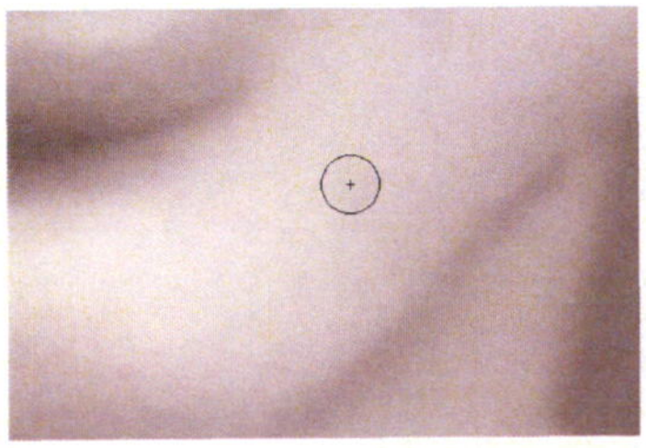

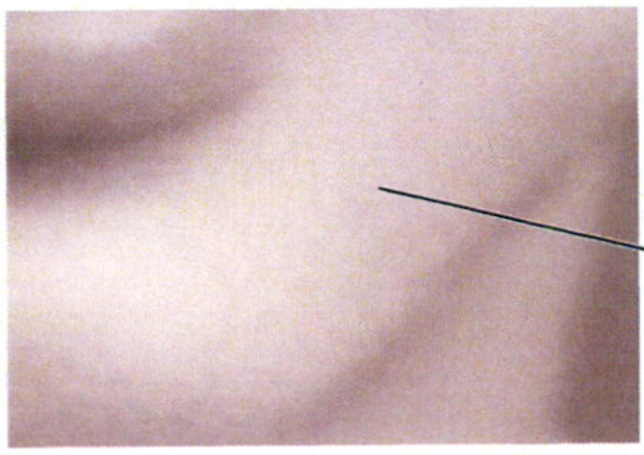

After clicking, the spot is healed using the source pixels.

8. **Save the file and continue to the next exercise.**

Aligning the Healing Source

When you work with the Healing Brush and Clone Stamp tools, you have the option to align the healing source to the cursor. If the Align option is turned off, the source starting point will be relative to the image; each successive click uses the same source point. If the Align option is turned on, the source starting point will be relative to the cursor.

A

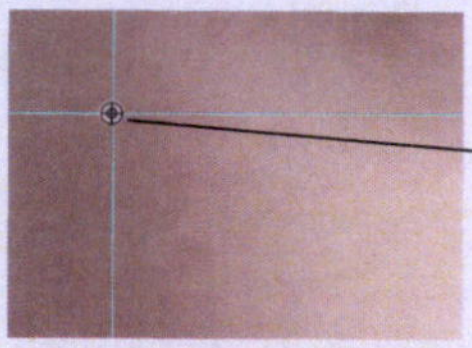

We first Option/Alt-clicked at the guide intersection to define the healing source.

B

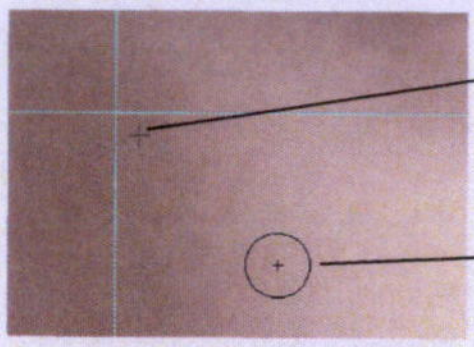

The crosshair shows the source of the healing.

This circle shows the cursor location where we clicked with the Healing Brush tool.

C

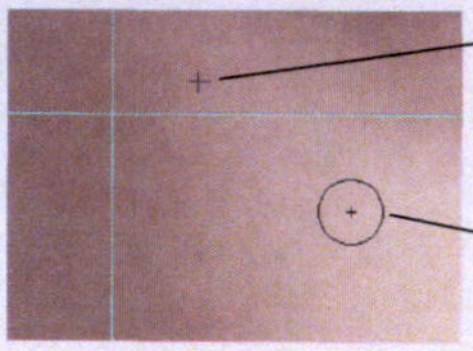

When the Aligned option is turned **on**, the source moves relative to the tool cursor.

Clicking farther to the right moves the source the same distance from its defined origin.

D

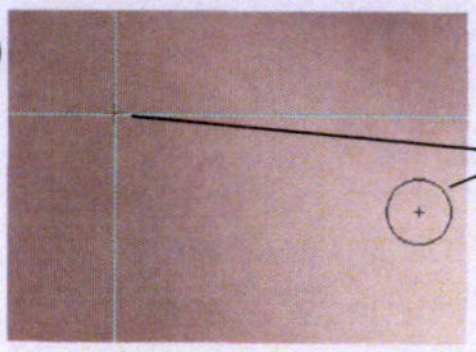

When the Aligned option is turned **off**, the source remains in the same position even when the Healing Brush tool is clicked farther right.

Clone out Major Damage

The client's image has definitely been improved by removing the grain and healing the small blemishes, but four major areas of damage still need to be fixed. In this exercise you will use the Fill dialog box to fix the damage in the image background, and then use the Clone Stamp tool to fix the scratch on the man's shoulder.

1. **With the file rossi.psd open, zoom into the top-right corner (where the corner has been ripped off).**

2. **Using the Rectangular Marquee tool, draw a selection around the torn-off corner.**

3. **With the new marquee active, choose Edit>Fill.**

   In the Fill dialog box, the Contents menu determines what will fill the active selection when you click OK. You can choose the active foreground or background color; any Color (selected in the Color Picker dialog box when you choose the Color option); white, gray or black; a defined pattern; or a specific state in the History panel. If you use the Content-Aware option, you allow Photoshop to evaluate the image and surrounding pixels to determine what should fill the selection.

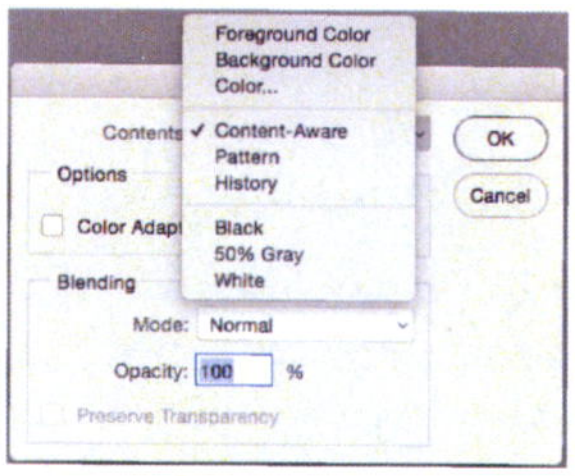

   In the case of this image, the backdrop is a slightly mottled gradient. The Content-Aware option is an excellent choice for fixing the torn-off corner.

4. **Choose Content-Aware in the Contents menu, then click OK.**

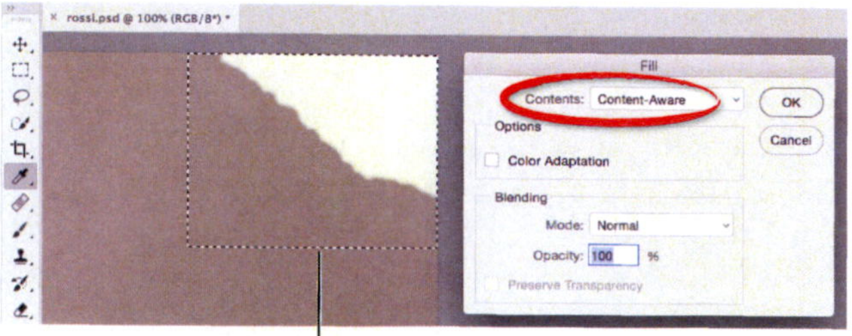

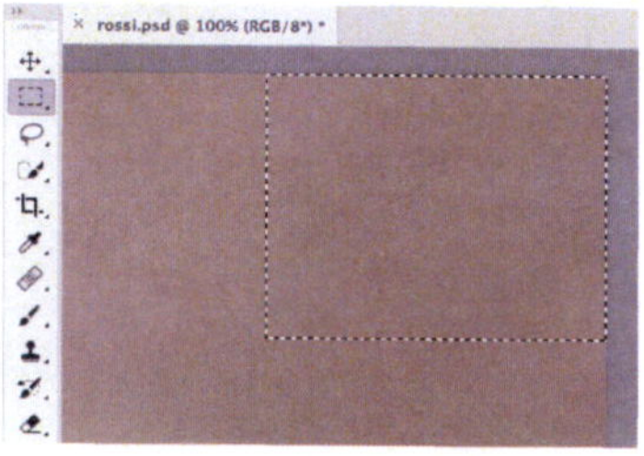

The damaged corner is inside the selection area.

5. **Choose Select>Deselect to turn off the active selection marquee.**

6. **Repeat the process from Steps 2–5 to remove the crease on the right edge and the water damage on the left edge of the image.**

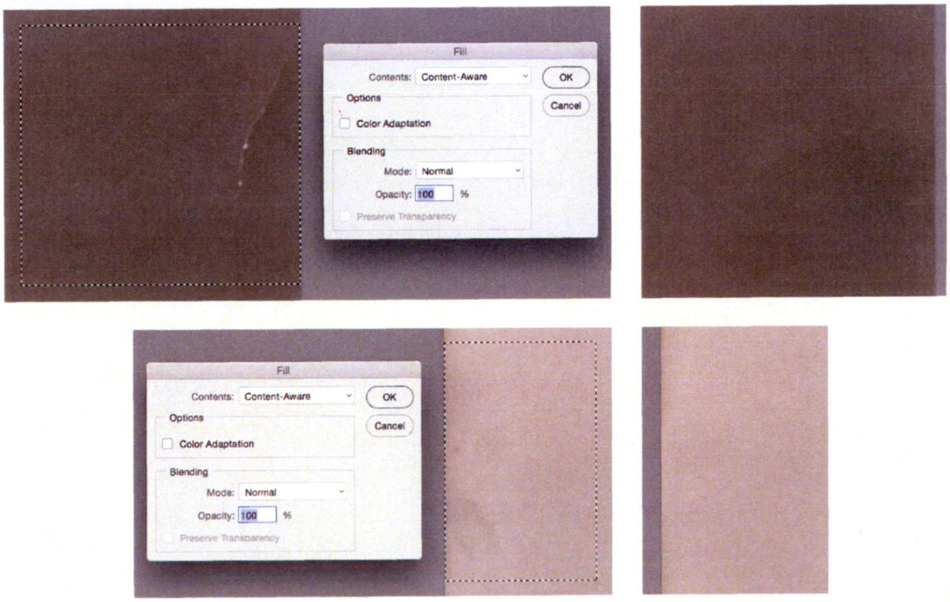

7. **Make the man's shoulder visible in the document window, then choose the Clone Stamp tool.**

   Content-Aware Fill works very well on areas of subtle shading, such as the backdrop in this image, or other areas where you do not need to maintain fine detail or edges in the selected area. If you try to use this option on a sharp edge, however, the Content-Aware Fill results are unpredictable. Other tools, such as the Clone Stamp tool, work better for retouching distinct edges.

   The Clone Stamp tool paints one part of an image over another part, which is useful for duplicating objects or removing defects in an image. When you are using the Clone Stamp tool, the Options bar combines brush options (brush size, blending mode, opacity, and flow) with healing options (alignment and sample source, which you used in the previous exercise).

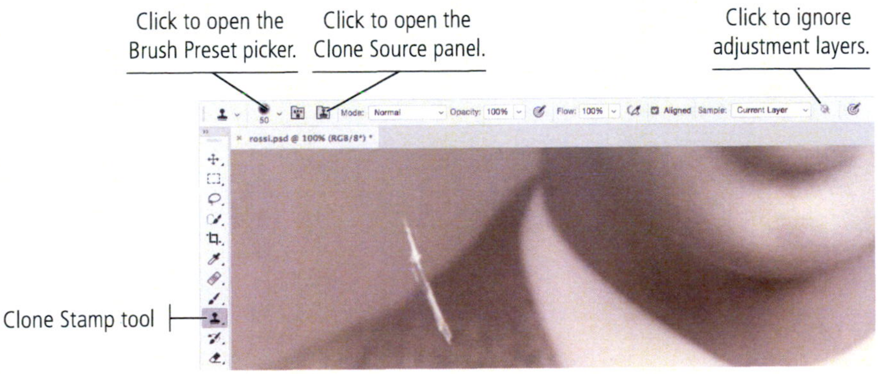

Note:

Press Command/Control-D to turn off a selection marquee.

8. **Open the Brush Preset picker in the Options bar. Define a 50-pixel brush with 50% hardness.**

   This size is large enough to cover the crease in the bottom-left corner of the image.

   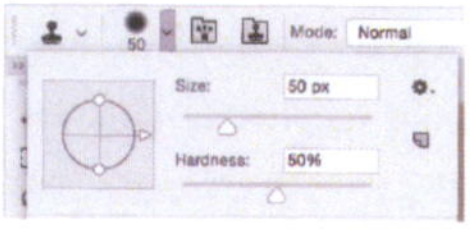

   When using the Clone Stamp tool, hard-edge brushes can result in harsh lines where you clone pixels; the reduced hardness creates a soft-edged brush, which will help to prevent hard edges in areas where you clone pixels.

9. **In the Options bar, make sure the Aligned option is turned on (checked).**

   As with the Healing Brush tool, you can define the source that will be cloned when you click with the Clone Stamp tool; the difference is that whole pixels are copied, not just their color values.

10. **Place the cursor over the edge you want to reproduce and Option/Alt-click to define the source.**

    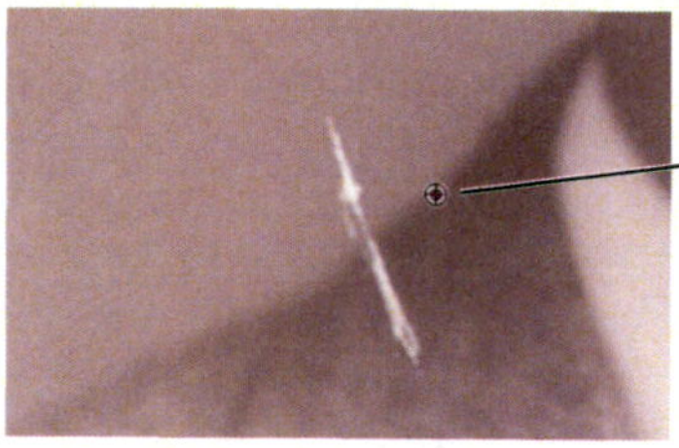

    Option/Alt-click to define the clone source.

11. **Place the cursor over the scratched pixels on the man's shoulder.**

    As you move the Clone Stamp tool cursor, the source pixels move along with the tool cursor to give you a preview of what will happen when you click.

12. **Click without dragging when the cloned pixels appear to align properly with the area behind the scratch.**

    Clicking without dragging clones a 50-pixel area. Because the brush we chose has 50% hardness, the center (where the shoulder edge is) is clear, but the outside parts of the brush are feathered into the surrounding area.

    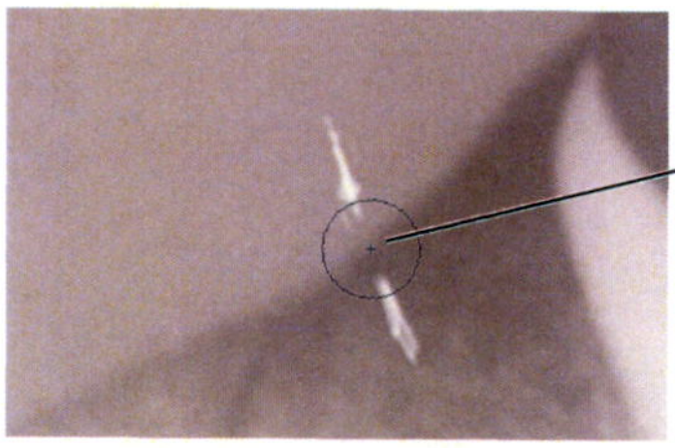

    Before clicking, use the cursor preview to align the cloned pixels to edge in the original.

13. **Choose the Lasso tool in the Tools panel. Draw a marquee around the scratches in the background, above the man's shoulder.**

    Be careful to avoid the man's shoulder in the selection area.

Note:

You can use the bracket keys to enlarge (]) or reduce ([) the Clone Stamp brush size.

Note:

When you are cloning, it's usually a good idea to clone in small strokes or even single clicks. This can help you avoid cloning in patterns or "railroad tracks" that do as much damage as good. When cloning large areas, it's also a good idea to frequently resample the clone source to avoid cloning the same pixels into a new noticeable pattern.

Note:

If you're not happy with the result of a clone, simply undo the action (Command/Control-Z, or using the History panel) and try again. Cloning — especially edges — often takes more than one try to achieve the desired result.

14. **Choose Edit>Fill. Choose Content-Aware in the Contents menu and click OK.**

Photoshop evaluates the image and determines what should be created inside the selection area. The fill might take a few seconds to process, so be patient.

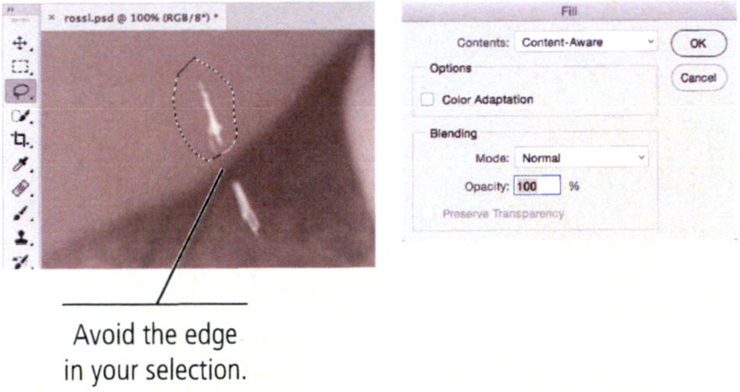

15. **Turn off the active selection (Select>Deselect).**

16. **Use the same method as in Steps 13–15 to remove the scratches from the man's coat.**

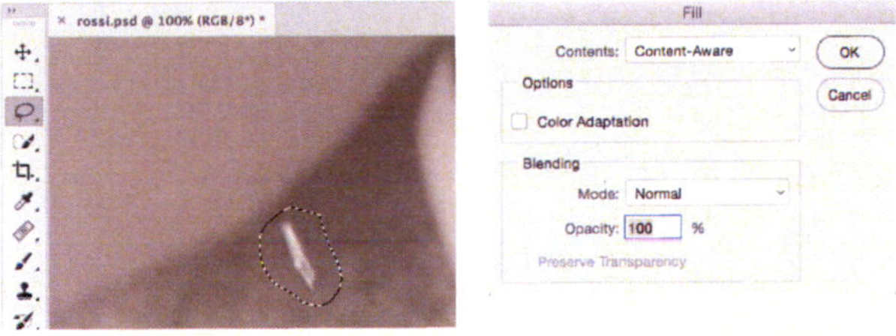

17. **Choose File>Save As. Change the file name to rossi-fixed.psd and save it in your WIP>MOAH folder.**

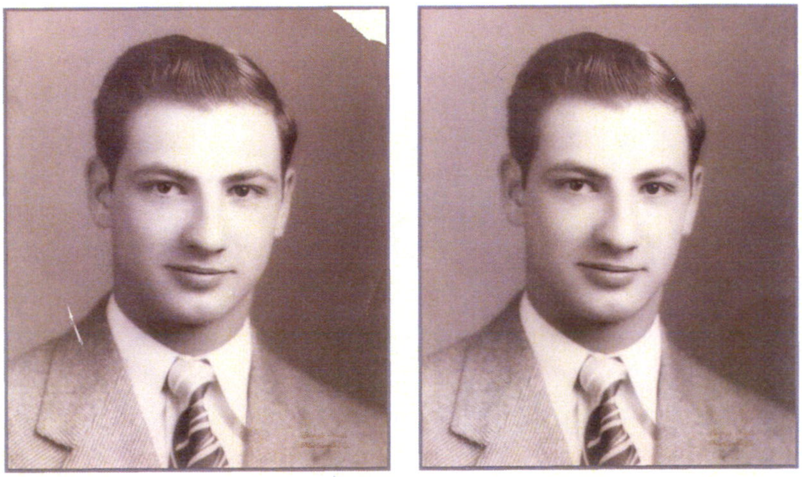

18. **Close the file and continue to the next stage of the project.**

The Clone Source Panel in Depth

The Clone Source panel (Window>Clone Source) allows you to store up to five sources for the Clone Stamp or Healing Brush tool. These sources can be from any layer of any open image, which allows you to create unique blended effects by combining pixels from multiple layers or multiple files.

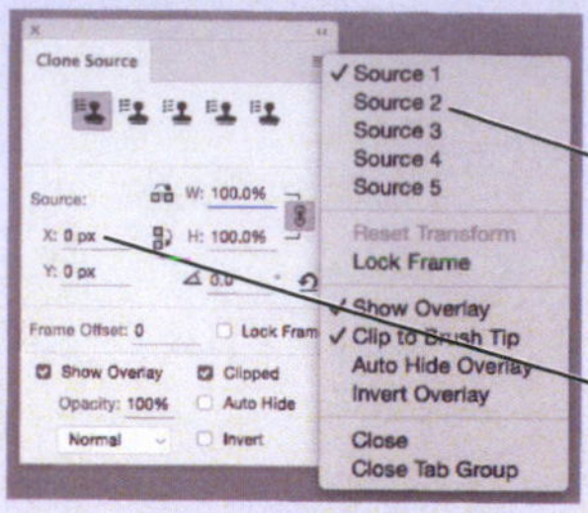

Store and access up to five sources from any layer of any open image.

Transform the offset, size, and angle of the clone source.

The Show Overlay options allow you to show (at the defined opacity) the source pixels on top of the area where you are cloning. For example, say you want to clone the parachutist onto the plane photo. You would first define a clone source in the parachutist image, then make the plane image active.

With the Show Overlay option checked, placing the Clone Stamp cursor over the plane image shows the parachutist on top of the plane image. When you click in the plane image with the Clone Stamp tool, that area of the parachutist image will be cloned into the plane image; the overlay allows you to preview the source areas that will be cloned into the plane image.

If the Auto Hide option is checked, the overlay is only visible when the mouse button is not clicked. The Invert option reverses the overlay into a negative representation of the source image. You can also change the blending mode of the overlay from the default Normal to Darken, Lighten, or Difference.

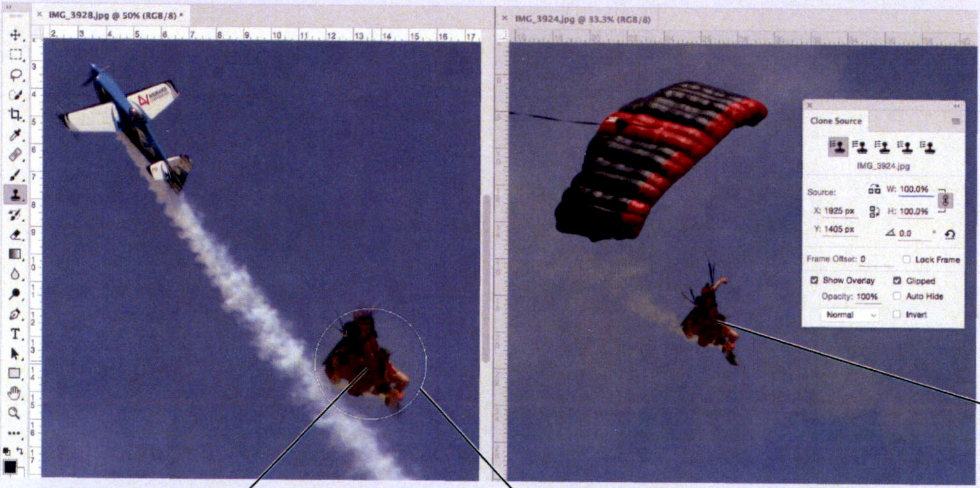

We defined a clone source here.

Using Show Overlay, the Clone Stamp cursor shows the pixels that will be cloned by clicking.

If the Clipped option is checked, the clone source appears only within the tool cursor area.

We turned off the Clipped option and reduced the opacity to 50% to show the entire source file over the image where the cloning is taking place.

Stage 2 Correcting Lighting Problems

Before you start correcting problems with lighting and color, you should understand the different parts of an image, as well as the terms used to describe these areas.

- **Highlights** are defined as the lightest areas of the image that include detail. Direct sources of light such as a light bulb or reflected sunlight on water are called **specular highlights**; they should not be considered the highlights of an image.
- **Shadows** are the darkest areas of the image that still contain some detail; areas of solid black are not considered shadow tones.
- The shades between the highlights and shadows are the **midtones** (or **gamma**) of the image.

Contrast and saturation play an integral role in reproducing high-quality images. **Contrast** refers to the tonal variation within an image; an image primarily composed of highlights and shadows is a high-contrast image, while an image with more detail in the midtones is a low-contrast image.

Contrast is closely linked to **saturation**, which refers to the intensity of a color or its variation away from gray. The saturation of individual colors in an image, and the correct saturation of different colors in relation to one another, affects the overall contrast of the image. If an image is under- or oversaturated, the contrast suffers — detail is lost and colors appear either muted or too bright.

Correct Problems with Brightness/Contrast

Depending on the image, several tools are available for correcting problems related to images that are either too dark or too light. The most basic adjustment option — Brightness/Contrast — can fix images that need overall adjustment to brightness, contrast, or both.

1. **Open the file `bezel.jpg` from your WIP>MOAH folder.**

   This image has an overall dark feel, probably caused by poor lighting or underexposure. The Brightness/Contrast adjustment can correct this problem.

2. **Choose Image>Adjustments>Brightness/Contrast and make sure the Preview option is checked.**

3. **Drag the Brightness slider to 35.**

   Increasing the overall brightness creates an immediate improvement in this image, although some areas of detail are still muddy.

Note:

Image adjustments can be applied directly to the image pixels or as non-destructive adjustment layers using the Adjustments panel. In this project, you edit the actual image pixels; you use the adjustment layer method in Project 6: Advertising Samples.

4. **Drag the Contrast slider to 15.**

Increasing the contrast brings out more detail in the overall object.

5. **Click OK to apply the change.**

6. **Save the file in your WIP>MOAH folder as a native Photoshop file named bezel-fixed.psd.**

7. **Close the file and continue to the next exercise.**

Correct Contrast and Tonal Range with Levels

The **tonal range** of an image is the amount of variation between the lightest highlight and the darkest shadow in a particular image. A grayscale image can contain 256 possible shades of gray. Each channel of a color image can also contain 256 possible shades of gray. To achieve the best contrast in an image, the tonal range of the image should include as many levels of gray as are available.

While the Brightness/Contrast option is a good choice for making basic adjustments, the Levels adjustment is the best approach for enhancing image detail throughout the entire tonal range. Using Levels, adjusting contrast is a three-step process:

- Determine the image's highlight areas (the lightest areas that contain detail).
- Determine the image's shadow areas (the darkest areas that contain detail).
- Adjust the gamma (the contrast in midtones of an image) to determine the proportion of darker tones to lighter tones.

1. **Open the file `drachma.jpg` from the WIP>MOAH folder.**

2. **Display the Histogram panel (Window>Histogram), and then choose Expanded View from the panel Options menu.**

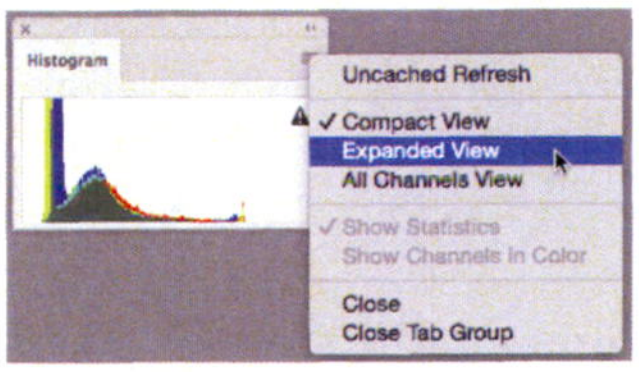

The Histogram panel shows the distribution of pixels — or more accurately the tonal values of those pixels — from the darkest to the lightest portions of an image, for the entire image or for individual color channels. The Histogram panel can help identify problems that need to be corrected.

When you first display the panel, it probably appears in Compact view, which shows only the graphs for the individual color channels and the composite image. In Expanded view, you can see more information about how pixels are distributed in the image (from shadows on the left to highlights on the right).

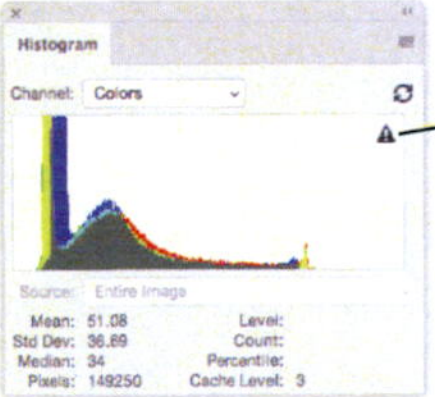

If you see a warning icon, click it to reset the cache.

- The **Mean** value is an average point of the brightness values. A Mean of 128 usually identifies a well-balanced image. Images with a Mean of 170 to 255 are light; images with a Mean lower than 90 are very dark.
- The **Standard Deviation** (Std Dev) value represents how widely the brightness values vary.
- The **Median** value shows the middle value in the range of color values.
- The **Pixels** value displays the total number of pixels used for the graphic displayed on the histogram.
- The **Level** statistic displays the intensity level of the pixels below the mouse cursor.
- **Count** shows the number of pixels in the area below the cursor.
- **Percentile** represents the percentage of pixels below or to the left of the cursor location. Zero represents the left edge of the image and 100% is the right edge.
- The **Cache Level** is determined by the Performance preferences and is related to the Cache Refresh icon (and Warning icon). The larger your cache, the more you can do before the image and the disk cache don't match. On the other hand, a larger cache requires more RAM for the application to run smoothly.

3. **In the Histogram panel, change the Channel menu to RGB.**

   The histogram — the chart that shows the distribution of tones — can display a single graph for the entire composite image (all channels combined) or for individual channels. The white space at the left and right side of the histogram indicate that some of the tones in the available range are not being used in this image.

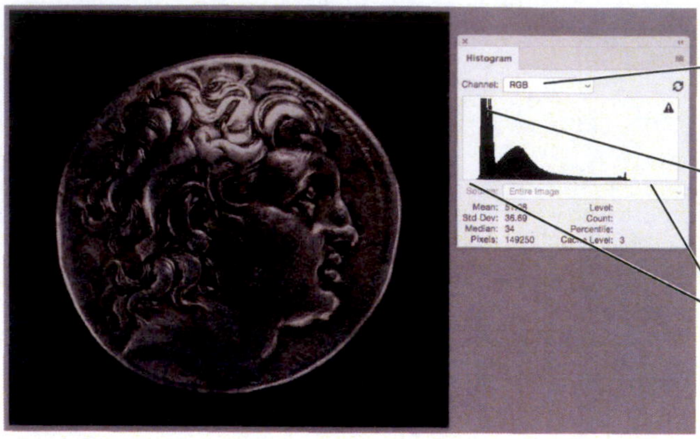

Choose from this menu to view and modify the histogram for individual channels.
These shadow values are pushing out of the "container," indicating a problem in the shadow tones.
The empty spaces on the left and right of the histogram indicate that some tones in the available range are not being used.

4. **If you see one, click the Warning icon in the upper-right corner of the Histogram panel to reset the cache.**

   Every time you zoom in or out of an image, Photoshop stores the results of the display in a **cache** (a drive location that keeps track of what you're doing). The image you're looking at on the histogram often doesn't match the results on the drive. The Warning icon shows there's a problem; clicking the icon resets the image and rereads the cache.

5. **Choose Image>Adjustments>Levels and make sure Preview is checked.**

   The Levels dialog box shows a histogram like the one shown in the Histogram panel.

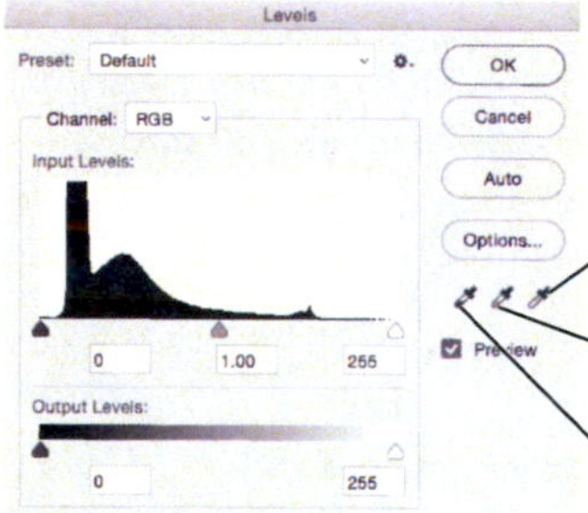

   Two sets of sliders control input levels and output levels. Each set has a black slider for adjusting the shadows and a white slider to adjust highlights. The Input Levels slider also has a gray triangle in the center of the slider bar for adjusting gamma or midtones.

   The Input sliders in the Levels dialog box correspond to the tonal range of the image. Any pixels that exist to the left of the Input Shadow slider are reproduced as solid black, and they have no detail; any pixels that exist to the right of the Input Highlight slider are reproduced as pure white.

6. **Move the Input Shadow slider to the right until it touches the left edge of the curve.**

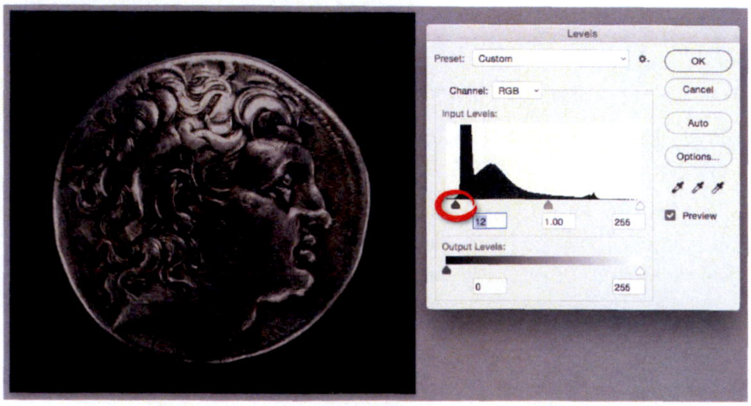

> ***Note:***
>
> *You can use the Channel menu to access and adjust the levels for a specific color channel.*

7. **Move the Input Highlight slider to the left until it touches the right edge of the curve.**

The two adjustments in Steps 6 and 7 extend the colors in the image to take advantage of all 256 possible tones.

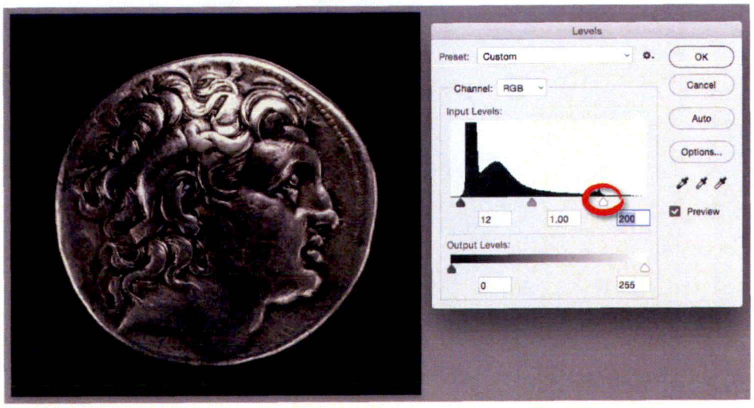

8. **Move the Input Gamma slider to the left until the middle box below the slider shows approximately 1.35.**

The Input Gamma slider controls the proportion of darker tones to lighter tones in the midtones of an image. If you increase gamma, you increase the proportion of lighter grays in the image; this effectively increases contrast in lighter shades and lightens the entire image. If you decrease gamma, you extend the tonal range of darker shades; this allows those areas of the image to be reproduced with a larger range of shades, which increases the contrast in darker shades.

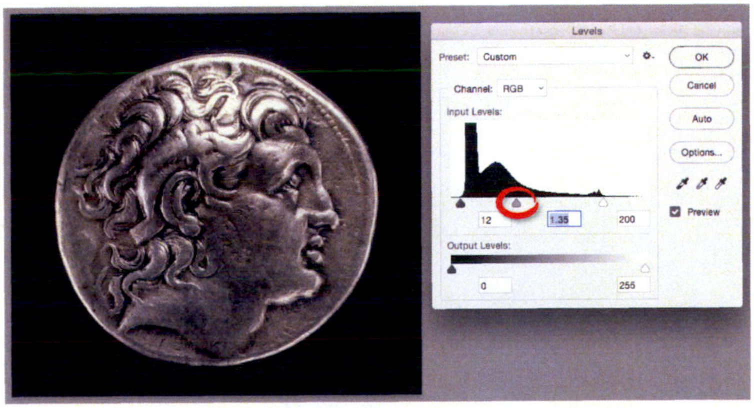

Dragging the Input Gamma slider extends the range between the midtone and the highlights, creating greater contrast and showing more detail throughout the image.

To decrease contrast in an image, you can adjust the Output sliders. This method effectively compresses the range of possible tones that can be reproduced, forcing all areas of the image into a smaller tonal range. Areas originally set to 0 are reproduced at the value of the Output Shadow slider; areas originally set to 255 are output at the value of the Output Highlight slider.

Note:

You can change input and output levels by moving the sliders, entering actual values in the boxes below the slider sets, or by using the eyedroppers to select the brightest and darkest points in the image.

9. **Click OK to close the Levels dialog box.**

10. **Save the file in your WIP>MOAH folder as a native Photoshop file named drachma-fixed.psd.**

11. **Close the file and then continue to the next exercise.**

PHOTOSHOP FOUNDATIONS

Identifying Shadows and Highlights

When you move the Shadow and Highlight sliders in the Levels dialog box, you change the **black point** and **white point** of the image — the points at which pixels become black or white. The goal is to find highlight and shadow points that maintain detail. Choosing a point that has no detail causes the area to turn totally white (highlight) or black (shadow) with no detail reproduced. In some images, it can be difficult to visually identify the black and white points in an image; in these cases you can use the Levels dialog box to help you find those areas.

If you press Option/Alt while dragging the Input Shadow or Input Highlight slider, the image turns entirely white or black (respectively). As you drag, the first pixels that become visible are the darkest shadow and the lightest highlight.

Once you identify the highlight and shadow points in the image, select the White Point eyedropper and click the highlight, and then select the Black Point eyedropper and click the shadow to define those two areas of the image.

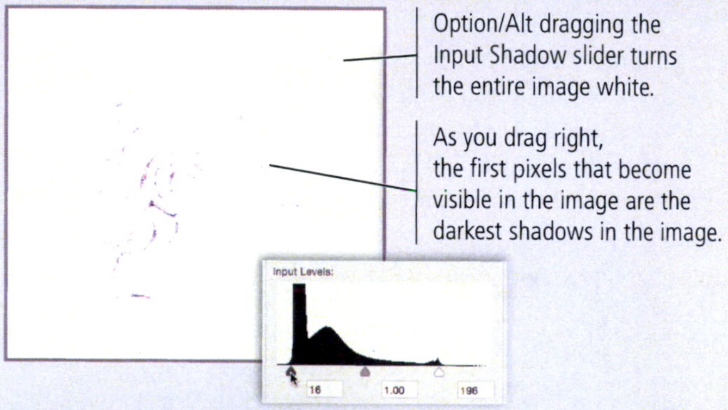
Option/Alt dragging the Input Shadow slider turns the entire image white.
As you drag right, the first pixels that become visible in the image are the darkest shadows in the image.
Input Levels:
16
1.00
196

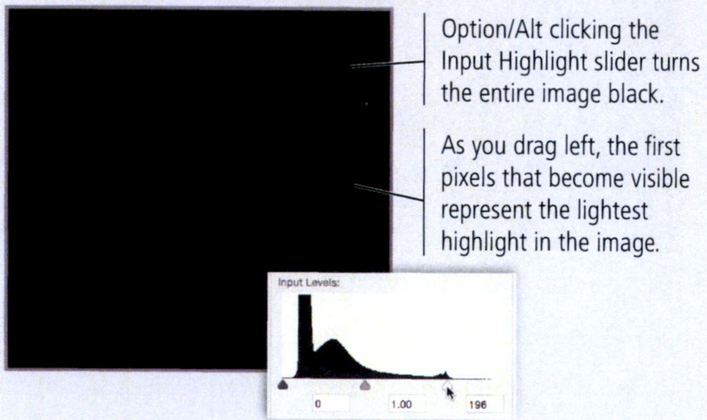
Option/Alt clicking the Input Highlight slider turns the entire image black.
As you drag left, the first pixels that become visible represent the lightest highlight in the image.
Input Levels:
0
1.00
196

The Gradient Map Adjustment

PHOTOSHOP FOUNDATIONS

The **Gradient Map adjustment** (Image>Adjustments>Gradient Map) enables you to create interesting artistic effects by mapping the tones of an image to the shades in a defined gradient.

In the Gradient Map dialog box, you can apply any defined gradient by clicking the arrow to the right of the gradient sample and choosing from the pop-up menu, or you can edit the selected gradient by clicking the sample gradient ramp. The **Dither** option adds random noise to the effect. If you check the **Reverse** option, image highlights map to the left end of the gradient, and image shadows map to the right end of the gradient, effectively reversing the gradient map.

The composite histogram of an RGB image starts at the darkest point and ends at the lightest point with 256 total possible tonal values. If you think of the gradient as having 256 steps from one end to the other, then you can see how the shades of the gradient map to the tones of the original image.

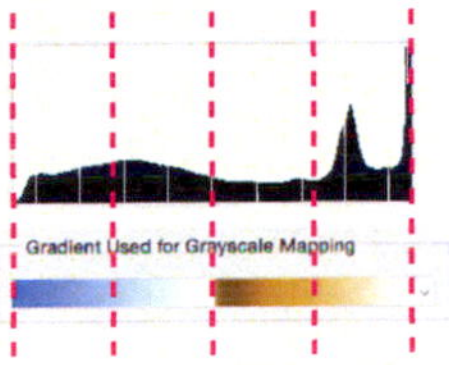

Correct Lighting Problems with the Exposure Adjustment

Many images are either over- or underexposed when photographed. If an image is underexposed, it appears dark and lacks detail in the shadows. If an image is overexposed, it appears too light and lacks detail in the highlights. You can use the Exposure adjustment to correct exposure — and thus, the overall detail and contrast in the image.

Keep in mind, however, that Photoshop cannot create information that doesn't exist. If you have an underexposed image with no detail in the shadow areas, Photoshop cannot generate that detail for you. Some problems are simply beyond fixing.

The Exposure dialog box is designed to make tonal adjustments to 32- and 64-bit HDR (high dynamic range) images, but it also works with 8-bit and 16-bit images. The Exposure adjustment works by performing calculations in a linear color space (gamma 1.0) rather than the image's current color space.

> ***Note:***
>
> *HDR refers to high-density range (32- or 64-bit) images.*

1. **Open vases.jpg from your WIP>MOAH folder.**

2. **Choose Image>Adjustments>Exposure and make sure Preview is checked.**

3. **Choose the White Point eyedropper in the dialog box, and then click the white area on the edge of the center vase.**

The eyedroppers in the Exposure dialog box adjust the image's luminance (or the degree of lightness, from white to black). By adjusting the luminance only, you can change the lightness of the image without affecting the color.

- Clicking with the Black Point eyedropper shifts the point you click to black (0 luminance).
- Clicking with the White Point eyedropper shifts the point you click to white (100 luminance).
- Clicking with the Gray Point eyedropper shifts the point you click to gray (50 luminance).

Click here with the White Point eyedropper to define the white area of the image.

Clicking with the White Point eyedropper changes the Exposure setting.

4. **Drag the Gamma Correction slider left to extend the midtone range, which increases contrast and brings out detail in the image. (We used a setting of 1.20.)**

The Gamma slider adjusts the image midtones. Dragging the slider left lightens the image, improving contrast and detail in the midtones and highlights. Dragging the slider right darkens the image, extending the range and increasing detail in the shadows.

Extending the Gamma Correction value into the shadow range brings out more detail in the midtones.

5. **Click the Offset slider and drag very slightly left to add detail back into the midtones and shadows.**

The Offset slider lightens (dragged to the right) or darkens (dragged to the left) the shadows and midtones of the image. The white point (highlight) remains unaffected, but all other pixels are affected.

Decreasing the Offset value adds detail back into the shadows.

6. **Click OK to finalize the adjustment.**

7. **Save the file as a native Photoshop file named `vases-fixed.psd` in your WIP>MOAH folder.**

8. **Close the file and continue to the next stage of the project.**

Stage 3 Correcting Color Problems

You can't accurately reproduce color without a basic understanding of color theory, so we present a very basic introduction in this project. Be aware that there are entire, weighty books written about color science; we're providing the condensed version of what you absolutely must know to work effectively with files in any color mode.

Before starting to color-correct an image, you should understand how different colors interact with one another. There are two primary color models — RGB and CMYK — used to output digital images. (Other models such as LAB and HSB have their own purposes in color conversion and correction, but they are not typically output models.)

Additive vs. Subtractive Color

The most important thing to remember about color theory is that color is light, and light is color. You can easily prove this by walking through your house at midnight; you will notice that what little you can see appears as dark shadows. Without light, you can't see — and without light, there is no color.

The **additive color** model (RGB) is based on the idea that all colors can be reproduced by combining pure red, green, and blue light in varying intensities. These three colors are considered the **additive primaries**. Combining any two additive primaries at full strength produces one of the **additive secondaries** — red and blue light combine to produce magenta, red and green combine to produce yellow, and blue and green combine to produce cyan. Although usually considered a "color," black is the absence of light (and, therefore, of color). White is the sum of all colors, produced when all three additive primaries are combined at full strength.

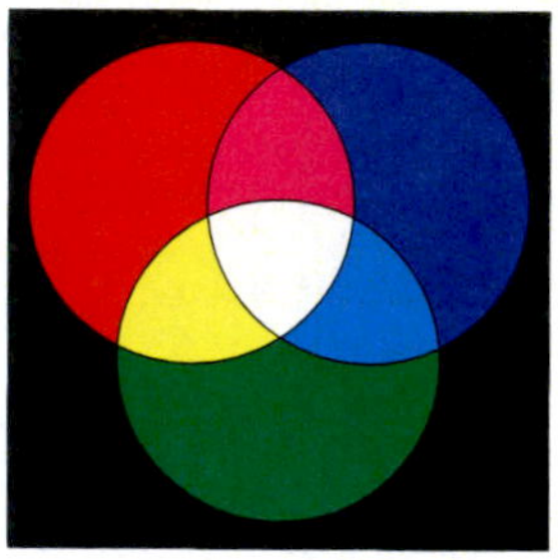

Additive color model

Subtractive color model

Reproducing color on paper requires **subtractive color theory**, which is essentially the inverse of additive color. Instead of adding red, green, and blue light to create the range of colors, subtractive color begins with a white surface that reflects red, green, and blue light at equal and full strength. To reflect (reproduce) a specific color, you add pigments that subtract or absorb only certain wavelengths from the white light. To reflect only red, for example, the surface must subtract (or absorb) the green and blue light.

Remember that the additive primary colors (red, green, and blue) combine to create the additive secondaries (cyan, magenta, and yellow). Those additive secondaries are also called the **subtractive primaries**, because each subtracts one-third of the light spectrum and reflects the other two-thirds:

- Cyan absorbs red light, reflecting only blue and green light.
- Magenta absorbs green light, reflecting only red and blue light.
- Yellow absorbs blue light, reflecting only red and green light.

> *Note:*
>
> *Additive color theory is practically applied when a reproduction method uses light to reproduce color. A computer monitor is black when turned off. When the power is turned on, light in the monitor illuminates at different intensities to create the range of colors you see.*

A combination of two subtractive primaries, then, absorbs two-thirds of the light spectrum and reflects only one-third. As an example, a combination of yellow and magenta absorbs both blue and green light, reflecting only red.

Color printing is a practical application of subtractive color theory. The pigments in the cyan, magenta, yellow, and black (CMYK) inks are combined to absorb different wavelengths of light. By combining different amounts of the subtractive primaries, it's possible to produce a large range (or gamut) of colors.

Understanding Color Terms

Many vague and technical-sounding terms are mentioned when discussing color. Is hue the same as color? The same as value? As tone? What's the difference between lightness and brightness? What is chroma? And where does saturation fit in?

This problem has resulted in several attempts to normalize color communication. A number of systems have been developed to define color according to specific criteria, including Hue, Saturation, and Brightness (HSB); Hue, Saturation, and Lightness (HSL); Hue, Saturation, and Value (HSV); and Lightness, Chroma, and Hue (LCH). Each of these models or systems plots color on a three-dimensional diagram, based on the elements of human color perception — hue, colorfulness, and brightness.

Hue is what most people think of as color — red, green, purple, and so on. Hue is defined according to a color's position on a color wheel, beginning from red (0°) and traveling counterclockwise around the wheel.

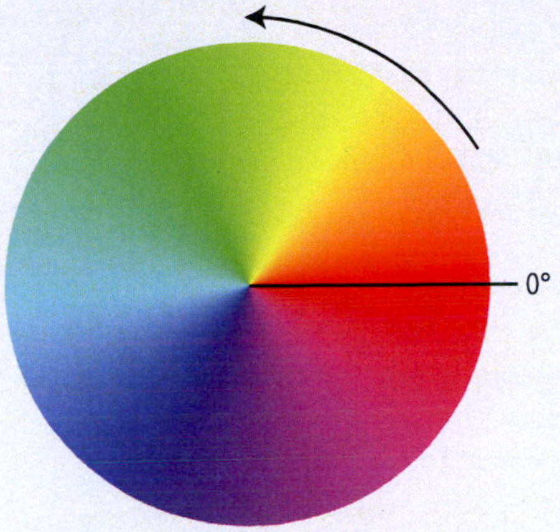

Saturation (also called "intensity") refers to the color's difference from neutral gray. Highly saturated colors are more vivid than those with low saturation. Saturation is plotted from the center of the color wheel. Color at the center is neutral gray and has a saturation value of 0; color at the edge of the wheel is the most intense value of the corresponding hue and has a saturation value of 100.

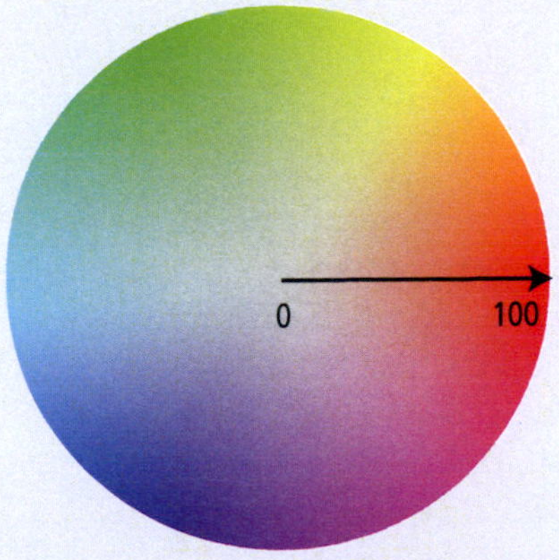

If you bisect the color wheel with a straight line, the line creates a saturation axis for two complementary colors. A color is dulled by the introduction of its complement. Red, for example, is neutralized by the addition of cyan (blue and green). Near the center of the axis, the result is neutral gray.

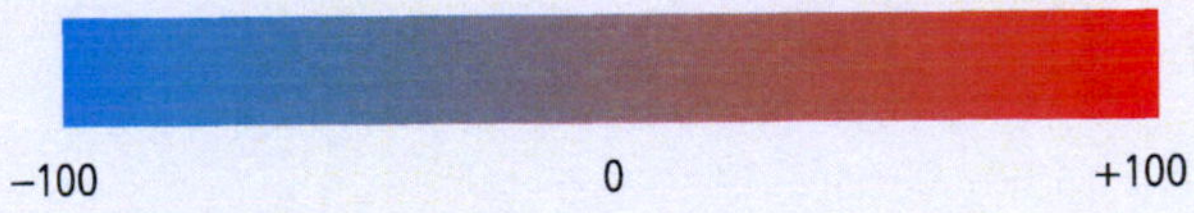

Chroma is similar to saturation, but chroma factors in a reference white. In any viewing situation, colors appear less vivid as the light source dims. The process of chromatic adaptation, however, allows the human visual system to adjust to changes in light and still differentiate colors according to the relative saturation.

Brightness is the amount of light reflected off an object. As an element of color reproduction, brightness is typically judged by comparing the color to the lightest nearby object (such as an unprinted area of white paper).

Lightness is the amount of white or black added to the pure color. Lightness (also called "luminance" or "value") is the relative brightness based purely on the black-white value of a color. A lightness value of 0 means there is no addition of white or black. Lightness of +100 is pure white; lightness of –100 is pure black.

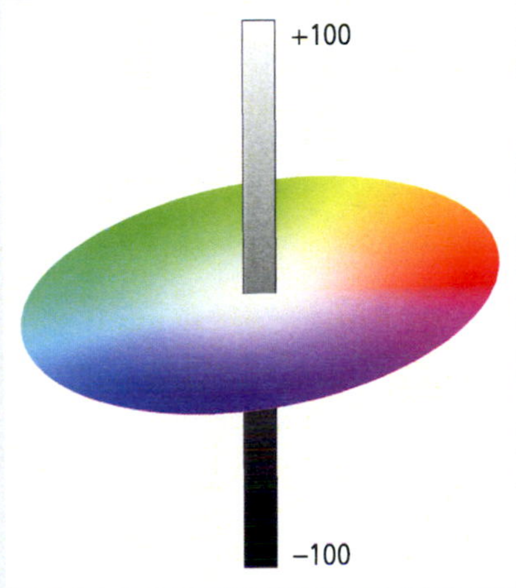

All hues are affected equally by changes in lightness.

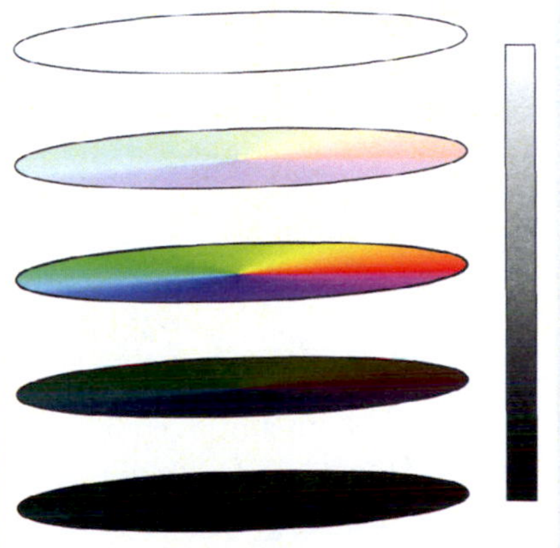

Although the RGB and CMYK models handle color in different ways, these two color models are definitely linked. RGB colors are directly inverse (opposite) to CMY colors, referring to the position of each color on a color wheel. The relationship between primary colors is the basis for all color correction.

Referencing a basic color wheel can help you understand how RGB colors relate to CMY colors. If you center an equilateral triangle over the color wheel, the points of the triangle touch either the RGB primaries or the CMY primaries. Adding together two points of the triangle results in the color between the two points. Red and blue combine to form magenta, yellow and cyan combine to form green, and so on.

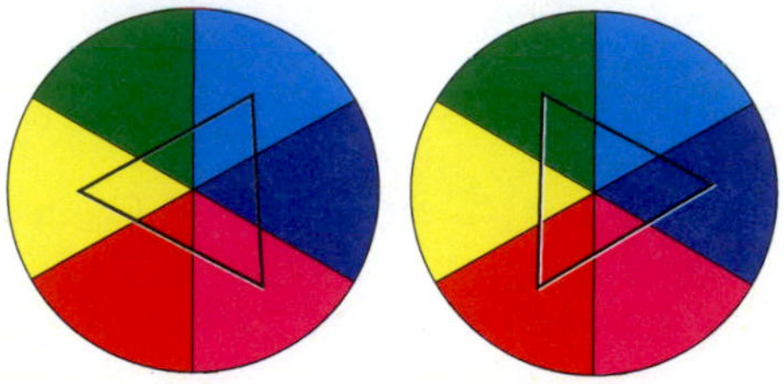

Opposite colors on the color wheel are called **color complements**. Using subtractive color theory, a color's complement absorbs or subtracts that color from visible white light. For example, cyan is opposite red on the color wheel; cyan absorbs red light and reflects green and blue. If you know green and blue light combine to create cyan, you can begin to understand how the two theories are related.

How does all this apply to color correction?

If you want to add a specific color to an image, you have three options: add the color, add equal parts of its constituent colors, or remove some of its complement color. For example, to add red, you can add red, add yellow and magenta, or remove cyan. Conversely, this means that to remove a color from an image, you can remove the color itself, remove equal parts of its constituents, or add its complement. To remove cyan, for example, you can remove cyan, remove blue and green, or add red.

Make sure you understand the relationships between complementary colors:

- To add red, add yellow and magenta or remove cyan.
- To add blue, add cyan and magenta or remove yellow.
- To add green, add cyan and yellow or remove magenta.
- To remove cyan, remove blue and green or add red.
- To remove yellow, remove green and red or add blue.
- To remove magenta, remove blue and red or add green.

Understanding Gray Balance

Understanding the concept of neutral gray is also fundamental to effective color correction. Once you correct the contrast (tonal range) of an image, many of the remaining problems can be at least partially corrected by correcting the **gray balance**, or the component elements of neutral grays.

In the RGB color model, equal parts of red, green, and blue light combine to create a shade of gray that is equal to the percentage of each component — R=0 G=0 B=0 creates pure black, while R=255 G=255 B=255 creates pure white. To correct an image in RGB mode, you should evaluate and correct the neutral grays so that they contain equal percentages of the three primary colors.

Using the CMYK color model, equal percentages of cyan, magenta, and yellow theoretically combine to produce an equal shade of gray — C=0 M=0 Y=0 creates pure white, while C=100 M=100 Y=100 theoretically creates pure black. In practice, however, the impurities of ink pigments — specifically cyan — do not live up to this theory. When you print an area of equal parts cyan, magenta, and yellow, the result is a muddy brown because the cyan pigments are impure. To compensate for the impurities of cyan, neutral grays must be adjusted to contain equal parts of magenta and yellow, and a slightly higher percentage of cyan.

Note:

Because white is a combination of all colors of light, white paper should theoretically reflect equal percentages of all light wavelengths. However, different papers absorb or reflect varying percentages of some wavelengths, thus defining the paper's apparent color. The paper's color affects the appearance of inks printed on that paper.

Note:

It might seem easiest to simply add or subtract the color in question, but a better result might be achieved by adding one color and subtracting another. For example, if an image needs less blue, simply removing cyan can cause reds to appear pink or cyan to appear green. Adding magenta and yellow to balance the existing cyan creates a better result than simply removing cyan.

Note:

An important point to remember is that any color correction requires compromise. If you add or remove a color to correct a certain area, you also affect other areas of the image.

Correct Color Cast with the Color Balance Adjustment

Color cast is the result of improper gray balance, when one channel is significantly stronger or weaker than the others. An image with improper gray balance has an overall predominance of one color, which is most visible in the highlight areas. The image that you will correct in this exercise has a strong yellow cast that needs to be removed.

1. **Open the file bust.jpg from your WIP>MOAH folder.**
2. **Display the Info panel (Window>Info).**
3. **If you don't see both RGB and CMYK color modes in the Info panel, choose Panel Options in the Info panel Options menu. In the resulting dialog box, choose Actual Color for the First Color Readout and CMYK Color for the Second Color Readout, then click OK.**

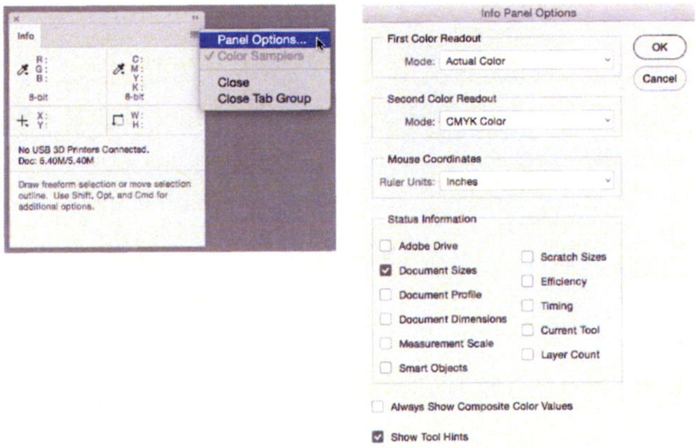

Note:

This exercise relies purely on numbers to correct gray balance. To see an accurate preview of image color on screen, you should calibrate your monitor and create a monitor profile that you can load into Photoshop.

4. **Choose the Color Sampler tool (nested under the Eyedropper tool).**
5. **In the Options bar, choose 3 by 3 Average in the Sample Size menu.**

   Instead of correcting based on individual pixel values, you can average a group of contiguous pixels as the sample value. Doing so prevents accidentally correcting an image based on a single anomalous pixel (a dust spot, for example).

Note:

The Color Sampler tool can place up to ten sample points per image.

6. **Click the cursor on the bust's right shoulder to place a color sample.**
7. **Click to add a second sample point to bust's left shoulder.**

   As you can see in the Info panel, the two samples show a significantly lower percentage of blue, which leads to a strong yellow color cast.

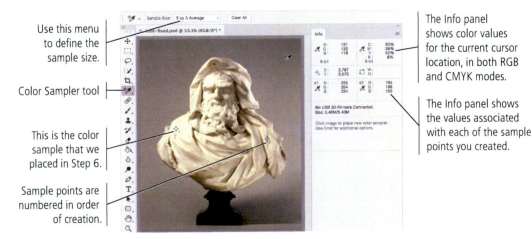

8. **Choose Image>Adjustments>Color Balance.**

Color Balance is a basic correction tool that can effectively remove overall color cast. The Color Balance dialog box presents a separate slider for each pair of complementary colors. You can adjust the highlights, shadows, or midtones of an image by selecting the appropriate radio button; the Preserve Luminosity check box ensures that only the colors shift, leaving the tonal balance of the image unchanged.

9. **Click the Highlights radio button in the Tone Balance section at the bottom of the Color Balance dialog box.**

10. **Drag the Yellow/Blue slider right until the right field shows +25.**

Remember, adding a color's complement is one method for neutralizing that color. Increasing blue in the highlight areas neutralizes the yellow color cast.

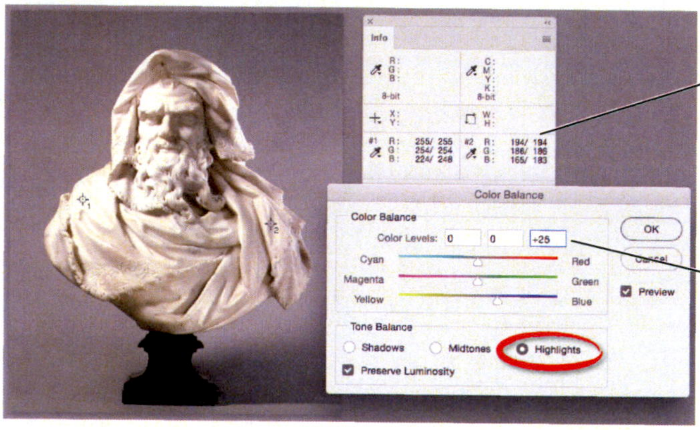

The values after the "/" show the result of the changes; these will become the actual sample values if you click OK.

These fields correspond to the three color sliders. The right field shows the Yellow/Blue adjustment.

11. **Click the Midtones radio button in the Tone Balance section at the bottom of the Color Balance dialog box.**

The focus of this image — the bust — is primarily occupies the highlight and midtone ranges. You are adjusting the color balance in both ranges to minimize the yellow cast.

12. **Drag the Yellow/Blue slider right until the right field shows +10.**

Remember, adding a color's complement is one method for neutralizing that color. Increasing blue in the midtone areas further neutralizes the yellow color cast.

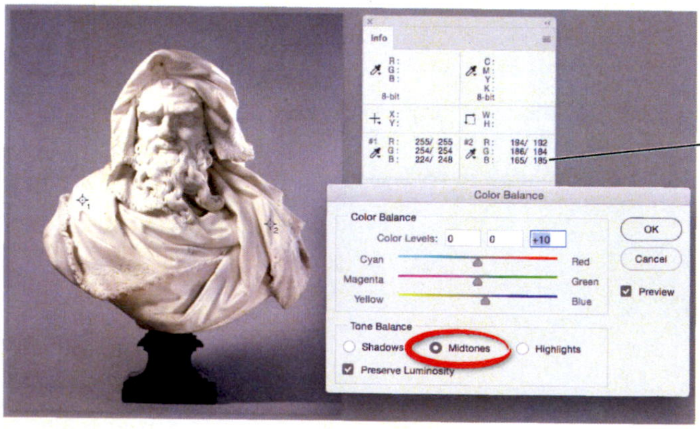

Changing the color balance brings the three values much closer to equal, removing the color cast.

13. **Click OK to apply the adjustment.**

> *Note:*
>
> *To delete an existing sample point, make the Color Sampler tool active, press Option/Alt, and click a point when the cursor icon changes to a pair of scissors.*

14. **Save the file in your WIP>MOAH folder as a native Photoshop file named bust-fixed.psd.**

15. **Close the file and continue to the next exercise.**

Correct Gray Balance with Curves

The Curves adjustment is the most powerful color-correction tool in Photoshop. If you understand the ideas behind curves, you can use this tool to remove color cast, enhance overall contrast, and even modify color values in individual channels.

The diagram in the Curves dialog box is the heart of the Curves adjustment. When you open the Curves dialog box, a straight diagonal line in the graph represents the existing color in the image.

The horizontal axis represents the input color value, and the vertical axis represents the output color value. The upper-right point is the maximum value for that color mode (255 for RGB images and 100 for CMYK images). The bottom-left corner of the curves grid is the zero point.

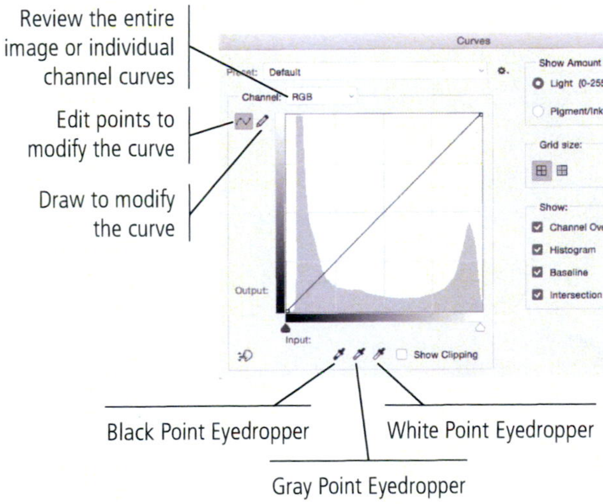

The color mode of the image determines the direction of the input and output scales. In both CMYK and RGB, 0 means "none of that color." However, remember the difference between the two different color modes:

- The additive RGB color model starts at black and adds values of each channel to produce different colors, so 0, 0, 0 in RGB equals black.
- The subtractive CMYK model starts with white (paper) and adds percentages of each ink (channel) to produce different colors, so 0, 0, 0, 0 in CMYK equals white.

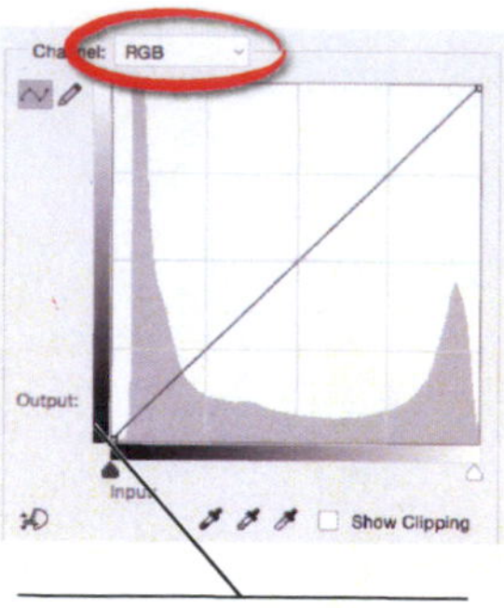

In RGB, the zero point represents the black point or image shadows.

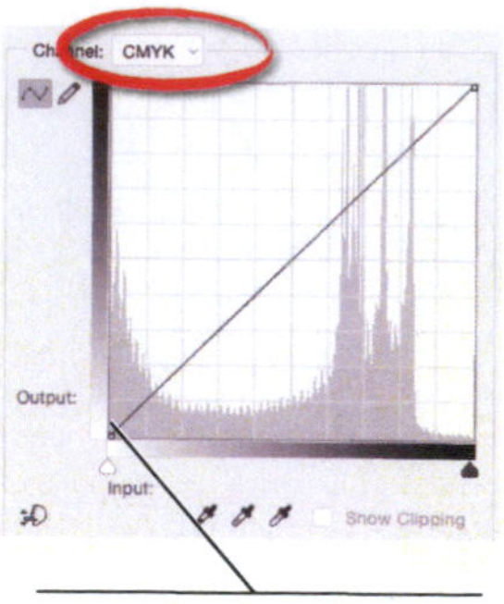

In CMYK images, the zero point represents the white point or image highlights.

Every curve is automatically anchored by a black point and a white point. (For RGB, the black point is at the bottom left and the white point is at the top right.) You can add points along the curve by simply clicking the curve. You can also move any point on the curve by clicking and dragging.

When you move points on the curve of an image (whether for the whole image or for an individual channel), you are telling Photoshop to, "Map every pixel that was [this] input value to [that] output value." In other words, using the following image as an example, a pixel that was 128 (the input value) will now be 120 (the output value). Because curves are just that — curves, and not individual points — adjusting one point on a curve changes the shape of the curve as necessary.

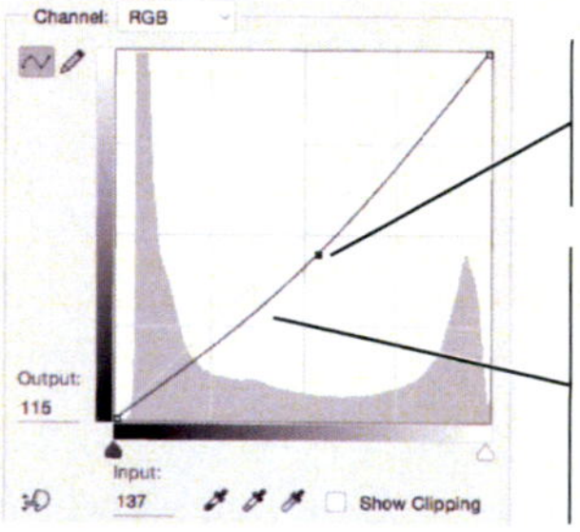

This point changes the input value of 137 to an output value of 115.

On either side of the adjusted point, the curve is adjusted to smoothly meet the other points on the curve (in this case, the black and white points).

Adjusting Curves On-Screen

PHOTOSHOP FOUNDATIONS

The On-Image Adjustment tool in the Curves dialog box allows you to make curve adjustments by interacting directly with the image (behind the dialog box).

When the On-Image Adjustment tool is active, clicking in the image places a point on the curve based on the pixel data where you clicked; you can then drag up or down within the image area to move that point of the curve (in other words, to change the output value of the selected input value).

You can add 14 points on a curve, and delete points by pressing Command/Control-delete.

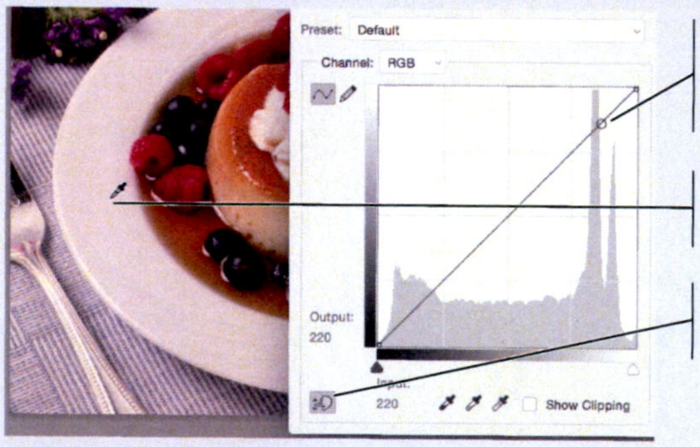

The open circle shows the curve point related to the cursor.

On-Image Adjustment tool cursor

The On-Image Adjustment tool is active.

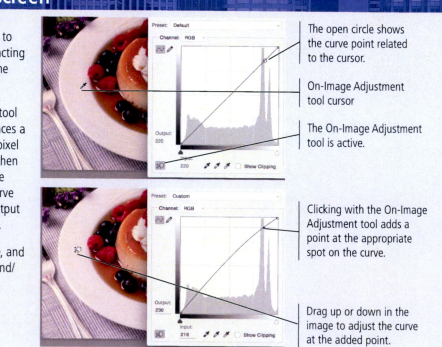

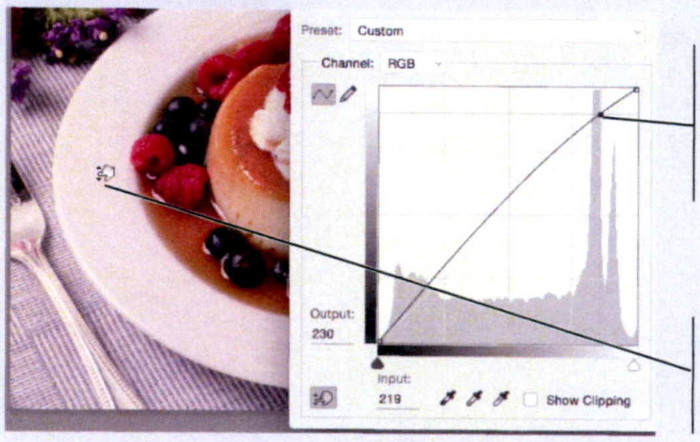

Clicking with the On-Image Adjustment tool adds a point at the appropriate spot on the curve.

Drag up or down in the image to adjust the curve at the added point.

1. **Open the file plaque.jpg from the WIP>MOAH folder.**

2. **Using the Color Sampler tool, place a sample point on the empty area outside the plaque.**

   Recognizable "neutral" areas — such as the surrounding area in this image — are the best places to look for global color problems; fixing these will also fix many problem areas that you might not immediately recognize.

   This image has a strong red cast that needs to be neutralized. You can correct cast by removing the cast color or adjusting the other two primaries; the goal is equal (or nearly equal) parts of red, green, and blue in the neutral areas.

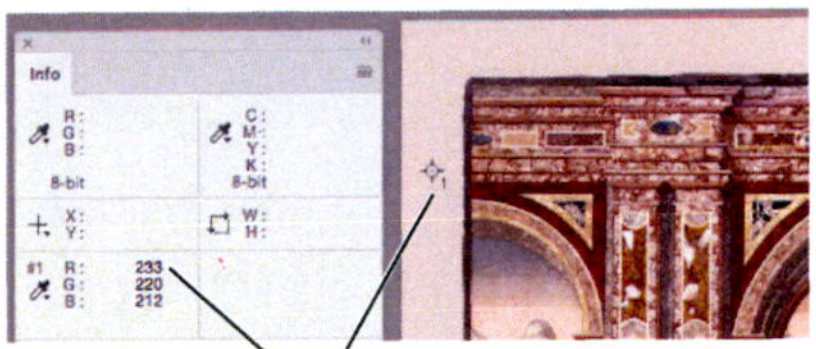

The sample shows a strong red cast in what should be a neutral area.

   In the Info panel, the sample values show that the red channel has a value of 233, the green channel has a value of 220, and the blue channel has a value of 212. To fix the cast in this image, you will use the middle of these values (the green channel) as the target and adjust the other two curves.

Note:

Your sample might be in a different place, showing slightly different values. Use the values you see on your screen, rather than the numbers in our screen shots, to complete the following steps.

3. **Choose Image>Adjustments>Curves and make sure the Preview option is checked in the Curves dialog box.**

4. **Choose Red in the Channel menu to display the curve for only the Red channel, and then click the line on the graph to place a point near the three-quarter grid intersection.**

   After you adjust a curve (including adding the point as in this step) the Info panel shows two values for the placed color sample. Numbers before the slash are the original values. Numbers after the slash are the values that result from changes in the Curves dialog box.

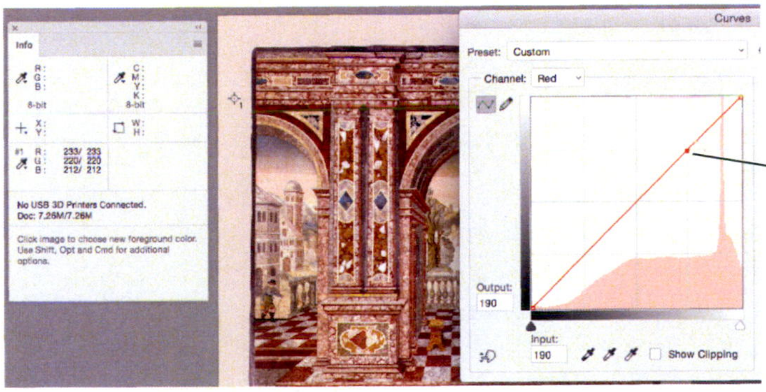

Click here to add a point to the curve.

5. **With the new point selected on the curve, type the original Red value in the Input field (ours is 233).**

6. **Type the target value in the Output field (ours is the Green value of 220).**

   In the Info panel, the number after the slash shows that the Red value for this sample will be equal to the Green value when you click OK.

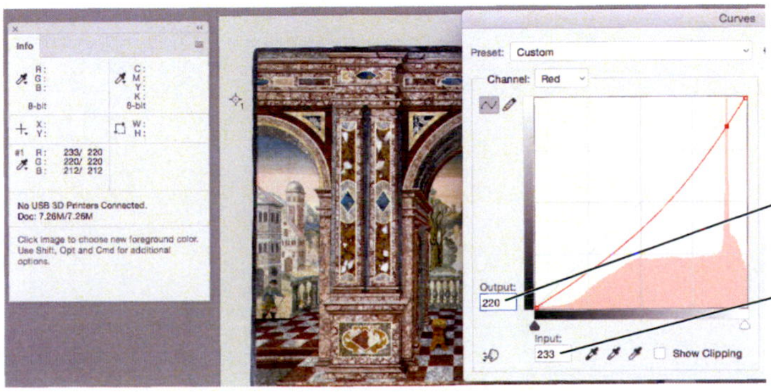

Type the target value in this field.

Type the original Red value in this field.

7. **In the Channel menu, choose the other channel that you need to adjust based on your sample values (ours is Blue). Add a point to the curve, and then adjust the input value to match your target output value (the original Green value, in our example).**

   Using our sample point, we adjusted the Input value of 212 to an Output value of 220.

   You can add the point anywhere along the curve; when you change the Input and Output values, the point automatically moves to that location along the curve.

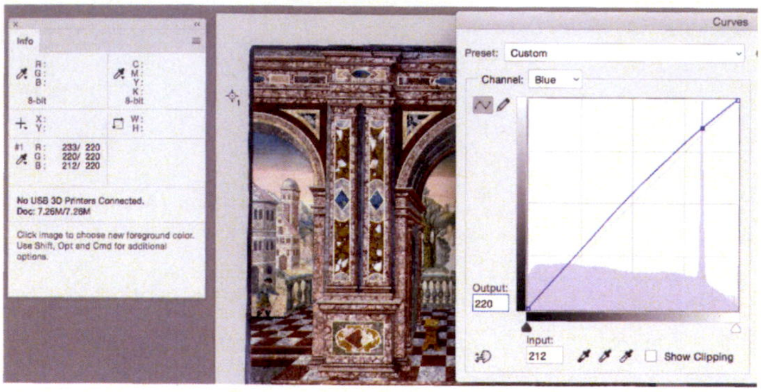

8. **Click OK to apply the changes and close the Curves dialog box.**

   You can see how simply correcting gray balance has a significant impact on the image:

9. **Save the file in your WIP>MOAH folder as a native Photoshop file named plaque-fixed.psd.**

10. **Close the file and continue to the next exercise.**

Correct Contrast with Curves

Remember, contrast is essentially the difference between the values in an image. By adjusting the points on the curve, you increase the tonal range between those points — which means you also increase the contrast in that same range.

In the following image, Point A has an Input value of 167 and an Output value of 182. Point B has an Input value of 87 and an Output value of 62. Mathematically:

- Original tonal range (Input values): 167 to 87 = 80 available tones
- New tonal range (Output values): 182 to 62 = 120 available tones

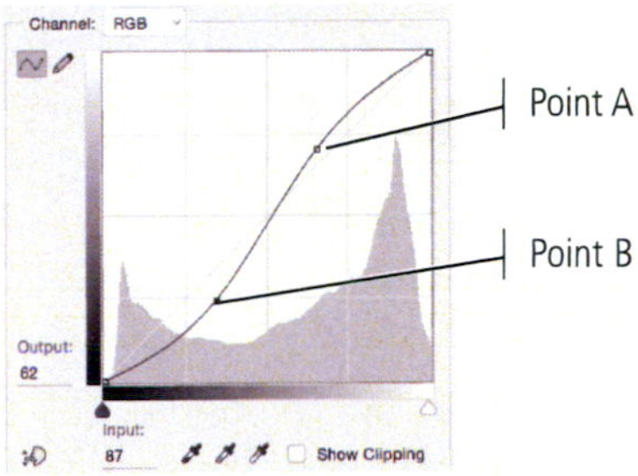

Making these two curve adjustments significantly increases the tonal range available for the image's midtones, which means the contrast in the midtones is also significantly increased. A steeper curve indicates increased tonal range and increased contrast. Notice, however, that the curves before Point B and after Point A are much shallower than the original curves, which means this change also significantly reduces the contrast in the shadow and highlight areas.

Points to Remember about Curves

Curves are very powerful tools, and they can be intimidating. To simplify the process and make it less daunting, keep these points in mind:

- Aim for neutral grays.
- You can adjust the curve for an entire image, or you can adjust the individual curves for each channel of the image.
- The horizontal tone scale shows the Input value, and the vertical tone scale shows the Output value.
- Changes made to one area of a curve affect all other areas of the image.
- The steeper the curve, the greater the contrast.
- Increasing contrast in one area inherently decreases contrast in other areas.

1. **Open the file tile.jpg from the WIP>MOAH folder.**

2. **Choose Image>Adjustments>Curves and make sure Preview is checked.**

3. **Activate the Show Clipping option, click the white point on the top-right corner of the graph, and then drag left until some pixels start to appear in the image (behind the dialog box).**

   We dragged the Input White point just past the point where the histogram shows the lightest highlights in the image. (You performed this same action in the Levels dialog box when you adjusted the Input Highlight slider.) The Input and Output fields show that any pixels with an Input value of 220 will be output as 255; in other words, anything with an Input value higher than 220 will be clipped to solid white.

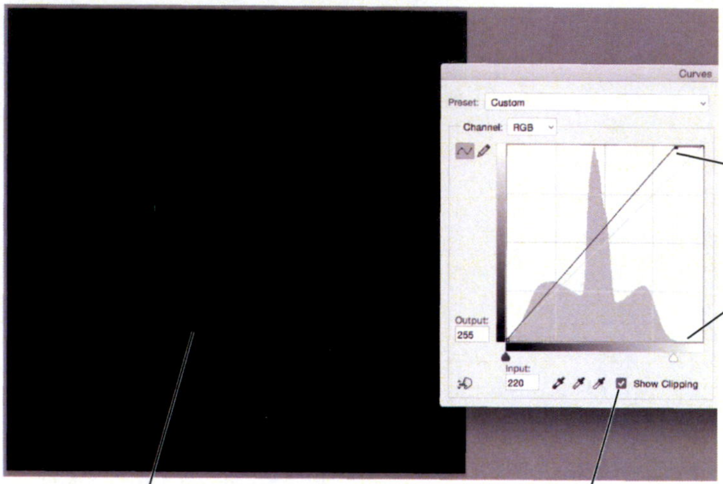

White point

The empty area to the right of the histogram shows that the image does not use the entire available tonal range.

These small specks identify the lightest areas that will be clipped by the adjustment.

Show Clipping is active.

4. **Turn off the Show Clipping option so you can see the actual image behind the dialog box.**

   Even this small change improved the image, but the midtones need some additional contrast. To accomplish that change, you need to steepen the curve in the middle of the graph.

5. **Click the curve to create a point at the quartertone gridline and drag it slightly to the right.**

   We adjusted the curve point from an Input value of 75 to an Output value of 65.

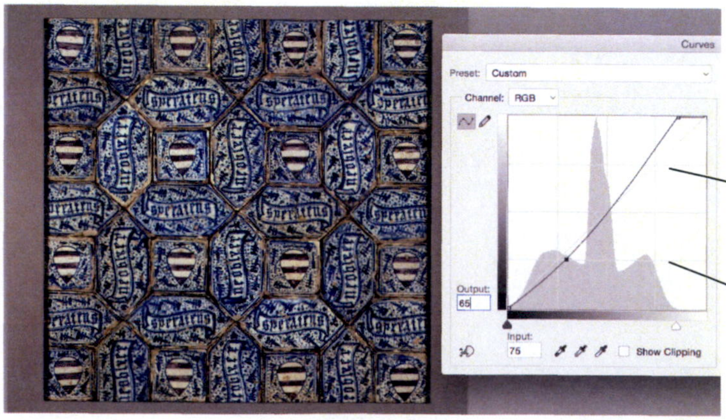

Three-quartertone gridlines

Quartertone gridlines

6. **Click the curve at the three-quartertone gridline and drag the point to the left.**

   We adjusted the Input value of 165 to an Output value of 190.

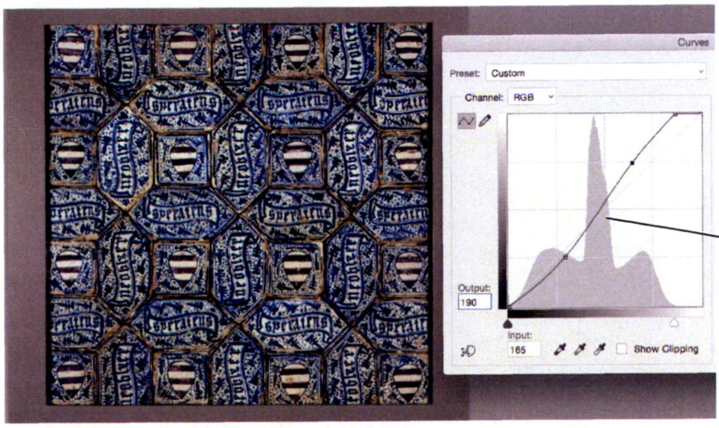

The adjusted points steepen the curve, increasing contrast between the two points.

Understanding Curve Display Options

Options on the right side of the dialog box allow you to control what is visible in the graph.

The Show Amount Of radio buttons reverse the input and output tone scales. Light is the default setting for RGB images; Pigment/Ink % is the default setting for CMYK images.

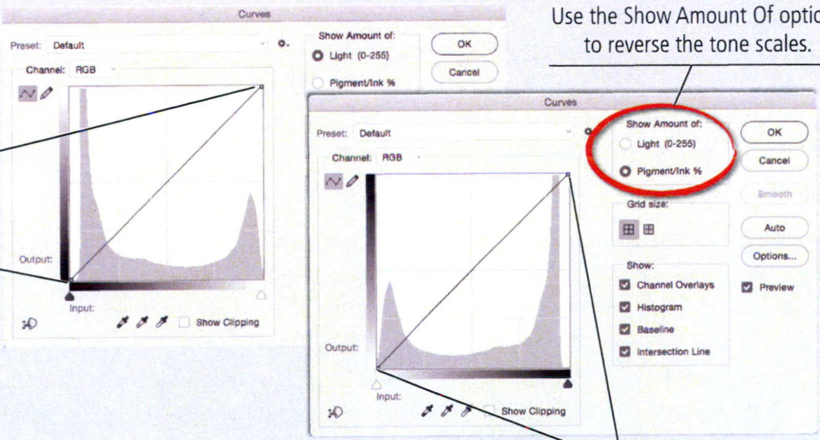

Use the Show Amount Of options to reverse the tone scales.

By default, the lightest point for an RGB image is in the top right.

The darkest point for an RGB image is in the bottom left.

For an RGB image, the lightest point moves to the bottom left and the darkest point moves to the top right.

The Show options determine what is visible in the actual graph:

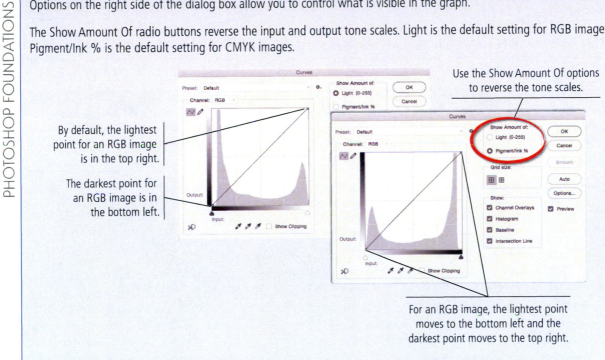

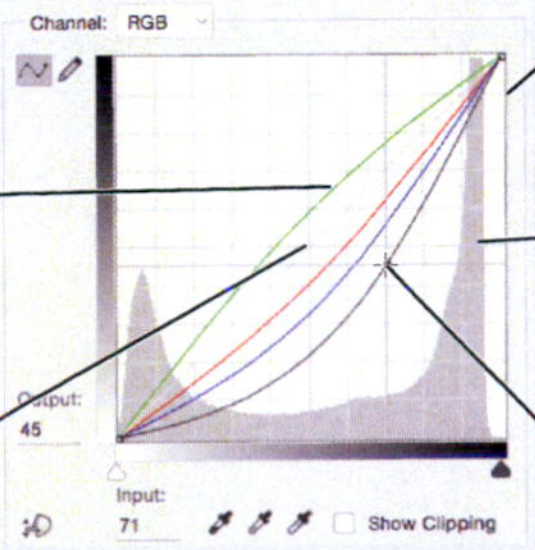

When the Channel Overlays option is checked, each channel is represented on the graph by a separate line.

When the Baseline option is active, the original curve is represented by a gray line.

Use the Grid Size options to show the grid in quartertone or 10% increments.

When the Histogram option is active, the image's tonal range is represented behind the graph.

When the Intersection Line option is active, crosshairs appear when you drag a point in the graph, which can help you more precisely adjust curve points.

7. **Click OK to apply the changes and close the dialog box.**

   Adjusting the contrast with curves improved the detail in the image and enhanced the overall image color.

8. **Save the file in your WIP>MOAH folder as a native Photoshop file named tile-fixed.psd.**

9. **Close the file and continue to the next stage of the project.**

Understanding Automatic Color Correction

PHOTOSHOP FOUNDATIONS

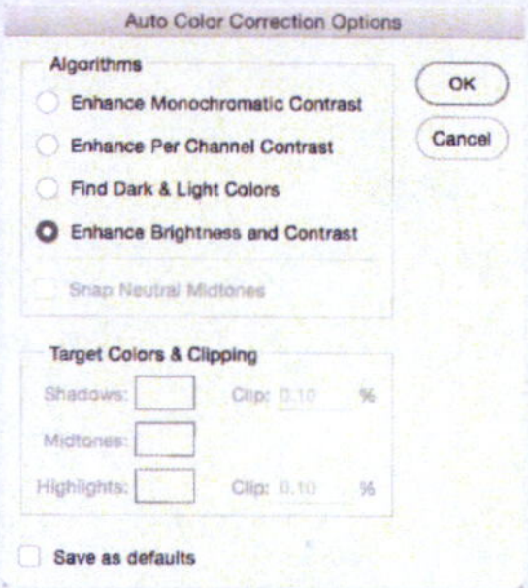

Clicking Options in the right side of the Curves dialog box opens the Auto Color Correction Options dialog box. (These settings apply if you click Auto in the Levels or Curves dialog box.)

The Algorithms options determine how Photoshop will adjust an image's tonal range:

- **Enhance Monochromatic Contrast** clips all channels identically, preserving overall color while making highlights appear lighter and shadows darker. This is effectively the same as choosing Image>Adjustments>Auto Contrast.
- **Enhance Per Channel Contrast** maximizes the tonal range in each channel by moving the darkest shadow to 0 (or 100 for CMYK images) and the lightest highlight to 255 (or 0 for CMYK images). The overall color relationship is not maintained, which might result in color cast in the adjusted image. This is effectively the same as Image>Adjustments>Auto Tone.
- **Find Dark & Light Colors** uses the average lightest and darkest pixels to maximize contrast and minimize clipping. When selected, you can also activate **Snap Neutral Midtones**; this finds an average neutral color, then adjusts midtone (gamma) values to make that color neutral. This is effectively the same as Image>Adjustments>Auto Color.
- **Enhance Brightness and Contrast** allows Photoshop to use content-aware monochromatic adjustments to produce smoother results across the entire tonal range.

The **Target Colors & Clipping** options are available when one of the first three algorithms is selected. You can define the target shadow, midtone, and highlight values by clicking the appropriate color swatch. The Clip fields determine how much of the darkest shadow and lightest highlight will be clipped. For example, a Shadow Clip setting of 1% means Photoshop will ignore the first 1% of the darkest pixels when adjusting the image.

The Match Color Adjustment

The Match Color adjustment (Image>Adjustments>Match Color) allows you to match colors between multiple RGB images, layers, or selections. In the Match Color dialog box, the Target shows the image, layer, or selection you are modifying. The changes are based on values from the source image and layer selected in the Image Statistics area. You can change the luminance or color intensity of the target image, fade the adjustment, and neutralize color cast caused by the adjustment.

The Destination Image Target is the active image (and selected layer, if applicable) when you open the dialog box. If the target image has an active selection area, you can check the Ignore Selection... option to apply the change to the entire target image instead of the selected area only.

- The **Luminance** slider affects the brightness in the target image; higher values lighten the image.
- The **Color Intensity** slider adjusts the color saturation in the target image; higher values increase the color saturation.
- The **Fade** slider changes the amount of adjustment applied to the target image; higher values (i.e., more fade) reduce the amount of the adjustment.
- The **Neutralize** check box automatically removes color cast in the target image.

In the Image Statistics section of the dialog box, choose the source image and layer to which the target will be matched. You can use the two check boxes to apply changes based on the selected area only (if the target or source image has an active selection area).

Stage 4 Preparing Images for Print

You might have noticed that all the images for this project are in the RGB color mode. Printing, however, relies on the CMYK mode to output color images.

Although a full discussion of color science and management can be extremely complex, and is beyond the needs of most graphic designers, applying color management in Photoshop is more intimidating than difficult. We believe this foundational information on color management will make you a more effective and practically grounded designer.

Understanding Gamut

Different color models have different ranges or **gamuts** of possible colors. The RGB model has the largest gamut of the output models. The CMYK gamut is far more limited; many of the brightest and most saturated colors that can be reproduced using light cannot be reproduced using pigmented inks.

This difference in gamut is one of the biggest problems graphic designers face when working with color images. Digital image-capture devices (including scanners and digital cameras) work in the RGB space, which, with its larger gamut, can more closely mirror the range of colors in the original scene. Printing, however, requires images to first be converted or **separated** into the CMYK color space.

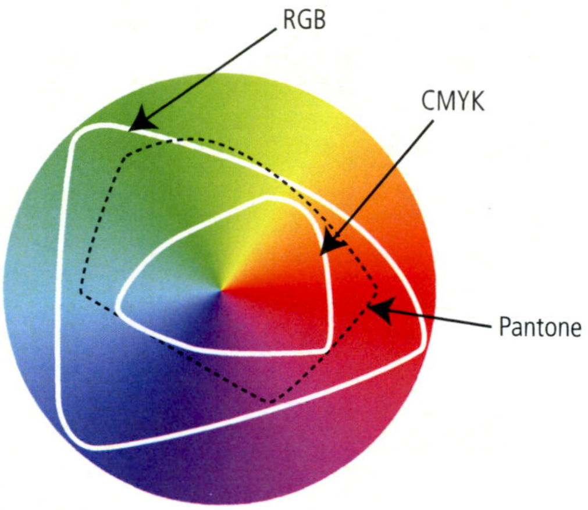

The usual goal in color reproduction is to achieve a color appearance equivalent to the original. Depending on the image, at least some colors in the RGB color model likely cannot be reproduced in the more limited gamut of the CMYK color model. These **out-of-gamut** colors pose a challenge to faithfully reproducing the original image. If the conversion from RGB to CMYK is not carefully controlled, **color shift** can result in drastic differences between the original and printed images.

Color Management in Brief

Color management is intended to preserve color predictability and consistency as a file is moved from one color mode to another throughout the reproduction process. Color management can also eliminate ambiguity when a color is only specified by some numbers. For example, you might create a royal purple in the Photoshop Color Picker; but without color management, that same set of RGB numbers might look more lilac (or even gray) when converted to CMYK for printing. A well-tuned color-management system can translate the numbers that define a color in one space to numbers that can better represent that same color in another space.

It's important to have realistic expectations for color management, and to realize that color management isn't a replacement for a thorough knowledge of the color-reproduction process. Even at its best, color management can't fix bad scans or bad photos — all it can do is introduce consistency and predictability to a process that otherwise rarely has either.

Color management relies on **color profiles**, which are simply data sets that define the reproduction characteristics of a specific device. A profile is essentially a recipe that contains the ingredients for reproducing a specific color in a given color space. The color recipes in profiles are known as **look-up tables** (LUTs), which are essentially cross-reference systems for finding matching color values in different color spaces.

Note:

Color shift can also result when converting from one type of CMYK to another, or (though less likely) from one version of RGB to another. Whatever models are being used, color management gives you better control over the conversion process.

Source profiles are the profiles of the devices (scanner, camera, or monitor in the case of original digital artwork) used to capture or generate the image. **Destination profiles** are the profiles of output devices used in the process. Most professional-level devices come with profiles you can install when you install the hardware; a number of generic and industry-specific destination profiles are also built into Photoshop.

LAB (or L*a*b*, or CIELAB) is a theoretical color space that represents the full visible spectrum. This device-independent color space can represent any possible color. By moving device-dependent RGB and CMYK colors into LAB as an intermediary space, you can convert color from any one space to any other space.

Note:

Color profiles are sometimes also called "ICC profiles," named after the International Color Consortium (ICC), which developed the standard for creating color profiles.

The **Color Management Module** (CMM) is the engine that drives color conversions via the LUT numbers. The engine doesn't do much other than look up numbers and cross-reference them to another set of numbers. The mechanics of color-managed conversions are quite simple. Regardless of the specific input and output spaces in use, the same basic process is followed for every pixel:

1. The CMM looks up the color values of a pixel in the input-space profile to find a matching set of LAB values.
2. The CMM looks up the LAB values in the output-space profile to find the matching set of values that will display the color of that pixel most accurately.

Color Management in Theory and Practice

PHOTOSHOP FOUNDATIONS

RGB and CMYK are very different entities. The two color models have distinct capabilities, advantages, and limitations. There is no way to exactly reproduce RGB color using the CMYK gamut because many of the colors in the RGB gamut are simply too bright or too saturated. Rather than claiming to produce an exact (impossible) match from your monitor to a printed page, the true goal of color management is to produce the best possible representation of the color using the gamut of the chosen output device.

A theoretically ideal color-managed workflow resembles the following:

- Image-capture devices (scanners and digital cameras) are profiled to create a look-up table that defines the device's color-capturing characteristics.
- Images are acquired using a calibrated, profiled device. The profile of the capturing device is tagged to every image captured.
- The image is opened in Photoshop and viewed on a calibrated monitor. The monitor's profile is defined in Photoshop as your working space.
- Photoshop translates the image profile to your working space profile.
- You define a destination (CMYK) profile for the calibrated output device that will be used for your final job.
- The image is converted from RGB to CMYK, based on the defined working space and destination profiles.

Notice that three of the "ideal workflow" steps mention a form of the word "calibrate." To **calibrate** something means to check and correct a device's characteristics. Calibration is an essential element in a color-managed workflow; it is fundamentally important to achieving consistent and predictable output.

You cannot check or correct the color characteristics of a device without having something to compare the device against. To calibrate a device, a known target — usually a sequence of distinct and varying color patches — is reproduced using the device. The color values of the reproduction are measured and compared to the values of the known target. Precise calibration requires adjusting the device until the reproduction matches the original.

As long as your devices are accurately calibrated to the same target values, the color acquired by your RGB scanner will exactly match the colors displayed on your RGB monitor and the colors printed by your desktop printer. Of course, most devices (especially consumer-level desktop devices that are gaining a larger market share in the commercial graphics world) are not accurately calibrated, and very few are calibrated to the same set of known target values.

Keeping in mind these ideals and realities, the true goals of color management are to:

- Compensate for variations in the different devices
- Accurately translate one color space to another
- Compensate for limitations in the output process
- Better predict the result when an image is reproduced

Understanding Color Modes

Bitmap color reproduces all pixels in the image as either black or white; there are no shades of gray.

Grayscale color reproduces all tones in the file as shades of gray. This type of image has only one channel (you were introduced to color channels in Project 1: Music CD Artwork, and will learn more in subsequent projects).

RGB creates color by combining different intensities of red, green, and blue light (collectively referred to as the "additive primaries"). Computer monitors and television sets display color in RGB, which has a **gamut** or range of more than 16.7 million different colors. An RGB file has three color channels, one for each of the additive primaries.

LAB color is device independent; the colors it describes don't depend upon the characteristics of a particular printer, monitor, or scanner. In theory, LAB bridges the gap between the various color models and devices; it is used in the background when converting images from one color space to another.

CMYK ("process") **color** is based on the absorption and reflection of light. Four process inks — cyan, magenta, yellow, and black — are used in varying combinations and percentages to produce the range of printable colors in most commercial printing. A CMYK file has four color channels, one for each subtractive primary and one for black.

Theoretically, a mixture of equal parts of cyan, magenta, and yellow would produce black. Pigments, however, are not pure, so the result of mixing these colors is a muddy brown (called **hue error**). To obtain vibrant colors (and so elements such as type can be printed cleanly), black ink is added to the three primaries. Black is represented by the letter "K" for "key color."

The problem with using RGB for print jobs is that the RGB colors eventually need to be converted to CMYK separations for a commercial printing press. Photoshop includes sophisticated tools that allow you to control this conversion.

Your client's catalog will be printed, which means the image files ultimately have to be in the CMYK color mode. In this stage of the project, you will learn how to control and correct for the conversion process from RGB to CMYK — a very common process in professional graphic design. (In a professional environment, you would actually have to convert all of the images you have used in this project; we are only working with one for the sake of illustration.)

Define Color Settings

Photoshop's color management system allows you to set up a fully managed color workflow — from input device through output device. You can use Adobe's predefined color settings or create custom settings that pertain to the equipment you use.

1. **With no file open in Photoshop, choose Edit>Color Settings.**

   The Color Settings dialog box defines default working spaces for RGB, CMYK, gray, and spot colors, as well as general color management policies.

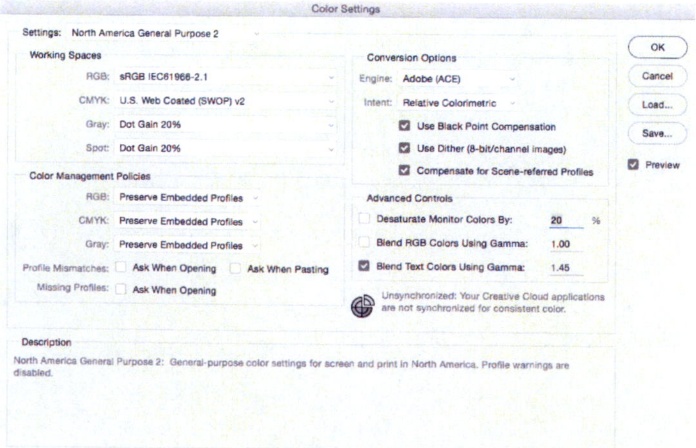

> **Note:**
>
> *Your default options might be different than what you see here, depending on what previous users have defined.*

2. Choose North America Prepress 2 in the Settings menu.

Photoshop includes four saved groups of options that are common in North America, which can be accessed in the Settings menu. You can also make your own choices and save those settings as a new preset by clicking Save, or you can import settings files created by another user by clicking Load.

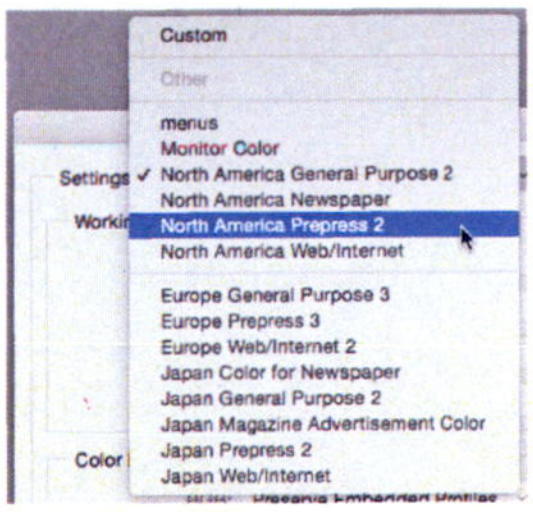

3. In the Working Spaces area, choose the RGB profile for your monitor. If your specific monitor isn't available, choose Adobe RGB (1998).

If you use a color-managed workflow, each color mode must be defined as a particular type of color space. Because there are different types of monitors, there are different types of RGB color spaces; the same is true of the other color spaces. The Working Space menus define exactly which version of each space is used to define color within that space.

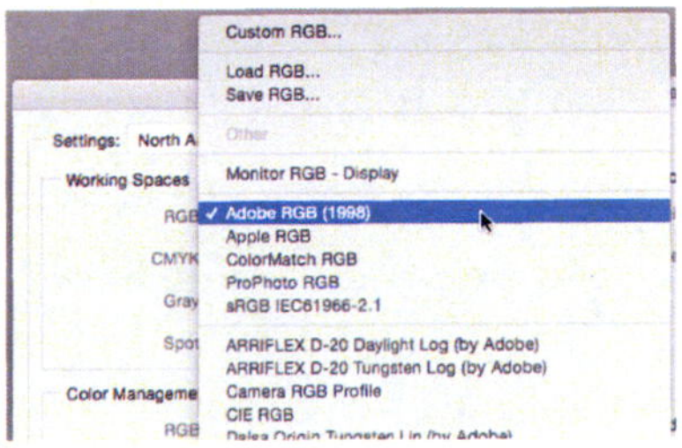

For color management to work properly, you must have accurate, device-specific profiles for every device in the workflow. However, you can use generic settings such as Adobe RGB (1998) in a "better-than-nothing" color environment — which is almost a direct contradiction to the concept of color management. We're showing you *how* to use the tools in Photoshop, but it's up to you to implement true color management by profiling your devices and using those profiles for specific jobs.

> *Note:*
>
> *In Photoshop, a* ***working space*** *is the default profile used for each of the different color modes.*

> *Note:*
>
> *When you choose a profile that isn't part of the saved settings, the Settings menu automatically changes to "Custom."*

4. In the CMYK menu, choose U.S. Sheetfed Coated v2.

There are many CMYK profiles — each different printer and press has a gamut unique to that individual device.

This is a United States industry-standard profile for a common type of printing (sheetfed printing on coated paper). In a truly color-managed workflow, you would actually use a profile for the specific printing press/paper combination being used for the job. Again, we're using the default profiles to show you how the process works.

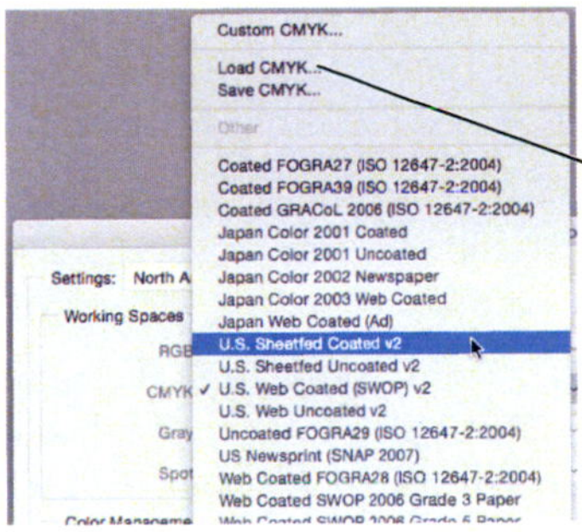

Use the Load CMYK option to access profiles that are supplied by your output provider.

> *Note:*
>
> *We assume this catalog will be printed on a sheetfed press. However, always ask your output provider what profile to use for a specific job.*

5. Leave the Gray and Spot working space menus at their default settings.

The Gray working space defines how grayscale images will translate when the images are printed. Gray working space options include:

- **Dot Gain** (of varying percentages). These options compensate for the spread of a halftone dot in a grayscale image.
- **Gray Gamma.** This option allows you to set the monitor's gamma to compensate for differences between the monitor's presentation of an image and the actual grayscale image on press.

The Spot working space is similar to the Gray working space, but you can only specify dot gain percentages (not gamma).

> *Note:*
>
> *If you convert an image's color space using the Image>Mode menu, Photoshop converts the image to the default working space for the mode you choose.*

6. **In the Color Management Policies area, make sure RGB is turned off; Preserve Embedded Profiles is selected for CMYK and Gray; and all three check boxes are selected.**

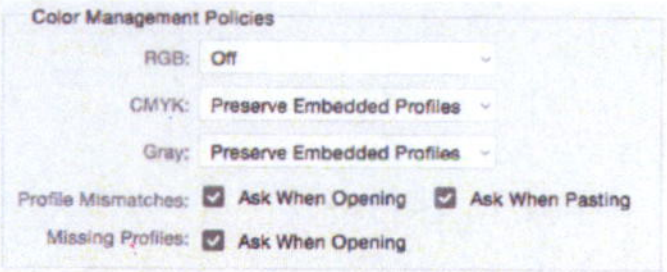

These options tell Photoshop what to do when you open an existing image. When an option here is turned off, color is not managed for that mode. If you choose Preserve Embedded Profiles, images that have a defined profile retain that profile; images with no profile use the current working space. If you choose Convert to Working Space, all images, even those with an embedded profile, are converted to the current working profile; images with no profile are assigned the current working profile.

For profile mismatches, you can display a warning when opening or pasting an image with an embedded profile that does not match the working profile. When an image doesn't have an embedded profile, you can display a warning by checking the Missing Profiles Ask When Opening option.

Note:

Web printing is done on larger presses and fed from huge rolls of paper, with the actual pages being cut off the roll only after the ink has been laid down. Although web presses are typically cheaper to operate for long print runs, they generally do not produce the same quality of color as their sheetfed counterparts.

Sheetfed presses place ink on sheets of paper that have already been cut to press-sheet size from a large roll of paper. Sheetfed presses are typically considered higher quality, with appropriately higher costs associated with the job.

7. **Review the options in the right side of the dialog box.**

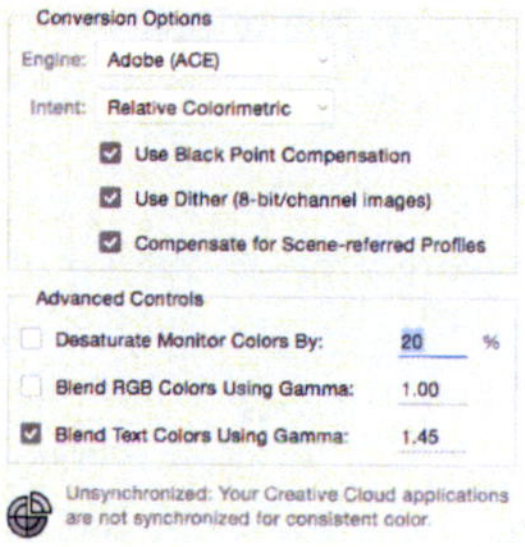

Engine determines the system and color-matching method used to convert between color spaces – **Adobe (ACE)** or Adobe Color Engine; **Apple CMM** (Macintosh only); or **Microsoft ICM** (Windows only).

The **Intent** menu defines how the engine translates source colors outside the gamut of the destination profile.

- **Perceptual** presents a visually pleasing representation of the image, preserving visual relationships between colors. All colors — including those available in the destination gamut — shift to maintain a proportional relationship within the image.
- **Saturation** compares the saturation of colors in the source profile and shifts them to the nearest-possible saturated color in the destination profile. The focus is on saturation instead of actual color value; this method can produce drastic color shift.
- **Relative Colorimetric** maintains any colors that are in both the source and destination profiles; source colors outside the destination gamut shift to fit. This method adjusts for the media whiteness of the media.
- **Absolute Colorimetric** maintains colors in both the source and destination profiles. Colors outside the destination gamut are shifted to a color within the destination gamut, without considering the white point of the media.

When **Use Black Point Compensation** is selected, the full range of the source space is mapped into the destination space. This method is most useful when the black point of the source is darker than that of the destination.

When **Use Dither** is selected, colors in the destination space are mixed to simulate missing colors from the source space. (This can result in larger file sizes for web images.)

Compensate for Scene-Referred Profiles relates to the increasingly popular use of Photoshop to perform color correction (and profile matching) for video enhancement.

Desaturate Monitor Colors is useful for visualizing the full range of color, including colors outside the monitor's range. When this option is deselected, colors that were previously distinct might appear as a single color.

Blend RGB Colors Using Gamma inputs a gamma curve to avoid artifacts. (A gamma of 1.00 is considered "colorimetrically correct.")

Blend Text Colors Using Gamma applies the defined gamma to text layers.

8. **Click Save in the Color Settings dialog box. In the resulting navigation dialog box, change the Save As/File Name field to museum.csf and click Save.**

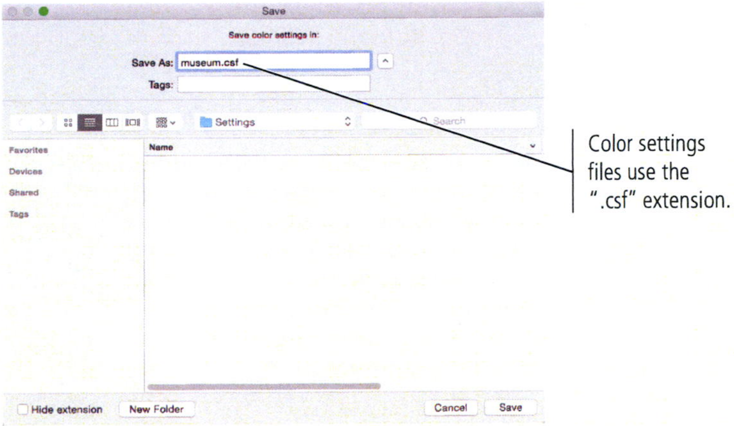

By default, custom color settings are saved in a Settings folder in a specific location where your system stores user preferences for different applications. Settings files saved in the application's default location are available in the Settings menu of the Color Settings dialog box.

If you are working on a shared computer or a network where you can't save to the system files, you might want to save the custom Color Settings file in your WIP folder. In this case, you would have to click the Load button to locate the CSF file.

9. **In the Color Settings Comment dialog box, type Use this option for Photoshop museum image adjustment project.**

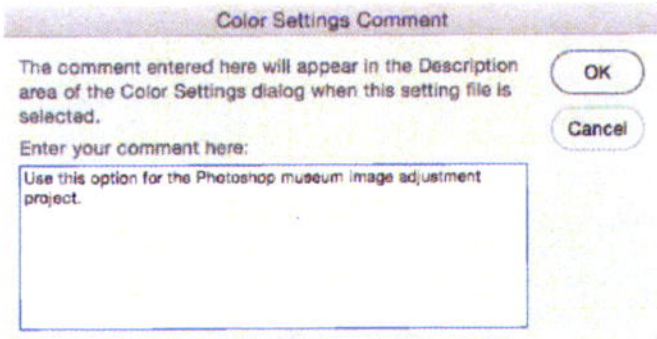

10. **Click OK to return to the Color Settings dialog box.**

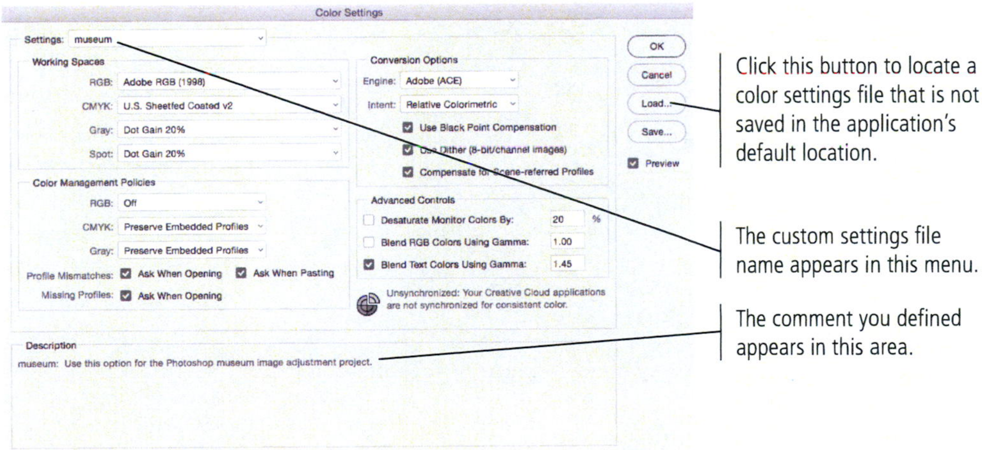

11. **Click OK to close the Color Settings dialog box and apply your settings, and then continue to the next exercise.**

Identify Out-of-Gamut Colors

Fortunately, Photoshop contains the necessary tools for previewing out-of-gamut colors, which means you can correct colors *before* converting an image. If you have no out-of-gamut colors, then there is nothing to shift, and you can be fairly confident that your color images will be reproduced as you intended.

1. **Open the file jar.jpg from the WIP>MOAH folder.**

2. **When you see the profile mismatch warning, choose Use the Embedded Profile and click OK.**

   Remember, color management relies on profiles to accurately translate color from one model to another. This dialog box shows you the starting point — the embedded image profile. As a general rule, you should use the embedded profile whenever one is available.

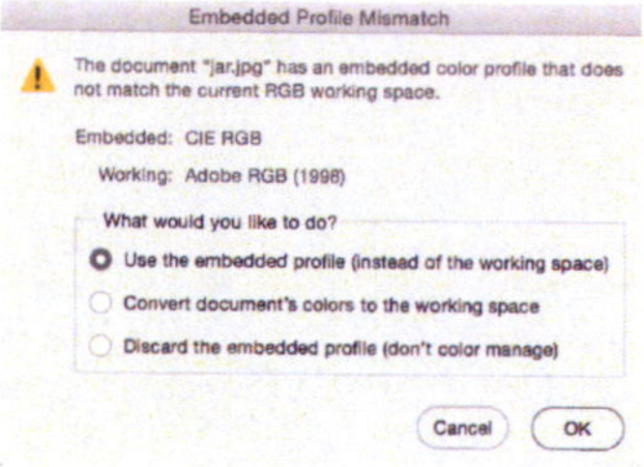
Embedded Profile Mismatch
The document "jar.jpg" has an embedded color profile that does not match the current RGB working space.
Embedded: CIE RGB
Working: Adobe RGB (1998)
What would you like to do?
Use the embedded profile (instead of the working space)
Convert document's colors to the working space
Discard the embedded profile (don't color manage)
Cancel
OK

3. **Choose View>Proof Colors to toggle that option on.**

   This toggle provides a quick preview of what will happen when the image is converted to the CMYK working-space profile — without affecting the actual file data. In this case, you do not see significant color shift, suggesting that the image will not need significant correction for four-color printing.

Original color

Proof color

4. **Choose View>Proof Colors again to toggle the option off.**

Note:

You can choose Edit>Assign Profile to define a specific profile for the active image.

Note:

Photoshop ships with a large collection of common profiles, which are meant to meet the needs of diverse manufacturing environments in which Photoshop is used for what's commonly called ***prepress*** *(the process of getting images ready to print).*

Note:

Command/Control-Y toggles the Proof Colors view on or off.

Shift-Command/Control-Y toggles the Gamut Warning View.

5. **Choose View>Gamut Warning.**

When the Gamut Warning is visible, any areas where color shift will occur are highlighted with a gray overlay. In this case, the highlight shows that only the brightest blue areas on the jar will be affected.

A gray highlight overlays areas where color shift will occur.

> ***Note:***
>
> *You can change the color of the gamut warning overlay in the Transparency & Gamut pane of the Preferences dialog box.*

6. **Continue to the next exercise.**

Adjust Highlight and Shadow Points for Print

For images that will be commercially printed, some allowance must be made in the highlight and shadow areas for the mechanics of the printing process. In CMYK images, shades of gray are reproduced using combinations of four printing inks. In theory, a solid black would be printed as 100% of all four inks, and pure white would be 0% of all four inks. This, however, does not take into consideration the limitations of mechanical printing.

Images are printed as a pattern of closely spaced dots called a **halftone**. Those dots create the illusion of continuous color. Different sizes of dots create different shades of color — larger dots create darker shades and smaller dots create lighter shades.

There is a limit to the smallest size dot that can be consistently reproduced. A 1% dot is so small that the mechanical aspect of the printing process causes anything specified as a 1% dot to drop out, resulting in highlights that lack detail and contrast. The **minimum printable dot**, then, is the smallest printable dot, and should be specified for highlights in a CMYK image. There is some debate over the appropriate highlight setting because different presses and imaging equipment have varying capabilities. To be sure your highlights will work on most printing equipment, you should define the highlight as C=5 M=3 Y=3 K=0.

Maximum printable dot is the opposite of minimum printable dot. Paper's absorption rate, speed of the press, and other mechanical factors limit the amount of ink that can be placed on the same area. If too much ink is printed, the result is a dark blob with no visible detail; heavy layers of ink also result in drying problems and a number of other issues.

Total ink coverage is the largest percentage of ink that can be safely printed on a single area, and therefore dictates the shadow dot you define in Photoshop. This number, similar to minimum printable dot, varies according to the ink/paper/press combination being used for a given job. The Specifications for Web Offset Publications (SWOP) indicates a 300% maximum value. Many sheetfed printers require 280% maximum, while the number for newspapers is usually around 240% because the lower-quality paper absorbs more ink.

Unless your images will be printed in a newspaper, 290% is an acceptable shadow for most applications. You can safely define shadows as C=80 M=70 Y=70 K=70. If you need to adjust a lower or higher number for specific projects, you can do so at any time.

1. **With `jar.jpg` open and the gamut warning visible, choose Image>Adjustments>Curves.**

2. **Double-click the White Point Eyedropper.**

3. **In the resulting Color Picker (Target Highlight Color) dialog box, change the CMYK values to C=5 M=3 Y=3 K=0 and click OK.**

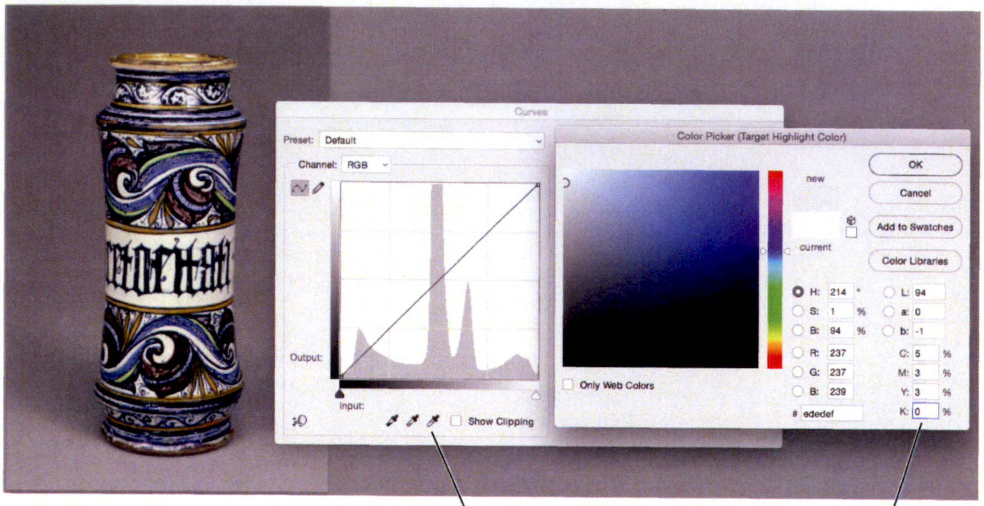

Double-click the White Point Eyedropper to open the Color Picker (Target Highlight Color) dialog box.

Change the Target Highlight Color in these fields.

4. **With the White Point Eyedropper selected, click the lightest highlight in the image where you want to maintain detail.**

We selected this area as the white point.

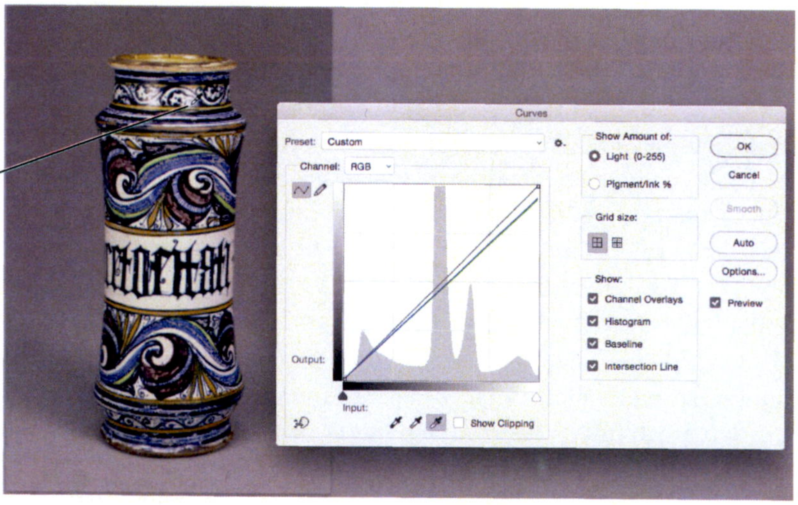

5. **Double-click the Black Point Eyedropper. Change the target CMYK values to C=80 M=70 Y=70 K=70, and then click OK.**

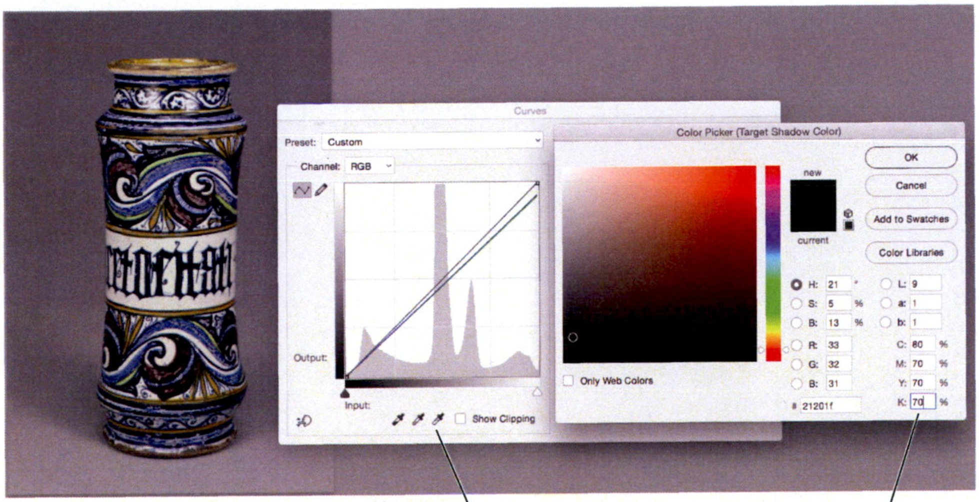

Double-click the Black Point Eyedropper to open the Color Picker (Target Shadow Color) dialog box.

Change the Target Shadow Color in these fields.

6. **With the Black Point Eyedropper selected, click the darkest area of the image where you want to maintain shadow detail.**

By defining the target highlight and shadow points in the image, you can see that the gray gamut warning is nearly gone in all but the brightest blue areas. As you saw when you used the Proof Colors option, the shift will be minimal; no further correction is required for this image.

Note:

You can turn the gamut warning off and on while the Curves dialog box is open.

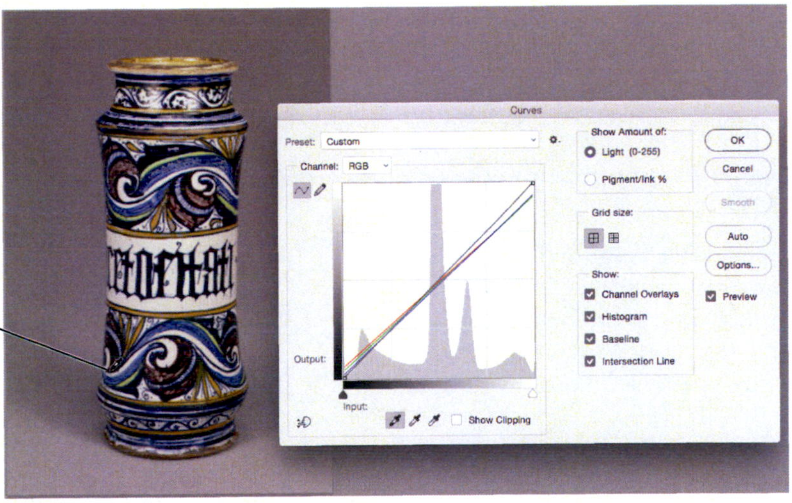

We selected this area as the black point.

7. **Click OK to apply your changes.**

8. **Click No in the warning message.**

If you change the target Black Point, Gray Point, or White Point Eyedropper values, Photoshop asks if you want to save the new target values as the default settings when you click OK to close the Curves dialog box.

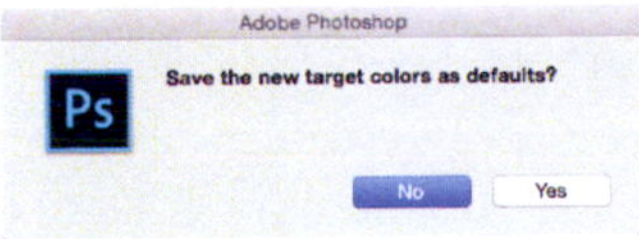

9. **Choose View>Gamut Warning to toggle that option off.**

10. **Continue to the next exercise.**

    Because the RGB gamut is so much larger than the CMYK gamut, you can expect colors to be far less brilliant (especially in the outer ranges of saturation) when corrected to the CMYK gamut. It's better to know this will happen and control it, rather than simply allowing the color management engine to shift colors where it deems best.

Converting Image Color Modes

Although many modern workflows convert RGB images to CMYK during the output process (called "on-the-fly" or "in-RIP conversion"), there are times when you need to manually convert RGB images to CMYK. This is a fairly simple process, especially if you have corrected your images to meet the requirements of the printing process.

1. **With the corrected jar image open from the previous exercise, choose Image>Mode>CMYK Color.**

   This menu option converts the image to the CMYK color mode using the current working space profile. Since you intentionally defined the working profile and corrected the image to that profile, you can safely use this menu option to convert the RGB image to CMYK.

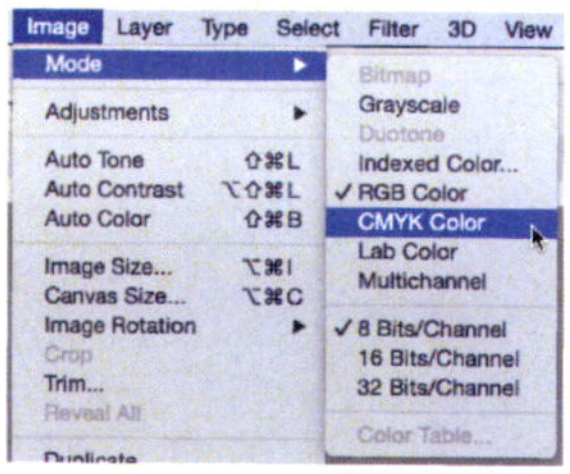

Note:

You can also convert an image to a different color model by choosing Edit>Convert to Profile and choosing any available profile in the Destination Space Profile menu.

2. **Click OK in the resulting warning dialog box.**

   If you had not completed the process in the previous series of exercises, you shouldn't convert the image color mode. Color mode is not something that should be simply switched on a whim; rather, it is the final stage of a specific process.

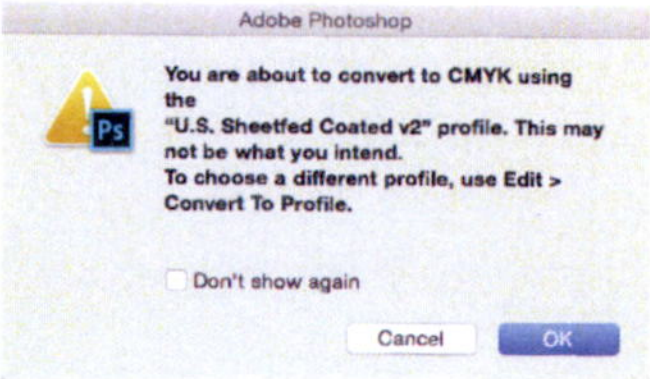

3. **Choose File>Save As. If necessary, navigate to your WIP>MOAH folder as the target location.**

4. **Change the Format/Save As Type menu to Photoshop, and then add -CMYK to the end of the existing file name.**

5. **Macintosh users: In the bottom half of the Save As dialog box, make sure the Embed Color Profile: U.S. Sheetfed Coated v2 option is checked.**

   Windows users: In the bottom half of the Save As dialog box, make sure the ICC Profile: U.S. Sheetfed Coated v2 option is checked.

   This image has been corrected and converted to the U.S. Sheetfed Coated v2 color profile. By embedding the profile into the Photoshop file, other applications and devices with color management capabilities will be able to correctly process the image color data in the file, based on the embedded profile.

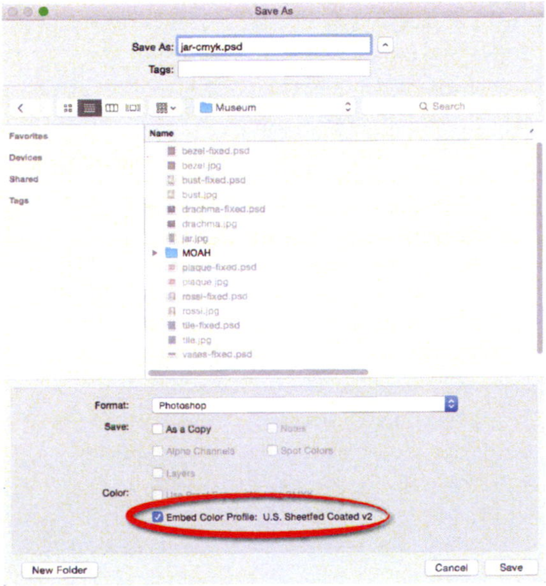

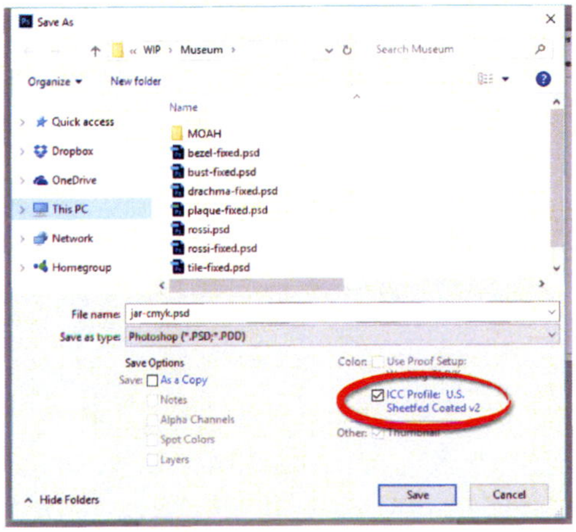

6. **Click Save.**

7. **Close the file, then continue to the final stage of the project.**

Converting Images to Grayscale

An RGB image has three channels and a CMYK image has four channels; each channel is a grayscale representation of the tones of that color throughout the image. A **grayscale image** has only one channel; the grayscale tones in that channel are the tones in the entire image. Choosing Image>Mode>Grayscale simply flattens the component color channels, throwing away the color information to create the gray channel.

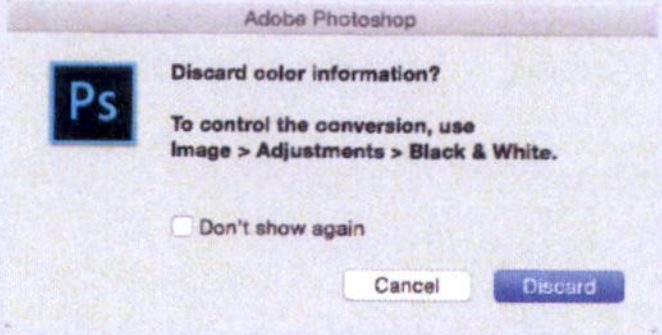

The **Desaturate** adjustment (Image>Adjustments> Desaturate) has a similar effect, but maintains the same number of channels as the original image. This adjustment averages the individual channel values for each pixel and applies the average value in each channel. (Remember, equal values of red, green, and blue combine to create a neutral gray value.)

If you need to convert a color image to grayscale, you might want to carefully consider which data to use for generating the gray channel. The **Black & White** adjustment (Image>Adjustments>Black & White) enables you to control the conversion process. In the Black and White dialog box, you can either choose one of the built-in presets, or you can drag the individual color sliders to determine how dark that color component will be in the resulting image.

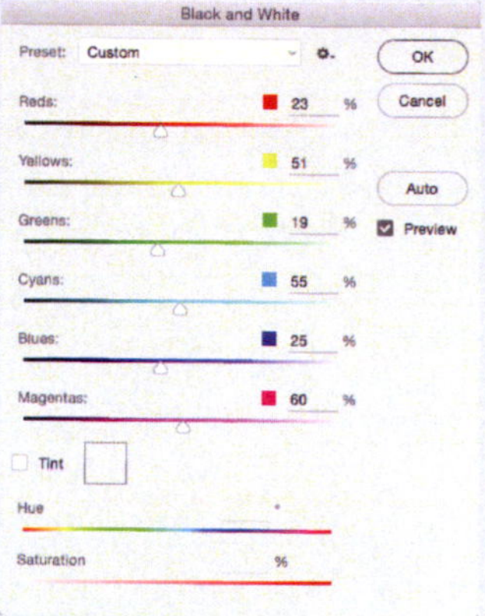

If you move the mouse cursor over the image, it changes to an eyedropper. You can click an area in the image to highlight the predominant color in that area. Click within the image and drag to dynamically change the slider associated with that area of the image.

Remember, equal parts red, green, and blue combine to create a neutral gray. Applying the Black & White filter maintains the existing color channels, with the exact same data in all three channels. Because the adjusted image is still technically in a color mode (not Grayscale), you can also use the Tint options in the Black & White dialog box to apply a hue or saturation tint to the grayscale image. After using the Black & White dialog box to control the conversion of colors to grayscale, you can safely discard the color data by choosing Image>Mode>Grayscale.

The Channel Mixer Adjustment

You can use the **Channel Mixer** adjustment to change the values of individual channels in an image, affecting overall color balance and contrast.

The **Output Channel** menu determines which channel you are changing; the Source Channels sliders determine how much of the original channels will be used to create the new output channel values.

Replacing 40% of the Blue channel with data from the Green channel reduces some of the yellow color cast.

The Constant slider adjusts the overall grayscale value of the output channel. Negative values add more black to the channel (reducing the target color in the overall image), and positive values add more white to the channel (increasing the target color in the overall image).

You can also use the Channel Mixer to control the conversion to grayscale. If you check the Monochrome option at the bottom of the dialog box, the output channel automatically changes to gray.

When the **Monochrome** option is checked, you can change the percentage of each component channel that will be used to generate the grayscale values. If the combined channel values are higher than 100%, Photoshop displays a warning icon next to the total.

The "Output Channel:Gray" option is deceptive, since there is no Gray channel in either an RGB or CMYK image. As with the Black and White adjustment, the Channel Mixer results in a color image with the same number of color channels that it had before you applied the adjustment. All the color channels have equal data, however, so you can safely discard color data by choosing Image>Mode>Grayscale.

Stage 5 Working with HDR Images

The human eye is extremely sensitive to subtle changes in light. In general, we can perceive detail in both light and dark areas — and areas in between — with a single glance. Camera sensors, on the other hand, are not so sensitive. If you look at most photographs, they typically have sharp detail in one of the ranges — highlights, midtones, or shadows, depending on the exposure and other settings used to capture the image. If a photograph favors highlights, details in shadow areas are lost (and vice versa).

To solve this problem, the concept of HDR (**high dynamic range**) images combines multiple photographs of different exposures into a single image to enhance the detail throughout the entire image — combining highlight, shadow, and midtone detail from various exposures to create an image more like what the human eye is capable of observing, rather than the more limited range that characterizes a digital camera's sensors.

The phrase "dynamic range" refers to the difference between the darkest shadow and the lightest highlight in an image.

- A regular 8-bit RGB photo has a dynamic range of 0–255 for each color channel (2^8 or 256 possible values). In other words, each pixel can have one of 256 possible values to describe the lightness of that color in that specific location.
- A 16-bit RGB photo allows 16 bits of information to describe the information in each pixel, allowing a dynamic range of 2^{16} or 65,536 possible values in each color channel.
- A 32-bit or HDR image allows 2^{32} possible values — more than 4 billion, which is signficantly larger than the visible spectrum of 16.7 million colors (thus, 32-bit dynamic range is sometimes referred to as "infinite").

Use Merge to HDR Pro

The last piece required to complete this project is an image of the new museum's exterior. The photographer suggested using high dynamic range (HDR) photo techniques to capture the most possible detail in the scene, and has provided you with five photos taken at the same time, using different exposure settings.

1. **With no file open, choose File>Automate>Merge to HDR Pro.**
2. **In the resulting Merge to HDR Pro dialog box, choose Folder in the Use menu and then click the Browse button.**

   This option makes it easy to identify the folder that contains all component images for the HDR merge.

3. **Navigate to WIP>MOAH>Museum, then click Open/OK.**

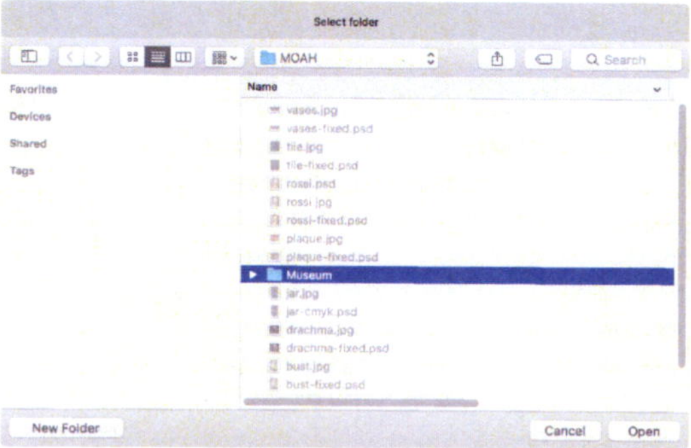

> ***Note:***
> *You can merge up to seven images with the Merge to HDR Pro utility.*

4. **Make sure the Attempt to Automatically Align Source Images box at the bottom of the dialog box is checked, then click OK.**

   Because you are merging multiple images into a single one, there is a chance that one or more images might be slightly misaligned. (Even using a tripod, a stiff breeze can affect the camera just enough to make the different exposures slightly different.) When Attempt to Automatically Align Source Images is checked, Photoshop compares details in each image and adjusts them as necessary to create the resulting merged image.

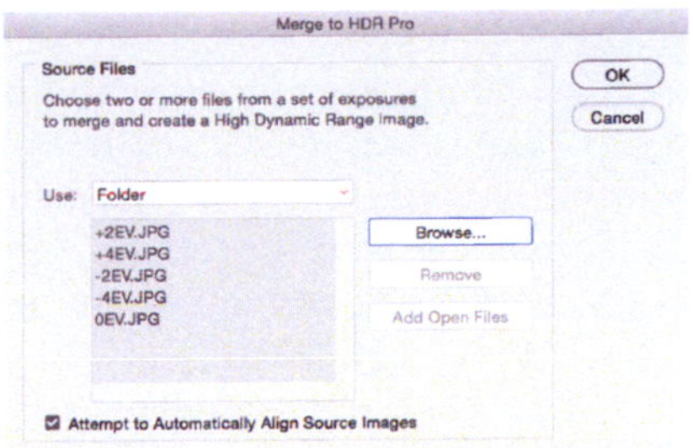

5. **If you don't see a histogram on the right side of the dialog box, open the Mode menu and choose 32 Bit.**

   The resulting dialog box shows each selected image as a thumbnail at the bottom. By default, all selected images are included in the merge. You can exclude specific exposures by unchecking the box for that image.

   If you work with HDR, you need to realize that most computer monitors are not capable of displaying 32-bit image depth. When you merge to a 32-bit image, you can use the White Point Preview slider to change the dynamic range that is visible on your screen, but this has no effect on the actual data in the file — it affects only the current display of the image data.

6. **Check the Remove Ghosts option on the right side of the dialog box.**

   When an HDR image contains movement, merging the individual exposures can blur the areas where that movement occurs. When you check Remove Ghosts, the software uses one of the exposures (highlighted in green) to define detail in the area of motion, such as the moving car in this image; you can change the key exposure by simply clicking a different image in the lower pane.

Note:

The merge process might take a minute or two to complete, so be patient.

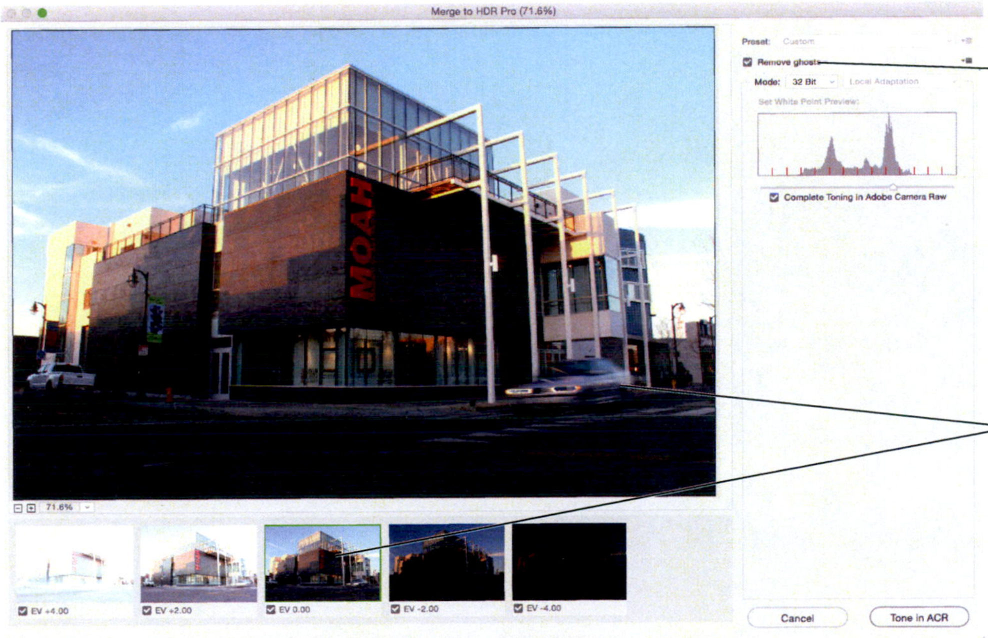

Check Remove Ghosts to eliminate blurring in areas that differ from one exposure to another.

When Remove Ghosts is checked, details in areas of movement are defined by the selected exposure.

7. **Open the Mode menu and choose 8 Bit.**

32-bit images can store a tremendous amount of information, which creates images with far more detail than you see in a conventional 8-bit photograph. However, one significant disadvantage of such images is that they cannot be separated for commercial printing. If you're going to use an HDR image in a print application — such as the cover of this catalog — you need to apply the process of **tone mapping** to define how the high dynamic range will be compressed into the lower dynamic range that is required by the output process.

8. **Leave the secondary menu set to Local Adaptation.**

You can use the other options to apply less specific tone mapping to the image. Equalize Histogram and Highlight Compression have no further options. The Exposure and Gamma option allows you to define specific values for only those two settings.

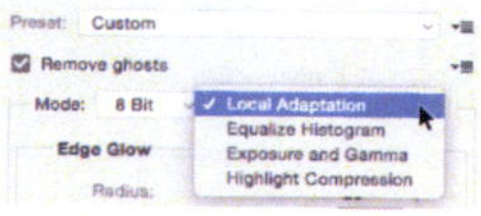

When the Local Adaptation method is selected, you can change the values for a number of specific options to map the tones in the HDR image to a lower dynamic range.

9. **Open the Preset menu and choose Surrealistic.**

The application includes a number of standard settings, including several variations of monochromatic, photorealistic, and surrealistic. Each preset changes the values of the Local Adaptation sliders to create the desired effect.

You can create your own presets by clicking the button to the right of the Preset menu and choosing Save Preset in the resulting menu.

10. Experiment with the different sliders until you are satisfied with the result.

Tone mapping is a largely subjective process, and different end uses can influence the settings that you apply to a specific image. You should understand the following information as you experiment with the various settings:

- **Radius** defines the size of the glowing effect in areas of localized brightness.
- **Strength** determines the required tolerance between tonal values before pixels are no longer considered part of the same brightness region.
- **Gamma** values lower than 1.0 increase details in the midtones, while higher values emphasize details in the highlights and shadows.
- **Exposure** affects the overall lightness or darkness of the image.
- **Detail** increases or decreases the overall sharpness of the image.
- **Shadow** and **Highlight** affect the amount of detail in those areas of the image. Higher values increase detail and lower values reduce detail.
- **Vibrance** affects the intensity of subtle colors, while minimizing clipping of highly saturated colors.
- **Saturation** affects the intensity of all colors from –100 (monochrome) to +100 (double saturation).

11. Click OK to finalize the process.

Because you chose 8 Bit in the Mode menu of the Merge to HDR Pro dialog box, the resulting image is an 8-bit RGB image (as you can see in the document tab).

Note:

The original exposures for this image were captured by Charlie Essers.

12. Save the file in your WIP>MOAH folder as a native Photoshop file named **museum-merged.psd**, then close it.

Project Review

fill in the blank

1. The _______________ filter blurs an image by a selected pixel radius.

2. _______________ is defined as random pixels that stand out from the surrounding pixels.

3. The _______________ blends colors from user-defined source pixels with colors in the area where you click.

4. The _______________ paints one part of an image over another part, which is useful for duplicating specific objects or removing defects in an image.

5. _______________ are direct sources of light such as a light bulb or reflected sunlight on water; they should not be considered the highlights of an image.

6. _______________ refers to the tonal variation within an image.

7. A _______________ is a visual depiction of the distribution of colors in an image.

8. _______________ is defined according to a color's position on a color wheel, beginning from red (0°) and traveling counterclockwise around the wheel.

9. _______________ (also called "intensity") refers to the color's difference from neutral gray.

10. _______________ (also called "luminance" or "value") is the amount of white or black added to the pure color.

short answer

1. Explain the concept of neutral gray.

2. List three important points to remember when working with curves.

3. Briefly explain the concepts of minimum printable dot and maximum ink coverage.

Portfolio Builder Project

Use what you learned in this project to complete the following freeform exercise.
Carefully read the art director and client comments, then create your design to meet the needs of the project.
Use the space below to sketch ideas; when finished, write a brief explanation of the reasoning behind your design.

art director comments

The director of the local tourism board recently saw your work for the museum, and has hired you to work on a new project about local architecture.

To complete this project, you should:

- ❑ Find at least 10 photos of different architectural styles throughout the Los Angeles metropolitan area.
- ❑ Use photo retouching techniques to clean up any graffiti and trash that is visible in the images.
- ❑ Use correction techniques to adjust the tonal range and gray balance of the images.
- ❑ Correct and convert all images based on the U.S. Sheetfed Coated v2 CMYK destination profile.

client comments

Over the next year, we're planning on publishing a series of promotional booklets to show tourists that L.A. is more than just Hollywood.

Each booklet in the series will focus on an 'interest area' such as fine art or — for the first one — architecture. The city has a diverse architectural mix, from eighteenth-century Spanish missions to 1920s bungalows to the Walt Disney Concert Hall designed by Frank Gehry in the 1990s.

We'd like at least 10 pictures of different landmarks or architectural styles, corrected and optimized for printing on a sheetfed press. If possible, we'd also like some historical images to include in a "building a metropolis" section on the first couple of pages.

Of course, Los Angeles is a large city, and cities have their problems — not the least of which are graffiti and garbage. We are trying to attract tourists, not turn them away. Make sure none of the images show any graffiti or blatant litter; if these problems are visible in the images you select, give them a good digital cleaning.

project justification

Project Summary

As with many other skills, it takes time and practice to master image correction techniques. Understanding the relationship between brightness and contrast, and how these two values affect the quality of reproduction in digital images, is the first and possibly most critical factor in creating a high-quality image. An image that has too much contrast (a "sharp" image) or not enough contrast (a "flat" image) translates to an unsatisfactory print.

A basic understanding of color theory (specifically complementary color) is the foundation of accurate color correction. Effective color correction relies on the numbers, rather than what you think you see on your monitor. As you gain experience in correcting images, you will be better able to predict the corrections required to achieve the best possible output.

Remove photographic grain with blur and sharpen techniques

Use the Healing Brush and Spot Healing Brush tools to correct scratches

Use the Clone Stamp tool to remove major damage

Use Merge to HDR Pro to find detail in multiple exposures

Correct minor problems with the Brightness/ Contrast adjustment

Correct lighting problems with the Exposure adjustment

Correct contrast with the Curves adjustment

Correct and convert an image using the defined destination CMYK profile

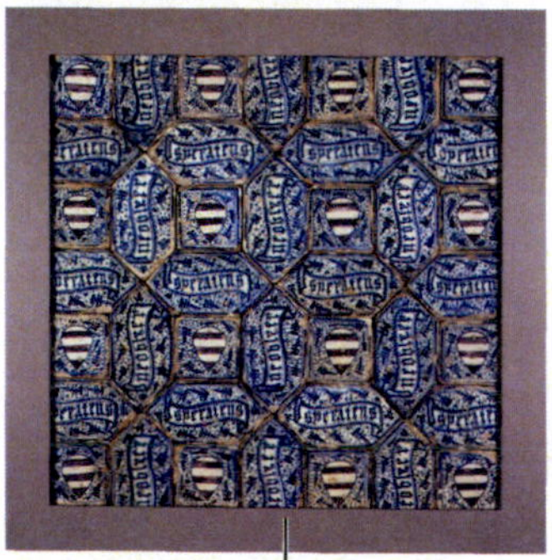

Correct contrast and tonal range using the Levels adjustment

Correct contrast and gray balance using the Curves adjustment

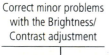

Correct overall color cast using the Color Balance adjustment

City Promotion Cards

Your client is the Redevelopment Authority for the city of Lancaster, in the California high desert (north of Los Angeles). You have been hired to create a series of promotional postcards featuring the improvements that have been made over the last two years, that will help drive tourism to the area.

This project incorporates the following skills:

- ❏ Creating new files
- ❏ Managing missing and mismatched profiles
- ❏ Working with content-aware tools
- ❏ Adding effects in the Blur Gallery
- ❏ Creating and managing different types of text layers
- ❏ Using paragraph styles to format text
- ❏ Working in 3D
- ❏ Creating layer comps

Antelope Valley
Poppy Festival
Join us the last weekend in April for two days of music, art, food and fun celebrating the state flower of California and the appearance of poppies in the Antelope Valley! Warm breezes replace the winter chill, jubilant laughter fills the air, and poppies burst into bloom blanketing hillsides in a sea of orange.
The California Poppy Festival kicks off spring in the Antelope Valley with a glorious array of celebrated performers, unrivaled activities and events, and mouth watering delicacies that are designed to delight, enchant, and amuse people of all ages.
www.poppyfestival.com
THE
BLVD
The downtown that once served as the heart of the Antelope Valley has been restored to its former glory, with a modern twist! Come see the dramatic transformation and explore more than 40 new shops and restaurants. Don't miss our annual special events, and the weekly farmer's market every Thursday.
www.theblvdlancaster.com

Project Meeting

client comments

We want to feature two of our proudest achievements in a postcard campaign that we're hoping will help drive tourism to the area.

In the past two years, more than $50 million in public and private funding has been spent revitalizing the downtown Lancaster area. The BLVD, Lancaster's new outdoor shopping and dining destination, is distinguished by its beautiful sidewalk streetscape and ramblas. The BLVD is lined with a unique mix of dining, shopping, arts, and entertainment venues.

The Poppy Festival is attended by more than 20,000 visitors over two days. It's an award-winning festival that celebrates California's state flower, which is fitting since we're also the home of the Antelope Valley Poppy Preserve.

The images you create will be used in digital advertising and on websites, but we also plan to print them for inclusion in a larger promotional package that we send to conference coordinators around the country.

art director comments

The client wants to create these files for both digital and print applications, so you should define the file size to meet the print specs:

Trim: 5″ high × 7″ wide

Bleed requirement: 0.125″ on all four sides

I want each postcard to include two images. The ones we have are excellent, but they will require some manipulation to work in the overall composition.

Although compositing type and images is typically done in a page layout application, there isn't a lot of text to include on these postcards. You can use the Photoshop type tools to do what you need, without requiring a separate file.

I'd also like to see two different versions of each postcard. The 3D options in Photoshop can create the appearance of depth even in a flat file — which might just be the "pop" that the client asked for.

When you're finished, save each version as a JPEG that we can email for approval.

project objectives

To complete this project, you will:

- ❑ Create a new color-managed file
- ❑ Apply content-aware scaling
- ❑ Use the Content-Aware Move tool
- ❑ Apply a tilt-shift blur effect
- ❑ Apply an iris blur effect
- ❑ Place and format point text
- ❑ Create and control area type
- ❑ Work with paragraph styles
- ❑ Create a solid-color fill layer
- ❑ Create a 3D postcard
- ❑ Create a 3D sphere
- ❑ Create layer comps

Stage 1 Creating New Files

The basic process of creating a new file is relatively easy. However, you have a number of options that affect what you will see when you begin working. The first stage of this project explores a number of these issues, including color management settings and controlling the background layer.

Create a New Color-Managed File

The Color Settings dialog box defines the default working spaces for RGB, CMYK, Gray, and Spot Color spaces. Once you've made your choices in the Color Settings dialog box, those working spaces are automatically applied when you create a new file.

1. **Download `Cards_PS18_RF.zip` from the Student Files web page.**
2. **Expand the ZIP archive in your WIP folder (Macintosh) or copy the archive contents into your WIP folder (Windows).**

   This results in a folder named **`Cards`**, which contains the files you need for this project. You should also use this folder to save the files you create in this project.

3. **In Photoshop, choose Edit>Color Settings.**
4. **In the resulting dialog box, choose the appropriate profile for your monitor in the Working Spaces: RGB menu.**
5. **Set all three Color Management Policies menus to Preserve Embedded Profiles, and check all three boxes for Profile Mismatches and Missing Profiles.**

   You can display a warning when opening or pasting an image with an embedded profile that does not match the working profile. You can also display a warning when opening an image that doesn't have an embedded profile.

Choose your monitor profile here.

Check all three of these options.

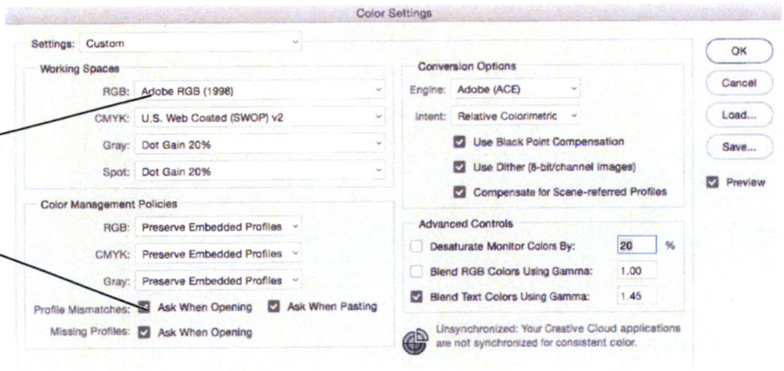

6. **Click OK to apply your changes.**
7. **Choose File>New.**

   You have several options for creating a new file:

   - Choose File>New;
   - Use the associated keyboard shortcut, Command/Control-N; or
   - Click the New button in the Start workspace.

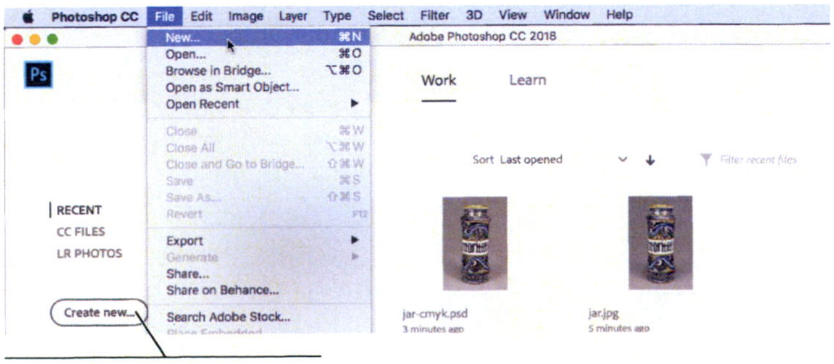

If the Start workspace is visible, click the New button to open the New Document dialog box.

8. **Click the Print option at the top of the resulting New Document dialog box.**

   The New Document dialog box presents a number of preset sizes and prebuilt starter templates, broken in to categories based on the intended output.

   When you choose the Print category, you see common page sizes such as Letter and Legal. Each preset includes a unit of measurement (for example, 8.5″ × 11″ in for the Letter preset or 210 × 297 mm for the A4 preset); the defined unit of measurement for each preset is automatically selected in the Preset Details section on the right side of the dialog box.

   The Photo, Print, and Art & Illustration presets all automatically default 300 Pixels/Inch resolution. The Web, Mobile, and Film & Video presets all default to 72 Pixels/Inch.

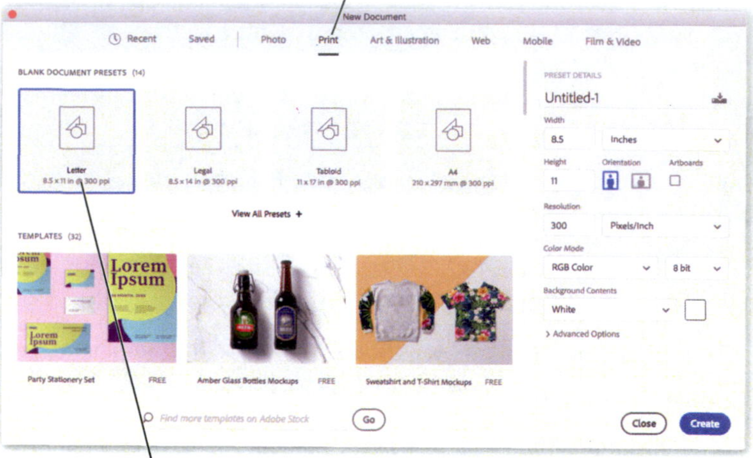

   The **color mode** defines the structure of the colors in your file. All presets in all categories default to the 8-bit RGB color mode. Although the file will eventually be printed, you are going to work in the RGB space to preserve the widest-possible color gamut during the development stage.

Note:

If you choose one of the templates at the bottom of the dialog box, the Create button changes to "Download" so you can download the necessary template files from Adobe Stock.

9. **In the Preset Details section, type festival in the Name field.**

   When you save the file, the file name defaults to the name you define here.

10. **Highlight the existing Width field value and then type 7.25.**

    Because this file will eventually be printed, you are defining the width to include the required bleed (1/8″) area on each side.

11. **Press Tab to highlight the Height field.**

    Like most applications, you can press Tab to move through the options and fields in a dialog box. Pressing Shift-Tab moves to the previous field in the dialog box.

12. **Change the highlighted Height field to 5.25.**

    Again, this size includes the require 1/8″ bleed for the top and bottom edges.

13. **Choose Transparent in the Background Contents menu.**

    You might need to scroll down in the Preset Details pane to be able to access the Transparent option in the Color Mode menu.

    If you choose White or Background Color in this menu, the new file will include a default locked Background layer. If you choose Transparent, the new file will have a default unlocked Layer 1.

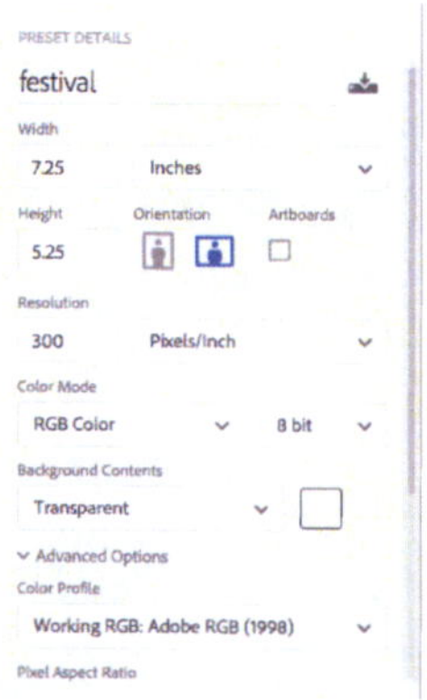

14. **Expand the Advanced options (if necessary) and choose Working RGB: [Profile Name] in the Color Profile menu.**

    This option defines the working RGB space that you selected in the Color Settings dialog box. (Options in the Pixel Aspect Ratio menu are primarily used for editing video. Since this is a print project, you don't want to alter the pixel ratio.)

15. **Click Create to create the new file.**

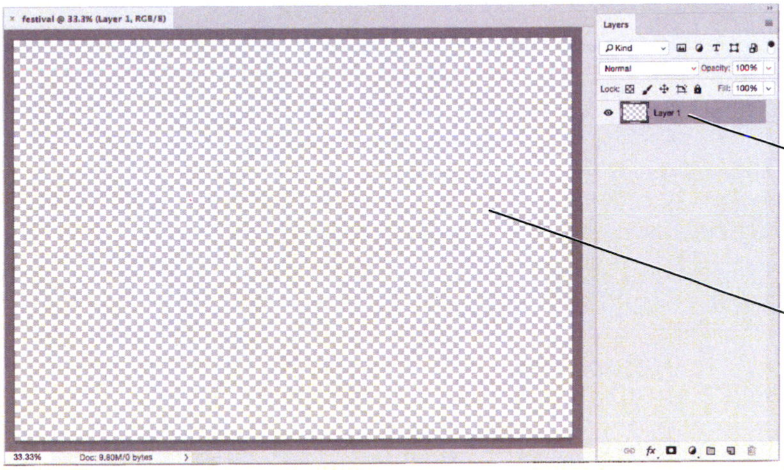

Because you chose Transparent in the Background Color menu, the new file has one regular layer and no locked Background layer.

The checked pattern identifies transparent areas.

16. **Choose File>Save As. Navigate to your WIP>Cards folder as the location for saving this file.**

Because you named the file when you created it (in the New dialog box), the Save As/File Name field is automatically set to the file name you already assigned. The extension is automatically added on both Macintosh and Windows computers.

17. **Make sure Photoshop is selected in the Format/Save As Type menu and click Save.**

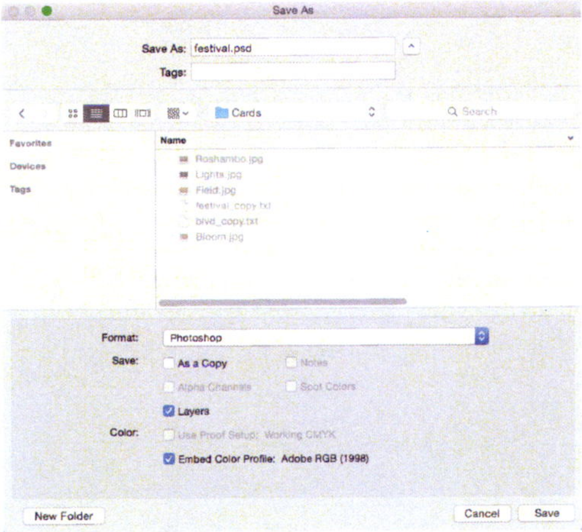

Note:

If you create a file using a profile other than the default working profile for that space, the document tab (or title bar, if you're not using the Macintosh Application frame) shows an asterisk next to the color space information.

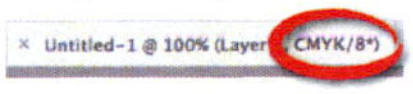

18. **Read the resulting warning message, then click OK.**

This warning appears as soon as a file has at least one regular layer. This file has no locked background layer, so the only layer is a regular layer by default.

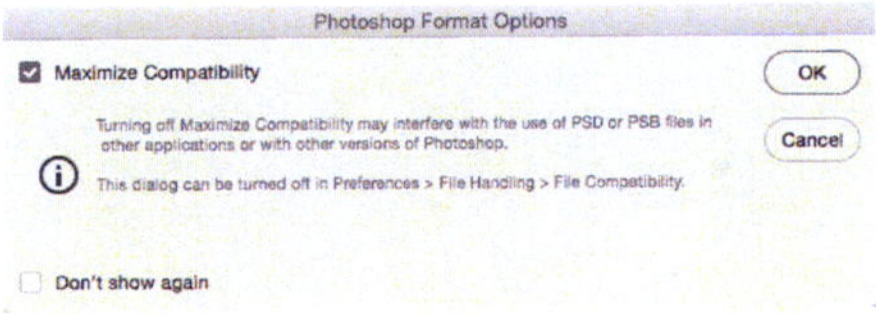

19. **Continue to the next exercise.**

Control the Background Layer

When you create a new file, the background of the canvas depends on your selection in the New dialog box. You should understand how that choice affects not only the color of the canvas, but also the existence (or not) of a background layer.

1. **With festival.psd open, make sure rulers are visible (View>Rulers).**
2. **Using any method you prefer, place ruler guides 0.125″ from each edge.**

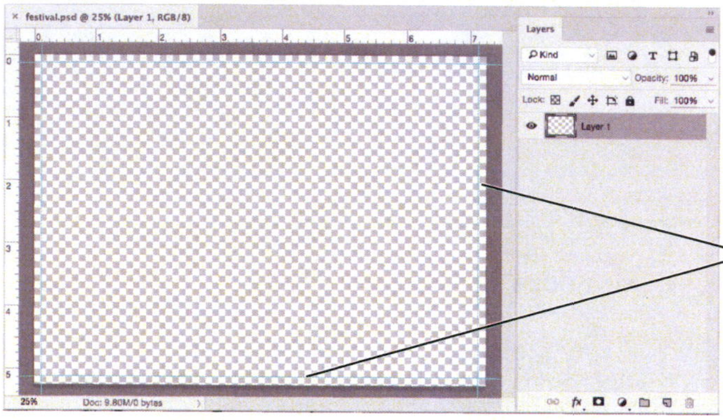

Place guides 1/8″ from each edge of the canvas.

3. **Save the file.**
4. **At the bottom of the Tools panel, click the Default Foreground and Background Colors button.**
5. **At the bottom of the Tools panel, click the Switch Foreground and Background Colors button.**
6. **With the default Layer 1 selected, choose Layer>Flatten Image.**

   When you flatten an image, all layers in the file are flattened into a locked Background layer. Because this file currently has only one layer, the new Background layer is simply a solid white fill. It is important to note that the defined Background color is not applied as the color of the resulting Background layer.

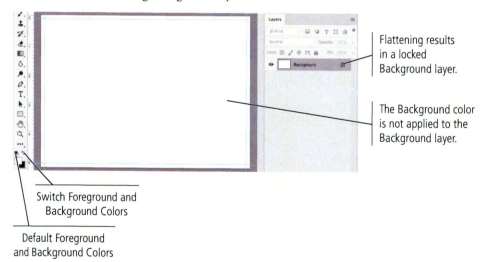

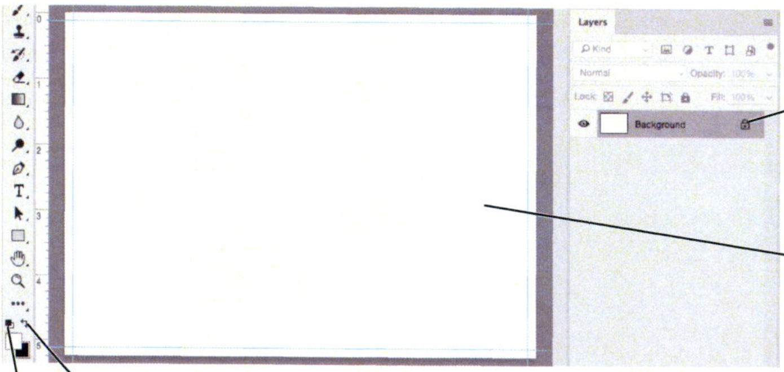

7. **With the Background layer selected, choose Edit>Fill.**

You can fill a selection with a number of options:

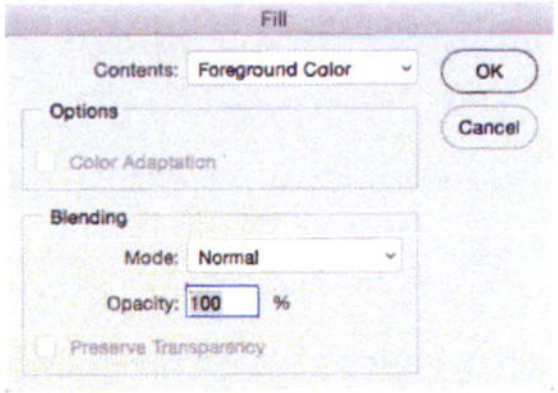

- Choose the defined foreground or background color.
- Choose Color to define a specific color in the Color Picker dialog box.
- Choose Content Aware to fill an area with pixels from surrounding image areas.
- Choose Pattern, and then choose a specific pattern in the pop-up menu.
- Choose History to fill the object with a specific history state (if possible).
- Choose Black, 50% Gray, or White.

You can also define a specific blending mode and opacity for the filled pixels. Using layers for different elements, however, is typically a better option than changing the fill transparency settings because you can adjust the layer blending mode and opacity as often as necessary.

Note:

Press Shift-Delete/ Backspace to open the Fill dialog box.

8. **In the Fill dialog box, choose Background Color in the Contents menu and then click OK.**

Because you did not draw a specific selection area, the entire selected layer (the Background layer) is filled.

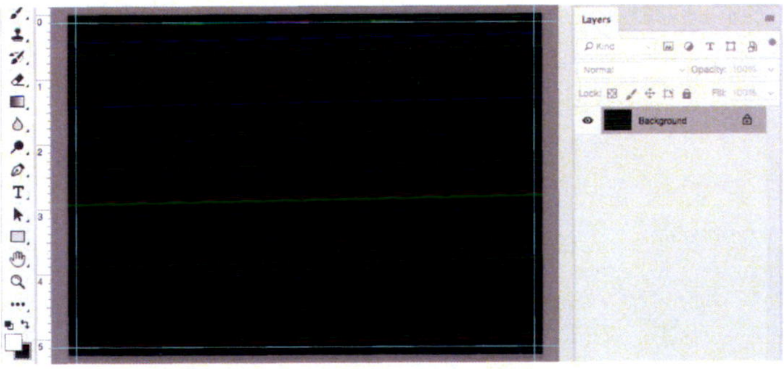

9. **Choose File>Save As. In the Save As dialog box, change the file name to blvd.psd and click Save.**

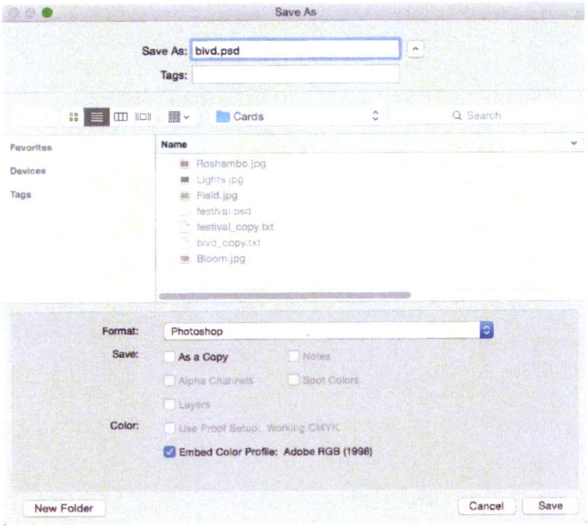

10. **Continue to the next exercise.**

Control Missing and Mismatched Profiles

In the Color Settings dialog box, you told Photoshop how to handle images with profiles that don't match your working profiles, as well as images that don't have embedded profiles. These issues become important any time you work with files from more than a single source — and especially with client-supplied images, which often come from a wide variety of sources.

1. **With `blvd.psd` open, open `Lights.jpg` from your WIP>Cards folder.**

   This image does not have an embedded profile, so (as you defined in the Color Settings dialog box) Photoshop asks how you want to handle the file.

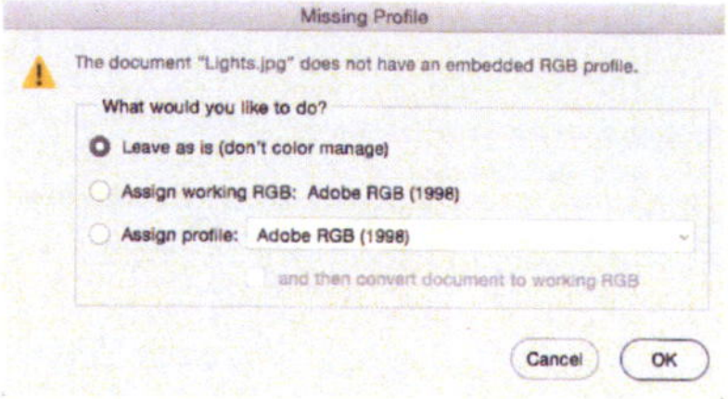

2. **Choose Leave As Is and click OK.**

Note:

It's quite common to find images that don't have embedded color profiles, especially when you work with older (legacy) files. In this case, color management will be imperfect at best since you don't know how the image was captured.

3. **With `Lights.jpg` open, chose Select>All. Choose Edit>Copy, then close the file.**

4. **With `blvd.psd` active, choose Edit>Paste.**

   Because the file's locked Background layer was selected, the pasted contents are added as a new layer, immediately above the existing (selected) layer. Remember, you can't paste content onto a locked layer.

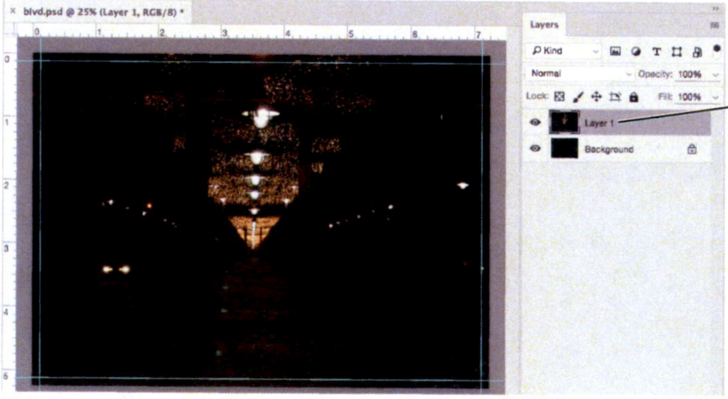

Note:

Refer back to Project 1: Music CD Artwork for a more detailed explanation of the Background layer.

5. **In the Layers panel, rename Layer 1 as `Lights`.**

6. **Choose File>Save. Click OK in the Maximize Compatibility warning.**

   As we already explained, this warning appears the first time you save a file that has at least one regular layer.

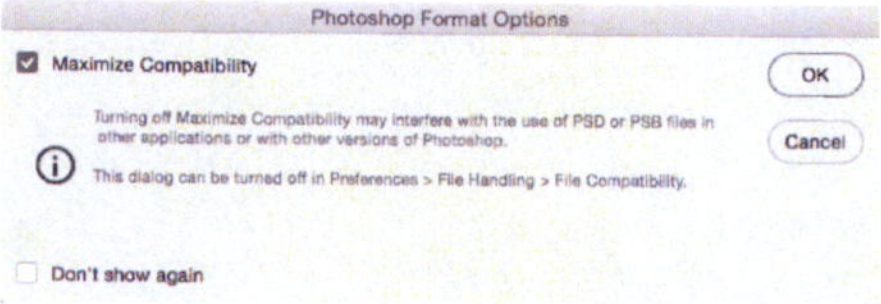

7. **Open the file `festival.psd` from your WIP>Cards folder.**

8. **Open the file Bloom.jpg, and read the resulting warning.**

   This file has an embedded profile, but it does not match your defined working RGB profile. Again, you told the application to show a warning when opening a file with a mismatched profile.

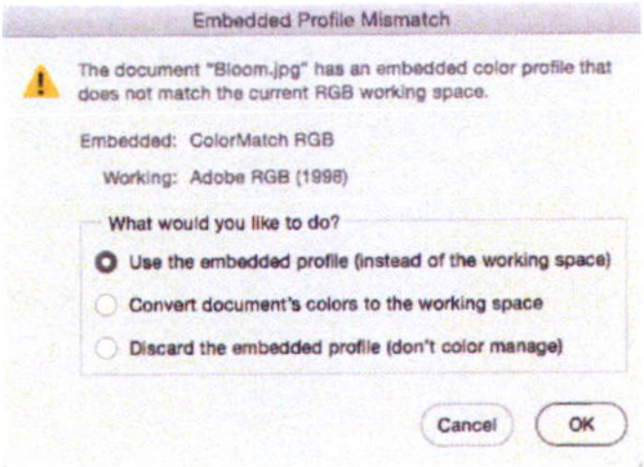
Embedded Profile Mismatch
The document "Bloom.jpg" has an embedded color profile that does not match the current RGB working space.
Embedded: ColorMatch RGB
Working: Adobe RGB (1998)
What would you like to do?
Use the embedded profile (instead of the working space)
Convert document's colors to the working space
Discard the embedded profile (don't color manage)
Cancel
OK

9. **Choose the option to use the embedded profile, then click OK.**

10. **Copy the contents of the file, then close it.**

11. **With festival.psd open, choose Edit>Paste.**

    In the Color Settings dialog box, you told the application to warn you if profiles do not match when you paste layer content. Photoshop cannot manage more than one profile for a single color space within the same file.

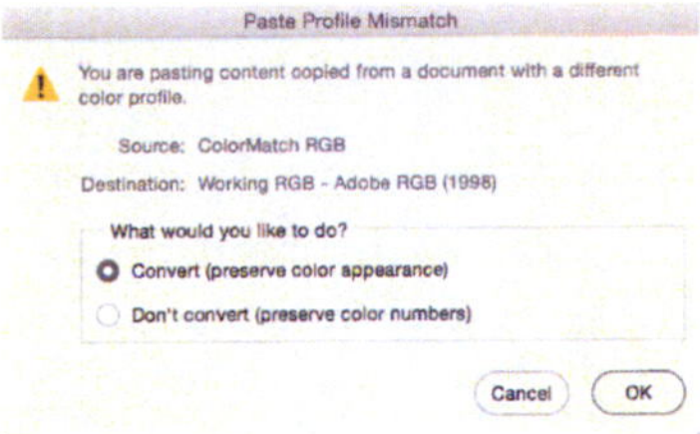
Paste Profile Mismatch
You are pasting content copied from a document with a different color profile.
Source: ColorMatch RGB
Destination: Working RGB - Adobe RGB (1998)
What would you like to do?
Convert (preserve color appearance)
Don't convert (preserve color numbers)
Cancel
OK

    The Convert option converts the pasted image colors to the color profile of the file where you're pasting, preserving the color appearance. The Don't Convert option preserves the color data (but not the actual profile) in the pasted information.

12. **In the Paste Profile Mismatch dialog box, choose the Convert option and then click OK.**

    Because this file has no Background layer, the pasted image is pasted into the active Layer 1.

Layers
Normal
Opacity: 100%
Fill: 100%
Layer 1

The pasted content is added to the selected Layer 1.

13. **In the Layers panel, rename Layer 1 as Bloom.**

14. **Save the file and continue to the next stage of the project.**

Stage 2 Manipulating Pixels

Before digital image-editing software, a photo was a photo. If you wanted a different angle or arrangement, you simply took another photo. Digital photo editing also makes it much easier to manipulate the actual content of an image — from scaling specific objects to a different size, to moving them to a new location, to changing the image's entire focal point. In this stage of the project, you will learn a number of techniques for changing the content in the client's supplied images to better meet the needs of the project.

Apply Content-Aware Scaling

When you scale a selection, you are stretching or squashing the pixels in that selection. This can produce the result you want, but it can also badly distort the image. Content-aware scaling intends to correct this problem by analyzing the image and preserving areas of detail when you scale the image.

1. **Make blvd.psd the active file.**

   The focus of this image is directly down the center. Because you are going to add type and other images to complete the entire postcard composition, you first need to move the image's focal point to create room for the textual elements.

2. **Choose the Move tool in the Tools panel.**

3. **With the Lights layer selected in the Layers panel, click in the document window to activate it. Press Shift, then click and drag to the left until the path in the image is approximately one-third of the way across the canvas.**

   As you can see, moving a layer's contents reveals the underlying layer. The right edge of the path image creates a harsh line.

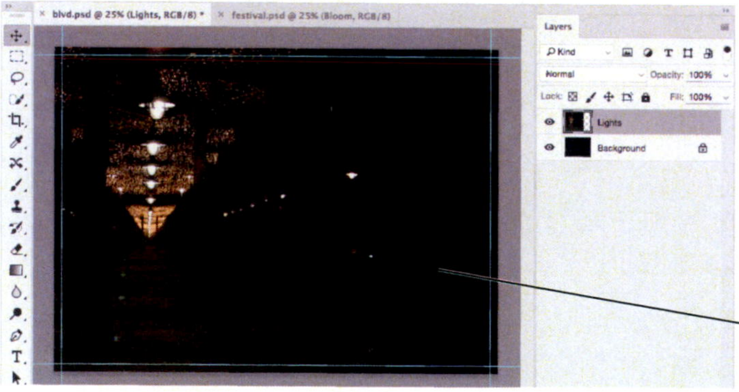

Just moving the layer reveals the content of underlying layers.

Note:

The black background color does not appear as clearly distinct in our screen shots; however, you should be able to see the edge on your monitor.

4. **Choose Edit>Undo Move.**

   Rather than simply moving the image to the position you want, you are going to scale it to fill the entire space — while moving the lighted path into the left half of the image.

5. **With the Lights layer still selected, choose Edit>Transform>Scale.**

   When you enter into transformation mode by calling any of the Transform submenu options, the selection (or entire layer, if you don't have a specific area selected) is surrounded by a bounding box and handles, which you can use to control the transformation. The Options bar also includes fields for numerically transforming the selection.

6. **Click the left-center handle on the image layer and drag left until the path in the image is approximately one-third of the way across the canvas.**

   It can be helpful to reduce the view percentage so you can see more area around the defined canvas.

   Transformations alter the pixels in the layer. As you can see, the lights are distorted by scaling the layer in only one direction.

Scaling in only one direction distorts the image content.

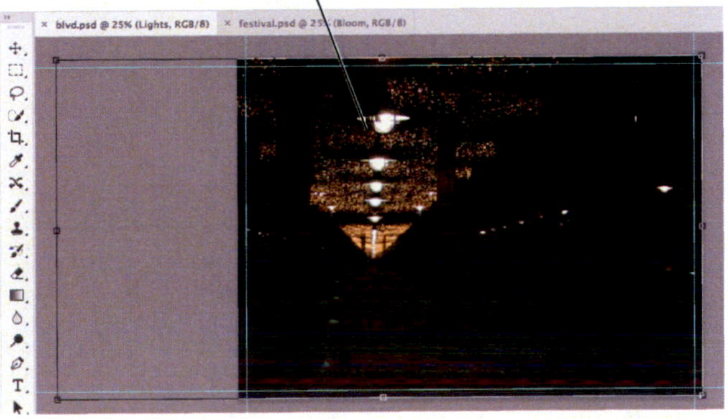

7. **In the Options bar, click the Cancel Transform button (or press ESC).**

   As long as the transformation handles remain visible, you can cancel any changes you made. By cancelling the transformation, the layer is restored to its original state.

8. **With the Lights layer selected, choose Edit>Content-Aware Scale.**

   Again, you see the transformation handles. The process is virtually the same as regular scaling, but identifies and tries to protect areas of detail when you scale the image.

9. **Click the left-center handle on the layer and drag left until the path in the image is approximately one-third of the way across the canvas.**

   As you can see, some distortion still occurs. However, the lights hanging over the path — the most obvious point of detail — are not noticeably distorted. Other areas of detail — the trees and bench, for example — are somewhat distorted, but not nearly as badly as they were from the regular scale transformation.

Content-aware scaling attempts to preserve areas of detail.

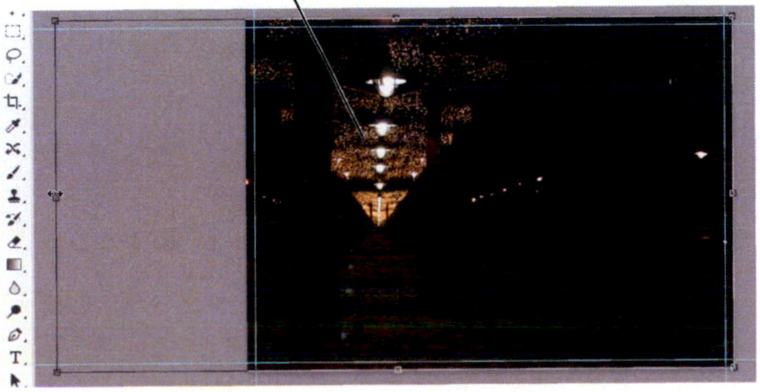

10. **Press Return/Enter to finalize the transformation.**

11. **Save the file and continue to the next exercise.**

PHOTOSHOP FOUNDATIONS

More about Content-Aware Scaling

Content-aware scaling identifies areas of detail when it determines what to protect. In some cases, though, the image focus might have little or no detail within the shape areas — the white bird in the following image, for example. To solve this problem, you can identify a specific mask area to protect when you use content-aware scaling.

Use this menu to protect a specific mask area.

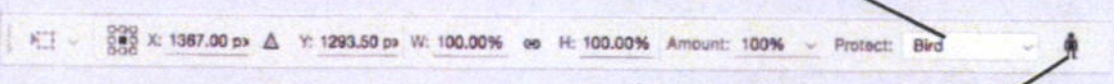

Click this button to protect skin tones from scaling.

Original image

Image scaled using Transform>Scale mode

Image scaled using Content-Aware Scale mode

Image scaled using Content-Aware Scale mode, but with the bird area protected by a mask.

Use the Content-Aware Move Tool

Photoshop makes it easy to move content around on the canvas. If an entire layer is selected, you can easily use the Move tool to move all the content on that layer to a different location. If you create a specific selection area using one of the marquee or lasso tools, you can also move only the selected area to another location on the active layer. It's important to realize, however, that this process actually removes the area under the original selection area, which might not be what you want. The Content-Aware Move tool allows you to move a selection and fill the original selection area with detail instead of leaving an empty hole.

1. **Make festival.psd the active file.**

   The main focus of the poppy image is nicely centered in the canvas. To make room for the other pieces of the composition, you need the flower to be on the right side of the image.

2. **Choose the Lasso tool in the Tools panel.**

3. **Draw a marquee that roughly selects the flower in the center of the image.**

Lasso tool
Draw a loose selection around the entire flower.

4. **Choose the Move tool in the Tools panel.**

5. **Click inside the selection area, then drag the selected area to the right side of the canvas.**

   When you use the Move tool with a specific selection marquee, you are moving all of the pixels within that selection area. The area of the original selection is removed from that layer, so you can see underlying layers (or transparent gray-and-white checkerboard, if there is no underlying layer).

   You should notice that the moved pixels remain on the same layer. As long as the selection marquee remains active, you can continue to move the selected pixels around the same layer without affecting the other pixels on that layer. If you deselect, however, the underlying pixels will be permanently replaced by the pixels you moved.

   To get around this problem, it's fairly common practice to move selected pixels to another layer before dragging with the Move tool:

   1. Make a selection.
   2. Choose Edit>Cut to remove the selected pixels from the original layer, or
   3. Choose Edit>Copy to keep the selected pixels on the original layer.
   4. Choose Edit>Paste to add the cut/copied pixels onto a new layer.

   If you leave the selection marquee in place before choosing Edit>Paste, the cut/copied pixels are pasted in the exact position as they were when you cut/copied them.

6. **Choose Edit>Undo Move to restore all the pixels to their original positions.**

7. **With the same marquee still selected, choose the Content-Aware Move tool (nested under the Spot Healing Brush tool).**

   You can draw a new marquee with the Content-Aware Move tool, but in this case it isn't necessary because you already defined the selection area with the Lasso tool.

8. **In the Options bar, make sure Move is selected in the Mode menu and the Transform On Drop option is selected.**

   When the Content-Aware Move tool is active, the Mode menu in the Options bar determines whether you will move or extend the selection area.

   The Adaptation menu determines how closely the software analyzes the structure and color of the image to create the final result. Structure is defined on a 1–7 scale, Color is defined on a 0–10 scale. Higher values mean stricter adaptation; they take longer to process, but can produce more accurate results.

   When the Transform On Drop option is active, releasing the mouse button results in a bounding box around the moved selection; you can use the bounding box handles to adjust the moved selection's size. The movement is not finalized until you press Return/Enter (or click the Commit Transform button in the Options bar). If Transform On Drop is *not* checked, the movement is finalized as soon as you release the mouse button.

9. **Click inside the selection area and drag the selected flower to the right side of the canvas.**

   Content-Aware Move tool
Transform On Drop is checked by default.
When you release the mouse button, bounding box handles are available to transform the moved selection.
Moving the selection does not reveal the underlying layers.

10. **Press Return/Enter to finalize the move.**

    The process might take a while to complete because Photoshop has to analyze and determine what pixels to create. Be patient.

    When the process is complete, the original selection area is filled with pixels that seamlessly blend into the surrounding area. The edges of the moved area are also blended into their new surrounding area.

    The original selection area is filled with information that blends into the image.
Edges of the moved selection area are blended into the surrounding image.

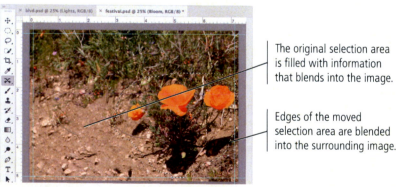

10. **Turn off the active selection (Select>Deselect).**

11. **Save the file and continue to the next exercise.**

More about the Content-Aware Move Tool

You can also use the Content-Aware Move tool in Extend mode to enlarge objects in a linear direction, as you can see in the images to the right.

Tighter selection marquees generally produce better results than a loose area that includes a lot of background pixels.

Original image

Image after extending the right building with the Content-Aware Move tool.

Apply a Tilt-Shift Blur Effect

Many of the Blur filters can be used for functional purposes, such as removing noise with the Gaussian Blur filter. Others have more artistic purposes, and include far more specific controls than a simple dialog box interface. Photoshop includes five sophisticated blur filters, which are controlled in a specialized workspace that contains only the tools you need to apply the filters.

1. **Make the `blvd.psd` file active, and make sure the Lights layer is selected in the Layers panel.**

2. **Choose Filter>Blur Gallery>Tilt-Shift.**

   The Tilt-Shift filter applies a linear blur out from a center line. You can use on-screen controls in the Blur Gallery to change the angle and position of the blur, as well as a number of other options.

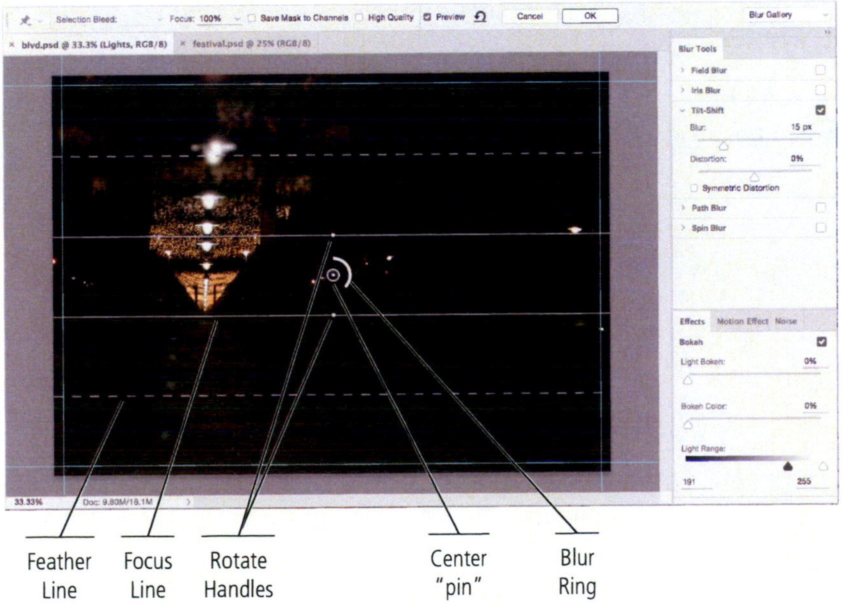

3. **Move the cursor over either Rotate Handle. Press Shift, then click and drag until the cursor feedback shows the angle of 90°.**

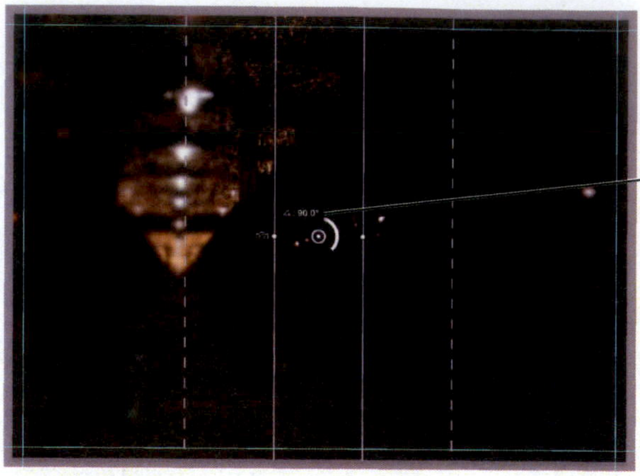

Heads-up display shows the blur rotation angle.

> *Note:*
>
> *Pressing Shift constrains the rotation to 22.5° increments.*

4. **Click the center "pin" of the blur control and drag left until the row of lights is between the two focus lines.**

   Anything between the two focus lines will be preserved without a blur.

5. **Click the Blur Ring and drag the white area until the cursor feedback shows the Blur: 20.**

   Changing intensity of the blur using the on-screen control applies the same change in the Blur field in the Blur Tools panel.

Drag the center point to move the blur center.

Drag the outer ring to change the blur intensity.

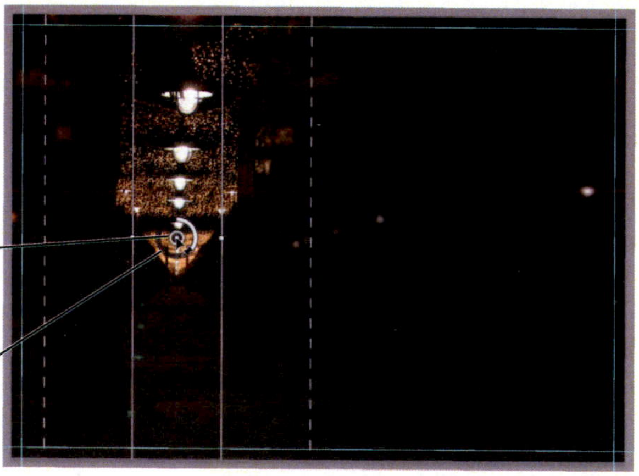

> *Note:*
>
> *The Distortion option defines the shape of the blur that is applied. You can also check the Symmetric Distortion option to apply the distortion amount to both sides of the blur.*

6. **Click the left Focus Line (the solid line) away from the Rotate Handle, and drag left until the line is close to the right side of the left palm tree.**

7. **Click the left Feather Line (the dotted line) and drag until the line is just past the left side of the same palm tree.**

The Feather Lines define the distance from unblurred (at the Focus Line) and completely blurred pixels.

Focus Line

Feather Line

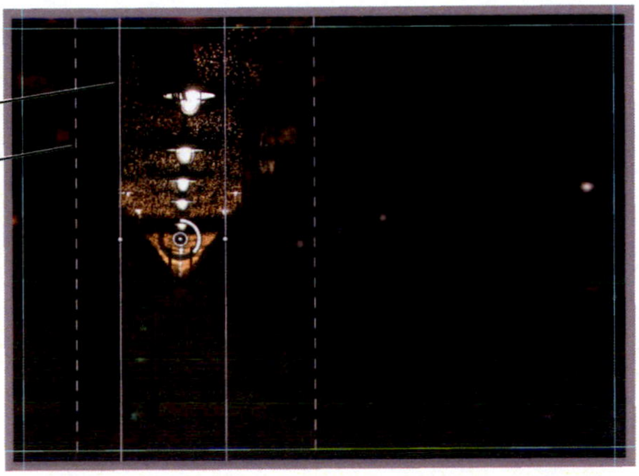

8. **Repeat Steps 6–7 to position the right Focus and Feather lines relative to the right palm tree.**

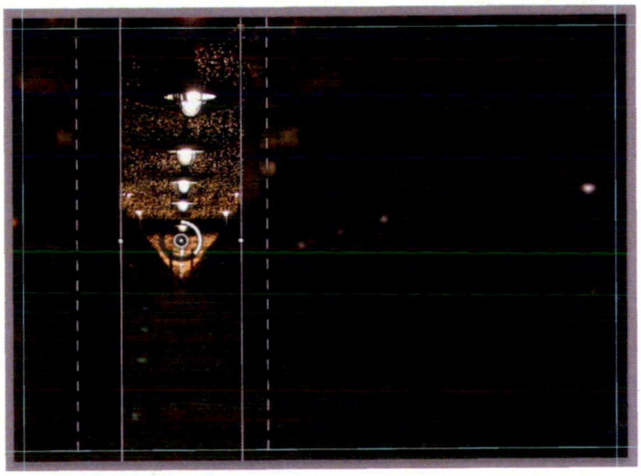

9. **Click OK in the Options bar to apply the blur.**

When you finalize the blur, the process can take a while to render. Be patient.

Because the Lights layer is a regular layer, the Blur Gallery filter is applied destructively. If you apply these filters to a Smart Object layer, they are remembered as Smart Filters and can be edited.

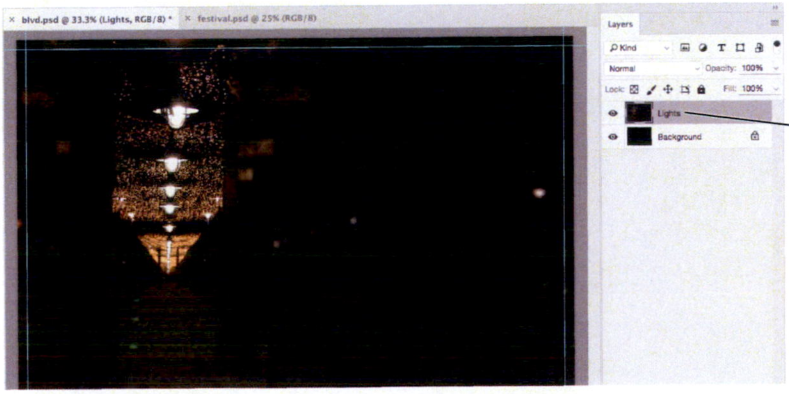

Blur Gallery filters destructively affect the regular layer.

10. **Save the file and continue to the next exercise.**

Note:

*In the Effects panel, you can control **bokeh** effects — the aesthetic qualities of blurred points of light — for a field, iris, or tilt-shift blur.*

***Light Bokeh** brightens blurred areas of an image.*

***Bokeh Color** changes the color of lightened areas in the image from neutral (0%) to colorful (100%).*

***Light Range** determines which brightness values are affected by the Light Bokeh.*

APPLY AN IRIS BLUR EFFECT

The Iris Blur filter mimics the effect of changing the aperture, focal length, and focus distance with a camera. The blur applies around a central point; you can use on-screen controls to define the shape and size of the blur.

1. **Make the festival.psd file active.**

2. **With the Bloom layer selected, choose Filter>Blur Gallery>Iris Blur.**

 The Iris blur is also controlled in the Blur Gallery interface.

Ellipse Handle Feather Handle Center "pin" Blur Ring Roundness Handle

3. **Click the center "pin" and drag to position the blur so it is approximately centered on the flower.**

 You can click away from the existing blur controls to add a new pin — which means you can define more than one focal point on the same layer.

4. **Click the right ellipse handle and drag left to change the width of the ellipse.**

 If you click the ellipse *away* from the handle, you can enlarge or shrink the existing ellipse without affecting its proportional shape.

Drag the pin to move the focal point of the blur.

Drag the Ellipse Handle to rotate or change the shape of the blur ellipse.

Drag the Ellipse to resize the blur without changing its shape.

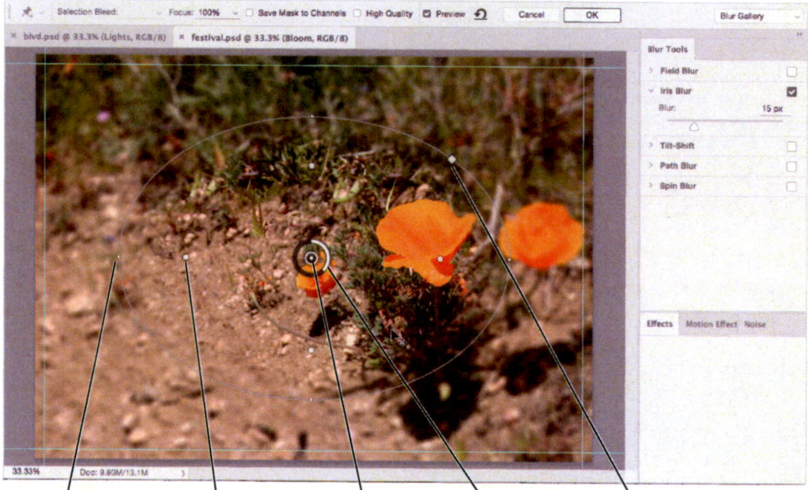

> *Note:*
>
> *You can apply a blur to only certain parts of a layer by drawing a selection marquee before opening the Blur Gallery. In this case, you can use the Selection Bleed option (in the Options bar) to determine how much the selected area blends with the unselected areas.*

> *Note:*
>
> *Click the Roundness Handle and drag to make the blur shape more or less rectangular.*

5. **Click the top Feather Handle and drag down until it is placed at the top edge of the center flower.**

The distance between the Feather Handle and the outer ellipse defines the length of the blur. When you click and drag one handle, all four move symmetrically.

6. **Press Option/Alt, then click the bottom Feather Handle and drag up to increase the blur distance on only the bottom of the flower.**

Pressing Option/Alt allows you to move one Feather Handle independently of the others.

Option/Alt-drag a Feather Handle to move it independently of the other handles.

7. **Click the Blur Ring and drag around to increase the intensity to 20 px.**

8. **Click OK in the Options bar to apply the blur.**

9. **Save the file and continue to the next stage of the project.**

Note:

You can use the Save Mask to Channels option (in the Blur Gallery Options bar) to create an alpha channel mask from the defined blur. Solid areas in the mask show areas that are unblurred; white areas of the mask show areas that are entirely blurred.

Note:

The Focus option in the Options bar defines the clarity of the area in the focus zone. For a Tilt-Shift blur, this is the area between the two Focus Lines. For an Iris blur, this is the area inside the Feather Handles.

More about the Blur Gallery

Field Blur

The Field Blur filter applies an overall blur that affects the entire layer. Changing the blur intensity changes the amount of blur that is applied to that layer.

You can also place multiple focus points to change the blur in different areas of the layer. In the image to the right, we applied a 25-px blur to the pin at the top of the image and a 0-px blur to the pin in the lower-left portion of the image. The 0-px pin prevents the blur from affecting the entire image, so the front of the bridge appears in focus.

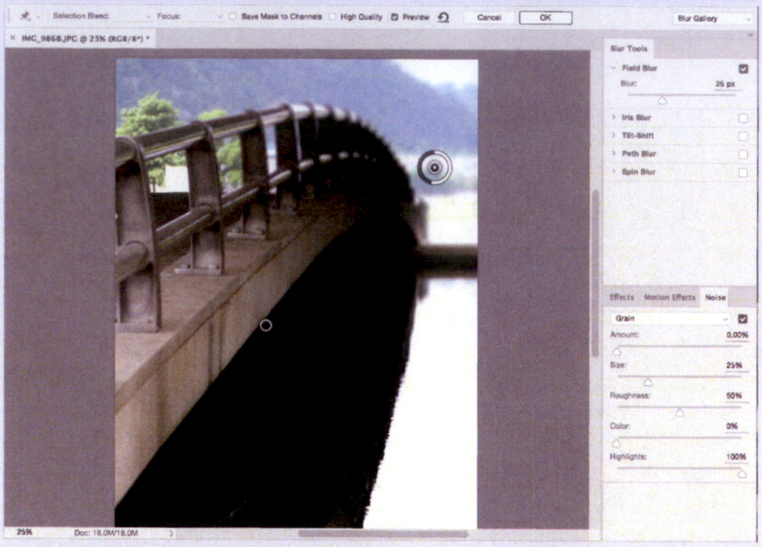

Spin Blur

The Spin Blur filter creates a rotational blur around a defined point. The blur angle controls the amount of blur that is applied.

You can click and drag the rotation point to move the blur's center point; if you Option/Alt-click and drag the rotation point, you can move it away from the center of the blur ring to create an off-center spin blur.

The feather handles define the outer edge of the area affected by the blur.

Clicking and dragging the blur ring away from the ellipse handles resizes the blur ring proportionally; you can also click and drag one of the ellipse handles to resize the blur ring in only one direction.

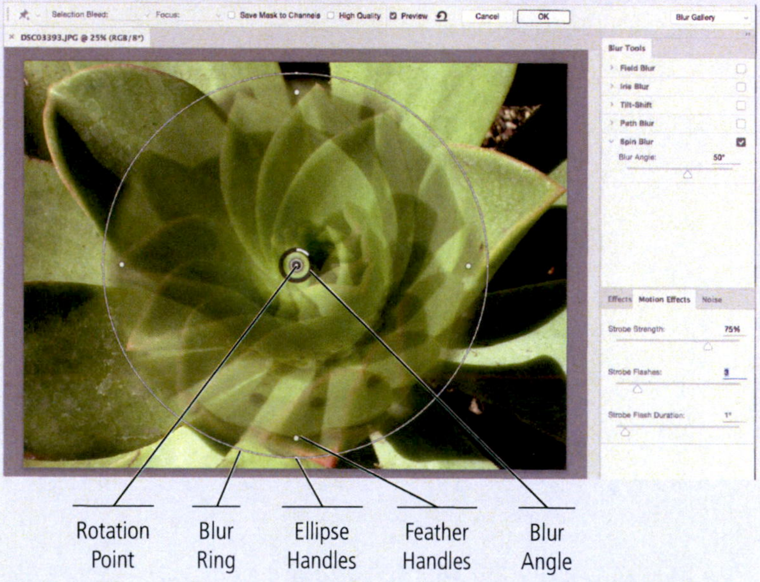

You can also use the Motion Effects panel to change the strength of the blur:

- Strobe Flashes defines the number of exposures that will be visible.
- Strobe Strength defines how much blurring is visible between strobe flash exposures. A setting of 0% (the default) means no strobe effect is visible; a setting of 100% results in very little blur between exposures.
- Strobe Flash Duration defines the length of the strobe flash exposure in degrees, which controls the distance of the blur around the blur circumference.

Applying a spin blur with an increased Stroke Strength effect creates the appearance of the blade in motion; because Strobe Flashes effect is set to 3, you can see three ghosted versions of the plant's center leaves in the image above.

More about the Blur Gallery (continued)

Path Blur

The Path Blur filter creates a motion blur based on a path that you define.

Clicking and dragging in the gallery window creates the initial blur path. You can click anywhere along the blue path to create a path midpoint and bend the path in a specific direction.

Each endpoint on the blur path can have a different speed, or the degree of blur that is applied at that point. If Edit Blur Shapes is checked in the Blur Tools panel, you can drag and/or bend the red arrow to change the direction of the blur that is applied along the blur path.

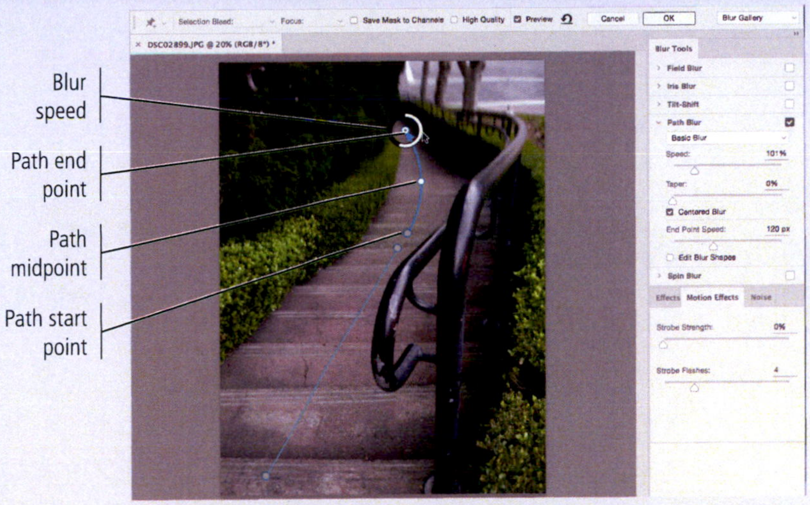

In the Blur Tools panel, you can use the top menu to define a basic blur or rear sync flash blur (this simulates the effect of a flash fired at the end of an exposure).

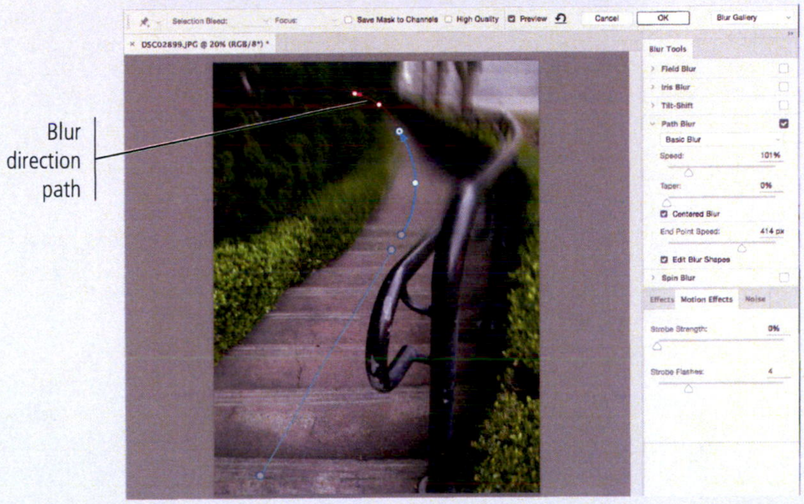

The Speed slider defines the overall blur amount for all defined blur paths.

The Taper slider adjusts the edge fading of blurs; higher values allow the blur to fade gradually.

The Centered Blur option creates stable blurs by centering the blur shape for any pixel on the defined path.

If you check the Edit Blur Shapes option, you can manipulate the red arrow for each end point on a blur path to change the direction and speed (length) of the selected blur.

In the Motion Effects panel, Strobe Flashes defines the number of exposures of the virtual strobe flash light. Strobe Strength defines how much blurring is visible between strobe flash exposures.

In the above images, we creates two separate blur paths. The first defines a curved blur that follows the shape of the lower stairs; the starting point has a rather high blur speed and the end point has a blur speed of 0 px. Because the 0-px blur speed does not eliminate all blurring at the end point, we added a second straight blur path with 0-px blur speeds at both ends to eliminate all blurring in that area of the image (at the top of the staircase).

Stage 3 Working with Type

Type is naturally a vector-based element. As long as you maintain type as vectors, the letter shapes can be resized and transformed without losing quality. And as you know, Photoshop can combine raster and vector objects into a single composition.

Many Photoshop jobs require some kind of type. Although Photoshop is not a typesetting tool by definition, its type capabilities are robust enough for creating and manipulating type in a variety of ways. To complete these postcards, you are going to create and format several type elements.

The Anatomy of Type

Before we jump into the exercises in this section, you should understand the terms that you will often hear when people talk about type:

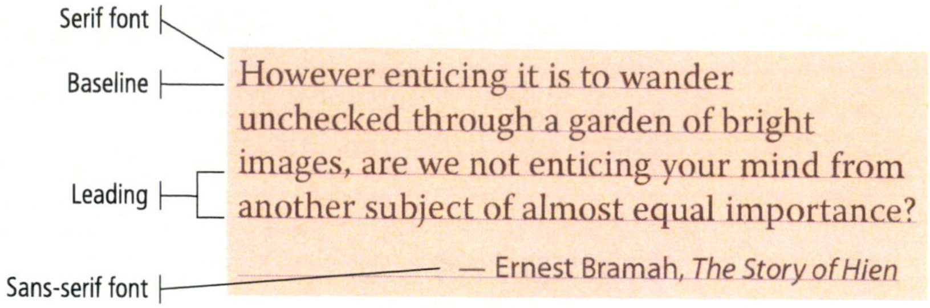

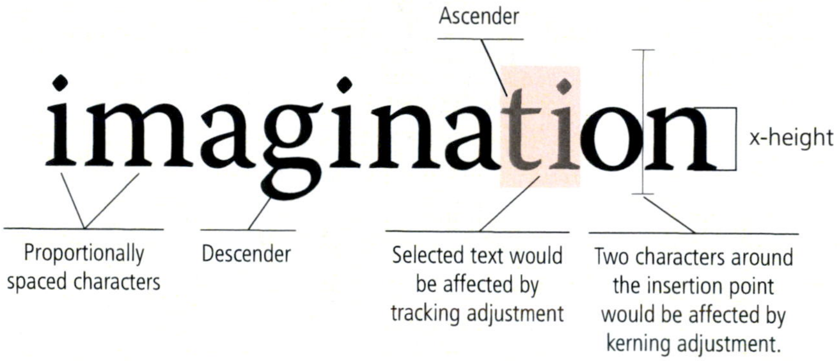

> ***Note:***
>
> *There are other types of special fonts, including script, symbol, dingbat, decorative, and image fonts. These don't fit easily into the serif/sans-serif distinction.*

Type is typically divided into two basic categories: serif and sans serif. **Serif type** has small flourishes on the ends of the letterforms; **sans-serif** has no such decorations (*sans* is French for "without"). The actual shape of letters is determined by the specific **font** you use; each **character** in a font is referred to as a **glyph**.

Fonts can be monospaced or proportionally spaced. In a monospace font, each character takes up the same amount of space on a line; in other words, a lowercase "i" and "w" will occupy the same horizontal width. In a proportionally spaced font, different characters occupy different amounts of horizontal space as necessary.

When you set type in a digital application, the letters rest on a non-printing line called the **baseline**. If a type element has more than one line in a single paragraph, the distance from one baseline to the next is called **leading** (pronounced "ledding"). Most applications set the default leading as 120% of the type size, but you can change the leading to any value you prefer.

The **x-height** of type is the height of the lowercase letter "x." Elements that extend below the baseline are called **descenders** (as in "g," "j," and "p"); elements that extend above the x-height are called **ascenders** (as in "b," "d," and "k").

The size of type is usually measured in **points** (there are approximately 72 points in an inch). When you define a specific type size, you determine the distance from the bottom of the descenders to the top of the ascenders (plus a small extra space above the ascenders called the **body clearance**).

Place and Format Point Type

You can create two basic kinds of type in Photoshop: point type and area type. **Point type** is created by simply clicking in the image window with one of the Type tools. A point type element can exist on one line or multiple lines. Point type can continue into apparent infinity without starting a new line; if you want to start a new line, you have to manually tell Photoshop where to create the break.

> ***Note:***
>
> *You must install the ATC fonts from the Student Files website to complete the rest of this project.*

1. **With festival.psd active, choose the Horizontal Type tool.**

   You can access the basic type options in the Options bar. Additional options are available in the Character and Paragraph panels.

2. **In the Tools panel, click the Default Foreground and Background Colors button.**

   Type automatically adopts the active foreground color.

3. **In the Options bar, change the Font Size to 28 pt.**

   If you define type settings before you create a type layer, those settings automatically apply to the layer you create.

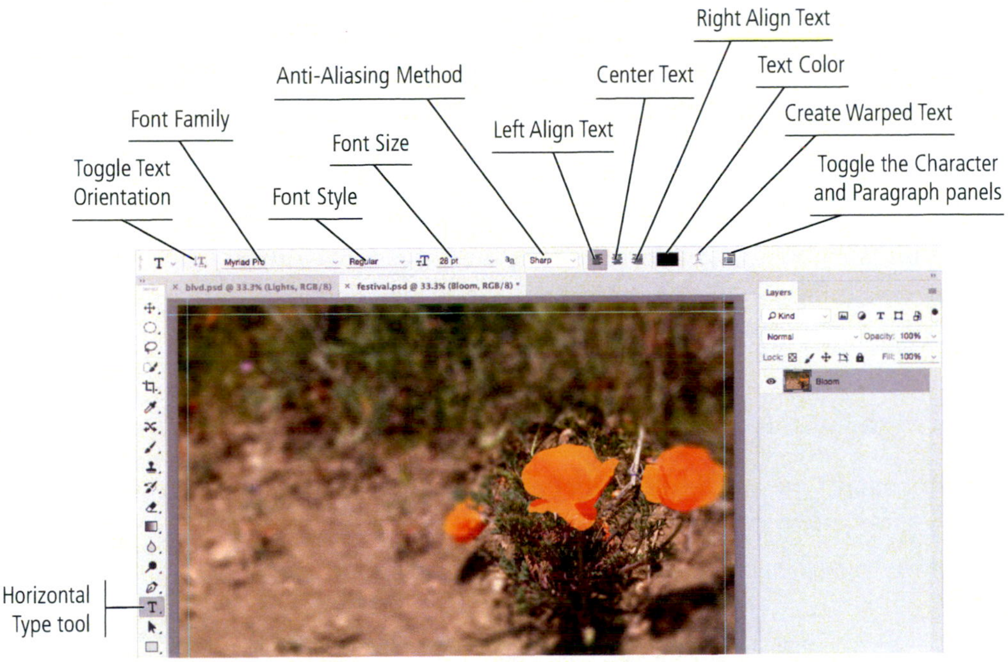

4. **Click anywhere in the canvas to create a type layer, then type Antelope Valley.**

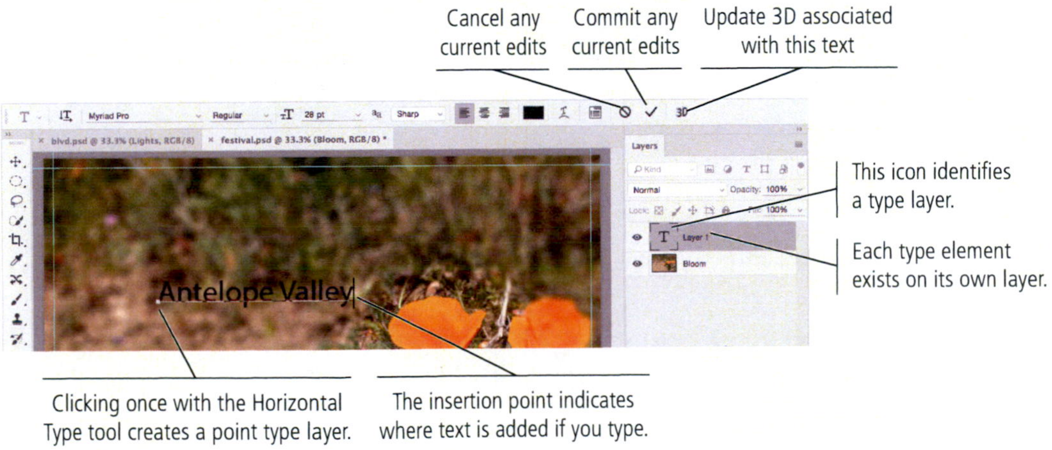

5. **In the Options bar, click the Commit button to finalize your changes to the active the Type layer.**

You can also choose a different tool, or select a different layer to finalize your changes.

6. **With the new type layer selected, click the Font menu to highlight it and type atc g.**

Typing in the Font menu returns a list of all fonts that contain the defined search string. The resulting font names do not need to exactly match the search string. In this case, any fonts that include the characters "atc" and the character "g" are returned.

7. **Move the mouse cursor over the first font in the resulting list.**

Photoshop includes a live font preview that automatically shows the selected text in the font where your mouse cursor is currently hovering.

Note:

If you're working with the insertion point flashing in a type layer, or you have characters on a type layer selected, you can't use the keyboard shortcuts to access different tools.

Note:

If you change the alignment of point type, the text moves around the origin point of the element.

Type in this field to search for specific fonts.

Click this button to show all fonts that are available on your computer.

After committing the edits, the type layer adopts its name based on the text in the layer.

Only fonts matching the search criteria appear in the resulting menu.

The active type layer changes to show the font that is active under the mouse cursor.

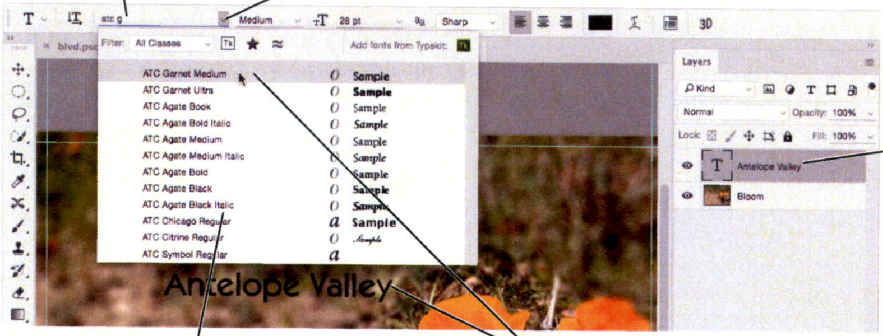

8. **Click ATC Garnet Medium in the menu to change the font of the active type layer.**

9. **Click with the Horizontal Type tool again (away from the existing type) to create a second type layer, then type Poppy Festival.**

Clicking places the insertion point in a new point type element, creating a new type layer.

The Type tools remember the last formatting options you defined.

Clicking again creates a separate type layer.

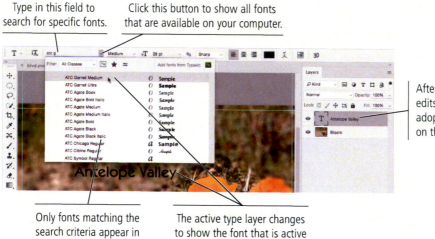

10. **With the insertion point flashing in the second type layer, choose Select>All.**

When the insertion point is flashing, this command highlights (selects) all of the text in the active type layer.

You can also click and drag to select specific characters, double-click to select an entire word, triple-click to select an entire line, or quadruple-click to select an entire paragraph.

11. **In the Options bar, change the Font Style to Ultra, and change the Font Size to 72 pt.**

If you type in the field, you have to Press Return/Enter (or click the Commit button) to finalize the new formatting. If you choose a defined size from the attached menu, you do not need to press Return/Enter.

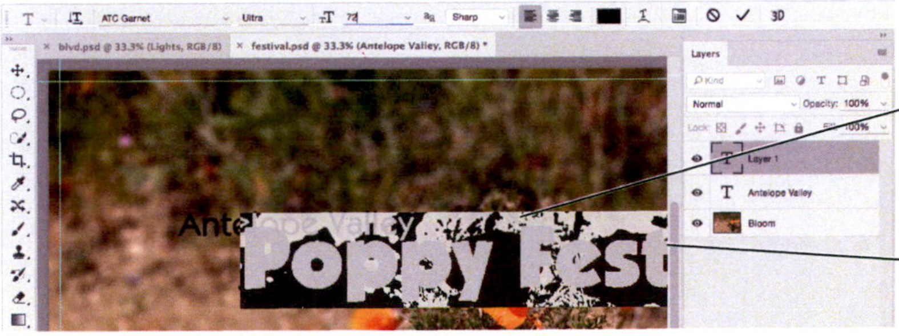

Character attributes such as font size affect all selected characters.

Point type exists on a single line unless you manually insert a line break.

12. **Press the Left Arrow key to deselect the characters and move the insertion point to the beginning of the type. With the insertion point still flashing in the type, press and hold Command/Control to access the type layer bounding box.**

Pressing Command/Control temporarily switches to the Move tool, so you can move a type layer without switching away from the Horizontal Type tool.

13. **Click inside the bounding box area and drag to move the type until it is centered horizontally on the canvas, approximately 0.25" from the top ruler guide.**

The pink smart guides identify when the dragged content is centered on the canvas. To find the correct position for the top edge of the type, you might want to turn on page rulers (View>Rulers).

Press Command/Control while the insertion point is flashing to access the layer's transformation bounding box.

Click inside the bounding box area and drag to move the layer content.

Smart Guides identify when the center of the object aligns to the center of the canvas.

14. **While still holding the Command/Control key, click the bottom-right bounding-box handle and drag down. Resize the type so it is approximately 1.25" high.**

Feel free to toggle rulers on and off as necessary while working on this (and all) projects.

Even though you resized the type layer (proportionally and disproportionally), it is still live type — you can still place the insertion point and edit as necessary.

Note:

You could accomplish the same thing by selecting the type layer with the Move tool active, then choosing Edit>Free Transform.

Drag the handles to resize or transform the type layer.

15. **When you finish resizing the type, release the Command/Control key.**

More About Working with Fonts

If you click the arrow to the right of the Font Family menu, you will see a menu that lists fonts that are available to Photoshop on your computer.

The top section of the menu lists the ten most **recent fonts**. By default, these appear in the order they were used (the most recently used appears at the top of the menu). In the Type pane of the Preferences dialog box, you can change the number of displayed fonts.

Each font listed in the Font menu includes a number of elements:

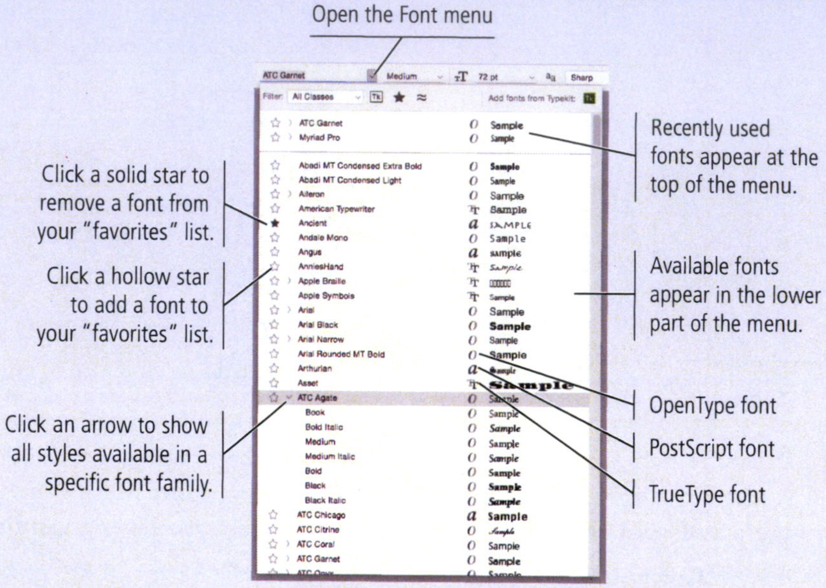

Open the Font menu
Click a solid star to remove a font from your "favorites" list.
Click a hollow star to add a font to your "favorites" list.
Click an arrow to show all styles available in a specific font family.
Recently used fonts appear at the top of the menu.
Available fonts appear in the lower part of the menu.
OpenType font
PostScript font
TrueType font

- You can use the star icons on the left side of the font menu to define "favorite" fonts. You can then use the button at the top of the menu to show only those fonts that you have marked as favorites.
- The font family names in each section appear in alphabetical order.

  An arrow to the left of a font name indicates that a specific font family includes more than one style. You can click the arrow to show all possible styles.

  If you apply a font that includes more than one style, the style you choose appears in the Font Style menu below the Font Family field. You can open the Font Style menu to change the style without changing the font family.

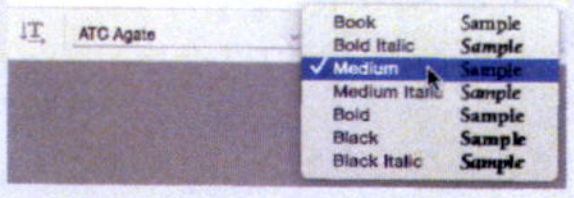

- An icon identifies the type of each font.

  PostScript (Type 1) fonts have two file components (outline and printer) that are required for output.

  TrueType fonts have a single file, but (until recently) were primarily used on the Windows platform.

  OpenType fonts are contained in a single file that can include more than 60,000 glyphs (characters) in a single font. OpenType fonts are cross-platform; the same font can be used on both Macintosh and Windows systems.
- A sample of each font appears at the right side of the menu. You can change the size of the sample in the Type>Font Preview Size menu.

The top of the Font menu includes options for filtering fonts. (If you have an individual-user subscription to Adobe Creative Cloud, you can also show only fonts that are installed through the Adobe Typekit website; see Project 5: Calendar Cover.)

Show only certain categories of fonts.

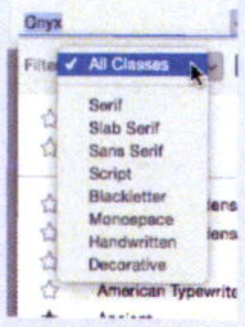

Show only fonts that are marked as favorites.

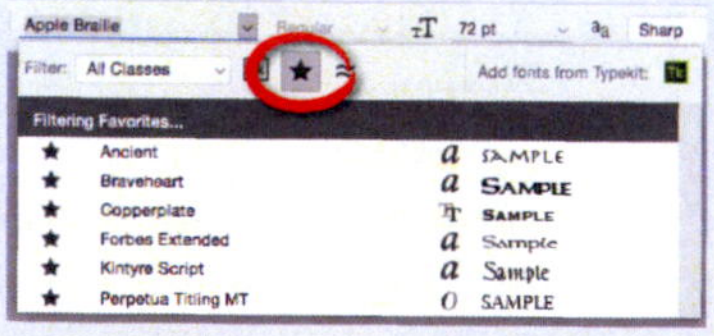

Show only fonts that are similar to the currently active font.

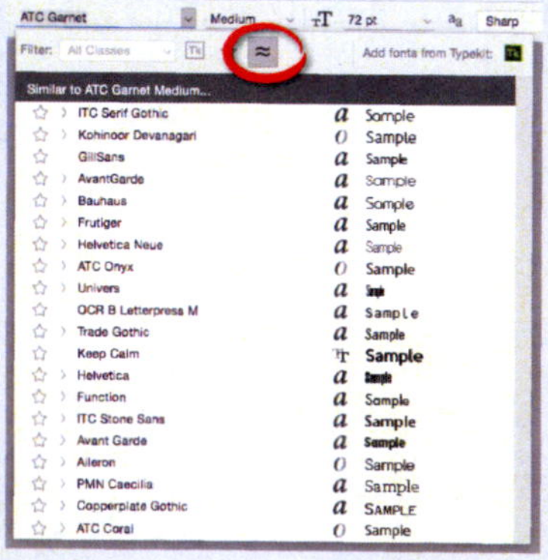

16. **Click to place the insertion point between the "F" and "e" in the word Festival.**

17. **In the Options bar, click the button to toggle open the Character and Paragraph panels.**

    You can also choose Window>Character or Type>Panels>Character to open the Character panel. Changes made in the Character panel apply only to selected text.

Click here to toggle the Character and Paragraph panels.

The Font Size shows the change that was created by scaling the type layer.

18. **In the Character panel, change the Kerning field to -30.**

    Kerning and tracking control the spacing between individual characters. **Kerning** adjusts the spacing between two specific characters (called a **kerning pair**). **Tracking** (also called range kerning) is applied over a range of selected type.

    Kerning values are based by default on the type **metrics** (the values stored in the font data). Professional-quality fonts include predefined kerning and tracking tables in the font data. The **Optical** option in the Kerning menu is useful for fonts that don't have built-in kerning values; Photoshop applies kerning based on how it perceives letter shapes.

    You should always check the letter spacing when you set headline type, use All Caps or Small Caps type styles, or apply any other artificial manipulation such as the stretching you applied in Step 11.

Note:

Kerning and tracking are largely matters of personal taste. In this project, you want the letters to be very tightly spaced, but not touching.

Kerning applies to the space between two characters, where the insertion point is placed.

19. **Continue adjusting the kerning between the letter pairs until you are satisfied with the results.**

20. **With the Horizontal Type tool still active, press and hold the Command/Control key to access the layer's bounding box handles, then Shift-drag the bottom-right handle until the right edge of the type is again 1/4" from the right ruler guide.**

    Reducing the tracking tightened the spacing between specific letter pairs, which reduced the overall width of the type layer. This transformation fixes that problem.

Note:

Press Option/Alt-Left Arrow to apply –20 kerning units or Option/Alt-Right Arrow to apply +20 kerning units at the current insertion point.

21. **Save the file and continue to the next exercise.**

The Character Panel in Depth

PHOTOSHOP FOUNDATIONS

All of the options that are available in the Options bar are also available in the Character panel. However, the Character panel includes a number of other options that control the appearance of type in your document.

Changes to character formatting affect only selected characters. If you make changes before typing, the changes apply to all characters you type from the insertion point.

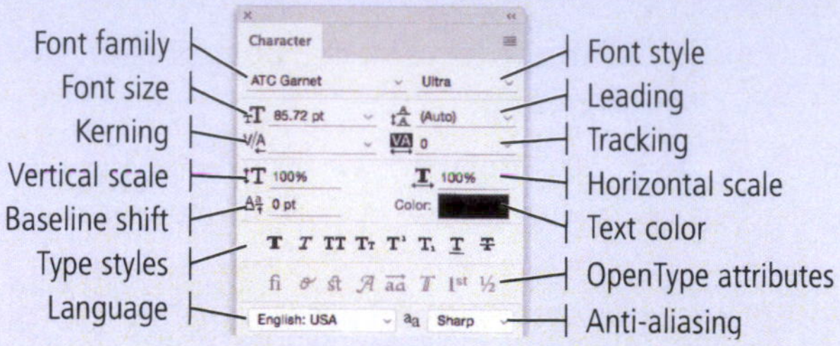

Anti-Aliasing Options for Type

Although type is vector-based, it will eventually be rendered (rasterized) at some point — even if that doesn't happen until the final output. Anti-aliasing produces smooth-edge type by partially filling the edge pixels, which allows the edges of the type to better blend into the background when the type is rendered. (Be aware that anti-aliasing small type might distort the letter shapes.) Photoshop supports five options for anti-aliasing type. The effects of each method are best viewed at higher zoom percentages.

None

Sharp

- None applies no anti-aliasing.
- Sharp creates the sharpest type.
- Crisp makes type appear slightly sharp.
- Strong makes type appear heavier.
- Smooth makes type edges appear very smooth.

Crisp

Strong

Smooth

Use the Move Tool with Type Layers

Type layers in Photoshop are similar to most other layers. You can drag and transform type layers using most of the same tools that you use to transform other kinds of layers. You can scale or skew type layers; change their opacity, fill, and blending mode; apply layer styles; and even add warp effects — while still maintaining the editable type.

1. **With festival.psd active, choose the Move tool.**

2. **In the Layers panel, click the Antelope Valley layer to select it.**

   Using the Move tool, you can move and manipulate type layers like any other layer, but you can't edit the actual type.

3. **In the Character panel, click the Color swatch to open the Color Picker for the text color.**

   The insertion point does not need to be flashing to change the formatting of the active type layer. Keep in mind, however, that any change you make while the insertion point is *not* flashing applies to all type in the layer. If you want to change the formatting of only some type on a layer, you first have to use the Type tool to select the characters you want to affect.

Note:

The only options you can't apply to live text are the Distort and Perspective transformations, custom warps (although you can use the built-in warp shapes), and filters. To use these features, you must rasterize the type layer.

4. **Move the Eyedropper cursor over a bright orange color in the poppy image and click to sample that color. Click OK to change the type color.**

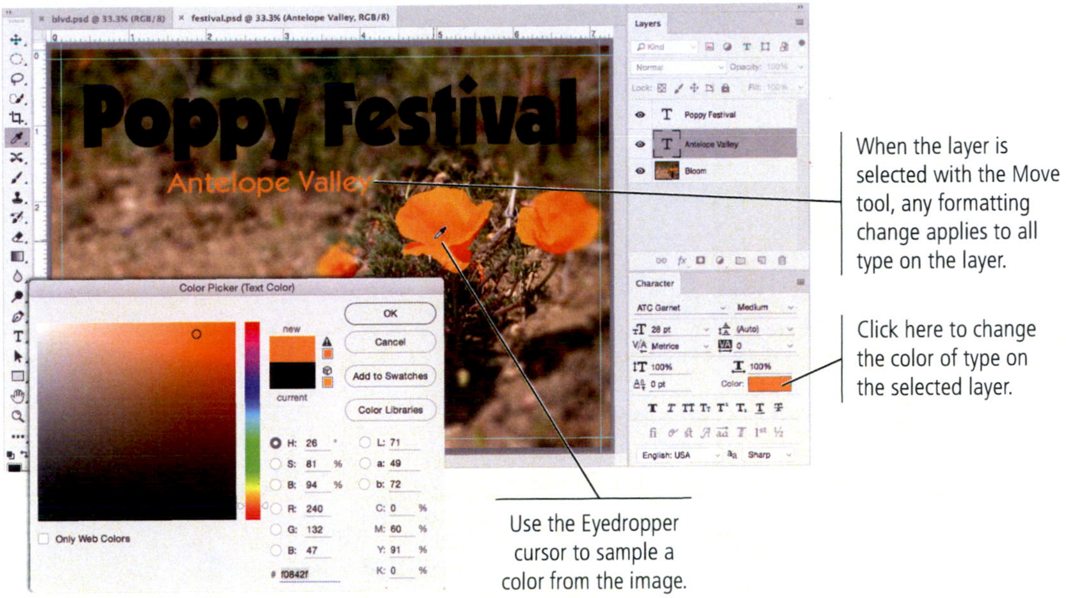

When the layer is selected with the Move tool, any formatting change applies to all type on the layer.
Click here to change the color of type on the selected layer.
Use the Eyedropper cursor to sample a color from the image.

5. **With the Auto-Select option turned off in the Options bar, click and drag to move the type so the first letter in the layer appears just above the "o" in the word "Poppy".**

   If you don't turn off the Auto-Select option, you would have to click exactly on the rather thin letters in the type. When this option is not checked, you can click anywhere in the canvas to drag the selected layer.

   As you can see, the 28-pt text is too large to fit in the space. The type runs directly behind the "F" in the word Festival because the Poppy Festival type layer is higher in the layer stacking order.

6. **In the Character panel, reduce the font size to 22 pt.**

   This layer uses left paragraph alignment, and the origin point of the layer remains in place when you change the formatting.

7. **Select the Poppy Festival type layer, then use the Character panel to change the type color to white.**

8. **Save the file and continue to the next exercise.**

Create Vertically Oriented Type

Although most type (in English, at least) is oriented left-to-right, row-to-row, there are times when you want to orient type vertically — each character below the next. You can use the Vertical Type tool to accomplish this goal, whether for foreign-language design or simply for artistic purposes.

1. **Make blvd.psd the active file, then choose the Vertical Type tool (nested under the Horizontal Type tool).**

2. **In the Options bar, choose ATC Garnet Ultra as the font, define the size as 72 pt, choose the Top Align Text option, and choose white as the type color.**

3. **Click to create a new type layer, then type BLVD.**

   When you use the Vertical Type tool, each letter appears below the previous one.

   As you can see, the left edges of the letters (especially B and L) do not align. Vertical type orientation does not recognize the edges of lettershapes for the sake of alignment.

   In the Options bar, paragraph alignment options affect the position of type relative to the point where you click. You can align the type below, centered on, or above the origin point. You cannot, however, align the left or right edges of the letters.

Vertically oriented type can be oriented above, centered, or below the point where you click.

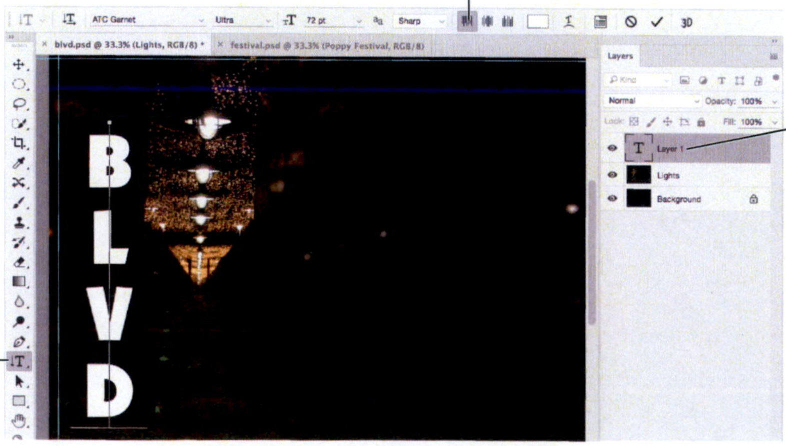

A new type layer is created just as it was when you used the Horizontal Type tool.

Vertical Type tool

4. **Click the new type layer in the Layers panel to select the layer (not the highlighted text), then choose Type>Orientation>Horizontal.**

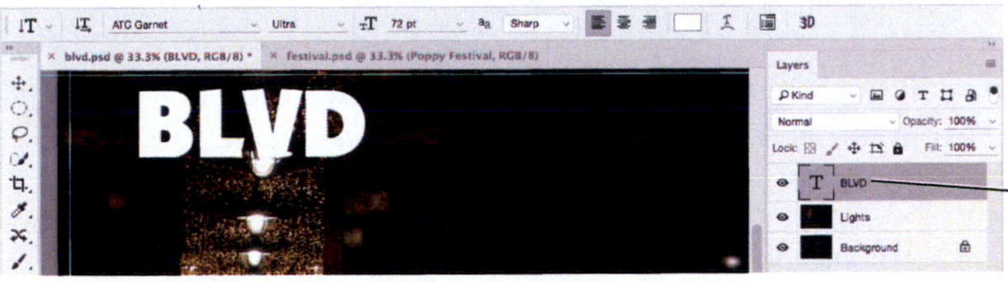

Select the actual type layer to change its orientation.

5. **Place the insertion point after the "B" and press Return/Enter to start a new paragraph.**

6. **Repeat this process to move each character onto a separate line.**

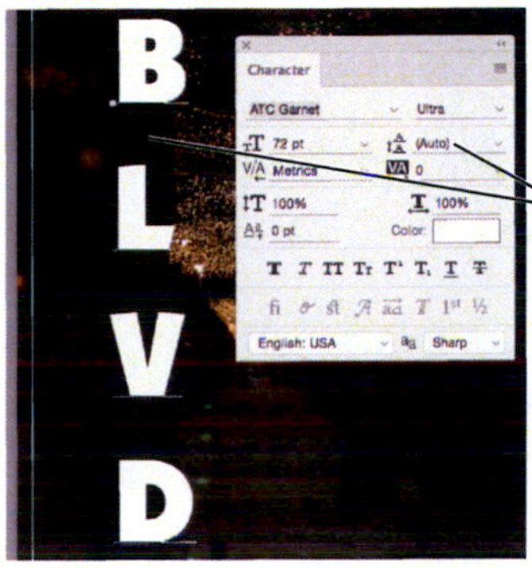

For horizontally oriented type, the default (auto) leading creates a large space from one baseline to the next.

7. **Place the insertion point before the "B". In the Options bar or Character panel, change the type size to 12 pt, then type THE and press Return/Enter.**

Changes to character formatting apply only to the insertion point (and the new type that you add from that point).

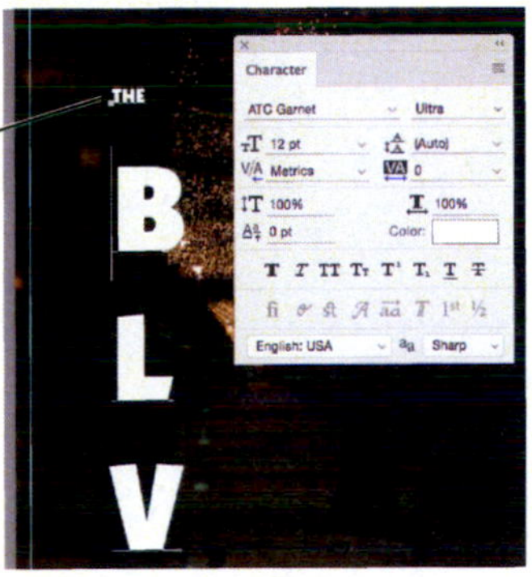

8. **Select the four letters in "BLVD". In the Character panel, change the Leading field to 55 pt.**

Although leading appears to apply to paragraphs, it is actually a character property. To change the leading for an entire paragraph, you have to select all characters in that paragraph.

Changes to character formatting apply only to the highlighted type.

Reduced leading reduces the space from one baseline to the next.

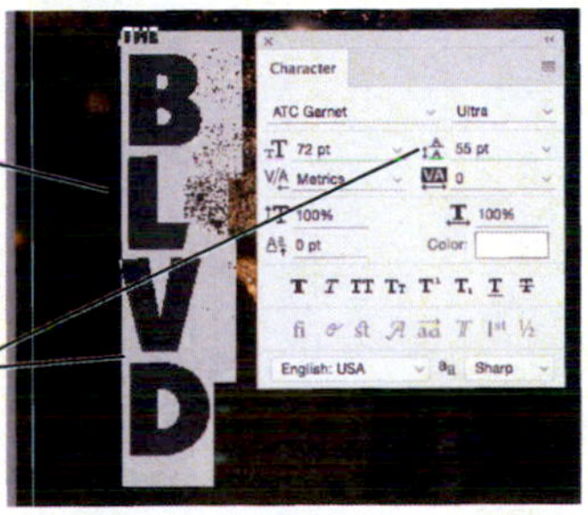

9. **Choose the Move tool. With the type layer selected, move the layer so the type begins in the top-left corner of the canvas, approximately 1/4″ from the ruler guides.**

10. **Choose Edit>Free Transform. Press Shift, then drag the bottom-right handle until the letters occupy the entire left side of the canvas. Leave approximately 1/4″ from the bottom ruler guide, as shown in the following image.**

11. **Press Return/Enter to finalize the transformation.**

Move the type to be approximately 1/4″ from the top-left corner.

Transform the type to occupy the entire left side, leaving a 1/4″ margin inside the ruler guides.

12. **Choose the Horizontal Type tool, then click to place the insertion point in the word "THE" (the first paragraph).**

13. **In the Paragraph panel, change the Indent Left Margin field to 4 pt.**

You can choose Window>Paragraph to open the Paragraph panel, or click the Toggle the Character and Paragraph Panels button in the Options bar.

The Indent values affect the position of the type relative to the layer's orientation point. This better aligns the "T" in "THE" with the left edge of the "B" in "BLVD."

When you work with point type, paragraph attributes apply to all type on a single line. If you have more than one paragraph — as you do in this type layer — you can apply different paragraph format options to each paragraph.

14. **Change the Add Space After Paragraph field to -3 pt.**

Leading affects the space from one baseline to the next, even within a single paragraph. The Space Before Paragraph and Space After Paragraph options relate to an entire paragraph. By reducing this value, you are closing up the space between the first paragraph ("THE") and the second paragraph ("B").

Paragraph formatting options apply to the entire paragraph where the insertion point is flashing.

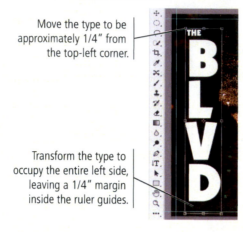

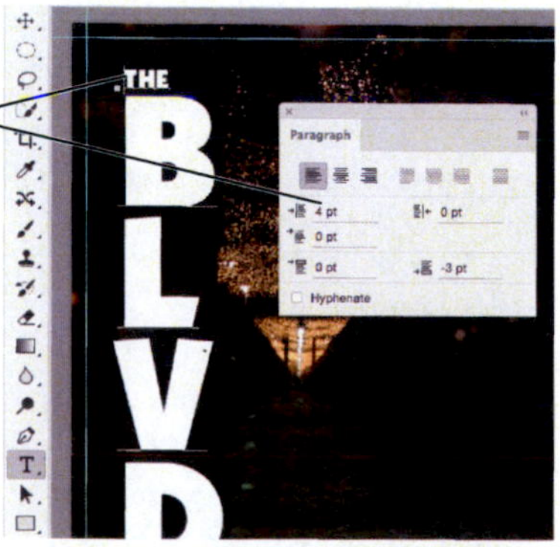

15. **Save the file and continue to the next exercise.**

The Paragraph Panel in Depth

You can change a number of paragraph attributes, including alignment and justification, indents, and space above and below paragraphs. The Justification options are only available when you work with area type (which you will do shortly), and some options are not relevant for point type that only occupies a single line.

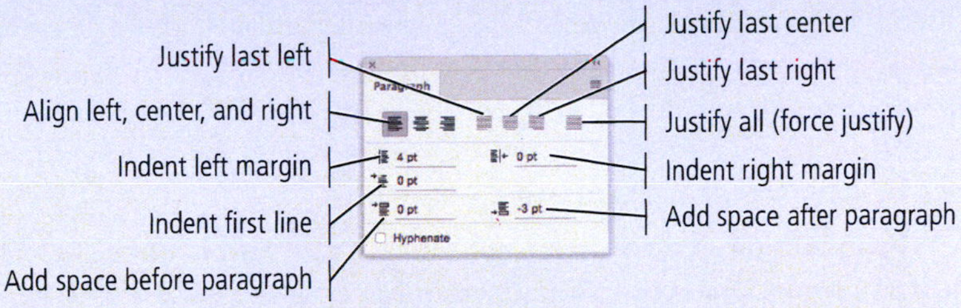

Hyphenation Options

When the Hyphenate option is selected, text in area type hyphenates automatically, based on the Hyphenation options in the Paragraph panel Options menu. You can control the minimum length of a word before it can be hyphenated, as well as the minimum number of characters that must appear before or after a hyphen. Formal rules of typography typically suggest that only words longer than six characters should be hyphenated, and at least three characters should exist before or after a hyphen.

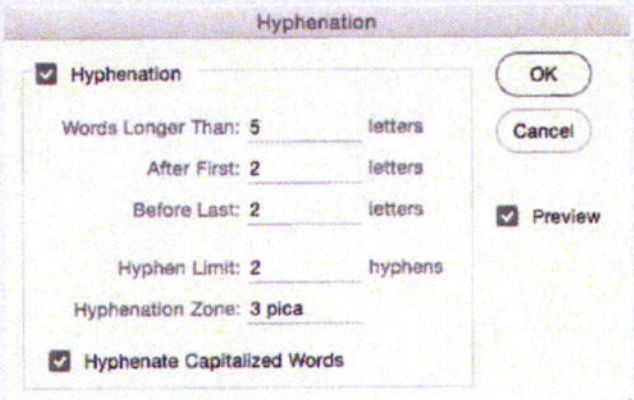

The **Hyphen Limit** field defines how many hyphens can appear at the ends of consecutive lines; formal rules of typography recommend limiting consecutive hyphens to three, and preferably no more than two.

The **Hyphenation Zone** determines the distance from the right edge of a type area where automatic hyphens can exist. If this field is set to 1/2″, for example, the automatic hyphen would have to fall within a half inch of the type area edge for a word to be automatically hyphenated.

The final option, **Hyphenate Capitalized Words**, can be turned off to prevent automatic hyphenation in proper names such as corporate or product names (many companies seriously frown on their trademarks being split across lines).

Justification Options

When you work with area type, you can justify paragraphs inside the type area. Justified type stretches horizontally to fill the width of the area. The last line of the paragraph can be aligned left, centered, or right, or it can be stretched based on your choice in the Paragraph panel. When text is justified, it's stretched based on the defined Justification options, which can be changed by choosing Justification in the Paragraph panel Options menu.

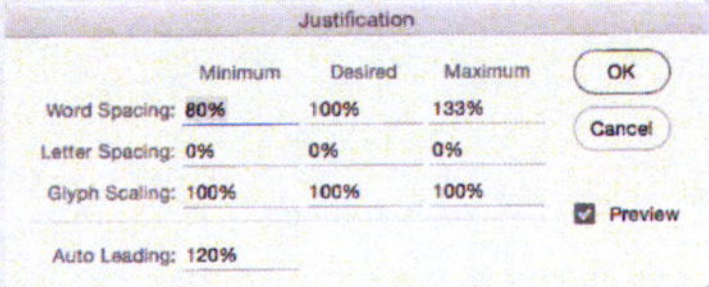

The Minimum and Maximum values define the acceptable spacing for justified paragraphs. The Desired value defines the *preferred* spacing for paragraphs:

- The **Word Spacing** fields control the space between words (anywhere you press the space bar). A 100% value means the word spacing remains the same when you justify a paragraph.
- The **Letter Spacing** fields control the space between letters, including kerning and tracking values. A 0% value means the letter spacing remains the same when you justify a paragraph.
- The **Glyph Scaling** fields control the width of individual characters. A 100% value means they are not stretched.

The **Auto Leading** field applies to both area type and point type that occupies more than one line. By default, automatic leading is set to 120% of the type size. You can change this automatic value, but it is usually better to change the leading for individual type instances instead of changing the default automatic value.

Create and Control Area Type

In many cases your clients will provide specific text to include in a design; that text might be part of an email message or saved in a word-processing file. If the client-supplied text is only a couple of words, it's easier to retype the text into your Photoshop file. But when the supplied text is longer, there's no point in making extra work by retyping what has already been typed.

The final type element you need for each postcard is a two- or three-paragraph blurb of promotional copy. You are going to create these as area-type layers so that you can better control the line breaks and alignment, and more easily fit them into a specific amount of space.

1. **On your desktop, double-click the file `festival_copy.txt` (in your WIP>Cards folder) to open the text file in a text-editing application.**

   You can't place or import external text files directly into a Photoshop file. If you want to use text from an external file, you simply open the file in a text editor, copy it, and paste it into a Photoshop type layer.

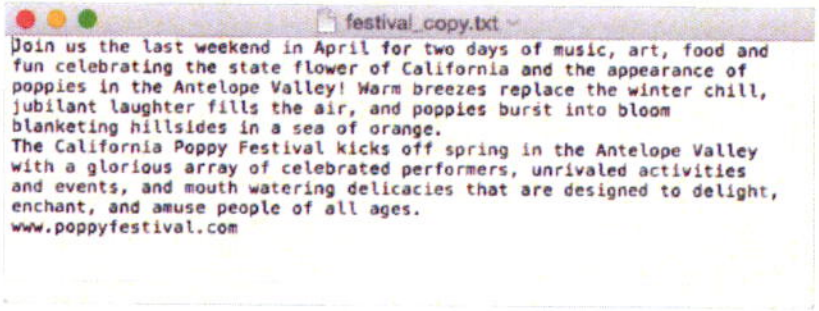
festival_copy.txt
Join us the last weekend in April for two days of music, art, food and fun celebrating the state flower of California and the appearance of poppies in the Antelope Valley! Warm breezes replace the winter chill, jubilant laughter fills the air, and poppies burst into bloom blanketing hillsides in a sea of orange.
The California Poppy Festival kicks off spring in the Antelope Valley with a glorious array of celebrated performers, unrivaled activities and events, and mouth watering delicacies that are designed to delight, enchant, and amuse people of all ages.
www.poppyfestival.com

> ***Note:***
>
> *We used Macintosh TextEdit as our word processor.*

2. **Select all text in the file, copy it, then close the file.**

3. **With `festival.psd` active in Photoshop, choose the Horizontal Type tool in the Tools panel.**

4. **In Photoshop, click below the "P" in "Poppy", and drag down and right to create a type area (as shown in the following image).**

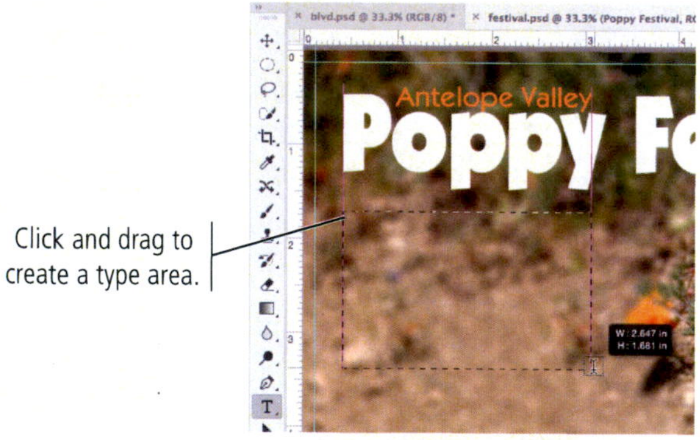
Click and drag to create a type area.
Antelope Valley
Poppy

   When you release the mouse button, you have a type area with bounding box handles that you can drag to change the area's shape.

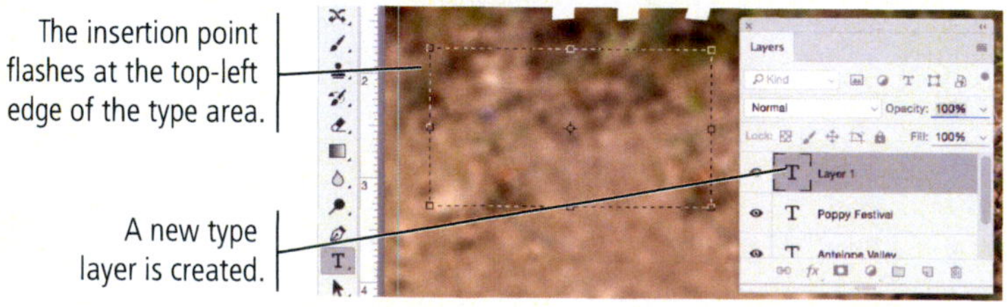
The insertion point flashes at the top-left edge of the type area.
A new type layer is created.
Layers
Normal
Opacity: 100%
Fill: 100%
Layer 1
Poppy Festival

> ***Note:***
>
> *If the insertion point is not flashing in the top-left corner of the area, make sure the Left Align Text option is selected in the Options bar.*

5. **With the insertion point flashing inside the new type area, use either the Options bar or Character and Paragraph panel to define the type formatting as follows:**

   Font Family: ATC Onyx
   Font Style: Italic
   Font Size: 11 pt.
   Leading: 14 pt.
   Type Color: white
   Paragraph Alignment: Left

6. **With the insertion point still flashing in the type area, choose Edit>Paste.**

   Because you defined the type formatting before you pasted the type, it is automatically formatted with the settings you defined.

7. **With the Horizontal Type tool still active, click the right-center bounding box handle of the type area and drag so the right edge of the area is between the "y" in Poppy and the "F" in Festival.**

   When you resize the type area by dragging the bounding box handles, you do not affect the type; you change the type *container*, which allows more (or less, depending on how you drag) of the type to show.

   Type also wraps within the type area. You don't have to manually define where new lines begin; simply press Return/Enter to start a new formal paragraph.

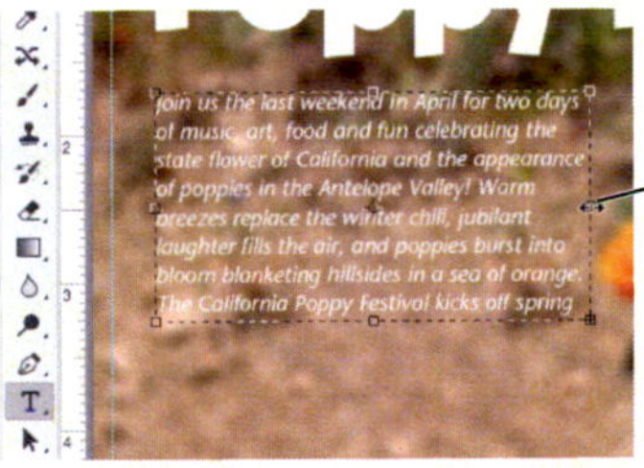

Dragging a type area handle with the Horizontal Type tool changes the size of the area without resizing the type.

8. **Click the bottom-center handle and drag down to the bottom ruler guide.**

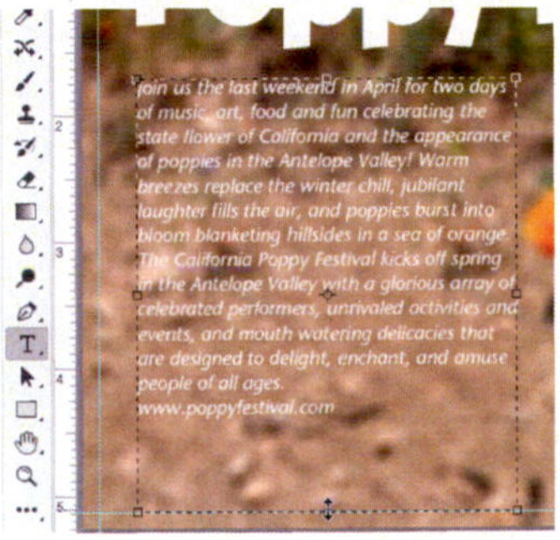

Note:

Make sure to use the Horizontal Type tool when you want to change the dimensions of a type area. If you press Command/Control-T or choose Edit>Free Transform, stretching or otherwise resizing the type area bounding box resizes the type it contains.

9. **Click and drag to select at least part of all three paragraphs in the area. In the Paragraph panel, change the Add Space After Paragraph field to 8 pt.**

   Paragraph formatting attributes apply to any paragraph that is even partially selected. If no characters are highlighted, any paragraph formatting changes apply to the paragraph where the insertion point is currently placed.

10. **Drag the top-center handle of the type area until the web address is approximately 1/4″ from the bottom guide.**

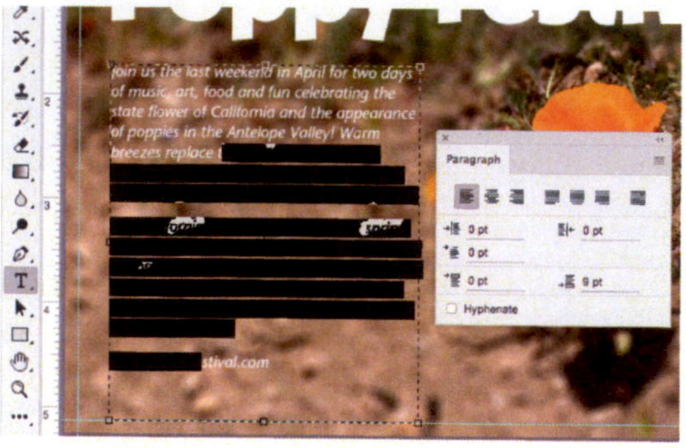

11. **Select the entire last paragraph in the area. In the Character panel, change the font to ATC Onyx Normal, and change the size to 13 pt. In the Paragraph panel, click the Center Text button.**

   Remember: character attributes such as font and size apply only to selected characters. To change these for the entire paragraph, you first have to select the entire paragraph.

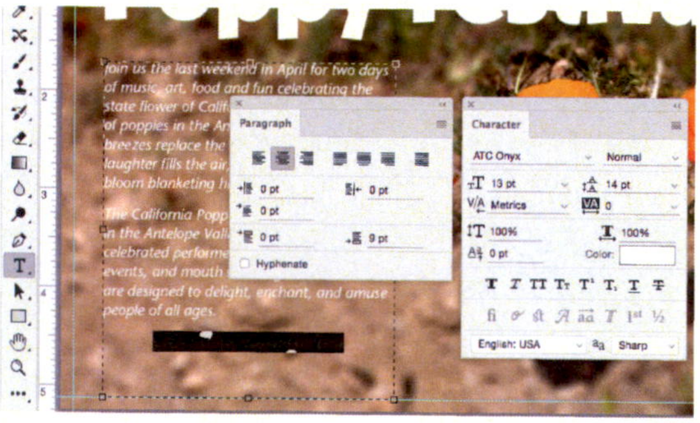

12. **Save the file and continue to the next exercise.**

Create Paragraph Styles

When you work with longer blocks of text, many of the same formatting options are applied to different text elements throughout the story (such as headings), or to different elements in similar pieces of a campaign. To simplify the workflow, you can use styles to store and apply multiple formatting options in a single click.

Styles also have another powerful benefit: when you change the options applied in a style, any text formatted with that style reflects the newly defined options. In other words, you can change multiple instances of non-contiguous text in a single process, instead of selecting each block and making the same changes repeatedly.

Note:

Photoshop also supports character styles, which can be used to store any character-formatting options that can be applied to selected characters.

1. **With festival.psd active, select the entire first paragraph in the type area.**

2. **Open the Paragraph Styles panel (Window>Paragraph Styles).**

   The Paragraph Styles panel shows that the selected type is formatted with the Basic Paragraph style. The plus sign next to the style name indicates that some formatting is applied other than what is defined by the style.

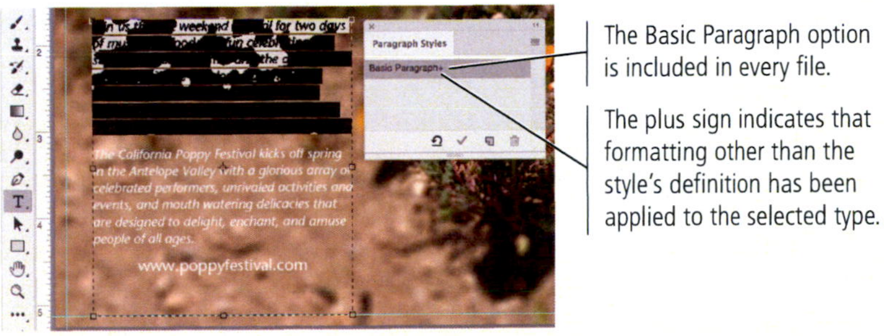
[redacted]
The California Poppy Festival kicks off spring in the Antelope Valley with a glorious array of celebrated performers, unrivaled activities and events, and mouth watering delicacies that are designed to delight, enchant, and amuse people of all ages.
www.poppyfestival.com
Paragraph Styles
Basic Paragraph+
The Basic Paragraph option is included in every file.
The plus sign indicates that formatting other than the style's definition has been applied to the selected type.

> ***Note:***
>
> *You can delete a style by dragging it to the panel Delete button. If the style had been applied, you would see a warning message, asking you to confirm the deletion (you do not have the opportunity to replace the applied style with another one, as you do in Adobe InDesign).*

3. **Click the Create New Paragraph Style button at the bottom of the panel.**

   When you create a new style, it defaults to include all formatting options that are applied to the currently selected type.

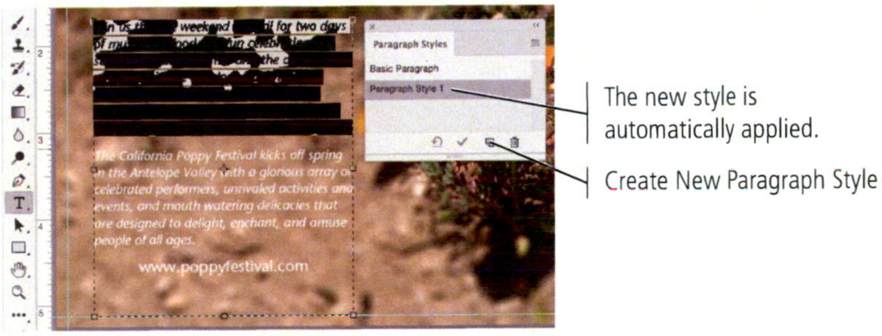
[redacted]
The California Poppy Festival kicks off spring in the Antelope Valley with a glorious array of celebrated performers, unrivaled activities and events, and mouth watering delicacies that are designed to delight, enchant, and amuse people of all ages.
www.poppyfestival.com
Paragraph Styles
Basic Paragraph
Paragraph Style 1
The new style is automatically applied.
Create New Paragraph Style

   If you have used type styles in InDesign or Illustrator, you need to be aware of a difference in the way you create styles based on existing formatting. In those applications, a new style adopts the formatting of the current insertion point, which means you do not have to select specific type to create a style.

   In Photoshop, however, you have to select at least part of a paragraph to create a style based on that paragraph's formatting. Also, you cannot select multiple paragraphs with the same formatting to create a style based on those options.

> ***Note:***
>
> *You can also choose Style Options in the panel Options menu to open this dialog box.*

4. **Double-click the new style in the panel to review the style's settings.**

   Double-clicking a style opens the Paragraph Style Options dialog box for that style, so you can edit the settings stored in the style. Different options are available in the right side of the dialog box depending on what is selected in the list of categories.

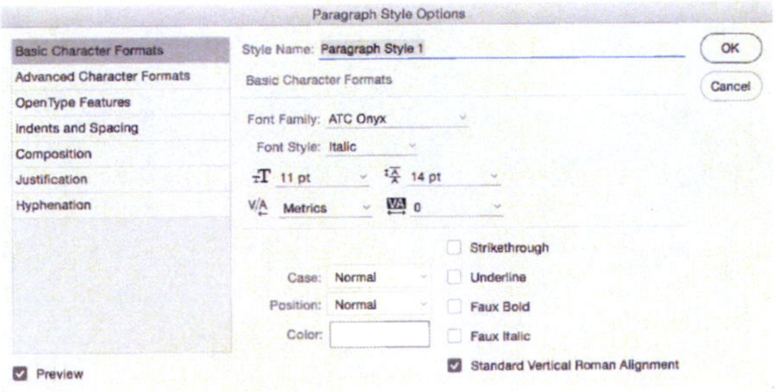
Paragraph Style Options
Basic Character Formats
Advanced Character Formats
OpenType Features
Indents and Spacing
Composition
Justification
Hyphenation
Style Name: Paragraph Style 1
Basic Character Formats
Font Family: ATC Onyx
Font Style: Italic
11 pt
14 pt
Metrics
0
Case: Normal
Position: Normal
Color:
Strikethrough
Underline
Faux Bold
Faux Italic
Standard Vertical Roman Alignment
OK
Cancel
Preview

   Checking the Preview option allows you to immediately see the effect of your changes in the layout before you finalize the changes.

5. **Change the style name to Body Copy and click OK.**

6. **Select the entire second paragraph, then click the Body Copy style in the Paragraph Styles panel to apply that style to the active paragraph.**

   This highlights another anomaly in the application. When you apply a style to type that already showed a plus sign, you have to click the Clear Override button to apply only the style's formatting to the selected type.

7. **With the same type selected, click the Clear Override button at the bottom of the Paragraph Styles panel.**

   This is an issue that you should be aware of; if you do not clear the overrides, later changes to the applied style might not correctly reflect in type formatted with the style. Whenever you work with styles, check the applied styles to see if a plus sign appears where you know it shouldn't.

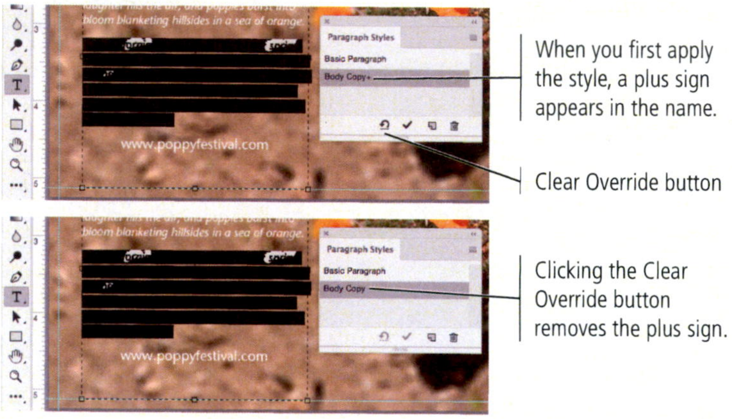

8. **Repeat this process to create a new paragraph style named Web Address based on the formatting of the last paragraph in the type area.**

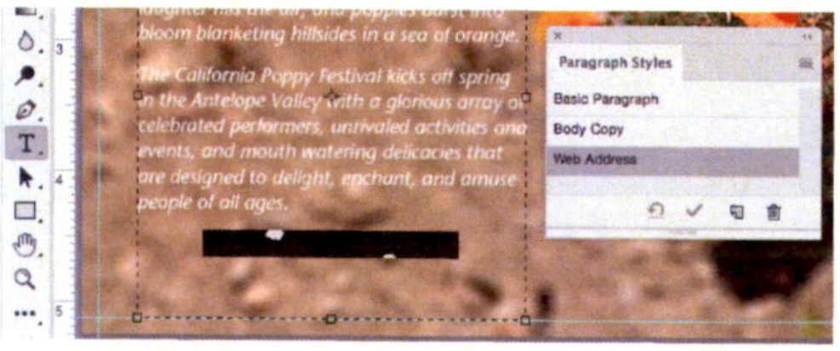

9. **Save the file and continue to the next exercise.**

> ***Note:***
> *You could also choose Clear Override in the Paragraph panel Options menu.*

> ***Note:***
> *If the applied style shows a plus sign in the name, you can click the Redefine button to change the selected style formatting to match the formatting of the current text selection.*

LOAD PARAGRAPH STYLES FROM ANOTHER FILE

Once you create styles, you can apply them to any text in the file, on any layer. You can also import styles from other Photoshop files so they can be used for different projects.

1. **On your desktop, open the file `blvd_copy.txt` (from your WIP>Cards folder) in a text editor application.**

2. **Select all the text in the file, copy it, then close the file.**

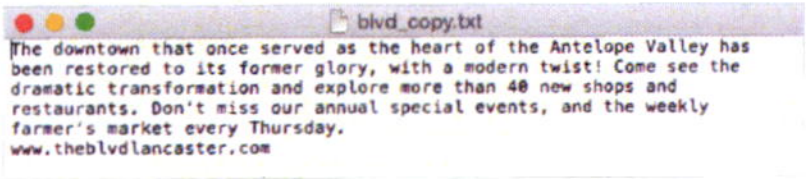

blvd_copy.txt
The downtown that once served as the heart of the Antelope Valley has been restored to its former glory, with a modern twist! Come see the dramatic transformation and explore more than 40 new shops and restaurants. Don't miss our annual special events, and the weekly farmer's market every Thursday.
www.theblvdlancaster.com

3. **In Photoshop, open the `blvd.psd` file if necessary. Using the Horizontal Type tool, click and drag to create a type area in the top-right corner of the canvas.**

4. **With the insertion point in the new area, paste the copy from Step 2.**

   The pasted type adopts the last-applied formatting options, which is not what you want. Because you already defined paragraph styles for the other card in this same campaign, you can load those styles and apply them to the type in this card.

5. **If necessary, adjust the handles of the area so all the type in the story appears in the type area.**

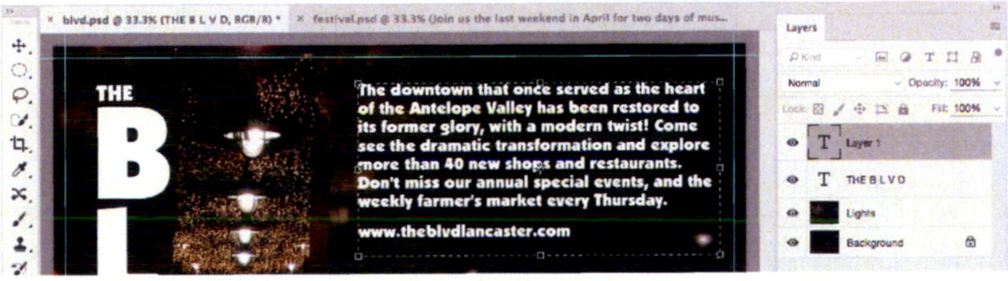

THE
B
The downtown that once served as the heart of the Antelope Valley has been restored to its former glory, with a modern twist! Come see the dramatic transformation and explore more than 40 new shops and restaurants. Don't miss our annual special events, and the weekly farmer's market every Thursday.
www.theblvdlancaster.com
Layers
Normal
Opacity: 100%
Fill: 100%
Layer 1
THE B L V D
Lights
Background

6. **In the Paragraph Styles panel Options menu, choose Load Paragraph Styles. Navigate to `festival.psd` (in your WIP>Cards folder) and click Open/Load.**

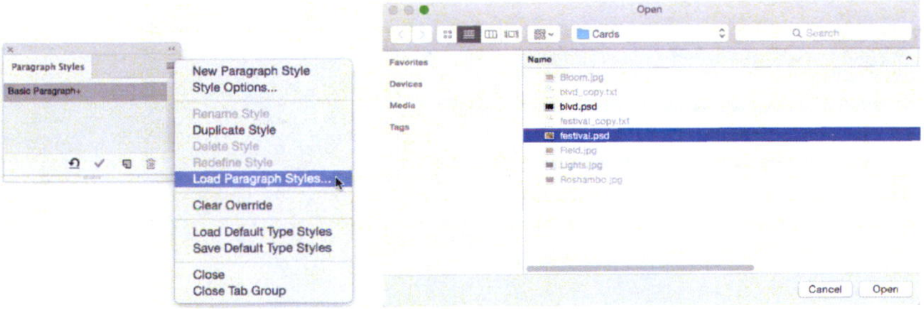

Paragraph Styles
Basic Paragraph+
New Paragraph Style
Style Options...
Rename Style
Duplicate Style
Delete Style
Redefine Style
Load Paragraph Styles...
Clear Override
Load Default Type Styles
Save Default Type Styles
Close
Close Tab Group
Open
Cards
Favorites
Devices
Media
Tags
Name
Bloom.jpg
blvd_copy.txt
blvd.psd
festival_copy.txt
festival.psd
Field.jpg
Lights.jpg
Roshambo.jpg
Cancel
Open

> ***Note:***
>
> *Loading styles from one Photoshop file to another is an all-or-nothing choice; you can't select certain styles to import.*

7. **Select the entire first paragraph in the type area. Click Body Copy in the Paragraph Styles panel, then click the Clear Override button.**

8. **Repeat Step 7 to apply the Web Address style to the second paragraph.**

9. **Adjust the type area handles until you are satisfied with the text appearance.**

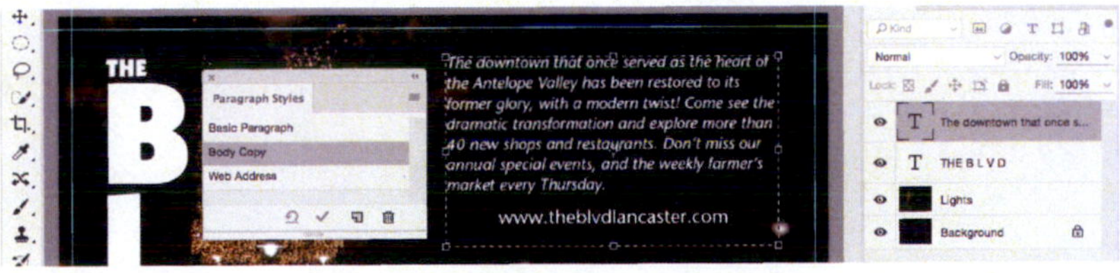

THE
B
Paragraph Styles
Basic Paragraph
Body Copy
Web Address
The downtown that once served as the heart of the Antelope Valley has been restored to its former glory, with a modern twist! Come see the dramatic transformation and explore more than 40 new shops and restaurants. Don't miss our annual special events, and the weekly farmer's market every Thursday.
www.theblvdlancaster.com
Normal
Opacity: 100%
Fill: 100%
The downtown that once s...
THE B L V D
Lights
Background

10. **Save the file and continue to the next stage of the project.**

More about Working with Type

In some cases, maintaining a type layer with live text is either unnecessary (e.g., you know the book title isn't going to change) or it prevents you from applying certain changes (e.g., you can't apply filters to a type layer). When you find an effect or change that won't work with live text, you must convert the type layer in one way or another.

You can simply rasterize a type layer by choosing Type>Rasterize Type Layer, which converts the editable, vector-based type to a regular pixel-based layer. Once rasterized, you can't edit the text, but you can apply filters and use the layer as a clipping mask.

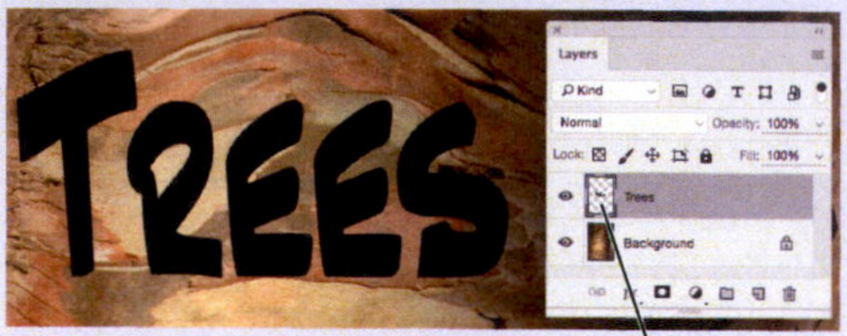

Rasterizing type results in a regular, pixel-based layer.

You should understand that type is fundamentally based on vectors. Rather than simply rasterizing type, you can convert a type layer to a vector-based shape layer by choosing Type>Convert to Shape. Converting a type layer to a shape means the type is no longer editable, but you can still manipulate the letterforms as you would any other vector shape layer. By converting type to a shape layer, you can use the Distort or Perspective transformation to create custom warps for the layer. You still can't apply filters, however, since filters only work on rasterized layers.

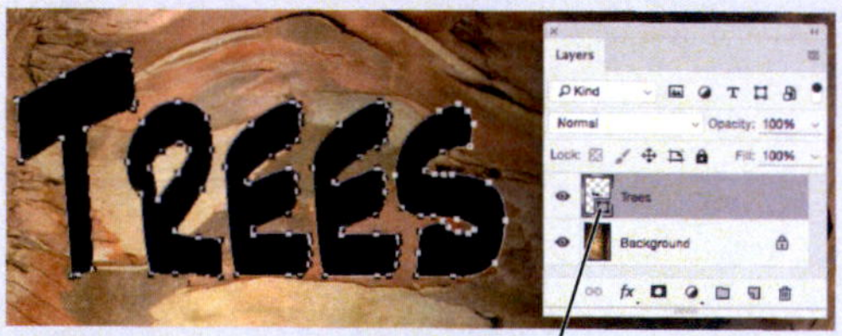

The resulting shape layer adopts the original text color as the fill color.

If you need to apply filters, custom warps, or transformations to type, but you want to maintain the type layer as live (editable) text, you can convert the type layer to a Smart Object in the layer's contextual menu. You can apply filters or transformations in the main document, but still edit the text in the Smart Object file.

Convert the type to a Smart Object in the master file.

The Smart Object file maintains the live type.

Finally, you can use the vector information of type to create a work path (Type>Create Work Path), which you can then save as a regular path in the Paths panel. In this case, the type layer is maintained as an editable type layer, but you can use the path for any purpose you choose.

The work path appears in the Paths panel.

The original type layer is maintained.

Creating Type Selections

You can use one of the Type Mask tools (horizontal or vertical) to create a selection in the shape of letters. When you click with one of these tools, you automatically enter a kind of Quick Mask mode; the letters you type are removed from the mask to show what will be selected. (If you press Command/Control while the red mask is visible, you can drag the type selection around in the image window.)

When you have finished typing, switching to the Move tool shows the marching ants that make up the type-shaped selection. No layer, path, or channel is automatically created when you use the Type Mask tools.

Horizontal Type Mask tool

Stage 4 Creating Style with Layers

In this and earlier projects, you have learned a number of techniques for manipulating layers — isolating specific areas, transforming selections, moving and scaling content while preserving image detail, modifying colors, retouching damage... the list is already extensive. To complete the rest of this project, you will learn several new techniques for adding visual interest to layers, including creating a solid-color overlay and applying layer effects.

Create a Solid-Color Fill Layer

A solid-color fill layer is exactly what it sounds like — a layer of colored pixels, which obscures all underlying layers. Like a vector shape layer (which you used in Project 2: Car Magazine Cover), the fill layer's thumbnail shows a swatch of the current fill color; you can double-click that swatch to change the color. A fill layer also has an attached (pixel-based) layer mask, which you can use to define where the fill color will be visible.

1. **With `festival.psd` open, select the Bloom layer in the Layers panel.**

2. **Click the Create New Fill or Adjustment Layer button at the bottom of the Layers panel and choose Solid Color in the resulting menu.**

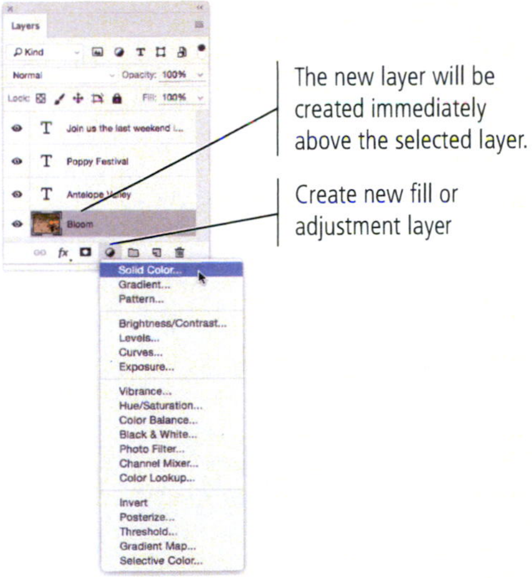

3. **Click OK in the Color Picker dialog box to accept the default color value.**

   The fill color defaults to the active foreground color. Don't worry if yours is different than what you see in our images; you will change the color in the next few steps.

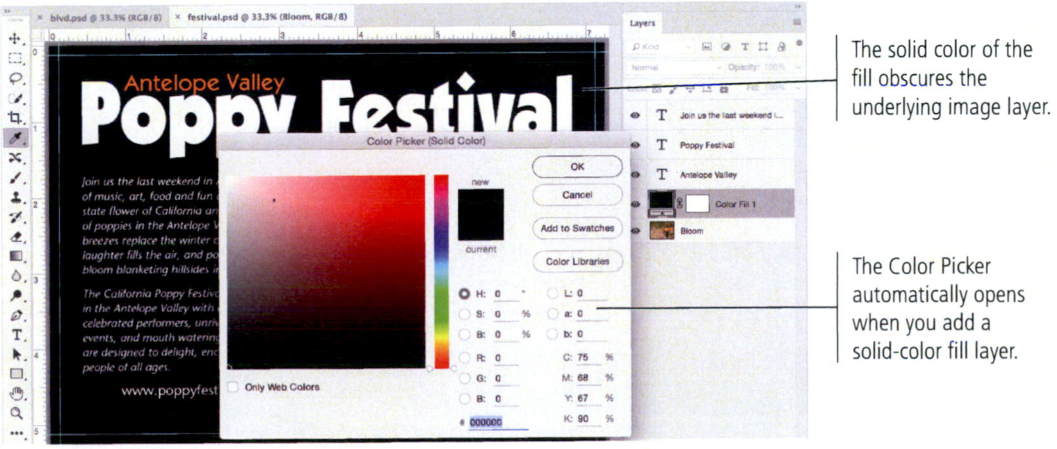

4. **In the Layers panel, click the eye icon to hide the Color Fill layer.**

   To sample a color from the underlying image, you first have to hide the fill layer.

5. **Double-click the Color Fill 1 layer's thumbnail to reopen the Color Picker dialog box.**

   You can change the Color Fill layer color even though it isn't currently visible.

6. **With the Color Picker dialog box open, click in the image (behind the dialog box) with the eyedropper cursor to sample a dark green area of the image as the layer's fill color.**

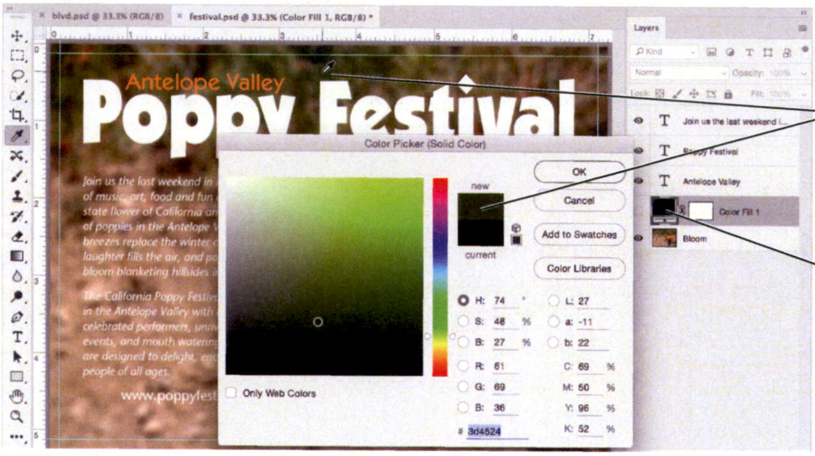

Because the Color Fill layer is hidden, you can sample a color from the underlying layer.

Double-click the color icon to change the layer's fill color.

7. **Click OK to close the Color Picker dialog box, then make the Color Fill layer visible again.**

8. **In the Layers panel, click to select the mask thumbnail for the Color Fill layer.**

   Fill and adjustment layers automatically include a mask, which you can use to define where the fill is visible. This is similar to the vector shape layers, where the vector path(s) define where the color is visible. The fill layer's mask, however, is pixel-based, which means it can include shades of gray.

   Remember from earlier projects: black areas of a mask are transparent and white areas are opaque. In this case, white areas of the mask result in full strength of the fill layer's color; shades of gray indicate varying degrees of the fill color.

Note:

You could have accomplished the same basic goal by creating a new layer, filling it with a solid color, then manually adding a pixel mask. When you add a solid-color fill layer, the mask is automatically added for you; you can also double-click the color swatch in the layer icon to change the color that fills the layer.

9. **Choose the Gradient tool in the Tools panel. Reset the foreground and background colors (so that white is the Foreground and black is the Background Color), then choose the Foreground to Background gradient in the Options bar.**

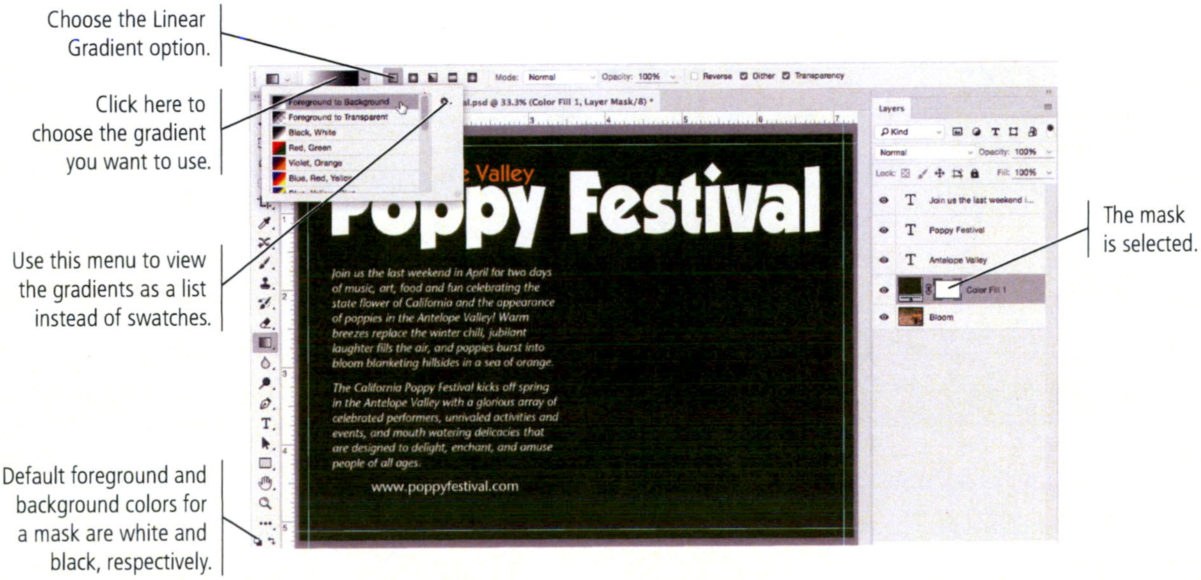
Choose the Linear Gradient option.
Click here to choose the gradient you want to use.
Use this menu to view the gradients as a list instead of swatches.
Default foreground and background colors for a mask are white and black, respectively.
The mask is selected.
Poppy Festival
We dragged the gradient from here...
www.poppyfestival.com

10. **Make sure the Linear Gradient option is selected. Click near the right edge of the type area, then drag right to the right edge of the canvas.**

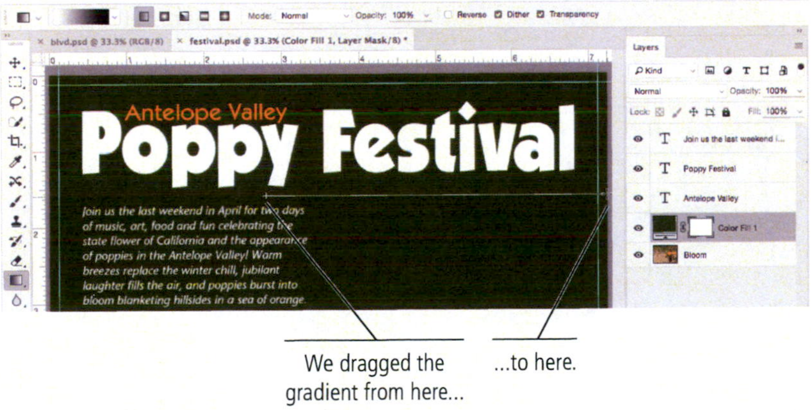

11. **Choose Multiply in the Blending Mode menu at the top of the Layers panel.**

Multiplying the dark color with the underlying image allows the white type to stand out more clearly against the background. The result, however, is too dark — almost entirely obscuring the underlying image.

Antelope Valley
Poppy Festival
Join us the last weekend in April for two days of music, art, food and fun celebrating the state flower of California and the appearance of poppies in the Antelope Valley! Warm breezes replace the winter chill, jubilant laughter fills the air, and poppies burst into bloom blanketing hillsides in a sea of orange.
The California Poppy Festival kicks off spring in the Antelope Valley with a glorious array of celebrated performers, unrivaled activities and events, and mouth watering delicacies that are designed to delight, enchant, and amuse people of all ages.
www.poppyfestival.com
Multiply
Opacity: 100%
Fill: 100%
Join us the last weekend
Poppy Festival
Antelope Valley
Color Fill 1
Bloom

The Multiply blending mode mixes the color of the fill layer with colors in the underlying layer.

12. **Change the layer's opacity to `70%`.**

Reducing the fill layer's opacity allows more of the underlying image to show through. You can type the new value in the field, use the attached menu, or use the scrubby slider for the field's label.

The **Opacity** percentage changes the opacity of the entire layer, including applied effects and styles. The **Fill** percentage changes the opacity of the actual layer pixels, but none of the applied effects or styles. In this case, the layer doesn't yet have any applied styles or effects, so both controls would have the same effect.

Note:

If the Opacity field is unavailable, check the Lock options. When you use the Lock All option, you can't change the layer opacity.

Antelope Valley
Poppy Festival
Join us the last weekend in April for two days of music, art, food and fun celebrating the state flower of California and the appearance of poppies in the Antelope Valley! Warm breezes replace the winter chill, jubilant laughter fills the air, and poppies burst into bloom blanketing hillsides in a sea of orange.
The California Poppy Festival kicks off spring in the Antelope Valley with a glorious array of celebrated performers, unrivaled activities and events, and mouth watering delicacies that are designed to delight, enchant, and amuse people of all ages.
www.poppyfestival.com
Multiply
Opacity: 70%
Fill: 100%
Join us the last weekend i...
Poppy Festival
Antelope Valley
Color Fill 1
Bloom

Reducing the fill layer's opacity reduces the darkness created by the multiplied colors.

Note:

When a layer is selected and the insertion point is not flashing in a Type layer, you can press the number keys to change the active layer's opacity in 10% increments:

1 = 10%	*6 = 60%*
2 = 20%	*7 = 70%*
3 = 30%	*8 = 80%*
4 = 40%	*9 = 90%*
5 = 50%	*0 = 100%*

13. **Select the Bloom layer in the Layers panel, then click the Lock All button at the top of the Layers panel.**

The Bloom layer is technically the postcard background, even though it is not a formal Background layer. By locking all properties, you prevent the layer from being moved, painted on, or otherwise edited.

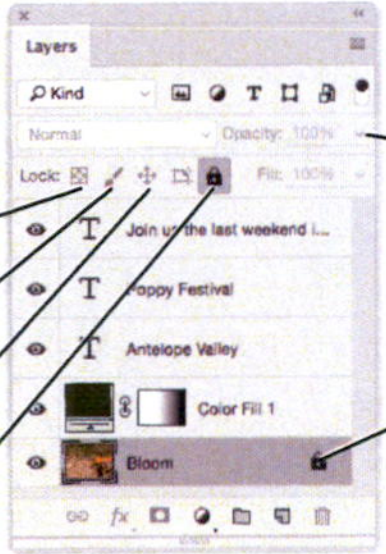

Lock transparent pixels
Lock image pixels
Lock position
Lock all
When the entire layer is locked, the opacity, fill, and blending mode options are not available.
The solid lock icon indicates that all properties of the layer are locked.

Note:

For all but type layers, you can lock three different attributes individually, or you can lock the entire layer at once.

14. **Select the three type layers, then click the Lock Position button.**

By locking the layers' positions, you prevent them from accidentally being moved as you continue working. Since only the position is locked, however, you can still apply effects that do not affect the position of the layer content.

You cannot, by definition, lock the image pixels or transparent pixels of a type layer. If you activate the Lock All button for a Type layer, you will not be able to apply styles to those layers in the next steps.

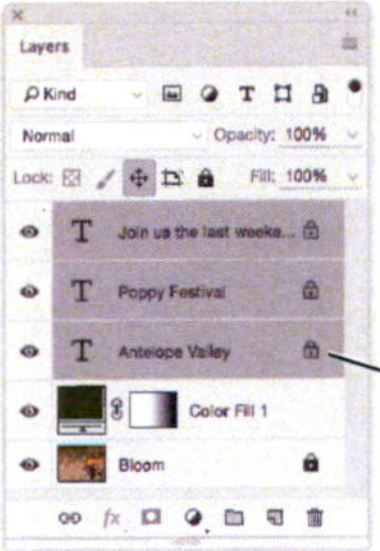

The hollow lock icon indicates that some, but not all, properties of the layer are locked.

15. **Save the file, then make blvd.psd active.**

16. **Choose File>Place Embedded. Select the file Roshambo.jpg (in your WIP>Cards folder) and click Place.**

17. **Click inside the bounding box of the placed image and drag to move the placed layer to the empty area in the bottom-right corner of the canvas. Press Return/Enter to finalize the placement.**

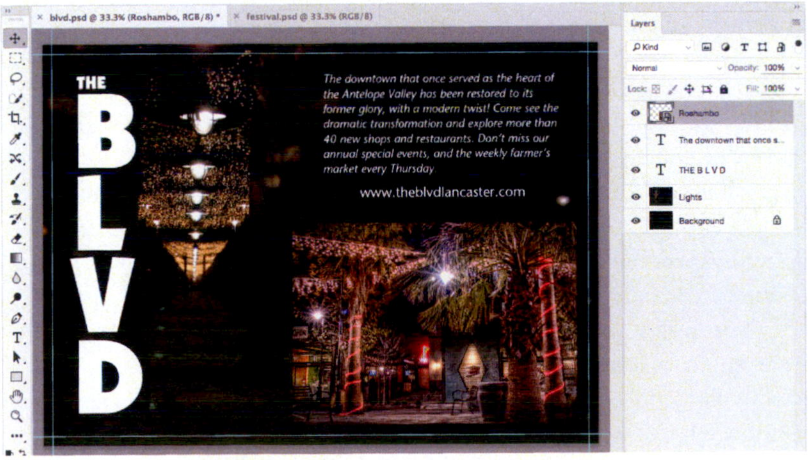

18. **Save the file and continue to the final stage of the project.**

Stage 5 Working in 3D

Photoshop includes the ability to create real-time, three-dimensional artwork, either from scratch or by importing wire frames and rendered artwork from industry-standard 3D applications such as Maya or 3D Studio Max.

The following is a brief introduction to Photoshop's 3D functionality. If you have never worked in real three dimensions before, you will almost certainly have to spend some extra time learning the related terminology. We also encourage you to experiment with the various 3D options until you are comfortable manipulating objects in digital space.

You should already be familiar with the concept of the X and Y axes. When you work with 3D files, you also need to understand the concept of the Z axis, which creates the illusion of depth.

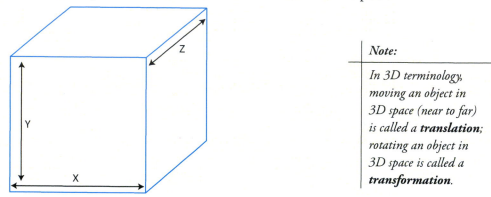

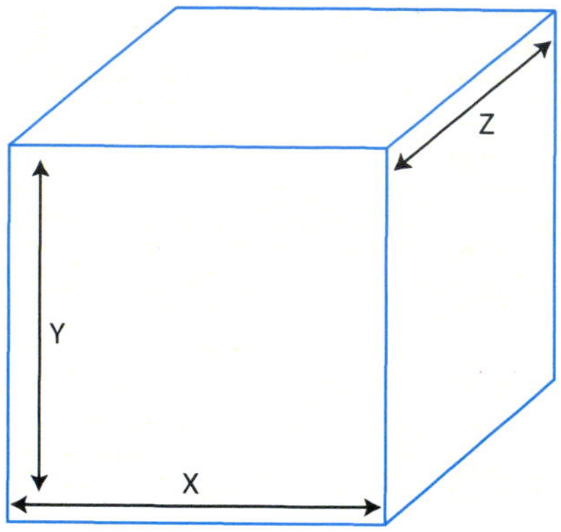

Note:

In 3D terminology, moving an object in 3D space (near to far) is called a ***translation****; rotating an object in 3D space is called a* ***transformation****.*

- **Meshes** (sometimes called **wireframes**) are the basic skeletons of three-dimensional objects. The mesh defines the underlying shape of the 3D object.
- **Materials** refer to the physical surface of an object (for example, the aluminum of a soda can or the felt of a fedora hat). Photoshop uses a number of texture-map characteristics to create the material appearance of a 3D object; you can also define existing two-dimensional Photoshop layers as the material for a mesh.
- **Lighting** affects the way highlights and shadows are created on and by a 3D object. Photoshop supports four different types of lighting (infinite, spot, point, and image) to create different lighting effects.
- **Camera position** refers to the point of view relative to the object. Photoshop includes the ability to move the camera around an object on all three axes.

To understand digital 3D modeling, you should try to think about the way you interact with the world at large. When you walk around a car, for example, you are able to see the different sides of the car; the front, back, and sides all have different appearances.

You should also understand that what you see depends not only on your position relative to an object, but also on the position of the object. For example, if you stand still but someone backs a car into a parking space, you see a different aspect of the same car.

Finally, what you see on a 3D object also depends on the position of the light. When the garage light shines behind you, for example, you might see your own reflection in the car's window. When the interior lights are on, you see more of the car's interior than your reflection.

It's important to keep these overall concepts in mind: 3D modeling considers the physical shape and position of an object, your position relative to the object, and the position of light sources relative to the object.

It is also important to realize that whole books are written about Photoshop's 3D features. The exercises in this stage were designed to introduce you to the possibilities relative to enhancing a static image such as the postcards in this project.

Create a 3D Postcard

Photoshop can open existing 3D files created in other applications and import 3D objects as new 3D Photoshop layers. You can also use built-in functionality to create some 3D objects from scratch. In this case, you're going to create a new 3D object from the simplest built-in shape preset — a postcard. In the final exercise of this project, you will use Layer Comps to export two separate versions of the file using these two separate layers.

Important note: If, after first launching the application, you saw a warning about insufficient vRAM, you will not be able to complete this stage of the project. Your finished project will consist of one version of each postcard, which you should save as flattened JPEG files for client approval.

1. **Open the Performance pane of the Preferences dialog box. Make sure the Use Graphics Processor option is checked and click OK.**

   If this option is not available (grayed out) on your computer, your video card and/or driver does not support OpenGL. If you cannot use OpenGL, your 3D options and functionality will be very limited and very slow; all processes will be performed (if possible) by the Photoshop application instead of the video card in your computer.

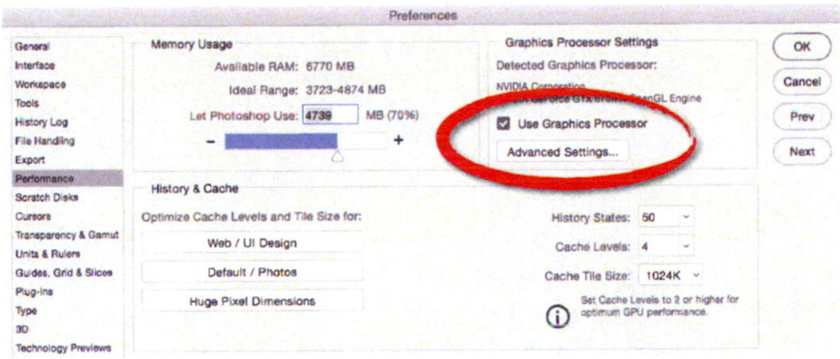

2. **With blvd.psd active, drag the Roshambo layer to the Create a New Layer button at the bottom of the panel.**

   This is an easy way to duplicate a layer. You could also Control/right-click the layer name and choose Duplicate Layer from the contextual menu.

   3D extrusions permanently change the layer to a special 3D layer; to maintain the original placed "flat" image and a 3D version of the placed image, you have to use two separate layers.

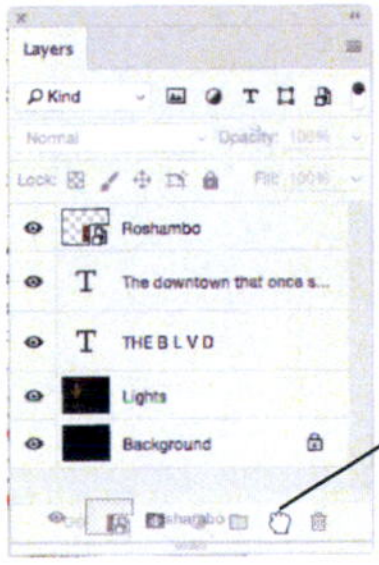

Drag a layer to the Create a New Layer button to duplicate the layer.

3. **Change the name of the Roshambo copy layer to Roshambo 3D.**

   This step is simply to make it easier to distinguish one layer from the other. You do not need to include the "3D" tag in a layer that you are using for 3D effects.

4. **Hide the Roshambo layer, then select Roshambo 3D as the active layer.**

5. **Choose View>Show>Guides to hide the ruler guides.**

   The 3D workspace has a number of on-screen controls. The ruler guides are no longer necessary, and would simply confuse the visual clarity of the 3D controllers.

6. **Choose 3D>New Mesh from Layer>Postcard.**

   Photoshop includes a number of prebuilt meshes, which you can add to any file. The most basic mesh — a "postcard" — is simply a two-sided representation of the selected layer. Just like a physical postcard, it has no real depth, but it can be moved in three dimensions to show different aspects of the card.

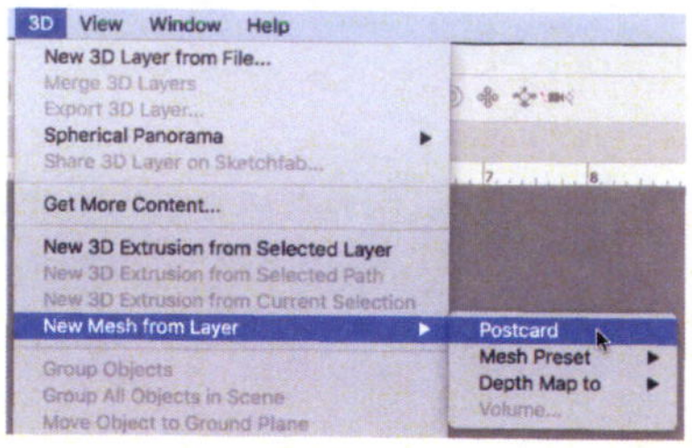

7. **Read the resulting message, then click Yes to automatically switch to the 3D workspace.**

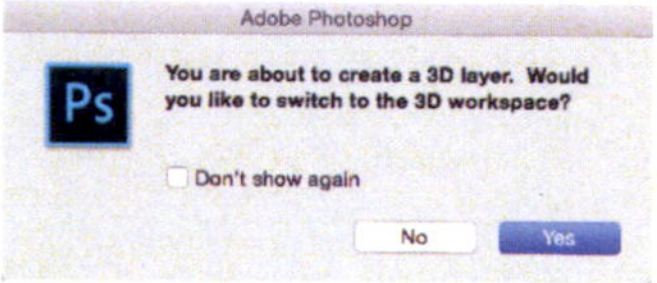

   Photoshop's built-in 3D workspace includes a number of tools that are useful in controlling a 3D layer. Some of these tools might be intimidating the first time you use the 3D workspace, but they will make more sense when you begin to manipulate the 3D object.

Note:

If you don't see the Secondary View panel, choose View>Show>3D Secondary View.

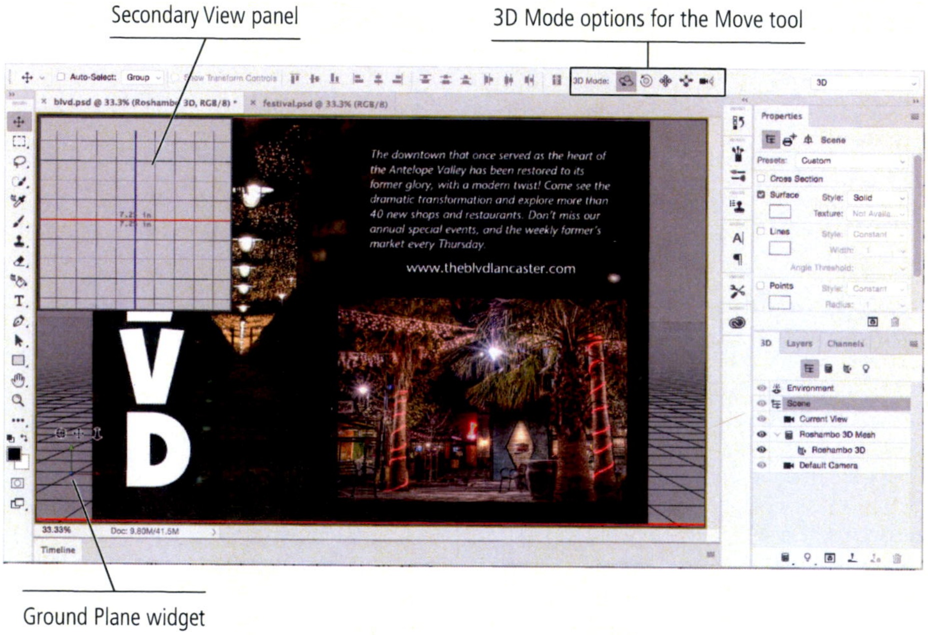

8. **With blvd.psd active, review the Roshambo 3D layer in the Layers panel.**

   When you create a 3D mesh from an existing layer, that layer shows a number of special attributes. The layer thumbnail includes a 3D icon, and the previous layer content is converted into a material for the active mesh.

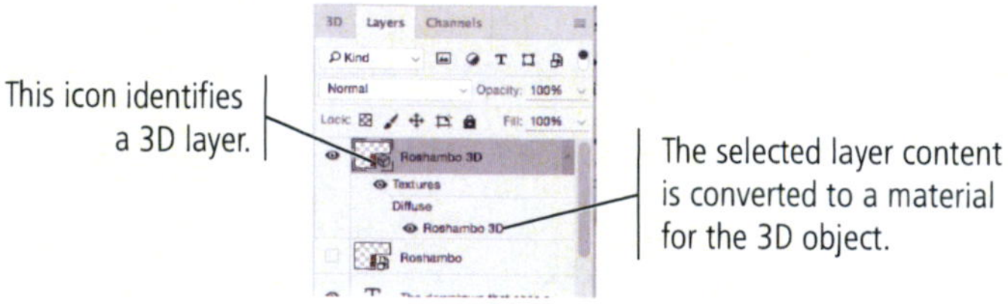

9. **Save the file and continue to the next exercise.**

Move an Object in 3D

One advantage to working with 3D is the ability to move objects in three directions — left or right, up or down, near or far. You can also rotate the mesh around any axis to change the visible portion of the object.

1. **With blvd.psd open, open the menu in the Secondary View panel and choose Default.**

   The Default view is the same as what you see in the main document window when you first create the 3D object.

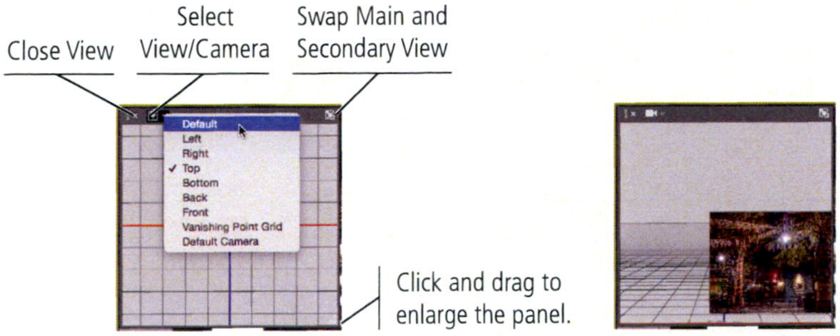

   This panel is a good way to review other aspects of a 3D object without affecting what appears on the canvas. In addition to the default options in the menu, you can also click and drag around the panel to change the secondary view. If you find a view you particularly like, you can click the Swap Main and Secondary View button in the top-right corner of the panel to replace the current view on canvas with what you see in the secondary view.

> *Note:*
>
> *Press Option and drag in the Secondary View panel to zoom in or out.*

2. **Click the Close View button in the top-left corner of the panel to hide the Secondary View panel.**

3. **In the Tools panel, make sure the Move tool is selected. Choose the Orbit the 3D Camera mode in the Options bar.**

   The 3D tool modes can be used to change various properties of the selected scene attribute (the current view or a specific mesh). The modes, from left to right, are:

   - **Orbit the 3D Camera.** Drag up-down to rotate the object around the X axis, or left-right to rotate around the Y axis. Press Option/Alt to rotate the object around the Z axis.
   - **Roll the 3D Camera.** Drag left-right to rotate the object around the Z axis.
   - **Pan the 3D Camera.** Drag left-right to move the object horizontally, or up-down to move the object vertically, without affecting its depth or rotation. Press Option/Alt and drag up-down to move the object along the X/Z axis (horizontally far to near).
   - **Slide the 3D Camera.** Drag left-right to move the object horizontally, or up-down to move the object on the X/Z axis (horizontally far to near). Press Option/Alt and drag up/down to move the object along the X and Y axes simultaneously.
   - **Zoom the 3D Camera.** Drag up-down to make the object proportionally larger or smaller. Press Option/Alt to scale the object along the Z axis only.

> *Note:*
>
> *You can toggle the visibility of all the 3D on-screen widgets in the View>Show submenu.*

> *Note:*
>
> *You can save a specific view preset by choosing Save in the Current View menu.*

4. **In the 3D panel, select Current View. In the document window, click the 3D Ground Plane and drag to reposition the ground plane.**

As you drag, you can see the ground-plane grid move. The red line in the grid represents the X axis and the blue line represents the Z axis.

You should also notice that the 3D object moves along with the ground plane. Basically, rotating the ground plane is like moving the camera to a different location; if you walk around an object with a camera in your hand, the visible area of the object changes with your relative position. In the Properties panel (3D Camera mode), the View menu automatically switches to "Custom View".

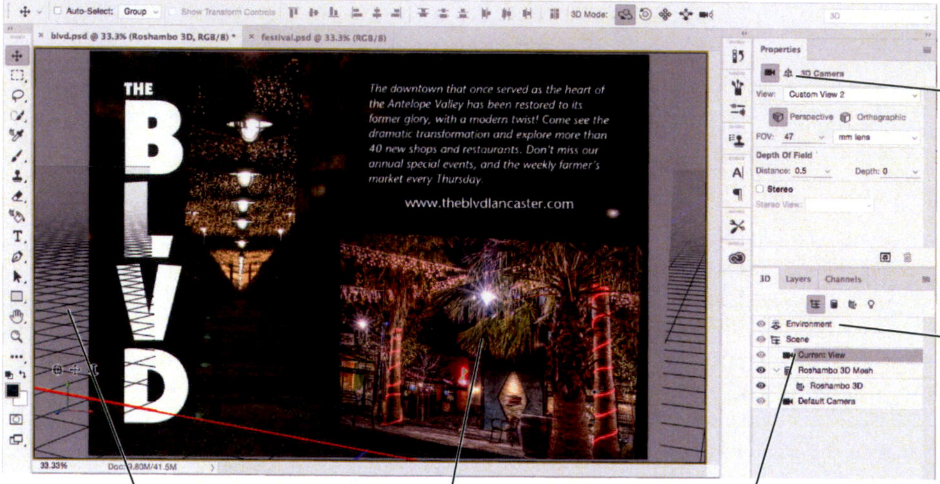
THE
BLVD
The downtown that once served as the heart of the Antelope Valley has been restored to its former glory, with a modern twist! Come see the dramatic transformation and explore more than 40 new shops and restaurants. Don't miss our annual special events, and the weekly farmer's market every Thursday.
www.theblvdlancaster.com
Properties
3D Camera
View: Custom View 2
Perspective
Orthographic
3D
Layers
Channels
Environment
Scene
Current View
Roshambo 3D Mesh
Roshambo 3D
Default Camera
Use these buttons to change modes in the Properties panel.
The 3D panel lists all elements of the selected 3D layer.
Click the Ground Plane and drag to move the current view.
The object also moves when you change the current view.
Current View is selected.

5. **With 3D Camera options visible in the Properties panel, choose Default in the View menu to reset the camera view.**

The Properties panel has a number of different modes, depending on what is selected in the 3D panel. The Coordinates mode shows the current position of the camera relative to its original (default) position.

It's important to realize that the changes you make — whether to the scene or to the mesh — are non-destructive; you can reposition either as much as you like, at any time.

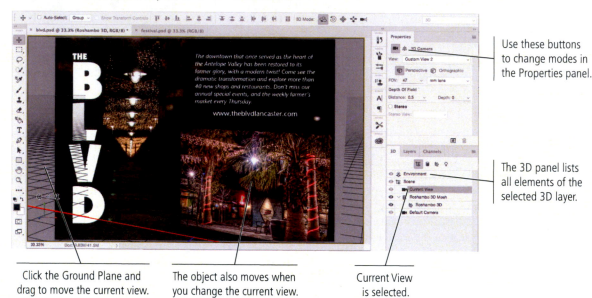

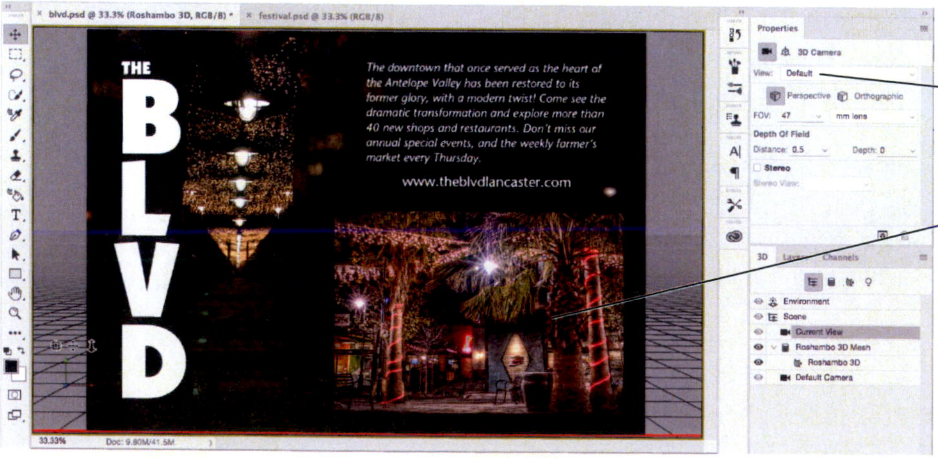
THE
BLVD
The downtown that once served as the heart of the Antelope Valley has been restored to its former glory, with a modern twist! Come see the dramatic transformation and explore more than 40 new shops and restaurants. Don't miss our annual special events, and the weekly farmer's market every Thursday.
www.theblvdlancaster.com
Properties
3D Camera
View: Default
Perspective
Orthographic
Environment
Scene
Current View
Roshambo 3D Mesh
Roshambo 3D
Default Camera
Use this menu to restore the default view.
The object returns to the default view, which is directly from the front.

6. **In the 3D panel, click the Roshambo 3D Mesh.**

   You could also simply click the mesh on the canvas to select the object.

The gray rectangle represents the edge of the mesh object.

When the mesh object is selected, the 3D Axis widget appears on screen.

You can apply virtually any changes to the object position using the 3D Axis widget. Each axis in the widget has three different controls:

- **Move On Axis** changes the position of the object along the selected axis.
- **Rotate Around Axis** changes the rotation of the object around the perpendicular axis. In other words, the control on the red (X) axis rotates the mesh around the green (Y) axis.
- **Scale Along Axis** changes the size of the object along the selected axis.

The active control is yellow.

Y Axis

X Axis

Z Axis

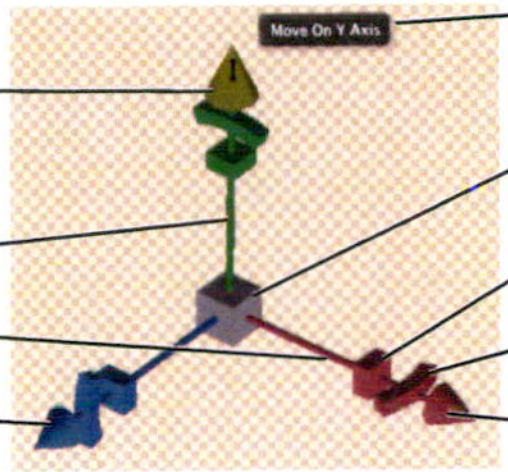

Cursor feedback shows the name of the active control.

Scale Uniformly

Scale Along Axis

Rotate Around Axis

Move Along Axis

You can also click the center cube in the widget and drag to scale the object uniformly (on all three axes).

7. **In the Properties panel, click the Coordinates button to show the numeric position of the mesh.**

8. **In the 3D Axis widget, click the Rotate Around Y Axis control (on the red axis) and drag right to rotate the mesh.**

   When you make changes using the on-screen controls, those changes are reflected in the Coordinates pane of the Properties panel. You can use either method to move, rotate, and scale the selected mesh.

Note:

Press V to cycle through the modes of the Properties panel.

Cursor feedback shows the specific transformation as you drag.

The gray mesh wireframe shows how the object is changing.

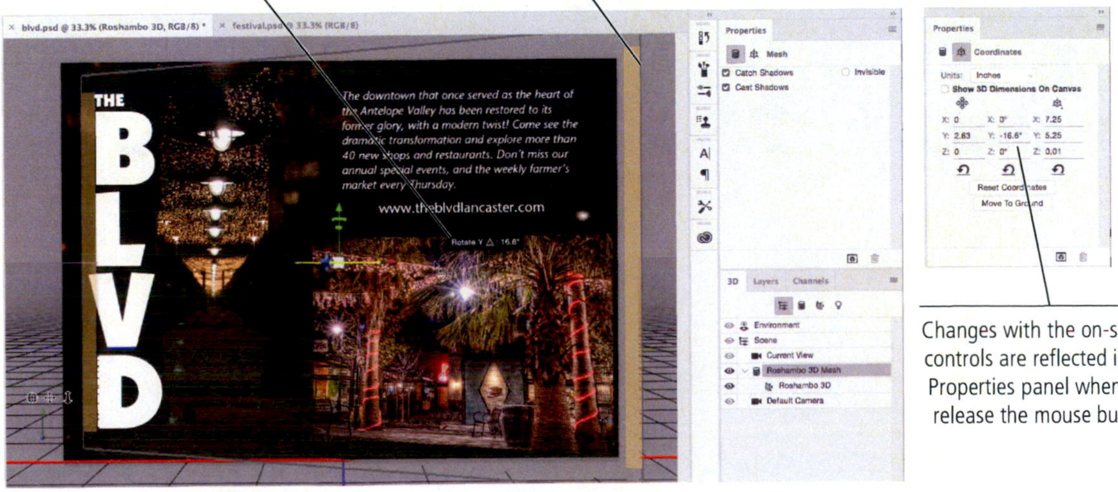

Changes with the on-screen controls are reflected in the Properties panel when you release the mouse button.

9. **Place the cursor over the center cube in the 3D Axis widget. Press Shift, then click and drag up to enlarge the icon.**

Before rotating the mesh in the previous step, it was difficult to see all of the controls in the widget. Making the icon larger makes it easier to access the individual controls.

former glory, with a modern
dramatic transformation and
40 new shops and restauran
annual special events, and th
market every Thursday.
www.theblvdlanc

Shift-drag the Scale Uniformly control to enlarge the widget.

> *Note:*
>
> *In the 3D Axis widget, the Y axis is green, the X axis is red, and the Z axis is blue.*

10. **In the Z Axis (blue) of the widget, click the Rotate Around X Axis control and drag up to rotate the mesh.**

This rotation tilts the mesh front to back.

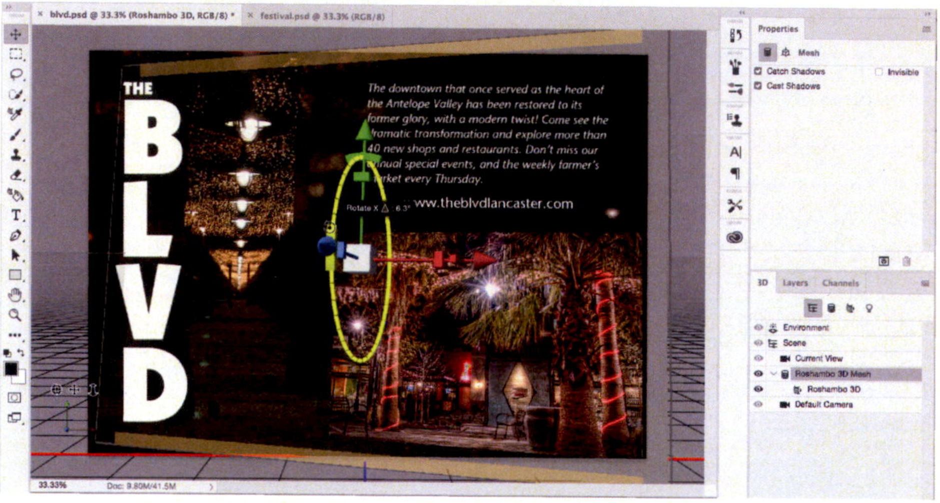
blvd.psd @ 33.3% (Roshambo 3D, RGB/8) *
festival.psd @ 33.3% (RGB/8)
THE
BLVD
The downtown that once served as the heart of
the Antelope Valley has been restored to its
former glory, with a modern twist! Come see the
dramatic transformation and explore more than
40 new shops and restaurants. Don't miss our
annual special events, and the weekly farmer's
market every Thursday.
www.theblvdlancaster.com
Properties
Mesh
Catch Shadows
Invisible
Cast Shadows
3D
Layers
Channels
Environment
Scene
Current View
Roshambo 3D Mesh
Roshambo 3D
Default Camera
33.33%
Doc: 9.80M/41.5M

11. **In the X Axis (red) of the widget, click the Move on X Axis control and drag right to move the mesh until the right edge of the image is past the canvas edge.**

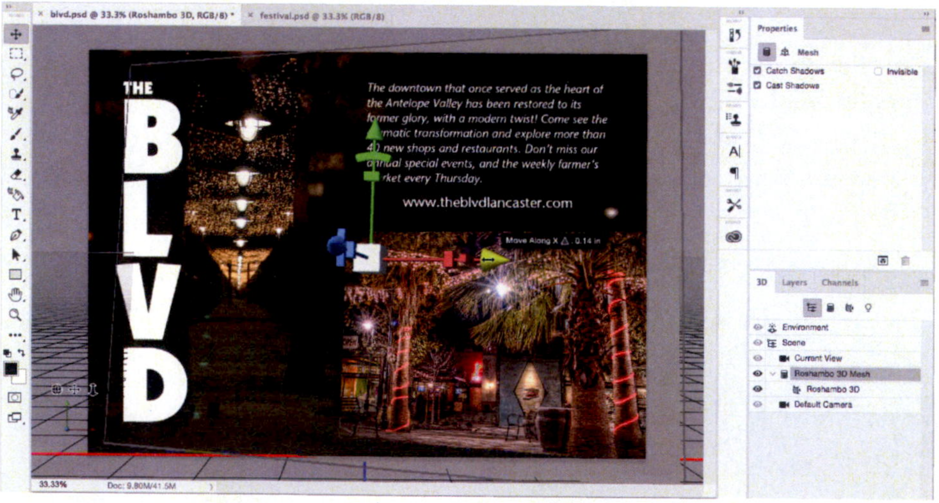
blvd.psd @ 33.3% (Roshambo 3D, RGB/8) *
festival.psd @ 33.3% (RGB/8)
THE
BLVD
The downtown that once served as the heart of
the Antelope Valley has been restored to its
former glory, with a modern twist! Come see the
40 new shops and restaurants. Don't miss our
market every Thursday.
www.theblvdlancaster.com
Move Along X
0.14 in
Properties
Mesh
Catch Shadows
Invisible
Cast Shadows
3D
Layers
Channels
Environment
Scene
Current View
Roshambo 3D Mesh
Roshambo 3D
Default Camera
33.33%
Doc: 9.80M/41.5M

12. **Click the Render button at the bottom of the Properties panel.**

While you work with the 3D mesh, the preview is simply an on-screen representation. Rendering the 3D creates the final, full-resolution version of your 3D object.

The complete rendering process takes a long time, depending on the power of your computer processor. Be patient! The status area at the bottom-left corner of your document window shows the time remaining to complete the rendering process.

Note:

You can press the ESC key to cancel the rendering process.

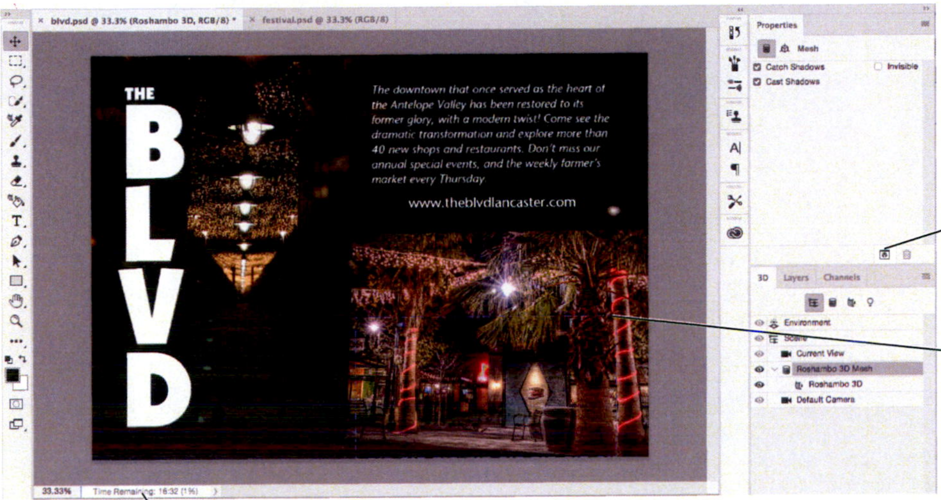

Render

This outline moves across the canvas while rendering is being processed.

Time remaining to complete the rendering process appears here.

13. **Save the file and continue to the next exercise.**

Create a 3D Sphere

In the previous exercises, you worked with a simple "flat" 3D object. Photoshop includes a number of more complex meshes that allow more flexibility and creativity than a simple postcard. In this exercise, you are going to add a sphere to the festival postcard, with another poppy image as the material on that mesh.

1. **With festival.psd active, create a new empty layer at the top of the layer stack. Change the name of the new layer to Globe.**

2. **In the 3D panel, choose Selected Layer(s) in the Source menu. Choose the Mesh from Preset option, then choose Sphere in the attached menu. Click Create at the bottom of the panel.**

This has the same general effect as choosing 3D>New Mesh from Layer>Mesh Preset>Sphere. You should try to be aware of your options for accomplishing any particular goal and determine which is best suited to your personal working preferences.

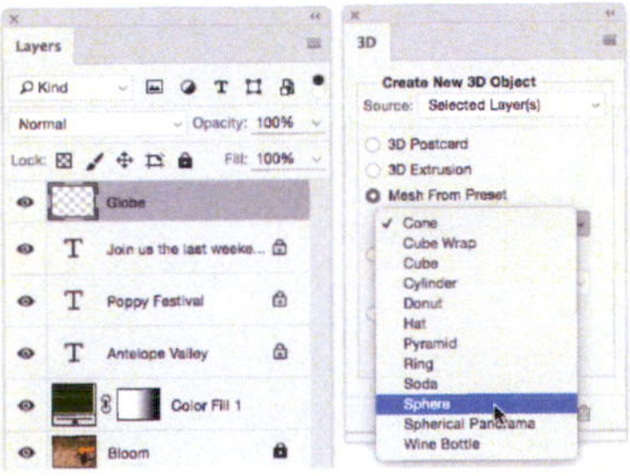

Note:

If you are not already using the built-in 3D workspace, you will be asked if you want to switch to that workspace before proceeding.

Understanding 3D Materials Properties

When a 3D object's material is selected in the 3D panel, the top section of the Properties panel defines four types of lights that affect the 3D object:

- **Diffuse** is the color of the surface material, or the file that makes up the reflective surface of the object.
- **Specular** defines the color of areas where the light is 100% reflected (specular highlights).
- **Illumination** is the color of surface areas where the material is transparent; this setting results in the effect of interior lighting, such as a painting on a light bulb.
- **Ambient** defines the color of ambient (environmental) light that is visible on reflective surfaces.

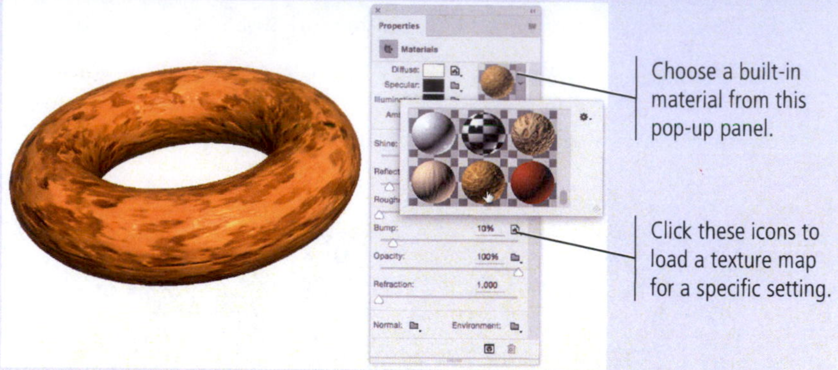

For each of the types of lighting, you can click the color swatch to change that light's color. For all but Ambient light, you can also use the attached menus to define an existing file (or create a new one) that will be used for that property.

The lower half of the panel defines additional material properties:

- **Shine** defines the dispersion of reflected light. Low values result in more apparent light, and high values result in less apparent light and cleaner highlights.
- **Reflection** increases the strength of reflected objects in the 3D object's surface.
- **Roughness** can be used to cause a surface to appear less polished. Higher roughness makes an object less reflective (think of a chrome bumper that has been scratched by sandpaper).
- **Bump** adds depth in the material surface without altering the actual object mesh. Lighter gray values in the defined texture map create raised areas, and darker gray values create flatter areas.
- **Opacity** determines the transparency of the surface material. If you define a map file for this setting, lighter areas in the map are less transparent, and darker areas are more transparent.
- **Refraction** is the change in light direction that occurs when light strikes a surface (think of the classic "bent pencil in a glass of water" example).
- **Normal** is similar to the Bump option, but can use an RGB image as the texture map file.
- **Environment** stores an image of the environment around the object, which can be seen in reflective areas of the object's surface.

You can load a file to apply as a mesh's surface (as you did in this project). You can also control an object's appearance using a **texture map**, which is (typically) a grayscale image in which different shades determine the strength of a particular setting.

If you choose Edit UV Properties in one of the Texture Map menus, you can control the scale, tiling, and offset of the repeat pattern for the selected texture map.

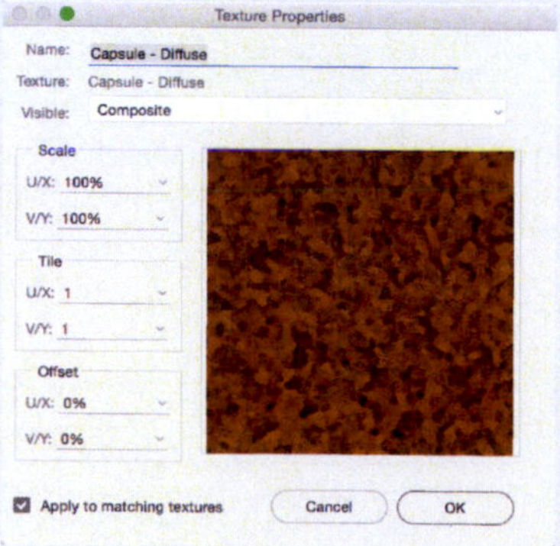

3. **If you get an Embedded Profile Mismatch warning, choose Convert Document's Colors to the Working Space, then click OK.**

4. **If necessary, close the Secondary View panel.**

   Although the 3D workspace elements all serve useful purposes, they can be distracting at times. You can turn specific interface elements off or on in the View>Show submenu.

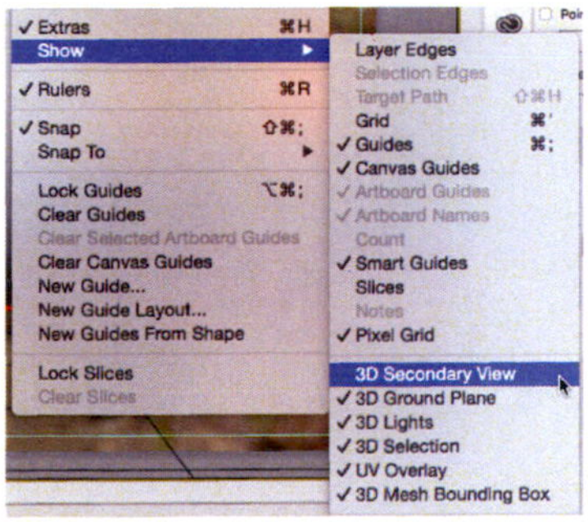

5. **In the 3D panel, select the Sphere_Material.**

6. **In the Properties panel, open the menu next to the Diffuse option and choose Replace Texture.**

Sphere_Material is selected.

7. **Navigate to `Field.jpg` (in your WIP>Cards folder) and click Open. If you see a warning about mismatched color profiles, use the embedded profile.**

The selected image becomes the material on the sphere surface.

8. **Click the sphere on the canvas to select the mesh object. Click one of the gray lines that represents the mesh edge, and drag to move the object to cover the poppy in the background image.**

   When the mesh is selected, it is surrounded on the screen by a cage that represents the outer 3D "box" shape. In addition to using the 3D Axis widget, you can also use the mesh cage to make specific changes; cursor feedback shows what you can accomplish by clicking a specific location on the mesh preview.

   In this case, you can use the mesh edge to drag the object without rotating or resizing it.

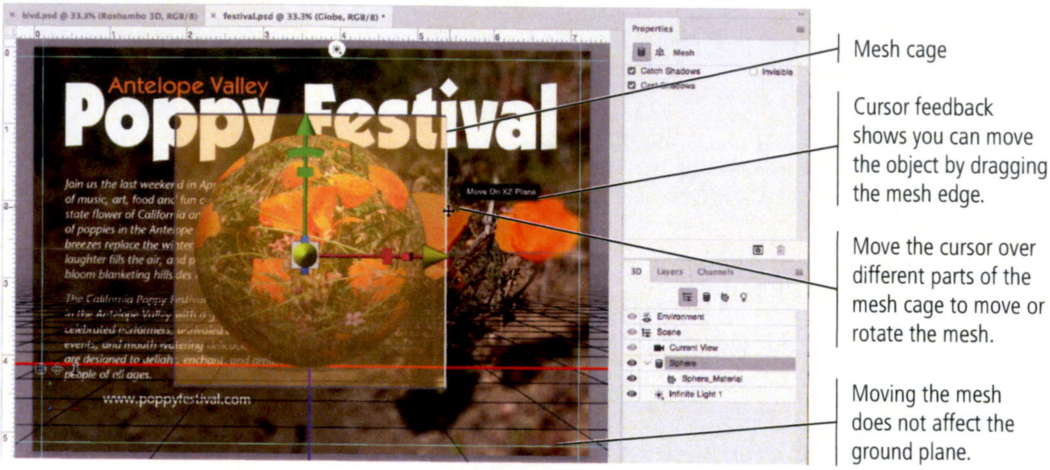
Antelope Valley
Poppy Festival
www.poppyfestival.com
Move On XZ Plane
Mesh cage
Cursor feedback shows you can move the object by dragging the mesh edge.
Move the cursor over different parts of the mesh cage to move or rotate the mesh.
Change the panel to Coordinates mode.
Moving the mesh does not affect the ground plane.

9. **In the Properties panel, click the Coordinates button to show the numeric position of the mesh object.**

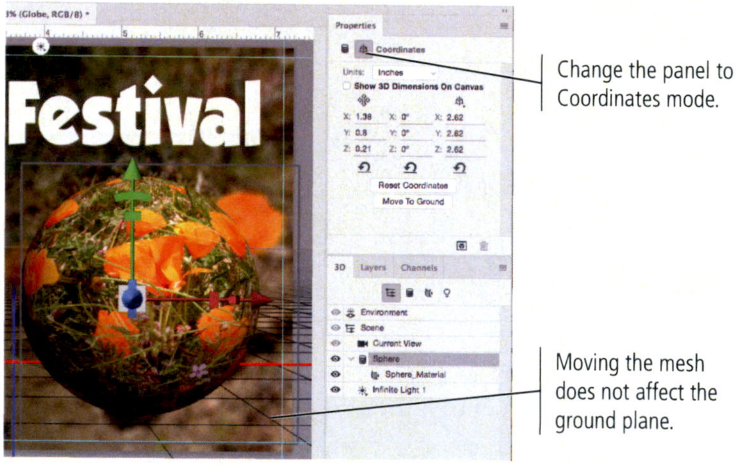

10. **Move the cursor near the vertical edge of the mesh cage. When the cursor feedback shows "Rotate Around Y Axis," click and drag right until the large cluster of poppies is visible on the sphere.**

    We liked the content that appears when the sphere is rotated approximately –26°, as you can see in the cursor feedback while dragging and in the Properties panel when you release the mouse button.

When you release the mouse button, the new Y rotation angle appears in the Properties:Coordinates panel.

11. **Move the cursor near the top horizontal edge of the mesh cage. When the cursor feedback shows "Rotate Around X Axis," click and drag down until you are satisfied with the image that appears on the sphere surface.**

12. **Click the Scale Uniformly control and drag up to enlarge the sphere proportionally.**

13. **In the Properties panel, show the Coordinates options and then click the Move to Ground button.**

This snaps the object to create the appearance of sitting on the ground plane, which is represented by the red line.

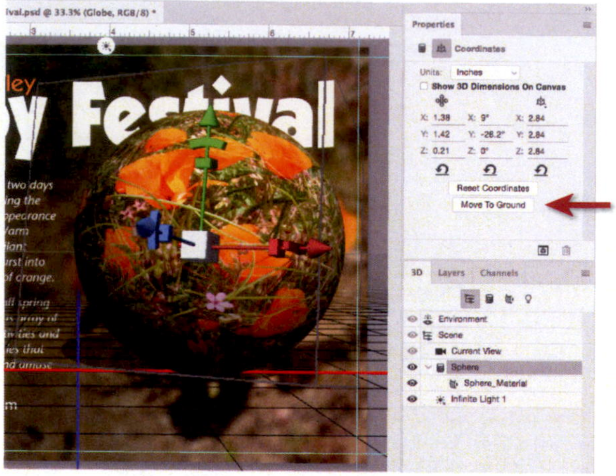

> ***Note:***
>
> *This button has the same effect as choosing 3D>Move Object to Ground Plane.*

14. **In the 3D panel, click the Current View to select it.**

15. **Choose the Pan the 3D Camera button in the Options bar.**

16. **Click and drag until the sphere is back in the same relative position as before you snapped it to the ground plane.**

When the Current View is selected in the 3D panel, you can drag the ground plane — basically, changing the view of the object without changing the actual mesh. The object retains its position relative to the ground plane so it does move, but the actual mesh and mesh texture do not change.

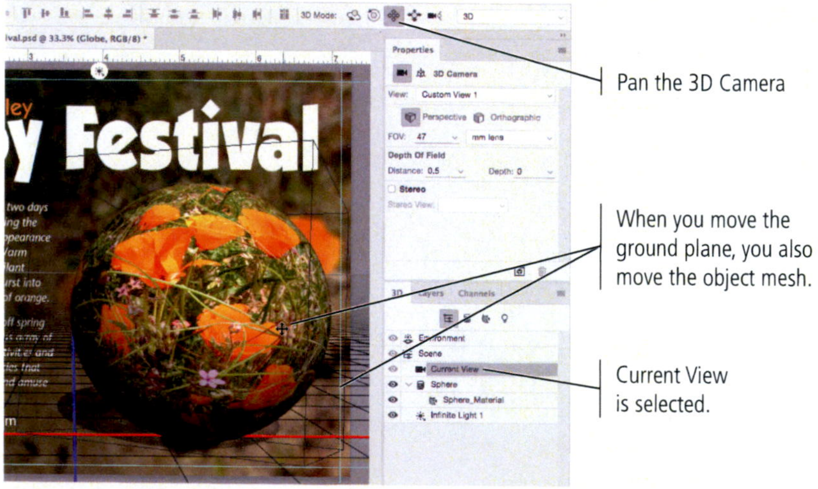
Pan the 3D Camera
When you move the ground plane, you also move the object mesh.
Current View is selected.

17. **Click the light widget at the top of the document window.**

The light sources related to a 3D object determine how shadows are cast. The Sphere preset mesh includes one infinite light source, which is a light that shines from a single point far away (like the sun).

> ***Note:***
>
> *You could also click the Infinite Light 1 option in the 3D panel to select the light.*

18. **Click the light handle in the on-screen preview and drag until the shadow on the bottom of the sphere is strongest on the bottom-right side of the mesh.**

This position better matches the shadow style that is applied to the type layers.

Click the light widget to select it.

Drag the light handle to change the direction of the light source.

Changing the light direction changes the shadows on the sphere, and that are cast on the ground plane.

You should notice that the shadow on the ground plane is far behind the sphere, and does not appear natural. This is the result of Step 7, when you moved the object mesh away from the ground plane.

19. **In the Properties panel, show the Infinite Light options. Change the light Intensity to 60% and change the Shadow Softness to 30%.**

Now that you can better see the shadow, you can make more informed changes. The Softness option creates a blurrier edge on the ground-plane shadow.

Click to show specific Infinite Light properties.

Use this option to change the strength of the light.

Use this option to soften the shadow edges.

20. **Select the Environment in the 3D panel. In the Properties panel, change the Ground Plane Shadows Opacity to 85%.**

    This darkens the shadow that is cast by the sphere onto the ground plane, but does not affect the shadow on the surface of the sphere.

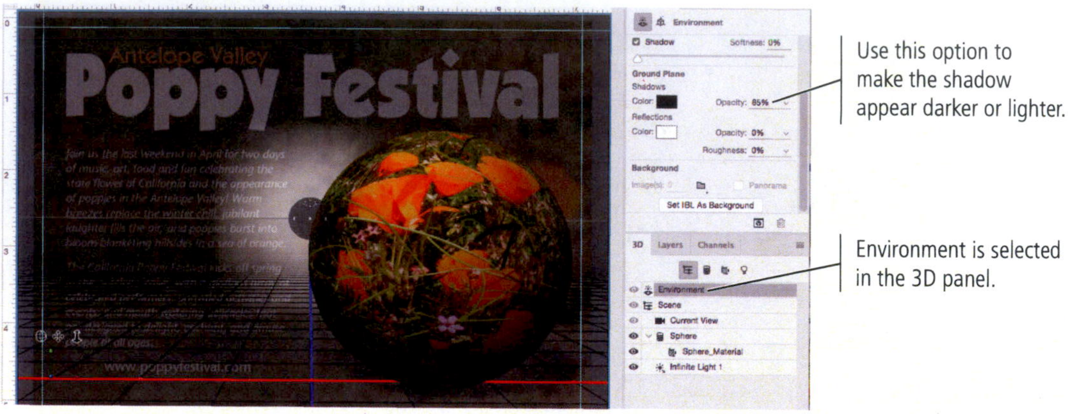
Antelope Valley
Poppy Festival
Use this option to make the shadow appear darker or lighter.
Environment is selected in the 3D panel.

21. **Click the Render button at the bottom of the Properties panel.**

    When the rendering is complete, the sphere edges and the ground-plane shadow show a distinct improvement over the working on-screen preview.

22. **Save the file, then continue to the final exercise of the project.**

Create Layer Comps

Layer Comps allows you to save multiple iterations of a file at one time. A layer comp can store the position and visibility of individual layers, as well as any effects applied. This feature is useful when you want to experiment with the position of specific layers, but you want to keep a record of earlier positions of the layers — or, as in this case, when you want to present two versions of a file: one version with a layer visible, and one version with a layer hidden.

It's important to know that layer comps do not store pixel information. Modifying the actual pixel data on a layer will not be undone by reverting to an earlier layer comp. To undo that kind of change, you must use the History panel and snapshots, assuming you haven't closed the file since you created the snapshots.

1. **With festival.psd open, select any layer other than the Globe layer.**

    Deselecting the 3D layer turns off all of the 3D visual aids (ground plane, etc.)

2. **Open the Layer Comps panel (Window>Layer Comps).**

    When no layer comps exist in the file, or you make changes that do not match what is saved as an existing layer comp, the panel shows the Last Document State as active. Buttons at the bottom of the panel enable a number of options:

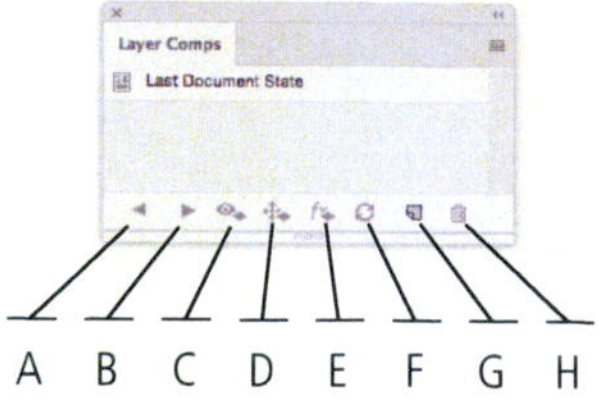

    A Apply Previous Selected Layer Comp
    B Apply Next Selected Layer Comp
    C Update Visibilities of Selected Layer Comps and Layers
    D Update Positions of Selected Layer Comps and Layers
    E Update Appearances of Selected Layer Comps and Layers
    F Update Layer Comp
    G Create New Layer Comp
    H Delete Layer Comp

3. **Click the Create New Layer Comp button at the bottom of the Layer Comps panel.**

4. **In the New Layer Comp dialog box, name the comp Final 3D. Make sure the Visibility option is checked, and then click OK.**

 When you choose the Visibility option, only the currently visible layers (in this case, all of them) will be included in the comp.

New Layer Comp button

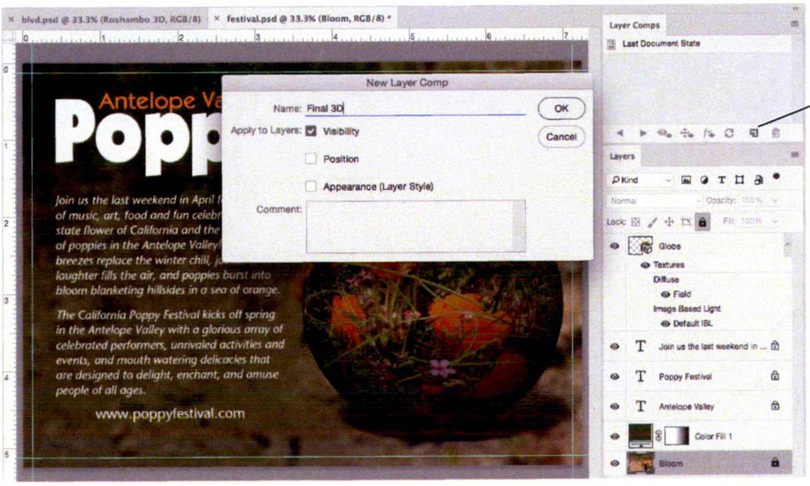

When you close the dialog box, the new comp has been added to the panel. It is active because you haven't made any changes to layers since saving the layer comp.

Icons to the right of the layer comp identify which attributes — visibility, position, and appearance — are stored in the layer comp. If an icon is grayed out, it is not part of that comp. You can click these icons to toggle each attribute on or off for a selected comp.

This icon shows the currently active comp.

Only the Visibility property is stored in this layer comp.

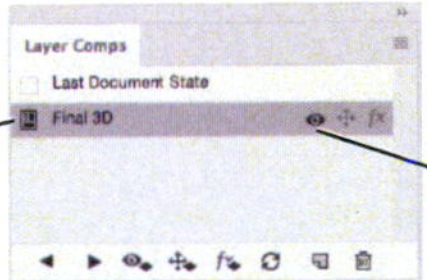

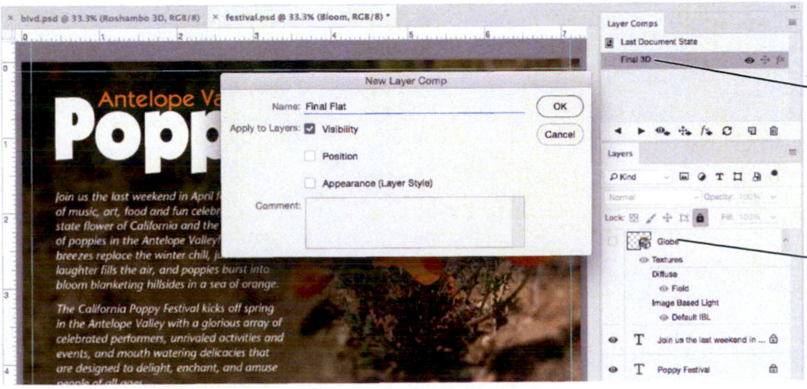

Note:

You can select a specific layer comp in the panel and click the buttons at the bottom of the panel to change the layer properties that are stored in that comp. The first three buttons affect only one attribute (visibility, position, or appearance); the Update Layer Comp button updates all three attributes at once.

5. **In the Layers panel, hide the Globe layer.**

 When you make changes in the file after creating a layer comp, the Active icon on the left side of the panel automatically switches to Last Document State.

6. **Create another new layer comp named Final Flat, again including only the layer visibility attributes in the comp.**

 Remember, you hid the Globe layer in Step 5; checking the visibility option means that layer will not be visible if you activate the Final Flat layer comp.

Last Document State is active because you changed something after saving the Final 3D layer comp.

The Globe layer is hidden.

7. **Choose File>Export>Layer Comps to Files.**

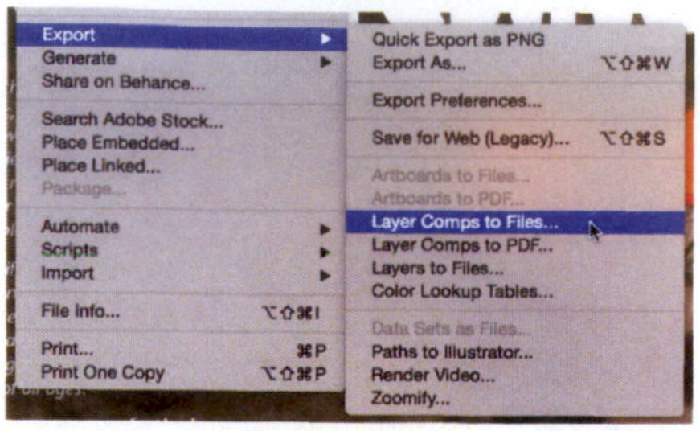

8. **In the Layer Comps to Files dialog box, make sure the WIP>Cards folder is selected in the Destination field, and make sure festival appears in the File Name Prefix field.**

   This script creates separate files for each layer comp. The target location defaults to the same location as the working file, and the file name defaults to the current file name.

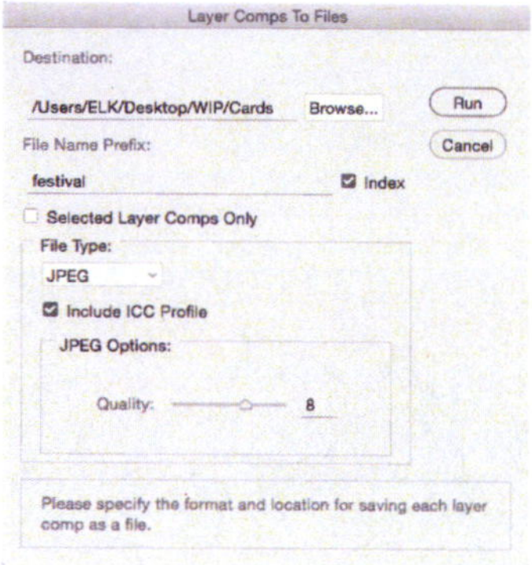

9. **Choose JPEG in the File Type menu, and leave the remaining options at their default values.**

10. **Click Run.**

    The process could take a while to complete; don't panic and don't get impatient. When the file is done, you will see the message shown here.

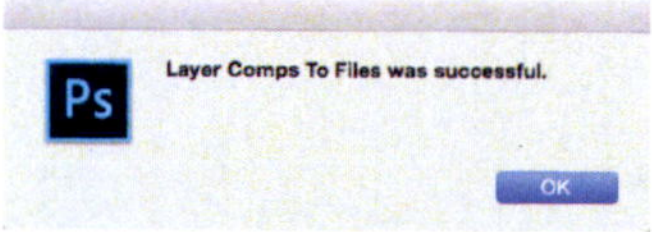

11. **Click OK to close the message, and then save and close the Photoshop file.**

12. **Repeat this process to create two versions of the BLVD postcard. Make sure you show the Roshambo layer when you create the "flat" layer comp. Also make sure the File Name Prefix field accurately reflects the files that you are exporting.**

    There appears to be a bug in the software; when you open this dialog box the second time, the file name defaults to the last-used option. If you don't change it to "blvd," you would overwrite the festival postcard versions.

13. **Save and close the blvd.psd file.**

Project Review

fill in the blank

1. _______________ identifies and tries to protect areas of detail when you scale the image.

2. _______________ allows you to move a selection, filling the original selection area with detail instead of leaving an empty hole.

3. A _______________ effect applies a consistent blur over the entire selected layer.

4. _______________ is created by simply clicking (without dragging) with one of the Type tools.

5. _______________ is the distance from one baseline to the next in a paragraph of type.

6. The _______________ tools can be used to create selections in the shape of individual characters or entire words.

7. _______________ describes the space between individual type characters (where the insertion point is placed).

8. _______________ cannot be applied to type layers; you must first rasterize a type layer to apply them.

9. A(n) _______________ light source shines as a single point from a seemingly far distance.

10. A(n) _______________ stores the visibility of specific layers at a given point.

short answer

1. Briefly describe the result of moving a selection with the Move tool.

2. Briefly explain the difference between point type and area type.

3. Briefly explain the concept of a material, as it relates to a 3D object.

Portfolio Builder Project

Use what you learned in this project to complete the following freeform exercise.
Carefully read the art director and client comments, then create your own design to meet the needs of the project.
Use the space below to sketch ideas; when finished, write a brief explanation of your reasoning behind your final design.

art director comments

As a freelance designer, you have been hired by the band Midnight Sun to create a logo and cover artwork for their forthcoming CD release.

To complete this project, you should:

- ❑ Design an interesting logotype for the band.
- ❑ Determine the appropriate size for the cover that is inserted into a CD jewel case.
- ❑ Locate or create artwork or images to illustrate the CD title.
- ❑ Create the CD cover art for commercial printing requirements.

client comments

We're originally from Alaska. We all had full-time jobs when we first started, so we practiced late at night (no surprise!) until we decided we would get more exposure in Seattle. Since we spent so much time awake in the middle of the night, we named the band Midnight Sun.

We haven't had much luck yet in finding a label, so we're going to self-publish an EP to help promote the band and, hopefully, raise some money. We're calling the disc "The Lower 48" because all of the songs are about our journey to where we are now.

We want the cover art to represent the type of music we play — primarily rock, but with other genres thrown in. Blues, hip hop, international beats, and even orchestrated undertones all make an appearance.

We have a very unique sound, but we're an eclectic group of people. We're hoping you can create cover art that says who we are without using a boring group photo.

project justification

Project Summary

Completing this project required a number of new skills for manipulating layer content — scaling and moving selections, applying blur effects, and working with layer styles. By now you should understand the difference between working with an entire layer and working with only a selected area, and be able to choose the appropriate tools to affect only what you want to change.

You also did a considerable amount of work with type, which can be either created from scratch or pasted from a text editor. Although the type controls in Photoshop are not quite as robust as those in formal page layout applications — which are specifically designed to create and control large blocks of type — they are certainly useful for a range of different applications.

You learned how to create both point and area type, as well as the different formatting options that are available for selected characters or entire paragraphs. You also worked with a number of tools that create unique artistic effects from a Photoshop type layer — sampling colors from an image to format type, applying styles to type layers, and changing layer opacity and blending modes.

Finally, you learned the basics of working with 3D objects. As we already stated, we didn't even come close to explaining everything there is to know about 3D. However, you did experiment with a number of the options that are most relevant to print designers.

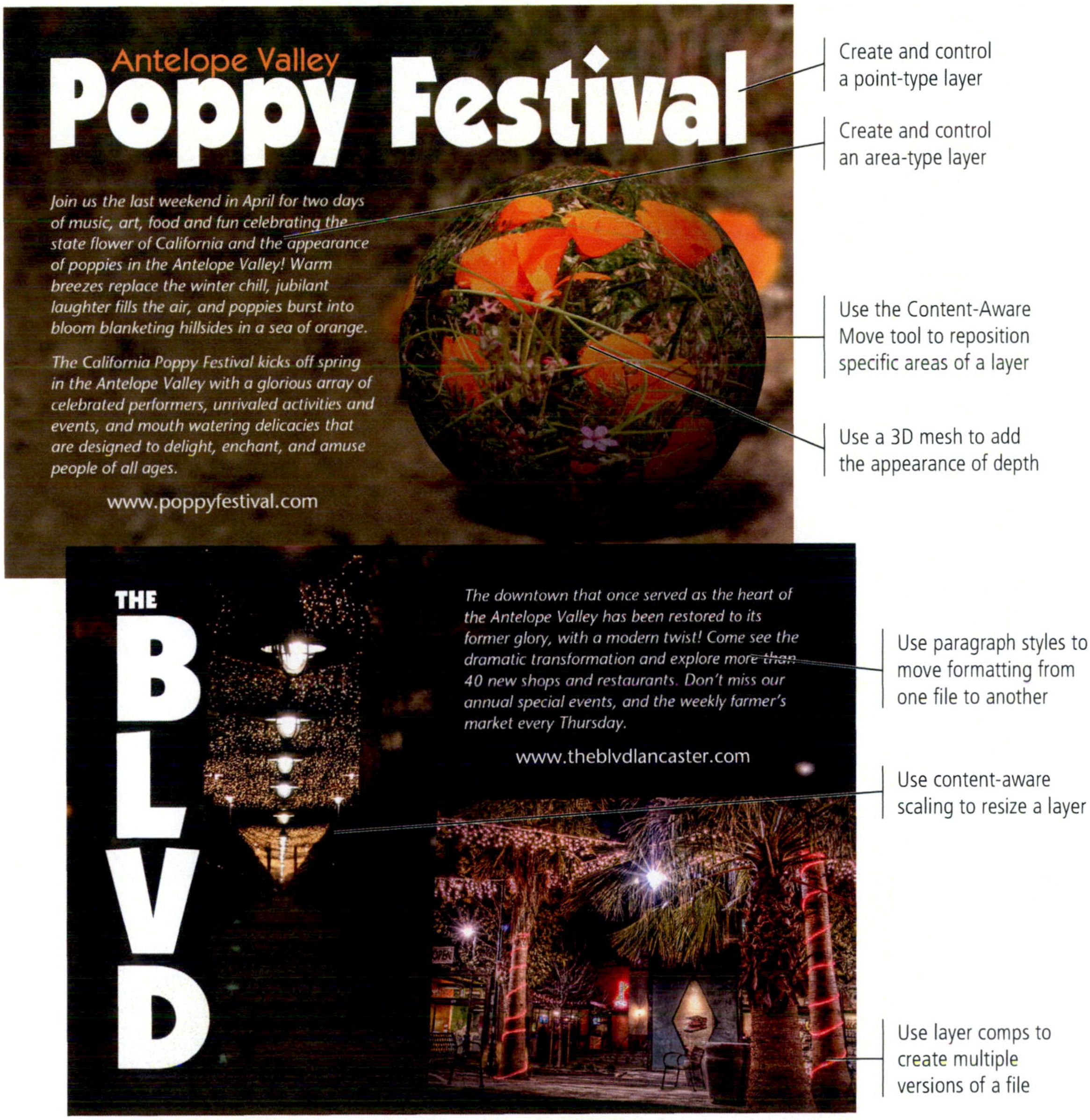

Antelope Valley
Poppy Festival
Join us the last weekend in April for two days of music, art, food and fun celebrating the state flower of California and the appearance of poppies in the Antelope Valley! Warm breezes replace the winter chill, jubilant laughter fills the air, and poppies burst into bloom blanketing hillsides in a sea of orange.
The California Poppy Festival kicks off spring in the Antelope Valley with a glorious array of celebrated performers, unrivaled activities and events, and mouth watering delicacies that are designed to delight, enchant, and amuse people of all ages.
www.poppyfestival.com
Create and control a point-type layer
Create and control an area-type layer
Use the Content-Aware Move tool to reposition specific areas of a layer
Use a 3D mesh to add the appearance of depth
THE BLVD
The downtown that once served as the heart of the Antelope Valley has been restored to its former glory, with a modern twist! Come see the dramatic transformation and explore more than 40 new shops and restaurants. Don't miss our annual special events, and the weekly farmer's market every Thursday.
www.theblvdlancaster.com
Use paragraph styles to move formatting from one file to another
Use content-aware scaling to resize a layer
Use layer comps to create multiple versions of a file

project 5

Calendar Cover

Your client is a performing arts center that is preparing to publish its schedule for the upcoming Fall/Winter season. The annual mailing drives a significant portion of season ticket subscriptions, so it is one of the most important pieces of their overall marketing campaign. Although your agency has been hired to produce the entire booklet, your job is to complete only the cover.

This project incorporates the following skills:

- ❑ Managing missing fonts
- ❑ Creating a complex mask
- ❑ Creating custom vector shapes
- ❑ Working with spot channels

Project Meeting

client comments

Our calendar mailings are the number one driver behind annual subscriptions. We send out the Spring/Summer schedule in early December, so it is in potential subscribers' hands before the holiday season.

We anticipate one of this year's biggest performances to be The Golden Fleece, which is a new symphony and ballet telling the story of Jason and the Argonauts. The Royal Ballet Company has committed to two weekends in the end of April for the performance, and we hope to sell out all six shows. We sent you an image from the ballet company's media files; we want that image to be featured prominently on the calendar cover.

Our calendars are printed on a six-color press. The sixth press unit runs a flood varnish, and we do have the budget to use a spot color on the other press unit if you think it will enhance the design.

art director comments

I already started work on the cover, but I need to move over to the interior layout so I want you to finish the cover. I used two different fonts in the file; if you don't have the ones I used, you can substitute similar fonts.

There are several tasks that remain to be completed on the cover image.

Create a banner shape that extends the entire width of the piece, behind the dancer but in front of the background images, to hide the bottom edge of the fireworks layer.

Create a complex selection to remove the main dancer from her background.

For the fifth color, we will use Pantone 8943 from the metallic ink set — metallic orange, which will work nicely as the orange in the client's logo. Be aware that using spot colors in Photoshop requires a few tricks and workarounds that are different from what you do when you work with regular image channels.

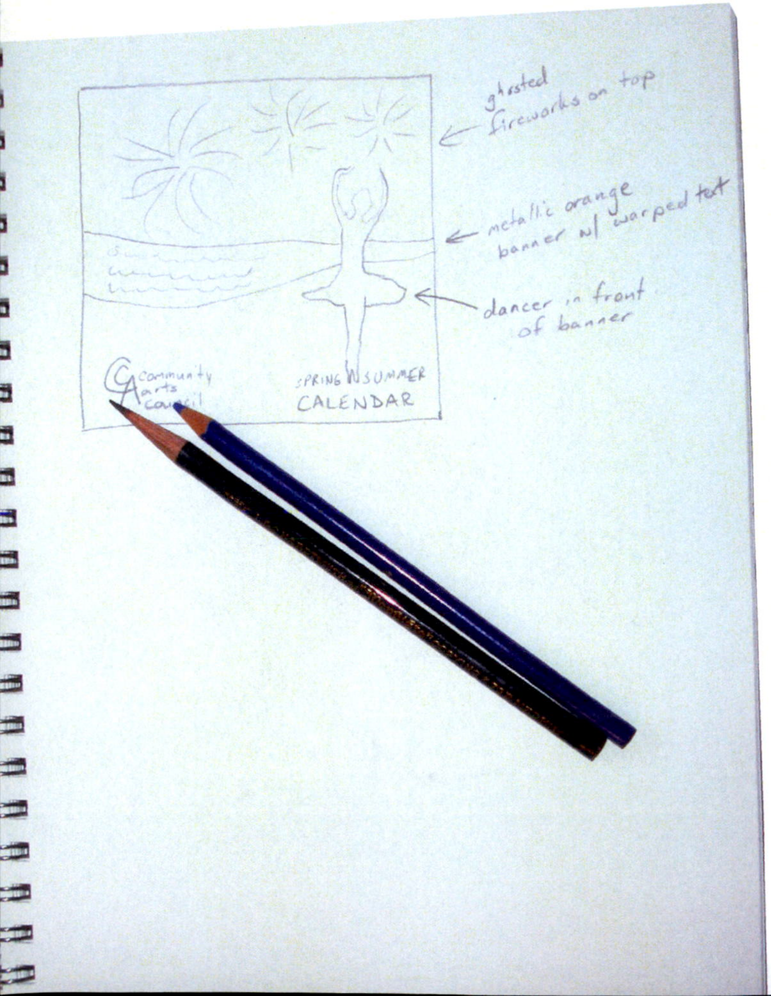

project objectives

To complete this project, you will:

- ❑ Manage missing fonts
- ❑ Create a custom shape layer
- ❑ Create warped text
- ❑ Manually edit an Alpha channel
- ❑ Use Select and Mask to refine a complex selection
- ❑ Define a new spot channel
- ❑ Copy layer information to a spot channel
- ❑ Save the file with spot-color information

Stage 1 Managing Missing Fonts

When you work with type in a Photoshop file, it is important to understand that fonts are external files of data that describe the font for on-screen display and for the output device. The fonts you use in a layout need to be available on any computer that will be used to open the file. Photoshop stores a reference to used fonts, but it does not store the actual font data.

Evaluate Project Requirements

Because this project includes a partially completed file, your first task is to evaluate the existing file and determine what needs to be accomplished.

1. **Download `Calendar_PS18_RF.zip` from the Student Files web page.**

2. **Expand the ZIP archive in your WIP folder (Macintosh) or copy the archive contents into your WIP folder (Windows).**

   This results in a folder named **Calendar**, which contains the file you need for this project. You should also use this folder to save the files you create in this project.

3. **In Photoshop, open the file `ballet-cover.psd` from the WIP>Calendar folder. If you get a missing profile warning, choose the option to leave it as is.**

4. **Read the resulting warning. If you see the dialog box on the left, click Next.**

   The first message window (below left) only appears the first time you encounter a missing-font problem.

   When you work with type in a Photoshop file, it is important to understand that fonts are external files of data that describe the font for on-screen display and for the output device. The fonts you use in a design need to be available on any computer that will be used to open the file. Photoshop stores a reference to used fonts; it does not store the actual font data.

   The application warns you if required fonts are missing when you open the Photoshop file. Each missing font is listed in the secondary Missing Fonts dialog box. You can use the menus attached to each missing font to define a specific font that should be used in place of the missing ones — the default font (typically Minion Pro Regular), or another font that has been used in the file and is available on your system.

> ***Note:***
>
> *You can choose Type>Resolve Missing Fonts to reopen the Missing Fonts dialog box at any time as you work on a Photoshop file.*

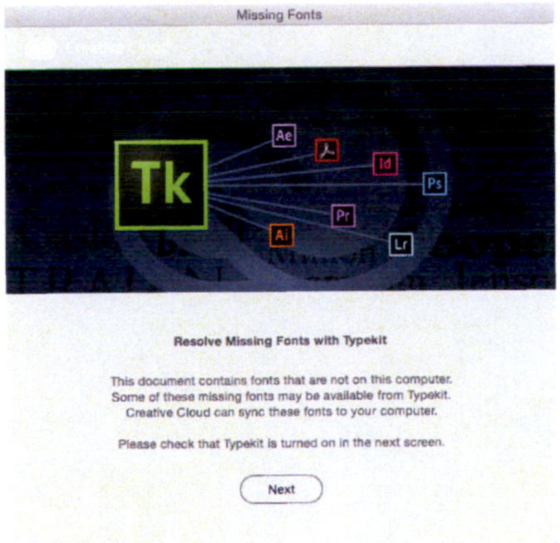

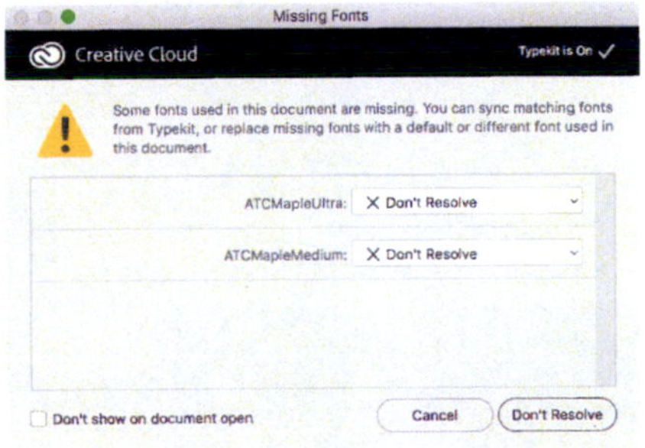

If missing fonts are available in the Typekit library, the dialog box automatically identifies the appropriate Typekit font in the menu. Clicking the Resolve Fonts button syncs the required Typekit fonts in your Creative Cloud account, making them available in your version of Photoshop.

5. **Click the Don't Resolve button to open the file without affecting the type layers.**

6. **Review the Layers panel for the open file.**

   If you click Cancel, the file opens without resolving missing font problems. Type layers with missing fonts appear normal in the document window.

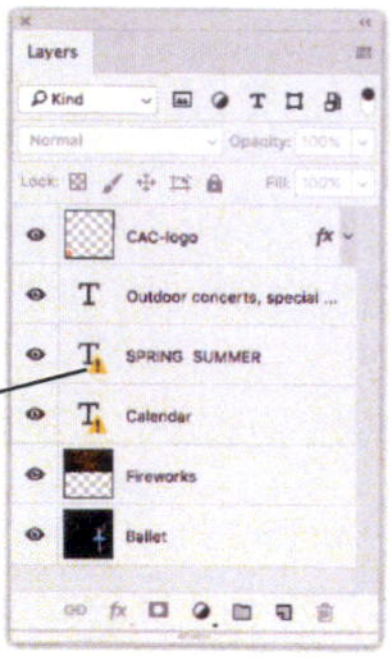

In the Layers panel, type layers with missing fonts show a warning icon.

7. **Choose the Horizontal Type tool in the Tools panel.**

8. **Click anywhere in the word "SPRING" at the bottom of the page to place the insertion point.**

   You do not need to first select a specific type layer to place the insertion point in an existing type layer.

9. **Read the resulting message, then click OK.**

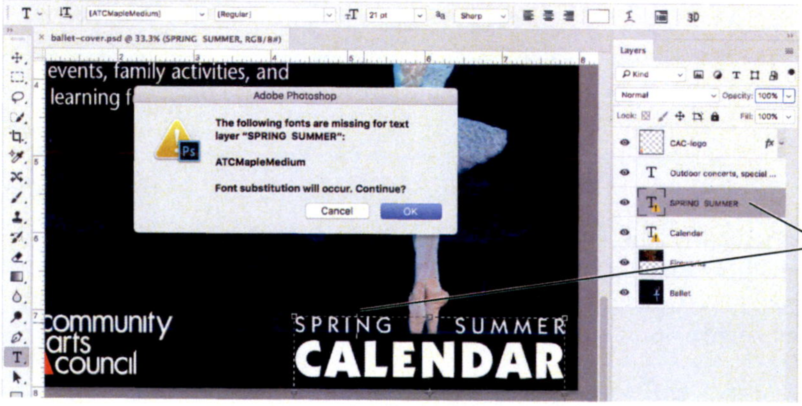

Clicking with the Horizontal Type tool places the insertion point in the type layer.

After dismissing the warning message, the missing font on the selected layer is replaced by the application's default font (typically Myriad Pro Regular).

10. Select all the type on the active layer and change the font to ATC Garnet Medium.

11. Click the Commit button in the Options bar to finalize the change and remove the insertion point from the active type layer.

After committing the change, the layer is still selected in the Layers panel but the insertion point is no longer flashing in the related type.

12. Repeat Steps 7–11 to change the "CALENDAR" type to the ATC Garnet Utra font.

14. Save the file, then continue to the next stage of the project.

Working with Adobe Typekit

Adobe Typekit is an online library of high-quality fonts. The Typekit Portfolio Plan, which provides access to the full font library and allows you to sync up to 100 fonts at a time to your desktop, is included in your individual user subscription to the Adobe Creative Cloud.

You can use the Typekit website to browse through a large number of available fonts, and even filter those fonts based on specific attributes and/or uses (for example, show only serif fonts that are available for desktop use). When you find fonts you want to use, you can sync them to your desktop through the Adobe Creative Cloud application; synced fonts will be available for use in any application on your device.

When Typekit fonts are available on your desktop, you can filter the application's font menus to show only fonts from Typekit in the menu.

Show Fonts from Typekit

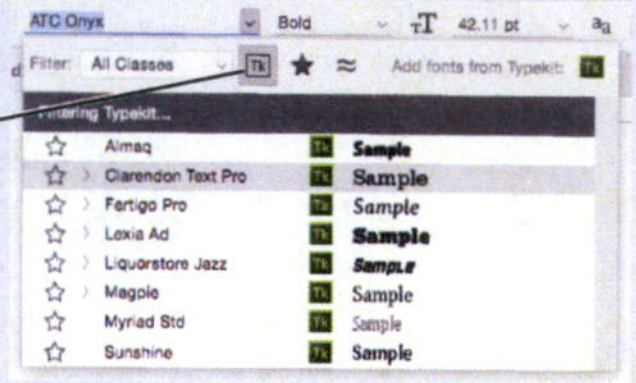

Verify your Adobe ID

To use Typekit fonts in an Adobe application, you must first verify that you are signed in using the username and password that is associated with your individual user subscription. (Typekit functionality is not available if you are working on a computer that has an Adobe software Device licenses instead of an individual user subscription.)

If you open the Help menu, you will see an option to either Sign In or Sign Out. If you see the words "Sign Out," the menu option also shows the email address (username) that is currently signed in.

If you see your own username, you are already signed in and can use the Typekit functionality. If you see a different username, you should choose the Sign Out option and then sign in with your own username. If you see the words "Sign In," you should choose that menu option and follow the on-screen directions to sign in with your own username.

If this option shows "Sign In," you are not yet signed in to your Creative Cloud account.

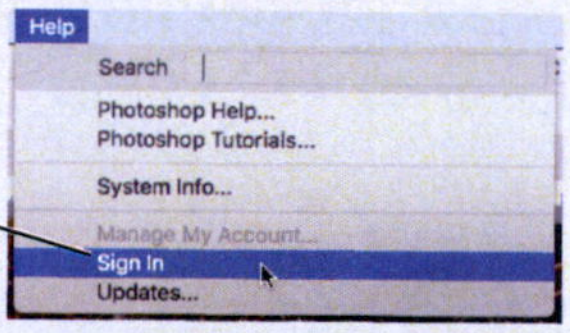

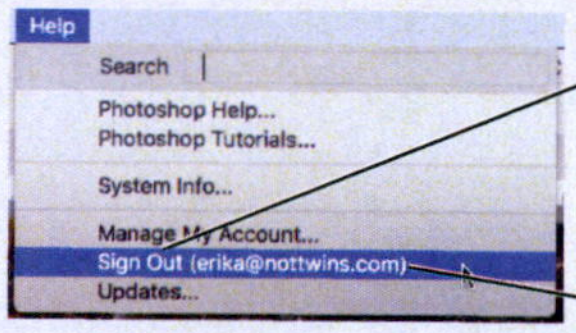

If this option shows "Sign Out," someone is already signed in to a Creative Cloud account.

This is the email (Adobe ID) that is currently signed in to the Adobe Creative Cloud.

Using the Adobe Creative Cloud Application

On Macintosh, the Adobe Creative Cloud application is accessed on the right side of the Menu bar at the top of the screen. On Windows, it is accessed on the right side of the Taskbar at the bottom of the screen.

Macintosh

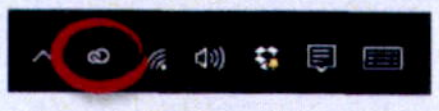

Windows

Font syncing through Adobe Typekit is managed through the Assets:Fonts pane of the application. Any fonts that are already synced in your account are listed in this pane. (If you have not yet synced fonts in your account, you see a default screen.)

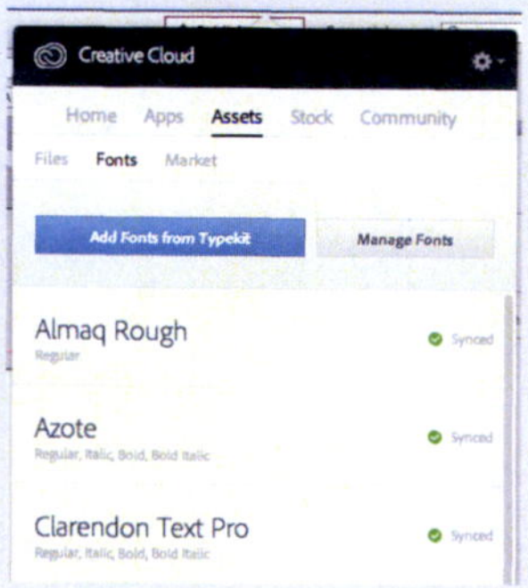

You can click Add Fonts from Typekit to sync additional fonts using the Typekit website. Clicking the Manage Fonts button open a website page showing which fonts are already synced in your account; you can use this page to unsync specific fonts.

You can also access the Typekit website by clicking the Add Fonts from Typekit button at the top of most Font menus in Adobe applications.

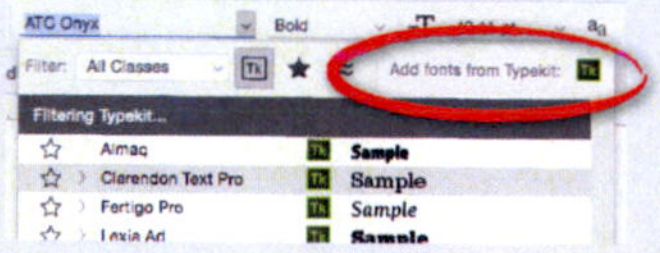

Working with Adobe Typekit (continued)

Installing Fonts from Adobe Typekit

Clicking any version of the Add Fonts from Typekit button launches your default browser and shows the Browse Fonts page of the Adobe Typekit website.

Because you launch the site from your Creative Cloud application, you are automatically logged in to your Typekit account.

If you are looking for a specific font, you can use the Search field in the top-left corner of the browser window.

On the right side of the browser window, you can use the buttons to filter the available fonts based on a number of criteria. (Filter buttons are toggles; when they are green, they are active. Active filters remain active until you turn them off.)

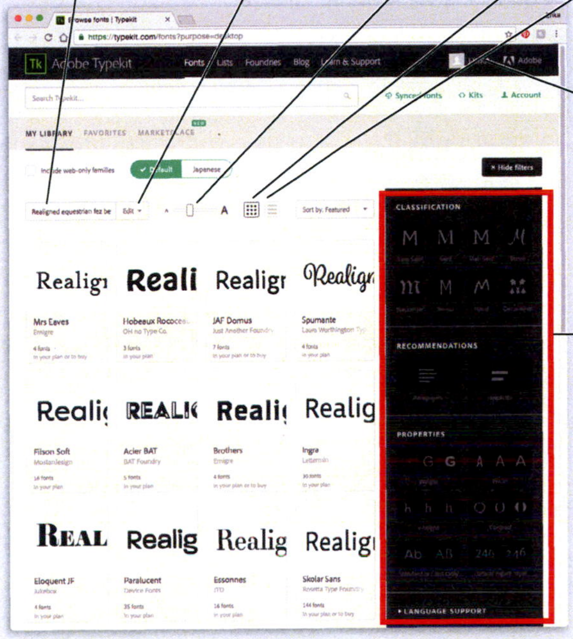
Type here to change the text in the font previews.
Choose pre-defined preview text in this menu.
Change the size of preview text.
Switch to Grid
Switch to List
Your name (associated with your Adobe ID) should appear here.
Use these options to filter fonts based on specific criteria.
Adobe Typekit
CLASSIFICATION
RECOMMENDATIONS
PROPERTIES
LANGUAGE SUPPORT

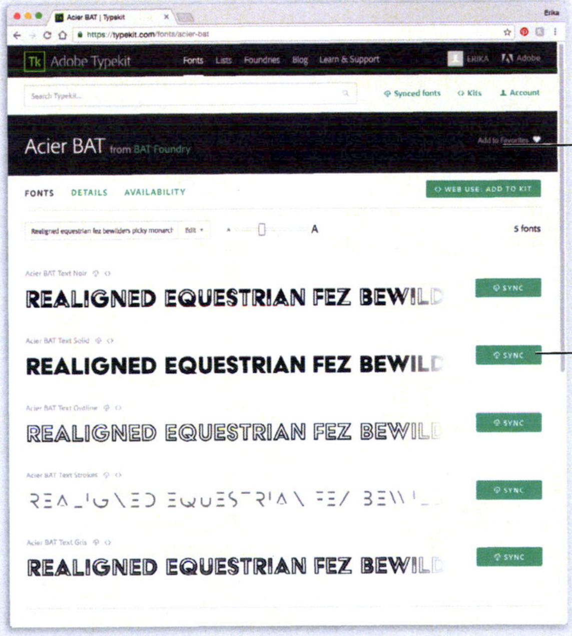
Click a font in the Browse screen to see the entire font family.
Click the Sync button to enable a specific font in your Creative Cloud account.
Acier BAT
REALIGNED EQUESTRIAN FEZ BEWILD

- **Classification** — Show only fonts that are sans serif, serif, slab serif, script, blackletter, mono, hand, or decorative.
- **Recommendations** — Show fonts that are best suited for paragraphs or headings.
- **Properties** — Show fonts that fit specific criteria, including:
  - Weight, or the thickness of strokes in the letterforms
  - Width of the individual letterforms
  - x-height, or the ratio of lowercase letter height compared to uppercase
  - Contrast, or the ratio of thin strokes compared to thick strokes in individual letterforms
  - Type case, or whether a font includes both upper- and lowercase or all capitals/small caps and all caps
  - Number positioning, which refers to whether numbers all align to the baseline or extend above or below the baseline
- **Language Support** — Show fonts that include special glyphs for non-Roman alphabetic characters and diacritical marks.

Clicking a preview in the list shows that font's details page, where you see all the available fonts in the family you selected. Clicking the Sync button makes that font available in your Creative Cloud account, so you can use it in any Adobe application where you are signed in.

Stage 2 Creating Custom Vector Shapes

The first stated goal of this project is to create a banner shape that hides the bottom edge of the fireworks layer content, and helps the call-to-action text stand out from the background image. This is easily accomplished using the custom shapes that are available in Photoshop's built-in libraries. In this stage of the project, you will create a custom banner shape and then adjust the existing text layer to make the two elements work together.

Create a Custom Shape Layer

Photoshop includes a number of built-in custom shape libraries, which make it very easy to add complex vector graphics into any Photoshop file. Like any other vector shape layer, the custom shapes can have specific defined fill and stroke colors; you can also access and edit the anchor points that make up the vector shape to best suit the job at hand.

1. **With `ballet-cover.psd` open, make the Fireworks layer active in the Layers panel.**

   New layers are created immediately above the previously selected layer. By first selecting the Fireworks layer, the shape layer you are about to create will automatically appear directly above the Fireworks layer.

2. **Choose the Custom Shape tool (nested under the Rectangle tool).**

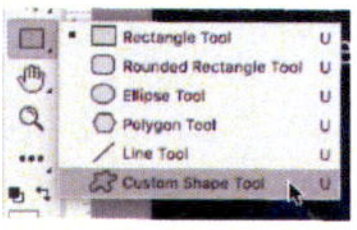

3. **In the Options bar, make sure the Shape option is selected.**

   Like the Pen tool, the shape tools (including the Custom Shape tool) can be used to create a vector-based shape layer, a path, or pixels of a solid color. In this case, you want to create a new shape layer.

4. **Click the arrow button to the right of the Shape menu to open the Custom Shape panel, and then show the Custom Shape panel Options menu.**

   You can change the display of the shapes in the panel, load shapes from external files, and access a number of built-in libraries.

5. **Choose Banners and Awards in the panel Options menu. Click OK when asked if you want to replace the current shapes with the new set.**

   You can choose from a large number of common and special shapes from the built-in shape libraries when you use the Custom Shape tool. You can always restore the default shape options by choosing Reset Shapes in the panel Options menu.

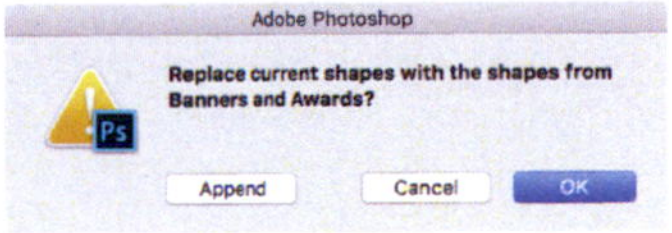

> *Note:*
>
> *Some users report seeing a message asking if they want to save changes to the current shapes before replacing them, even if they did not make changes to the default set. This is a minor bug in the software. If you see this message, click No.*

6. **In the Custom Shape panel (on the Options bar), choose the Flag shape.**

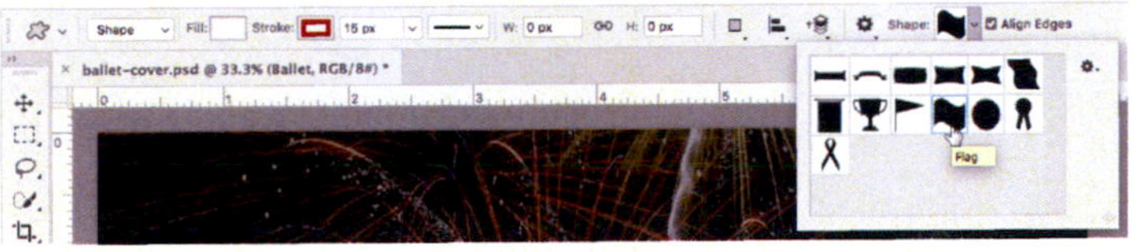

7. **Click the Stroke swatch in the Options bar and choose the No Color option.**

8. **Click the Fill swatch in the Options bar. Click the button to open the Color Picker, then use the Eyedropper cursor to sample the color in the logo (in the bottom-left corner).**

   Ultimately, the shape you are creating will be moved to a spot channel to reproduce the banner in a specific color of ink, so it really doesn't matter what color you use in this step. We're working with the logo color because both the logo and the banner will eventually be created with the same spot color.

Click here to open the Color Picker...

...then click to sample the logo color.

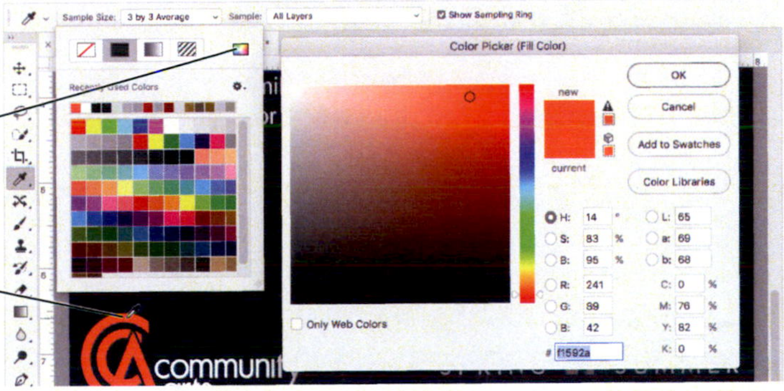

9. **In the document window, click and drag to draw the custom banner shape bottom across the entire canvas, covering the edge of the Fireworks layer content (behind the "call to action" text).**

   The Custom Shape tool creates a vector path based on the shape you select. Because you chose the Shape layer option in Step 3, the new shape layer is added to the Layers panel.

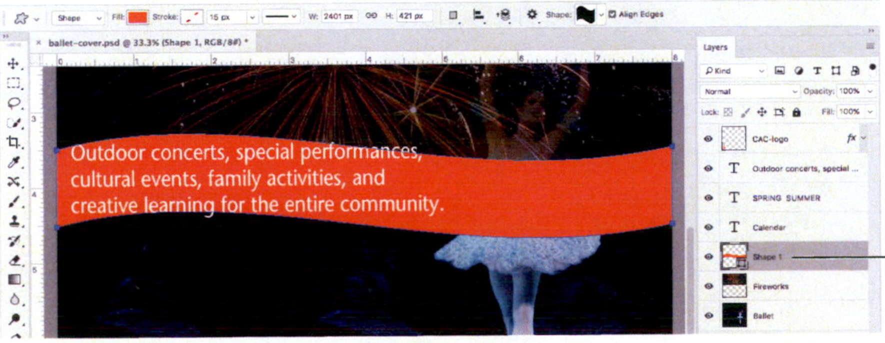

The shape layer is added immediately above the previously selected layer.

10. **Save the file and continue to the next exercise.**

Create Warped Text

In this exercise, you are going to warp the call-to-action text so it appears to follow the contour of the banner shape you created in the previous exercise. This is easily accomplished with the built-in Warp Text options that change the shape of text without rasterizing it.

1. **With `ballet-cover.psd` open, choose the Horizontal Type tool in the Tools panel.**
2. **In the Layers panel, click to select the "Outdoor concerts..." type layer.**
3. **In the Options bar, click the Create Warped Text button.**

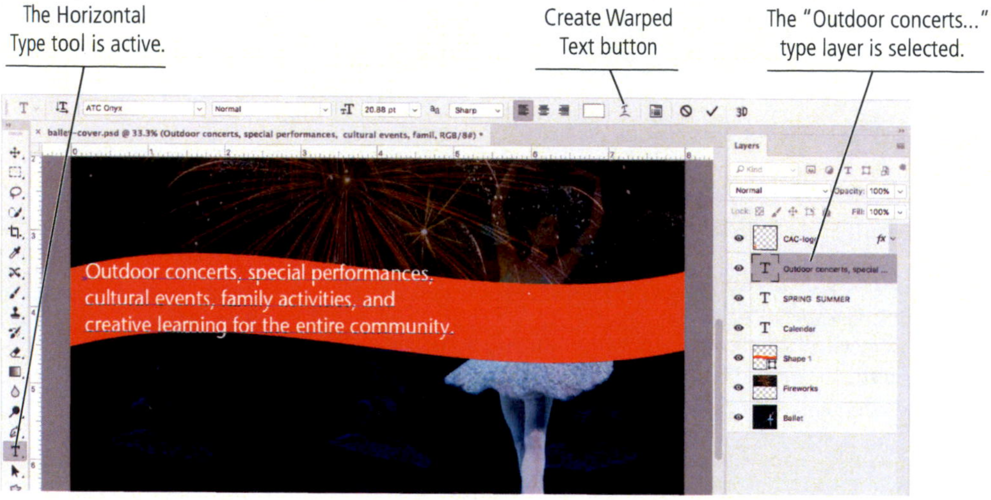

4. **In the Warp Text dialog box, choose Rise from the Style menu.**

   Photoshop includes 15 built-in warp styles. The icon next to each style name suggests the result of applying that style. As long as text remains editable, your warping options are limited to this list of predefined shapes. If you work with rasterized text (or any other pixel-based selection), you can also create custom warps.

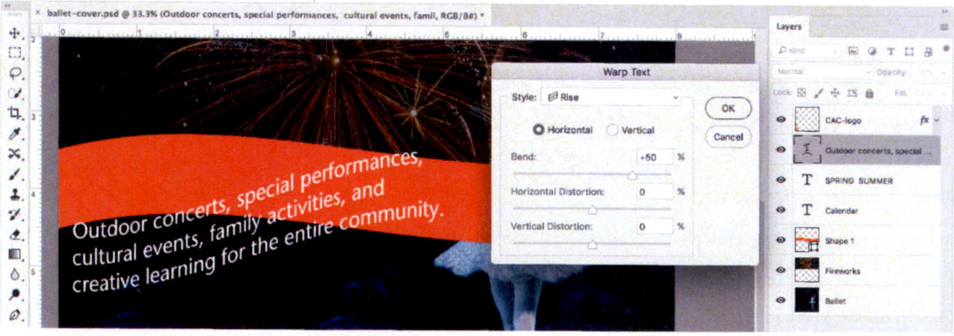

5. **Define a `-40` Bend and `-25` Horizontal Distortion value.**

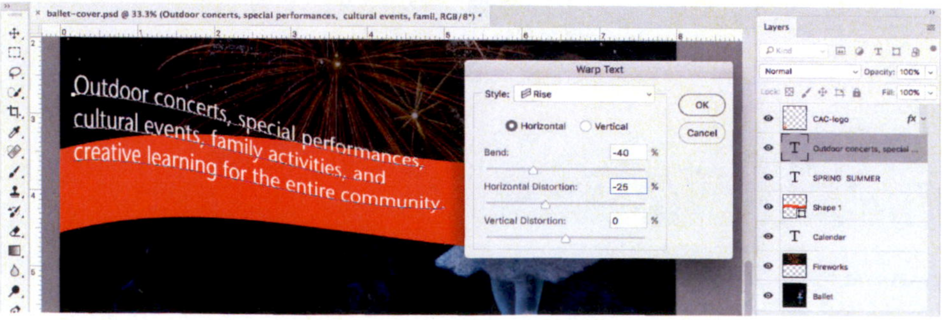

6. **Click OK to close the Warp Text dialog box.**

7. **In the Layers panel, click the Shape 1 layer to select it.**

8. **Using the Direct Selection tool, adjust the shape's anchor points and handles to better match the shape and contour of the warped text.**

   Make sure the shape entirely obscures the bottom edge of the Fireworks layer content.

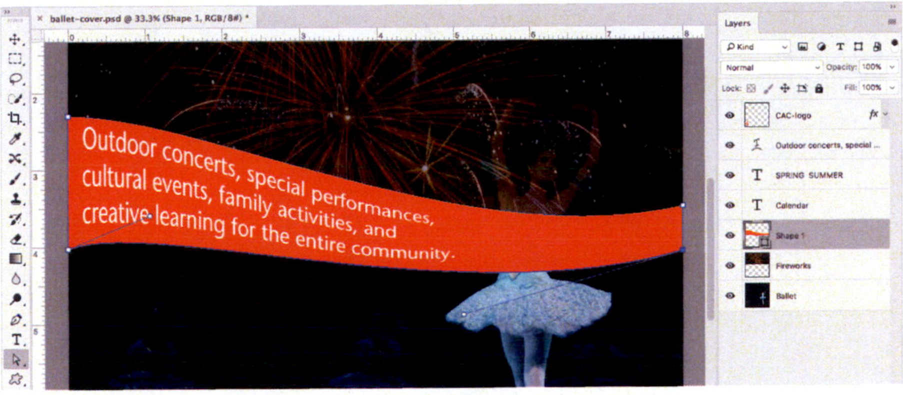

9. **Save the file and continue to the final stage of the project.**

Stage 3 Creating a Complex Mask

You should already understand a number of different ways to make selections, from basic shape selections with a marquee to color-based selections using the Color Range options. There are some images, however, that defy these tools. Specifically, images with various colors with thin lines and complex edges can be difficult to isolate. The background photo for this project is a perfect example. Although you could manually (and painstakingly) create the selection you need, Photoshop includes several tools that make it much easier to select and isolate complex image areas. You will use those options in this stage of the project.

Select the Focus Area

To accomplish the first state goal of this project, you are going to create a mask that allows the dancer in the foreground to appear in front of other objects, including a custom shape layer that you will create later in the project. There is usually more than one way to accomplish a specific task in Photoshop, and making a complex selection is no exception. In this exercise, you will use the new Select Focus Area option to complete this task.

1. **With `ballet-cover.psd` open, hide all but the Ballet layer.**

2. **Make the Ballet layer active in the Layers panel.**

3. **Choose Select>Focus Area.**

   This function automatically evaluates the image and determines areas that are in focus. You can adjust the In-Focus Range parameter to broaden or narrow the selection; a range of 0 selects the entire image, while high range (near the right side of the slider scale) selects only the parts of the image that are in clearest focus. If the selection area has noise, you can use the Image Noise Level slider control to control how that noise affects the selection.

4. **With the Preview option checked in the resulting dialog box, open the View Mode menu and choose On Layers.**

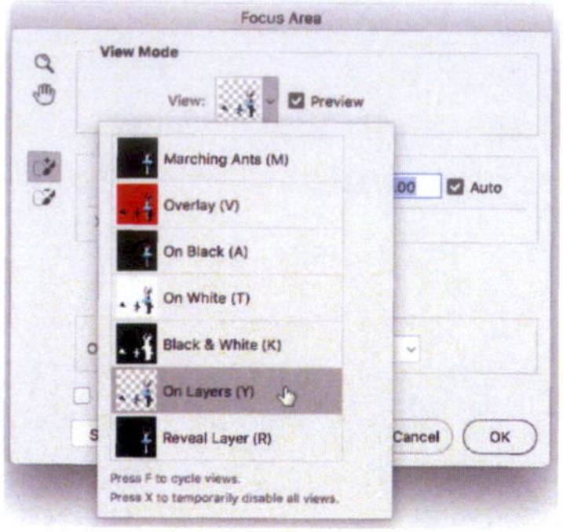

The preview options allow you to change the way your image appears in the document window while you refine your selection with the dialog box tools. On Layers shows the transparent checkerboard pattern behind the selected areas.

When there is a clear focal point in an image, the Focus Area tool produces excellent results with very little intervention. As in the case of the image you are using in this project, however, you should understand that many photos will defy 100% automatic selections. You can still use the Focus Area selection as a starting point and then make whatever adjustments are necessary using other tools.

5. **Select the Focus Area Subtract Tool in the left side of the dialog box.**

   This tool allows you to paint on the image to remove areas from the current selection.

6. **Click and drag down the dark selected area to the right of the dancer's legs.**

   When you release the mouse button, the software identifies contiguous areas of similar focus and color to remove from the selection.

7. **Continue painting with the Focus Area Subtract Tool to remove as much of the dark background that touches the front dancer as possible.**

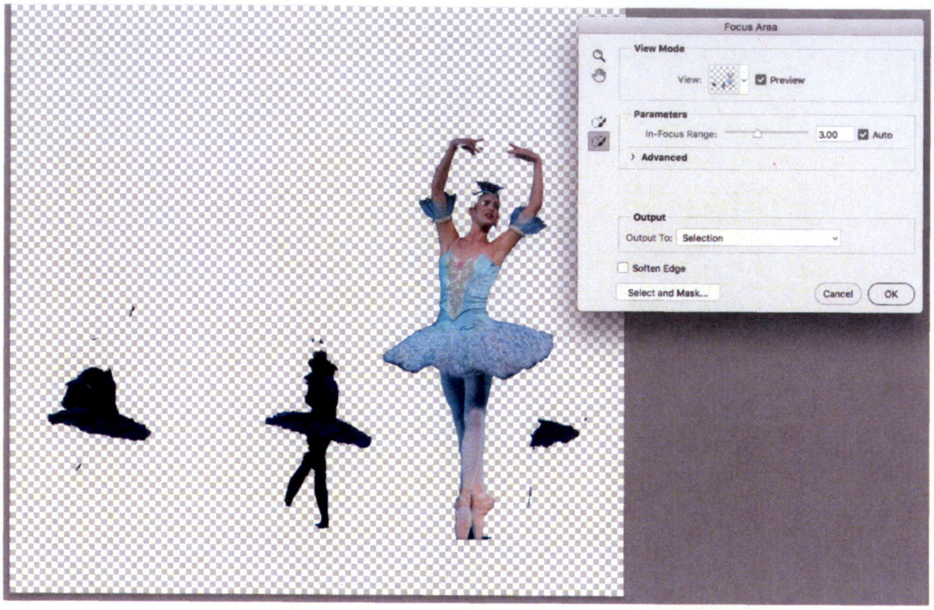

8. **At the bottom of the Focus Area dialog box, choose the New Layer with Layer Mask option in the Output To menu.**

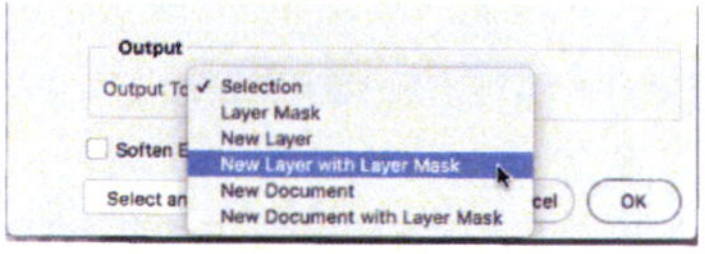

Your ultimate goal is to place the logotype layer group between the foreground and background elements in this image. The foreground elements need to exist on a separate layer to accomplish this goal, so you are using the dialog box to automatically create a new layer that shows only the selected foreground elements.

Note:

If you double-click an alpha channel icon in the Channels panel, you change the visible mask's opacity in the Layer Mask Display Options dialog box.

9. **Click OK to finalize your selection.**

Because you chose the New Layer with Layer Mask option in the Output To menu, the unselected areas are now masked on the new Ballet copy layer.

A new masked layer is the result of the Focus Area selection.

10. **Save the file and continue to the next exercise.**

Erase and Paint the Alpha Channel

Although automatic results are usually a good start, you should almost never rely entirely on the software to accomplish your goals. Most automatic features will require at least some manual adjustment or intervention.

We intentionally chose the Backstage image you are using in this project to highlight this point. The foreground elements are not entirely in clear focus (especially around the dancer's tiara), so the Focus Area dialog box was not able to create a perfect selection. The image color also made it difficult to clearly differentiate selected and unselected areas from the Quick Mask overlay.

Now that you have created the initial mask, you can use other tools to fine-tune the mask and determine exactly what will be visible on the layer. In this exercise, you will use painting tools to add to and subtract from the existing layer mask.

1. **With `ballet-cover.psd` open, make sure the Ballet copy layer is selected in the Layers panel and then open the Channels panel.**

   This file uses the CMYK color mode, so you have four channels — one for each of the four process color. When a masked layer is selected, the Channels panel also includes an alpha channel that contains the selected layer's mask.

2. **In the Channels panel, click the empty space to the left of the Ballet copy Mask to make it visible in the document window.**

Some areas need to be added to the mask.
Click here to show the mask in the document window.

3. **If your mask channel is not semi-transparent, double-click the Ballet copy Mask channel to open the Quick Mask Options dialog box. Set the Opacity field to 50%, then click OK.**

   Mask opacity remembers the last-used settings. Turning on Quick Mask mode gives you access to a Quick Mask channel in the Channels panel. You need access to that channel in order to change the options related to mask channels.

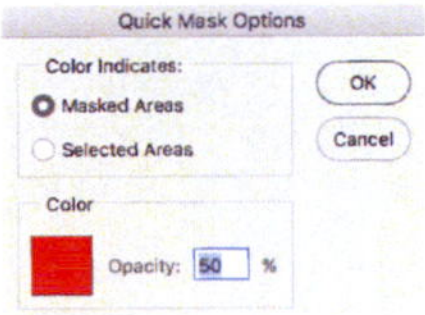

4. **In the Layers panel, click the Ballet copy layer mask icon to select the mask.**

   You must select the actual mask in the panel before you can paint to edit the mask.

5. **In the Tools panel, click the button to restore the default foreground and background colors to black and white (respectively).**

   You have to paint with black to add to a mask (hide areas), or paint with white to subtract from a mask (reveal areas).

6. **Select the Brush tool in the Tools panel. In the Options bar, choose a 100-px brush with 100% hardness, 100% opacity, and 100% flow.**

Open the Brush Preset Picker to define the brush size and hardness.

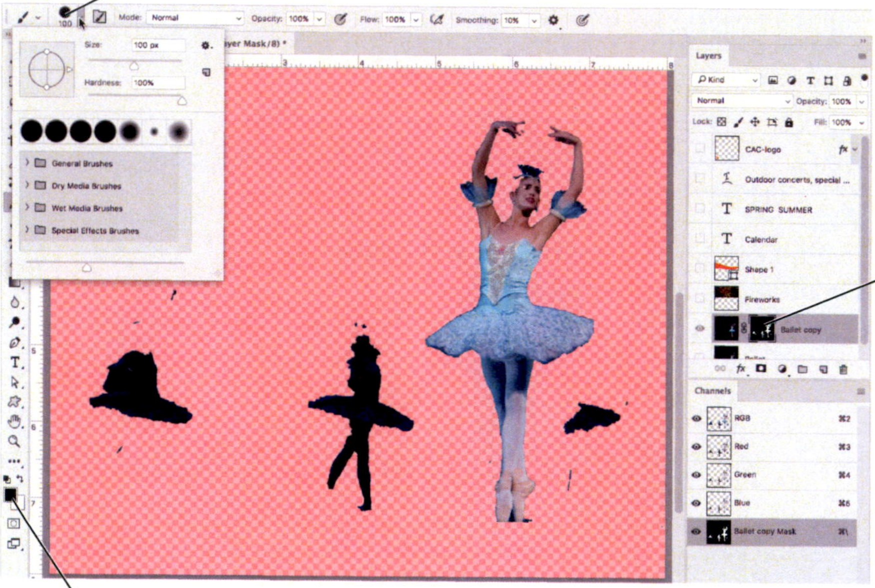

Make sure the actual mask is selected.

Paint with black to add to the mask area.

7. **Click and drag over any isolated background areas that are not masked.**

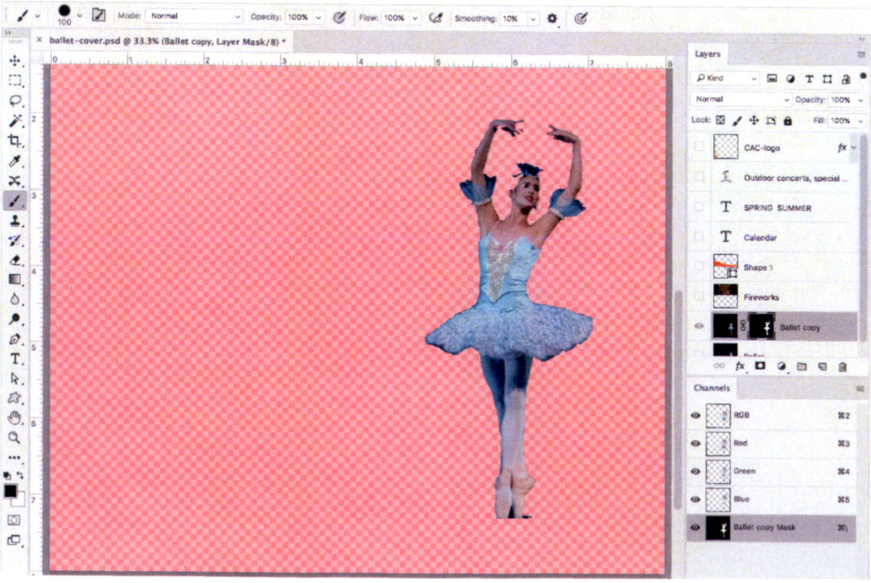

8. **Zoom in to the dancer's feet. Continue painting with the Brush tool to add to the mask area (remove the background pixels around the feet).**

   Zoom in or out, and use the bracket keys to reduce ([ ) or enlarge ( ]) the brush size as necessary.

   When using any tool that has a brush size, you can press the Left Bracket key ([ ) to dynamically decrease the brush size or press the Right Bracket key ( ]) to increase the brush size.

   Don't worry about the dark artifact pixels that surround most of the selection at this point; you will use another technique to refine the selection edge.

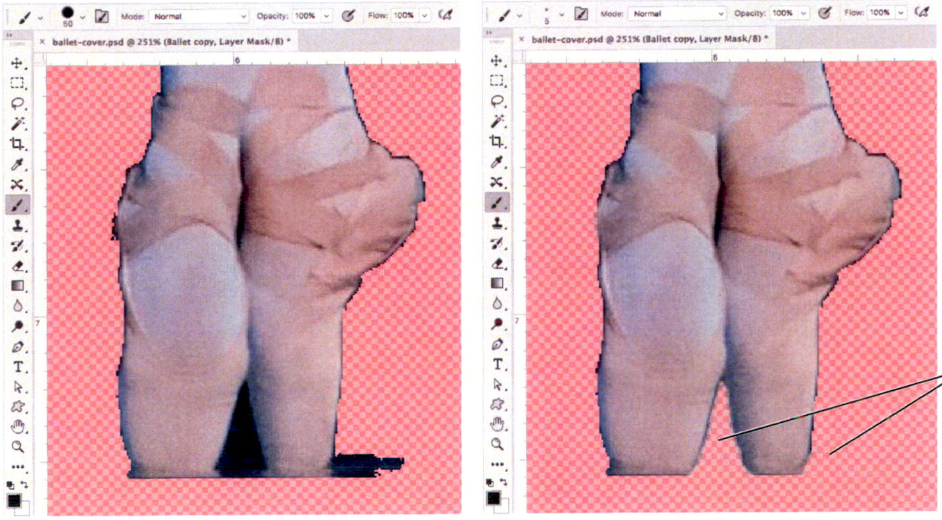

9. **Zoom in to the dancer's head.**

   This is an excellent example of a case in which algorithms are no substitute for human subjectivity. The dancer's dark hair blends into the dark background in the original image. The automatic selection algorithms used in the Focus Area utility are not able to determine the difference between the two areas. You have to use your best judgment to define the area where the dancer's hair ends.

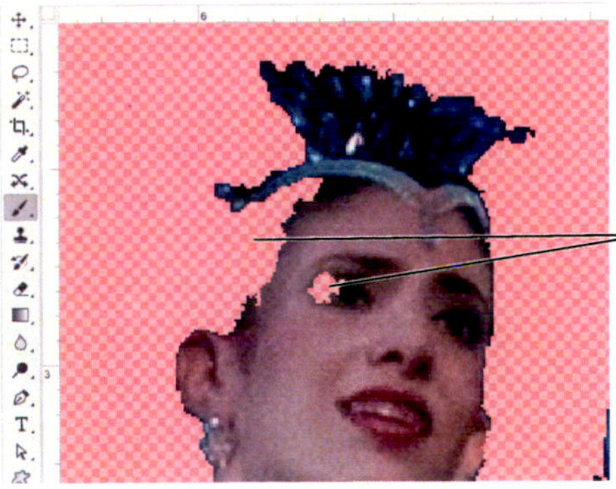

Some areas need to be removed from the mask.

10. **Click the Switch Foreground and Background Colors button at the bottom of the Tools panel.**

    Remember, paint with white to remove areas from the mask.

11. **Paint to the layer mask with white to remove any areas of the dancer's face and head from the mask.**

Again, feel free to change the brush size as necessary to accomplish your goal.

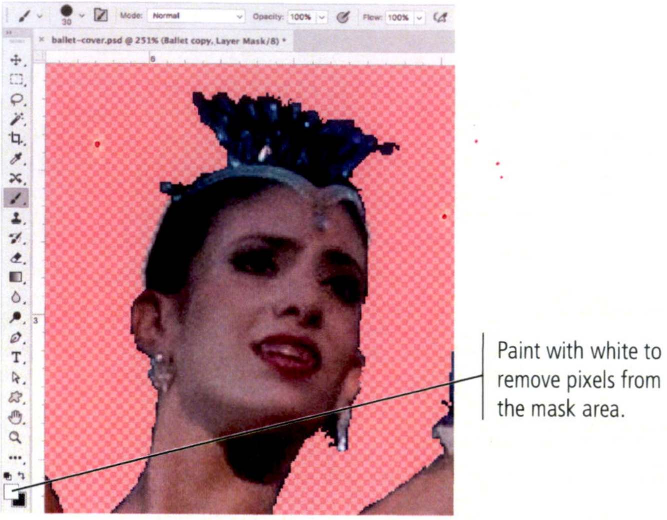

12. **In the Channels panel, click the eye icon to hide the Ballet copy Mask channel.**

The mask channel can be confusing when you use various view methods in the Select and Mask workspace, which you will do in the next few steps.

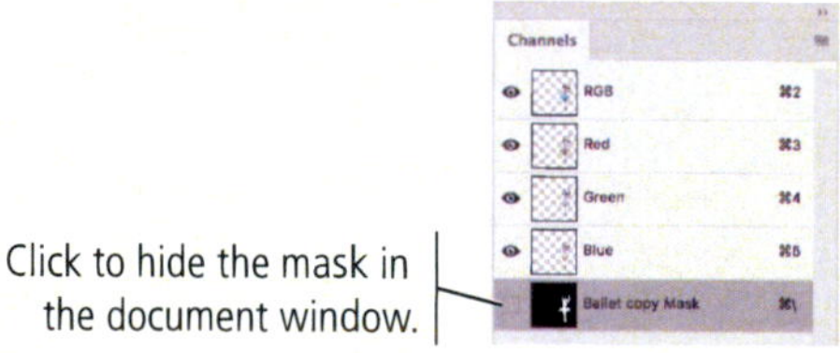

13. **With the mask selected in the layers panel, click the Select and Mask button in the Properties panel.**

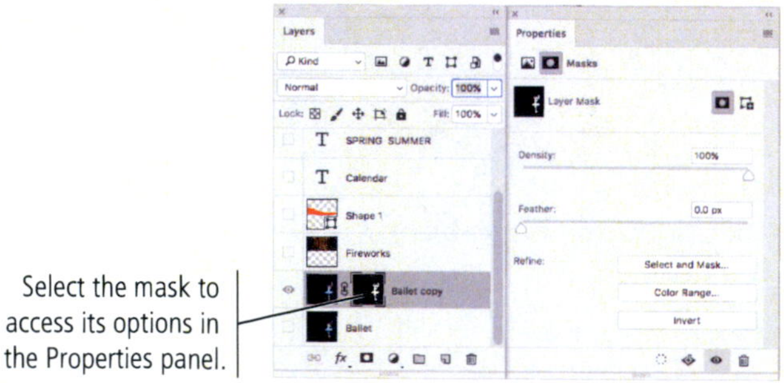

14. **Choose the On Layers option in the View Mode menu.**

 The Select and Mask workspace provides more sophisticated tools for refining a complicated mask like the one you are creating in this project.

Use the On Layers view mode.

Dark edge pixels surround most of the visible area.

15. **On the right side of the workspace, change the Edge Detection Radius value to 1 px.**

 Increasing the Radius value results in a slightly softer edge, removing most of the dark artifact pixels that resulted from the Focus Area selection.

Increase the Radius value to 1 px.

The dark pixels are removed from the selection edge.

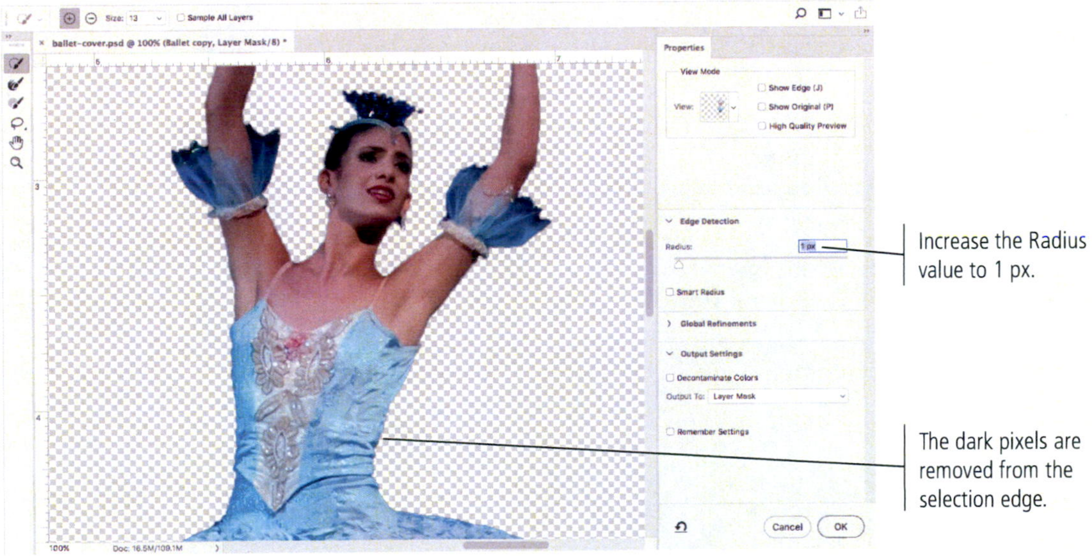

16. **Choose the Onion Skin view mode and set the transparency to 25%. Review the rest of your selection.**

 Different viewing modes have different uses. With the Onion Skin mode, the masked areas appear partially transparent; this allows you to see what you still need to add or remove from the mask.

 In our example, part of the dancer's hand is masked. You can use the Brush tool directly in the Select and Mask workspace to paint — either adding to or removing from the mask.

17. **Choose the Brush tool in the top-left corner of the workspace, and choose the option to add to the selected area.**

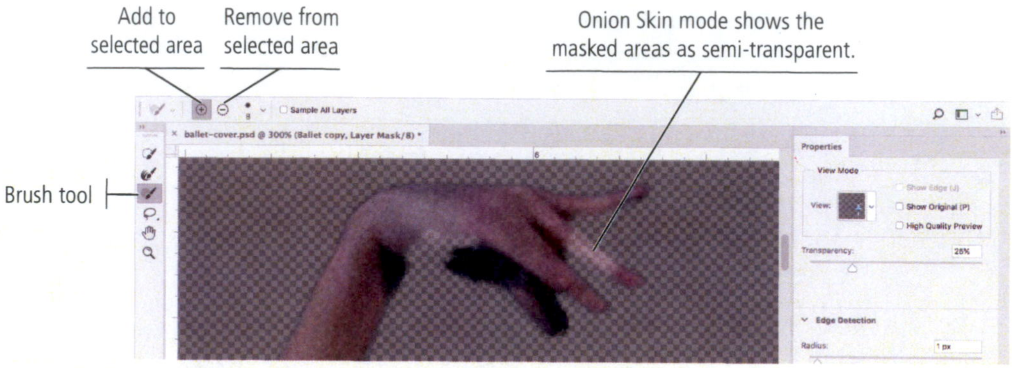

18. **Paint over any areas that need to be added to the selection.**

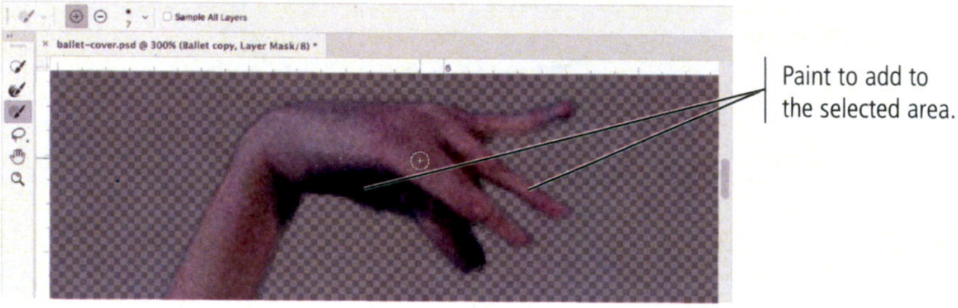

19. **Make sure Layer Mask is selected in the Output To menu, then click OK to finalize the revised mask.**

20. **In the Layers panel, make all layers visible. Click the Ballet copy layer and drag it above the Shape 1 layer.**

The dancer in the foreground, which you isolated from the background using a variety of techniques, now appears in front of the custom shape banner and the fireworks.

21. **Save the file and continue to the next stage of the project.**

Stage 4 Working with Spot Channels

Spot colors are frequently used to produce a special look, to match an exact color, or to highlight a certain aspect of a job (for example, with varnish or some other special coating). Spot-color inks are opaque, so they produce the desired result with a single printing unit instead of by combining varying percentages of the four process inks. If you want to create a certain look, or if a color must be the same on every printed job, a spot color is usually the best choice. You should be aware, however, that adding spot color to a process job adds to the cost, and budgets are usually a consideration when designing a print project.

Every designer should own a set of spot-color guides, such as the ones produced by Pantone. (Pantone is the most common spot-color system in the United States, but ask your printer which one they use before building spot colors in any design.) These printed spot-color guides usually show coated and uncoated samples. Some also show the process-color combination that produces the closest possible match to the spot ink. If you want to approximate a special ink color, you can use those ink percentages to designate the process color in a layout or illustration program.

Note:

Spot colors are typically selected from printed swatch books that show the exact color of the ink. Don't rely on the on-screen previews when you select a spot color.

Define a New Spot Channel

To work with spot colors in Photoshop, you have to create a new channel to include the information for that ink. Anything printed in the spot color needs to be placed or copied onto the spot channel.

1. **With ballet-cover.psd open, click at the bottom of the Layers panel to deselect all layers in the file.**

2. **Choose Edit>Color Settings. Choose U.S. Sheetfed Coated v2 in the CMYK Working Space menu, then click OK.**

   Before you create the required spot color channel, you will convert the file to the CMYK color mode for printing. When you make the conversion, the file is converted to whatever is defined as the working CMYK space.

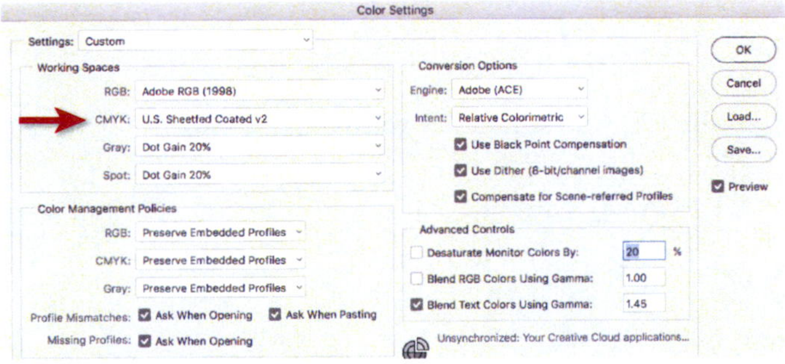

3. **Choose Image>Mode>CMYK Color. Read the resulting message, then click Don't Merge.**

   As the warning suggests, changing the color mode of a file can affect the appearance of individual layers. You are given the option to flatten the file before converting the colors.

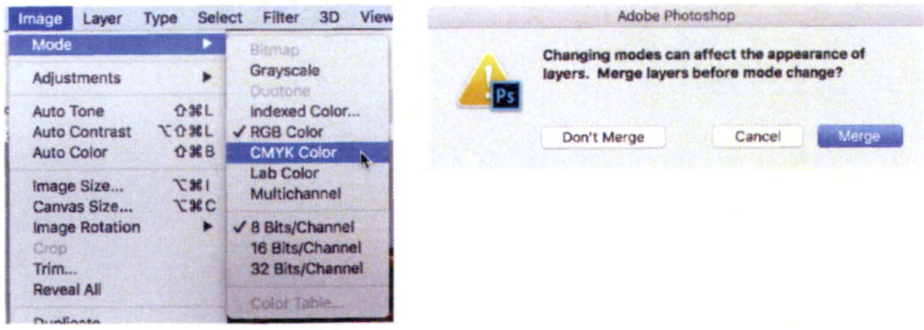

4. **Read the resulting warning, then click OK.**

Because you already defined the destination profile you want to use, you can safely click OK to dismiss the warning.

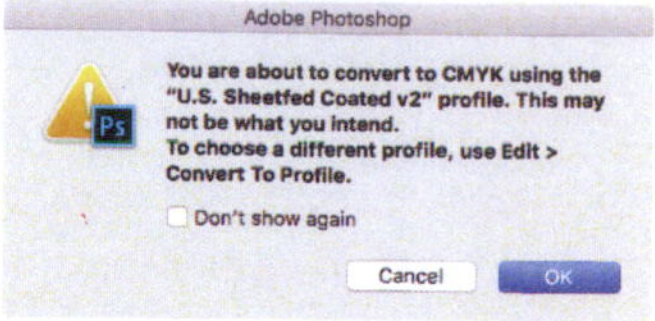

5. **Open the Channels panel Options menu and choose Panel Options.**

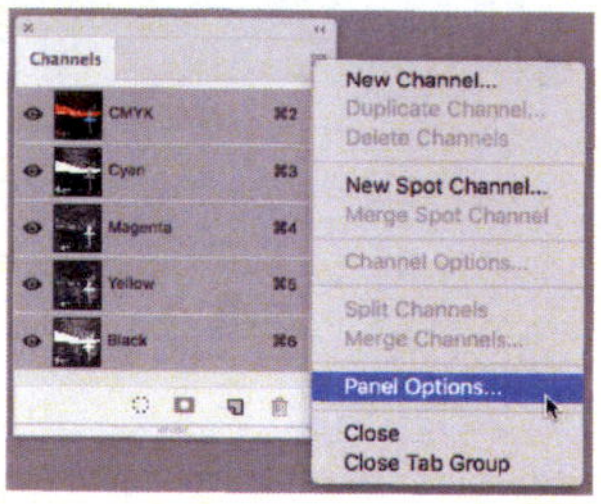

6. **In the resulting dialog box, select the large thumbnail and then click OK.**

The larger thumbnail makes it easier to see the channel contents in the panel.

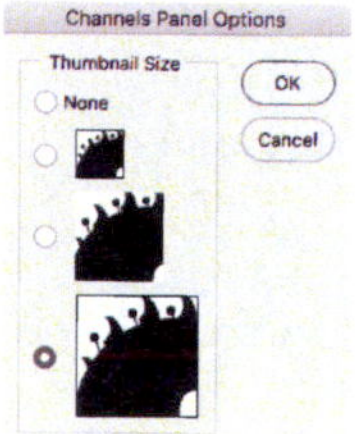

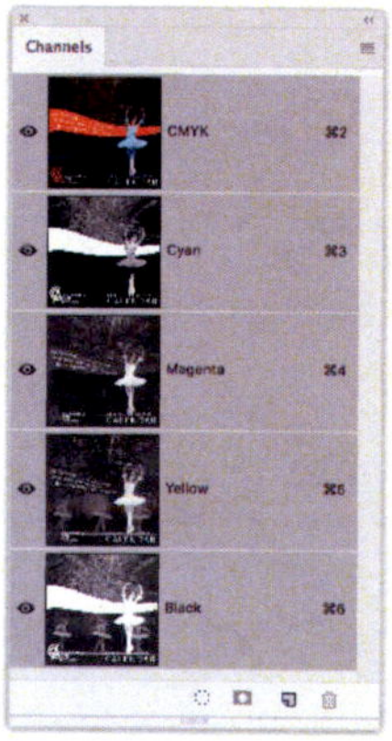

7. **Display the Channels panel. Open the Channels panel Options menu and choose New Spot Channel.**

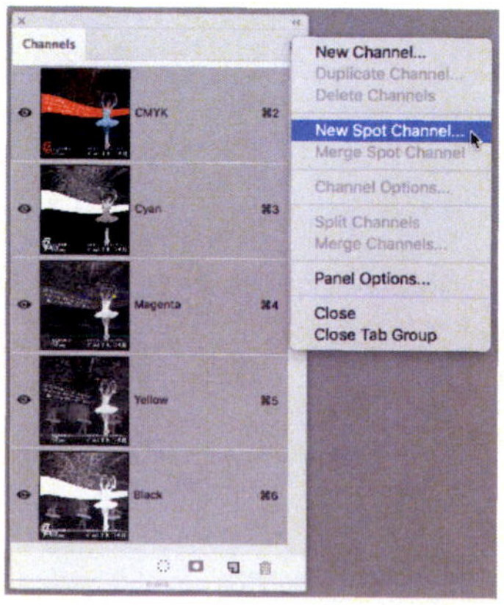

8. **In the New Spot Channel dialog box, click the Color swatch to open the Color Picker (Spot Color) dialog box.**

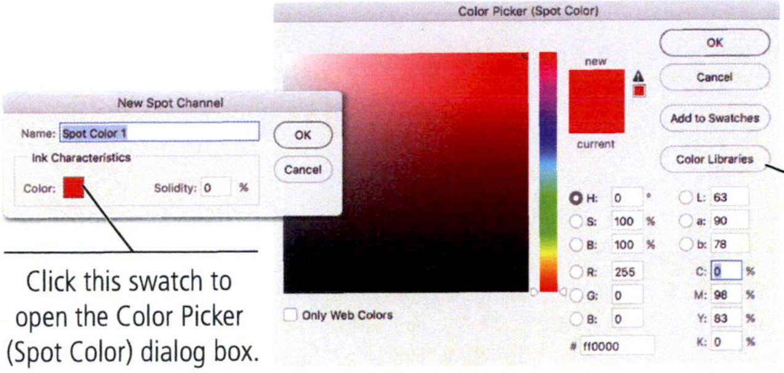

Click this swatch to open the Color Picker (Spot Color) dialog box.

Click this button to access the built-in spot-color libraries.

9. **Click the Color Libraries button to access the built-in spot-color libraries.**

10. **In the Book menu, choose PANTONE+ Metallic Coated. Type 8843 to scroll quickly to the color that the client selected for this job.**

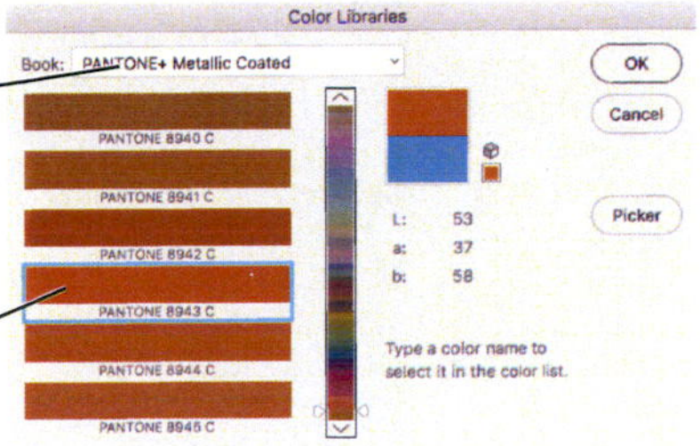

Choose the color library in this menu.

Scroll through the swatches or type a number to access the specific color you want to use.

Note:

This is the color your art director defined in the original project meeting.

11. **Click OK to return to the New Spot Channel dialog box.**

12. **Set the Solidity to 100%.**

Solidity for a spot channel is similar to layer opacity. If the ink channel is not entirely opaque (with a 100% Solidity value), CMYK elements under the spot areas will be visible through the spot ink. In this case, you want the spot-ink areas to completely obscure underlying CMYK elements, so you have to use a 100% Solidity value.

Note:

Double-clicking a spot-color channel thumbnail on the Channels panel opens the same dialog box you see when you first create a new spot channel.

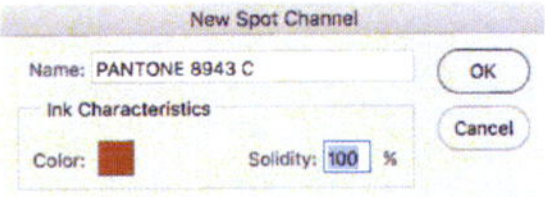

13. **Click OK to add the new spot channel to the file.**

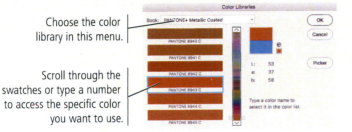

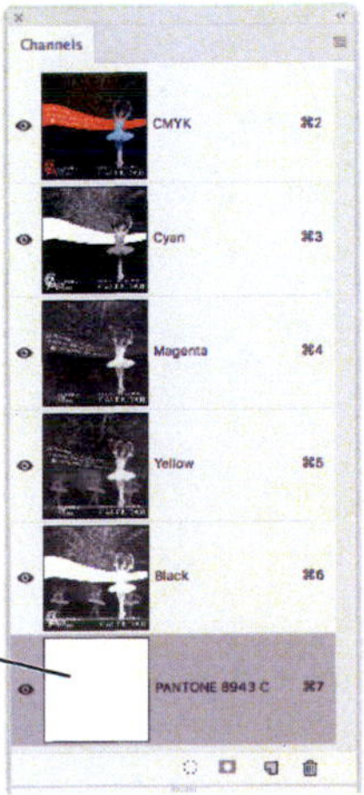

The newly added Pantone spot-color channel doesn't contain anything yet.

14. **Save the file and continue to the next exercise.**

Copy Layer Information to a Spot Channel

There is no easy way to map specific layer content to a specific spot channel. To ensure that specific objects print in a spot color, you have to manually cut the content from its layer and paste the content directly onto the appropriate spot-color channel. It is also important to understand that there are certain limitations to working with spot colors in Photoshop. You can't apply effects to a spot channel (such as the drop shadow behind the client's logo in the bottom-left corner). You also can't store vector information on a spot channel, which means vector shape and type layers must be rasterized if you place that content on a spot channel.

1. **With `ballet-cover.psd` open, drag the CAC-logo layer in the Layers panel to the Create a New Layer button to duplicate the layer.**

   You are duplicating the layer so that the original will be available later in case you need to make changes.

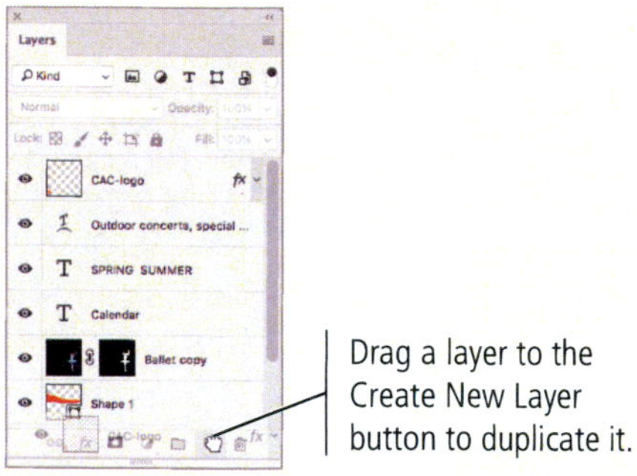

2. **Hide the original CAC-logo layer, then expand the effects listing for the CAC-logo copy layer.**

3. **Control/right-click the Drop Shadow effect for the CAC-logo copy layer and choose Create Layer from the contextual menu.**

   As we stated at the beginning of this exercise, you can't apply effects to spot-channel content. To maintain the drop shadow after the banner has been moved to the spot channel, you have to create an independent layer from the drop shadow effect.

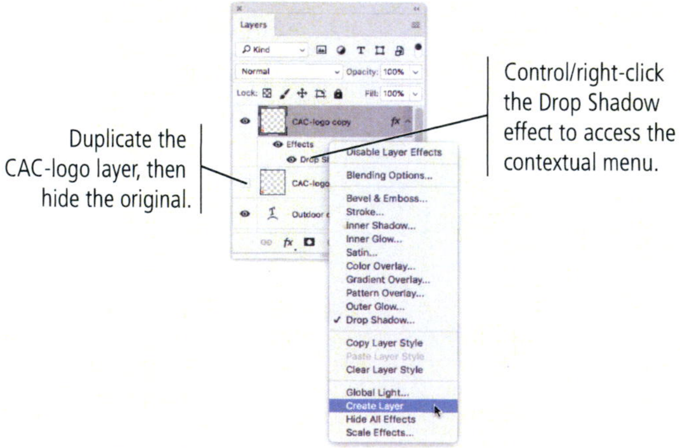

Duplicate the
CAC-logo layer, then
hide the original.
Control/right-click
the Drop Shadow
effect to access the
contextual menu.

4. **If you see a warning about effects not being reproduced by layers, click OK.**

   Drop shadows can be reproduced with layers, so you can dismiss the warning.

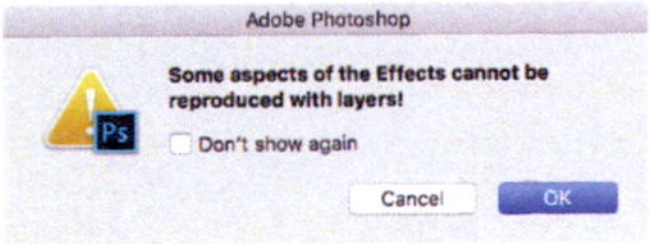

5. **Using the Lasso tool, draw a marquee that surrounds only the orange elements of the client's logo.**

6. **Make sure the CMYK (composite) channel is selected in the Channels panel and the CAC-logo copy layer is selected in the Layers panel.**

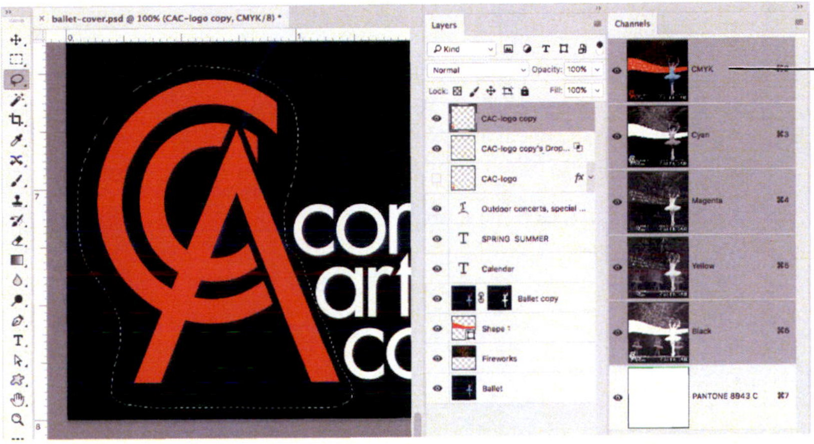
Make sure the CMYK channel is selected.

7. **Choose Edit>Cut.**

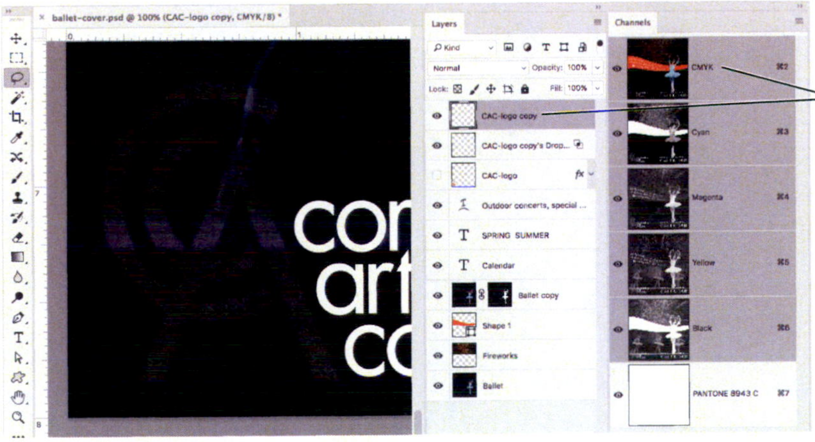
The pixels inside the previous marquee are removed from the CAC-logo copy layer and the CMYK channel.

8. **Select the PANTONE 8943 C channel in the Channels panel, then choose Edit>Paste Special>Paste in Place.**

This command places the pasted content in the exact position where it was when you cut it, but on the selected Pantone 8943 C channel.

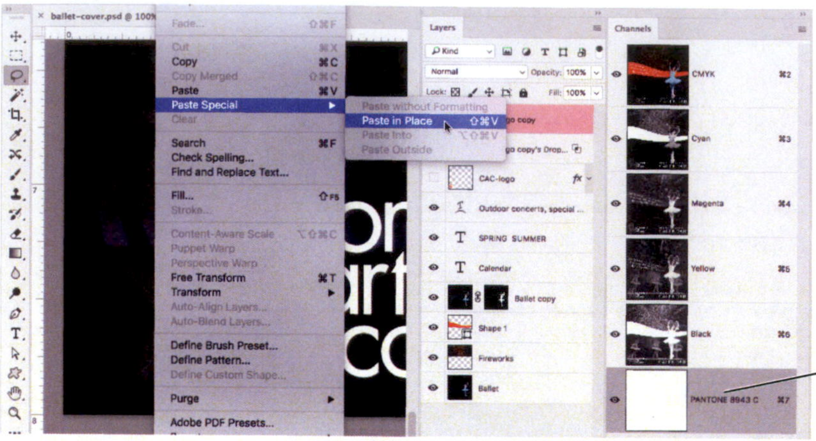

The PANTONE 8943 C channel is selected.

You should notice that the pasted content is not at full strength because the original orange color maps to a medium gray on the spot channel.

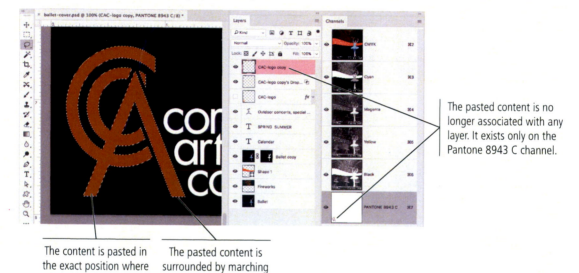

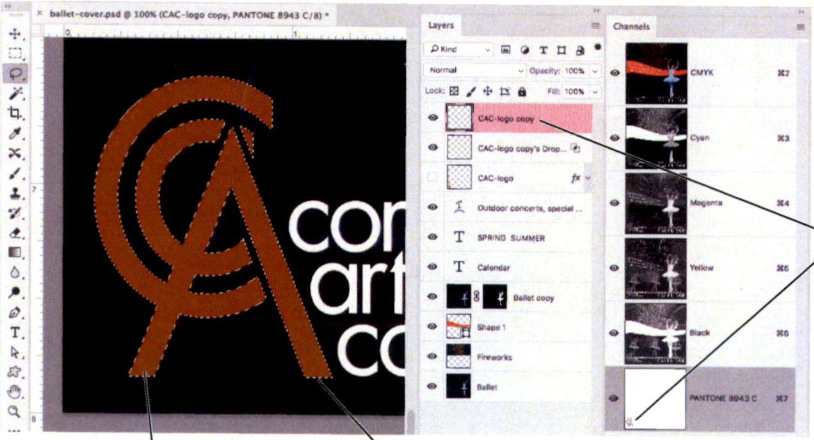

The pasted content is no longer associated with any layer. It exists only on the Pantone 8943 C channel.

The content is pasted in the exact position where it was when you cut it.

The pasted content is surrounded by marching ants in the image.

9. **Deselect the active selection area.**

Press Command/Control-D to deselect.

10. **In the Layers panel, drag the Shape 1 layer to the Create a New Layer button to duplicate the layer. Hide the original Shape 1 layer.**

11. **Control/right-click the Shape 1 copy layer and choose Rasterize Layer from the contextual menu.**

    To move part of this object to the spot-color channel, you first have to rasterize the vector object.

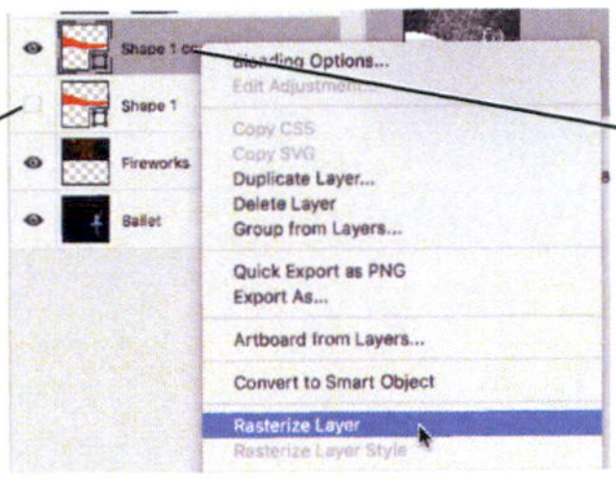

12. **With the rasterized layer selected, choose Select>Color Range.**

13. **Click the Eyedropper cursor anywhere in the orange banner shape.**

    The Color Range dialog box makes selections based on all visible layers. Because the Ballet copy and Outdoor content... type layers are visible, the area selected excludes the type and the space where the dancer's torso appears in front of the banner.

    If you selected the entire shape area (including the area behind the type and the dancer), the content pasted onto the spot-color channel would be printed over the CMYK separations — obscuring both the type and the dancer's torso.

    The logo is also not selected; it is no longer the same orange color as the banner since you removed it from the original layer and pasted it onto the spot-color channel.

14. Click OK to finalize the selection.

15. With the CMYK channels selected in the Channels panel, choose Edit>Cut to remove the selected pixels from the active layer.

16. Choose the PANTONE 8943 C channel in the Channels panel, then choose Edit>Paste Special>Paste in Place.

17. Deselect the active selection area.

Press Command/Control-D to deselect.

The selected area from Step 14 — the rasterized banner, excluding the area behind the dancer — is pasted in place onto the spot-color channel.

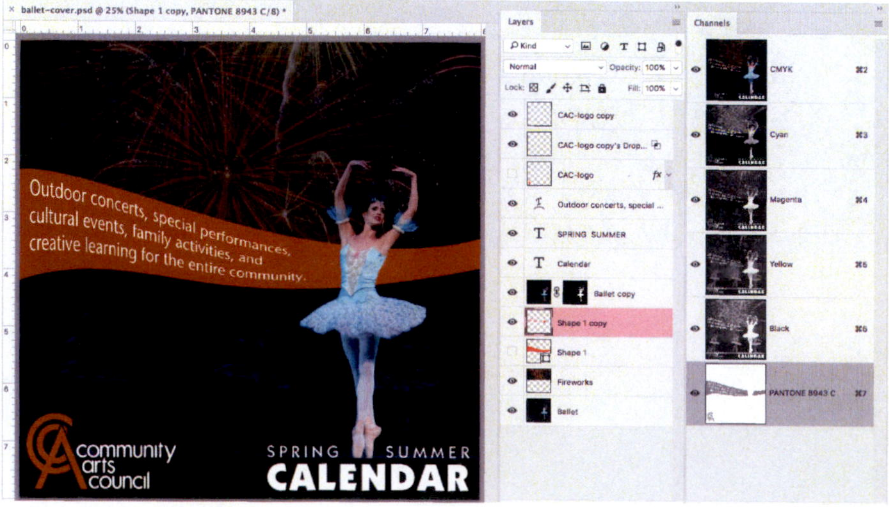

18. **Press Command/Control, and click the thumbnail for the PANTONE 8943 C channel.**

This method results in a selection that includes all pixels on the channel.

> *Note:*
>
> *The same method works in the Layers panel: Command/Control-click a layer thumbnail to select all pixels on that layer.*

19. **With all the pixels on the spot-color channel selected, choose Edit>Fill. Choose Black in the Contents menu, make sure the Mode is set to Normal, set the Opacity to 100%, and then click OK.**

Remember, each channel is a grayscale representation of one color separation. When you pasted the banner pixels onto the channel, the original orange was converted to a shade of gray as part of that channel data. For the banner to be at full strength of the spot color, it must be filled with solid black on the channel.

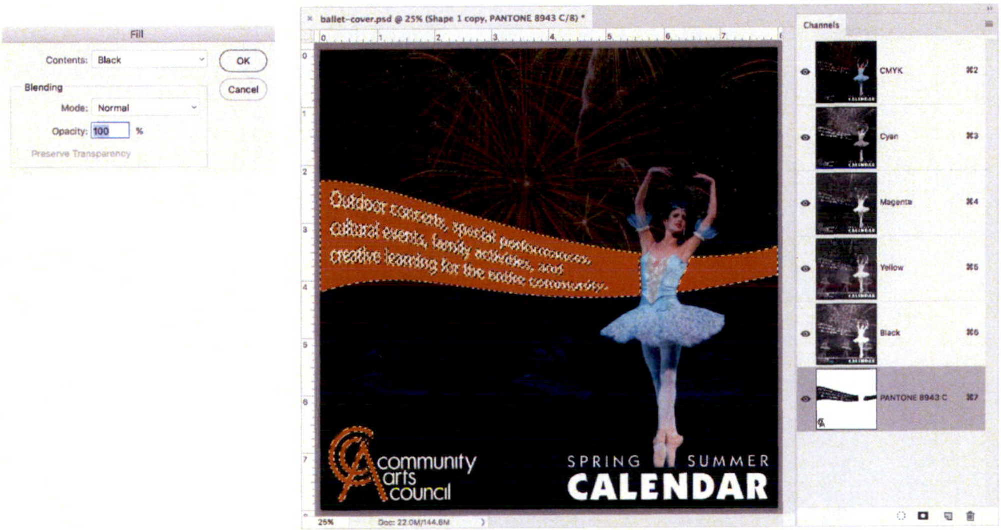

20. **Deselect the active selection area.**

21. **In the Channels panel, hide the CMYK channels and review the contents of the Pantone 8943 C channel.**

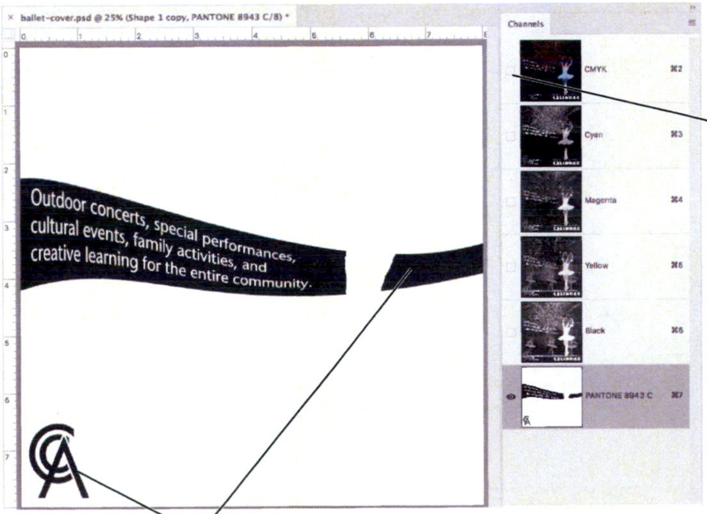

Click here to hide the CMYK layers.

The logo and banner should reproduce as full strength of the spot ink, so they appear as solid black on the spot-color channel.

22. **Show the CMYK channels again, then save the file and continue to the final exercise.**

Save the File without Spot-Color Information

When you use spot colors, you have to use a file format that can store the spot-channel information. The native Photoshop format (PSD) obviously stores the spot channels, and that format will be used for most print-based applications. A smaller file, such as JPEG, is usually preferred for digital distribution. However, JPEG does not support spot-color channels. If a file has spot channels, you need to merge the spot color data into the primary channels before saving a JPEG file; if you omit this step, information on the spot channels will simply be removed.

1. **With `ballet-cover.psd` open, select the PANTONE 8943 C channel in the Channels panel.**

2. **Open the Channels panel Options menu and choose Merge Spot Channel.**

   This command moves the spot channel data into the primary color channels. The software creates a nearest-possible color match for any spot color that is outside the primary color gamut.

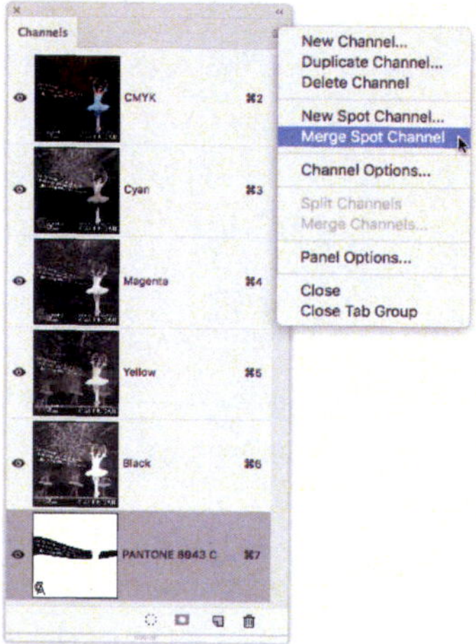

3. **Read the resulting message, then click OK.**

   Merging the spot channel requires the entire file to be flattened, which means you lose all individual layer data and future editability. You should take this step only after a file is absolutely finished, and always save it with a different name so you can preserve editability in the original, unmerged file.

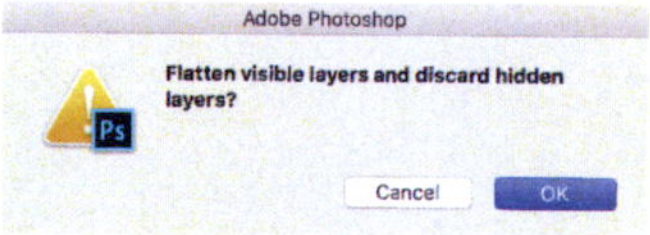

4. **With the merged file open, choose File>Save As.**

5. **Choose JPEG in the Format/Save As Type menu, then click Save.**

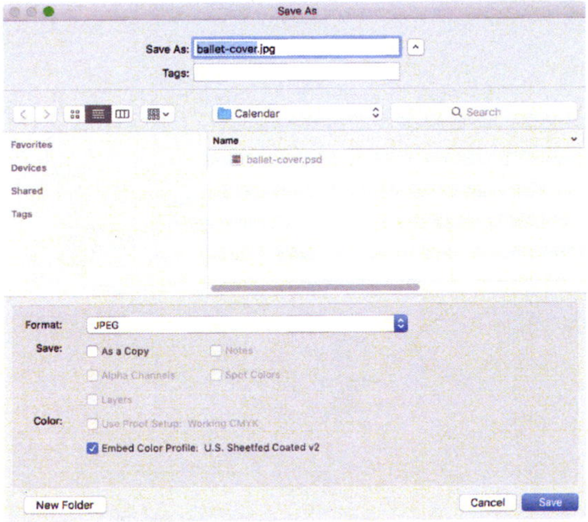

6. **In the JPEG Options dialog box, set the Quality field to 10 and then click OK.**

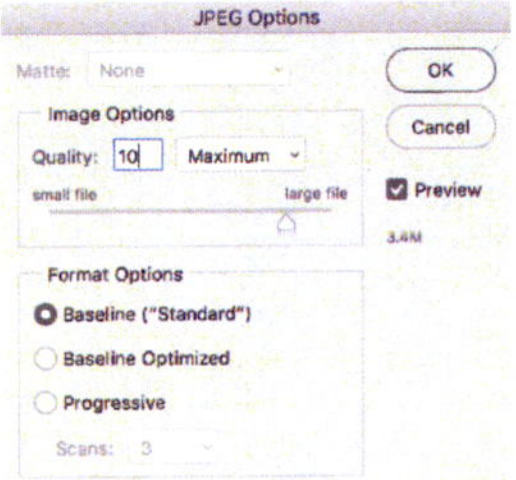

7. **Close any open file.**

Note:

Spot color information can also be saved in the PDF, EPS, or DCS file formats.

Understanding Duotones

Spot colors are sometimes used to print monotone, duotone, tritone, and quadtone images. **Monotones** are grayscale images printed with one ink (typically not black). **Duotones**, **tritones**, and **quadtones** are grayscale images printed with two, three, and four inks (respectively).

Of the four types of images, duotones are the most common. In many cases, duotones are printed with black ink for the shadows and midtones and one other color for the highlights. This technique produces an image with a slight tint that adds visual interest to images in a two-color print job. In Photoshop, duotones are treated as single-channel, 8-bit grayscale images. You can convert any 8-bit grayscale image by choosing Image>Mode>Duotone.

Choose Monotone, Duotone, Tritone, or Quadtone in this menu.

Click these icons to change the curve associated with each ink.

Click a swatch to change the colors of the duotone.

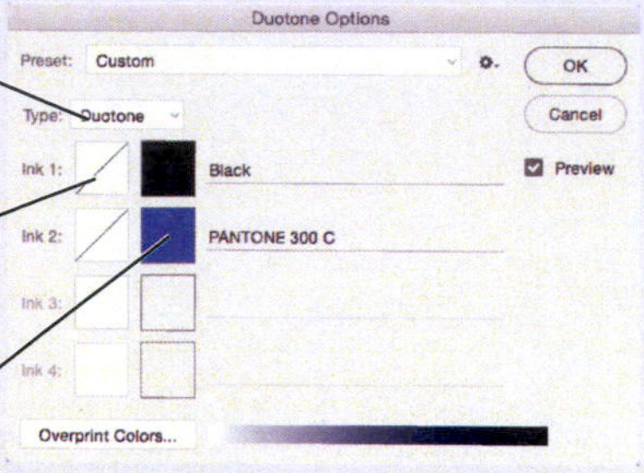

In a duotone image, you can't access the individual ink channels in the Channels panel. You can, however, manipulate the channels through the curves in the Duotone Options dialog box.

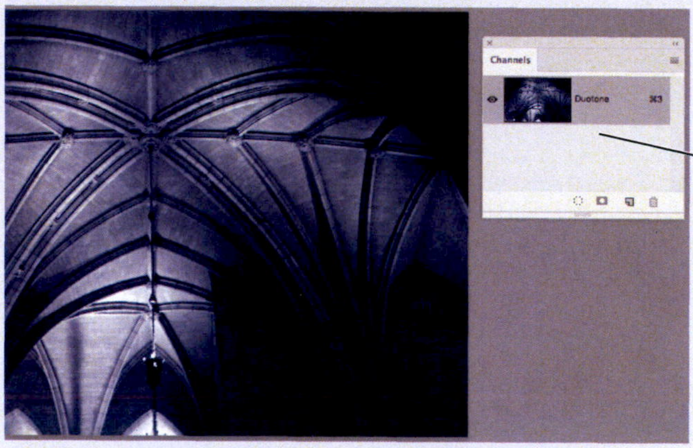

You can't use the Channels panel to access the individual inks in a duotone image.

Each ink has a curve that specifies how the color is distributed across shadows and highlights. This curve maps each grayscale value in the original image to a specific ink percentage. The default curve (a straight diagonal line) indicates that the grayscale values in the original image map to an equal percentage of ink. For example, a 50% midtone pixel becomes a 50% tint of the ink.

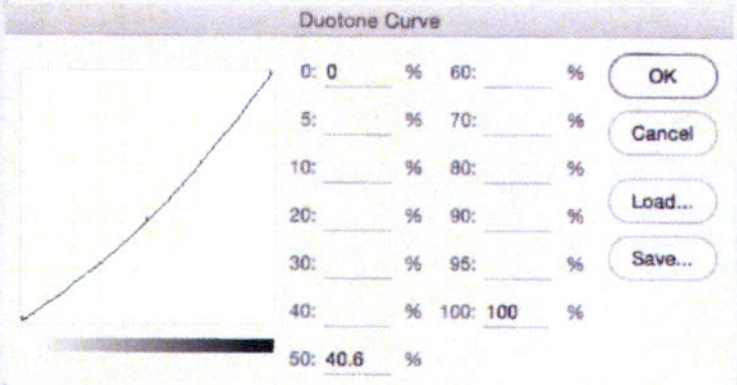

If you need direct access to the individual channels in a duotone, you can convert it to Multichannel mode (Image>Mode> Multichannel).

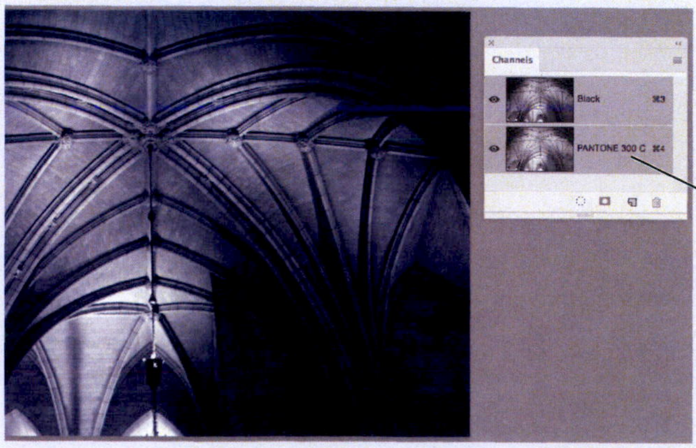

After converting to Multichannel mode, the individual ink separations are available in the Channels panel.

Project Review

fill in the blank

1. True or False: Used fonts are embedded into the Photoshop file so that they will be available for any user who opens the file. ________________

2. The ________________ option adjusts the degree of clarity that is selected by the Focus Area dialog box.

3. True or False: An Alpha channel visible in the document window is always 100% opaque. ________________

4. Paint with ________________ on a mask to remove from the mask area.

5. Paint with ________________ on a mask to add to the mask area.

6. The Custom Shape tool can be used to create ________________ from built-in or external libraries.

7. ________________ are special inks used to print specific colors, often those that are outside the CMYK gamut.

8. A ________________ is an image with only two channels, typically black and one other spot color.

9. Spot-color information is stored in a ________________; it is not associated with any Photoshop layer.

10. Images with spot color channels should be saved in the ________________ format.

short answer

1. Briefly describe the relationship between a layer mask and an Alpha channel.

2. Briefly explain the process of painting directly on a channel.

3. Briefly explain why spot colors are used in commercial graphic design.

Portfolio Builder Project

Use what you learned in this project to complete the following freeform exercise.
Carefully read the art director and client comments, then create your design to meet the needs of the project.
Use the space below to sketch ideas; when finished, write a brief explanation of the reasoning behind your design.

art director comments

The publisher you work for is creating a new title, SportsXtreme magazine, which will feature extreme sports such as BMX, sky diving, and whitewater rafting. As the in-house designer, you will be in charge of creating cover concepts for each edition of the magazine.

To complete this project, you should:

- ❑ Design an 8.25″ × 10.75″ cover concept that can be repurposed for each edition of the magazine.
- ❑ Create a nameplate that includes the magazine title, as well as the issue number, volume number, and date of the issue.
- ❑ Find or create artwork and images to illustrate each of the first two planned issues.
- ❑ Include placeholder text for three article titles on the cover.

client comments

Extreme sports are a big business, so we're going to publish this magazine to capitalize on a very large market. The target demographics in this area are very favorable for marketing companies, and we've already presold enough advertising space to make each issue at least 96 pages.

Each issue will focus on a variety of sports, but will have a main cover story that features a specific event. The first two issues will highlight skateboarding and wind surfing (respectively).

I want you to create a cover concept for the new magazine that will appeal to people who are interested in extreme sports — something bright, exciting, and dynamic that will speak to their adrenaline-junkie nature.

project justification

Project Summary

This project highlighted a number of aesthetic and technical issues associated with building a unified composition from a set of disparate elements. Many on-the-job projects include complex selections such as the one you created in this project. Although the tools available in Photoshop make the process far easier than painting every pixel by hand, you should be prepared to do some manual clean-up to perfect the fine details of a selection mask. Patience and attention to detail separate great work from average work.

Create a custom vector shape layer
Warp a type layer
Use a complex selection to isolate an image element from its photographic background
Outdoor concerts, special performances, cultural events, family activities, and creative learning for the entire community.
community arts council
SPRING SUMMER
CALENDAR
Rasterize effects and shape layers
Copy elements from regular layers to a spot-color channel

project 6

Advertising Samples

You are the in-house designer for a printing company, so your client is the new accounts manager, who is pitching your company's new large-format printing services to a potential customer. She asked you to morph an existing sample ad onto a number of different photos to help promote the company's new "Advertise Anywhere!" services.

This project incorporates the following skills:

- ❑ Patching a photo to remove unwanted elements
- ❑ Replacing specific colors in a photo to change the appearance of an object
- ❑ Using adjustment layers to change hue and saturation values for specific objects in a photo
- ❑ Adjusting an image's shadows and highlights to correct bad lighting
- ❑ Transforming a layer using one- and two-point perspective
- ❑ Warping a layer around irregular, non-flat surfaces
- ❑ Applying lighting effects to unify composite images

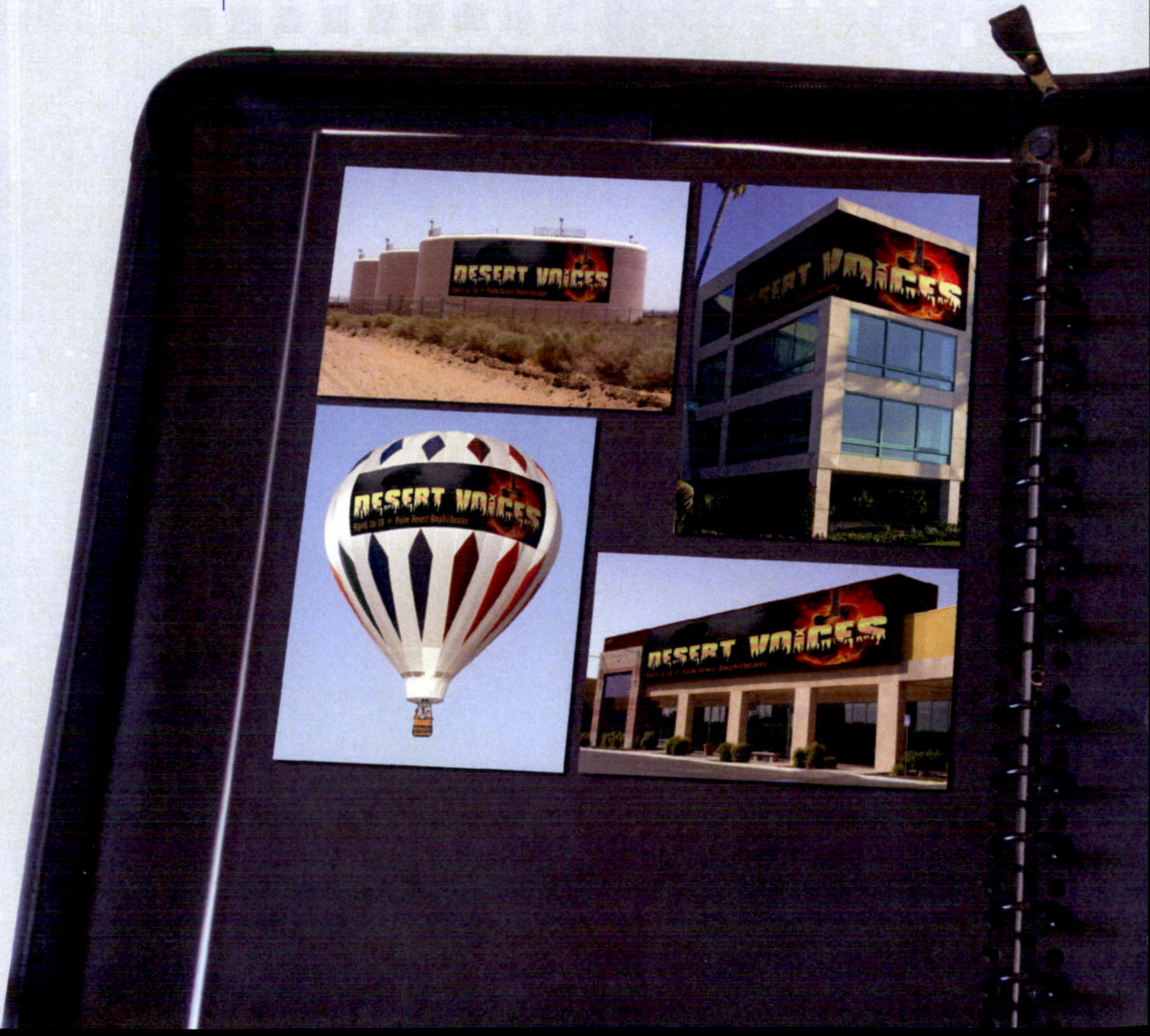

Project Meeting

client comments

Our new "Advertise Anywhere!" campaign is designed to help our clients promote their products by placing large ads in unusual places — on a bench, on the paint strips in parking lots, wrapped around a city bus, and in other non-traditional locations. The promoter for the annual air show, which draws more than 250,000 people every year, is very interested, but wants to see some samples. He asked me to do a presentation in two weeks for his marketing committee. If they like what they see, this contract could evolve into a bigger contract with the entire network.

We already created a sample ad for the air show, and I asked my assistant to gather some photos to use in the presentation. We have pictures of two local buildings, as well as two less common examples — a large water tank by the freeway and a hot air balloon.

art director comments

Since the "Advertise Anywhere!" program is new for our company, the owner is excited about presenting to the first potential client. All the pictures they want to use need some help to make them as attractive as possible.

In the water tank photo, there's a bunch of litter I want you to remove.

The bright yellow in the balloon is going to detract attention from the sample ad. Remove the yellow from the balloon body and mute the other colors a bit so the sample ad stands out.

One of the building photos isn't bad, but it's been painted since we took the photo. To personalize the presentation, convert the brown front façade to dark red and clean up any marks.

If you place the ad onto the office building as it is now, most of the ad will end up in dark shadows. Adjust the photo's overall lighting before you wrap the ad around the building.

project objectives

To complete this project, you will:

- ❑ Use the Patch tool to replace one area of an image with pixels from another area
- ❑ Use the Replace Color adjustment to change selected colors in an image
- ❑ Use adjustment layers to apply color changes to specific areas of an image
- ❑ Use the Shadow/Highlight adjustment to correct a shadow-filled image
- ❑ Use Free Transform mode to match a layer to the perspective in the background image
- ❑ Use the Vanishing Point filter to wrap a layer in perspective around a sharp corner
- ❑ Create a custom warp transformation to morph a sample ad onto a round shape
- ❑ Use the Lighting Effects filter to unify composited images

Stage 1 Cleaning and Adjusting Images

Photoshop includes a number of tools for creating irregular composite images — such as warping a flat ad around the shape of a water tank along the desert highway, or placing an ad on a hot-air balloon floating in the distance. Before you composite the images for this project, however, you need to do some clean-up work on the background photos. The best approach is to fix the images first, and then morph the ad onto the corrected files.

Remove Unwanted Image Elements

The Healing Brush and Spot Healing Brush tools are excellent choices for cleaning up marks and blemishes, and the Clone Stamp tool can effectively copy pixels from one location to another. As you have probably already noticed, there is usually more than one way to accomplish the same type of task — and retouching an image is no exception. The Patch tool can be used to replace one area with another and blend the area edges for smoother results.

1. **Download Outdoors_PS18_RF.zip from the Student Files web page.**

2. **Expand the ZIP archive in your WIP folder (Macintosh) or copy the archive contents into your WIP folder (Windows).**

   This results in a folder named **Outdoors**, which contains the files you need for this project. You should also use this folder to save the files you create in this project.

3. **In Photoshop, open tanks.jpg from the WIP>Outdoors folder. If you get a warning about a mismatched color profile, choose the option to use the embedded profile.**

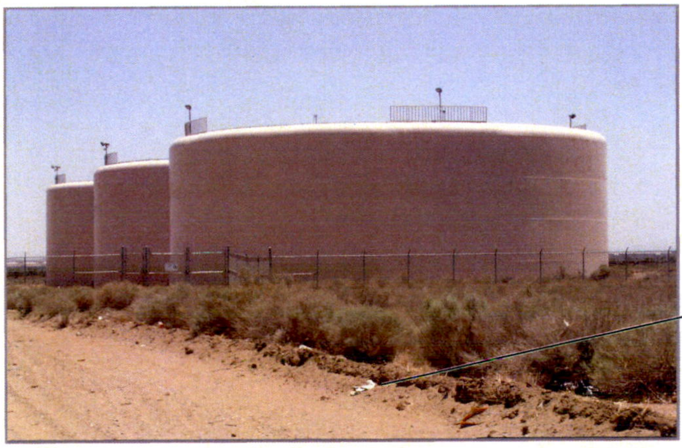

This image will make a better client sample without the annoying litter along the edge of the road.

4. **Zoom in to the large white object in the bottom center of the image.**

5. **Choose the Patch tool in the Tools panel (nested under the Spot Healing Brush tool).**

   If you don't see the Patch tool, look in the Edit Toolbar (...) menu at the bottom of the Tools panel, or call the default Essentials workspace to reset all tools to their default positions in the Tools panel.

   The Patch tool allows you to repair a selected area with either a texture, with pixels from another specified area, or with a pattern. It matches texture, lighting, and shading of the sampled pixels to the source (selected) pixels. This option gives you more control than the Content-Aware Fill dialog box because you choose the area to be filled *and* the pixels that will be used to fill that area.

6. **Using the Patch tool, draw a selection marquee that entirely surrounds the piece of trash.**

   Because of the texture and detail in the surrounding area, the other repair tools are not the best choices for removing this object from the roadside. The Patch tool, on the other hand, allows you to sample pixels from other areas of the image and blend them smoothly over the selected area.

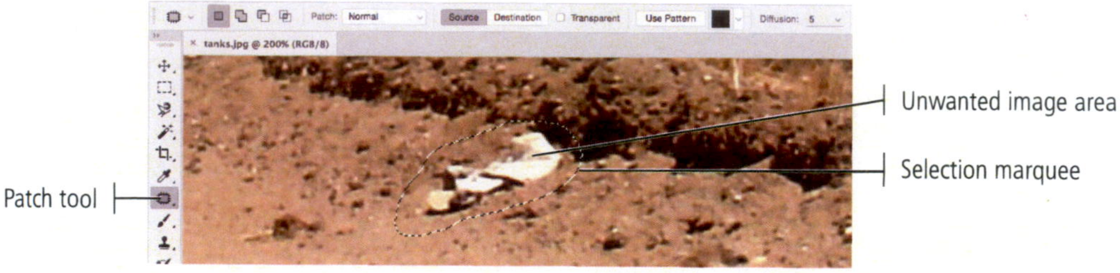

7. **In the Options bar, open the Mode menu and choose Content-Aware.**

   When the Mode menu is set to Normal (the default), you have two additional options: Source and Destination; these buttons define what the selection marquee represents.

   - If Source is active, the original marquee represents the area that will be patched.
   - If Destination is active, the original selection marquee represents the pixels that will be copied to another area.

   If the Mode menu is set to Content-Aware, Photoshop evaluates the image pixels and fills the original selection marquee with content from the area you drag to (similar to the Source option in Normal mode). In Content-Aware mode, you can determine how closely the software analyzes the Structure (on a scale of 1–7) and Color (on a scale of 1–10) of the image to create the final result. Higher structure and color values mean the patched pixels will more closely resemble the detail in the patching pixels; they take longer to process, but can produce more accurate results.

8. **Place the Patch tool cursor inside the selection marquee, then click and drag to the left. When you are satisfied with the preview, release the mouse button.**

   The pixels inside the second marquee (where you drag to) are used to fill the original location. This tool shows a dynamic preview; as you drag the marquee, the original selection changes to show the result that will be created when you release the mouse button.

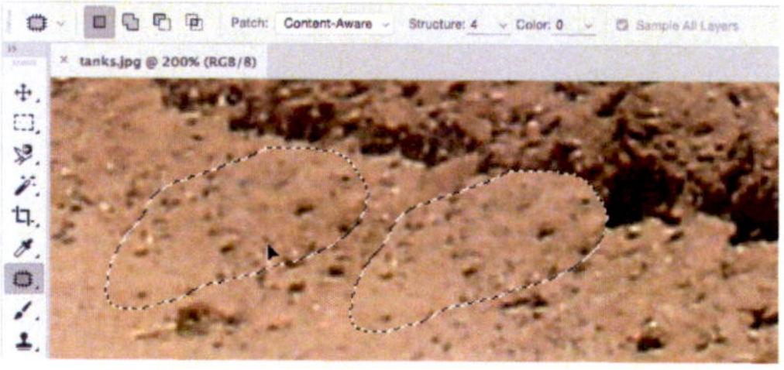

   When you release the mouse button, the Patch tool blends the selection edge smoothly into the surrounding area, preventing unwanted harsh edges around the patch.

9. **Press Command/Control-D to turn off the selection marquee so you can better review your results.**

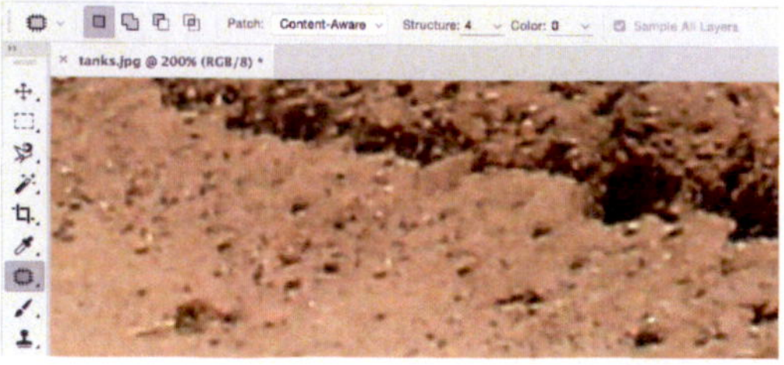

Note:

If you aren't satisfied with the result, undo the patch selection and try again. However, keep in mind that deselection is considered a step, so you can't use the one-process Undo command. You have to use the History panel to go back two steps and restore the original pixels, or use the Step Backward command (Command-Option-Z/Control-Alt-Z).

10. **Using the same technique, remove the rest of the litter from the foreground of this image.**

> *Note:*
>
> *When using the Patch tool, use the smallest selection area possible to achieve the best results.*

11. **Save the file as a native Photoshop file named tanks-clean.psd in your WIP>Outdoors folder.**

12. **Close the file, than continue to the next exercise.**

Replace Colors in Parts of an Image

The Replace Color adjustment allows you to select and replace a specific range of colors in an image. This adjustment option is a simple method for making overall changes to hue, saturation, or lightness in selected areas without having to experiment with layer blending modes.

1. **Open the file studio.jpg from the WIP>Outdoors folder. If you get a warning about mismatched profiles, choose the option to use the embedded profile.**

On the actual building, this façade has been repainted a deep red.

The fresh paint removed these white streaks.

2. **Choose Image>Adjustments>Replace Color.**

3. **Using the Eyedropper tool from the Replace Color dialog box, click in the image (behind the dialog box) to select the brown stucco façade of the building.**

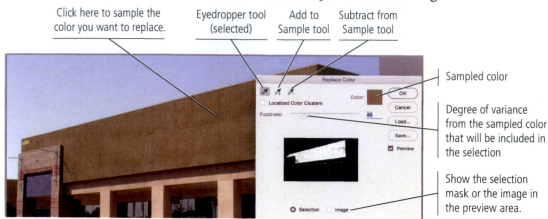

4. **Drag the Fuzziness slider right to increase the selection tolerance.**

   As you increase the fuzziness, you can see other areas of the image being added to the selection. Various areas in this image share many of the same earth tones, which means you can't select the façade color without affecting some other areas of the image — at least, not without a couple of extra steps.

5. **Click Cancel to close the Replace Color dialog box.**

6. **In the Layers panel, Control/right-click the Background layer and choose Duplicate Layer from the contextual menu. Click OK in the Duplicate Layer dialog box to accept the default layer name.**

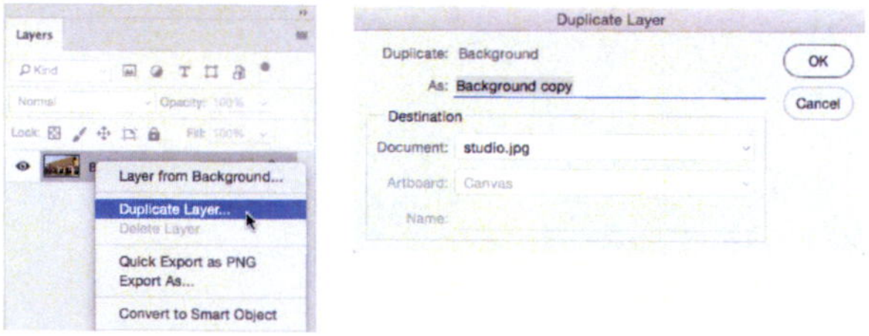

7. **With the Background Copy layer selected in the Layers panel, choose Image>Adjustments>Replace Color.**

8. **Click in the image to sample the same brown as the selection color, and then move the Fuzziness slider all the way to the right.**

   The preview shows that a large portion of the image is selected, including areas that you don't want to change. That's okay, since you'll use a layer mask to eliminate those areas from the duplicate layer.

Note:

When you Control/right-click a layer and select Duplicate Layer, you can use the Destination options to place the duplicate layer in the stack for the current (open) image, any open image, or a new image.

9. **In the lower half of the dialog box, experiment with the Hue, Saturation, and Lightness sliders until you find a dark red color.**

Much of the building has some shade of brown, so full Fuzziness selects most of the building face.

Use these options to change the color of the selected pixels.

> *Note:*
>
> *You can also click the Result color swatch and define a replacement color in the Color Picker dialog box.*

10. **Click OK to apply the change to the selected layer.**

11. **Using any method you prefer, draw a selection marquee around the edges of the façade (as shown in the following image).**

Since this selection has straight edges, the Polygonal Lasso tool will do a fine job of creating the selection. You could also draw a work path with the Pen tool, and then make a selection based on the work path.

> *Note:*
>
> *It's important to understand that image adjustments apply to the selected area or layer only. These adjustments do not apply to all layers in an image.*

12. **With the selection active (you can see the marching ants), click the Add Layer Mask button at the bottom of the Layers panel.**

When you add a layer mask with an active selection, the areas outside the selection are automatically masked.

Add Layer Mask button

13. **Zoom in to the edges of the façade and make sure the mask covers exactly what you want it to cover. Use the Brush and/or Eraser tool to clean up the mask edges if necessary.**

Remember, when you paint on a mask, black adds to the mask and white removes areas from the mask. You should also make sure to select the mask in the Layers panel (instead of the layer thumbnail) before painting on the mask, or you will mistakenly paint on the actual image layer.

14. **In the Layers panel, Control/right-click the Background Copy layer name and choose Merge Down from the contextual menu.**

Merge Down combines the selected layer with the next layer down in the Layers panel. **Merge Visible** combines all visible layers into a single layer. **Flatten Image** combines all layers into the Background layer, giving you the option to discard hidden layers.

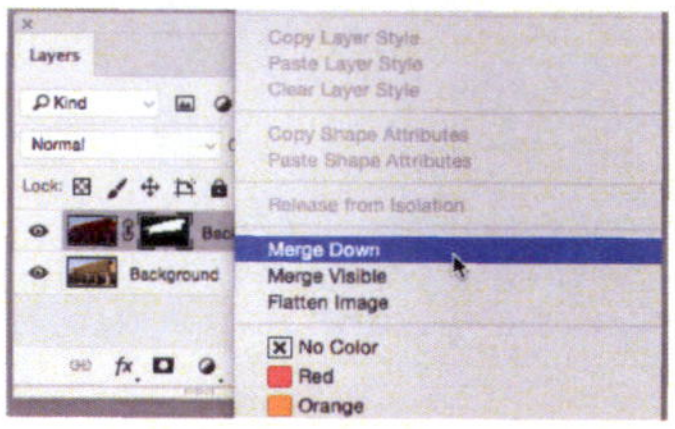

Because the next layer down is the Background layer, merging the selected layer down combines the Background Copy layer into the Background layer.

Note:

In this step, our goal is to teach you about the options for flattening image layers. In many cases, however, it is a better idea to leave the masked layer intact in case you need to make changes later.

15. **Use any technique you prefer to remove the white streaks from the building's façade.**

The Replace Color function only affected areas of color within the selected range (Step 8). These spots are drastically different than the selected brown shades, so they still need to be corrected.

We used a combination of the Spot Healing tool to clean up the spots on the face and the Clone Stamp and Patch tools to clean up the edges.

16. **Save the file as a native Photoshop file named studio-clean.psd in your WIP>Outdoors folder.**

17. **Close the file, then continue to the next exercise.**

Understanding the Selective Color Adjustment

The **Selective Color** adjustment (Image>Adjustments>Selective Color) allows you to change ink values in specific colors or neutrals without affecting other colors.

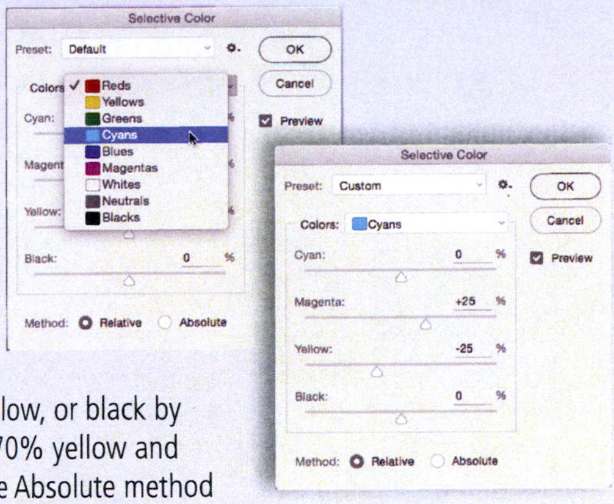

For example, if water looks too yellow, you should remove yellow to produce a more inviting blue color. If you reduce the overall amount of yellow, however, you might affect other areas such as the pier and island in the image shown below. The Selective Color option allows you to adjust the yellow component of only blues or cyans (for example), so you can fix the water without affecting other areas.

The Relative method changes the existing amount of cyan, magenta, yellow, or black by its percentage of the total. For example, if you start with a pixel that is 70% yellow and remove 10%, 7% is removed from the yellow (10% of 70% = 7%). The Absolute method adjusts the color in absolute values. If you start with a pixel that is 70% yellow and remove 10%, the yellow pixel is set to 60%.

Water in the original image has a strong yellow cast.

Adjusting ink percentages of only the cyans made the water more inviting without affecting the pilings in the foreground.

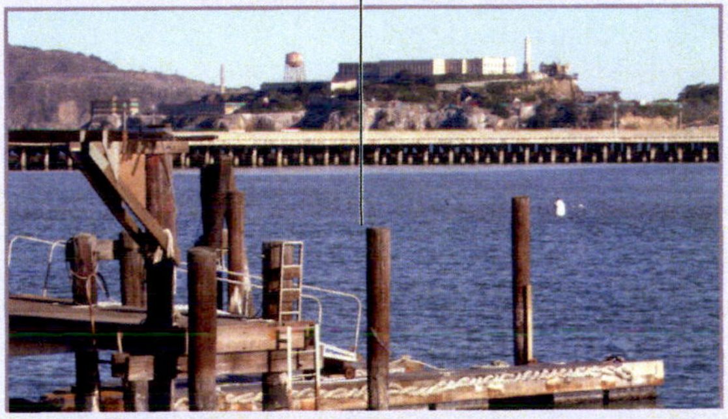

The Preset menu at the top of the Selective Color dialog box is useful if you need to make the same adjustment to multiple images — for example, you know photos from a particular digital camera always have a yellow cast in the blue areas. (The same Preset options are available in all adjustment dialog boxes.)

Adjust Hue and Saturation with an Adjustment Layer

Correcting the previous image highlighted one of the potential drawbacks of using image adjustments: you might change areas you don't want to change, requiring a workaround (in this case, a duplicate layer with a mask) to achieve the effect you want.

The process you used in the previous exercise is so common that Photoshop includes built-in options for creating adjustment layers, which effectively achieve the same result that you accomplished manually in the previous exercise. An adjustment layer is an empty layer containing an adjustment (such as a Levels or Curves adjustment) that modifies the layers below it.

1. **Open the file balloon.jpg from the WIP>Outdoors folder. If you get a warning about mismatched color profiles, choose the option to use the embedded profile.**

   The art director wants this yellow balloon to be white, so it doesn't distract from the sample ad. The Hue/Saturation adjustment, which allows you to change the Hue, Saturation, and Lightness values of specific primary colors, is perfectly suited for changing this yellow balloon to white.

2. Open the Adjustments panel and click the Hue/Saturation button.

The Hue/Saturation adjustment can be extremely useful for shifting the Hue, Saturation, or Lightness value of an entire image or for selected primary colors.

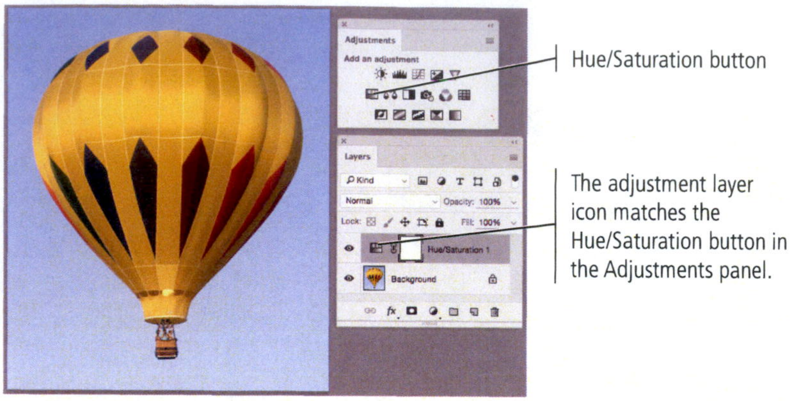

Adding an adjustment layer creates a new layer on top of the currently selected layer (in this case, the Background layer). This allows you to easily show or hide the adjustment, apply multiple adjustments to the same layer, or even delete an adjustment from the file without permanently changing the pixels on the original layer. The adjustment from an adjustment layer is not permanent unless you merge the adjustment layer with one or more underlying layers.

Keep in mind that adjustment layers affect all underlying layers. If you want an adjustment layer to affect only the next layer down, Control/right-click the adjustment layer and choose Create Clipping Mask from the contextual menu.

> **Note:**
>
> *You can use adjustment layers for most of the adjustments available in the Image>Adjustments menu. (For some reason, a few adjustments — including the Replace Color adjustment you used in the previous exercise — have been left out of this panel.)*

> **Note:**
>
> *You can add adjustment layers using either the Adjustments panel or the menu at the bottom of the Layers panel.*
>
> *You can also choose from the Layer>New Adjustment Layer submenu.*

More about Adjustment Layers

PHOTOSHOP FOUNDATIONS

Adjustment layers are another way to apply many of the same adjustments that are available in the Image> Adjustments menu. The difference is that adjustment layers are non-destructive; rather than permanently affecting the pixels in your image, adjustment layers store the adjustment settings, so you can change the settings or toggle the adjustment on or off at any point in your workflow.

You can add an adjustment layer using the buttons in the Adjustments panel, or the menu at the bottom of the Layers panel. Once an adjustment layer is added, you can use the Properties panel to change the settings of the adjustment.

Icons in the Adjustments panel match the icons that identify an adjustment layer.

Brightness/Contrast	Hue/Saturation	Invert
Levels	Color Balance	Posterize
Curves	Black & White	Threshold
Exposure	Photo Filter	Selective Color
Vibrance	Channel Mixer	Gradient Map
	Color Lookup	

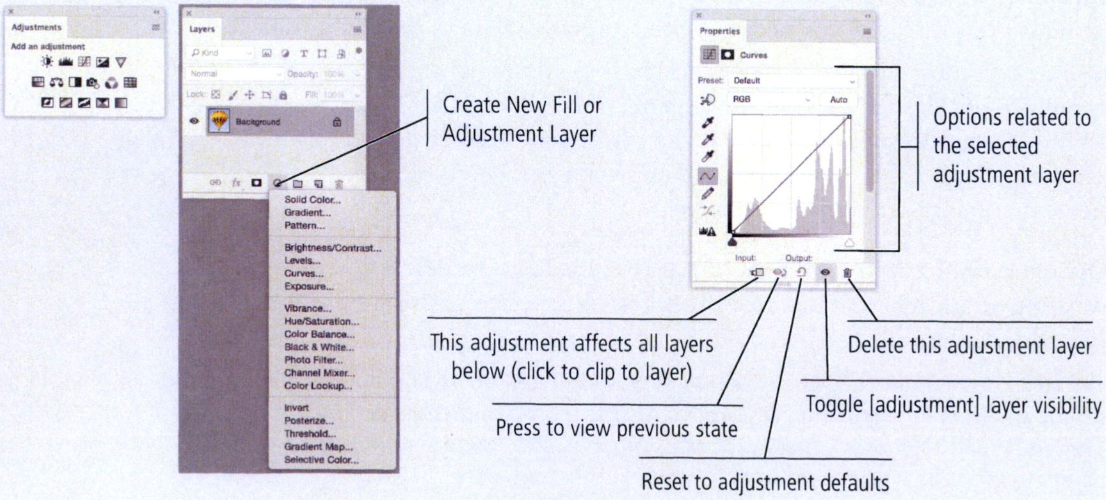

3. **In the Properties panel, choose Yellows in the Edit menu (which defaults to Master) and drag the Lightness slider all the way to the right.**

   When an adjustment layer is selected in the Layers panel, the Properties panel contains options specific to the selected adjustment layer.

   Since the balloon was pure yellow, increasing the yellow lightness to +100 converts the yellow parts of the balloon to pure white.

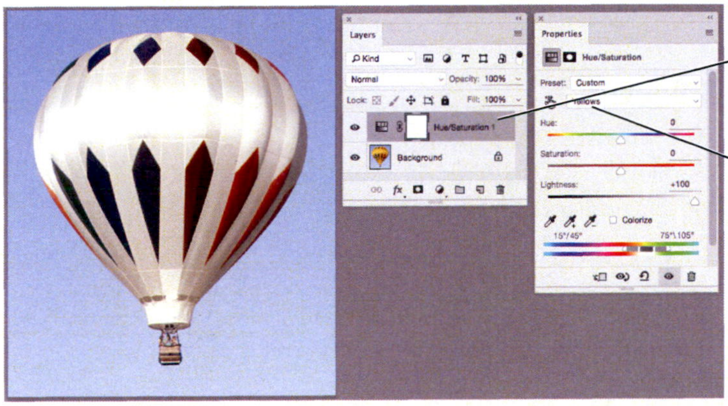

Select the adjustment layer to show related settings in the Properties panel.

Choose from this menu to adjust the entire image, or specific primary colors.

> *Note:*
>
> *Lightness is the position of a color along the black/white scale. Lightness of 0 adds no white or black to the hue. Lightness of –100 is solid black (obscuring all other color). Lightness of +100 is pure white (removing all color).*

4. **In the Layers panel, click the Adjustment Layer Mask thumbnail to select it.**

   Adjustment layers automatically include a layer mask, which allows you to isolate portions of an image for correction. Adjustment layers are also helpful for experimenting with corrections without permanently affecting the underlying layer.

5. **Choose the Brush tool in the Tools panel. Open the Brush Preset picker in the Options bar and define a 70-pixel brush with 100% hardness.**

6. **Click the Default Foreground and Background Colors button in the Tools panel, then click the Switch Foreground and Background Colors button.**

   This sets the foreground color to black, which you must use on an adjustment layer mask to protect certain areas from the adjustment.

> *Note:*
>
> *You can change the opacity, order, or blending mode of an adjustment layer, just as you can with a regular layer.*

7. **With the adjustment layer mask selected in the Layers panel, paint over the area of the basket to protect that area from the increased Lightness setting for yellows.**

Click here to open the Brush Preset picker.

The Brush tool is active.

Black is the active foreground color.

The adjustment layer mask is selected.

Painting on the mask restores the original color in the basket.

8. **Save the file as a native Photoshop file named `balloon-clean.psd` in your WIP>Outdoors folder. Click OK in the Photoshop Format Options dialog box when asked to maximize compatibility.**

   You were not asked to maximize compatibility with the previous files, because all of those still have only one layer.

9. **Close the file and continue to the next exercise.**

Adjust Image Shadows and Highlights

The Shadows/Highlights adjustment is well suited for correcting highlight and shadow areas of an image. (Photoshop calculates the changes based on the values of surrounding pixels.) Using the basic settings, you can adjust the values of shadows and highlights independently.

1. **Open the file `office.jpg` from the WIP>Outdoors folder. If you get a warning about mismatched profiles, choose the option to use the embedded profile.**

This overall image is extremely dark; most of the building is in shadows.

2. **Choose Image>Adjustments>Shadows/Highlights.**

3. **Reduce the Shadow Amount value to 15% to lighten the shadows in the image.**

   An Amount value of 0% means no change will be applied to that area; larger values result in lighter shadows or darker highlights.

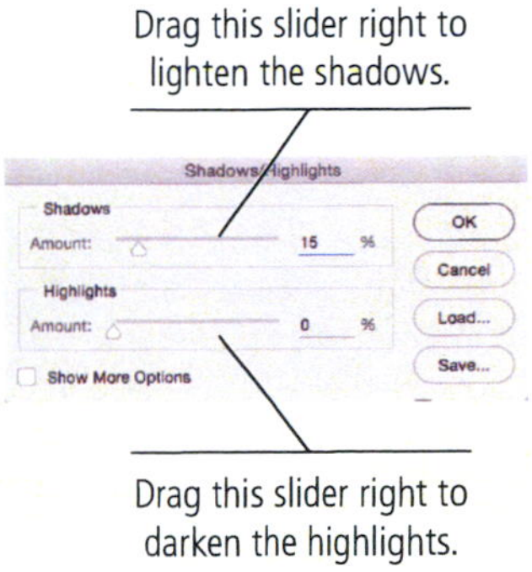

4. **Click OK to apply the change.**

5. **Save the file as a native Photoshop file named office-clean.psd in your WIP>Outdoors folder.**

6. **Close the file, then continue to the next stage of the project.**

Extended Control for Shadows/Highlights Adjustments

PHOTOSHOP FOUNDATIONS

When the **Show More Options** box is checked in the Shadows/Highlights dialog box, you can fine-tune the adjustments for both shadows and highlights, as well as modify the options for color correction and midtone contrast.

Tone defines the part of the tonal range that will be modified by the adjustment. Set to 100%, the adjustment will be applied to half of the tonal range. Smaller values restrict the adjustment to smaller regions of the related area (shadows or highlights).

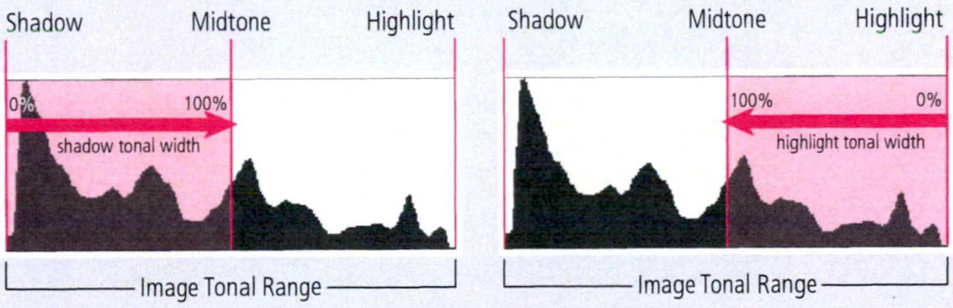

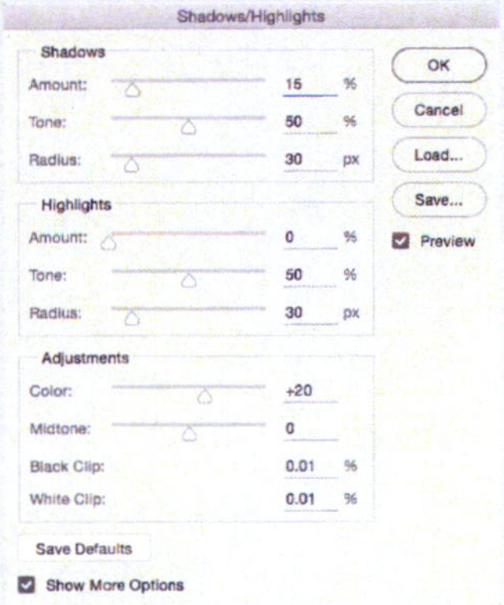

Radius controls the size of the area around each pixel that is used to determine whether a pixel is in the shadows or highlights.

Color fine-tunes the colors in areas that are changed by your choices in the Shadows and Highlights sections of the dialog box. Higher values tend to produce more saturated colors.

Midtone adjusts the contrast in the midtones, similar to the Input Gamma slider in the Levels dialog box.

Black Clip and **White Clip** determine how much of the extreme shadows and highlights are clipped, just as with the Clip options in the Auto Color Correction Options dialog box.

Painting Image Correction Tools

In addition to the tools you have used throughout this book, a number of tools in the Tools panel can be used to make basic corrections.

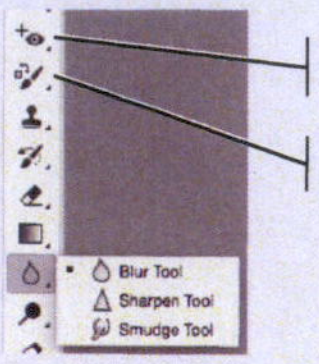

The **Red Eye tool** removes the red-eye effect caused by flash photography.

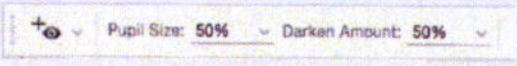

In the Options bar, the **Pupil Size** menu controls the size of the area affected by the tool. The **Darken Amount** option sets the darkness of the correction.

The **Blur tool** softens hard edges and reduces detail.

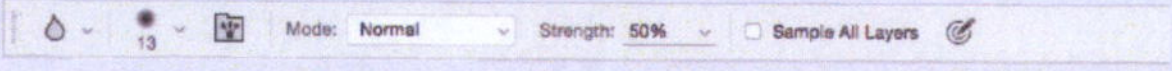

The **Sharpen tool** increases contrast at edges to increase apparent sharpness.

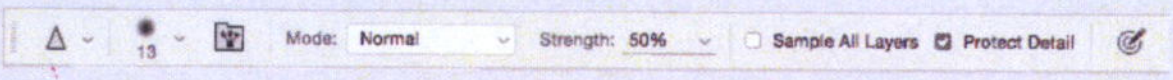

The **Smudge tool** allows you to push pixels around in an image, as if you were dragging your finger across wet (digital) paint.

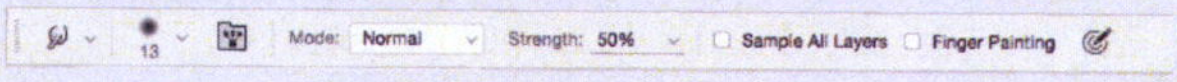

All three of these tools use a selected brush preset to affect the image. You can choose a specific blending mode, as well as the strength of the effect as you paint a brush stroke. Multiple brush strokes increase the tool's effect.

If the **Sample All Layers** option is checked, you can affect the selected layer using data from all layers in the file. For the Smudge tool, the Finger Painting option adds the foreground color to the beginning of the brush stroke.

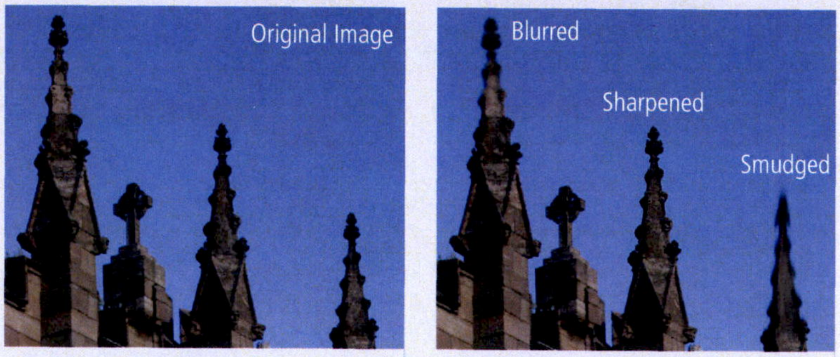

The **Color Replacement tool** attempts to simplify replacement of specific colors in your image. You can define the brush you want to use, and then paint over a targeted color to replace it with the foreground color.

You can replace the color, or you can choose Hue, Saturation, or Luminosity in the Mode menu. The sampling options determine how color will be replaced:

- **Continuous** samples colors as you drag.
- **Once** replaces color only in areas of the color that you first click.
- **Background Swatch** replaces only areas of the current background color.

The Limits menu determines how the tool's effect can be constrained:

- **Discontiguous** replaces the sampled color under the brush tip.
- **Contiguous** replaces color contiguous with the color under the brush tip.
- **Find Edges** replaces connected areas of the sampled color, attempting to preserve the sharpness of shape edges.

Tolerance defines how much variance from the sample will be affected. The **Anti-alias** option smoothes edges of the affected areas.

The Color Replacement tool works best for images with high-contrast edges.

Painting Image Exposure and Saturation

The **Dodge** and **Burn tools** are used to lighten or darken areas of an image (respectively). These tools are based on traditional photographic techniques for exposing specific areas of a print. Photographers hold back light to lighten an area on the print (**dodging**) or increase the exposure to darken areas on a print (**burning**).

You define a brush in the Options bar, as well as the image range you want to affect (highlights, midtones, or shadows) and the degree of exposure.

The original image shows the view through a guard house window at Alcatraz Island in San Francisco Bay.

The post on the left was painted with the Dodge tool to lighten the shadows and reveal details in the concrete.

The foliage at the bottom opening was painted with the Burn tool to darken the shadows, effectively removing all detail in that area.

The **Sponge tool** changes the color saturation of an area. As with the Dodge and Burn tools, you can define a specific brush to use. You can also define the mode of the Sponge tool — Saturate or Desaturate — and the flow rate for the effect.

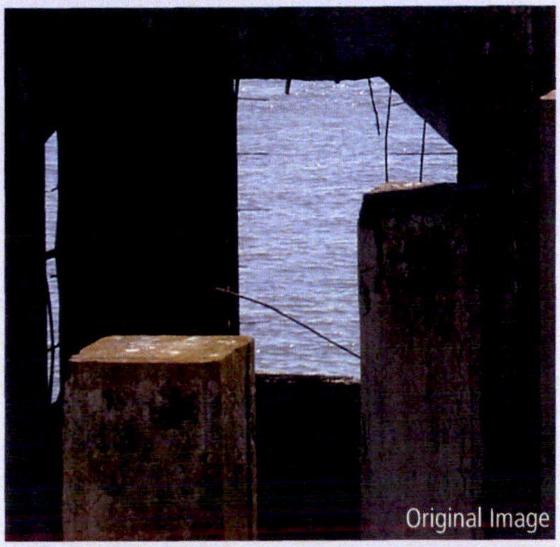

The opening in the wall was painted with the Sponge tool in Saturate mode to enhance the blue of the water.

Stage 2 Working in Perspective

Many compositing jobs will be straightforward copy-and-paste jobs — putting multiple images together, possibly adjusting size, clipping edges, or blending edges into other elements — such as the work you completed in the earlier projects of this book.

Other jobs are more complex, especially jobs that require you to make one object appear to be a seamless part of another image. When your goal is to merge one element with another existing image, you need to pay close attention to details such as size, angle, and depth so the composited element appears to blend naturally with the background image.

Transform the Perspective of a Layer

Basic transformations such as scale, rotation, skew, and perspective can all be accomplished in Free Transform mode. For skewing a flat ad onto a flat surface, Free Transform mode is the simplest choice.

> *Note:*
>
> *Whenever you open a file throughout the rest of this project, maintain the embedded profile if you get a warning about mismatched profiles.*

1. **Open the file studio-clean.psd from your WIP>Outdoors folder.**
2. **Choose File>Place Embedded. Select the file banner.tif from the WIP>Outdoors folder and click Place.**

   The Place Embedded command adds the selected file as a Smart Object layer.

3. **Using the Options bar, scale the layer to 73% proportionally, and then drag the banner so that its top-right corner is near the top-right corner of the studio façade.**

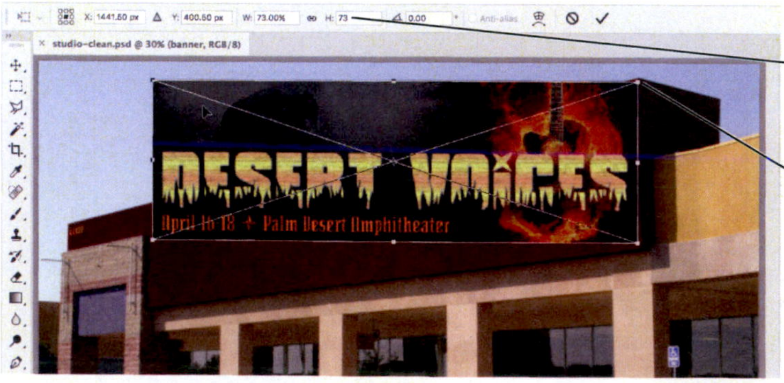

Use the W and H fields to resize the banner graphic to 73% of its original size.

Position the top-right corner near the top-right corner of the façade.

4. **Command/Control-click the center-left transformation handle and drag down to skew the layer. Align the bottom-left corner of the banner to the bottom-left corner of the building façade (as shown here).**

   Simply dragging a center handle stretches or shrinks the selection. Pressing the Command/Control key allows you to skew a selection instead of changing its horizontal or vertical size.

Press Command/Control and drag the center handle to skew the selection.

Note:

Press Shift while Command/Control-dragging to skew the object exactly vertical or exactly horizontal.

5. **Command/Control-click the top-left transformation handle and drag down to distort the perspective of the layer.**

   Simply dragging a corner handle stretches or shrinks the selection. Pressing the Command/Control key allows you to distort the image's shape, which affects perspective when you drag straight corners in this manner.

Press Command/Control and drag the corner handle to alter the perspective of the selection.

Note:

Press Shift while Command/Control-dragging to constrain the movement of the transformation handle to 45° angles.

6. **If necessary, adjust the bottom corner handles so that the banner fits entirely within the front of the façade.**

7. **When you're satisfied with the position, size, and perspective of the banner, press Return/Enter to finalize the transformation.**

8. **Apply a slight drop shadow to the banner layer (Layer>Layer Style>Drop Shadow). We used the following settings:**

Blend Mode:	**Multiply Black**	**Distance:**	**10**
Opacity:	**75%**	**Spread:**	**0**
Angle:	**125°**	**Size:**	**5**

Note:

We used the 125° angle for the drop shadow to approximate the angle of shadows that already exist in the image.

9. **Save the file as studio-ad.psd in your WIP>Outdoors folder. Click OK when asked to maximize compatibility.**

10. **Close the file, and then continue to the next exercise.**

Free Transform Options

You can transform any layer or selection using the options in the Edit>Transform menu or by choosing Edit>Free Transform. (Most of the options in the Edit>Transform submenu — Scale, Rotate, Skew, and Distort — can also be applied using the Free Transform option, making these choices redundant.)

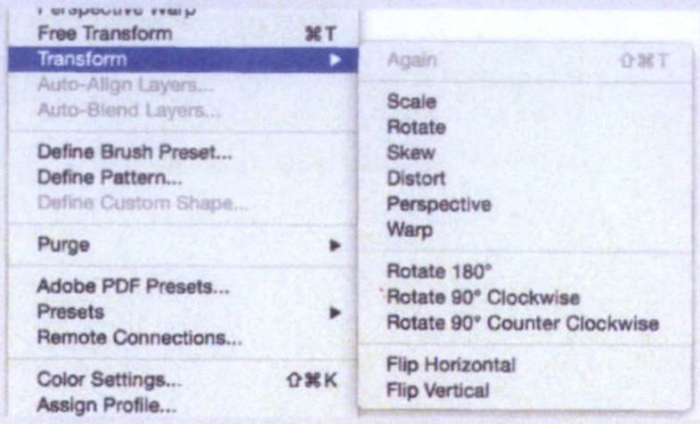

When you choose Edit>Free Transform, the selection is surrounded by handles that allow you to control the transformation. Use the following images as a guide for controlling your transformations.

Click a center handle to stretch or shrink the selection in one direction.

Command/Control-click a center handle to skew the selection.

Click slightly outside a corner handle to rotate the selection.

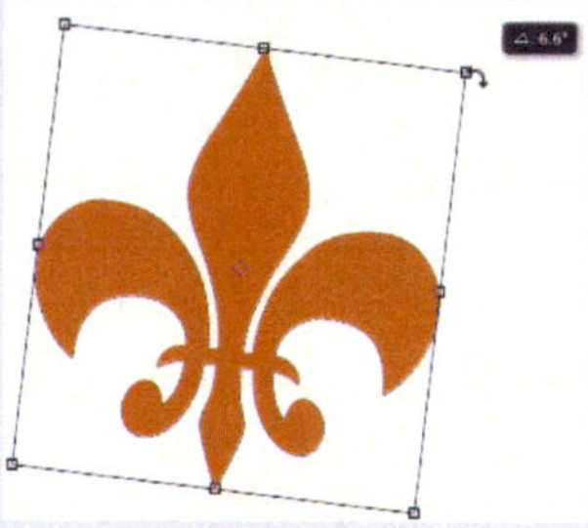

Click a corner handle to stretch or shrink the selection horizontally and vertically at the same time.

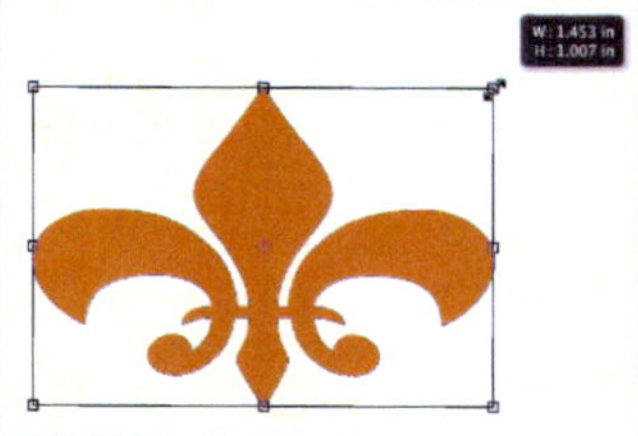

Command/Control-click a corner handle to distort the selection.

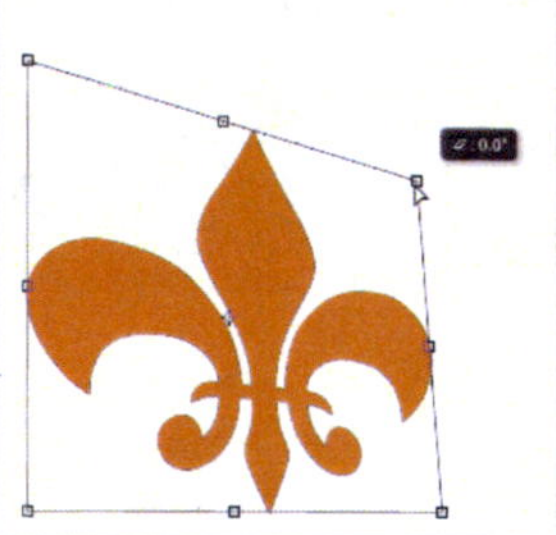

Press Option/Alt while making any free transformation to apply it equally on both sides of the selection center.

Pressing Shift with any of the transformations constrains the transformation to 45-degree increments. For example, if you press Shift while skewing a selection, the skew will be constrained to exactly horizontal or vertical.

If you choose Edit>Transform>Perspective, dragging a corner handle has the same effect as pressing Command-Option-Shift/Control-Alt-Shift when working in Free Transform mode. Dragging a side handle has the same effect as pressing Command/Control-Shift when in Free Transform mode.

The advantage to Perspective transformation mode is that you don't have to use the modifier keys. The disadvantage is that you can't change anything other than the horizontal or vertical skew and the reflective horizontal or vertical distortion of the selection.

Drag a corner handle to shrink or expand that side of the selection around the center point.

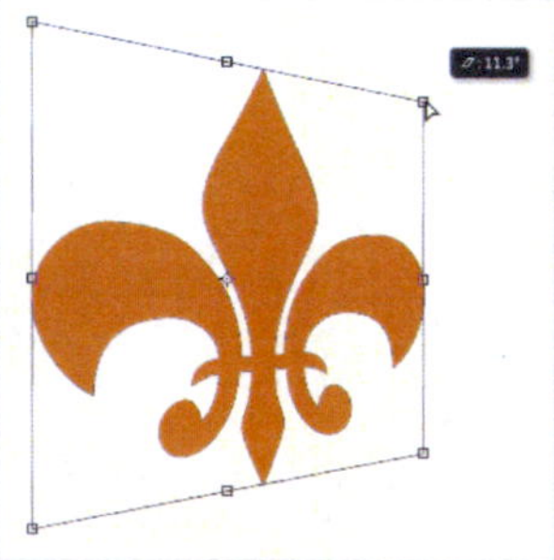

Drag a center handle to skew the selection.

Apply a Perspective Warp

In the next exercise, you are going to place the banner ad in perspective around the office building. Before you do that, however, you are going to use the powerful Perspective Warp utility in this exercise to straighten the lines in the photo and reduce some of the distortion caused by the photographer's angle relative to the building.

1. **Open the file `office-clean.psd` from the WIP>Outdoors folder.**

2. **With the Background layer selected in the Layers panel, choose Edit>Perspective Warp.**

3. **If you see a pop-up message, read it and then click the Close button.**

   When you enter Perspective Warp mode for the first time, Photoshop shows helpful tips for using the filter. If someone else has already closed these messages, you can reshow them by clicking the Reset All Warning Dialogs in the General pane of the Preferences dialog box.

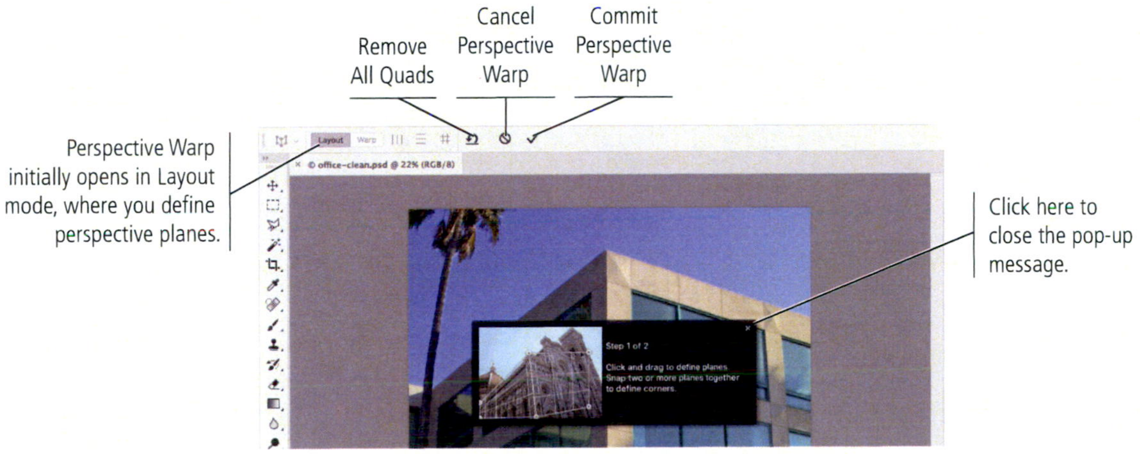

Remove All Quads

Click here to close the pop-up message.

4. **Click anywhere in the document window to create a perspective plane grid.**

   Photoshop's Help materials sometimes refer to perspective planes as quads. We use the term "planes" to maintain consistency throughout our discussion of perspective.

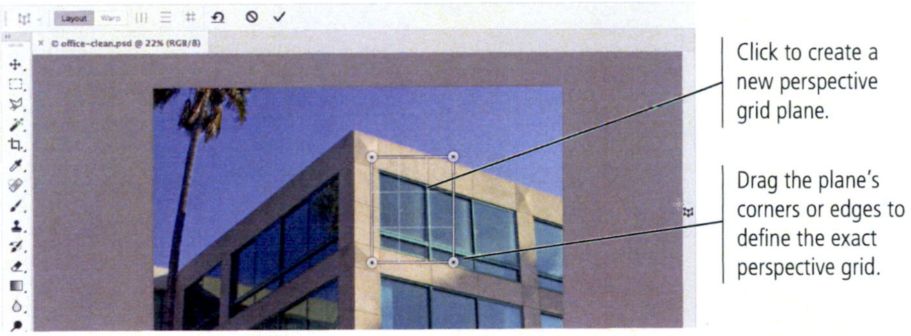

Click to create a new perspective grid plane.
Drag the plane's corners or edges to define the exact perspective grid.

5. **Click and drag the four corners of the perspective plane to match the apparent corners on the right side of the building.**

6. **At the bottom of the image, make sure all visible pieces of the building are included inside the plane grid. (Use the following image as a guide.)**

   Anything outside the grid boundaries will not be transformed when you later warp the perspective grid. To avoid unusual results, you must include the entire bottom edge of the building — including the pillars — inside the perspective warp grid.

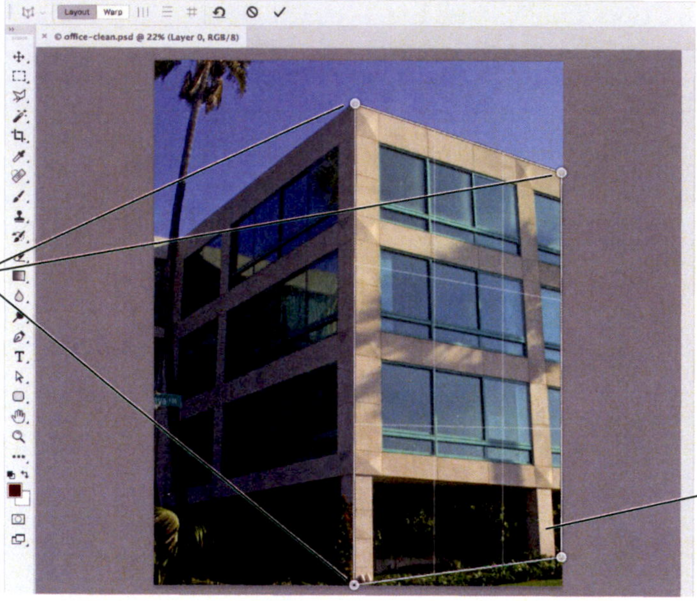
Drag the corners to apparent corners in the image.
Make sure the pillars are inside the defined plane grid.

7. **Click again to create a second perspective plane.**

8. **If you see a pop-up message, read it and then click the Close button to dismiss the message.**

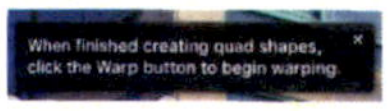

Click again to create a second plane grid.

9. **Click the top-right corner of the second grid. Drag that point up and right until you see a gray line along the left edge of the first plane grid.**

   Photoshop identifies and connects the edges of adjacent planes if you drag one edge near enough to another. The highlight (which might be difficult to see) indicates that releasing the mouse button will automatically connect the two planes along that line; you don't need to drag the bottom-right corner because it automatically snaps into place.

10. **Click and drag the left corners of the second plane to match the apparent corners in the image. Again, use the following image as a guide.**

    We dragged the bottom-left corner to the image's bottom-left corner so that the entire image foreground will be included in the warp. If you exclude any part of the shrubbery or palm tree, your end result could produce some unnaturally twisted vegetation..

11. **In the Options bar, click the Warp button. If you see a pop-up message, read it and then click the Close button to dismiss the message.**

Step 2 of 2
Move warp pins to manipulate perspective.

12. **Click the top-left corner on the left plane grid. Drag left until the vertical lines of the building appear to be truly vertical.**

Use the canvas edge as a guide for an exact 90° vertical line.

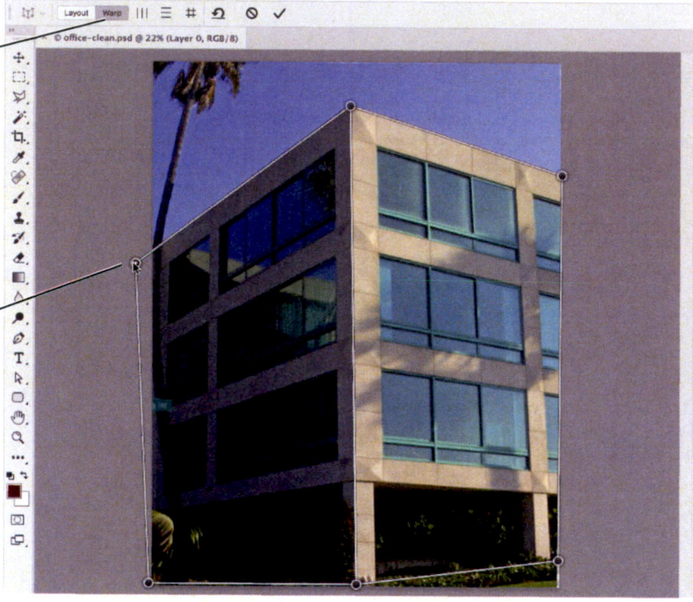
Layout
Warp
office-clean.psd @ 22% (Layer 0, RGB/8)
You are now working in Warp mode.
Drag the top-left grid corner until this line appears to be exactly vertical.

Note:

Three buttons in the Options bar can be used to (from left) automatically straighten near vertical lines; automatically level near horizontal lines; or auto warp to horizontal and vertical.

Layout
Warp

13. **Repeat Step 12 for the top-right corner on the right plane grid.**

You can drag any perspective grid corner to warp the image inside the plane grid.

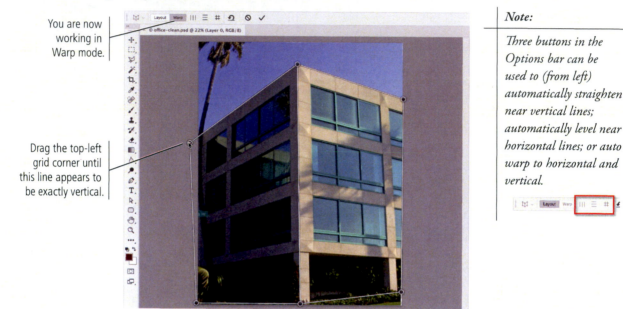

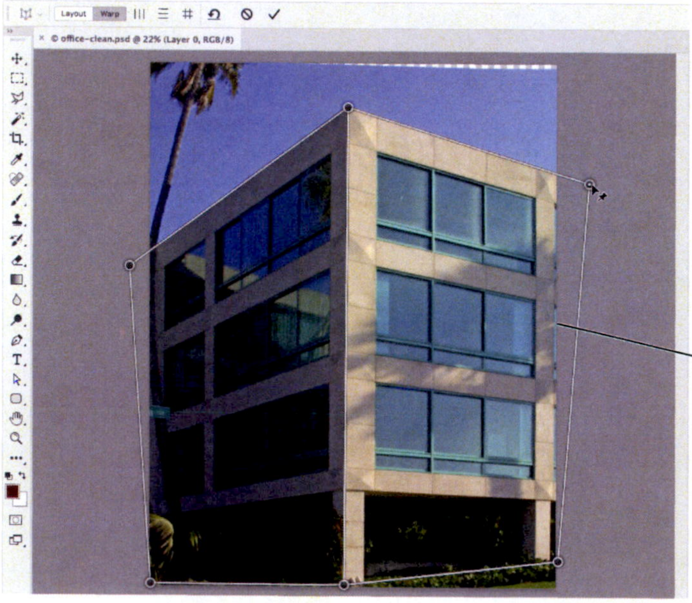
Layout
Warp
office-clean.psd @ 22% (Layer 0, RGB/8)
Drag the top-right grid corner until this line appears to be exactly vertical.

Note:

You can Shift-click an edge of the perspective plane to straighten that edge. The affected edge remains locked at a 90° angle unless you Shift-click the same edge again to unlock it. (Straight edges appear yellow in the document window.) Keep in mind that this action straightens the edge line in the perspective grid, and does not pay any attention to apparent lines in the actual image content.

14. **Click the Commit button in the Options bar (or press Return/Enter) to finalize the warp.**

    The Remove Warp button restore the image and any perspective planes to their original state; Perspective Warp mode remains active so you can readjust the warp. The Cancel Perspective Warp button cancels the entire process and exits Perspective Warp mode.

15. **Choose the Crop tool in the Tools panel. In the Options bar, make sure the Delete Cropped Pixels option is checked.**

16. **Drag down the top-center handle of the crop area until the visible area does not include any transparent pixels.**

    Pay particular attention to the top corners when you crop the image; you don't want any "empty" areas where there should be blue sky.

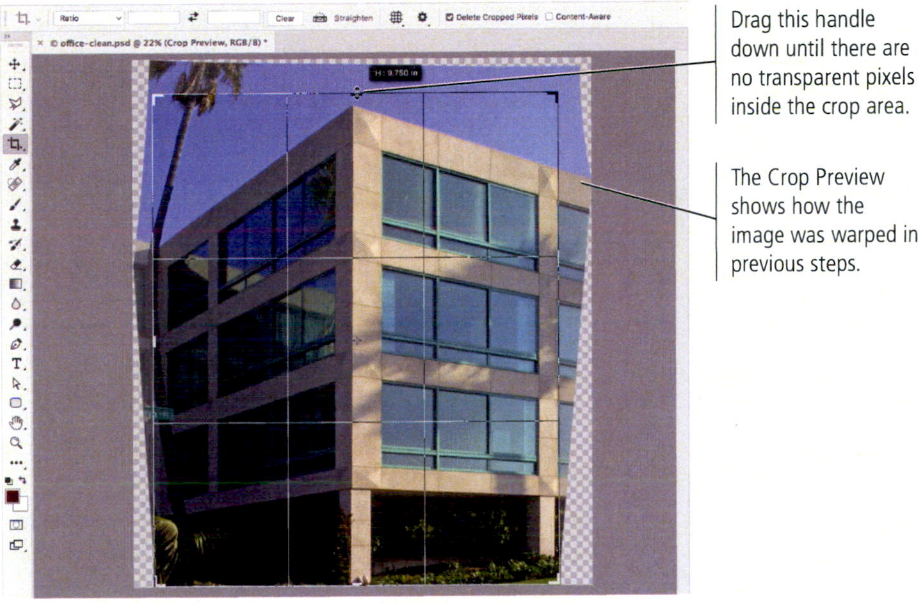
Ratio
Clear
Straighten
Delete Cropped Pixels
Content-Aware
office-clean.psd @ 22% (Crop Preview, RGB/8) *
H: 9.750 in
Drag this handle down until there are no transparent pixels inside the crop area.
The Crop Preview shows how the image was warped in previous steps.

17. **Click the Commit button in the Options bar (or press Return/Enter) to finalize the crop.**

18. **Save the file. Click OK when asked maximize file compatibility.**

19. **Continue to the next exercise.**

Use the Vanishing Point Filter

The studio image used **one-point perspective** — an artistic principle in which all lines in an image ultimately meet at a single invisible vanishing point outside the edges of the image. To effectively merge one image into another, the new image must be adjusted to use the same vanishing point as the original. The Free Transform option is usually enough to combine images in one-point perspective.

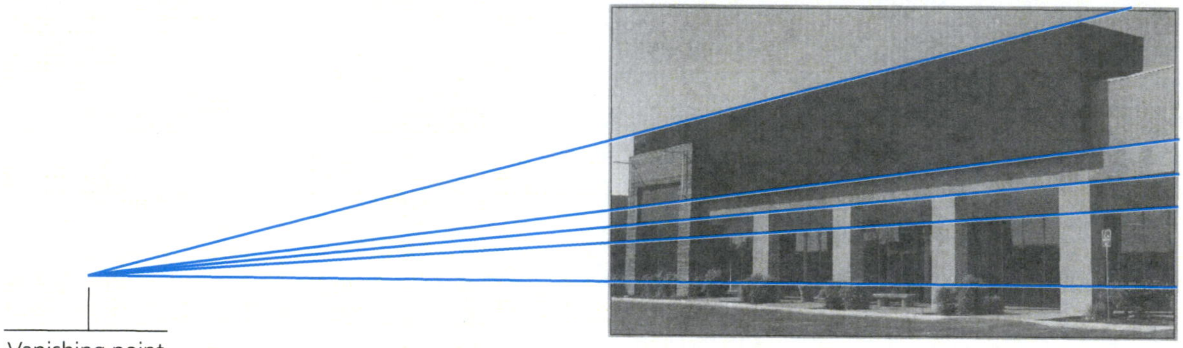

Many images have more than one side (or plane), where lines go off in two different directions. This type of image has **two-point perspective** because there are two different vanishing points. Combining images in two-point perspective (such as wrapping a selection around a corner) is a bit more difficult to manage using the Free Transform option. Fortunately, the Vanishing Point filter makes the process relatively easy — once you understand how it works.

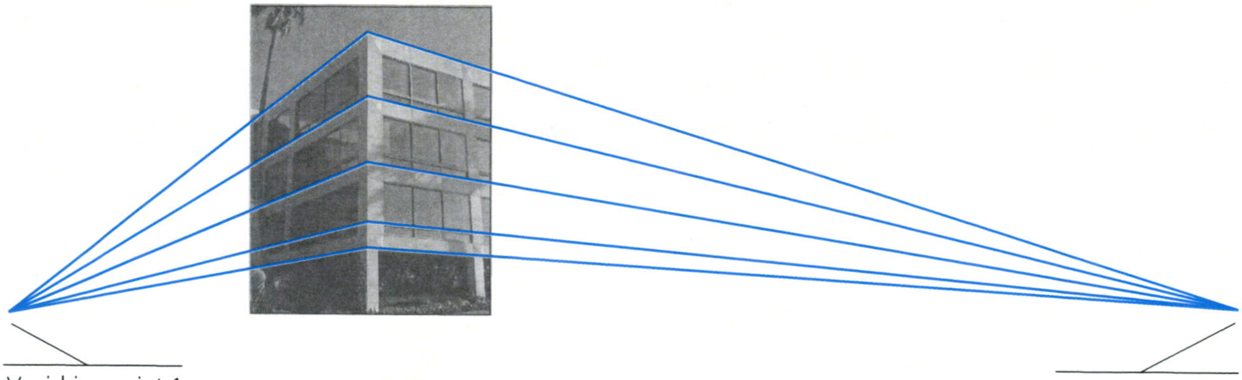

1. **Open the file `banner.tif` from the WIP>Outdoors folder. If you get a warning about mismatched profiles, choose the option to use the embedded profile.**

2. **Select the entire banner file (Command/Control-A) and copy it to the Clipboard.**

   The object that you want to put into perspective — whether from the active file or any other file — needs to be copied before you open the Vanishing Point filter. In this case, you can't place the banner artwork into the office file for the filter to work properly.

Vanishing Point Controls

The **Vanishing Point** dialog box might seem intimidating at first, but it's fairly easy to use once you understand the tools. Most of these tools perform the same functions as in the main Photoshop interface; the Marquee tool, however, is the most notable difference.

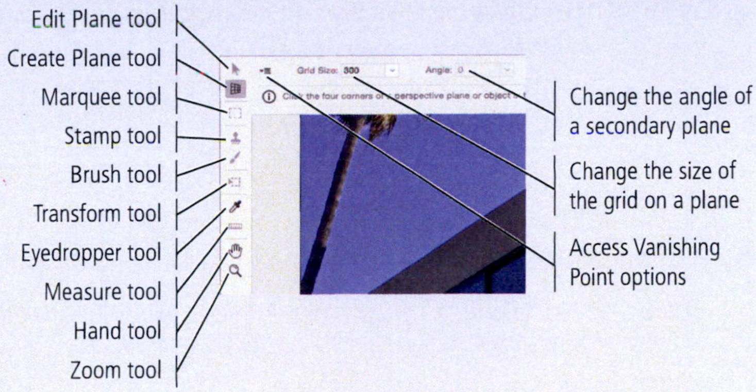

In addition to pasting a selection from the Clipboard, you can use the Marquee tool to make selections within the perspective planes in the Vanishing Point dialog box. Once you've drawn a selection, a number of options become available above the preview.

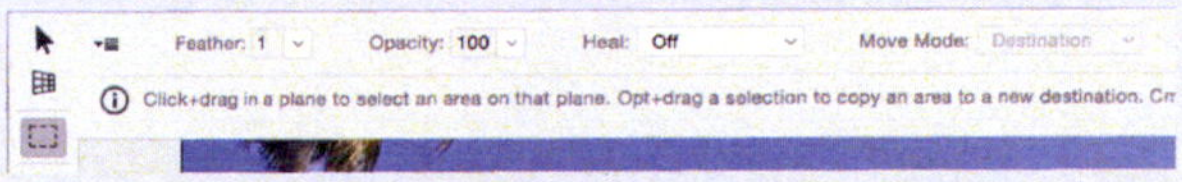

- The **Feather** option defines how many pixels at the selection edges are blurred to help smooth the transition from the copied pixels to the original pixels.
- The **Opacity** option allows you to adjust the opacity of moved pixels, which is useful if you aren't building the filter onto a new layer.
- The **Heal** menu defines the blending mode for moved pixels, which is also useful if you aren't building the filter onto a new layer.
- The **Move Mode** menu is similar to the Patch tool Source and Destination options.
  - If **Destination** is selected, clicking inside a selection marquee and dragging moves the marquee to a new position, maintaining the same perspective defined in the plane. (You can press Command/Control and drag from inside a Destination mode marquee to fill the selection with pixels from another area.)
  - If **Source** is selected, clicking inside a selection marquee and dragging fills the marquee with pixels from the destination area.
- Once you have moved pixels into a selection, you can use the **Transform** tool to rotate or scale the selection, as well as flip it horizontally or vertically using the check boxes that appear over the preview image.

Using the Marquee tool, we defined the original selection to be large enough to fit the entire window.

With the marquee in Destination Move mode, we dragged the marquee to the place we wanted to create a new window. The size of the marquee is altered to match the defined perspective plane.

We then switched to Source Move mode and dragged back over the original selection to create a second window.

3. **Close the banner file.**

4. **With `office-clean.psd` open, add a new empty layer to the file and make sure it is selected in the Layers panel.**

   The results of the Vanishing Point filter will become part of the selected layer. If you don't add a new layer before using the filter, the sample ad will be automatically flattened into the background.

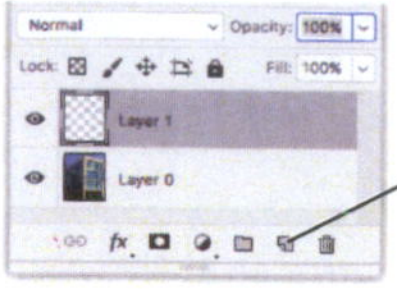

5. **Choose Filter>Vanishing Point.**

   The Vanishing Point filter has its own interface, where you can define the perspective in an image and place other selections onto those planes.

6. **With the Create Plane tool selected (it is by default), set the Grid Size to 300 pixels.**

7. **Click at the top corner where the two sides of the building meet to anchor the plane.**

8. **Release the mouse button and move the cursor to the right. Click again at the edge of the building above the second window.**

   Don't hold down the mouse button (click-and-drag) to create a perspective plane.

9. **Use the lines in the image to draw the rest of the perspective plane (as shown in the following image).**

   The Create Plane tool defines the first perspective plane of the image. When you define the perspective plane, make sure you follow the path of lines in the image so the vanishing point of your plane matches the vanishing point in the image.

   When you define the third corner of the plane, lines automatically connect the first and third points with the mouse cursor. Simply click to anchor the fourth corner point.

10. **With the Edit Plane tool selected, drag the top-, bottom-, and right-center handles in toward the center of the concrete surrounding the first section of windows, so the plane edges are about halfway between the surrounding windows. (Leave the left edge at the building corner.)**

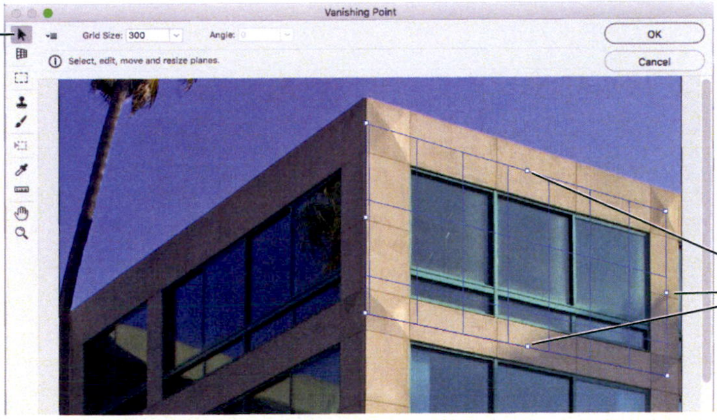
Edit Plane tool
Vanishing Point
Grid Size: 300
Angle:
OK
Cancel
Select, edit, move and resize planes.
Drag the top, right, and bottom handles in toward the center of the concrete blocks surrounding the first bank of windows.

11. **Press Command/Control, click the left-center handle, and then drag left to create a secondary plane that is perpendicular to the first plane.**

    If you click the handle before pressing the Command/Control key, this step won't work. Make sure you press the modifier key before you click and drag the handle.

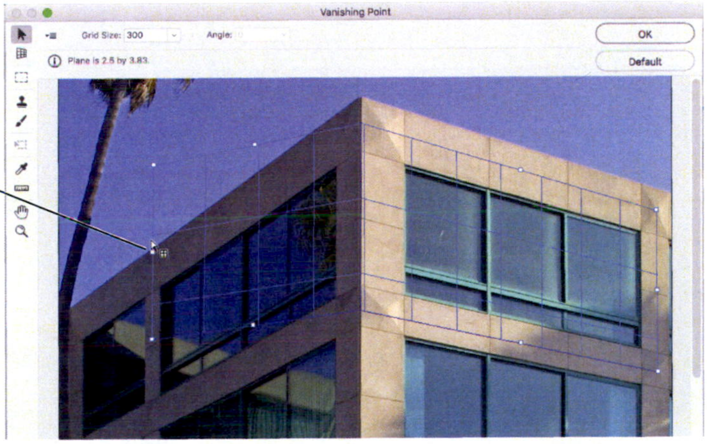
Press Command/Control, and then drag this handle to add a secondary plane.
Vanishing Point
Grid Size: 300
Angle:
OK
Default
Plane is 2.5 by 3.83

12. **Drag the top- and bottom-corner handles on the left side of the secondary plane until the plane more closely matches the perspective of lines on the left face of the building.**

Drag these handles up or down to adjust the perspective of the secondary plane.
Vanishing Point
Grid Size: 300
Angle: 270
OK
Cancel
Select, edit, move and resize planes.

13. **Press Command/Control-V to paste the copied pixels from the Clipboard (the banner file that you copied in Step 2).**

The pasted pixels appear in the top-left corner of the preview, surrounded by a selection marquee.

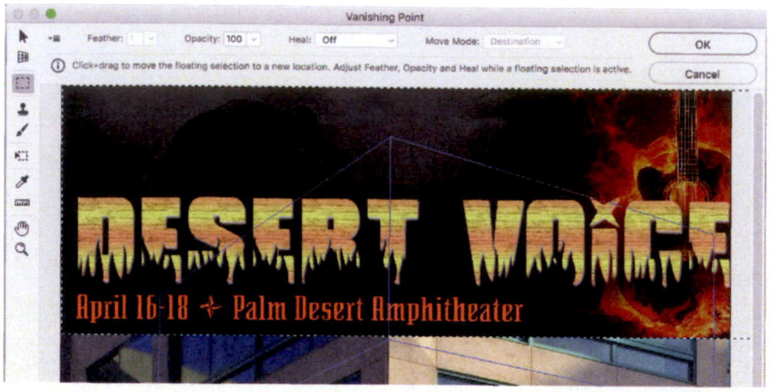

14. **Click inside the selection marquee and drag onto any part of the perspective plane. Drag the selection until the top-left corner of the ad matches the top-left corner of the plane.**

The selection is dropped into the perspective plane, cleanly wrapped around both sides of the building.

15. **Select the Transform tool in the left side of the Vanishing Point filter dialog box.**

16. **Open the Settings and Commands for Vanishing Point menu. Turn off the Clip Operations to Surface Edges option (it should be unchecked).**

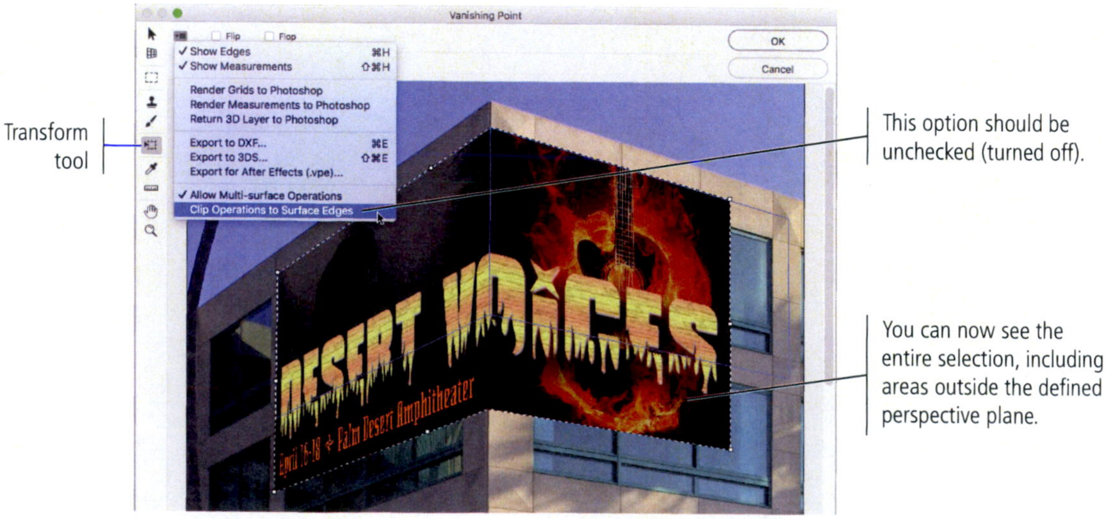

17. **Drag the bottom-right handles of the selection until all of the banner fits within the defined plane edge.**

The perspective planes still produce a very good result, even though you are scaling out of proportion to fit the banner within the allowed space.

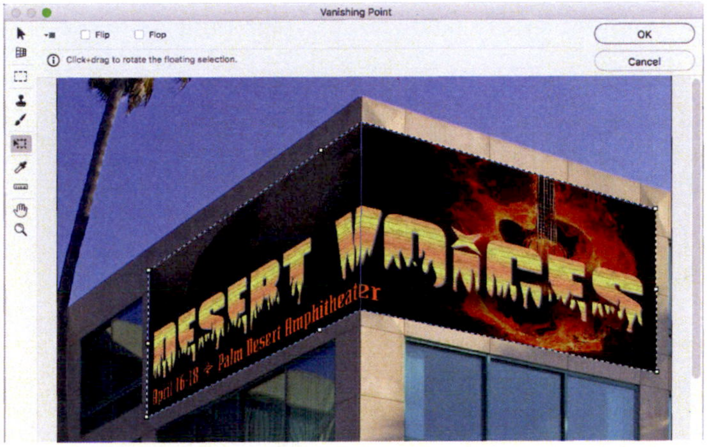

18. **Reactivate the Clip Operations to Surface Edges option, and then click OK to apply the Vanishing Point filter.**

19. **Apply a drop shadow using the following settings:**

Blend mode:	**Multiply Black**	**Distance:**	**5**
Opacity:	**75%**	**Spread:**	**0**
Angle:	**40°**	**Size:**	**10**

Note:

The 40° angle helps match the drop shadow angle to the apparent light source in the office image.

20. **Save the file as a native Photoshop file named office-ad.psd in your WIP>Outdoors folder. Click OK if asked to maximize compatibility.**

21. **Close the file, and then continue to the next exercise.**

Warp the Sample Ad

Linear perspective, such as the two examples you just created, is fairly easy to adjust (especially using the Vanishing Point filter). However, the world is not entirely linear; objects with curves also have depth and perspective. Compositing onto rounded objects is slightly more complicated than linear perspective, but you can accomplish the task with patience and attention to detail.

1. **Open the file `tanks-clean.psd` from your WIP>Outdoors folder.**

2. **Place the banner.tif file as an embedded Smart Object layer into the tanks file.**

3. **Scale the placed ad to 35% and position it in the center of the front water tank (above the top of the fence).**

4. **With the banner layer selected, choose Edit>Transform>Warp.**

   When you warp anything other than text, you have more options and better control over the warp.

Cancel Transform

Commit Transform

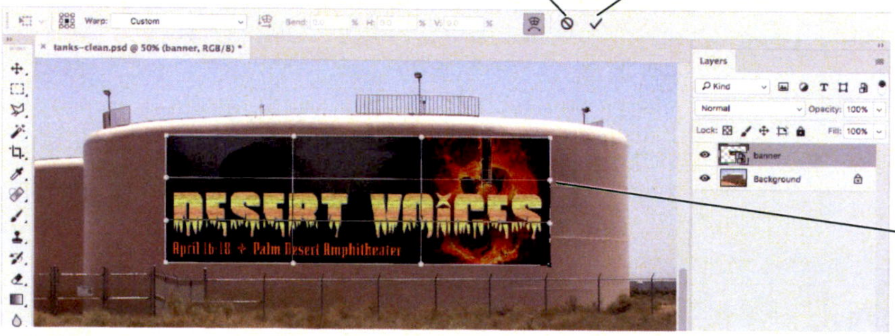

When warping anything other than text, a grid and handles appear for controlling the warp.

5. **In the Options bar, choose Arc Upper from the Warp menu.**

   As for warping text, the same predefined warp options are available for warping an object.

   The background image — the water tank — is only slightly curved. A minor Arc Upper warp should be enough to add perspective to the ad layer.

The default Bend value (50%) is obviously too much for compositing these two images.

6. **Experiment with Bend values until you're satisfied with the result. (We used a 5% bend.)**

   The Bend value changes only the edges affected by the warp you apply; in the case of Arc Upper, only the top edge changes when you modify the Bend value.

7. **In the Options bar, click the Commit button to finalize the transformation (or press Return/Enter).**

8. **Apply a drop shadow to the layer using the following settings:**

Blend mode:	**Multiply Black**	**Distance:**	**2**
Opacity:	**75%**	**Spread:**	**0**
Angle:	**90°**	**Size:**	**5**

Note:

The 90° angle helps match the drop shadow angle to the apparent light source in the tanks image.

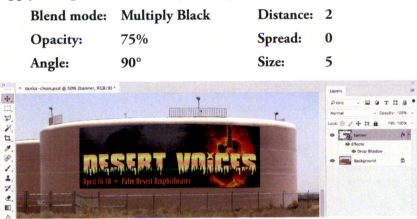

9. **Save the file as a native Photoshop file named tanks-ad.psd in your WIP>Outdoors folder. Click OK when asked to maximize compatibility.**

10. **Close the file, then continue to the next exercise.**

Apply a Custom Warp

In some cases, the predefined warp styles are adequate. In other cases — such as warping the ad around the balloon in this exercise — the existing styles do not work. In these cases, Photoshop provides a powerful toolset for defining custom warp shapes.

1. **Open the file balloon-clean.psd from your WIP>Outdoors folder.**
2. **Place the banner.tif file into the balloon file as an embedded Smart Object.**
3. **Scale the banner layer to 40% proportionally and position it as shown in the following image:**

4. **Choose Edit>Transform>Warp. Apply the Arch warp to the ad layer with a 12% bend.**
5. **If necessary, drag the layer (still in Warp Transform mode) so the banner appears within the white area (as shown here).**

   As you can see, this warp shape is flat; it does not reflect the roundness of the balloon.

6. **Choose Custom in the Warp menu on the Options bar.**

   Anchor points (and their attached handles) are now visible at the corners of the warped shape; you can move these points and handles to adjust the exact shape of the warp to better align it to the balloon's shape.

These handles control the warp curves between points on the grid.

7. **Drag the corner points on the left side of the warp grid to be directly inside the second seam line on the balloon.**

8. **Drag the handles on the left side of the grid to bloat the left edge of the ad layer.**

   Handles on a warp grid are just like handles on a vector path (created with the Pen tool). Curves follow the direction in which you drag the connected handles.

9. **Repeat Steps 7–8 for the right side of the ad.**

10. **Adjust the top and bottom handles to fit the edges vertically within the area between the color patches.**

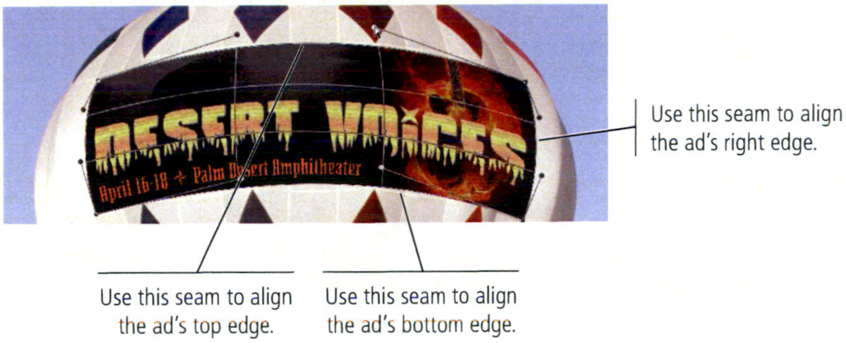

11. **Press Return/Enter to finalize the transformation, and then apply a drop shadow using the following settings:**

Blend mode:	**Multiply Black**	**Distance:**	**3**
Opacity:	**75%**	**Spread:**	**0**
Angle:	**120°**	**Size:**	**5**

12. **Save the file as a native Photoshop file named balloon-ad.psd in your WIP>Outdoors folder. Click OK when asked to maximize compatibility.**

13. **Close the file, then continue to the next stage of the project.**

Note:

The 120° angle helps match the drop shadow angle to the apparent light source in the balloon image.

Stage 3 Working with Lighting

Photoshop provides extremely powerful tools for creating one composite image from a number of separate components. Although the tools and techniques for doing this type of work are fairly mechanical, some degree of human judgment is required to ensure the separate pieces blend together seamlessly.

In extreme cases of mismatched lighting, a composited image might contain both one person in a photo squinting into the bright sunlight and everyone else in cooler shadows. Of course, not all lighting problems are this obvious, but even subtle differences can make good technical composites appear "off" to even the casual observer. Whenever you composite images, you need to be careful that the lighting is consistent across the entire composition.

The lighting in the original photo is evenly lighting the surface, so the composited ad is fine as is.

The shadows on this side of the building should also affect the composited ad.

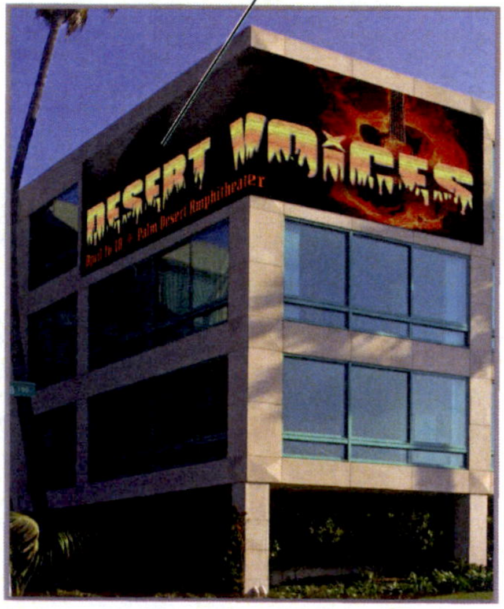

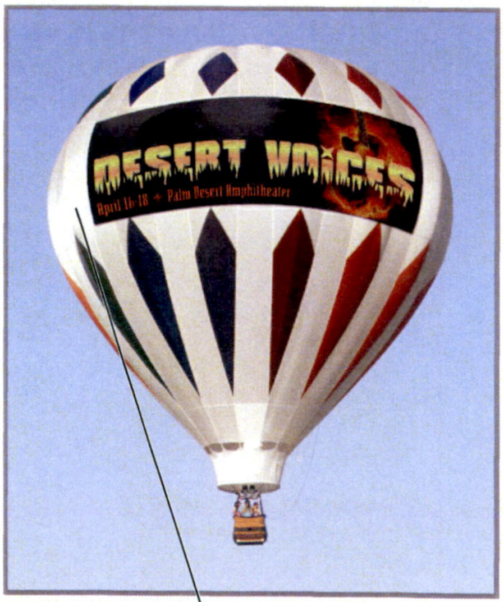

The bright sun glare on this spot of the balloon should also affect the composited ad.

This ad is too bright for the apparent position of the sun (directly overhead).

The **Lighting Effects** filter allows you to create different lighting effects in RGB images. The filter opens a separate gallery-like interface, with only the tools you need to apply lighting effects:

- **Options bar** for adding light sources, controlling the overall preview, and cancelling or finalizing the filter.
- **Preview area**, which includes widgets for all applied light sources.
- **Properties panel**, which defines a number of settings for the selected light.
- **Lights panel**, which lists all light sources that exist on the current layer.

The Lighting Effects filter supports three basic types of light sources. The appearance of different light widgets indicates the way each type casts light:

- **Point lights** shine in all directions, such as light that shines from a light bulb.
- **Spot lights** cast an elliptical beam of light, such as the beam from a flashlight.
- **Infinite lights** shine in a single direction from a far distance, such as the sun.

You can select a specific light by clicking in the Lights panel, or simply clicking the related light's widget in the preview area. When a specific light is selected in the preview area, you can use the on-screen controls to change various properties of the selected light.

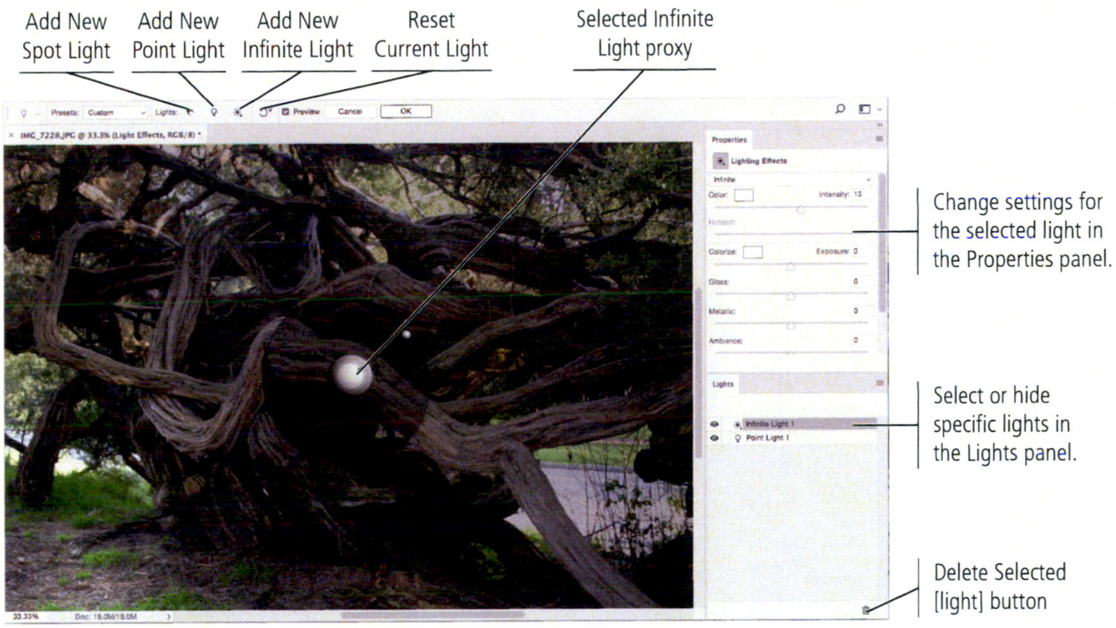

In addition to the options that you can change with the on-screen widgets, you can define a number of other light settings in the Properties panel.

- Clicking the **Color** swatch opens the Color Picker dialog box, where you can define a specific color for the selected light source.
- **Exposure** decreases or increases the lighting effect.
- **Gloss** simulates the effect of different photographic finishes, from low (matte) to high reflectance (gloss).
- **Metallic** determines the metallic or reflective quality of the light.
- **Ambience** adds the effect of a second diffuse light source that evenly affects the entire image. You can define the color of ambient light by clicking the **Colorize** swatch.
- **Texture** defines a specific channel to use as a texture map, which is a method for creating the appearance of texture in an image based on tones in the selected channel. When a channel is selected, the **Height** field increases or decreases the bumpiness of the resulting texture.

Apply a Point Lighting Effect

Point light shines in all directions from a single source point. This is a good option when you want to place a highlight point and blend the shadow away from that spot — as in the case of the balloon ad.

1. **Open the Performance pane of the Preferences dialog box. Make sure the Use Graphics Processor option is checked and click OK.**

   If this option is not available (grayed out) on your computer, your video card and/or driver does not support OpenGL. If you cannot use OpenGL, you will not be able to use the Lighting Effects filter.

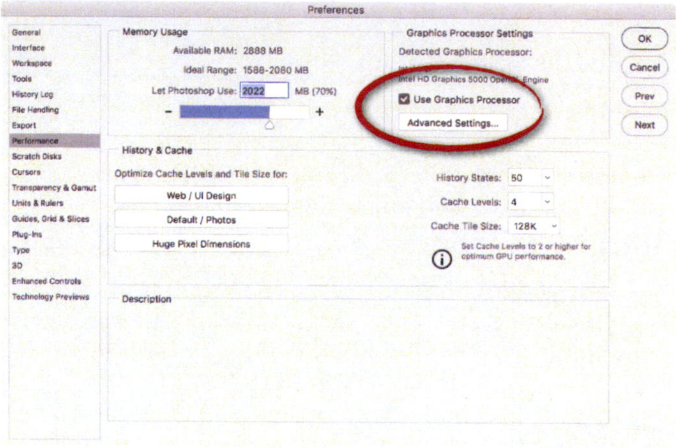

2. **Open balloon-ad.psd from your WIP>Outdoors folder.**

3. **With the banner layer selected in the Layers panel, choose Filter>Render> Lighting Effects.**

4. **In the Options bar, choose Default from the Preset menu.**

   Photoshop includes a number of default lighting styles, which you can apply to any image. The default light source is a single spot light.

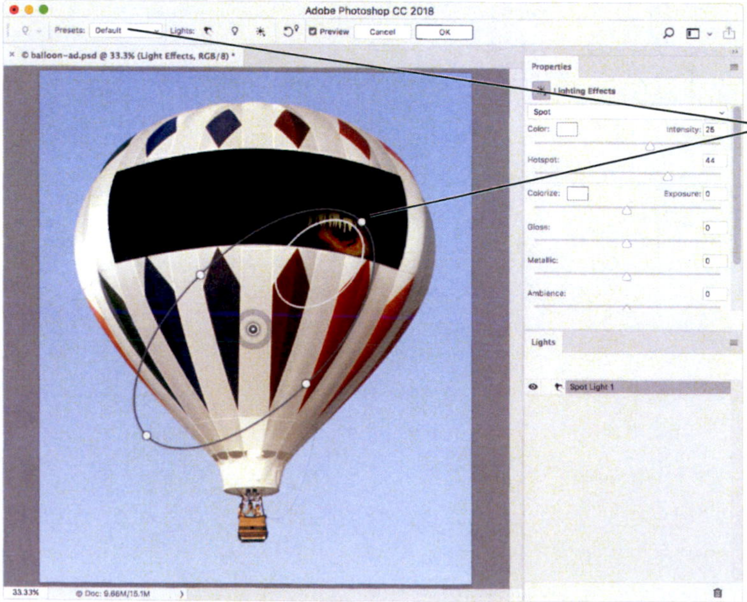

The Default light source is a single spot light in the center of the image.

> *Note:*
>
> *You can also save your own lighting styles by clicking Save in the Preset menu; all defined light sources (and their properties) will be saved in the style, so you can call it again later for another image.*

5. **With the only light selected in the Lights panel, choose Point in the menu at the top of the Properties panel.**

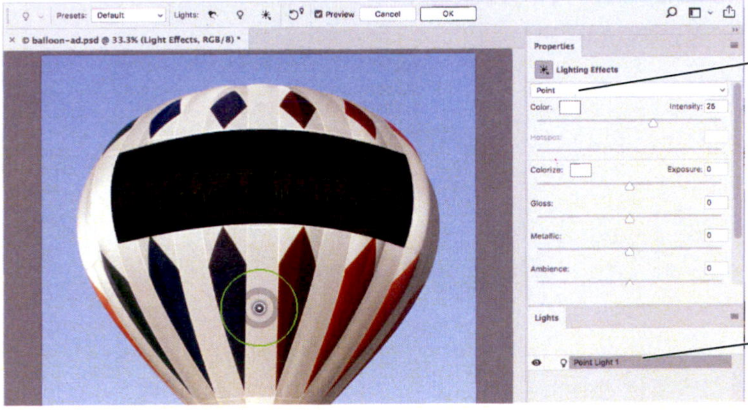

Use this menu to change the type of the selected light.

Click an item in this panel to select a specific light source.

6. **Place the cursor over the center point of the light widget. When the cursor feedback shows "Move", click and drag the light to the left center of the banner.**

   For a point light, you can simply drag the center point to reposition the light's position.

   Unfortunately, at the time of this writing, the HUD controls do not dynamically move while you are dragging. When you release the mouse button, the light widget appears at the point where you dragged to.

Cursor feedback shows what you can do with different parts of the light widget.

Click the center point of a Point light to move it.

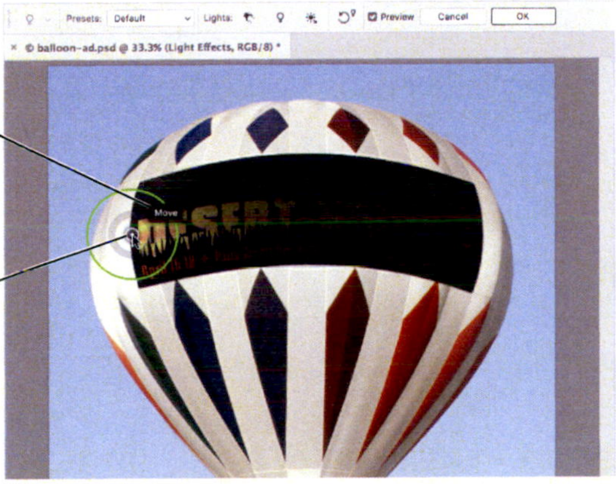

7. **Move the mouse cursor over the green line that surrounds the point light source. When the cursor feedback shows "Scale," click and drag out to enlarge the light source.**

   Again, the HUD scale control does not dynamically move while you are dragging.

The Scale control turns yellow when it is being changed.

8. **In the Options bar, click the button to add a new Point light.**

9. **In the Lights panel, make sure only the Point Light 2 is selected.**

   Both lights might remain selected when you add a new one. Simply click the Point Light 2 item in the list to select only that light.

10. **In the preview area, move the second point light to the bottom-center of the banner.**

11. **Move the cursor to the heavy black circle around the light point. When the cursor feedback shows "Intensity," click and drag left until the heads-up display (HUD) shows Intensity: 10.**

    Intensity determines how bright the light appears; full intensity (100) is the brightest light, while negative values (down to –100) remove light.

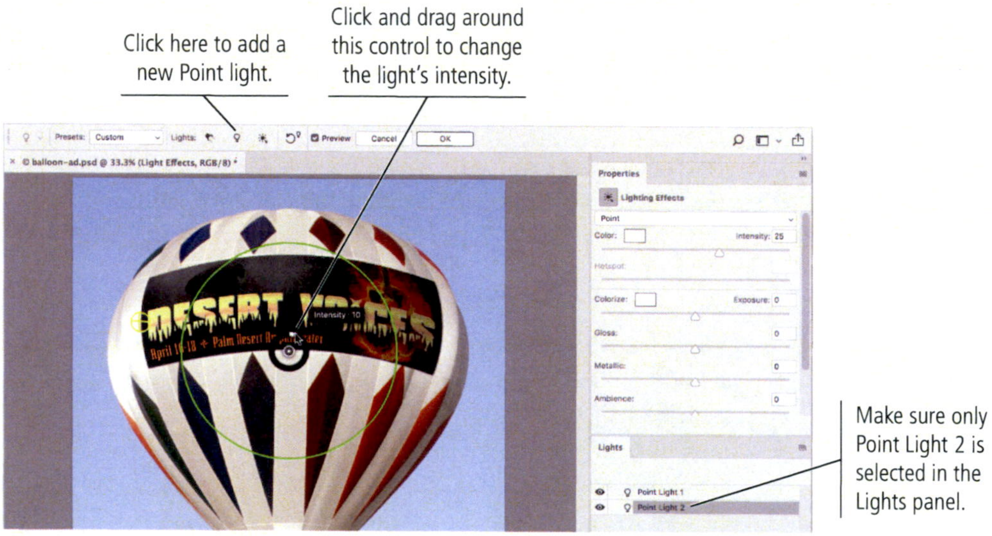

Click here to add a new Point light.
Click and drag around this control to change the light's intensity.
Make sure only Point Light 2 is selected in the Lights panel.

12. **In the Options bar, toggle the Preview checkbox off and then back on.**

    When you turn off the preview, you toggle the visibility of all lights at once. You can also use the Lights panel to turn individual lights off and on.

    The change is subtle, but you should be able to see how the two light sources change the banner to more realistically match the lighting that exists in the balloon photo.

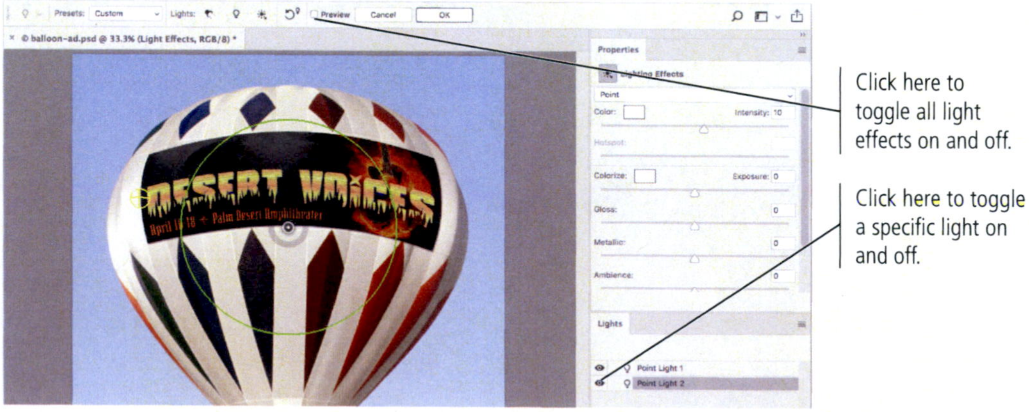

Click here to toggle all light effects on and off.
Click here to toggle a specific light on and off.

13. **Click OK in the Options bar to apply the lighting effect.**

    In the Layers panel, you can see that the Lighting Effects have been applied as a Smart Filter. You can turn the effect off or on using the eye icon, or double-click the Lighting Effects item in the panel to reopen the filter interface and change the applied lighting.

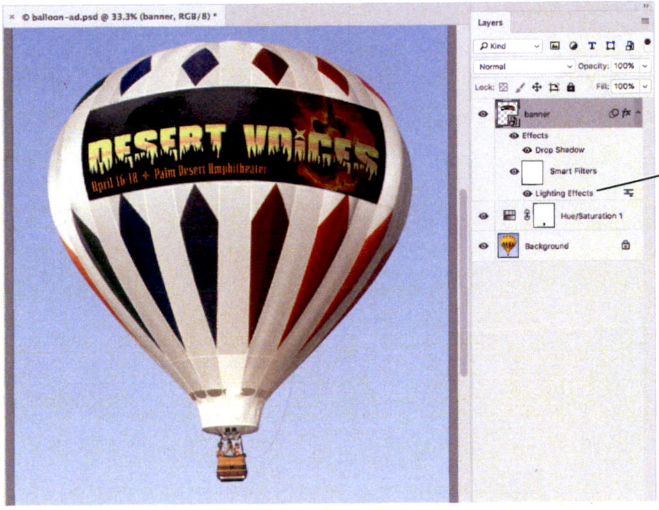

Lighting Effects are applied as a Smart Filter.

14. **Save the file as a native Photoshop file named balloon-final.psd in your WIP>Outdoors folder. Click OK when asked to maximize compatibility.**

15. **Close the file and continue to the next exercise.**

Apply an Infinite Light Lighting Effect

The light in the water tank photo is striking the top of the tanks; without adjusting the lighting that affects the banner ad, it seems unnaturally bright. To correct this problem, you are going to use the Lighting Effects filter to position the "sun" that is striking the banner layer from the correct position.

1. **Open the file tanks-ad.psd from your WIP>Outdoors folder.**

2. **Make sure the banner layer is selected in the Layers panel, then choose Filter>Render>Lighting Effects.**

    The Lighting Effects filter defaults to the last-used settings. If you continued directly from the previous exercise, your layer has two Point lights.

3. **In the Options bar, make sure the Preview option is checked.**

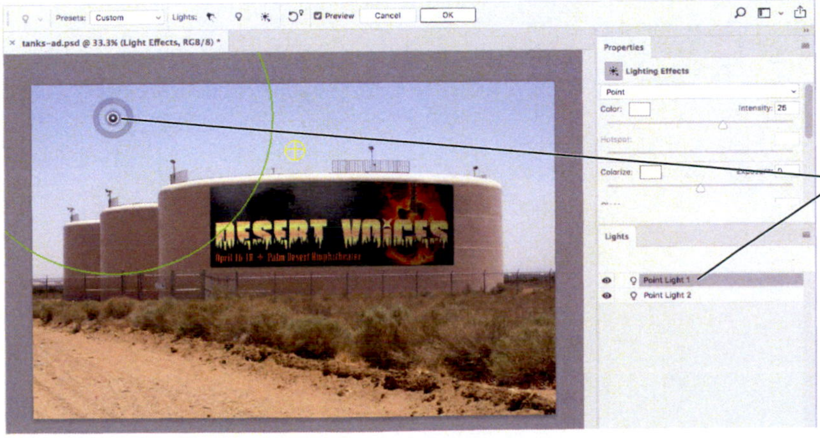

When you open the Lighting Effects filter, the last-applied lights are still in place.

4. **In the Lights panel, click the Point Light 2 and then click the panel's Delete button.**

   You can delete all but one light source from a layer.

5. **With Point Light 1 selected in the Lights panel, choose Infinite from the menu at the top of the Properties panel.**

   Infinite light shines from far away, so the overall light angle remains the same throughout an image. The widget in the preview area identifies the position of the light.

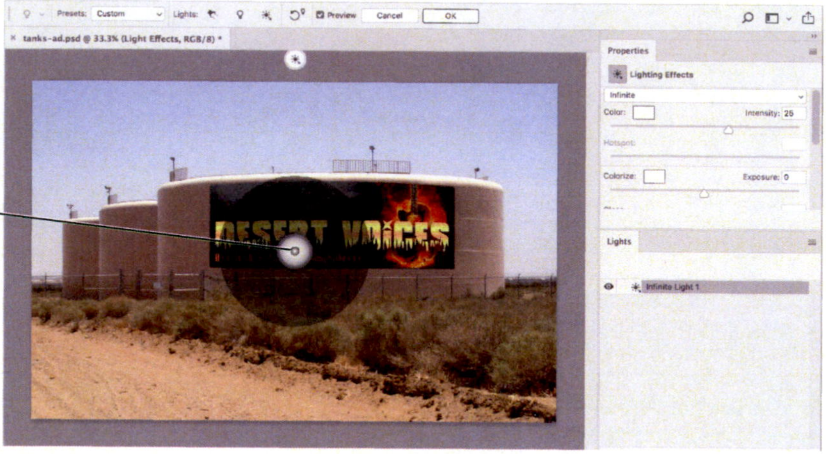

An Infinite light defaults to shine from directly in front of the image.

6. **Click the light source handle and drag up to rotate the light source.**

   By dragging the light's handle, you are directing the angle of the infinite light — think of positioning the sun relative to the photo. You have to try to think in three dimensions when you reposition an infinite light; use the open hemisphere as a guide.

7. **Move the cursor over the Intensity control, then click and drag to change the light's intensity to 30.**

   You can see that the infinite light actually darkens the banner layer — which is what you need to make the two layers blend together into a more natural composite.

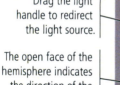

Drag the light handle to redirect the light source.

The open face of the hemisphere indicates the direction of the light source.

Drag around the Intensity widget to change the light's intensity.

8. **Click OK in the Options bar to apply the filter.**

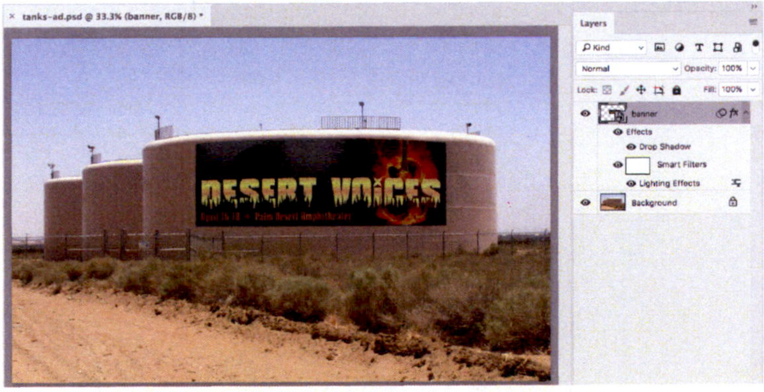

9. **Save the file as a native Photoshop file named tanks-final.psd in your WIP>Outdoors folder. Click OK when asked to maximize compatibility.**

10. **Close the file, then continue to the next exercise.**

Apply a Spot Light Lighting Effect

Spot lights cast an elliptical beam of light from a specific direction. This type of light is a good choice for lighting the right half of the office building ad, while leaving the left half of the ad in shadow.

1. **Open the file office-ad.psd from your WIP>Outdoors folder.**

2. **Make sure Layer 1 is selected in the Layers panel and choose Filter>Render>Lighting Effects.**

   Remember, you didn't place the banner into this file; instead, you pasted the banner into the Vanishing Point filter. In this file, the banner exists on Layer 1.

3. **With the existing light selected in the Lights panel, choose Spot in the menu at the top of the Properties panel.**

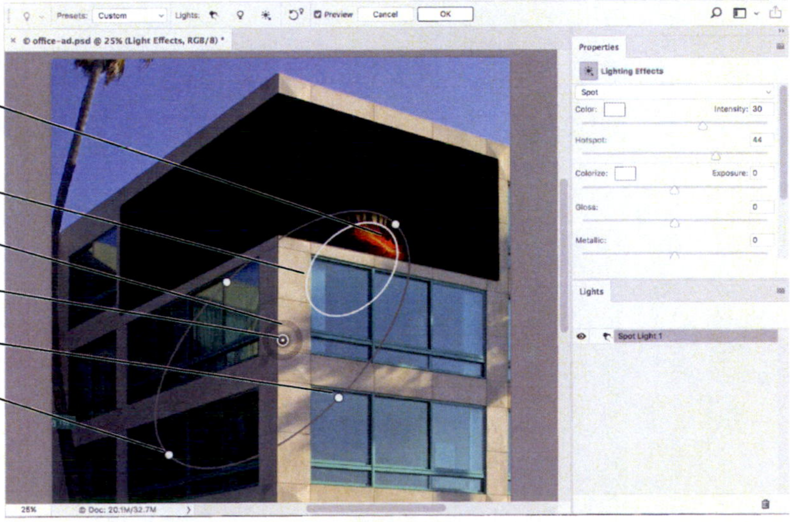

4. **Move the cursor outside the darker gray line. When you see "Rotate" in the cursor feedback, click and drag until the light is approximately horizontal.**

   If you click outside the darker (outside) gray line, you can rotate the light. You can also use the handles on that line to scale the width and length of the light.

   The lighter (inside) gray line defines the hotspot angle of the light.

Click anywhere outside this line to rotate the light.

5. **Click the Move control of the light widget and drag to the corner of the building, near the bottom of the banner area.**

   As with a point light, you can easily reposition the light by dragging the center point in the widget control.

Click the Move control and drag to position the center point of the lighting effect.

6. **Click the right Scale Width handle and drag out past the edge of the canvas.**

Click the handle on either end of the oval to change the scale width.

7. **Click the top Scale Length handle and drag up to the top edge of the canvas.**

Click the handle on either side of the oval to change the scale length.

8. **Click the Intensity control and drag to change the Intensity to 40.**

   The light striking the right side of the building is relatively bright, so you are increasing the banner's light intensity to more closely match.

Click and drag this control to change the light's intensity.

9. **Click the Hotspot Angle control and drag until the left edge of the hotspot angle is past the building corner.**

   Changing the hotspot angle increases the area that is affected by the light. Again, think of holding a flashlight — if you shine it directly at your feet, the spot is a small circle; if you shine it farther away, the beam becomes more elliptical and illuminates a larger area.

   Extending the hotspot angle extends the light to the left side of the ad — artificially, but it helps to meet both goals of highlighting your company's capabilities and making the two separate layers blend more naturally together.

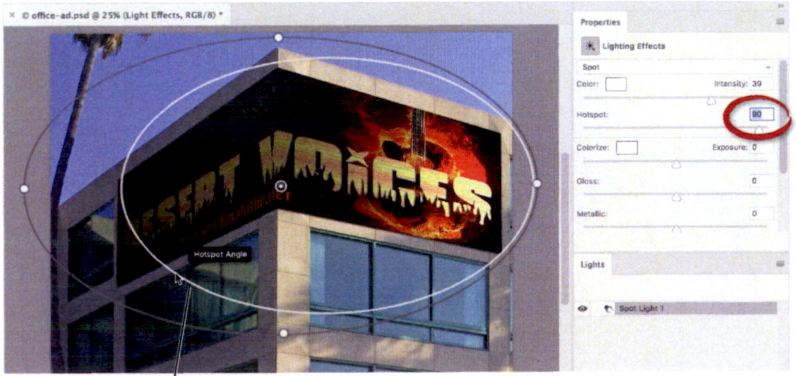

Click and drag this line to extend the light's hotspot.

Note:

Some users report difficulty selecting the hotspot angle line in the on-screen widget. If that is the case, you can use the Hotspot slider/field in the Properties panel to adjust the hotspot angle.

11. **Click OK in the Options bar to apply the lighting effect.**

    Because the layer containing the banner image is a regular layer and not a Smart Object layer, the lighting effect is not applied as a smart filter. It is applied destructively, which means you cannot edit the applied settings.

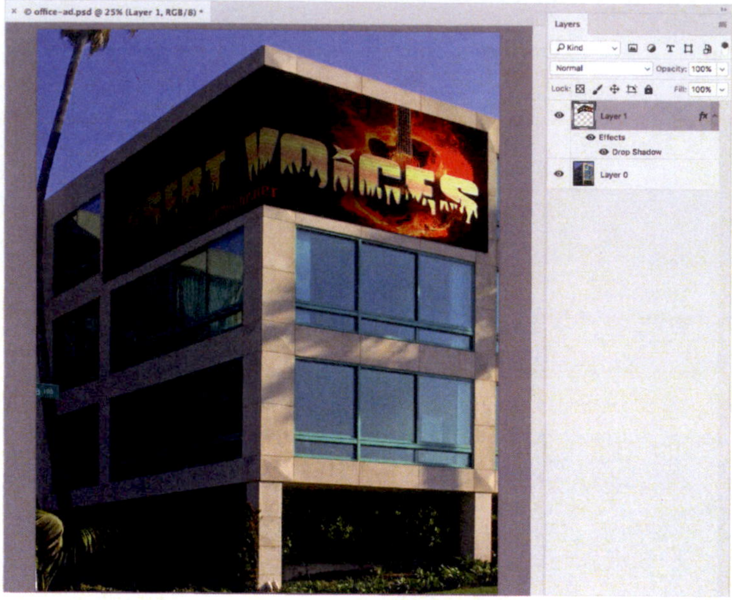

12. **Save the file as a native Photoshop file named** **office-final.psd** **in your WIP>Outdoors folder. Click OK when asked to maximize compatibility.**

13. **Close the file.**

The Rendering Filters

The **Clouds** filter (Filters>Render>Clouds) fills the currently selected layer with a random cloud-like pattern that varies between the foreground and background colors. The **Difference Clouds** filter (Filters>Render>Difference Clouds) does the same thing but returns a cloud pattern that looks as though it were affected by the Difference blending mode. Because these filters replace the content of the current layer, they are best applied on a separate layer that you can mask and blend to create the look you want.

The Clouds filter is applied to a separate layer behind the masked foreground layer. The clouds are a mixture of the defined foreground and background colors.

The Difference Clouds filter is applied to the same layer. The resulting colors are the effect of the Difference blending mode applied to the foreground and background colors.

The **Fibers** filter (Filters>Render>Fibers) fills the currently selected layer with a pattern that looks like woven fibers of the foreground and background colors. The Variance option controls how the colors vary (a low value produces long streaks of color, and a high value results in very short fibers). The Strength option controls how each fiber looks; low strength produces a loose weave, and high strength produces a tighter weave. The Randomize button changes the pattern randomly; you can keep clicking the button to generate new patterns until you find one that you like.

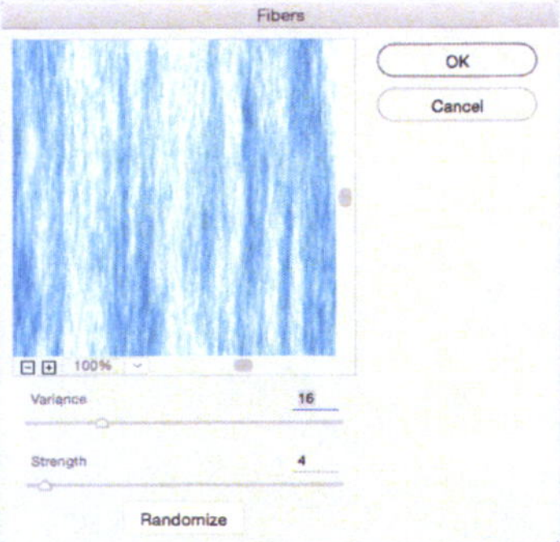

The **Lens Flare** filter (Filters> Render>Lens Flare) simulates the refraction caused by shining a bright light into a camera lens. You can drag the crosshair in the small preview image to change the position of the flare center, change the brightness of the flare, and define the type of lens to simulate.

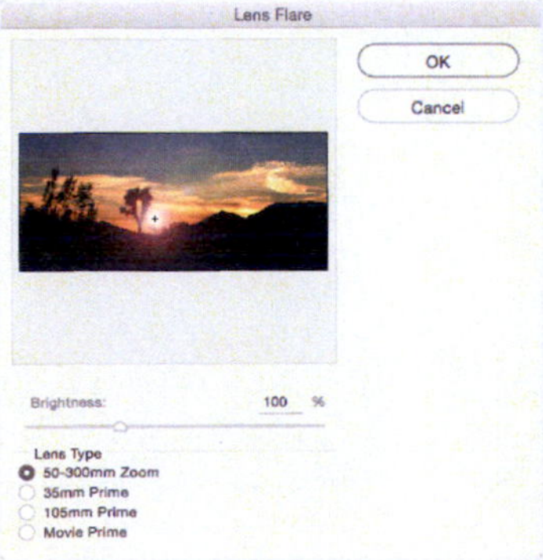

Project Review

fill in the blank

1. When using the Patch tool, choose the ______________ option to select an area that will be copied to another area (where you drag the marquee).

2. The ______________ adjustment allows you to change the ink values in specific primary colors or neutrals without affecting other colors.

3. The ______________ adjustment allows you to change the Hue, Saturation, and Lightness values of specific primary colors.

4. The ______________ tool attempts to simplify replacement of specific colors in your image; you can paint over a targeted color to replace it with the foreground color.

5. The ______________ tool mimics a process used in traditional photo development, and is used to lighten an area of a photograph.

6. In ______________ perspective, all lines in an image move toward a single spot on the horizon.

7. The ______________ provides an easy interface for transforming layer content onto a perspective plane.

8. The ______________ transformation can be used to distort a flat rectangular object into a custom shape, such as around the side of a balloon.

9. A(n) ______________ light source casts an elliptical beam of light, such as the beam from a flashlight.

10. A(n) ______________ light source shines light in all directions from directly above the image.

short answer

1. Briefly explain the advantages to using adjustment layers rather than applying adjustments to regular layers from the Image>Adjustments menu.

2. Briefly explain the concept of a vanishing point.

3. Briefly explain the three types of lighting that can be created using the Lighting Effects filter.

Portfolio Builder Project

Use what you learned in this project to complete the following freeform exercise.
Carefully read the art director and client comments, then create your own design to meet the needs of the project.
Use the space below to sketch ideas; when finished, write a brief explanation of your reasoning behind your final design.

art director comments

Your company's sales manager has another potential client for the Advertise Anywhere! program, and would like to build a personalized presentation similar to the one you did for the Nighttime News show.

To complete this project, you should:

- ❑ Build a sample ad for the Go Green clean energy initiative.
- ❑ Find background images on which you can composite the sample ad.
- ❑ Clean up or adjust the background images as necessary to create the best possible samples.
- ❑ Composite the sample ad onto the different backgrounds; adjust perspective and lighting as necessary to make the samples appear as natural as possible.

client comments

The director of the Go Green clean energy initiative saw the Nighttime News ads that we placed around the city, and called the show's marketing director to find out where they were created. I just got off the phone with her, and we have a meeting scheduled next week to present some ideas for advertising the Go Green campaign.

I need you to create a sample ad at the same size as the news show sample. It should include imagery that supports the idea of clean energy — hydroelectricity, windmills, or whatever. The only text for the ad should be the words 'Go Green!' and the website address (www.ggenergy.org).

For the background images, find a variety of different types of images. Methods of public transportation, buildings, and large outdoor signs are all good options, but we also want to highlight the 'anywhere' part of Advertise Anywhere! services. Get creative with these sample backgrounds — think up unusual locations where ads might be seen by large numbers of people.

project justification

Project Summary

Compositing images such as the ones in this project is part skill (applying necessary corrections), part judgment (determining the perspective and light source in the background images), and part experimentation (exploring the transformation and filter options to find the best possible solution to the specific problem). Being able to manipulate images — including the correction and transformation tools you used to create these samples — will be invaluable during your graphic design career.

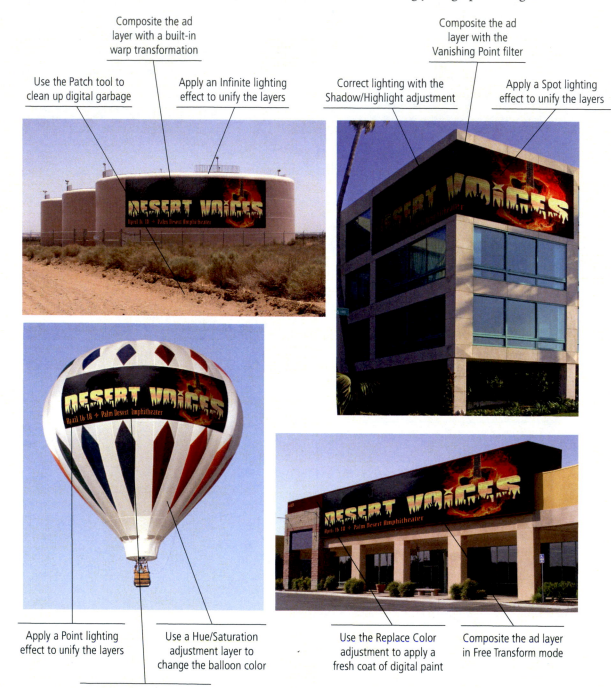

Composite the ad layer with a built-in warp transformation
Use the Patch tool to clean up digital garbage
Apply an Infinite lighting effect to unify the layers
Composite the ad layer with the Vanishing Point filter
Correct lighting with the Shadow/Highlight adjustment
Apply a Spot lighting effect to unify the layers
DESERT VOICES
Apply a Point lighting effect to unify the layers
Use a Hue/Saturation adjustment layer to change the balloon color
Composite the ad layer with a custom warp transformation
Use the Replace Color adjustment to apply a fresh coat of digital paint
Composite the ad layer in Free Transform mode

project 7

House Painting

Your client, a real estate developer, is planning a new pre-sales campaign for the company's latest master plan community. He has line-art sketches of the completed houses, but he wants color "paintings" to show prospective buyers what the finished houses might look like. You were hired to create a full-color digital rendering based on one of the artist's black-and-white sketches.

This project incorporates the following skills:

- ❑ Converting an image from bitmap to RGB color mode
- ❑ Loading a custom swatch panel to access approved colors
- ❑ Using fill and stroke techniques to create the basic shapes in the artwork
- ❑ Using hard and soft brushes to create detail in the painting
- ❑ Using brush blending modes to achieve special effects such as deep shadows
- ❑ Creating and applying custom patterns to create large areas of consistent texture
- ❑ Setting brush options to randomize brush strokes and paint "natural" scenes

Project Meeting

client comments

In three months we break ground on a new master planned community targeted for middle-income families. We are installing an on-site sales office soon so we can start preselling, and we want to be able to show potential buyers what finished houses will look like.

Our architect gave us pen-and-ink renderings, but we want something more realistic — like a painting — in color. If you can create a painting, we can print several copies to frame and hang around the office. When we get closer to building the houses, we might also launch a direct mail sales campaign and do some other print advertising. It depends on how many plots we can presell.

We have worked with an environmental designer to create the community master plan and have finalized everything from the site map to the stucco and trim colors that will be used for the finished houses. I showed your art director swatches of the paint chips, and we're hoping you can use those to create the actual painting.

art director comments

Most people in our field will tell you that high-quality art is part creativity and part technique. Your role in this project is to provide technique, since the actual artwork was already drawn by the architect.

The client isn't sure what he's going to do with the final artwork. He knows it's going to be printed, definitely as a framed print in the sales office, possibly in brochures and newspapers, and probably on his website as well.

With all these possible uses, you need to produce a versatile file that can support many file formats. The RGB color space is larger than CMYK, so create the painting in RGB and start with high enough resolution for print.

The large-format output company has switched to an all-PDF workflow for output. They don't accept any native application files, so you'll have to save the final painting as a high-resolution PDF file. The service rep also said their output devices convert color on the fly, and they get better results from RGB images than images already converted to CMYK.

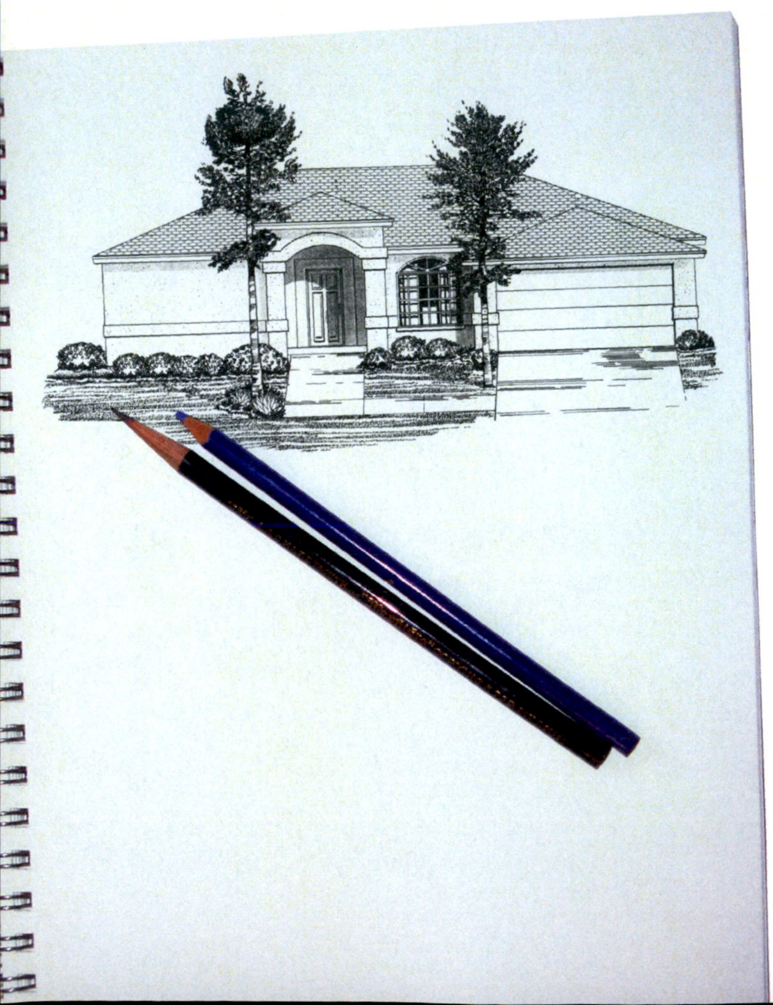

project objectives

To complete this project, you will:

- ❑ Convert a bitmap image to RGB
- ❑ Import custom swatches
- ❑ Create fill shapes
- ❑ Fill areas with the Paint Bucket tool
- ❑ Use hard- and soft-edge brushes
- ❑ Clone repeating drawing elements
- ❑ Create texture with a faux-finish brush
- ❑ Use opacity and blending modes to create deep shadows
- ❑ Define and save a custom pattern
- ❑ Change brush settings to paint random elements
- ❑ Create and save a brush preset
- ❑ Export a PDF file for print

Stage 1 Filling Solid Areas

This project differs from the ones you have completed so far. In this project, you use Photoshop to create original artwork — that is, rather than compositing images and text to create a finished job, you use Photoshop tools to create the actual pixels that make up the finished artwork.

Some of the skills you learn in this project (including painting with brushes) are normally used by creative designers to develop original digital artwork — starting with nothing other than an idea. By starting with an existing line-art drawing, however, you can use the same tools and techniques to build a full-color artistic rendering, even if you don't have the natural painting ability of da Vinci.

The easiest way to start a painting such as this one is to create the basic shapes that make up the object you are painting. You can make a basic selection and simply fill it with a color, use the Paint Bucket tool to fill areas of similar color, or use brushes and painting techniques to color specific areas. When you combine these techniques with Photoshop layers, you can also use transparency and blending modes to create images that appear as though they were painted with a traditional canvas and brushes.

Import Custom Swatches

The Swatches panel stores colors that you use frequently; you can access a color by simply clicking a swatch in the panel. You can use swatches from a number of built-in libraries commonly used in the graphics industry, or you can create custom swatch libraries that can be shared with other Adobe applications.

Rather than randomly picking colors for the various elements of the house, you will use a set of custom swatches based on the color scheme defined in the community master plan.

1. **Download Houses_PS18_RF.zip from the Student Files web page.**

2. **Expand the ZIP archive in your WIP folder (Macintosh) or copy the archive contents into your WIP folder (Windows).**

   This results in a folder named **Houses**, which contains the files you need for this project. You should also use this folder to save the files you create in this project.

3. **In Photoshop, display the Swatches panel (Window>Swatches).**

   Photoshop includes a default set of swatches chosen from the various built-in libraries.

4. **In the Swatches panel Options menu, choose Replace Swatches. If you see a message asking you to save current swatches, click No.**

   You can create a new swatch, change the panel view, manage visible swatch sets, or open built-in swatch libraries.

Note:

You can always restore the default swatches by choosing Reset Swatches in the panel Options menu.

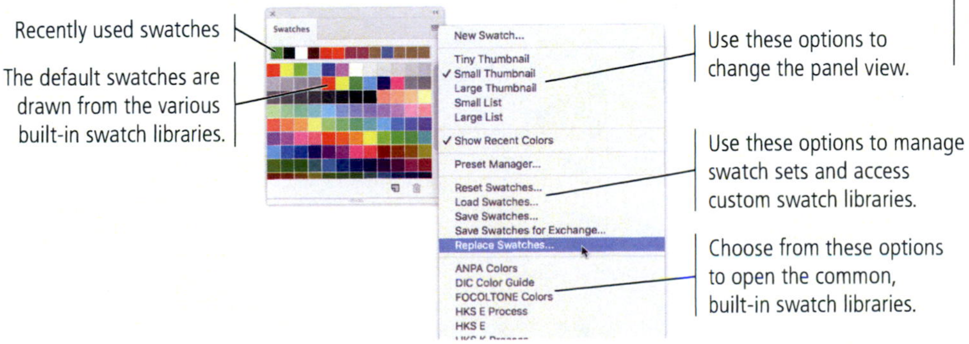

5. **Windows users: Choose Swatch Exchange (*.ASE) in the Files of Type menu.**

6. **Navigate to the file home color.ase in the WIP>Houses folder, then click Open/Load.**

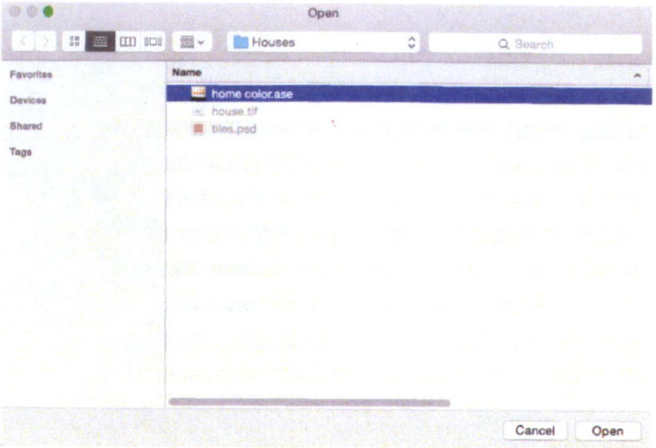

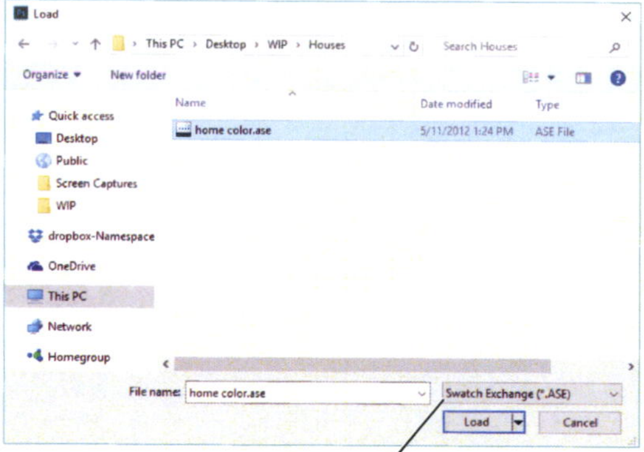

On Windows, you have to choose Swatch Exchange in the Files of Type menu.

The ASE extension identifies an Adobe Swatch Exchange file, which is a special format for sharing swatch libraries between Adobe applications.

You can save custom swatch sets to be used in other Adobe applications by choosing Save Swatches for Exchange in the Swatches panel Options menu. To save a swatch library for only Photoshop, you can use the Save Swatches command to save the swatch library with the ".aco" extension.

7. **Using the Swatches panel Options menu, change the panel to Small List view.**

Because you chose Replace Swatches in the panel Options menu in Step 2, the new panel contains only the swatches from the ASE file. These swatches were created specifically for this project, using basic names that will make it easier to complete the house painting.

8. **Click the bottom/right corner of the panel and drag down until you can see all the swatches in the imported library.**

Click and drag this corner to resize the panel.

9. **Continue to the next exercise.**

Note:

If you are sharing swatches between applications, Photoshop doesn't recognize pattern swatches, gradient swatches, or the Registration swatch from Illustrator or InDesign, nor does Photoshop transfer "book color" references such as HSB, XYZ, duotone, Monitor RGB, opacity, totally ink, or webRGB from within the application.

Create Fill Shapes

In this exercise, you use standard selection tools to paint the front walls of the house — large and relatively simple areas that you can fill with "stucco" colored paint.

1. **Open the file house.tif from the WIP>Houses folder. If you get a warning about a mismatched color profile, choose the option to use the embedded profile.**

2. **In the Layers panel, unlock the Background layer.**

3. **Double-click the unlocked Background layer name to highlight it, then type Sketch to rename it. Press Return/Enter to finalize the new name.**

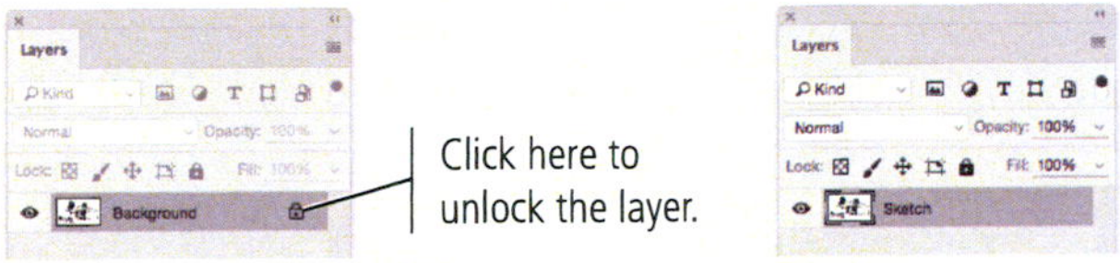

4. **In the Layers panel, click the Lock All icon to lock the renamed Sketch layer.**

   You're going to use this layer as a template for your painting. Locking the layer prevents you from accidentally moving or altering the original artwork.

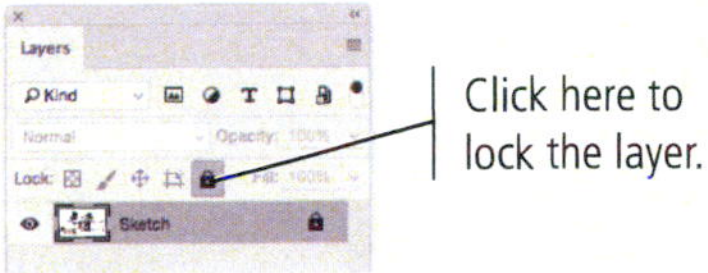

Layers
Sketch
Click here to lock the layer.

5. **Create a new layer named Walls, and make it the active layer.**

6. **Use the Rectangular Marquee tool to draw a selection around the front of the garage face (including the pillars to the sides of the garage door).**

   Don't worry if your selection covers parts of the bushes and doesn't include the pieces that stick out from the basic rectangular shape. You will refine the selection in the following steps, and you will paint the bushes on higher layers later in this project.

   We outlined the selection with a red overlay to make it more visible in these images. Yours will be visible as "marching ants" in the document window.

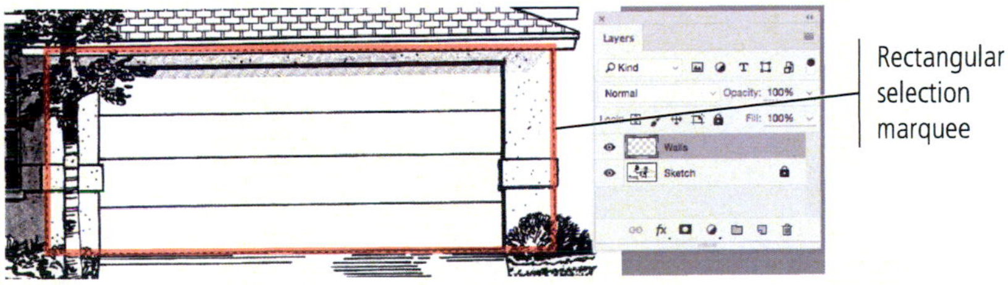

7. **Using the Add to Selection and Subtract from Selection options, draw additional selection marquees to select the entire face of the house.**

   Zooming in might make it easier to refine the selection, especially in the smaller areas where the house shape extends slightly.

Note:

As hard as we tried to get this image exactly square on the scanner bed, no scans are perfect. There's a chance that the straight lines, paths, and guides you create in Photoshop will not exactly match the horizontal, vertical, or angled lines in your scans. A very slight difference is nothing to worry about. The finished product will look fine because the original scan will ultimately be deleted.

8. **Click the Stucco 2 swatch in the Swatches panel to define that swatch as the foreground color.**

Clicking a color in the Swatches panel changes the active foreground color.

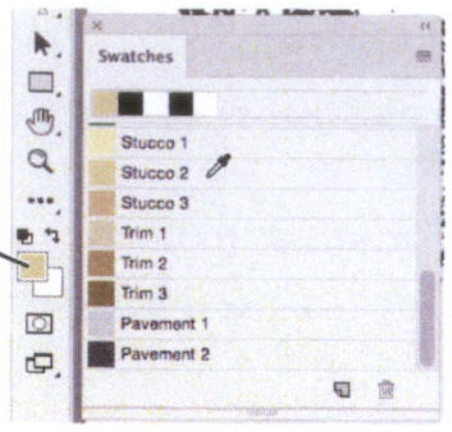

9. **Choose Edit>Fill. Choose Foreground Color in the Contents menu of the Fill dialog box.**

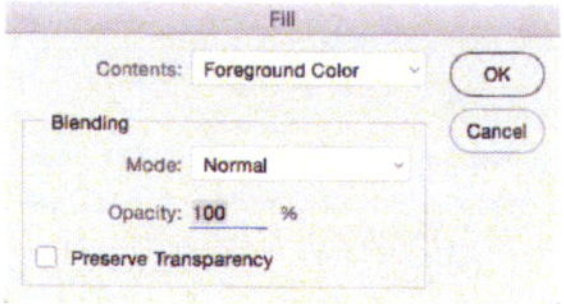

10. **Click OK to fill the wall selection.**

11. **With the Walls layer selected in the Layers panel, change the Opacity setting to 80%.**

    The finished artwork will be at full opacity. While you're working, however, it helps to see through various layers.

    Semi-transparent fills make it possible to see and continue painting the elements of the original artwork. When you're finished with the project, you can return this layer to 100% opacity. If you had changed the fill opacity to 80% in the Fill dialog box, you would be unable to change it back to 100%.

12. **Turn off the current selection (Select>Deselect).**

13. **Save the file as a native Photoshop file named house-working.psd in your WIP>Houses folder. When asked, click OK in the Photoshop Format Options dialog box to maximize file compatibility.**

14. **Continue to the next exercise.**

Fill Areas with the Paint Bucket Tool

The Paint Bucket tool has the same basic functionality as the Fill dialog box — you click the tool cursor to fill an area with the current foreground color. In the Options bar, you can choose the color, blending mode, and opacity of the fill.

1. **With `house-working.psd` open, hide the Walls layer and add a new layer named `Front Trim` at the top of the layer stack.**

2. **Choose the Paint Bucket tool (nested under the Gradient tool) in the Tools panel. In the Options bar, type `30` in the Tolerance field, and activate the Contiguous and All Layers options.**

   Unlike the Fill dialog box, the Paint Bucket tool creates fills based on the defined sample tolerance (like the settings used to create a selection based on a color range).

   In addition to the fill color, blending mode, and opacity, the Options bar includes settings for tool tolerance and anti-aliasing, as well as whether to fill only contiguous pixels within the defined tolerance. The All Layers option allows you to sample pixels from all visible layers instead of only the selected layer.

3. **Change the foreground color to the Trim 1 swatch.**

4. **Click the Paint Bucket tool on a white area of the trim board on the left side of the house.**

   The Paint Bucket tool fills areas with the selected foreground color. Because the Contiguous option is checked in the Options bar, only the area inside the "board" edges is filled.

   The tool's cursor can be confusing. Watch the top of the pointer in the cursor — not the drop of paint falling from the bucket — to identify the area that will be filled.

Use these settings to determine the sensitivity of the Paint Bucket tool.
Use the arrow tip to determine which area will be filled.

5. **Click inside each of the trim areas in the front of the house. (Use the following image as a guide for the areas you should fill.)**

   Make sure you click on both sides of the trees, and don't forget the window sill. In some segments, you might need to click several times to fill the primary shapes.

6. **Zoom into the trim on the right side of the window.**

   Because of the way the illustrator created shadows, you need to use a slightly different method to fill in the shadowed pieces of trim.

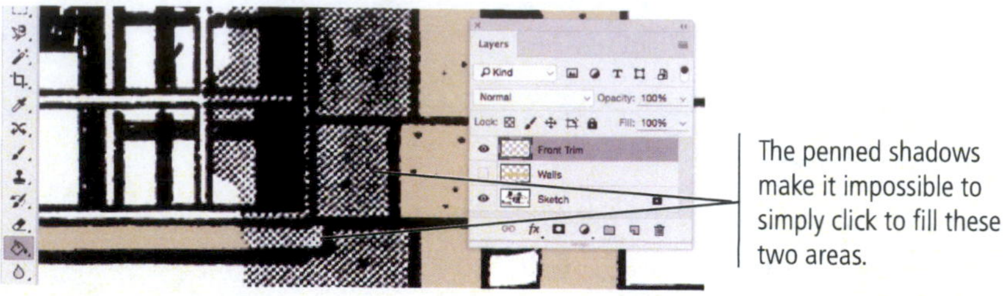

The penned shadows make it impossible to simply click to fill these two areas.

7. **Draw a rectangle marquee around the shadowed trim. Select the Paint Bucket tool, turn off the All Layers option in the Options bar, then click inside the selection marquee.**

8. **Repeat Step 7 to fill the shadowed section of the window sill.**

9. **Turn off the active selection, then hide the Sketch layer.**

   Because of the points used to create texture in the sketch, the Paint Bucket tool did not fill all the shapes. That's okay, though, because you will later use the empty spots to create texture of your own. Also, don't worry about the areas where trees and bushes cover the house; you're going to paint trees that will cover those areas.

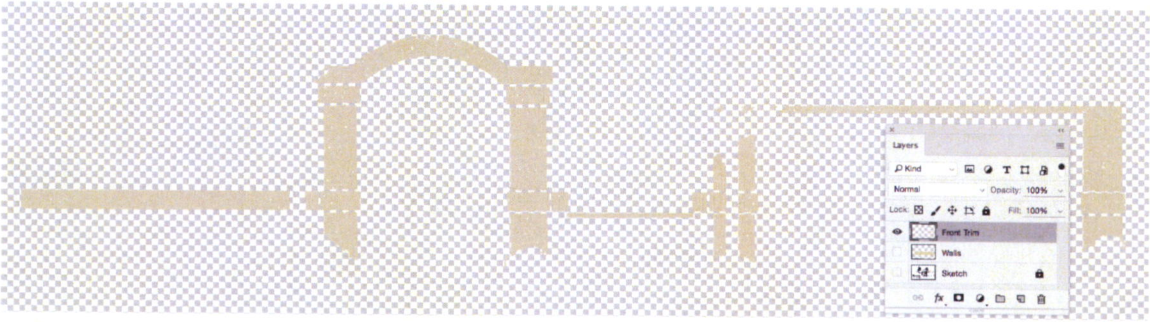

10. **Show the Sketch layer again.**

11. Create a new layer named **Fascia** at the top of the layer stack. Select the new layer as the active one.

12. Using the Paint Bucket tool with the All Layers option active, fill the upper parts of the fascia boards with the Trim 2 swatch.

13. Fill the lower parts of the fascia boards with the Trim 3 swatch.

14. Create a new layer named **Garage Door** at the top of the layer stack and select it. Use the Paint Bucket tool with the All Layers option active to fill the four panels on the garage door with the Doors 3 swatch.

Because of the sketched shading, you might need to increase the tool's tolerance to fill most of the top garage door panel. Alternatively, you can use the selection marquee technique to fill the appropriate area.

15. Create a new layer named **Pavement** at the top of the layer stack and select it. Use the Polygonal Lasso tool to draw a marquee around the driveway area, then use the Paint Bucket tool to fill the selected area with the Pavement 1 swatch.

In the sketch, the driveway area doesn't have a solid edge, so simply clicking with the Paint Bucket tool would fill most of the layer with gray. If you have defined a selection area, clicking inside the selection marquee only fills the selected area.

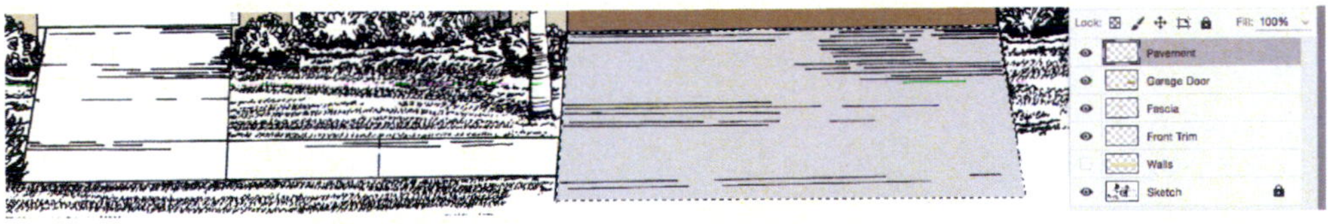

16. Turn off the active selection area, then use the Paint Bucket tool to fill in the remaining areas of sidewalk.

You don't need to draw a selection marquee for the sidewalk because the lines in the sketch form solid edges that limit the results from clicking with the Paint Bucket tool.

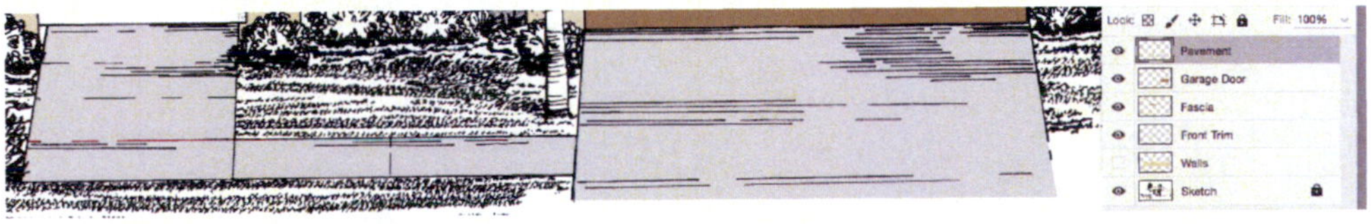

17. Deselect any active marquee, then save the file and continue to the next stage of the project.

Stage 2 Painting with Brushes

Filling a selection area is one of the more basic techniques for painting in Photoshop. To create complex custom artwork, you can use Photoshop brushes in the digital workspace just as you would use traditional brushes on canvas. The built-in brushes come in hundreds of shapes and sizes; combining these brushes with options such as opacity, flow, and blending mode provides an almost infinite array of choices for painting pixels in a Photoshop layout.

As you might have guessed, there is far more to using brushes than what you have already learned throughout this book's earlier projects. Painting the house in this project requires several different types of brushes, as well as controlling the brush options to complete various areas of the painting.

When you choose the Brush tool, you must first select a specific brush. You can choose one of the built-in brush presets from the Options bar, or you can define your own brush by changing the Size and Hardness settings in the Brush Preset Picker. You can also use the Options bar to a number of settings that affect how a specific brush works.

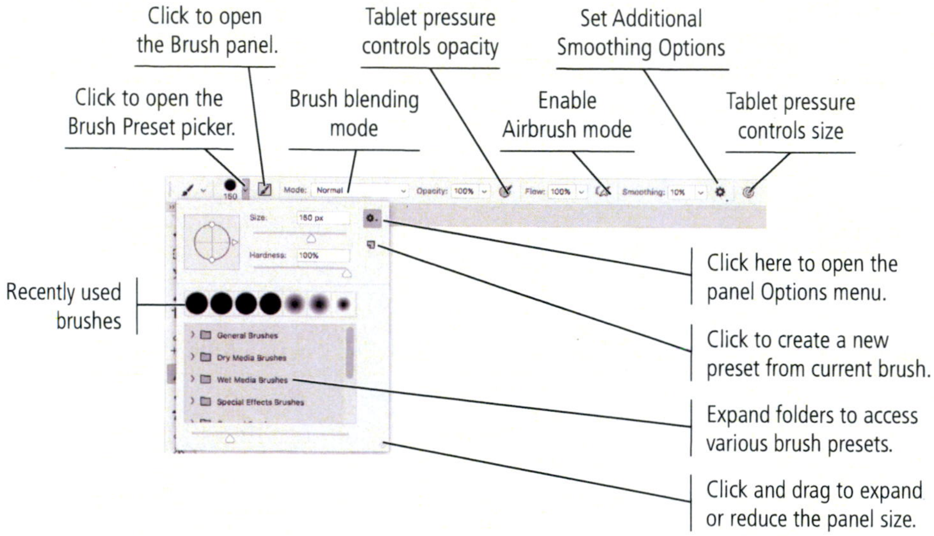

Tablet pressure controls opacity

Tablet pressure controls size

Click to create a new preset from current brush.
Expand folders to access various brush presets.
Click and drag to expand or reduce the panel size.

> ***Note:***
>
> *In addition to the hundreds of built-in Photoshop brushes, you can access over 1,000 free brushes from award-winning illustrator Kyle T. Webster by choosing Get More Brushes in the Brush Preset Picker Options menu.*

You learned about blending modes and opacity in an earlier project. The other brush options require a little bit of explanation.

- **Size** is the size of the brush tip, measured in pixels.
- **Hardness** is the percentage of the brush that's completely opaque. For example, a Hardness setting of 50% for a brush with a 10-pixel diameter means 5 pixels in the brush center are hard, and the remaining diameter has a feathered edge.

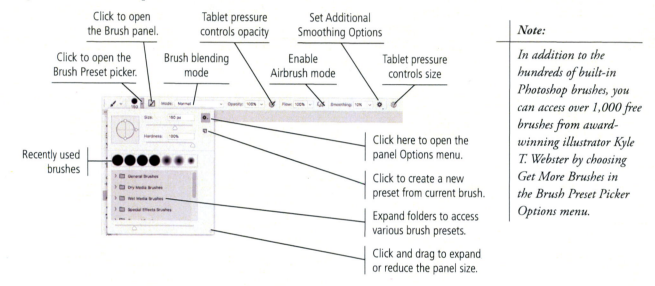

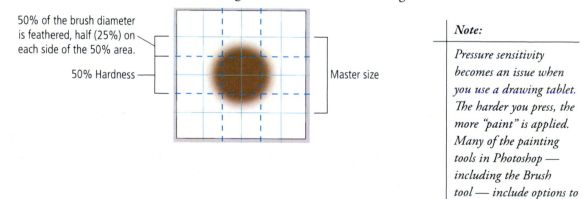

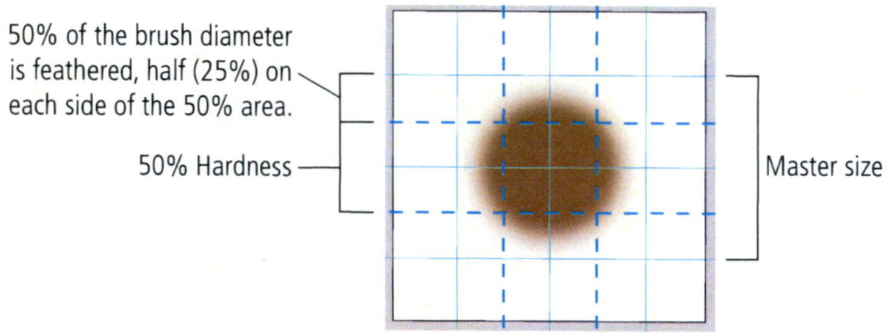

50% of the brush diameter is feathered, half (25%) on each side of the 50% area.
50% Hardness
Master size

> ***Note:***
>
> *Pressure sensitivity becomes an issue when you use a drawing tablet. The harder you press, the more "paint" is applied. Many of the painting tools in Photoshop — including the Brush tool — include options to allow pressure sensitivity while you paint.*

- **Flow** sets the rate at which color is applied as you paint repeatedly over the same area. As you continue painting over the same area (while holding down the mouse button), the amount of color "builds up."

  In the following example, we set the brush color to C=100 M=50, with a Flow setting of 50%. Each successive click moved the color values 50% closer to the brush color.

  Contrary to what many people think, the Flow setting does not apply hard percentages of the brush color. The first click resulted in 25% magenta, or 50% of the brush color value. The second click produced 38% magenta, which is the result of adding 50% of the difference between the first click (25% magenta) and the brush color (50% magenta) — or one half of the difference between 25 and 50 (25 / 2 = 12.5).

  For the third click, 50% of the difference between 38 (the previous value) and 50 (the brush value) is added: 50 – 38 = 12 / 2 = 6 + 38 = 44

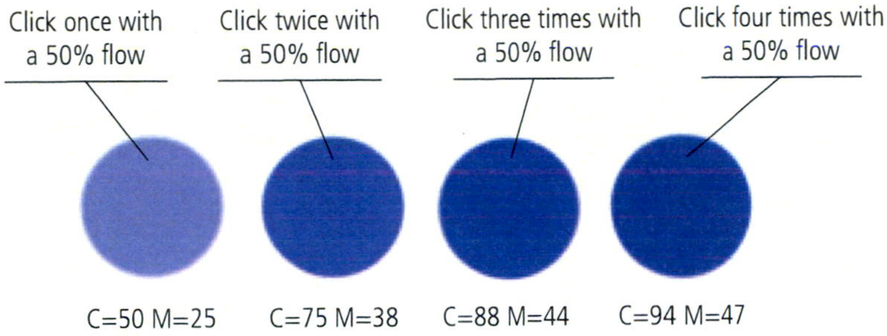

Click once with a 50% flow
Click twice with a 50% flow
Click three times with a 50% flow
Click four times with a 50% flow
C=50 M=25
C=75 M=38
C=88 M=44
C=94 M=47

- **Airbrush mode** simulates painting with an airbrush. If you hold down the mouse button or move the cursor back and forth over the same area, more color builds up in the same location. (Brush hardness, opacity, and flow options control how fast and how much "paint" is applied.)

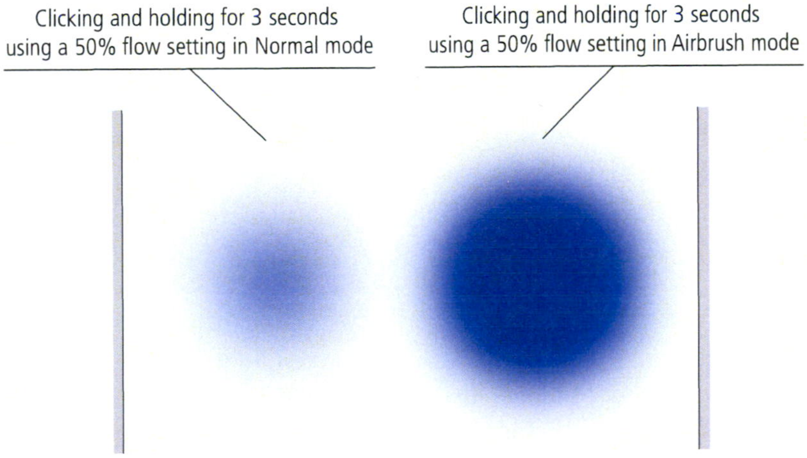

Clicking and holding for 3 seconds using a 50% flow setting in Normal mode
Clicking and holding for 3 seconds using a 50% flow setting in Airbrush mode

Note:

Press the Left Bracket key ([ ) or Right Bracket key ( ]) to decrease or increase (respectively) the current brush diameter to the next predetermined size.

Press Shift-[to decrease brush hardness, and press Shift-] to increase the brush hardness in 25% increments.

Note:

Color values are always whole numbers, which is why the magenta value is rounded to 38 instead of the mathematical 50% value of 37.5.

Note:

Press a number key to define the brush opacity setting in increments of 10% (e.g., pressing 6 sets the opacity to 60%).

Note:

Press Shift and a number key to define the brush flow setting in increments of 10% (e.g., pressing Shift-6 sets the flow to 60%).

- **Smoothing** helps to prevent jags on a brush stroke that result from slight jumps of a mouse cursor or stylus. Higher smoothing (up to 100%) values result in smoother brush strokes. You can click the Set Additional Smoothing Options button to control the way Photoshop applies smoothing.

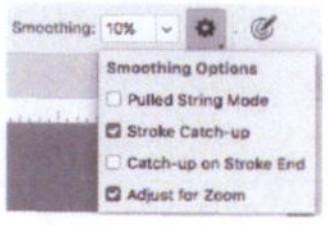

> ***Note:***
>
> *Smoothing is available when using the Brush, Pencil, Mixer Brush, or Eraser tool.*

When **Pulled String Mode** is active, clicking reveals a pink "safe zone"; increasing the Smoothing value increases the size of the safe zone. Cursor movement within the safe zone does not add to the stroke; the pink leash ("string") curves to show the movement. If you drag past the safe-zone area, leash is straightened and cursor movement adds to the stroke you are creating.

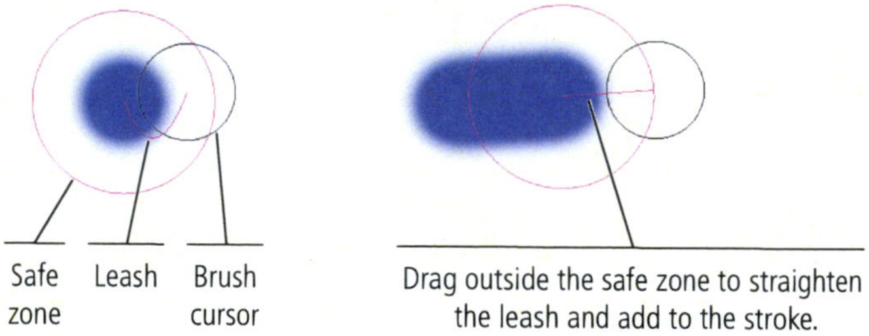

Safe zone
Leash
Brush cursor
Drag outside the safe zone to straighten the leash and add to the stroke.

The pink leash is visible by default whenever Smoothing is enabled. You can turn it off, and change its color, in the Cursors pane of the Preferences dialog box.

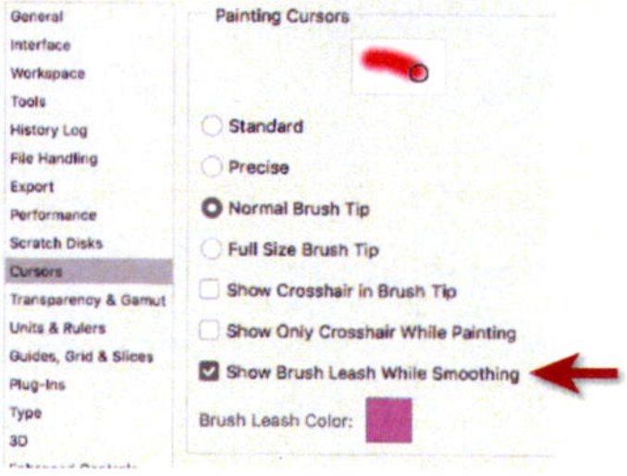

If you turn off Pulled Strong Mode, you can use the Catch Up options to control how strokes are created when you drag faster than the software is able to paint.

If **Stroke Catch Up** is active, the stroke you're painting will extend to current the position of the cursor if you pause while dragging. If this option is not active, the stroke painting ends when you pause; it does not necessarily extend to match the current cursor position.

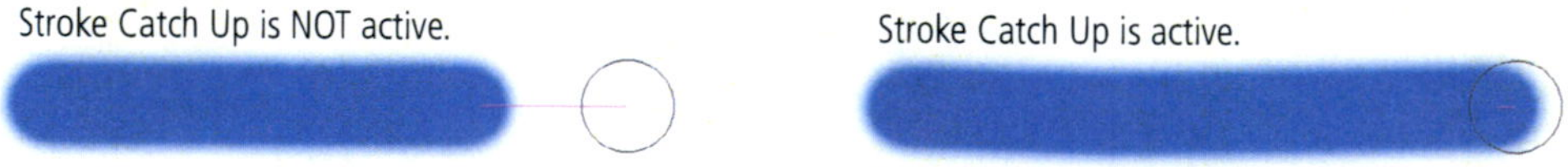

Stroke Catch Up is NOT active.
Stroke Catch Up is active.

Catch-Up On Stroke End is similar to Stroke Catch Up, but relates to how a stroke is finished when you actually *release* the mouse cursor. In the following examples, the top image shows point where we released the brush cursor; the bottom image shows the resulting stroke after releasing the mouse button.

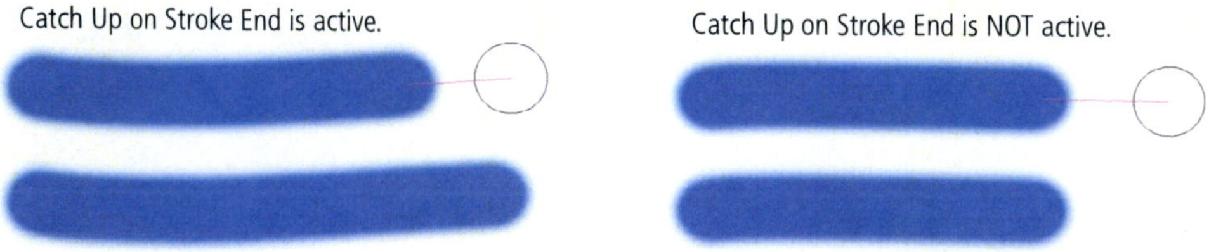

Catch Up on Stroke End is active.
Catch Up on Stroke End is NOT active.

If **Adjust For Zoom** is active, zooming in decreases smoothing and zooming out increases smoothing.

Use Hard Brushes

The brush Hardness setting allows you to paint either sharp lines or soft, feathered edges. Most painting projects — including this one — require a combination of hard- and soft-edge brushes.

1. **With `house-working.psd` open, create two new layers at the top of the layer stack — one named `Front Door` and one named `FD Panels`. Make sure the FD Panels layer is higher in the layer stack.**

   The Front Door layer will hold the overall door area; the FD Panels layer will hold the painted lines that form the shapes of the raised panels within the front door.

2. **Open the Cursors pane of the Preferences dialog box (in the Photoshop menu on Macintosh or the Edit menu on Windows).**

3. **In the Painting Cursors area, choose the Full Size Brush Tip option and activate the Show Crosshair in Brush Tip option. Click OK to apply the change.**

   The Full Size Brush Tip option changes the cursor to include the entire brush area, including the feathered part of soft-edge brushes.

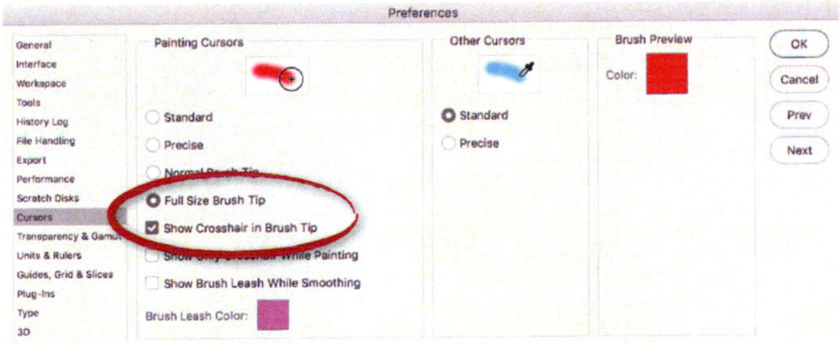

> *Note:*
>
> *When using the Brush tool, you can activate Caps Lock on your keyboard to temporarily switch to the Precise cursor mode. If you are already in Precise cursor mode, activating the Caps Lock key switches to the Normal Brush Tip cursor.*

4. **Make the Front Door layer active, then draw a rectangular selection around the front door. Make sure all door edges, but not the door frame, are included in the selection (see the image after Step 6).**

5. **Change the foreground color to the Doors 3 swatch, then choose the Paint Bucket tool in the Tools panel. Uncheck the All Layers option in the Options bar.**

   If the All Layers option is selected, clicking with the Paint Bucket tool would sample from the Sketch layer, and some of the selected area wouldn't be entirely filled.

6. **With the Front Door layer active, click the Paint Bucket tool inside the selection marquee.**

   Since the active layer (Front Door) has no current content, the Tolerance setting is irrelevant. The entire selection area fills with the Doors 3 color.

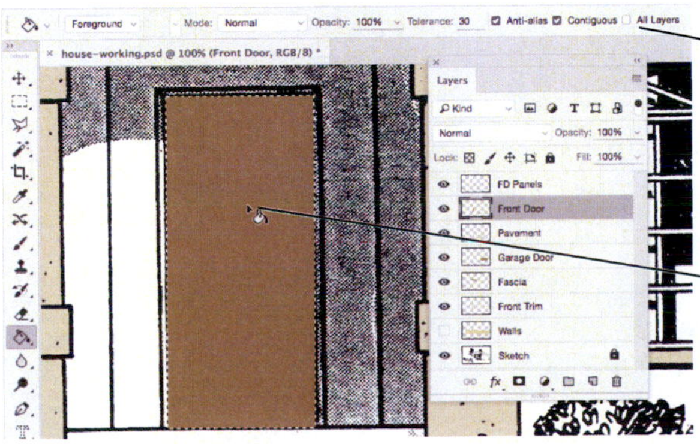

7. **Deselect the active selection marquee. Change the Front Door layer Opacity value to 50% so you can see the underlying sketch.**

8. **Make the FD Panels layer active, and then choose the Brush tool in the Tools panel.**

9. **Change the foreground color to the Doors 4 swatch.**

10. **In the Options bar, click the Brush button to open the Brush Preset Picker. Set the brush size to `10 px` and the Hardness to `100%`.**

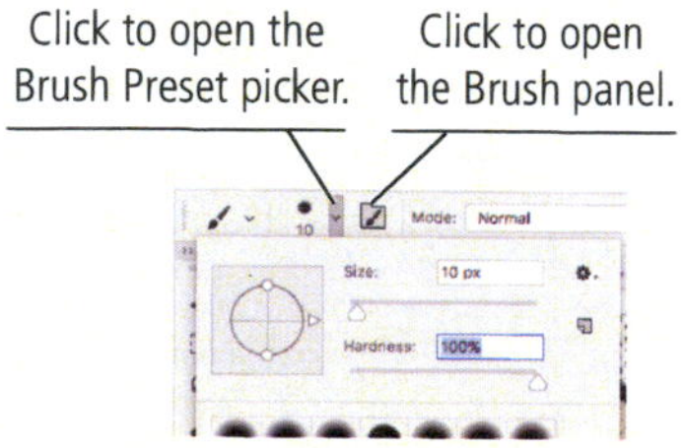

Click to open the Brush Preset picker.
Click to open the Brush panel.

11. **Press Return/Enter to close the Brush Preset Picker.**

12. **Place the cursor over the inset line on the top-left panel of the front door.**

    The default brush cursor shows the size of the selected brush tip. In this case, the 10-pixel brush is clearly wider than the line you want to paint.

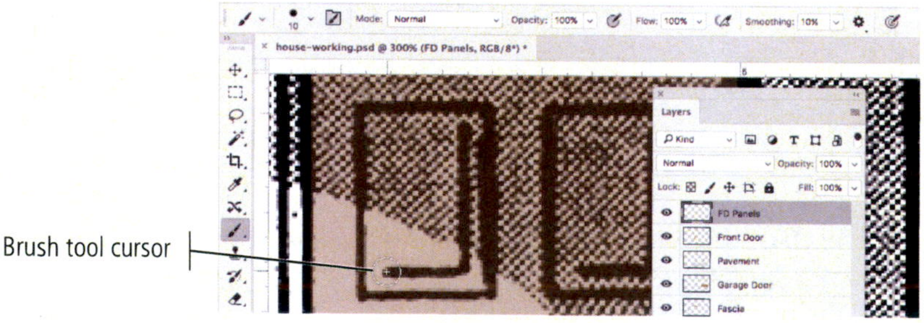

Brush tool cursor

> ***Note:***
>
> *Zooming in helps when you're working on the smaller details of a painting (such as the door inset panels).*

13. **Press [six times to reduce the brush size to 4 pixels.**

    You can press [and] to decrease or increase the brush size to the next defined preset. Under ten pixels, the key shortcuts change the brush size by 1 pixel at a time.

14. **Click at the top of the panel inset, press Shift, and then click at the lower-right corner of the panel inset.**

15. **Press Shift and click at the lower-left corner of the panel inset.**

    Pressing Shift and then clicking again connects the first and second points with a straight line of the brush color. You can also press Shift while dragging to paint a perfectly horizontal or vertical line.

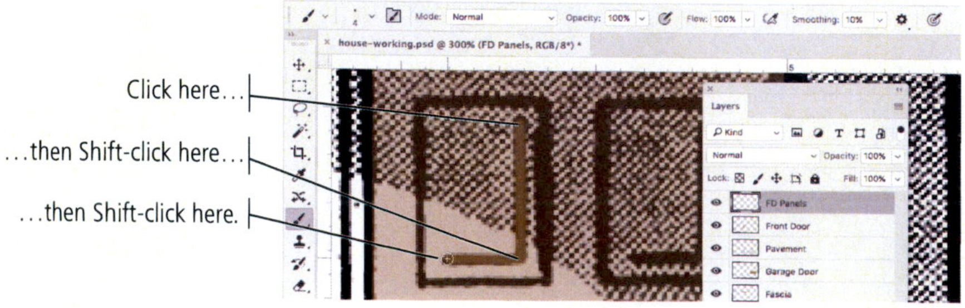

Click here...
...then Shift-click here...
...then Shift-click here.

16. **Save the file and continue to the next exercise.**

Use Soft Brushes

Painting with a hard brush results in colored pixels edged by white pixels. In the real world, however, there are very few perfectly hard edges with no variation in shades. Soft-edge brushes are far more useful for creating artwork that includes the subtle color variations found in a real object.

1. **With `house-working.psd` open, draw a rectangular selection marquee around the front door panel where you painted the inset.**

   Always remember that when you have an active selection, you can only affect the area inside the selection.

2. **Make sure the FD Panels layer is selected and Doors 4 is the current foreground color.**

3. **Choose the Brush tool. Using the Options bar, open the Brush Preset Picker and change the brush Size to `15 px` and the Hardness to `0%`. Press Return/Enter to finalize your selections and close the Brush Preset Picker.**

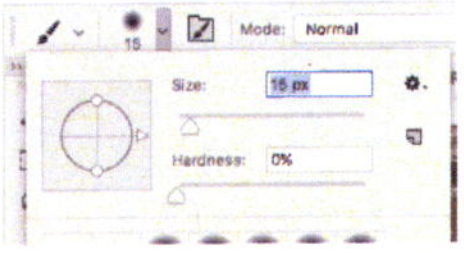

4. **Place the cursor so the crosshairs are exactly on top of the selection marquee.**

5. **Click at the top-right corner of the selection marquee, press Shift, and drag down to paint the panel's right edge.**

   Even though half the cursor is outside the selection marquee, areas outside the marquee are not painted; the reduced hardness results in a softer edge to the brush stroke.

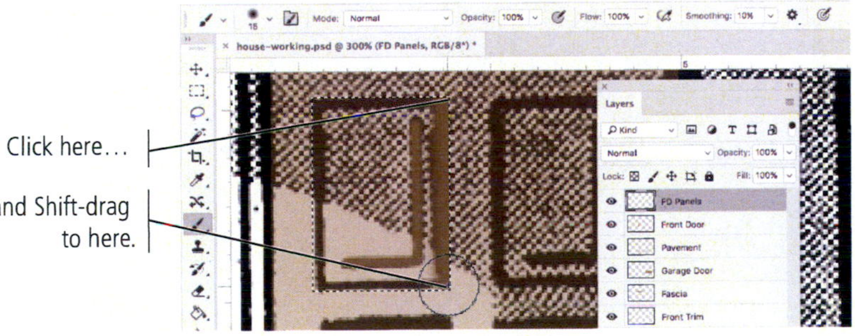
Click here…
…and Shift-drag to here.

   These screen shots show the art at 300%, which naturally causes even hard edges to appear soft. However, you should be able to see the difference between the hard-edge line and the soft-edge line.

6. **Using the same technique, paint a stroke at the top edge of the panel.**

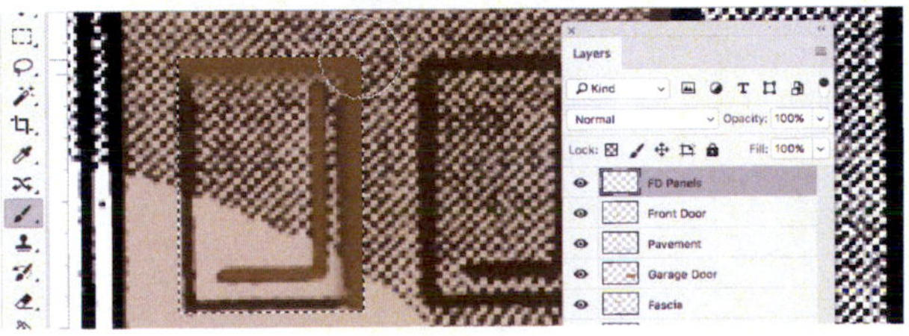

7. **Change the foreground color to Doors 2, and reduce the brush size to `10 px`. Paint the left and bottom edges of the panel.**

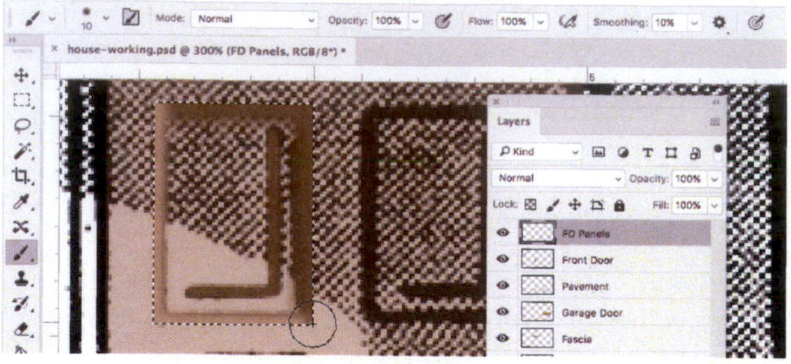

8. **Turn off the active selection.**

9. **Use the same processes outlined in this and the previous exercise to create the lower-left inset panel of the door.**

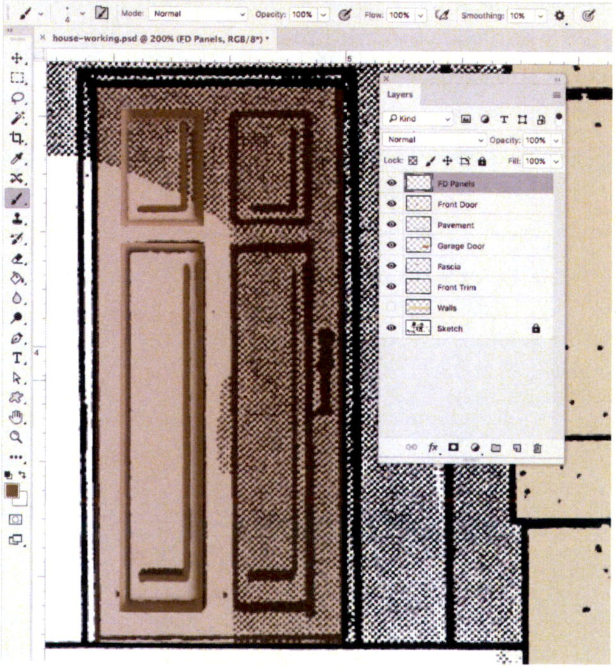

10. **Deselect the active marquee, save the file, and then continue to the next exercise.**

Paint Strokes around Selections

When you're painting something like this house, you start with spaces defined by sharp, black lines drawn on white paper. In the case of the bitmap scan provided by your client, there are plenty of lines to define the objects in the drawing. But as you can guess, real-world objects rarely contain sharp black lines.

In addition to the techniques you have already applied, a number of other options can be used to paint color into a digital file. In this exercise, you will use the Stroke dialog box to outline the front door.

1. **With house-working.psd open, make sure the FD Panels layer is selected.**
2. **With the Move tool active, press Option/Alt-Shift, and then click-drag right.**

   This method of copying a selection (or layer, if there is no specific selection marquee) is called **cloning**. When you clone an entire layer, the result is a copy of the existing layer. If you clone a selection marquee, the cloned content becomes part of the active layer.

> ***Note:***
>
> *Press Option/Alt and click-drag to clone the current selection.*
>
> *Press Shift to constrain movement to 45° increments.*

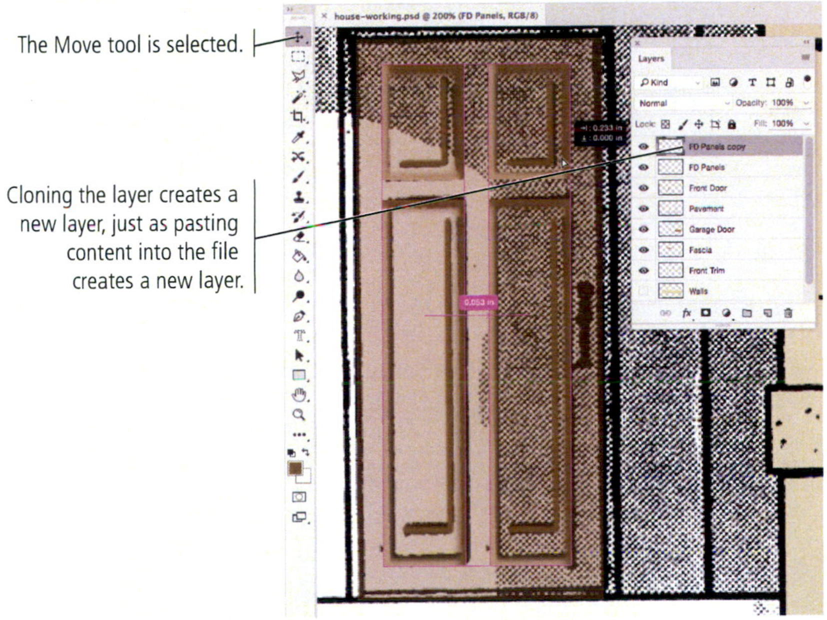

The Move tool is selected.
Cloning the layer creates a new layer, just as pasting content into the file creates a new layer.

3. **Use a small hard brush with a black foreground color to create the door handle on the Front Door layer.**
4. **Change the Front Door layer opacity back to 100%.**
5. **Select the FD Panels copy, FD Panels, and Front Door layers. With all three layers selected, click the Create a New Group button at the bottom of the panel.**

   You could also merge the selected layers into a single layer using the Merge Layers command. However, that option permanently flattens the merged layers, so you can no longer edit the individual component layers. In many real-world projects, professionals often prefer to maintain individual components as long as possible in case changes need to be made at a later time.

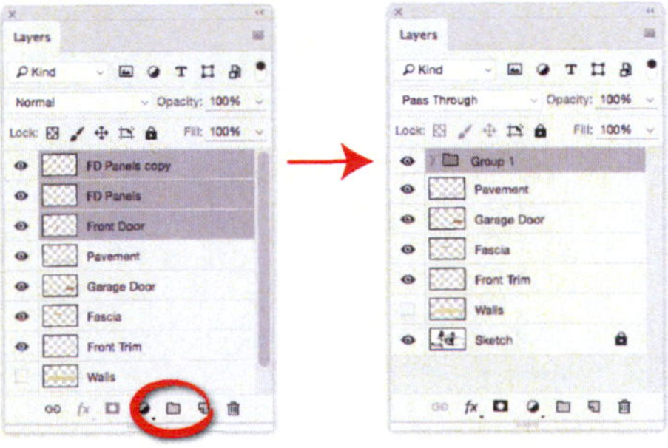

6. **Rename the new layer group Front Door.**

7. **In the Layers panel, expand the Front Door layer group. Click the Front Door layer (not the layer group) to make it the active layer.**

8. **Press Command/Control, then click the layer thumbnail for the Front Door layer (not the layer group).**

   This shortcut makes a new selection that encompasses all pixels on the layer you click.

   You could also use the Magic Wand tool to select the unpainted area of the layer, then choose Select>Inverse to invert the active selection.

Only the front door is selected.

9. **Change the foreground color to the Doors 4 swatch.**

10. **Choose Edit>Stroke. In the Stroke dialog box, set the Width value to 3 px and the Location to Center. Leave the Blending Mode menu set to Normal, then click OK to apply the stroke.**

    The Stroke dialog box is similar to the Fill dialog box, except you use it to define the stroke for the current selection.

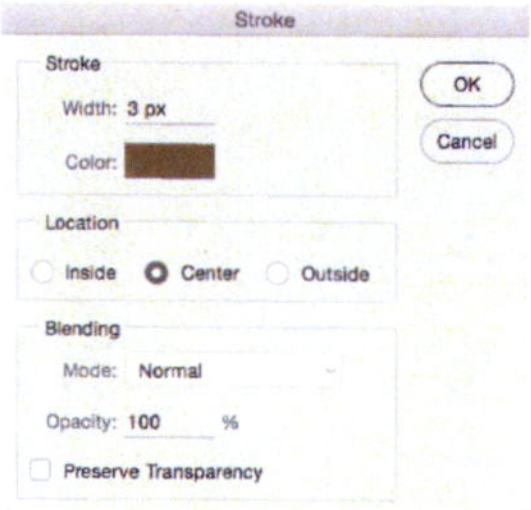

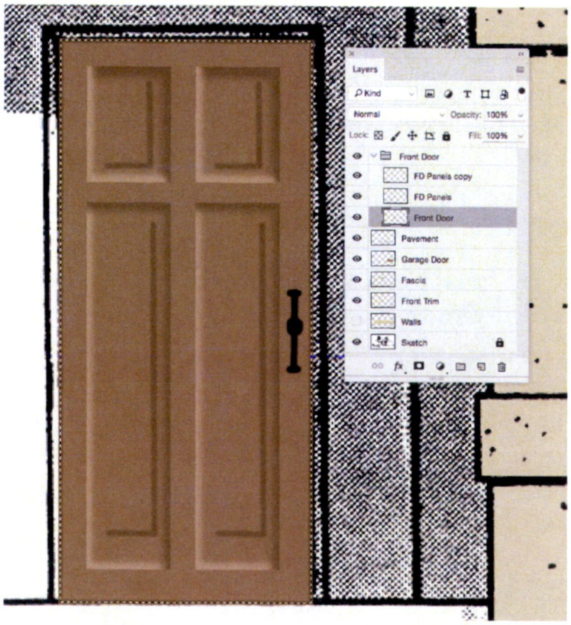

11. **Using the Rectangular Marquee tool, draw a new selection area around the outer door area. Use the Stroke dialog box to apply a 5-px stroke to the new selection.**

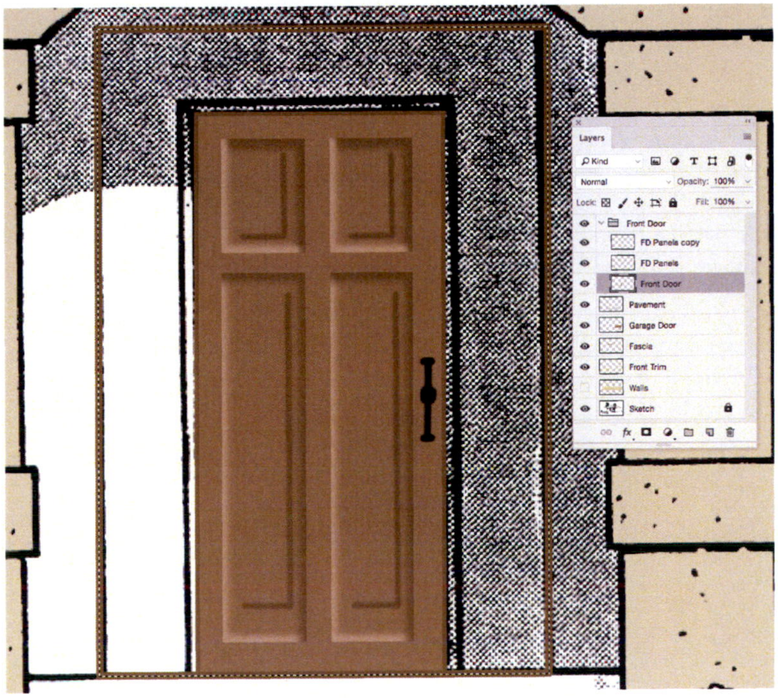

> *Note:*
>
> *The Location value of the stroke determines the placement of the stroke width in relation to the selection marquee.*

Inside
Center
Outside

12. **Deselect the current selection.**

13. **Choose the Brush tool, and define a 5-px brush with 100% hardness.**

14. **Place the cursor over the bottom-left corner of the stroke created in Step 11. Click, then Shift-drag left to create the line that marks the top of the stoop.**

    Use the brush cursor preview to align the brush with the existing stroke.

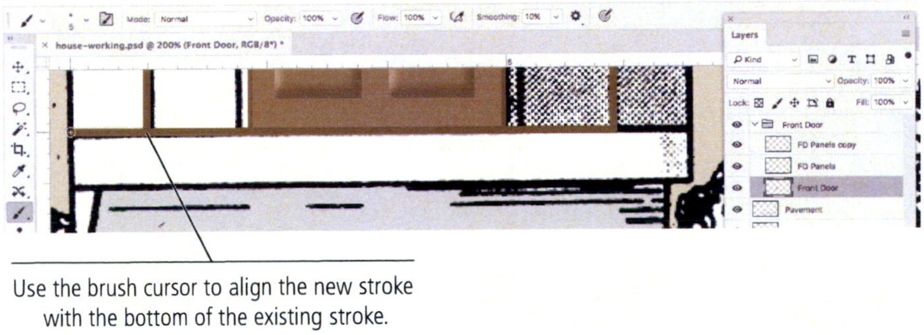

Use the brush cursor to align the new stroke with the bottom of the existing stroke.

15. **Repeat Step 14 to create the line on the right side of the door.**

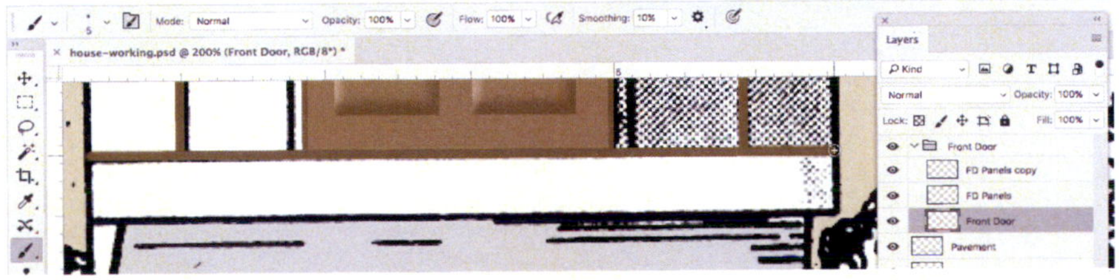

16. **In the Layers panel, collapse the Front Door layer group.**

17. **Save the file and continue to the next exercise.**

Apply Strokes to Closed Paths

The window on the front of the house includes a bit more detail than most other elements in this painting. To create this detail, you will use a combination of methods to add strokes to both closed and open paths.

1. **With house-working.psd open, create a new layer named Window at the top of the layer stack. Hide all layers but the Window and Sketch layers, and make the Window layer active.**

2. **Choose the Pen tool. In the Options bar, choose Path in the left menu. Open the Set Additional... menu and make sure the Rubber Band option is not checked.**

   When the Rubber Band option is checked, you will see a preview of the line you are drawing when you move the mouse cursor. Because you are only creating basic shapes in this exercise, the feature is not useful and can actually become confusing (especially drawing over a black-and-white image layer such as the sketch you are using here).

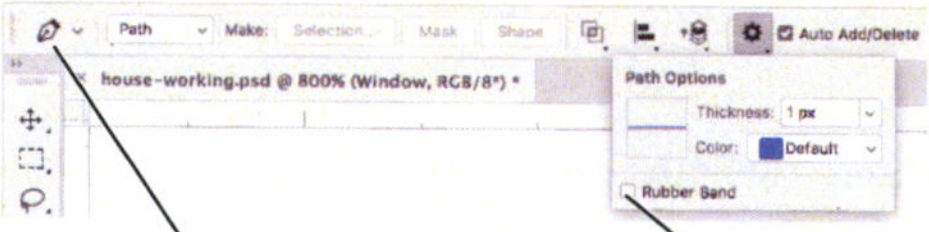

Use this option to create a path with the Pen tool.

Make sure the Rubber Band option is not active.

3. **Draw the top curved portion of the window.**

   The Pen tool makes it easier to draw a path that matches the window curve. You can then use this path to create a selection that you can use to apply a stroke. (We highlighted the path in red here to show you what path you need to create; your path will not have a colored stroke.)

Draw this path.

The path is stored in the Paths panel as a work path.

4. **With the work path selected in the Paths panel (Window>Paths), click the Load Path as Selection button at the bottom of the panel.**

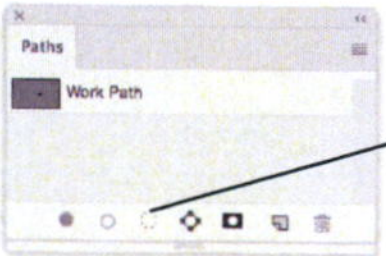

Load Path as Selection

5. **Choose Edit>Stroke. Apply a 6-px black stroke centered on the selection marquee and click OK.**

It's obscured by the sketch, but the selection is already outlined with a 6-px black stroke.

6. **Immediately choose Edit>Stroke again, and apply a 3-px white stroke centered on the selection marquee.**

7. **Turn off the active selection marquee.**

8. **Use the same 6-px-black/3-px-white sequence of strokes to create the outer frame of the square window.**

   In this case, you can simply use the Rectangular Marquee tool to draw the selection.

9. **Turn off any active selection, then hide the Sketch layer and review your work.**

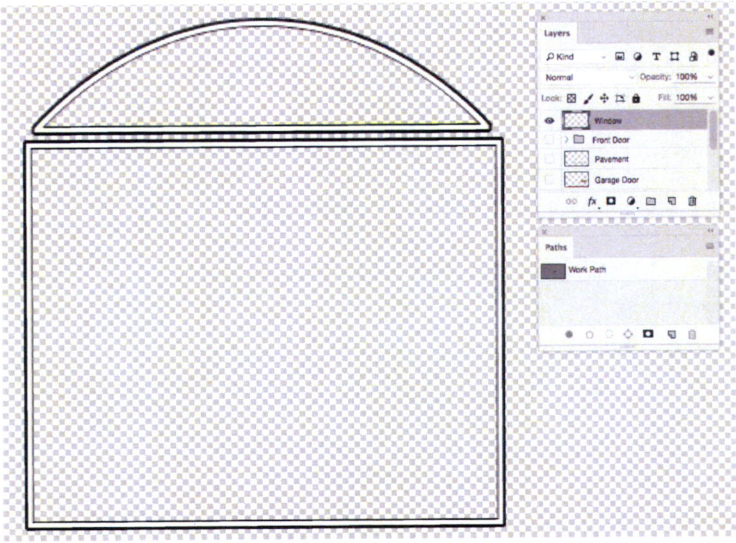

10. **Save the file and continue to the next exercise.**

Apply Strokes to Open Paths

The rest of the window lines are basically straight lines, which are easy to create; however, these lines do not create closed shapes from which you can make a selection, so you will use a slightly different technique to create the inner lines of the window.

1. **With `house-working.psd` open, show the Sketch layer, and then create a new layer immediately above the Window layer.**

   You will use this layer as a temporary workspace, so it isn't necessary to name it.

2. **Choose the Pencil tool (nested under the Brush tool in the Tools panel), and then reset the default foreground and background colors.**

3. **In the Options bar, open the Brush Preset Picker and change the size to 5 px. Press Retun/Enter to close the picker.**

   The Pencil tool is similar to the Brush tool, except it only creates hard edge. In the Options bar, you can select a brush preset from any of the available hard-edge brushes; you can also define the blending mode, opacity, and smoothing to use for the stroke.

The Pencil tool is active.

Reset the default foreground and background colors.

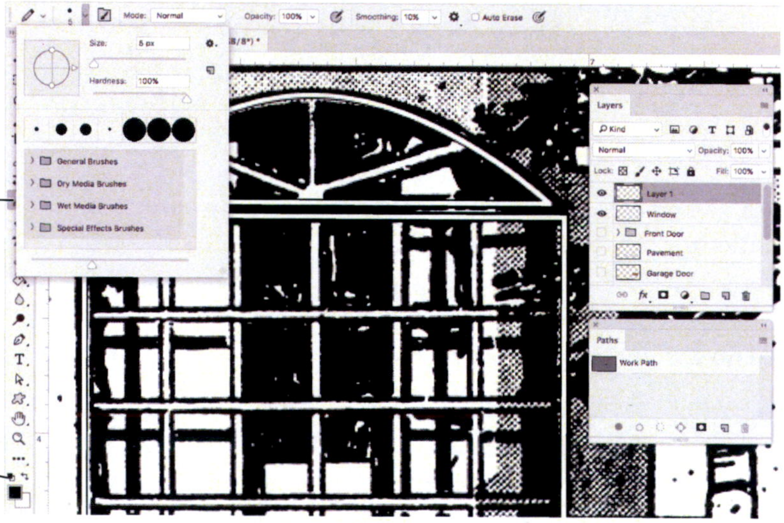

   Although you are not going to use the Pencil tool to actually draw, you need to set the tool's attributes so that you can apply those settings to a path in the next few steps.

4. **Use the Pen tool in Path mode to draw a horizontal line that represents the top horizontal division of the window.**

   Because this is an open path (i.e., it doesn't create an actual shape), creating the black-and-white effect requires a slightly different method.

5. **With the work path selected in the Paths panel, choose Stroke Path from the panel Options menu.**

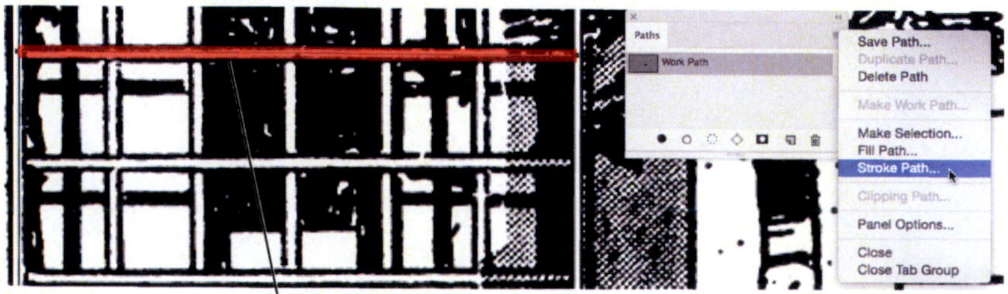

Using the Pen tool, draw this line as the path.

Note:

*If **Auto Erase** is checked in the Options bar, the Pencil tool paints based on the defined foreground and background colors, relative to the color of pixels under the tool cursor. If you draw over an area that contains the foreground color, that area is erased to the background color. If you draw over an area that does not include the foreground color, the Pencil tool simply applies the foreground color.*

6. **In the resulting Stroke Path dialog box, choose Pencil, and then click OK.**

   Using this method, you can define a specific tool to use for the stroke. The current characteristics of the selected tool will be applied, which is why you set the Pencil tool options in Steps 2 and 3.

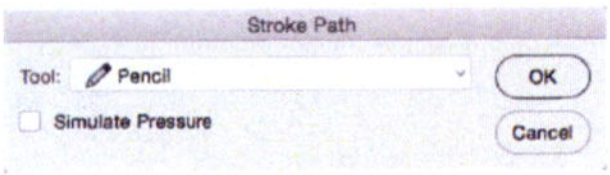
Stroke Path
Tool: Pencil
Simulate Pressure
OK
Cancel

7. **Choose the Pencil tool again, change the brush size to 3 px, and then swap the foreground and background colors.**

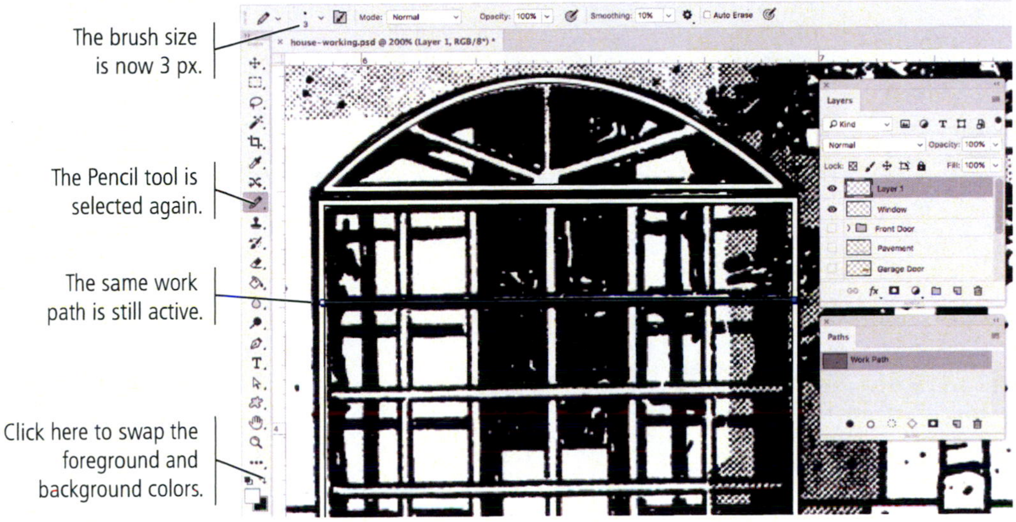
The brush size is now 3 px.
The Pencil tool is selected again.
The same work path is still active.
Click here to swap the foreground and background colors.

8. **With the work path still selected in the Paths panel, choose Stroke Path from the panel Options menu.**

9. **Choose Pencil in the resulting dialog box and click OK.**

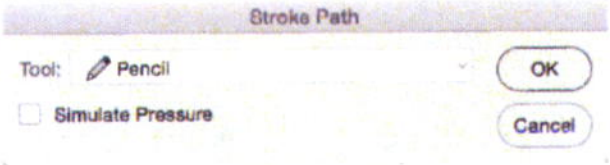
Stroke Path
Tool: Pencil
Simulate Pressure
OK
Cancel

10. **Click the empty area of the Paths panel to turn off the work path.**

11. **Hide the Sketch layer and review your work.**

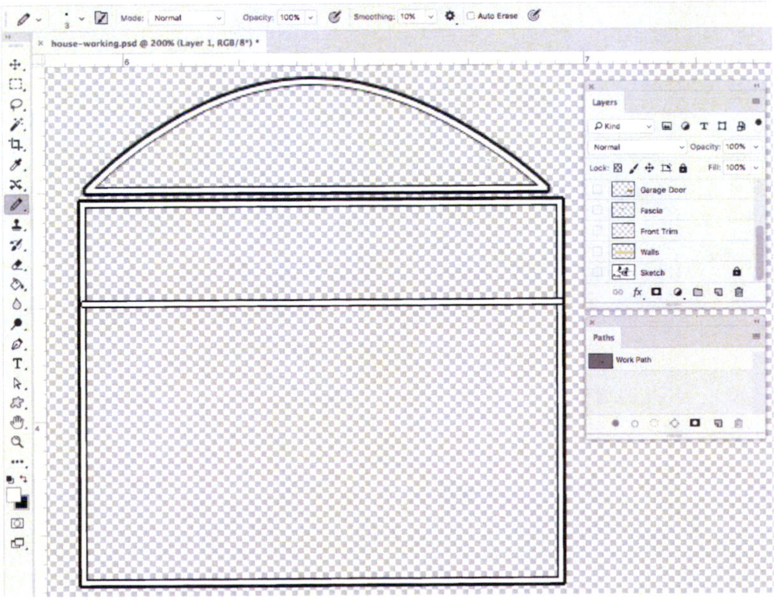

12. **Select the Move tool. With the Layer 1 layer active in the Layers panel, press Option/Alt-Shift, and then click and drag down to clone the horizontal line.**

If you had not deselected in Step 10, this step would create the cloned line on the existing Layer 1 instead of creating a new layer.

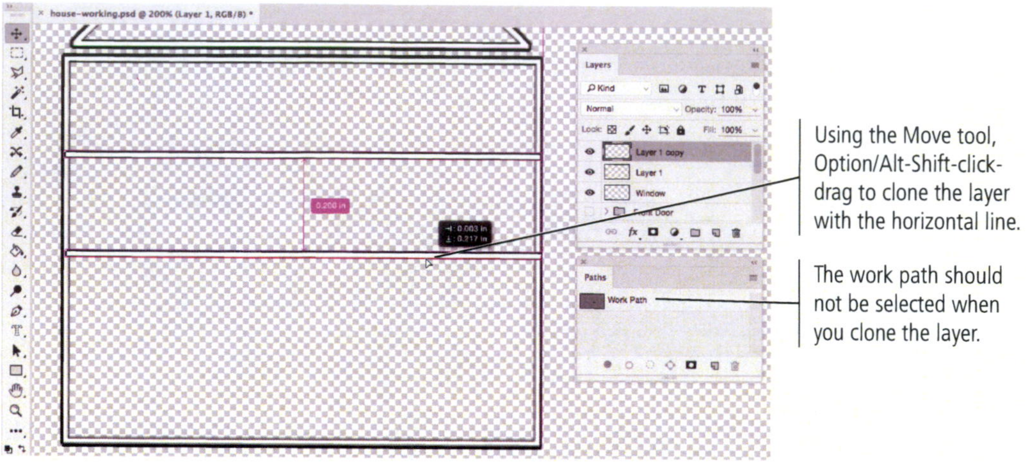

Using the Move tool, Option/Alt-Shift-click-drag to clone the layer with the horizontal line.
The work path should not be selected when you clone the layer.

13. **Repeat Step 12 to create the remaining horizontal line.**

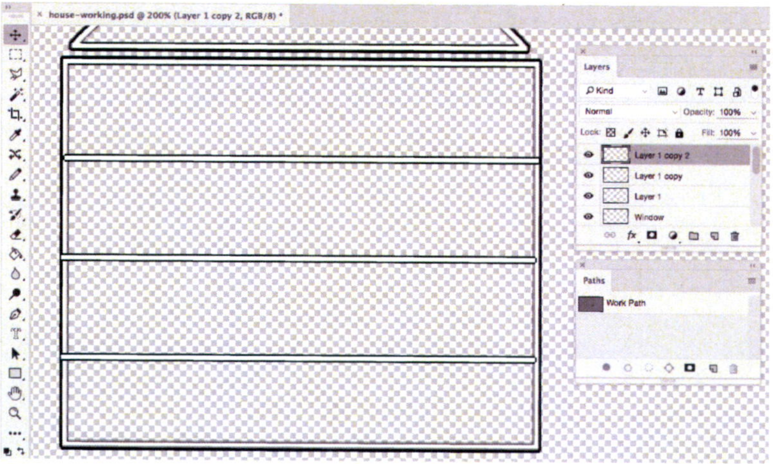

14. **Use any method you prefer to create the remaining lines of the window, including the lines in the arched window area.**

Whenever possible, clone elements to save yourself work. For example, you could clone one of the layers with a horizontal line, then transform (rotate and scale) that clone to create a vertical line — which you can then clone to create all the necessary vertical lines.

You can use the same process to create the angled lines in the arched window, rotating the layers as necessary to approximate the correct angles.

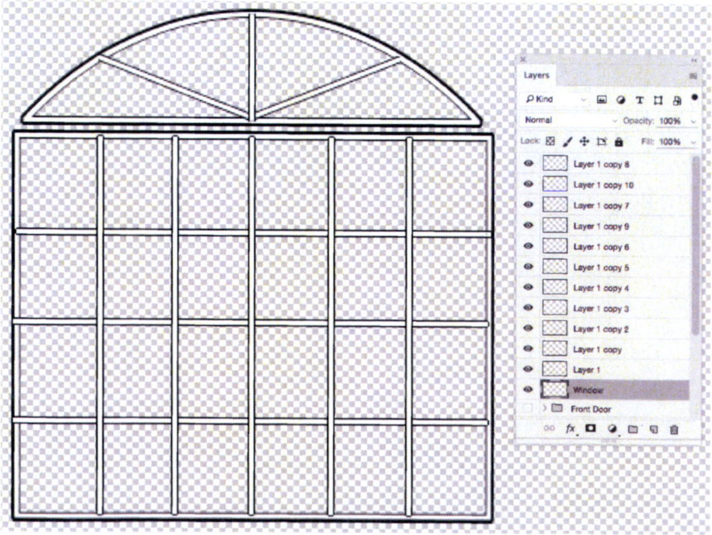

15. **Move the Window layer to the top of the layer stack.**

This hides the ends of the open lines behind the closed paths. If any line ends are visible, select the appropriate layer with the Move tool and use the Arrow keys to nudge it into place.

16. **Select all temporary layers and the Window layer. Open the Layers panel Options menu and choose Merge Layers.**

The topmost layer attributes — including the name — are applied to the merged layer. The entire element is now contained on the single Window layer.

As with the Front Door layer, you might prefer to store the component layers in a layer group, so you could more easily make changes to the component layers at a later point. In this case, it really isn't necessary, so you are merging all the component layers into a single Window layer.

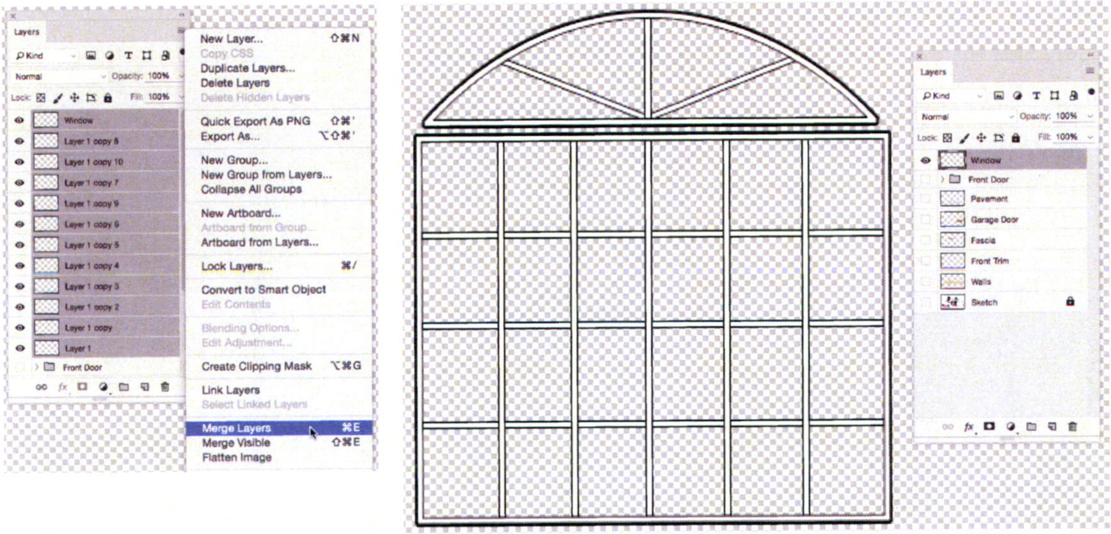

17. **Save the file and continue to the next exercise.**

> *Note:*
>
> *The document tab displays the name of the active layer. This tab can be very helpful when you're working on complex files with multiple layers.*
>
> 
>

Paint Behind Existing Color

The Behind blending mode is only available when you are creating pixels (painting, adding a fill or stroke to a selection, and so on). This blending mode adds new pixels behind the existing pixels; any existing pixels that are fully opaque will entirely hide the new pixels. This technique is extremely useful for filling spaces and lining edges of existing areas. In this exercise, you will use the Behind method to create the lines that surround the garage door panels.

1. **With house-working.psd open, hide all but the Sketch and Garage Door layers, and then select the Garage Door layer as the active layer.**

2. **Change the foreground color to the Doors 4 swatch.**

3. **Choose the Brush tool and define a 25-px brush size with 100% hardness. In the Options bar, open the Blending Mode menu and choose Behind.**

4. **Click and drag across the top dividing line in the garage door.**

Use a 25-px hard round brush.

Choose the Behind blending mode.

Click and drag across this line.

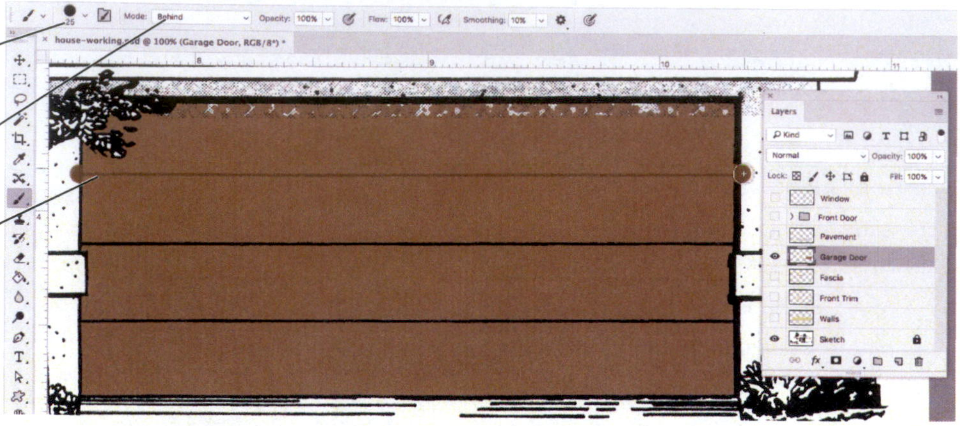

5. **Repeat Step 4 to fill in the other dividing lines in the door, the space above the door, and the space on the right and left sides of the door.**

6. **Show the Front Trim layer, then drag it to the top of the layer stack.**

   The Behind blending mode only applies to the active layer; other layers are obscured by painted areas. To create the appropriate effect, you have to change the layer stacking order so the trim appears in front of the entire Garage Door layer.

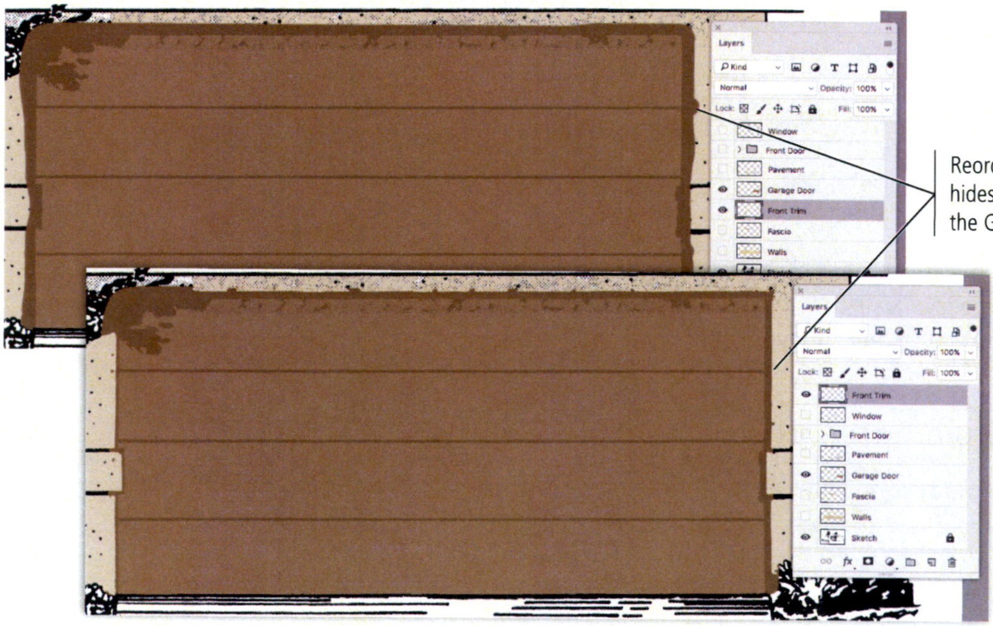

Reordering the layers hides overpainting on the Garage Door layer.

7. **Save the file and continue to the next exercise.**

Modify Selections to Fill Behind Color

Much of the remaining work is more of the same — you need to fill in the empty areas and apply a stroke around the house trim, fascia, and pavement. You could accomplish this with brushes, carefully painting individual strokes as necessary to all the different pieces. However, another method based on selections can accomplish the same general result in a fraction of the time.

1. **With `house-working.psd` open, make sure the Front Trim layer is selected.**

2. **Create a selection that contains only the filled area of the Front Trim layer.**

   To accomplish this, simply Command/Control-click the Front Trim layer thumbnail in the Layers panel.

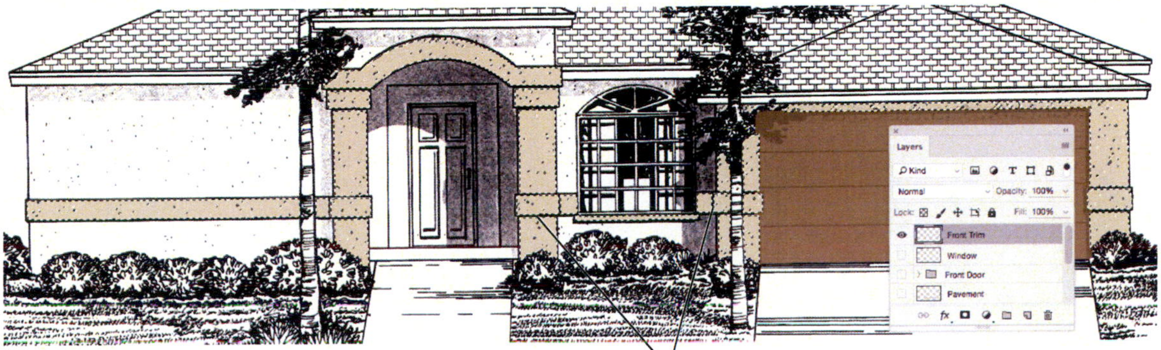

The selection excludes all of the inner areas.

3. **Choose Select>Modify>Expand. In the resulting dialog box, type 4 in the field and click OK.**

   This enlarges the original selection area by 4 pixels. When you fill the enlarged selection, the result will be an apparent edge around the objects on the Front Trim layer.

Expanding the selection includes most of the inner areas of the trim.

4. **Choose Select>Modify>Feather. In the resulting dialog box, type 3 in the field and click OK.**

   Feathering the selection creates a softer edge, which will result in more natural shadows.

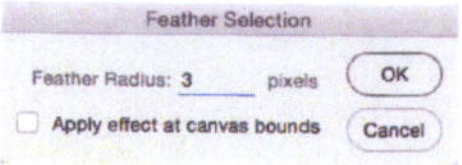

5. **Set the foreground color to Doors 4 if it is not already.**

6. **With the selection active, choose Edit>Fill. In the Fill dialog box, choose Foreground Color in the Contents menu and choose Behind in the Blending Mode menu, then click OK.**

   The Behind blending mode in this dialog box has the same effect as painting with the Brush tool using the Behind blending mode.

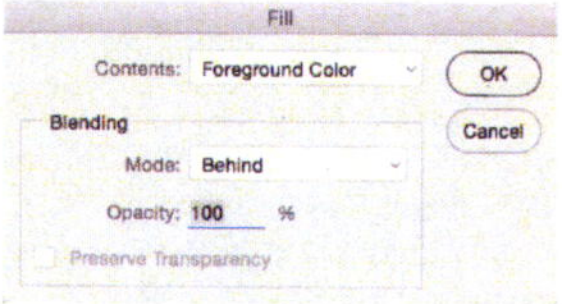

7. **Deselect the active selection, then hide the Sketch layer and review the results.**

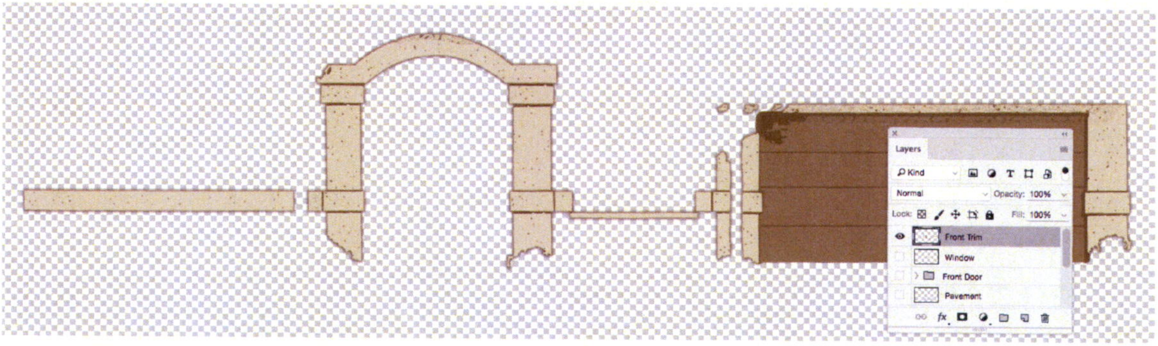

8. **Show the Fascia layer, and then drag it to the top of the layer stack.**

9. **Repeat Steps 2–7 for the Fascia layer using the same Doors 4 color.**

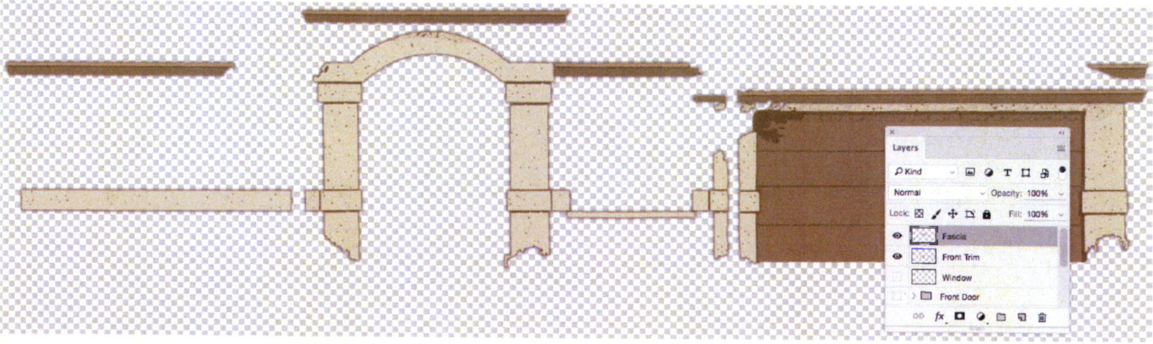

10. **Show the Pavement layer, and then drag it below the Garage Door layer.**

11. **Repeat the same general process (without the feathering) for the Pavement layer, using the Pavement 2 swatch as the fill color.**

We did not feather this selection before filling it because pavement typically does not have a softened edge.

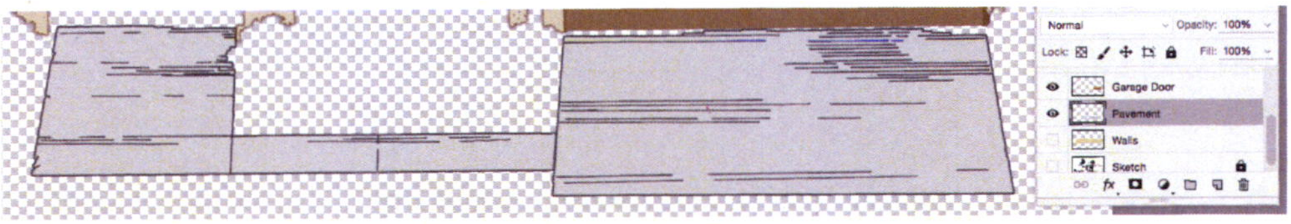

12. **Deselect any active marquee.**

13. **Choose the Brush tool and define a hard round brush. Using the Behind blending mode, fill in the pavement areas that were not filled in by Step 11.**

Click-Shift-click to create straight lines that connect the two points where you click; this method allows you to cleanly paint the pavement edges. You can then more easily fill in the empty areas.

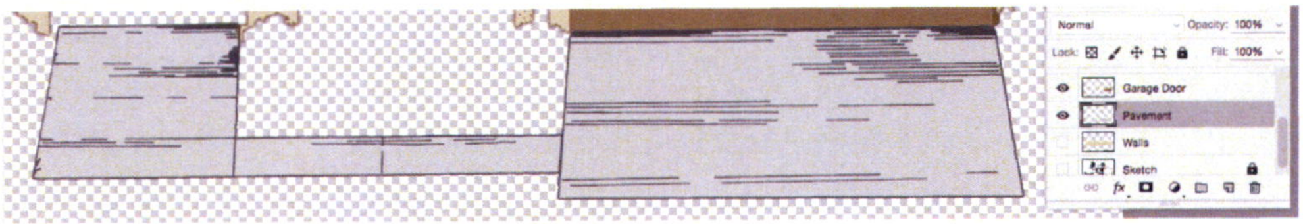

14. **Save the file and continue to the next exercise.**

Painting with the Mixer Brush

PHOTOSHOP FOUNDATIONS

The **Mixer Brush** simulates realistic painting techniques such as mixing colors on a canvas, combining colors on a brush, and varying paint wetness across a stroke.

In the Options bar, the **Current Brush Load** shows what color is currently loaded in the brush. You can click the swatch to open the color picker, or Option/Alt click the screen to sample a load color from the existing image.

If you click the arrow button to the right of the Current Brush Load swatch, you can choose **Clean Brush** to empty all color from the brush, or choose **Load Brush** to fill the brush with the defined load color. **Load Solid Colors Only** prevents the brush from loading multiple "paint" colors.

If **Load Brush After Each Stroke** is toggled on, the brush load is restored to full capacity after each stroke.

If the **Clean Brush After Each Stroke** option is toggled on, the brush is restored to only the load color after each stroke. When this option is toggled off, the brush "picks up" and holds color from the canvas.

The **Wet** setting defines how much paint the brush picks up from the canvas; higher settings produce longer streaks.

The **Load** setting defines the amount of paint loaded in the reservoir. At low values, strokes dry out more quickly.

The **Mix** setting defines the ratio of canvas paint to reservoir paint. At 100%, all paint is picked up from the canvas; at 0%, all paint comes from the reservoir.

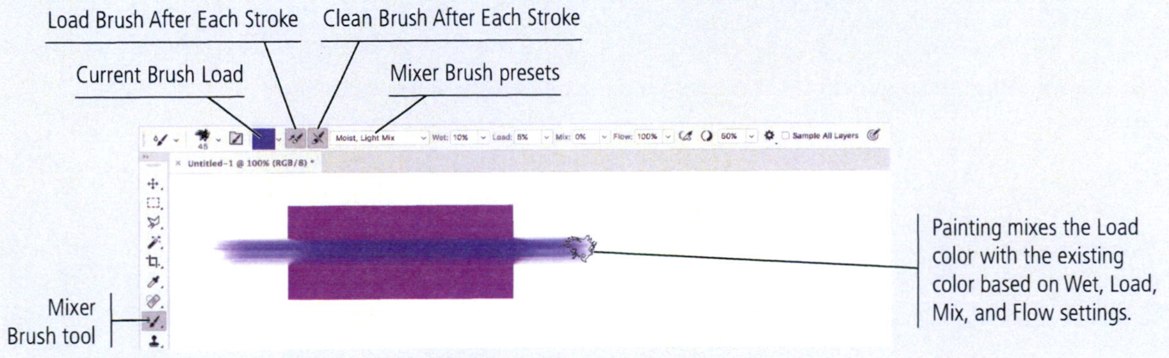

Create Texture with a Faux Finish Brush

Textures can be sampled from other images, copied and pasted into place, and created from scratch using combinations of brush styles and options. In this exercise, you use a textured brush to turn what are now simple brown walls into realistic-looking stone.

1. **With house-working.psd open, hide all but the Walls layer. Change the Walls layer opacity to 100%.**
2. **Command/Control-click the Walls layer thumbnail to select all pixels on that layer.**

3. **Choose the Brush tool. In the Options bar, set the brush blending mode to Normal.**
4. **Open the Brush Preset Picker from the Options bar, and then open the panel Options menu.**
5. **Choose Legacy Brushes in the menu.**

   The 2018 version of Photoshop CC introduced a whole new method of creating and managing custom brushes. The four default sets, which appear at the bottom of the Brush Preset Picker by default, are a very limited set random brushes. You still have access to hundreds of predefined brushes that were available in previous versions of the software, in addition to more than a thousand that are now available to download from the Adobe website by choosing Get More Brushes.

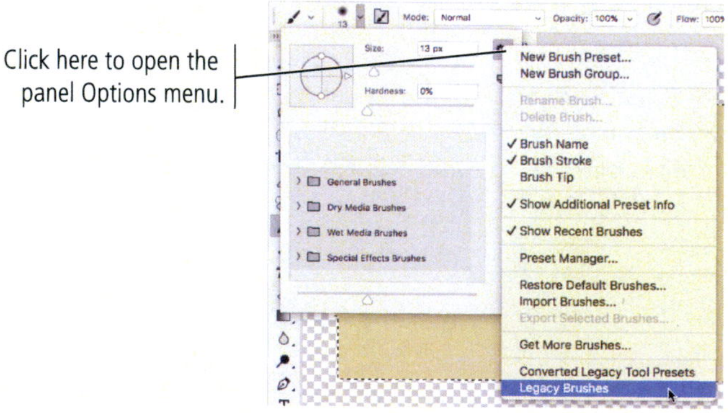

6. **In the warning message, click OK to replace the current brushes with the new set.**

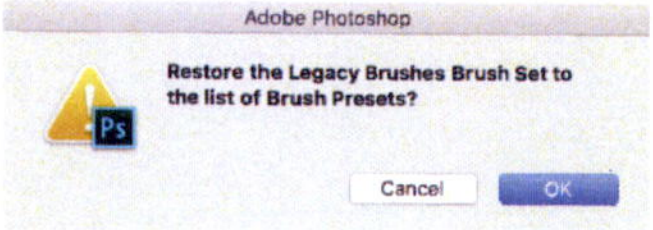

7. **In the Brush Preset Picker, expand the length of the panel so you can see more options, then expand the Legacy Brushes folder.**

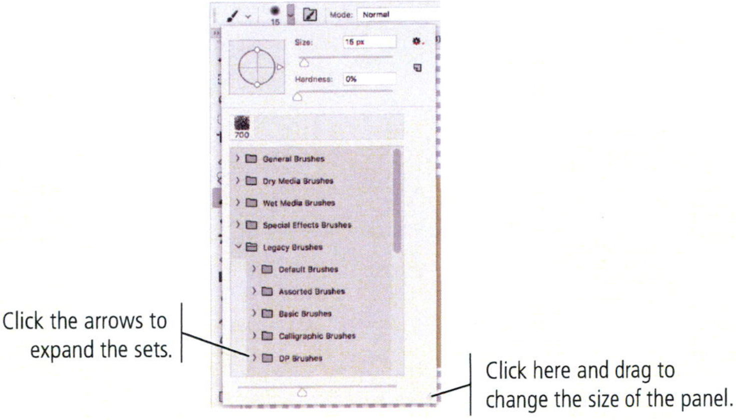

8. **Expand the Faux Finish Brushes in the panel, then scroll through the list until you find the Stencil Sponge - Wet brush.**

   The list of brushes includes a preview of the brush stroke that will be created. You can use the slider at the bottom of the panel to change the size of the brush previews.

9. **Select the Stencil Sponge – Wet preset. Make the brush size large enough to cover the highest part of the fill in the Walls layer.**

   A 700-px brush is large enough to cover the entire area in one brush stroke.

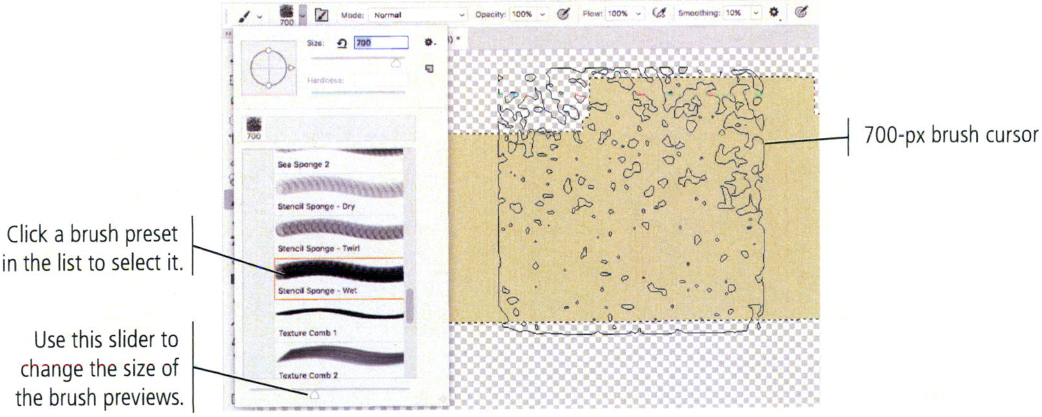

10. **Change the foreground color to the Stucco 3 swatch, and then click and drag from left to right to paint the texture into the selection area.**

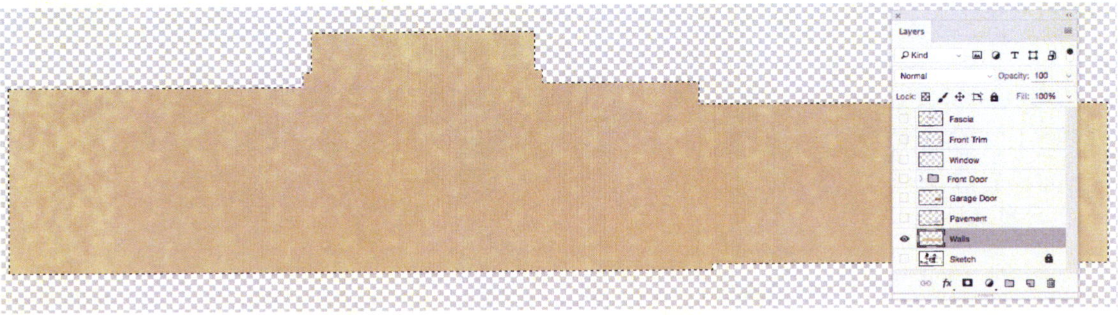

11. **Deselect off the active selection, save the file, and continue to the next exercise.**

Use Opacity and Blending Modes to Create Shadows

In many cases, it works well to paint on a separate layer and adjust the layer's blend options (blending mode and opacity). In other cases, however, adjusting the settings for the specific brush makes it easier to create subtle elements such as the shadows on the front of the house.

1. **With house-working.psd open, make all layers visible.**

2. **Reduce the Walls layer opacity to 50% so that you can see the sketch through the walls.**

3. **Create a new layer named House Shadows immediately below the Front Trim layer.**

4. **Choose the Brush tool and set the foreground color to Doors 3.**

5. **Using the Brush Preset Picker in the Options bar, choose the Soft Round brush in the General Brushes set, and set the size to 100 px.**

Expand the General Brushes set to access the basic round options.

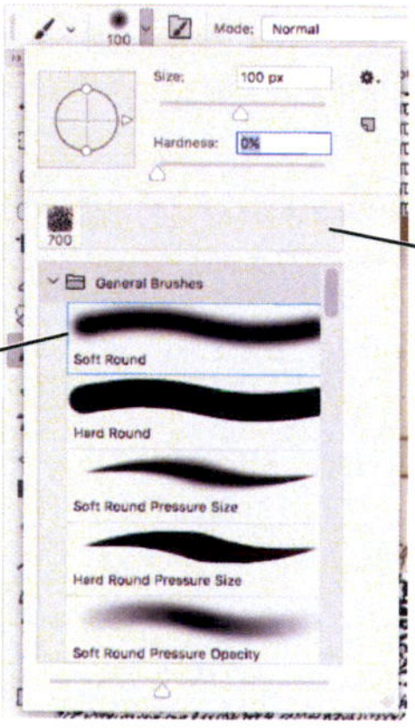

Recently used brushes appear here.

6. **In the Options bar, define the following options:**

Blending Mode:	**Multiply**
Opacity:	**25%**
Enable Airbrush-Style Build-Up Effects:	**Active**

7. **Use the shadows in the Sketch layer as a guide to paint the shadow strokes on the House Shadows layer.**

Because you are using Airbrush mode, each successive brush stroke applies more color. Use multiple strokes to build darker shadows near the house edges that cast the shadows.

Using reduced brush opacity and the Multiply blending mode, you can build darker shadows without completely obscuring the color and texture of the wall — just as actual shadows appear in real life.

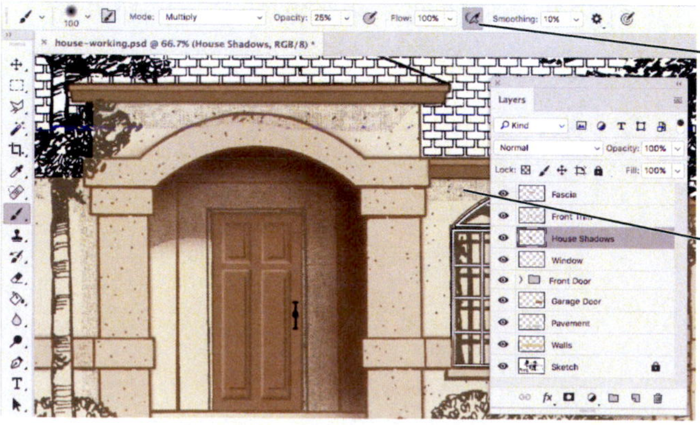

Enable Airbrush-Style Build-up Effects

The shadows on the sketch define where you need to paint.

8. **Hide the Sketch layer and review your results.**

   It can be helpful to frequently toggle the visibility of the Sketch layer as you paint in the shadows, so you can see where your shadows still need work.

9. **Continue painting the shadows until you are satisfied with your result.**

10. **Create a new layer named Window Inside below the Window layer. Fill the window area with black, and set the layer opacity to 35%.**

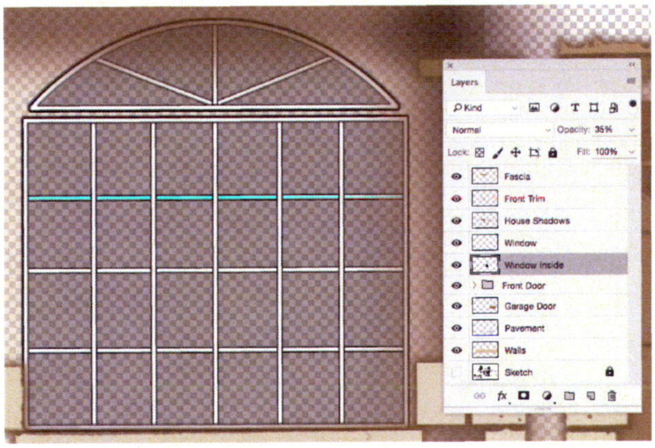

11. **Create another new layer named Window Shadows below the Window layer but above the Window Inside layer.**

12. **Use a soft round brush with a low Flow setting, and use black as the foreground color to paint the shadows that fall inside the house. Change the brush size, flow, and opacity as necessary to create the shadows.**

    We used a 20-px brush with 50% hardness, Normal blending mode, 100% opacity, and 25% flow for the horizontal lines and a slightly smaller brush size for the vertical lines.

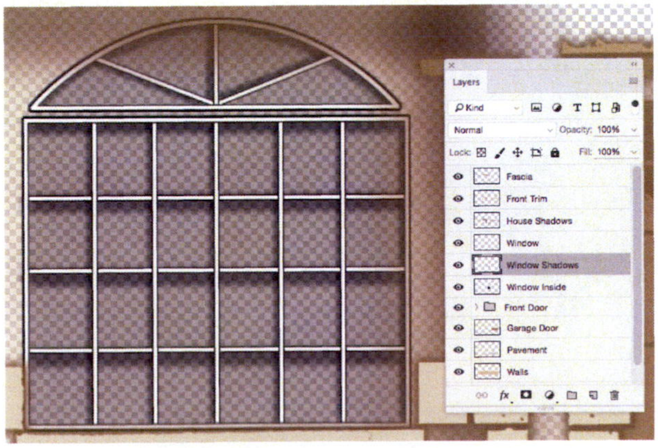

13. **Show all layers, and set the Walls layer to 100% opacity.**

14. **Save the file and continue to the next stage of the project.**

Painting Back in Time

The **History Brush tool** allows you to restore specific areas of an image back to a previous state. In the Options bar, you can choose the brush preset and brush settings that you want to use. When you paint with the History Brush tool, areas where you paint return to the target state or snapshot in the History panel. (The same effect can be achieved using any of the regular Eraser tools with the Erase to History option active.)

In the image shown here, we opened a file and made a Levels adjustment to lighten the image. We then applied some painting and touch-ups, as well as a filter to make the image look like a line-art drawing. In the final step, we selected the adjusted, unfiltered state and used the History Brush tool to restore only the top floors back to the photographic pixels.

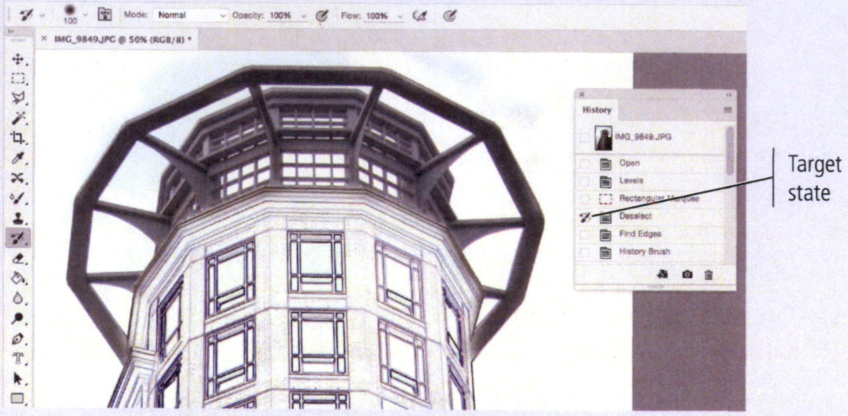

The **Art History Brush tool** paints with stylized strokes, using the targeted history state (or snapshot) as the source data for the painting. (We can't say the tool "restores" the data, because results from the artistic style of the brush could hardly be called "restorative.")

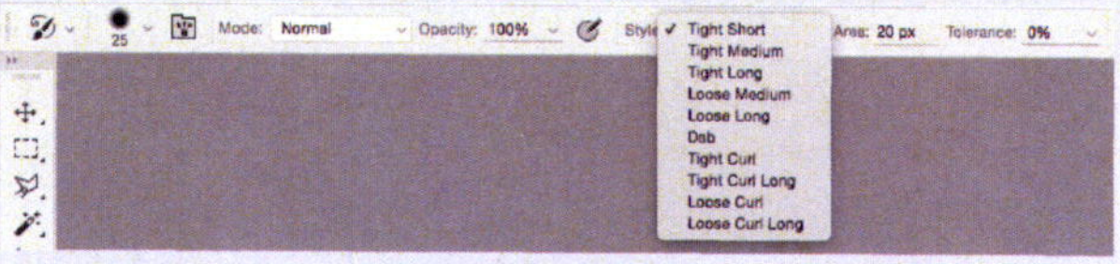

In the Options bar, you can define the brush preset, blending mode, and opacity, as well as a specific style that will be used for the brush marks. The Area option defines the area that will be covered with the brush marks; larger area values result in a greater area covered, as well as more brush marks created by the stroke. Tolerance limits the area where brush strokes can be applied; higher tolerance values limit painting to areas that significantly differ from colors in the targeted state of the snapshot.

In the series of images shown here, we targeted the original image snapshot in the History panel, and then restored the top floors by using the Art History Brush with different style settings.

Restored with the Tight Short style

Restored with the Loose Medium style

Restored with the Dab style

Restored with the Tight Curl style

Stage 3 Working with Patterns

The only element of the house left to paint is the roof. Manually drawing every shingle would take hours, and it would be difficult (if not impossible) to create the uniformity that is an actual part of real roofing shingles. A better solution is to use a pattern fill. Unfortunately, the built-in Photoshop pattern sets do not include a roof tile pattern, so in this exercise, you will create your own. Fortunately, you can create a pattern from anything you can paint.

Define a Pattern from Existing Artwork

The trick to creating a good repeating tile is placing or creating elements in such a way that apparent edges align properly when the pattern is tiled. Once you have defined the tile, creating and applying the pattern is fairly easy.

1. **Open the file tiles.psd from the WIP>Houses folder. If you receive a color profile mismatch warning, use the embedded profile.**

   This file was created as a 1-inch square. Each edge of the square has half of the blurred lines that make up the tile edges.

2. **Choose Edit>Define Pattern.**

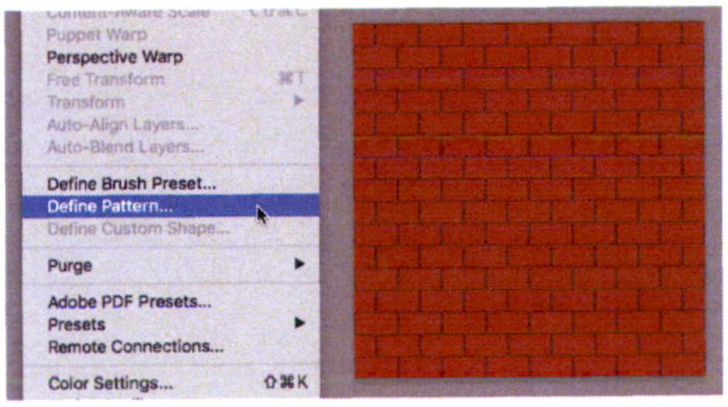

3. **In the Pattern Name dialog box, type Shingles and click OK.**

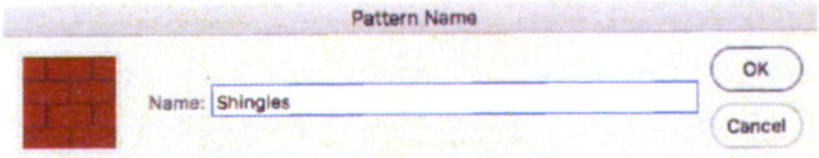

Understanding the Pattern Stamp Tool

PHOTOSHOP FOUNDATIONS

The **Pattern Stamp tool** (nested under the Clone Stamp tool) is used to paint patterns onto selected areas of an image. In the Options bar, you can define the specific brush settings and the pattern you want to apply.

The Impressionist option creates an artistic interpretation of the pattern; you have no control over the results, other than the specific brush and options being used.

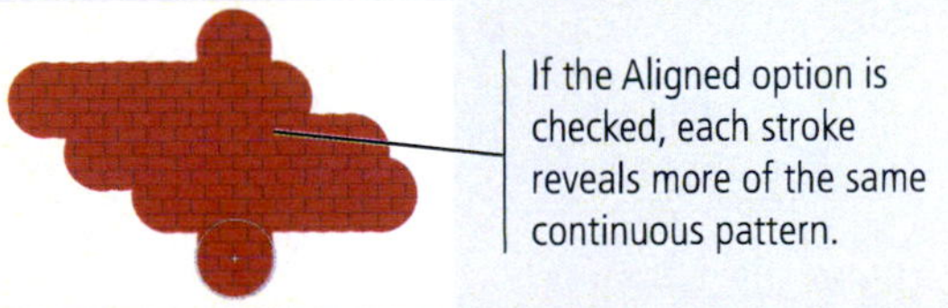
If the Aligned option is checked, each stroke reveals more of the same continuous pattern.

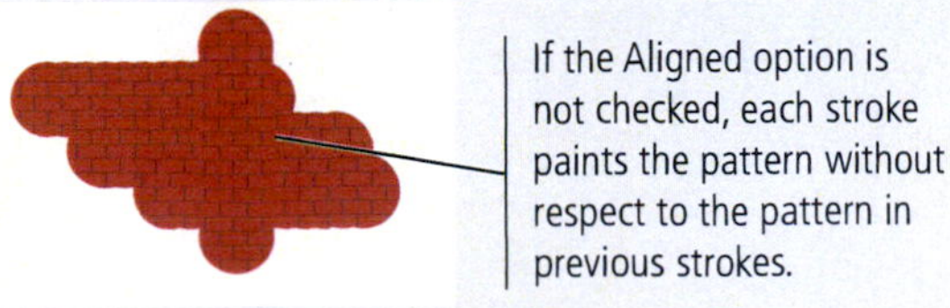
If the Aligned option is not checked, each stroke paints the pattern without respect to the pattern in previous strokes.

If the Aligned option is checked, the pattern is basically locked to the layer; clicking and dragging reveals the part of the pattern that exists where you drag. Think of the Aligned option this way: The entire layer is theoretically "filled" with the selected pattern; when you paint with the Pattern Stamp tool, the pattern fill is revealed in those areas where you paint — in other words, the pattern is aligned in each successive stroke.

When the Aligned option is not checked, each stroke of the Pattern Stamp tool paints the pattern onto the selected layer. The pattern is not aligned from one stroke to the next.

4. **Close the tiles image without saving it.**
5. **Make the house-working.psd file active in the document window.**
6. **Create a new layer named Roof 1 at the top of the layer stack.**
7. **Using the Polygonal Lasso tool, draw a selection around the main roof area.**

   You might have to make some assumptions in the top corners, where the sketched trees obscure the roof corners.

Don't worry if the selection covers some of the house; you will fix potential problems later.

8. **Choose Edit>Fill, and choose Pattern in the Contents menu. Open the Custom Pattern menu and choose the Shingles pattern.**

   This pattern you created was added to the existing options in the Patterns panel.

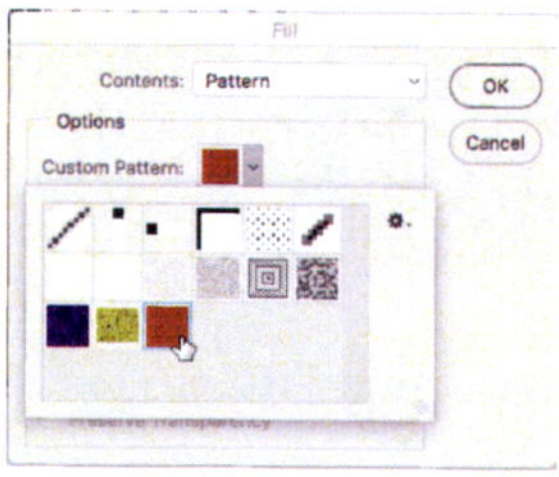

9. **Make sure the Blending Mode menu is set to Normal and the Opacity is set to 100%, then click OK to fill the selection area with the pattern.**

   As you can see, the lines on the pattern tile align seamlessly in the pattern fill.

10. **Deselect the active selection, then hide the Roof 1 layer.**

11. **Use the same process to create the two remaining sections of the roof, each on its own layer (named Roof 2 and Roof 3).**

Use the Polygonal Lasso tool to make a selection, then use the Fill dialog box to add the pattern fill.

12. **Show the Roof 1 layer.**

With all three roof sections showing, you can now see two problems. First, the main roof is obscuring the porch covering and fascia. Second, all three pieces of the roof were created with the same pattern, so all three pieces merge seamlessly together.

13. **Drag the Fascia and Front Trim layers to the top of the layer stack.**

It's common to lock, hide, and move layers as necessary when working on a complex assignment like this one. At times, the position of specific layers becomes critical, as does making sure you're working on the correct layer. When you work on a complex file, plan your work and then carefully follow those plans.

14. **Set the Roof 1 layer opacity to 50% so you can see the underlying layers.**

15. **Using the Rectangular Marquee tool, draw a selection marquee around the area of the house that is obscured by the Roof 1 layer content.**

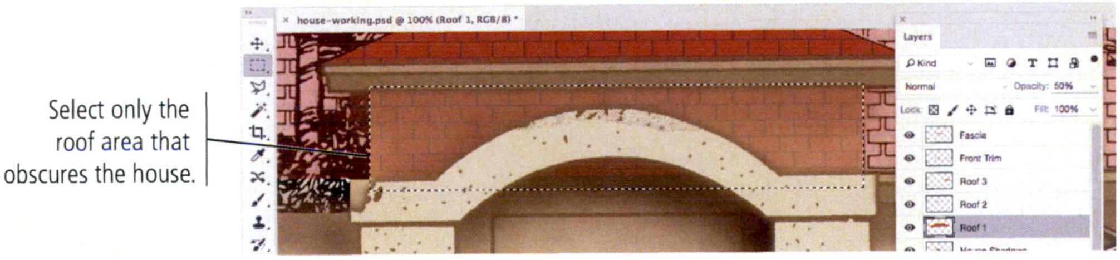

16. **With the Roof 1 layer selected, press Delete/Backspace to remove all pixels inside the selection area.**

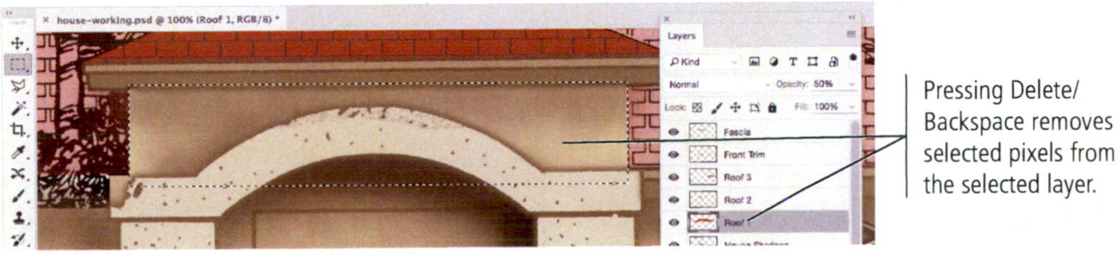

17. **Restore the Roof 1 layer to 100% opacity.**

18. **Use any method you prefer to add a dark, soft edge around each roof section. Sample the dark color in the tile pattern to use as the edge color.**

    You can use the Paint Behind method with a soft-edge brush, or use the modified-selection fill technique you used for the front trim.

19. **Save the file and continue to the next exercise.**

Save Custom Patterns

You never know when a particular pattern or other asset might be useful. By default, when you quit Photoshop you lose any custom assets unless you intentionally save them. Since you have taken the time to create the pattern for a tiled roof, it's a good idea to save it so you can use it again later.

1. **With house-working.psd open, choose Edit>Presets>Preset Manager.**

   You can use the Preset Manager to control built-in and custom assets, including brushes, swatches, gradients, styles, patterns, contours, custom shapes, and tools.

2. **Choose Patterns in the Preset Type menu.**

3. **Shift-click to select all patterns except the custom pattern you created.**

   Your panel might have more or fewer than the patterns shown in our screen shots. Select everything except the shingle pattern.

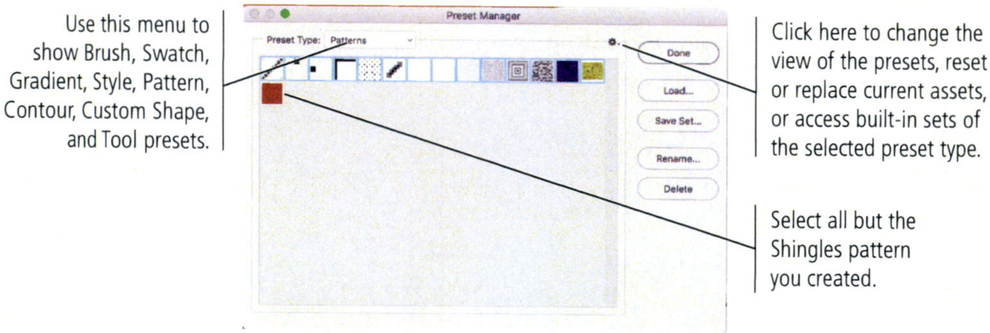
Use this menu to show Brush, Swatch, Gradient, Style, Pattern, Contour, Custom Shape, and Tool presets.
Preset Manager
Preset Type: Patterns
Done
Load...
Save Set...
Rename...
Delete
Click here to change the view of the presets, reset or replace current assets, or access built-in sets of the selected preset type.
Select all but the Shingles pattern you created.

4. **Click Delete to remove the selected patterns from the dialog box.**

   You're deleting these patterns from the panel only. You can always load them again by choosing from the available sets in the Patterns panel Options menu.

Erasing Pixels

The **Eraser tool** removes pixels where you click. If you erase from the Background layer or in a regular layer with transparency locked, the background color shows through where you erased.

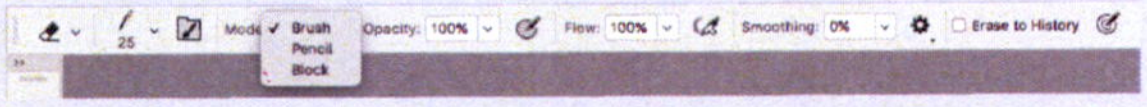

If the **Erase to History** option is checked, dragging with the Eraser tool (in any mode) reveals the selected state in the History panel.

- The default Block mode simply erases the area under the square cursor; you can't control the size, shape, opacity, or flow of the tool. When using the Eraser tool, the opacity setting determines the strength of the tool; 100% opacity entirely erases pixels.
- If you choose Brush mode, you can define the specific brush preset, opacity, and flow, as well as use the Eraser brush in Airbrush mode.
- If you choose Pencil mode, you can define the specific brush and opacity; Pencil mode does not offer flow control or Airbrush mode.

The **Magic Eraser tool** (nested under the Eraser tool) works on the same principle as the Magic Wand tool. Clicking with the tool erases all pixels within the defined tolerance.

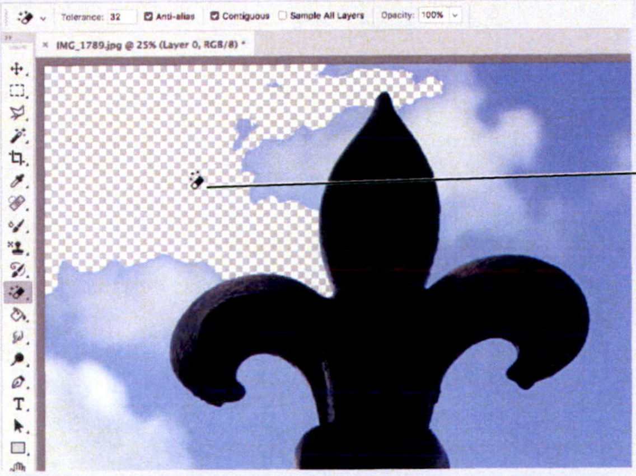

Clicking with the Magic Eraser tool removes all pixels within the defined tolerance.

The **Background Eraser tool** (nested under the Eraser tool) erases pixels while attempting to maintain the edges of an object in the foreground. The Background Eraser samples color at the brush center, and deletes that color where it appears inside the brush. In the Options bar, you can define the brush size and settings. You can also specify different sampling and tolerance options to control the range of pixels that are affected.

The sampling options determine how color will be replaced:

- **Continuous** samples colors as you drag.
- **Once** erases color only in areas containing the color that you first click.
- **Background Swatch** erases only areas containing the current background color.

The Limits menu constrains the tool's effect:

- **Discontiguous** erases the sampled color where it occurs under the brush.
- **Contiguous** erases colors that are contiguous with the color immediately under the brush tip.
- **Find Edges** erases connected areas of the sampled color, attempting to preserve edge sharpness.

Tolerance defines how much variance from the sample will be affected. If the **Protect Foreground Color** option is checked, pixels of the defined foreground color in the Tools panel will be protected from erasure.

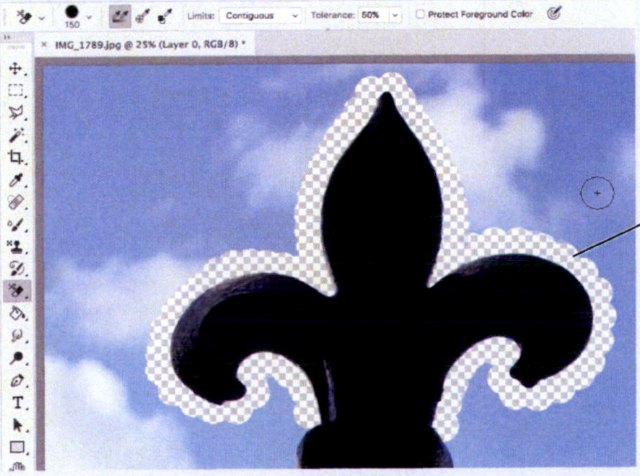

Clicking and dragging with the Background Eraser tool removes pixels within the defined tolerance.

5. **Select the remaining pattern swatch and click the Save Set button.**

6. **In the Save/Save As dialog box, name the set Portfolio Patterns.pat and click Save.**

   When you save a custom pattern set, the Save/Save As dialog box defaults to the application's Presets>Patterns folder. The extension (".pat") is automatically added for you.

   If you are using a shared computer, you might not be able to save files in the application's default location. If this is the case, navigate to your WIP>Houses folder to save the Portfolio Patterns.pat file.

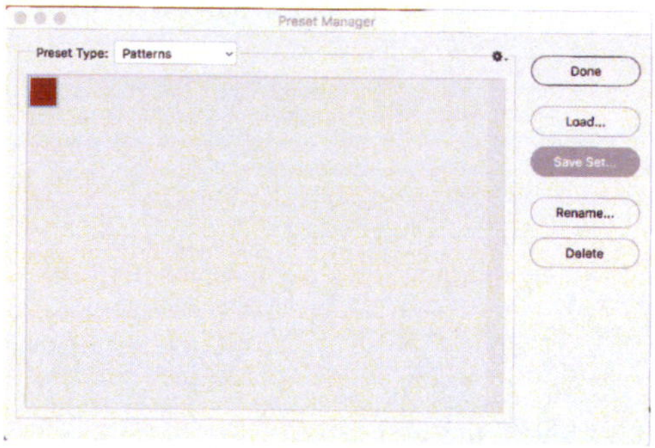

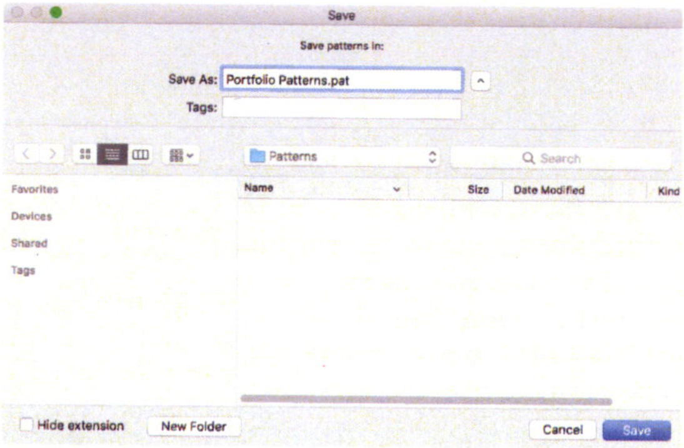

   After a pattern set has been saved, you can access those patterns again by clicking the Load button in the Preset Manager or by opening the Patterns panel Options menu.

7. **Click Done to close the Preset Manager, and then continue to the next stage of the project.**

Stage 4 Painting Nature

Some elements of this painting are far less structured than the house. The trees, bushes, grass, and other natural elements can't be created by filling and painting with basic brushes — or at least, you can't make them look natural with the tools you have learned so far. These elements should be painted more randomly so they look as natural as possible.

Use a Filter to Create Trees

When it comes to painting the landscaping, it helps to have an eye for art in general (more so than for any other component of this project). That's not to say, however, that you need to be Michelangelo to finish this project. The easiest place to start is with a built-in filter for creating the trees in the painting.

1. **With house-working.psd open, create a new layer named Tree 1 at the top of the layer stack. Hide all other layers except the Sketch layer.**

   You're going to use a series of different layers to create the various landscaping elements. Doing so will allow you to control the different pieces, including rearranging or merging them together as necessary to create the best possible result. These layers should be on top of the layer stack because most of the trees and bushes are in the sketch foreground (i.e., in front of the house).

2. **Using the Rectangular Marquee tool, draw a selection that roughly encompasses the tree on the left side of the sketch.**

   Drawing a selection marquee before calling the Tree filter limits the area in which the filter artwork can exist.

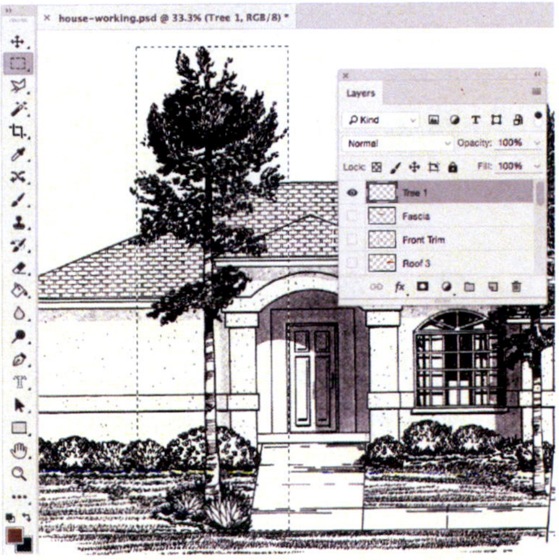

3. **With the Tree 1 layer selected, choose Filter>Render>Tree.**

   This filter does exactly what its name suggests — creates realistic trees using built-in artwork and randomizing settings.

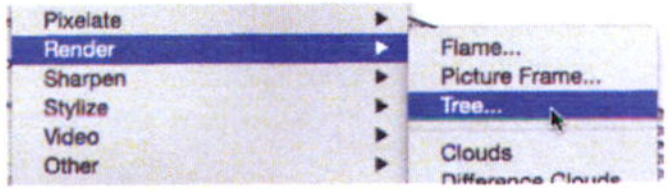

4. **Open the Basic Tree Type menu and review the options.**

   You can choose from a variety of specific species — for example, you need to create a pine forest or a ginko garden, or simply choose a tree with the look you want to achieve.

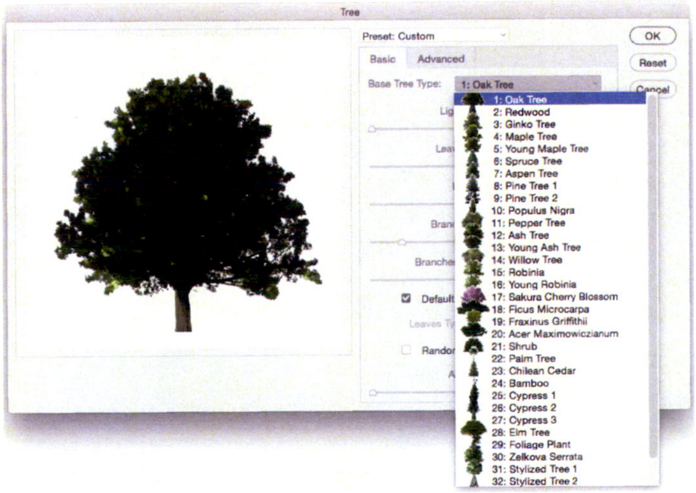

5. **Choose Populus Nigra in the Basic Tree Type menu.**

   We chose this option because it has the tall and narrow characteristics of the one in the sketch. The preview window on the left side of the dialog box shows what the resulting artwork will look like when you click OK.

6. **Experiment with the settings in the lower half of the dialog box until you are satisfied with the results.**

- **Light Direction.** Changing this value moves the apparent light source left (0) to right (180).
- **Leaves Amount.** Increasing this value adds more leaves, while decreasing it reduces the number of leaves. A value of 0, for example, would create a winter tree with no leaves at all.
- **Leaves Size.** Smaller size values results in smaller leaves, almost creating the look of a tree beginning to bud in early Spring.
- **Branches Height. Increasing** this value moves the first protruding branches father up the tree trunk.
- **Branches Thickness.** Increasing this value results in a thicker trunk and branches throughout the artwork.
- **Default Leaves.** Each tree uses a specific leaf shape as the default; for example, maple trees use a maple leaf shape. If you uncheck the Default Leaves option, you can change the shape that will be used for the leaves in your resulting tree.
- **Randomize Shapes.** If checked, this option randomly creates the tree artwork regardless of your other settings.
- **Arrangement.** When Randomize Shapes is not checked, you can increase this value to adjust the shape of branches and leaves in the resulting artwork.

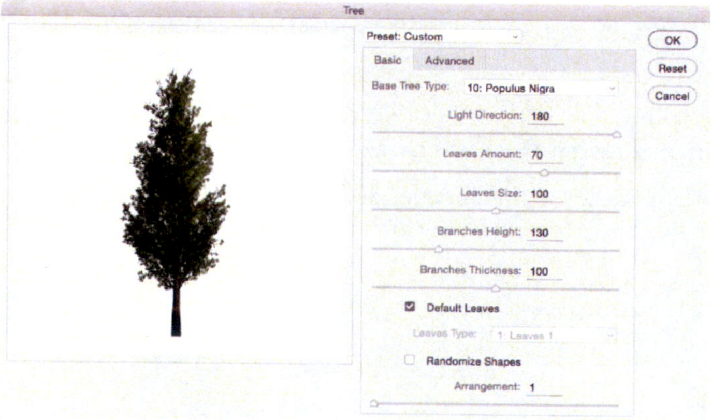

7. **Click OK to create the new tree artwork.**

The resulting artwork is scaled to fit inside the marquee that you drew before you called the filter. If you don't first make a selection area, the artwork would fill the most available space based on the dimensions of the tree you define in the filter dialog box.

8. **Turn off the active selection, then choose Edit>Free Transform. Use the bounding-box handles to adjust the size of the tree artwork to better match the sketched tree. Press Return/Enter when you are satisfied with the result.**

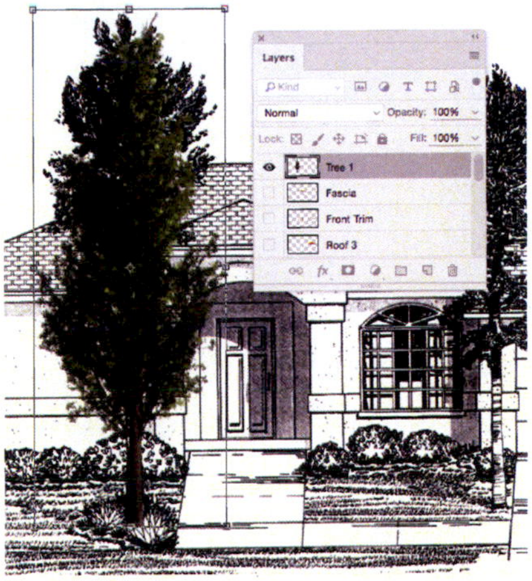

9. **Create another new layer named `Tree 2`. Repeat this same general process to create the second tree in the sketch.**

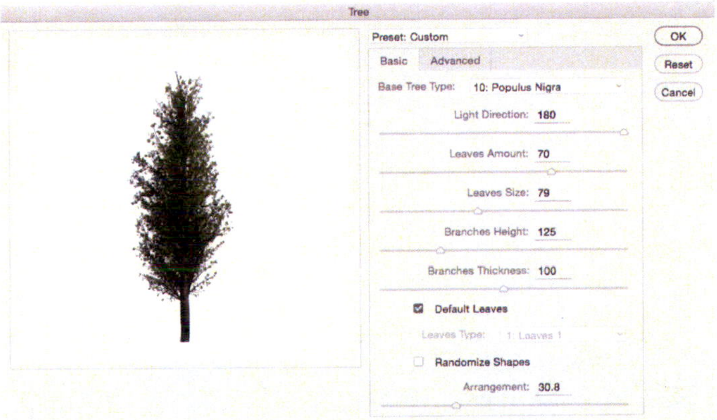

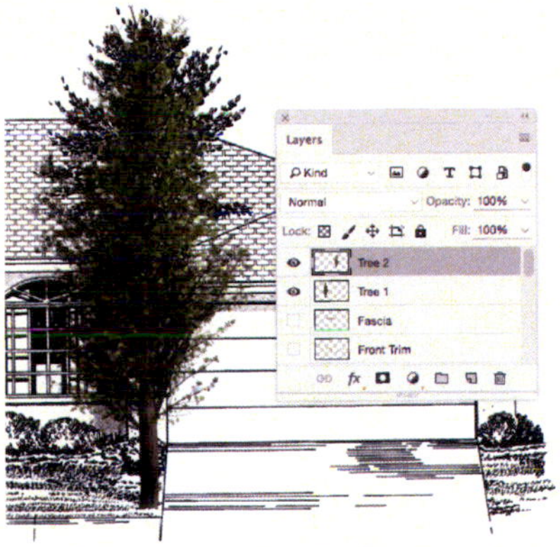

10. **Save the file, then continue to the next exercise.**

Change Brush Settings to Paint Random Elements

The randomness of shapes, colors, and textures occurring in nature simply cannot be painted using basic lines, regardless of the brush size, flow, opacity, and other options. For this reason, we can't provide specific step-by-step instructions to create every required brush stroke in this exercise. To create the shrubs and grass, we can only provide advice on how to select the best tool settings for the job. Every person will end up with different results.

1. **With `house-working.psd` open, create a new layer named `Shrubs` immediately below the Tree 1 layer. Make the Shrubs layer active.**

2. **Select the Brush tool. In the Options bar, choose Normal in the Mode menu, and set the Opacity and Flow to 100%.**

3. **In the Brush Preset Picker choose the Stencil Sponge-Twirl brush in the Faux Finishes set (inside the Legacy Brushes set).**

   This brush is the starting point; you will change the settings based on this selected preset.

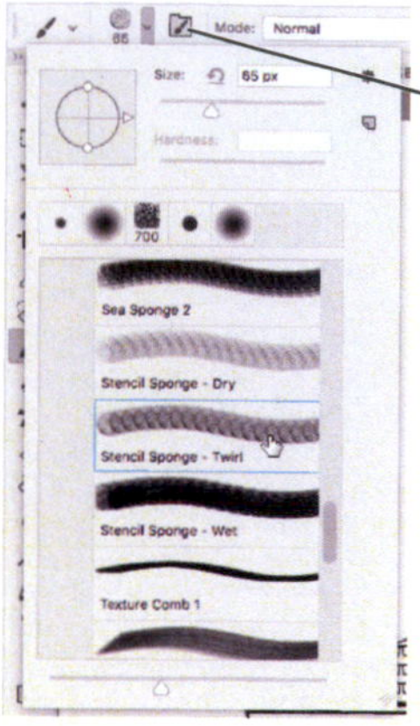

Click to open the Brush panel.

4. **In the Options bar, click the button to open the Brush Settings panel.**

5. **Choose Brush Tip Shape in the list of options. Set the Size to `40 px`, change the Angle to `30°`, and set the Roundness to `50%`.**

   Leaves are rarely straight up and down, so your brush strokes shouldn't be either.

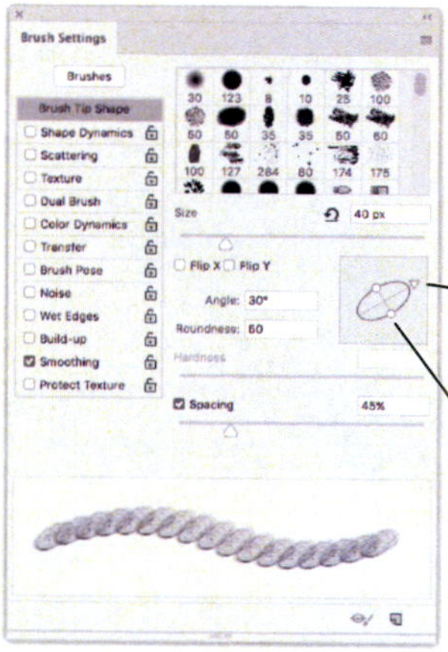

Drag the arrowhead to rotate the angle of the brush.

Drag these handles in (or out) to change the brush roundness.

6. **Select Shape Dynamics in the list on the left. Change all the Jitter sliders to `50%`, and then set all the Control menus to Off.**

   Real shrubbery has leaves in many different shapes and sizes. By jittering all these settings, you allow Photoshop to randomize the brush marks that will create the leaves.

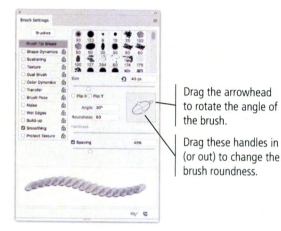

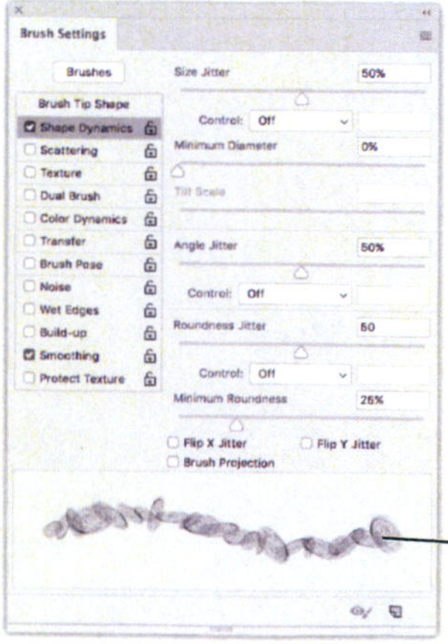

Notice the new preview, which dynamically shows the results of your settings.

7. **In the Scattering options, allow Photoshop to scatter the marks along both axes using a 150% setting.**

By scattering along both axes, you get a more random result than if brush marks only move perpendicularly from the brush stroke. Watch the preview to evaluate the results of different scatter values.

8. **Set the Count value to 2 to limit the number of brush marks in the same area.**

You can use multiple brush strokes to build up more marks in the same space.

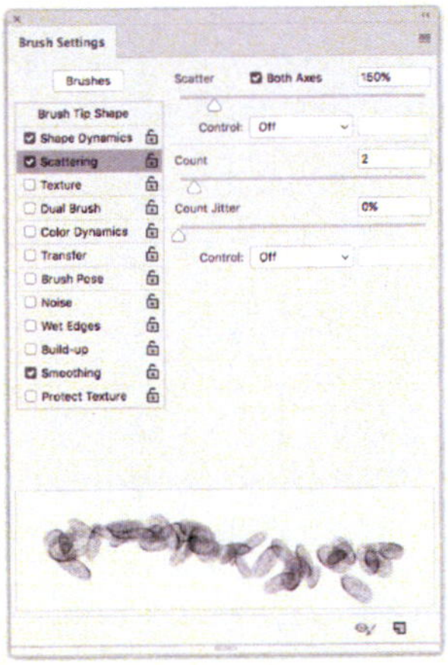

9. **In the Color Dynamics options, check the Apply Per Tip option, and apply a 100% Foreground/Background Jitter setting.**

You could manually vary the colors by frequently switching the foreground color, but this option speeds the process by varying the colors in a single brush stroke without choosing new paint colors.

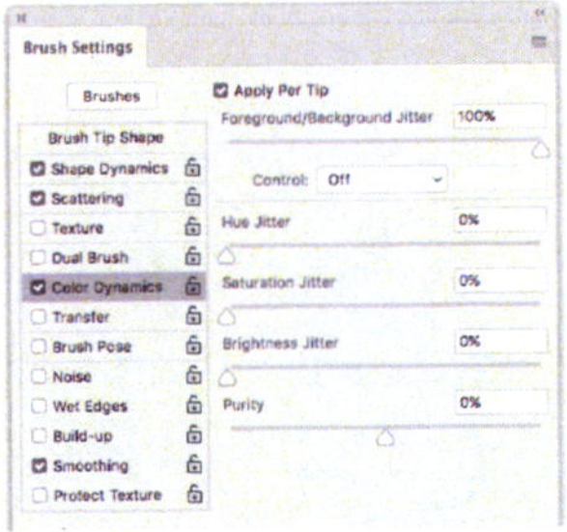

10. **In the Transfer options, apply 15% opacity jitter.**

A slight variation in the stroke opacity will further increase the randomness of the brush marks. Because some marks will be semi-transparent, overlapping areas will produce an even broader range of color without manually changing the brush color.

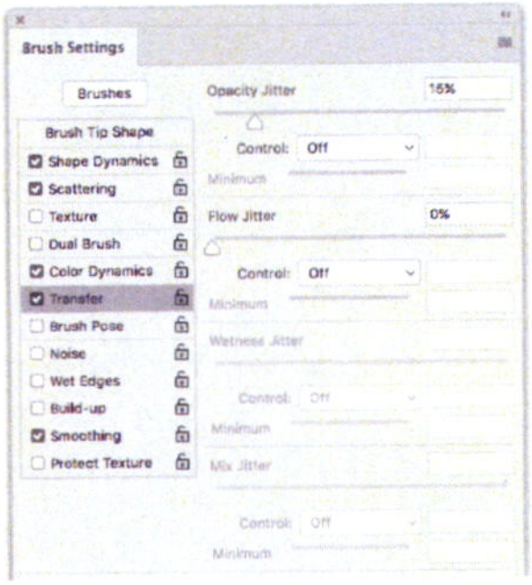

Brush Settings

Using the Brush Settings panel, you can control an extensive array of brush settings. Clicking a category in the left side of the panel shows the related options. The bottom area of the panel shows a dynamic preview of your choices.

Brush Tip Shape

Size controls the diameter (in pixels) of the brush.

Flip X and **Flip Y** change the direction of a brush tip on the X (horizontal) or Y (vertical) axis.

Angle defines the angle for an elliptical brush.

Roundness controls the ratio between the short and long axes of the brush; 100% creates a round brush, 0% creates a linear brush, and middle values create elliptical brushes.

Hardness controls the size of the brush's hard center. (This is the same as the Hardness setting in the Options bar.)

Spacing controls the distance between brush marks in a stroke. The spacing is a percentage of the brush diameter.

Shape Dynamics

Size Jitter varies the size of brush marks in a stroke, based on the maximum percentage defined here. You can also use the Control menu to vary the size of brush marks:

- Off provides no control over the variation.
- Fade varies the size of brush marks between the initial diameter and the minimum diameter in a specified number of steps (from 1 to 9999).
- Pen Pressure, Pen Tilt, Stylus Wheel, and Rotation vary the size of brush marks when using a drawing tablet/pen.

Minimum Diameter defines the minimum brush (as a percentage of brush diameter) when Size Jitter is used.

Tilt Scale specifies the scale factor for brush height when Pen Tilt is active in the Control menu.

Angle Jitter varies the angle of brush marks in a stroke (as a percentage of 360°). The Control menu specifies how you control the angle variance of brush marks:

- Off, Fade, Pen Pressure, Pen Tilt, and Stylus Wheel have the same meanings as for Size Jitter (above).
- Initial Direction bases the angle of brush marks on the initial direction of the brush stroke.
- Direction bases the angle of brush marks on the overall direction of the brush stroke.

Roundness Jitter varies the roundness of brush marks in a stroke (as a percentage of the ratio between the brush height and width).

Minimum Roundness specifies the minimum roundness for brush marks when Roundness Jitter is enabled.

Flip X Jitter and **Flip Y Jitter** allow the flip behavior (when enabled) to be randomized.

Scattering

Scatter controls how brush marks are distributed in a stroke. If Both Axes is active, brush marks are distributed radially; if Both Axes is not active, brush marks are distributed perpendicular to the stroke path.

Count defines the number of brush marks applied at each spacing interval.

Count Jitter varies the number of brush marks for each spacing interval, based on the defined maximum percentage.

Texture

Textured brushes use patterns to make strokes look as though they were painted on paper or canvas. After you choose a pattern, you can set many of the same options that are available when applying a texture effect to a layer.

Invert reverses the high (light) and low (dark) points in the texture; when Invert is selected, the lightest areas are the low points and the darkest areas are the high points.

Scale defines the size of the pattern texture as a percentage of the original pattern size.

Texture Each Tip applies the selected texture to each brush mark, rather than to the brush stroke as a whole.

Mode defines the blending mode that combines the brush and the pattern.

Depth defines how deeply color affects the texture. At 0%, all points receive the same amount of color, which obscures the texture; at 100%, low points are not painted.

Minimum Depth specifies the minimum depth to which color can penetrate.

Depth Jitter varies the depth (when Texture Each Tip is selected), based on the maximum percentage defined here.

Dual Brush

A dual brush combines two brush tips. The second brush texture is applied within the stroke of the primary brush; only areas where both brush strokes intersect are painted.

Mode defines the blending mode that will combine marks from the two brushes.

Size defines the diameter of the dual tip (in pixels).

Spacing defines the distance between the dual-tip brush marks in a stroke as a percentage of the brush diameter.

Scatter determines how dual-tip brush marks are distributed in a stroke. (See Scattering above.)

Count defines the number of dual-tip brush marks at each spacing interval.

Brush Settings (continued)

Color Dynamics

Color dynamics determine how the color of paint changes over the course of a stroke.

Apply Per Tip allows color dynamics to change across a single brush stroke. If this option is not checked, the color is varied only between multiple strokes with the same brush.

Foreground/Background Jitter varies between the foreground and background colors.

Hue Jitter varies the hue in a stroke; lower percentages create less hue variation across the stroke.

Saturation Jitter varies the saturation in a stroke; lower percentages create less saturation variation across the stroke.

Brightness Jitter varies the brightness in a stroke; lower percentages create less brightness variation across the stroke.

Purity increases or decreases the saturation of the color, between –100% and 100%. (At –100%, the color is fully desaturated; at 100%, the color is fully saturated.)

Transfer

Opacity Jitter varies the opacity of color in a stroke, up to the opacity value defined in the Options bar.

Flow Jitter varies the flow of color in a brush stroke.

Wetness Jitter varies the wetness setting of a Wet Mixer brush.

Mix Jitter varies the mixing quality of a Wet Mixer brush.

Brush Pose

These options allow you to define settings that mimic the behavior of a drawing tablet/stylus — Tilt X, Tilt Y, Rotation, and Pressure — if you are using a mouse. If you are using a digital drawing tablet, you can check the Override options to prevent stylus properties from affecting the brush stroke.

Other Brush Options

Noise adds randomness to brush tips that contain shades of gray (e.g., soft tips).

Wet Edges causes paint to build up along the edges of the brush stroke, creating a watercolor effect.

Build-up applies gradual tones to an image, simulating traditional airbrush techniques (this is the same as the Airbrush button in the Options bar).

Smoothing, which creates smoother curves in brush strokes, is most useful if you are using a drawing tablet.

Protect Texture applies the same pattern and scale to all textured brushes to simulate a consistent canvas texture throughout the entire image.

11. **In the Tools panel, set the foreground color to the Foliage 2 swatch and the background color to the Foliage 1 swatch.**

12. **With the Shrubs layer active, click with the brush and drag to paint the shrubs in the sketch. Use multiple brush strokes to add a greater variety of color throughout the shrubs.**

    The settings you applied allow you to easily create a random set of brush marks, differing in size, angle, roundness, position, color, and opacity.

    As you paint, don't forget about the History panel. You can step back up to 20 brush strokes, or you can create new History snapshots at regular intervals so you can return to earlier stages of your work.

13. **Show all layers in the file and review your work. Paint shrubs over any areas where the house is not perfectly painted.**

14. **Save the file and continue to the next exercise.**

Create a Brush Preset

As with custom patterns, you must save custom brush presets if you want to be able to use them again later (after quitting and relaunching Photoshop). You have a lot of leaves to paint in this image, so it's a good idea to save the brush you defined in the previous exercise.

1. **With `house-working.psd` open, open the Brush Settings panel Options menu and choose New Brush Preset.**

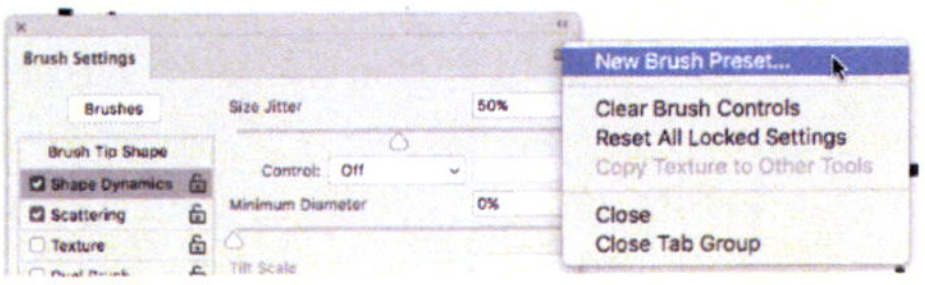

2. **In the Brush Name dialog box, name the new preset `Shrubbery`. Check the Include Tool Settings and Include Color options, then click OK.**

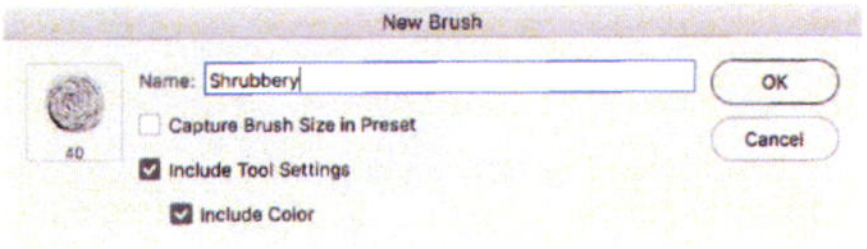

3. **Choose Edit>Presets>Preset Manager.**

4. **With Brushes showing in the dialog box, select only the brush preset you just created.**

   Your Shrubbery brush is the only one not yet stored in a set.

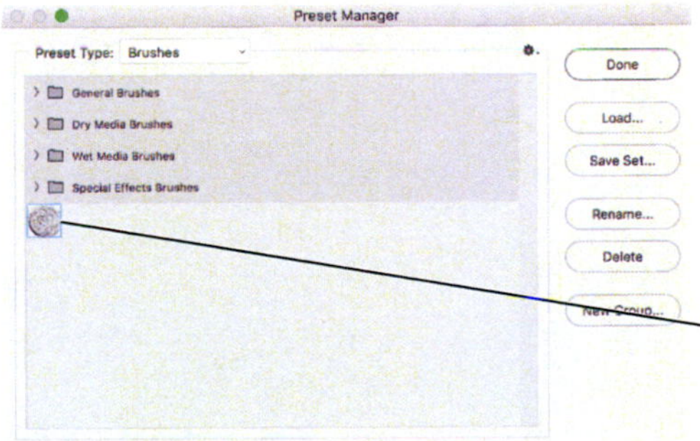

Select only the brush preset that you just saved.

5. **Click Save Set. Name the new set `Portfolio Brushes.abr` and click Save.**

   New brush sets are saved by default in the Presets>Brushes folder in your Photoshop application folder. The extension ".abr" is automatically added.

   If you are using a shared computer, you might not be able to save files in the application's default location. If this is the case, navigate to your WIP>Houses folder to save the Portfolio Brushes.abr file.

6. **Click Done to close the Preset Manager.**

> *Note:*
>
> *If you changed your Brush Settings panel or quit Photoshop since the previous exercise, you might have to go back and re-create the Shrubbery brush for this exercise to work properly.*

7. **Open the Brushes panel (Window>Brushes).**

The standalone Brushes panel is very similar to the Brush Preset Picker that you access in the Options bar. As you can see here, the Shrubbery brush does not yet appear in a set.

8. **Click the Shrubbery brush to select it, then click the panel's Delete button. Click OK when asked to confirm the deletion.**

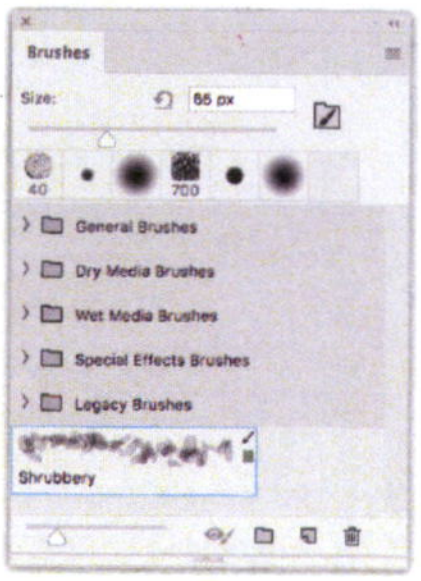

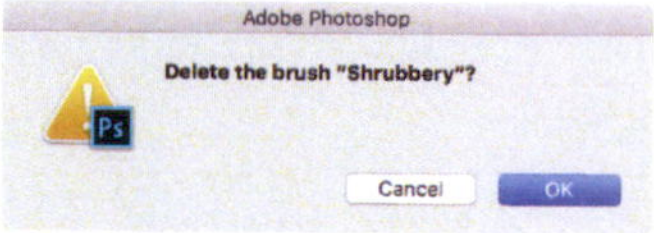

9. **Open the Brushes panel Options menu and choose Import Brushes. Select Portfolio Brushes.abr and click Open/Load.**

Deleting a brush or brush set from the panel does not delete it from your system. You can reload saved brush presets at any time.

Although the navigation dialog box defaults to application's default storage location for brush presets, you can navigate to any folder where you have saved an Adobe Brushes (.abr) file.

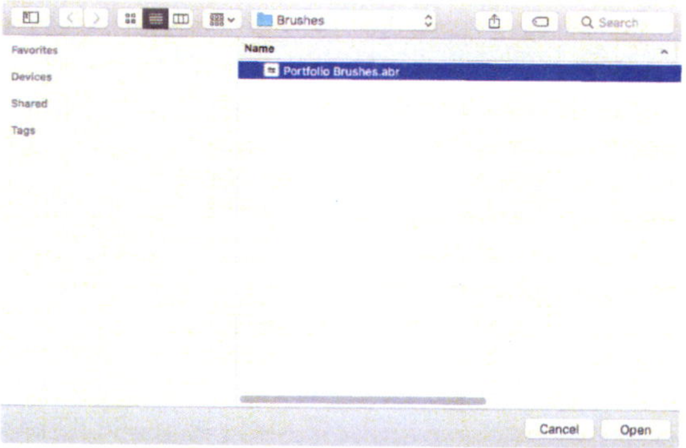

The Tool Presets Panel in Depth

Just as saving a custom brush preset allows you to access that brush again later, tool presets allow you to save and reuse settings for any Photoshop tool. **Tool presets** can be accessed in the Options bar or in the Tool Presets panel (Window>Tool Presets). The structure of the panel Options menu offers the same options as other asset panels — you can control what is visible in the panel, load and save custom sets of tool presets, and access built-in sets of tool presets.

To save your own tool presets, simply choose New Tool Preset from the panel Options menu or click the Create New Tool Preset button at the bottom of the panel. The new tool preset will include whatever tool and options are currently selected.

Click here to access tool presets.

View presets for all tools or for only the currently selected tool.

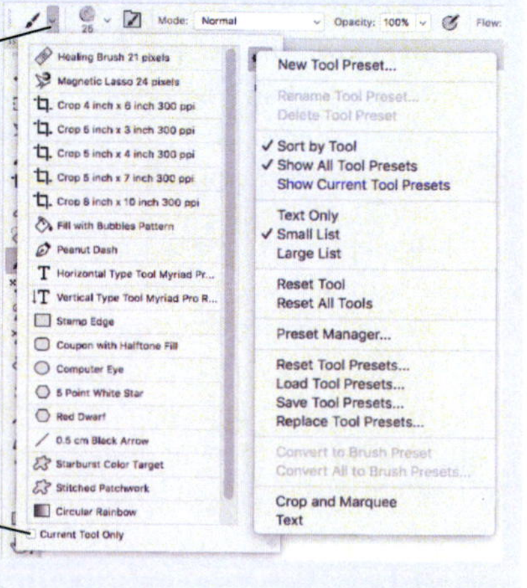

10. **In the Brushes panel, expand the Portfolio Brushes set.**

After importing the brushes file, your saved brush appears in a folder with the name you defined when you saved the set.

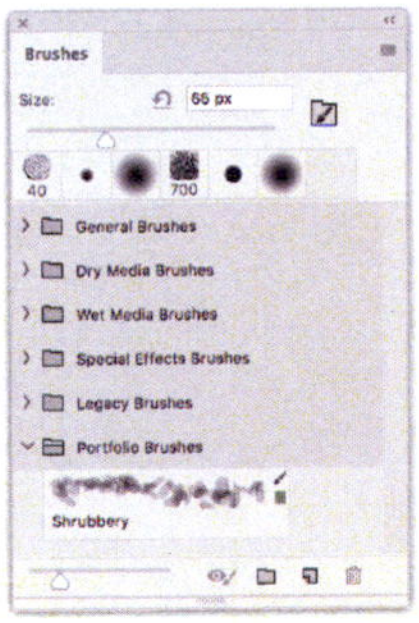

11. **Continue to the next exercise.**

Finish the Painting

Using the skills and techniques you just learned, paint the rest of the landscaping in the image. Keep the following tips in mind as you paint these elements.

1. **Create, rearrange, and merge layers as necessary to produce the best result.**

   You should experiment with the different brush settings as you paint these elements. Use layers liberally as you create the various elements so you can easily turn off or delete objects and try again.

2. **Grass — especially new sod — has far less randomness than leaves.**
   - **Choose foreground and background colors that are only slightly different (try Foliage 6 and Foliage 7).**
   - **Start with a brush preset that looks like a blade of grass (try one of the veining brushes in the Faux Finish Brushes set).**
   - **Use a small brush size with a small amount of size and angle jitter, and allow the marks to flip horizontally (Flip X Jitter option).**
   - **Experiment with different settings for foreground/background and opacity jitter.**

3. **When you're finished, add a new layer immediately above the Sketch layer, and fill it with solid white.**

4. **Save the file as house-final.psd in your WIP>Houses folder and continue to the final exercise.**

Working with Bristle Brushes

PHOTOSHOP FOUNDATIONS

Bristle tips let you create highly realistic, natural-looking brush strokes. In the Brush panel, you can set the following brush tip shape options:

- Shape defines the arrangement of bristles.
- Bristles defines bristle density.
- Length defines bristle length.
- Thickness defines the width of individual bristles within the brush.
- Stiffness defines bristle flexibility (lower values are more flexible).
- Angle defines the brush tip angle when painting with a mouse.
- Spacing defines the distance between the brush marks in a stroke. (When unchecked, cursor speed determines spacing.)

The Bristle Brush Preview appears in the top-left corner of the document window.

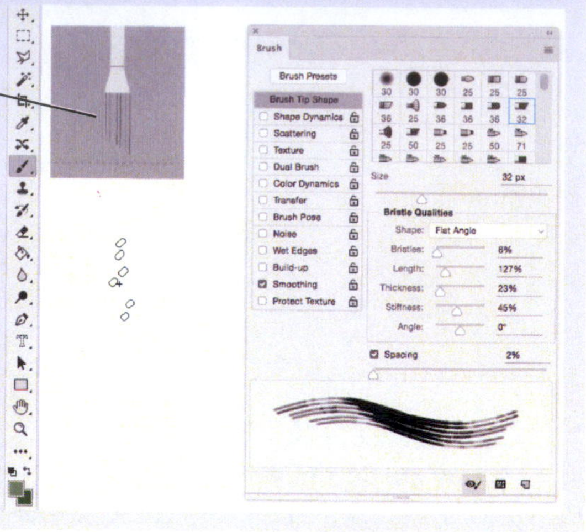

Export a PDF File for Print

The Portable Document Format (PDF) was created by Adobe to facilitate cross-platform transportation of documents, independent of the fonts used, linked files, or even the originating application. The format offers a number of advantages:

- Data in a PDF file can be high or low resolution, and it can be compressed to reduce file size.
- PDF files are device-independent, which means you don't need the originating application or the same platform to open and print the file.
- PDF files are also page-independent, which means a PDF document can contain rotated pages and even pages of different sizes. (You can't create multi-page PDF files in Photoshop, but you can combine individual pages created in Photoshop using Adobe Acrobat.)

1. **With house_final.psd open, choose File>Save As. Navigate to your WIP>Houses folder as the target destination.**

2. **Choose Photoshop PDF in the Format/Save As Type menu, and uncheck the Layers check box.**

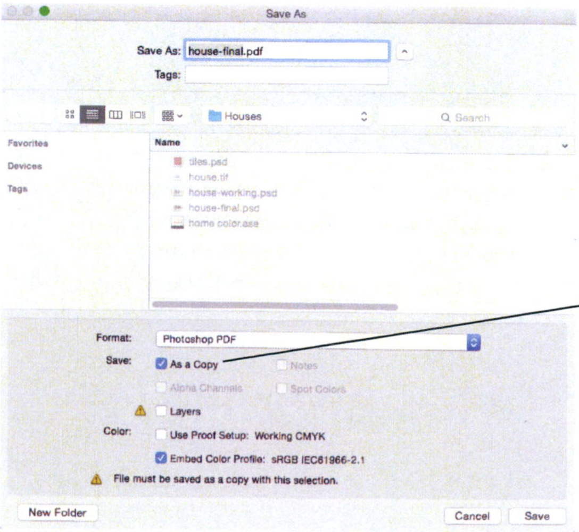

The As a Copy option is checked when you turn off the Layers option; since you are saving as a different format with a different file name, nothing else changes.

3. **Click Save, and then click OK in the warning message.**

   Before the PDF is saved, you have to define the settings that will be used to generate the PDF file. Some options (such as color profile information) can be changed in the Save Adobe PDF dialog box; those choices will override the selections in the Save As dialog box.

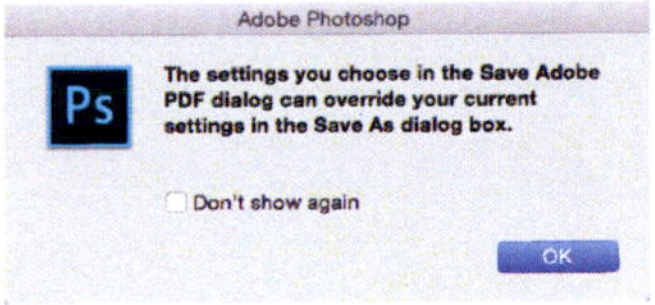

4. **Choose High Quality Print in the Adobe PDF Preset menu.**

   The Adobe PDF Preset menu includes six PDF presets (in brackets) that meet common output requirements. Other options might also be available if another user created custom presets in Photoshop or another Adobe application.

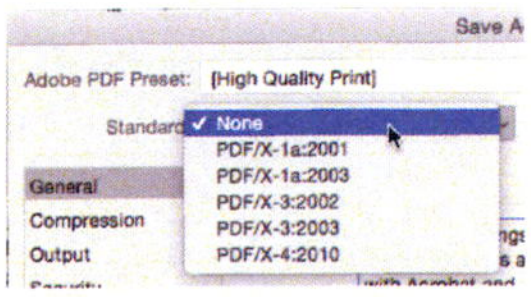

   Because there are so many ways to create a PDF, the potential benefits of the format are often undermined. The PDF/X specification was created to help solve some of the problems associated with bad PDF files entering the prepress workflow. Ask your output provider whether you should apply a PDF/X standard to your files.

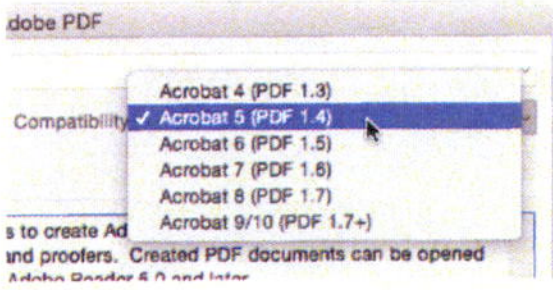

   The Compatibility menu determines which version of the PDF format you create. This is particularly important if your file uses transparency. PDF 1.3 does not support transparency, so the file will require flattening. If you save the file to be compatible with PDF 1.4 or later, the transparency information will be maintained in the PDF file; it will have to be flattened later in the output process (after it leaves your desk).

5. **In the General pane, uncheck all but Optimize for Fast Web Preview.**

   As soon as you change an option away from the defined preset, the menu changes to [High Quality Print] (Modified).

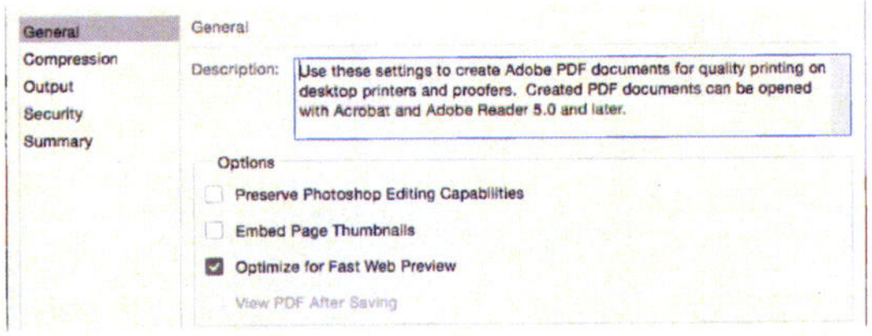

6. **Review the Compression options.**

   The Compression options determine what data will be included in the PDF file. If you're creating a file for commercial print, resolution is more important than file size. If your goal is a PDF for use on the web, file size and image quality are equally important.

   You can define a specific compression scheme for color, grayscale, and monochrome images. Different options are available, depending on the image type:

   - ZIP compression is lossless, which means all file data is maintained in the compressed file.
   - JPEG compression options are lossy, which means data is discarded to create a smaller file. When you use one of the JPEG options, you can also define an Image Quality option (from Low to Maximum).

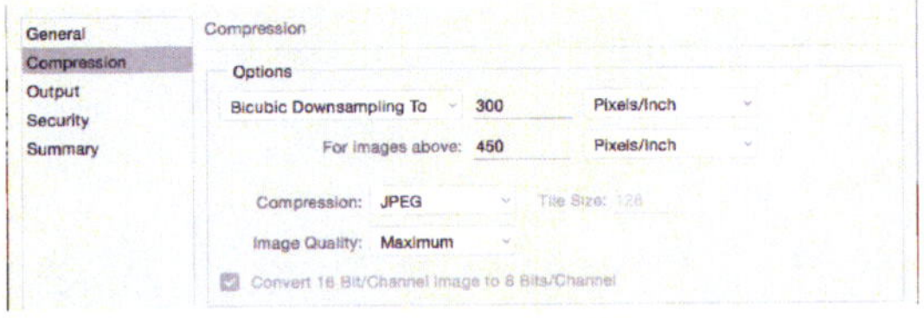

7. **Click Save PDF. When the process is finished, close the Photoshop file.**

Note:

Since you chose the High Quality Print preset, these options default to settings that will produce the best results for most commercial printing applications.

Note:

The Output options relate to color management and PDF/X settings. Ask your output provider if you need to change anything for those options.

Project Review

fill in the blank

1. The ______________ dialog box can be used to change the resolution of an image without affecting its physical size.

2. The ______________ command can be used to share color swatches between Photoshop and other Adobe applications.

3. The ______________ tool is used to fill areas with a solid color or pattern by clicking the area you want to fill.

4. ______________ is the percentage of a brush's diameter that is completely opaque.

5. The ______________ brush mode option is useful for filling gaps left by other painting methods.

6. The ______________ removes pixels from an image while attempting to maintain edges of an object in the foreground.

7. The ______________ can be used to restore specific areas of an image back to a previous state.

8. The ______________ tool is similar to the Brush tool, but can only create hard edges.

9. The ______________ tool is used to paint with patterns, either painting a stroke of the pattern or revealing more of the solid pattern with each brush stroke.

10. ______________ store specific settings for a specific tool; they can be accessed in the menu on the left end of the Options bar.

short answer

1. Briefly explain the difference between the Size, Hardness, and Flow settings when using the Brush tool.

2. Briefly explain how layers made it easier to complete this complex project.

3. Briefly explain three advantages of the PDF file format.

Portfolio Builder Project

Use what you learned in this project to complete the following freeform exercise.
Carefully read the art director and client comments, then create your own design to meet the needs of the project.
Use the space below to sketch ideas; when finished, write a brief explanation of your reasoning behind your final design.

art director comments

As part of the annual International Classic Surfing Competition, the Honolulu Marketing Group (a major event sponsor) is holding a surfboard decoration contest.

To complete this project, you should:

- ❑ Use the file **surfboard.psd** (in the **Boards_PS18_PB.zip** on the Student Files web page) as the basis for your work.
- ❑ Create a custom digital painting to decorate the surfboard shape.
- ❑ If necessary, rotate the surfboard canvas to paint your design vertically.

client comments

This year is the 30th anniversary of the Classic, and we're planning a contest for people to submit personal, custom surfboard designs.

In addition to people who will paint actual surfboards and send photos, we're allowing people to create virtual entries using the surfboard vector shape in the provided file.

There isn't really a theme, but we will divide the entries into several groups: fantasy, graffiti-style, abstract, and realistic. The winner of each category will win a $250 gift certificate from the ATC Board Company and be entered in the best-of-show judging round.

The best-of-show winner will receive an all-expenses-paid trip for two to Honolulu to attend the International Classic, as well as a custom surfboard handpainted with the winning design.

project justification

Project Summary

Drawing and painting from scratch requires some degree of creativity and natural artistic talent; however, learning the technical aspects of drawing and painting will help you as you complete many different types of projects — and might even help you to develop and refine natural artistic skills.

Creating original artwork in Photoshop — including artwork that starts as a black-and-white pen sketch — can be a time-consuming and sometimes repetitive process. If you learn how to use the painting and drawing tools, you will have a unique advantage when you need something unique. Mastering these skills also gives you an advantage because few people take the time to learn the intricacies of creating original digital artwork.

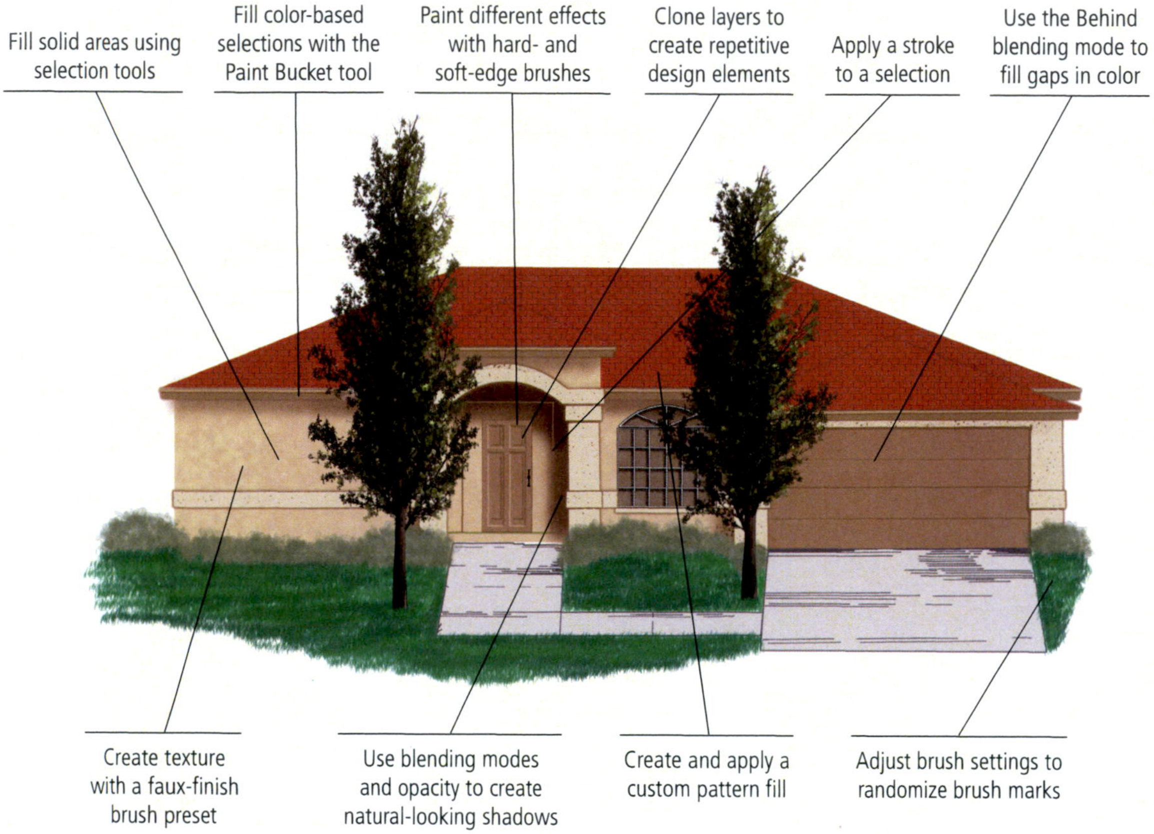

Fill solid areas using selection tools
Fill color-based selections with the Paint Bucket tool
Paint different effects with hard- and soft-edge brushes
Clone layers to create repetitive design elements
Apply a stroke to a selection
Use the Behind blending mode to fill gaps in color
Create texture with a faux-finish brush preset
Use blending modes and opacity to create natural-looking shadows
Create and apply a custom pattern fill
Adjust brush settings to randomize brush marks

project 8

Photographer's Web Page

Your client is a photographer in the San Francisco Bay area who has hired your agency to create a new website interface. Your job is to take the first draft and add a number of finishing touches to add visual appeal to the overall site. You must then generate the required pieces that will be used by a web developer to create the functioning HTML file.

This project incorporates the following skills:

- ❑ Using actions and batches to automate repetitive processes and improve productivity
- ❑ Adding depth and visual interest with 3D extrusion and puppet warping
- ❑ Generating image assets from Photoshop layers and layer groups, as required by the HTML developer
- ❑ Communicate design intent using cascading style sheets

Project Meeting

client comments

I really like the general idea that you created. I sorted through some photos and selected six that I want to include as the thumbnails at the bottom of the page. I think they're a good representation of the type of photography I enjoy most.

My only real complaint is that the top part is rather bland. Right now everything is just too horizontal. I don't have a real logo at this point but, is there anything you can do with the word "Metro" to make it a bit more visually interesting? And maybe something to make the longer filmstrip less horizontal too.

art director comments

All of the client's points are reasonable, and you can use Photoshop's built-in tools to meet each of her specific goals.

First, you need to scale down her images to make them fit as thumbnails into the space at the bottom of the layout. I also think it would be a nice touch to convert them to grayscale so the variety of color isn't too distracting in the main interface. Keep in mind, though, that you need to keep the original color images because the web developer will need them for the actual slideshow widget.

For the top, I want you to bend the filmstrip a bit. That will break the horizontal syndrome, and create a sort of frame around her studio name. You can also use the 3D functionality to add some depth to the studio name itself.

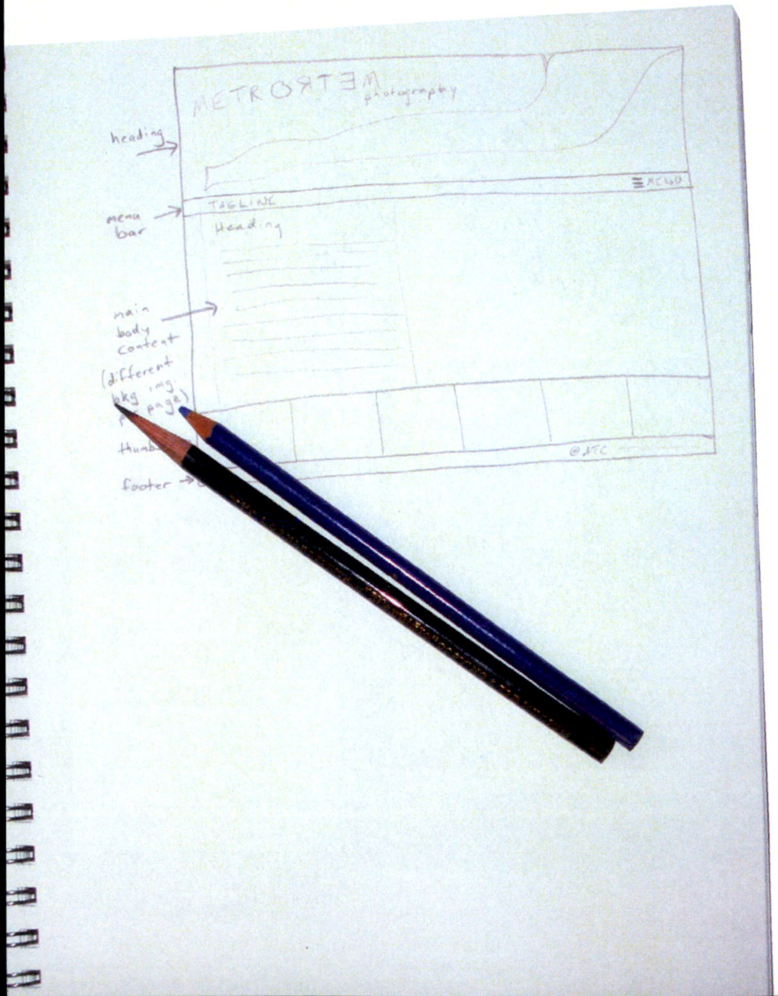

project objectives

To complete this project, you will:

- ❑ Review the initial site design
- ❑ Save an action set
- ❑ Create a new action
- ❑ Batch-process files
- ❑ Place and align thumbnails on the page
- ❑ Extrude a text layer to 3D
- ❑ Use Puppet Warp to transform a layer
- ❑ Generate image assets from layers
- ❑ Copy CSS for text and shape layers

Stage 1 Automating Repetitive Tasks

Actions are some of the most powerful (yet underused) productivity tools in Photoshop. In the simplest terms, actions are miniature programs that run a sequence of commands on a particular image or selected area. An action can initiate most of the commands available in Photoshop — alone or in sequence — to automate repetitive and potentially time-consuming tasks.

Running an action is a fairly simple process: highlight the appropriate action in the Actions panel and click the Play button at the bottom of the panel. Some actions work on an entire image, while others require some initial selection. If you use the actions that shipped with the Photoshop application, the action name tells you (in parentheses) what type of element the action was designed to affect; in most cases, however, you can run an action on other elements without a problem.

The Actions Panel in Depth

PHOTOSHOP FOUNDATIONS

The default **Actions panel** (Window>Actions) shows the Default Actions set, which contains several pre-built actions. A folder icon indicates an **action set**, which is used to create logical groupings of actions. You can expand an action set to show the actions contained within that set, and you can expand a specific action to show the steps that are saved in that action; any step in an action marked with an arrow can be further expanded to see the details of that step.

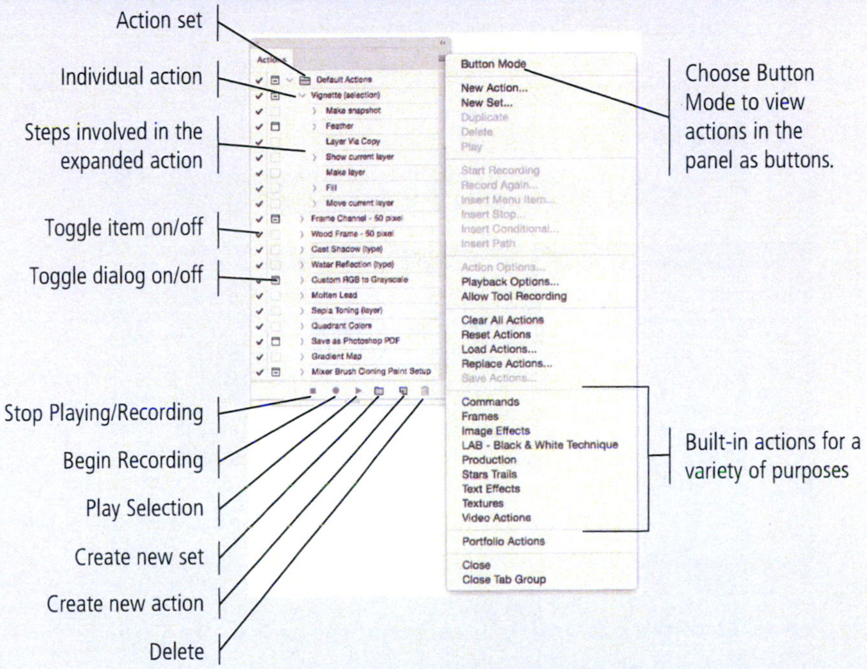

The left column of the Actions panel shows a checkmark next to each action set, individual action, and step within an expanded action. All elements of pre-recorded actions are active by default, which means that playing an action initiates each step within the action. You can deactivate specific steps of an action by clicking the related checkmark. (If the checkmark next to an action is black, all elements of that action are active. If the checkmark is red, one or more steps of that action are inactive.)

Modal Controls

The second column in the Actions panel controls the degree of user interaction required when running an action. If an icon appears in this column, the Photoshop dialog box relevant to that step opens when the action runs. These are called **modal controls**; the action pauses until you take some required action. You can deactivate modal controls for:

- An entire action set by clicking the dialog box icon next to a set name
- An individual action by clicking the icon next to the action name
- A single step by clicking the icon next to the step

If the modal controls are turned off, Photoshop applies the values that were used when the action was recorded. This increases the automatic functionality of the action, but also offers less control over the action's behavior.

Some actions require a certain degree of user interaction, in which case the modal controls can't be entirely deactivated. In this case, the dialog box icon appears grayed out in the panel, even when the remaining modal controls are turned off. (If an action shows a black dialog box icon, all modal controls within the action are active. If an action shows a red dialog box icon, one or more modal controls within the action have been turned off.)

Button Mode

Choosing Button Mode in the panel Options menu makes running an action one step easier. Each action is represented as a colored button, which you can simply click to run the action.

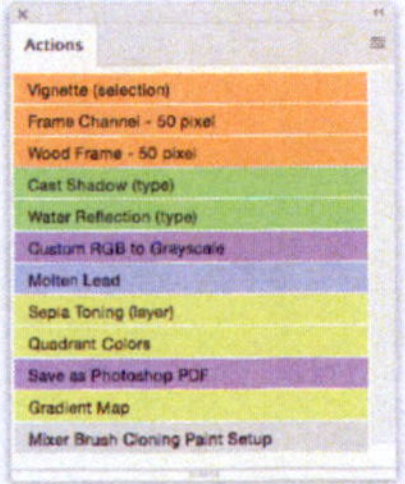

Review the Initial Site Design

Because this project starts from a partially completed file, your first task is to evaluate the existing file and determine what needs to be accomplished.

1. **Download `Metro_PS18_RF.zip` from the Student Files web page.**
2. **Expand the ZIP archive in your WIP folder (Macintosh) or copy the archive contents into your WIP folder (Windows).**

   This results in a folder named **Metro**, which contains the files you need for this project.

3. **Open the `metro-site.psd` file from the WIP>Metro folder. If you get a warning about missing or mismatched color profiles, choose the option to use the embedded profile.**
4. **Review the existing design and layer structure.**

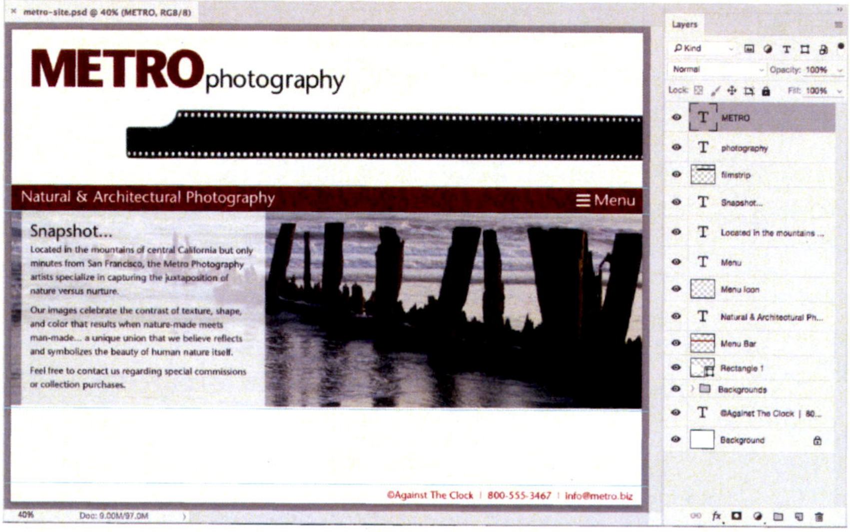

5. **Zoom in to the bottom-right corner of the canvas, then choose the Ruler tool (nested under the Eyedropper tool).**
6. **If you don't see the blue guides, choose View>Show>Guides.**
7. **Click the third horizontal ruler guide from the top of the canvas. Hold down the mouse button and drag down until the tool cursor snaps to the fourth ruler guide.**

   In the Options bar, you can see that the space between guides is 245 pixels high. This is the measurement you need when resizing the gallery images in the next exercise.

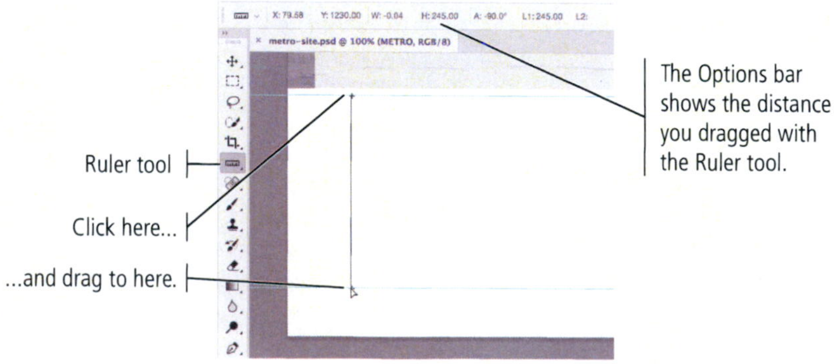

Ruler tool
Click here...
...and drag to here.
The Options bar shows the distance you dragged with the Ruler tool.

8. **Close the file, and then continue to the next exercise.**

Save an Action Set

Whenever you need to perform the same task more than two times, it's a good idea to automate as much of the process as possible. This project requires you to create thumbnails from nine images. Creating a single "negative" thumbnail for this project requires at least five steps:

1. Open the file (any number of clicks, depending on the default location in the Open dialog box).
2. Resize the image to a specific height to fit into the designated space in the site layout (at least two clicks, possibly three if the Resample check box is active, as well as typing the new dimensions).
3. Convert the reduced image to black-and-white.
4. Save the file in a new folder with a revised file name (any number of clicks, depending on the default location in the Save dialog box), as well as typing the new file name.
5. Close the file.

This process can be streamlined by using an action, which you have to record only once.

Note:

It's important to remember when creating actions that, "just because you can, doesn't mean you should." There are many powerful tools in Photoshop that require human judgment and intervention if they are to be effective. Color correction, for example, is different for every image, and should never be left entirely to a computer to implement.

1. In Photoshop with no file open, open the Actions panel (Window>Actions).

2. Choose Clear All Actions from the Actions panel Options menu.

Rather than editing an existing action set, you are going to create your own action set to store the action you define. If you did not clear the existing actions, the set you define would include all of the default actions as well as the one you create.

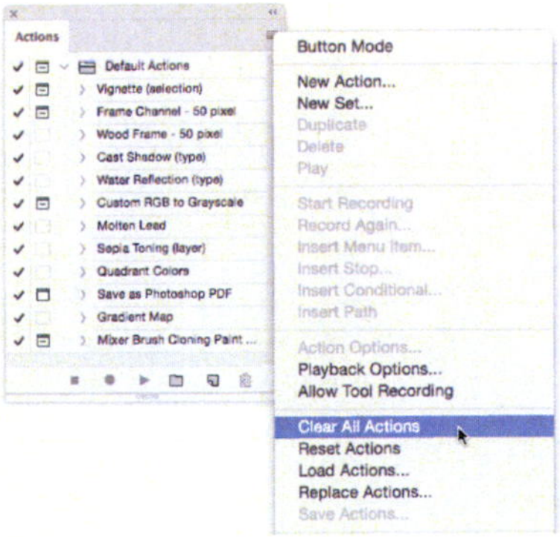

3. Click OK in the warning message dialog box.

Clear All Actions removes everything from the Actions panel. You can also remove a specific action or set from the panel by highlighting the item in the panel and clicking the Delete button, or by choosing Delete from the Actions panel Options menu. These commands remove the actions or sets from the panel, but they do not permanently delete saved actions or sets. If you delete an action from one of the built-in sets, you can reload the set to restore all items that originally existed in the set.

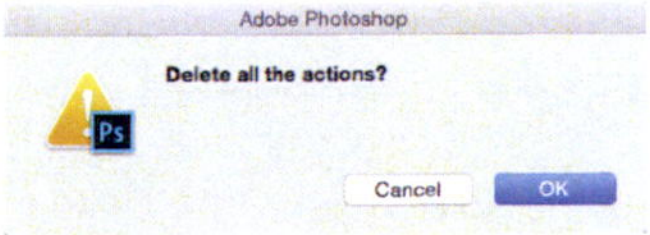

4. Click the Create New Set button at the bottom of the Actions panel.

Note:

*You can add actions to the Actions panel by choosing a defined set or by choosing **Load Actions** in the panel Options menu.*

***Reset Actions** restores the default set to the Actions panel. You have the option to replace the existing actions or append the default set to the current sets.*

***Replace Actions** replaces the current action sets with whatever set you load in the resulting dialog box.*

5. **In the New Set dialog box, name the new set Portfolio Actions, and then click OK.**

You can name the set whatever you prefer, but the action set name should indicate what the set contains, whether it's a set of actions for a specific type of project, for a specific client, or any other logical group.

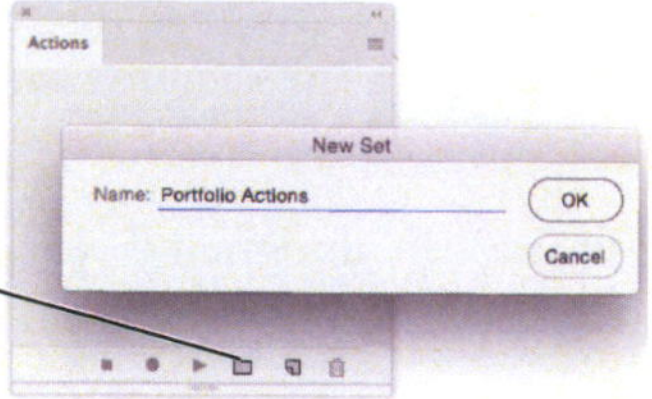

6. **Continue to the next exercise.**

Create a New Action

Recording an action is a fairly simple process: open a file, click the Record button in the Actions panel, and perform the steps you want to save in the action. Click the Stop button to stop recording, either permanently when you're done or temporarily if you need to do something else in the middle of creating the action. (If you stop recording, you can later select the last step in the existing action and start recording again by clicking the Record button.)

1. **In Photoshop, open windmill.jpg from your WIP>Metro>images folder. If you get a profile mismatch warning, use the embedded profile.**

When you apply this action in the next exercise, you can determine how color profile problems are managed by the automated batch processing.

Note:

You can change the name, keyboard shortcut, and/or button color of any action by selecting it in the Actions panel and choosing Action Options from the panel Options menu.

2. **Open the Actions panel if necessary, then click the Create New Action button at the bottom of the Actions panel.**

3. **In the New Action dialog box, type Create Web Thumbnail in the Name field.**

By default, new actions are added to the currently selected set. You can add the action to any open set by choosing from the Set menu. The Function Key menu allows you to assign a keyboard shortcut to the action, so an "F" key (with or without modifiers) can initiate that action. The Color menu defines the color of the button when the Actions panel is viewed in Button mode.

Note:

As with any user-defined element, you should use descriptive names for your actions.

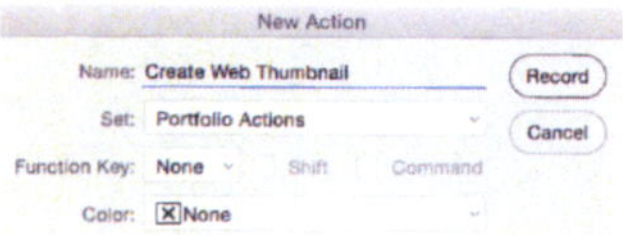

4. **Click Record to close the dialog box.**

   In the Actions panel, the Record button automatically becomes red, indicating that you are now recording; anything you do from this point forward is recorded as a step in the action until you intentionally stop the recording by clicking the Stop button at the bottom of the Actions panel.

The red button indicates that the action is currently being recorded.

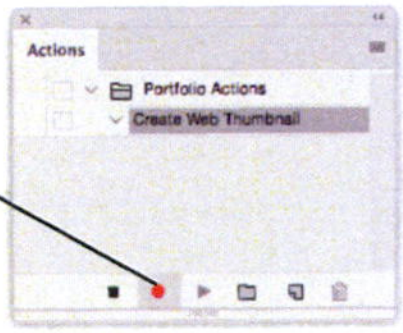

5. **With windmill.jpg open, choose Image>Image Size.**

6. **Make sure the Resample option is checked.**

   You want the thumbnails to be proportionally sized, and you want them to remain at 72 ppi.

7. **With the Constrain Aspect Ratio option active, choose Pixels in the Height Units menu and then change the Pixel Dimensions height to 245 pixels.**

   Because the Resample option is active, reducing the number of pixels results in a proportionally smaller document size.

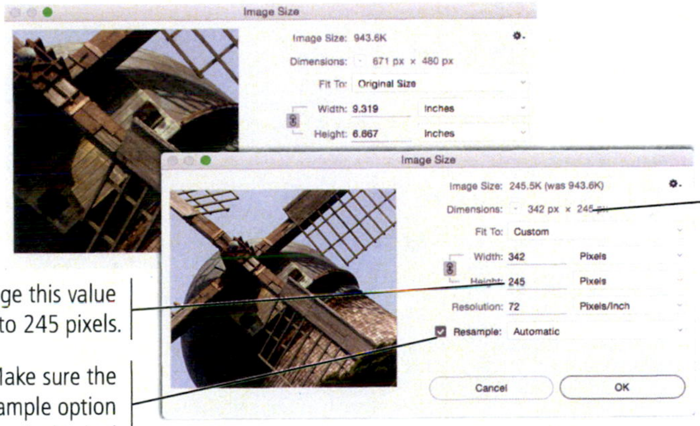

The image's physical dimensions are reduced proprtionally.

Change this value to 245 pixels.

Make sure the Resample option is checked.

8. **Click OK to close the Image Size dialog box and apply the change.**

9. **Choose Image>Mode>Grayscale. Read the resulting warning, then click Discard.**

   You are converting to the small thumbnails to grayscale simply for aesthetic purposes, so you don't need to control the precise conversion.

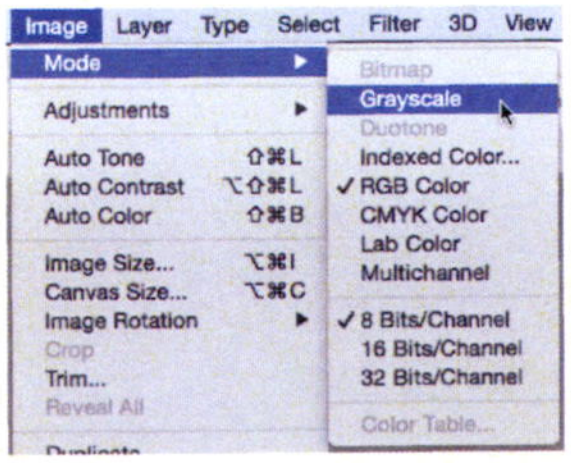

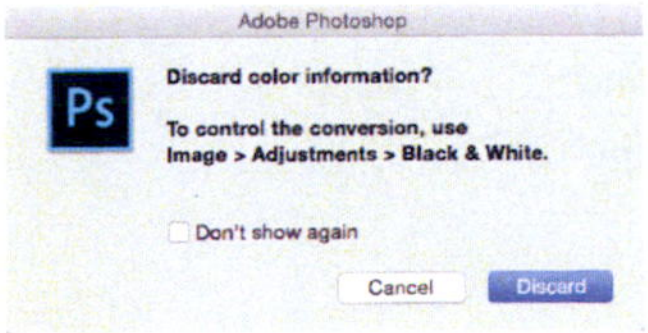

10. **In the Actions panel, click the Stop Playing/Recording button.**

11. **Expand the Image Size item in the Create Web Thumbnail action.**

The open image has been resized to 245 pixels high.

Pixel color data has been converted to grayscale.

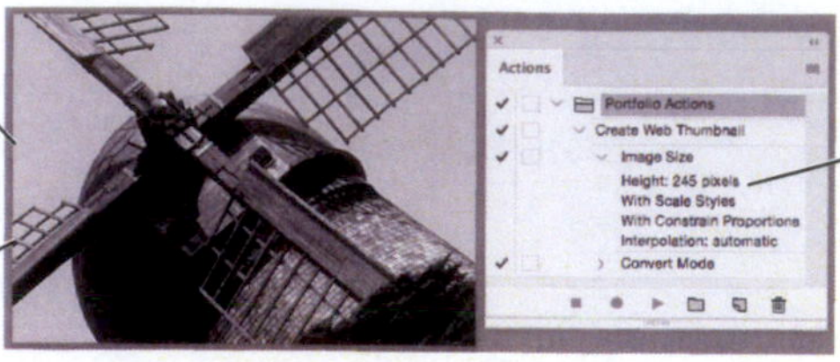

The two things you did in Steps 5–9 are included in the action.

12. **Click Portfolio Actions in the Actions panel to select the set, then choose Save Actions in the panel Options menu.**

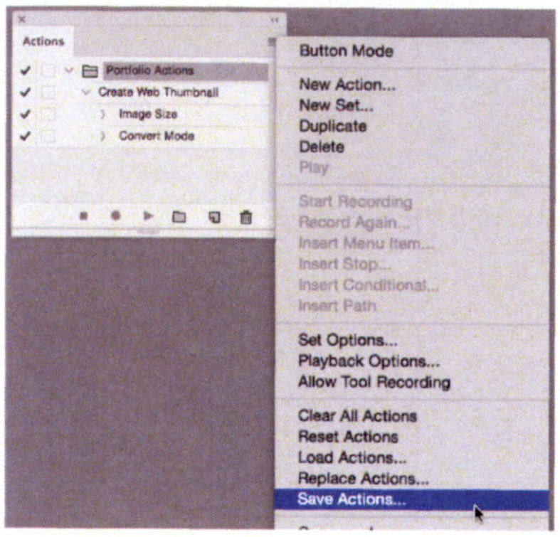

13. **In the Save dialog box, review the options and then click Save.**

Action sets are saved by default in the Photoshop>Presets>Actions folder with the extension ".atn" (which is automatically added for you). If you are using a shared computer, you might not be able to save files in the application's default location. If this is the case, navigate to your WIP>Metro folder to save the Portfolio Actions.atn file.

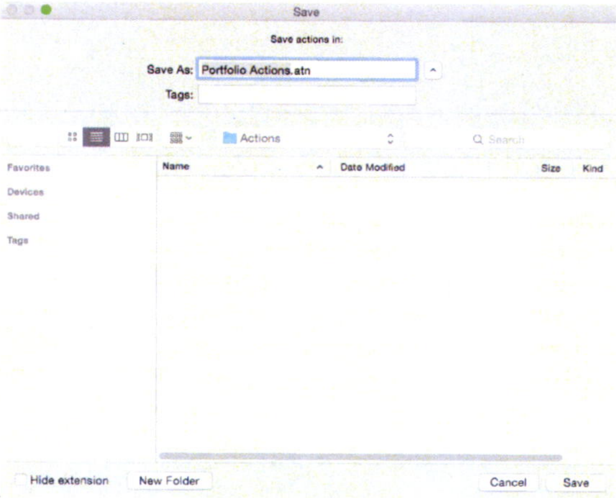

If you make changes to a set — whether you delete an existing action from the set or add your own custom actions — without saving the altered set, you will have to repeat your work the next time you launch Photoshop.

14. **Close the windmill.jpg file without saving.**

You don't need to save the changes since this file will be processed when you run the action on the entire images folder.

15. **Continue to the next exercise.**

Note:

The default file name is the same as the set name that you defined when you created the set.

Note:

Action sets are stored by default in the Presets>Actions folder in the Photoshop Application folder on your computer. You can also load an action from another location, such as when someone sends you an action that was created on another computer.

Inserting Action Stops and Menu Options

Action Stops

When you record actions, you can insert an intentional pause by choosing **Insert Stop** from the Actions panel Options menu. When you insert a stop, the Record Stop dialog box allows you to type a message — for example, specific instructions or reminders to the user — that displays when the action runs.

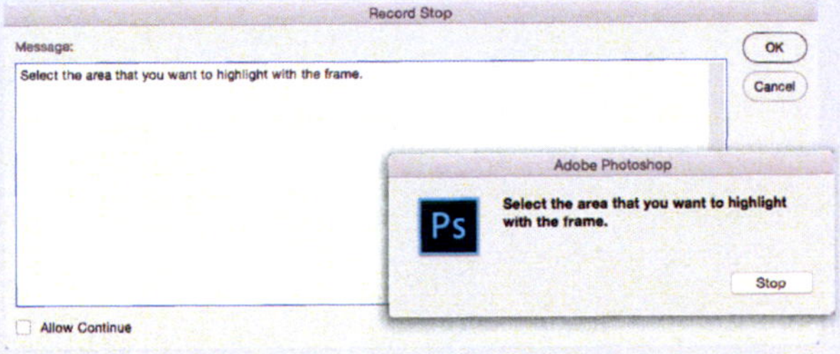

When a user runs the action and the action reaches a stop, the message you entered into the Record Stop dialog box appears. The user must click Stop, perform the required step, and then click the Play button in the Actions panel to complete the rest of the action. (If you check the Allow Continue option when you define the Stop, the resulting message includes a Continue button; if the user clicks Continue, the action resumes.)

Menu Items

You can cause an action to open a specific dialog box or execute a menu command by choosing **Insert Menu Item** from the Actions panel Options menu. When the Insert Menu Item dialog box appears, you can make a selection from the application menus, and then click OK. When a user runs the action, the specified dialog box opens or the menu command executes.

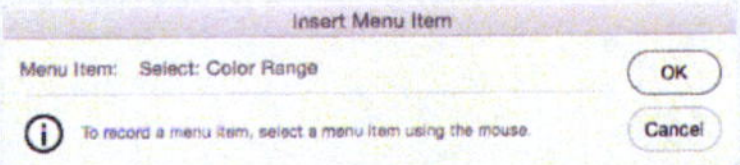

When you insert a menu item that opens a dialog box (such as Select>Color Range), you are adding a modal command that can't be turned off. When a user runs the action, even with modal commands turned off, the dialog box opens and requires user interaction. Although an action can automate many steps in a repetitive process, there are still some things that can't be entirely automatic.

Conditional Actions

You can also define steps in an action that occur if a specific condition is met by choosing **Insert Conditional** from the Actions panel Options menu. In the Conditional Actions dialog box:

- If Current defines the condition that will be evaluated. You can choose from the available list conditions.
- Then Play Action menu defines what will occur if the condition is true. You can choose any action that exists in the same set as the action you are recording.
- Else Play Action defines what happens if the condition is *not* true. You can choose any action that exists in the same set as the action you are recording.

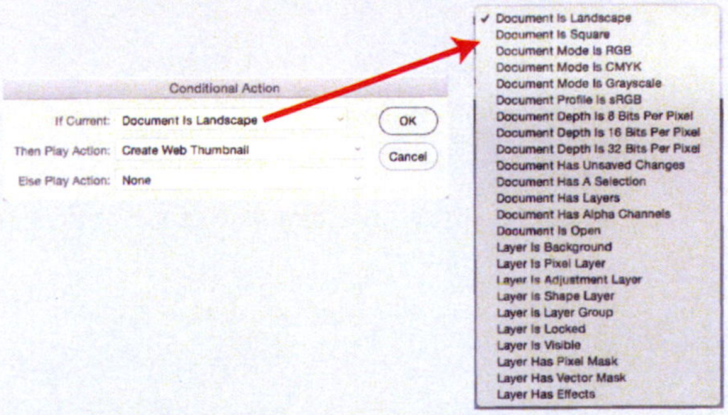

Batch-Process Files

The ability to batch-process files further enhances and automates productivity. If you have a large group of files that all require the same adjustments, you can build an action, set up a batch, and go to lunch (or, depending on your computer processor and number of files, go home for the night).

For example, when we write the Portfolio books, we take screen shots in RGB mode at 100%. Before the books are laid out for print production, the screen shots are converted to the U.S. Web Coated (SWOP) v2 CMYK profile and resized (not resampled) to 40%. As you have probably noticed, there are a lot of screen shots in these books. Rather than sitting for several days and modifying each file (or even sitting for one full day and running an action on each file), we set up a batch that converts all screen shots for an entire book in about 25 minutes.

1. **In Photoshop, choose File>Automate>Batch.**

   At the top of the Batch dialog box, the Set and Action menus default to the active selection in the Actions panel. In this case, there is only one available choice, so the Create Web Thumbnail action is already selected. You can choose to run a batch for any action in any open set.

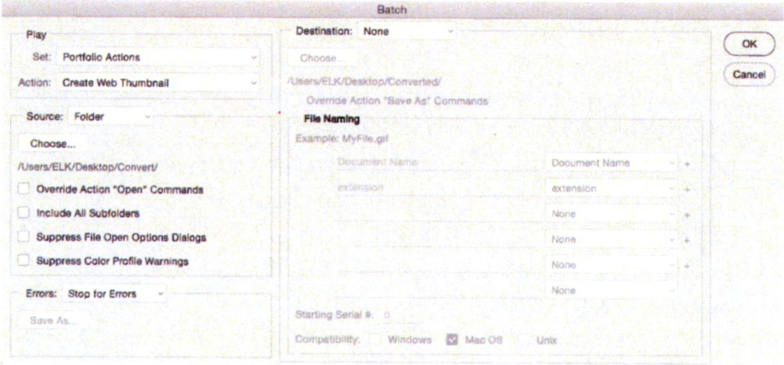

2. **Choose Folder in the Source menu.**

   The Source menu allows you to choose which files are batched:

   - **Folder** processes a complete group of images arranged within a single folder on your computer.
   - **Import** acquires and processes a group of images from a scanner or digital camera.
   - **Open Files** processes all files currently open in the application.
   - **File Browser** processes files selected in the File Browser.

   When Folder is selected, you can also choose to override "Open" commands that are recorded in the selected action, include subfolders within the selected folder, and suppress color profile warnings for the files being processed.

3. **Click the Choose button and navigate to the WIP>Metro>images folder and click Choose/OK to return to the Batch dialog box.**

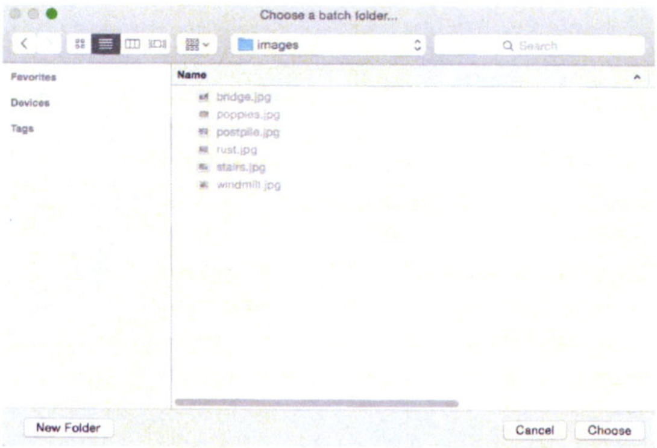

4. **Make sure the Suppress Color Profile Warnings option is checked to prevent the batch from stopping if color management policies are violated.**

   This is a matter of some debate, but when processing images for the web, color management is not considered as critical as it is for print.

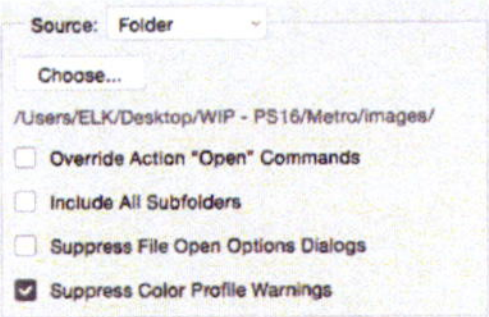

5. **Choose Folder in the Destination menu.**

   The Destination menu in the Batch dialog box presents three options:

   - **None** simply means that the action will be run. If the action saves and closes the files, those commands will be completed. If the action does not save and close the files, you might end up with a large number of open files and eventually crash your computer.
   - **Save and Close** saves the modified file in the same location with the same name, overwriting the original file.
   - **Folder** allows you to specify a target folder for the files after they have been processed. This option is particularly useful because it saves the processed files as copies of the originals in the defined folder; the original files remain intact.

6. **Click the Choose button (in the Destination area), navigate to the WIP>Metro>thumbnails folder, and click Choose/OK.**

7. **In the File Naming area, open the menu for the first field and choose document name (lowercase) from the menu.**

   The File Naming fields allow you to redefine file names for the modified files. You can choose a variable from the pop-up menu, type specific text in a field, or use a combination of both. The example in the File Naming area shows the result of your choices in these menus.

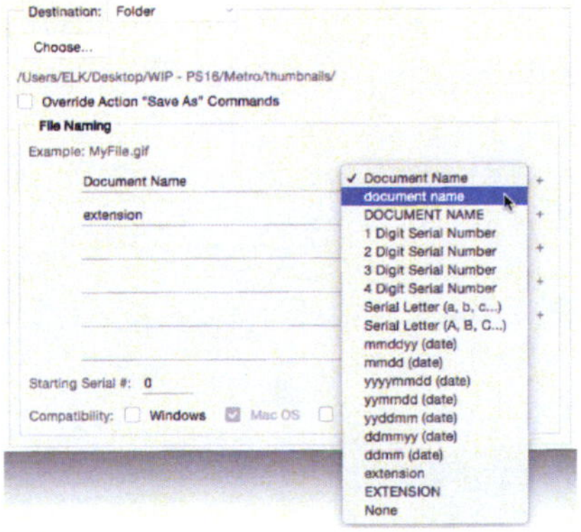

8. **In the second field (below "document name"), type -thumb.**

   This identifies the images as thumbnails, differentiating them from the full-size images with the same names.

9. **Choose extension (lowercase) from the menu for the third field.**

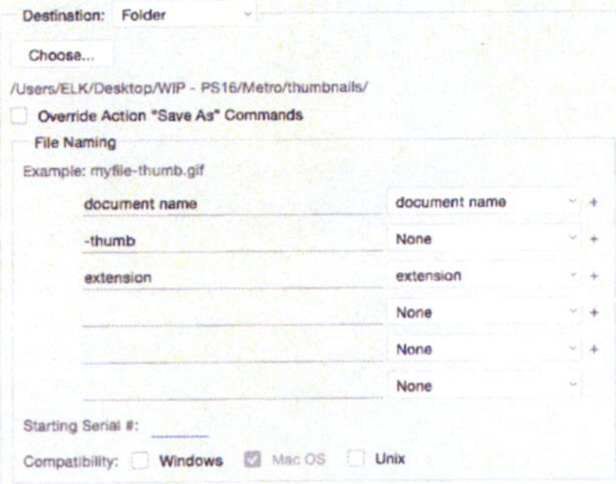

Note:

*You can create a **droplet** from an action, which allows you to run the action using a basic drag-and-drop technique (as long as Photoshop is running). The Create Droplet dialog box (File>Automate>Create Droplet) presents most of the same options as the Batch dialog box, with a few exceptions. Clicking Choose at the top of the dialog box allows you to define the name of the droplet and the location to save it. The dialog box does not include Source options because the source is defined when you drag files onto the droplet.*

Note:

These options are only available when Folder is selected in the Destination menu.

Note:

*The Errors section of the Batch dialog box determines what happens if an error occurs during a batch. **Stop for Errors** (the default setting) interrupts the batch and displays a warning dialog box. **Log Errors to File** batch-processes every file and saves a record of all problems.*

10. **Click OK to run the batch.**

When the process is complete, you will have six thumbnail images in your WIP>Metro>thumbnails folder.

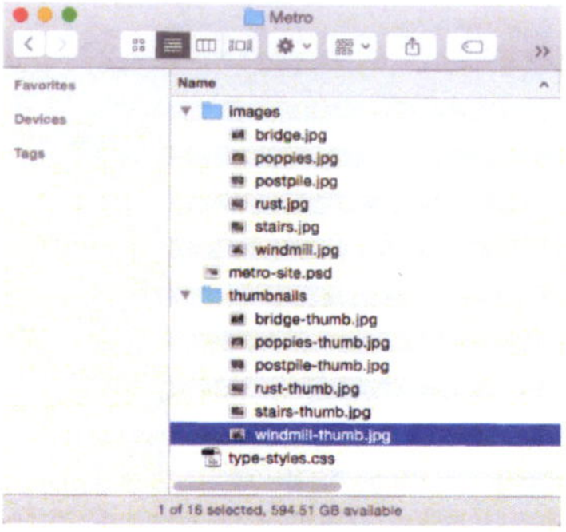

11. **Continue to the next exercise.**

Place and Align Thumbnails on the Page

Now that the thumbnail images have been created, you can arrange them in the gallery file so it can be animated, sliced, and saved for the web.

1. **Open the file metro-site.psd from the WIP>Metro folder. If you receive a missing profile warning, choose the option to use the embedded profile.**

2. **In the Layers panel, select the Background layer to make it active.**

   New layers are automatically added above the previously selected layer. In this case, the new layers will be added directly above the Background layer.

3. **On your desktop, navigate to the WIP>Metro>thumbnails folder. Select all six files in the folder and drag them onto the Photoshop document window.**

Drag multiple files from the desktop to the Photoshop document window to place more than one at a time.

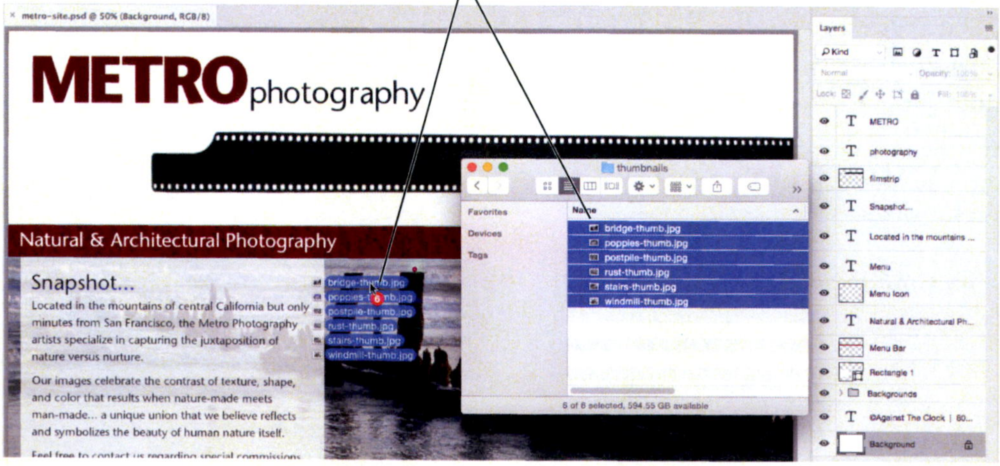

4. **Make the Photoshop application active again.**

The first dragged file shows the crossed diagonal lines, indicating that you need to finalize the placement.

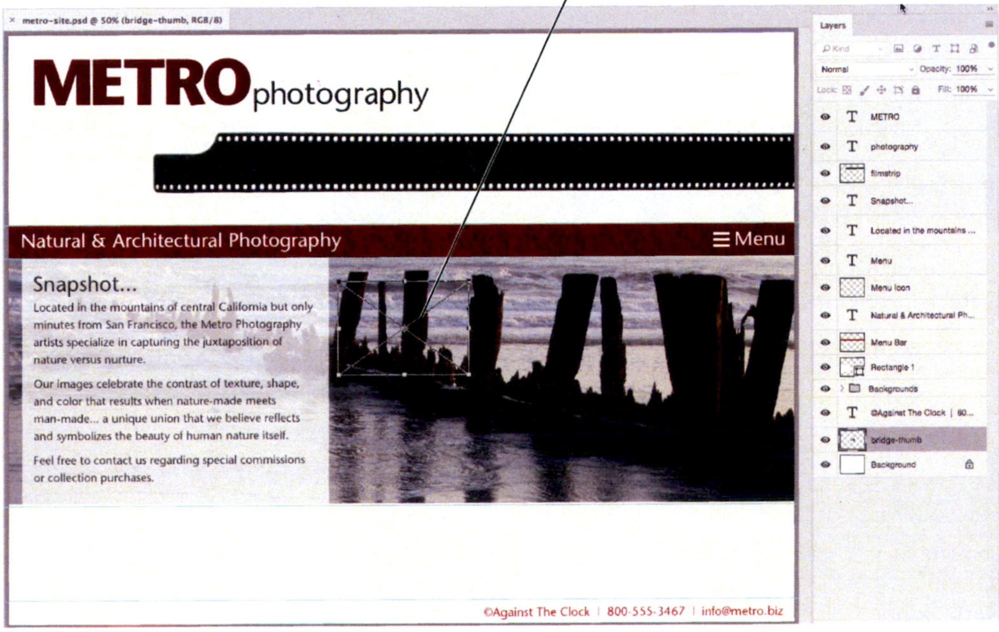

5. **Press Return/Enter six times to finalize the placement of each image.**

This method make this process of placing multiple files far easier than using the File>Place Embedded command, which only allows placement of a single image at once.

6. **Choose the Move tool. In the Options bar, make sure the Auto-Select option is not checked.**

By turning off Auto-Select, you can click anywhere in the document window to move the contents of the selected layer. Turning this option off prevents you from accidentally moving the content of a different layer.

7. **In the Layers panel, select the windmill-thumb layer.**

When Auto-Select is not active, the Move tool moves the content of whatever layer is active in the Layers panel.

8. **Make sure the Snap option is toggled on in the View menu.**

9. **Open the View>Snap To submenu and make sure Document Bounds is active.**

When the Snap options are turned on, arranging layers relative to one another is fairly easy (as you will see in the next few steps).

Make sure Snap is toggled on.

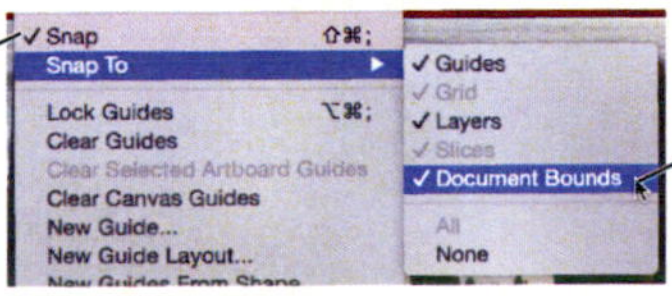

Make sure the Document Bounds option is toggled on.

10. **Click inside the document window and drag down and right until the windmill-thumb layer content snaps to the right canvas edge and the third and fourth horizontal ruler guides.**

If guides are not visible, choose View>Show>Guides.

Placed images are centered in the document window.
The new layers exist below the images in the Background layer group.
When Auto-Select is not checked, you can move the contents of layers that are not initially visible.
Drag the windmill-thumb layer content until it snaps to the right canvas edge and the blue ruler guides.

11. **Select the bridge-thumb layer in the layers panel, then drag it to the left side of the canvas between the third and fourth ruler guides.**

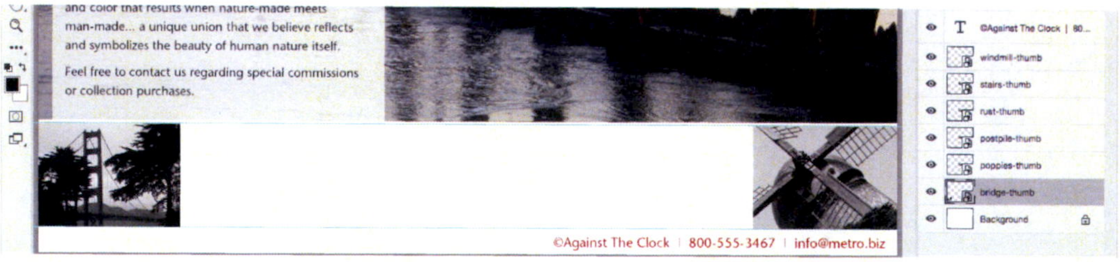

12. **In the Layers panel, Shift-click to select all six thumbnail image layers.**

When multiple layers are selected in the Layers panel, a number of alignment options become available in the Options bar. These are very useful for aligning or distributing the content of multiple layers relative to one another.

13. **In the Options bar, click the Align Bottom Edges button, then click the Distribute Horizontal Centers button.**

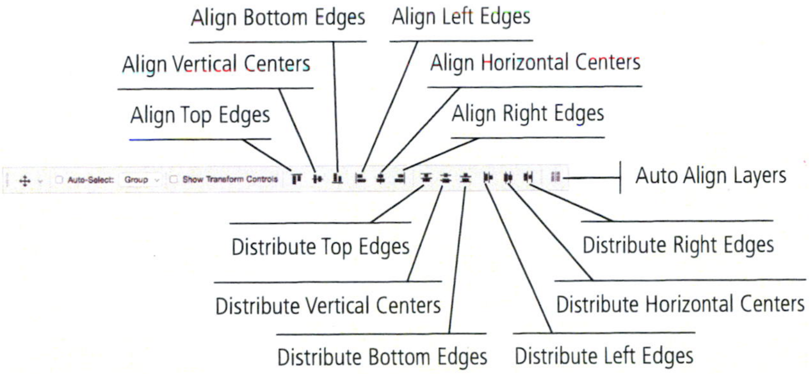

Aligning the bottom edges moves the four previously hidden layers to match the bottom-most edge of all selected layers — in this case, the bottom edge of the windmill and bridge images.

The Distribute Horizontal Centers option places an equal amount of space between the horizontal center point of each selected layer. The centers of the six thumbnail images are now exactly spaced in relation to one another.

14. **Save the file and continue to the next stage of the project.**

Stage 2 Editing Layers for Visual Effect

At the meeting, your client asked for some way to break up the horizontal uniformity in the top half of the interface design. Photoshop offers a number of tools for distorting layers, from simple scaling to the Free Transform mode to the Liquify filter. If you completed the other projects in this book, you have already used all of these techniques to fulfill specific project goals. In this stage of this project, you will learn two more methods for transforming layer content — 3D extrusion and puppet warping — to achieve effects that can't easily be created with other methods.

Extrude a Text Layer to 3D

If you completed Project 4: City Promotion Cards, you already experimented with some of the 3D options that are built into Photoshop. In addition to wrapping an object around a mesh shape, you can also create three-dimensional shapes from certain types of layer content — specifically, text.

Important Note: If you see a message about insufficient vRAM when you first launch the application, you will not be able to complete this exercise. You must have at least 512 MB vRAM to work with Photoshop's 3D features.

> ***Note:***
>
> *We are only touching the surface of what you can do when you work in three dimensions; our goal is to show you some of the options that will be useful for creating 3D effects in a 2D medium such as print or web design.*

1. **With metro-site.psd open, hide the filmstrip and photography layers.**
2. **Select the METRO layer in the layers panel and then select the Horizontal Type tool.**

The Horizontal Type tool is active.

Click here to make a 3D extrusion from the active text layer.

The METRO type layer is selected.

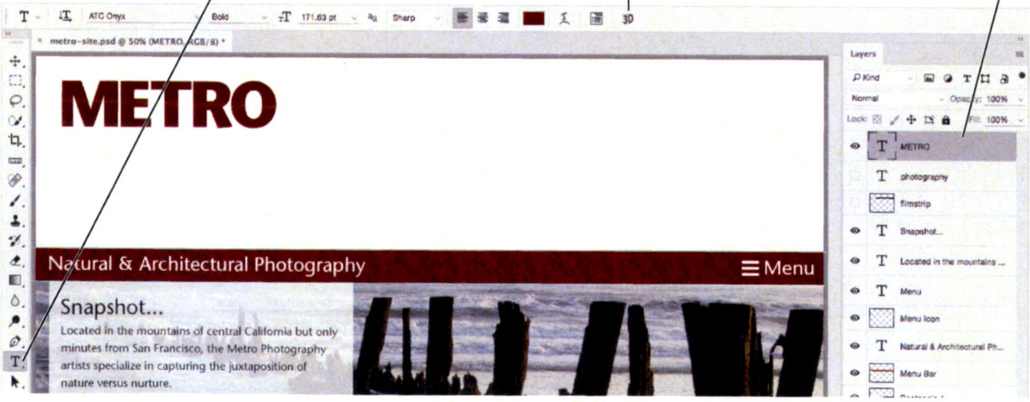

3. **Click the 3D button in the Options bar.**

   You don't need to place the insertion point to apply 3D effects to a type layer. Simply select the layer you want to affect in the Layers panel and make sure the Horizontal Type tool is active.

4. **Read the resulting message and then click Yes.**

   To work effectively with 3D objects, you need (at least) the Layers panel, the 3D panel, and the Properties panel. The built-in 3D workspace automatically shows those panels.

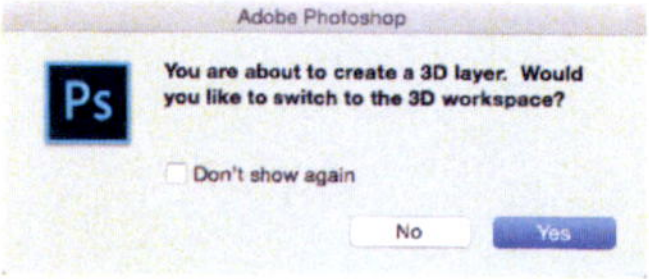

   When you create a 3D layer from the existing Type layer, Photoshop automatically asks if you want to switch to that workspace.

5. **Click the word "Metro" in the top-left corner of the canvas to select it.**

6. **Open the View>Show submenu. Make the following choices in the submenu:**

3D Secondary View	**Not Active**
3D Ground Plane	**Not Active**
3D Lights options	**Not Active**
3D Selection	**Active**
UV Overlay	**Not Active**
3D Mesh Bounding Box	**Active**

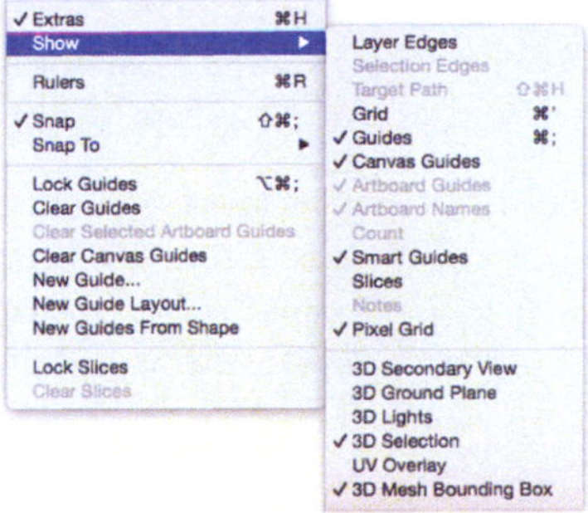

You're only manipulating a single word of type, so most of the 3D view tools aren't particularly helpful in this instance. The Selection and Mesh Bounding Box options, however, can be very helpful for manipulating the 3D shape on screen.

Because 3D Selection options are showing, you can use on-screen proxies to change a number of settings.

Move the mouse over various parts of the on-screen mesh to change different properties.

Options related to the new 3D layer are available in the 3D and Properties panels.

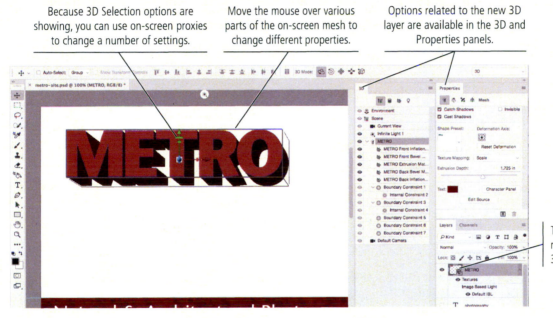

The Type layer now shows the 3D layer icon.

If you completed Project 4: City Promotion Cards, you were already introduced to some of the 3D capabilities that are available in Photoshop. As you complete this exercise, keep in mind that the 3D panel lists all of the elements that make up a 3D object:

- The **Environment** is everything around the 3D object.
- The **Scene** is basically everything that makes up the 3D effect.
  - **Current View** defines properties of the camera, or the perspective from which the scene is being viewed.
  - **Light** defines the specific light sources that shine on the 3D model. (These are the same light sources that you used in Project 6: Advertising Samples.)
  - **[Object Name]** defines properties related to the actual 3D model, including:
    - Materials, which are the appearances of the surfaces
    - Constraints, which are the shapes that make up the 3D mesh

7. **Select the Metro object in the 3D panel, then review the options in the Properties panel.**

   When the 3D type object is selected, the Properties panel has four modes:

   - Mesh options relate to the overall 3D shape. You can change how the mesh casts and catches shadows, and choose a shape preset to distort the 3D mesh.

     At the bottom of the Properties panel, you can use the Text swatch and Character Panel buttons to make changes to the type formatting. Clicking the Edit Source button opens a separate file with the live type layer — which means you can edit the text (and its formatting) even after converting it to a 3D layer.

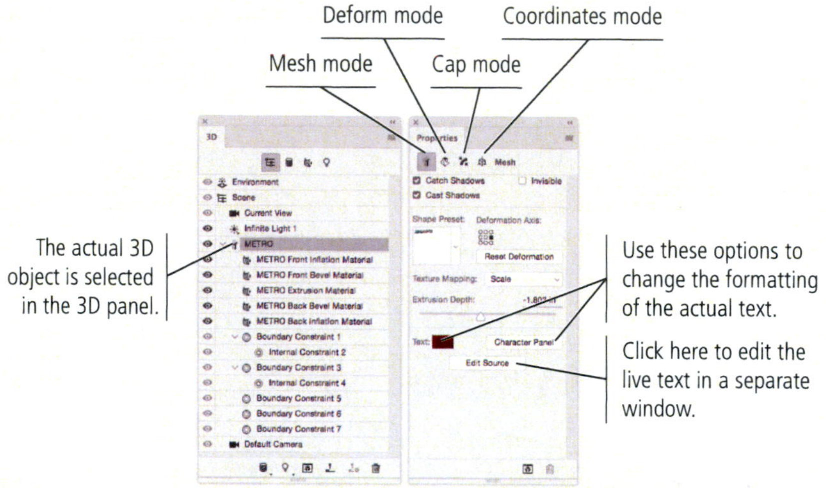

Deform mode
Coordinates mode
Mesh mode
Cap mode
The actual 3D object is selected in the 3D panel.
Use these options to change the formatting of the actual text.
Click here to edit the live text in a separate window.

   - Deform options control the depth, twist, taper, bend, and shear of the 3D extrusion.
   - Cap options control the beveling and inflation effects that are applied to the front and/or back surfaces of a 3D shape.
   - Coordinates options are the same as for the Scene, but apply only to the selected object.

Note:

Press V to toggle through various modes of the Properties panel.

8. **Click the Deform button at the top of the Properties panel, then place the mouse cursor over the Bend control of the on-screen Deform proxy.**

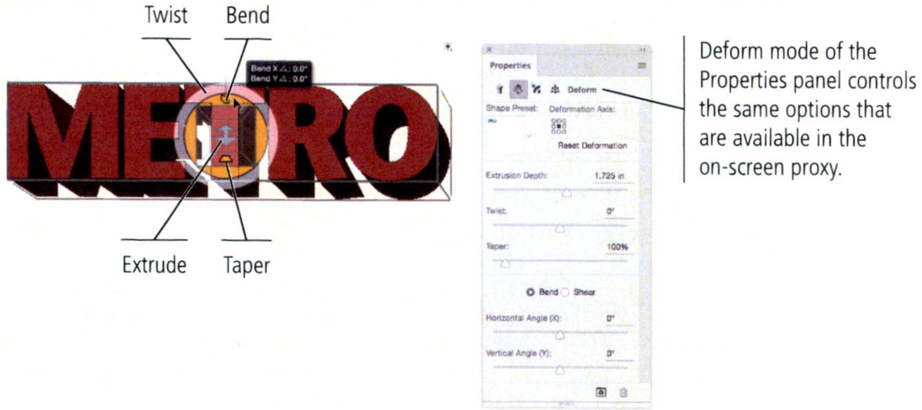

9. **Click and drag right until the cursor feedback shows (approximately) Bend X: 180°.**

   Dragging right or left changes the horizontal bend (Bend X). Dragging up or down changes the vertical bend (Bend Y).

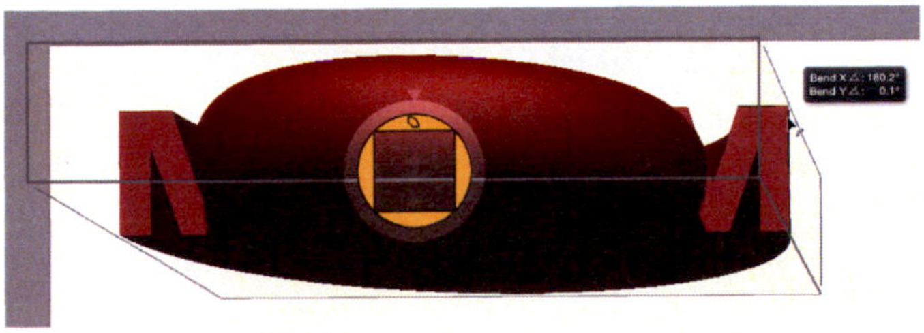

> *Note:*
>
> *In either the Mesh or Deform properties, you can apply a predefined group of shape options using the Shape Preset menu. Different presets change the Extrude options, which define the shape that is created.*

10. **In the Properties panel, click the right-center point in the Deformation Axis proxy.**

    You might have to reselect the Deform button at the top of the panel after changing the bend value. This appears to be a minor bug in the software that requires selecting the Deform button again after making any change to the object's properties.

    The registration point defines the origin of the bend or shear. As you can see in this example, the bend is now applied around the right-center point of the original object.

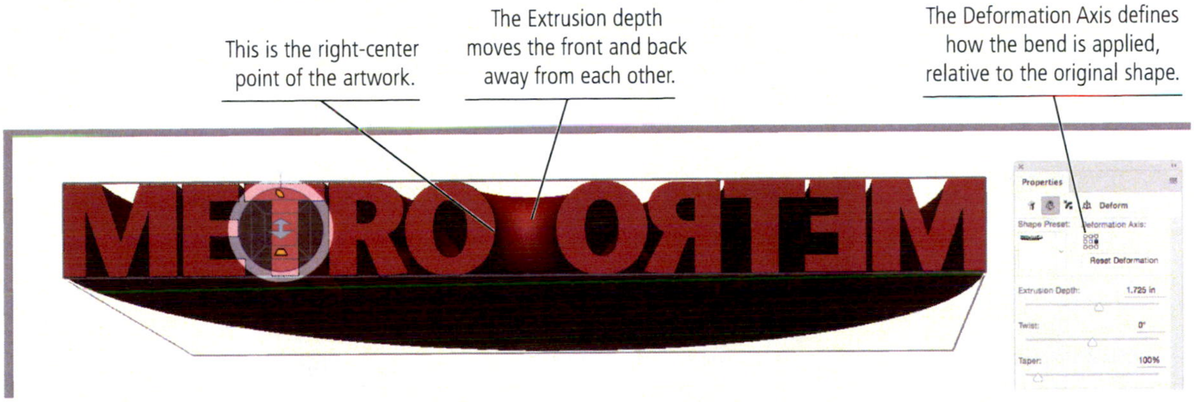
This is the right-center point of the artwork.
The Extrusion depth moves the front and back away from each other.
The Deformation Axis defines how the bend is applied, relative to the original shape.

11. **Place the cursor over the Extrude control of the on-screen Deform proxy. Click and drag down until the two "o" shapes overlap, as shown in the following image.**

    Changing the Extrusion Depth moves the front and back sides closer together or farther apart.

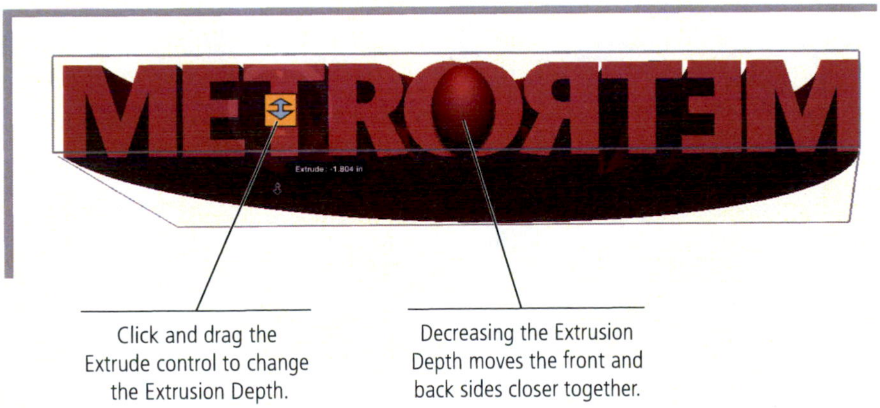
Click and drag the Extrude control to change the Extrusion Depth.
Decreasing the Extrusion Depth moves the front and back sides closer together.

12. **With the Metro object still selected in the 3D panel, click the Cap button at the top of the Properties panel.**

Cap properties control the same options that are available in the on-screen proxy.

13. **Place the mouse cursor over the Front Bevel Width control in the on-screen Cap proxy. Click and drag right to apply a 15% bevel.**

Bevel options change the contour map for the front and/or back of the shape. The Inflate options can be used to create a bubble effect.

14. **In the Properties panel, choose Front and Back in the Sides menu.**

Note:

Sometimes the 3D panel changes automatically to select the scene instead of the object; this appears to be a bug in the software. You should make sure the correct element is selected in the 3D panel.

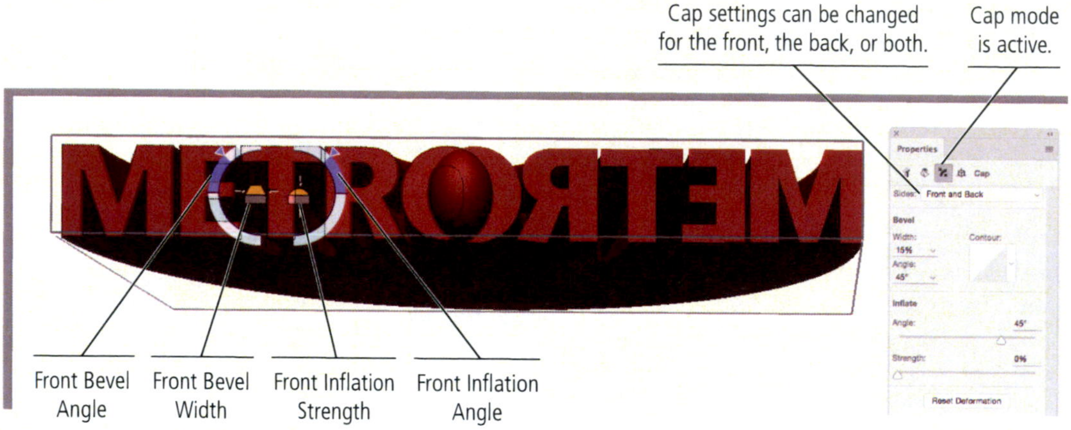

Cap settings can be changed for the front, the back, or both.
Cap mode is active.

Front Inflation Strength
Front Inflation Angle

15. **In the 3D panel, click METRO Extrusion Material to select only that mesh.**

When a specific material is selected, you can change the color and texture that apply to the selected material.

16. **In the Properties panel, open the Material Picker. Scroll down to find the No Texture option, then click it to remove the texture from the extrusion mesh.**

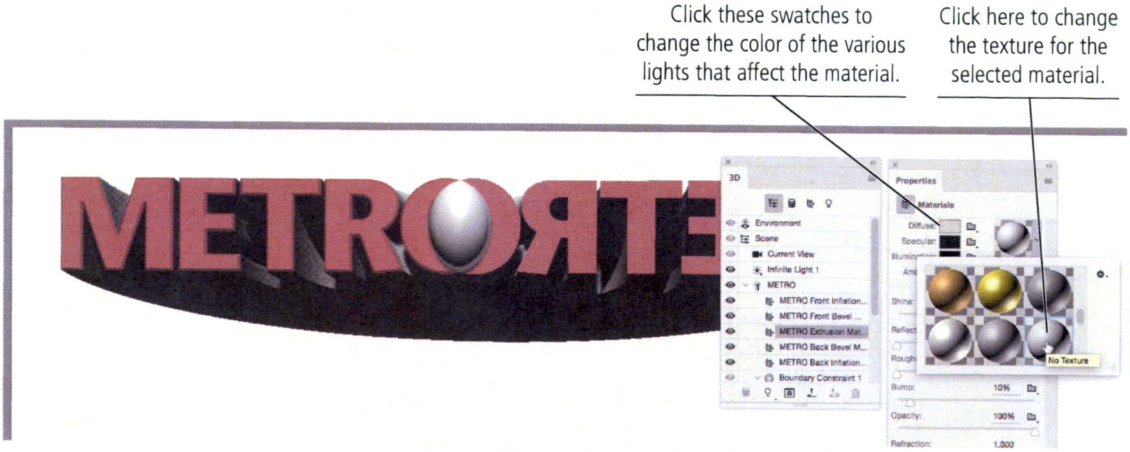

Click these swatches to change the color of the various lights that affect the material.
Click here to change the texture for the selected material.

In the Properties panel, the color of various lights changes the appearance of the selected material:

- **Diffuse** is the color of the surface material, or the file that makes up the reflective surface of the object.
- **Specular** defines the color of specular highlights (i.e., areas where the light is 100% reflected).
- **Illumination** is the color of surface areas where the material is transparent; this setting results in the effect of interior lighting, such as a painting on a light bulb.
- **Ambient** defines the color of ambient light that's visible on reflective surfaces.

17. **In the 3D panel, click the METRO object to select it.**

18. **Make the Move tool active in the Tools panel. Move the cursor near the front-top edge of the 3D object cage until the cursor feedback shows "Rotate Around X Axis"**

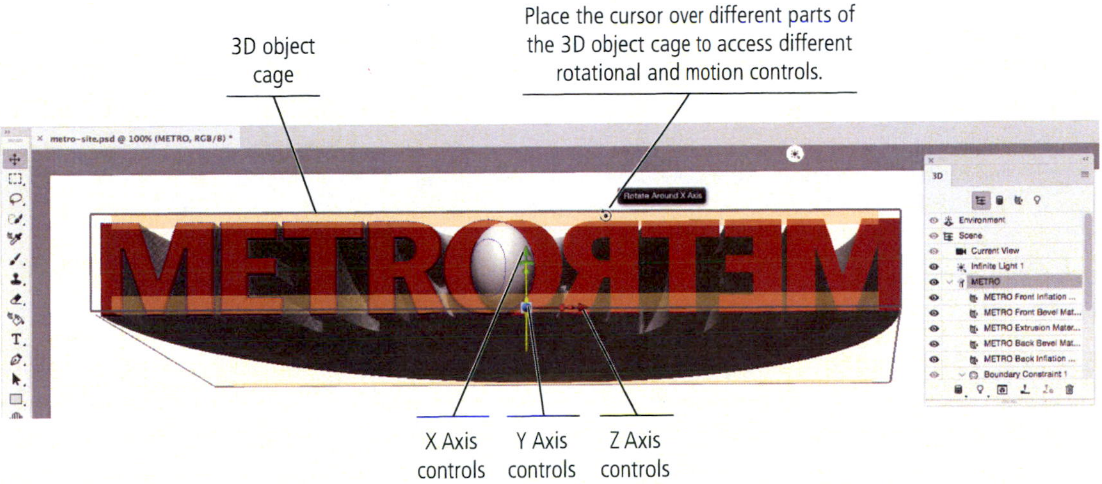

19. **Click and drag down to rotate the image around the X axis, so you can see the top edge of the 3D extrusion (use the following image as a guide).**

20. **Move the cursor near the right-top edge of the object cage until the cursor feedback shows Rotate Around Z Axis.**

21. **Click and drag left slightly to rotate the object around the Z axis (use the following image as a guide).**

22. **Move the Metro type layer closer to the top and left edges of the canvas.**

23. **In the Layers panel, make the "photography" type layer visible.**

    You hid these layers earlier to better focus on the 3D object. Now you need to scale the 3D object to fit into the available space, so you have to make those layers visible again.

24. **Using the Move tool, drag the "photography" type layer until the "h" ascender sits between the T and E on the reversed "METRO" (as shown here).**

25. **Save the file and continue to the next exercise.**

Use Puppet Warp to Transform a Layer

Puppet Warp provides a way to transform and distort specific areas of a layer without affecting other areas of the same layer. It is called "puppet" warp because it's based on the concept of pinning certain areas in place and then bending other areas around those pin locations — mimicking the way a puppet's joints pivot. In this exercise, you use puppet warping to bend and distort the top filmstrip image layer.

Note:

Puppet warping can be applied to image, shape, and text layers, as well as layer and vector masks.

1. **With metro-site.psd open, make the filmstrip layer visible.**

2. **Control/right-click the filmstrip layer in the Layers panel. Choose Convert to Smart Object from the contextual menu.**

   By first converting this layer to a Smart Object, you can apply the puppet warp non-destructively.

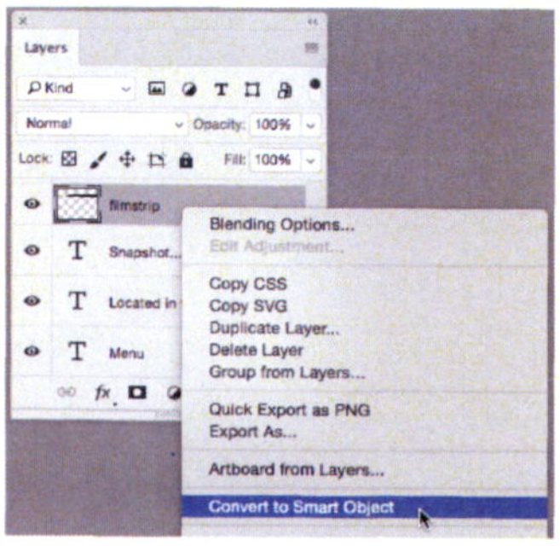

3. **With the filmstrip Smart Object layer selected in the Layers panel, choose Edit>Puppet Warp.**

   When you enter Puppet Warp mode, a mesh overlays the active layer content. This mesh represents the joints in the shape that can bend when you warp the layer content.

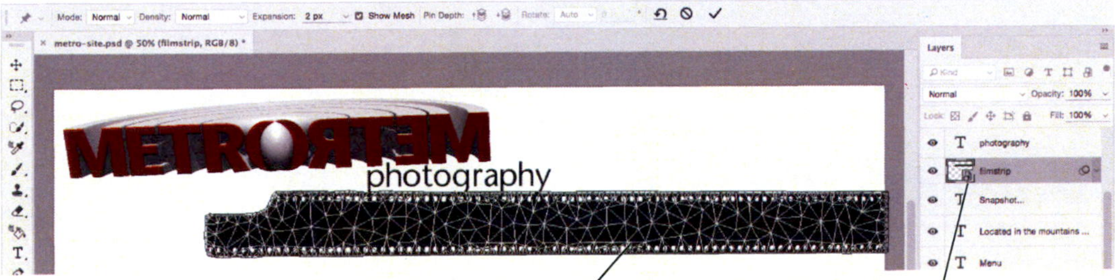

This mesh shows the area that can be warped.

The filmstrip layer is now a Smart Object layer.

4. **In the Options bar, make sure Show Mesh is checked and choose Fewer Points in the Density menu.**

   In the Options bar, you can change the mesh density from the default Normal to show Fewer Points or More Points.

Use this menu to change the number of points in the applied mesh.

5. **Click the mesh near the center of the filmstrip art to place an anchoring pin.**

   Clicking the mesh places a pin, which anchors the layer at that location.

6. **Click the top-right corner of the mesh and, without releasing the mouse button, drag up above the top edge of the image.**

   Clicking and dragging places a new pin and rotates the image around the location of the existing pin. Because you have placed one other pin on the layer, the entire shape rotates around the first pin location.

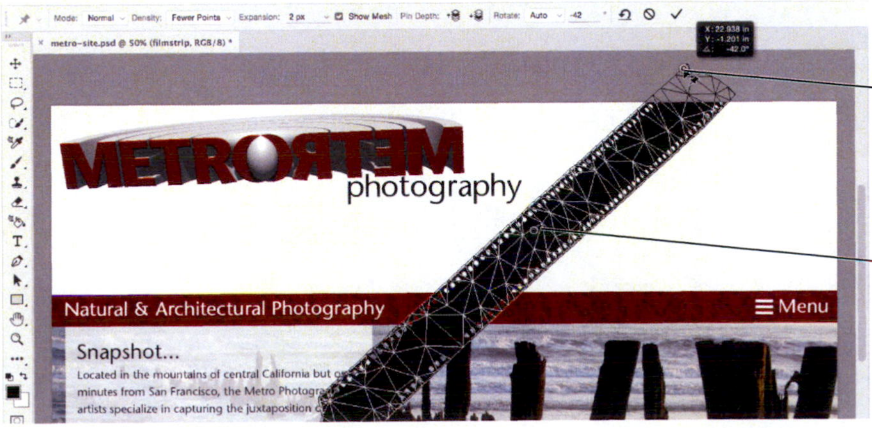

Clicking and dragging places a new pin, and rotates the layer around the existing pin.

This is the pin you placed in Step 4.

7. **Click near the left-center edge of the filmstrip image and drag up to move the filmstrip end back into the heading area.**

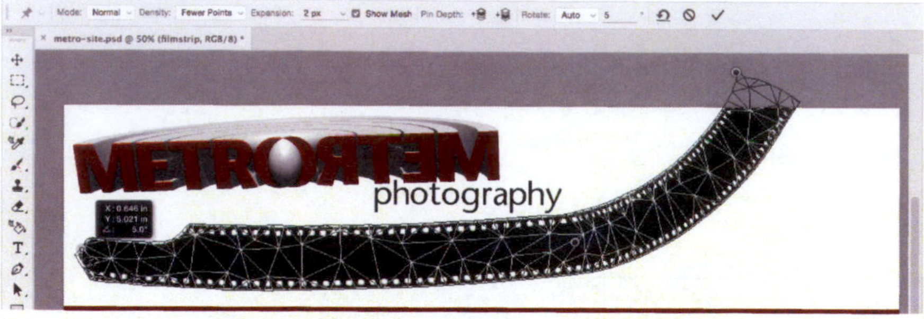

Note:

Pressing Command/Control-Z while working in Puppet Warp mode undoes the last action you performed inside the puppet warp mesh. You can only undo one action; after you finalize the warp, the Undo command undoes the entire warp — everything you did since you entered Puppet Warp mode.

8. **Add another pin to the bottom-right corner of the filmstrip. Drag the new point until the filmstrip edge is past the canvas edge (as shown here).**

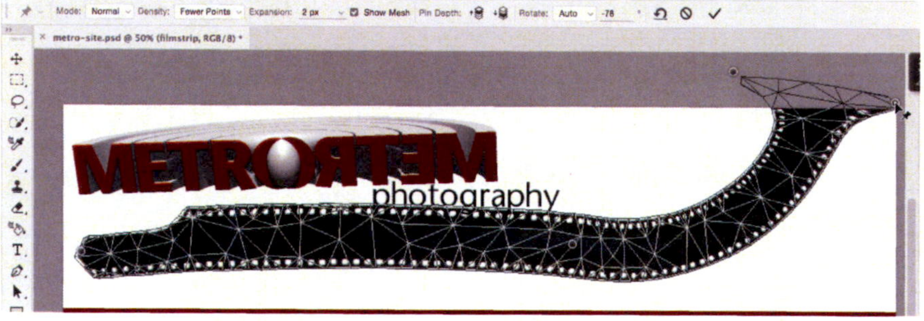

9. **In the Options bar, choose the Distort option in the Mode menu.**

   As you can see, Distort mode warps the object based on the position and angle of existing pins.

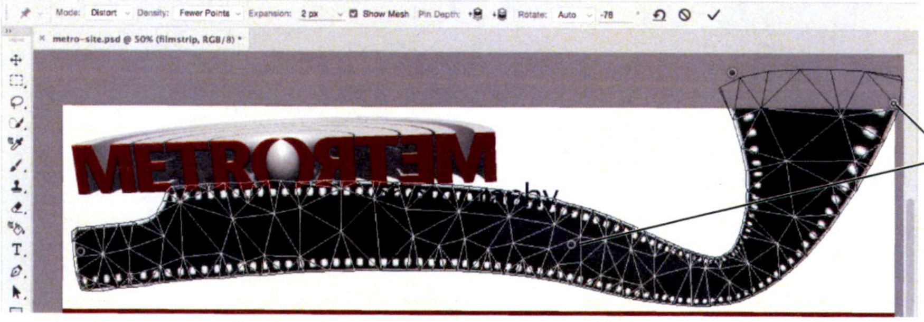

In Distort mode, the layer content distorts based on the position and angle of pins.

10. **Click the center pin and drag left to change the distorted shape.**

    This changes the distortion between the center pin and the pins on the either end of the filmstrip. The bend on the right end of the filmstrip is reduced.

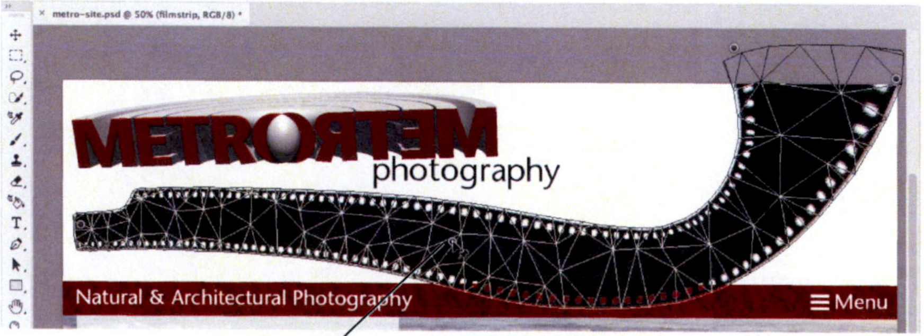

Moving a pin changes the overall shape distortion.

11. **Continue manipulating the filmstrip warp until you are satisfied with the result. Keep the following points in mind:**
    - **Click to add new pins at any point in the process.**
    - **Option/Alt click an existing, selected pin to remove it from the mesh.**
    - **Press Option/Alt to change the selected pin from an Auto rotation angle to a Fixed rotation angle.**
    - **With a specific pin selected, press Option/Alt, then click the rotation proxy and drag to change the angle of that pin.**
    - **Uncheck the Show Mesh option to get a better preview of your warp.**

    Our solution is shown here.

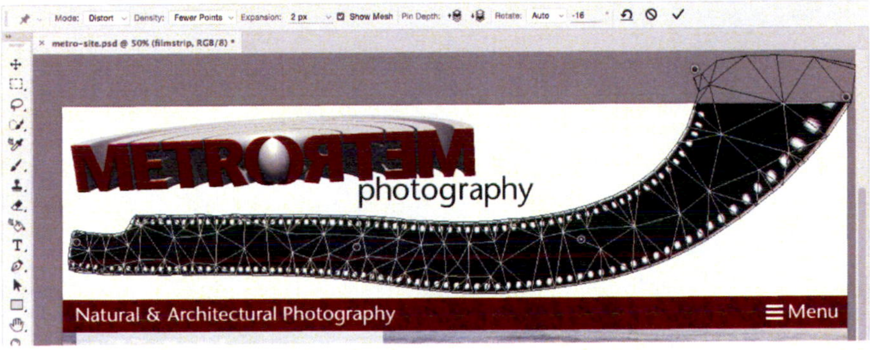

12. **Press Return/Enter to finalize the warp.**

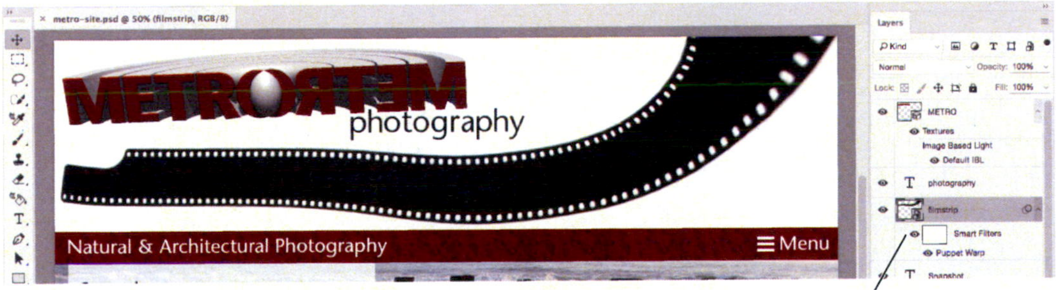

Because you converted the layer to a Smart Object, you can double-click the Puppet Warp effect to change the warp settings.

13. **Save the file, then continue to the next stage of the project.**

Note:

The Expansion option in the Options bar determines how far the mesh extends beyond the edge of the layer content.

Note:

If you warp a layer so that the mesh overlaps, you can use the Pin Depth buttons in the Options bar to show pins on underlying layers.

Stage 3 Generating Web-Ready Assets

It is common practice to create the look and feel of a website in Photoshop, and then hand off the pieces for a programmer to assemble in a web design application such as Adobe Dreamweaver. In the second half of this project, you complete a number of tasks to create the necessary pieces for the final website, including the different styles that will be used to properly format various elements in the resulting HTML page.

This site is a very simple example, using only a few elements to illustrate the process of properly mapping Photoshop objects to create the pieces that are necessary in an HTML page; we kept the site design basic to minimize the amount of repetition required to complete the project. The skills and concepts you complete in this project would apply equally to more complex sites.

Define a New Artboard

Responsive design is a term used to describe how page layouts change based on the size of display being used to show a specific web page. This technique typically requires different settings for various elements (type size, alignment, etc.), and even different content that will — or will not — appear in different-size displays (for example, removing thumbnail images from extra-small or phone display sizes).

Although this is not a book about web design, you should understand that responsive design technology generally recognizes four different display sizes:

Display size	Designation	Display Width
Extra-small for phones	xs	< 768 pixels
Small for tablets	sm	768–991 pixels
Medium for desktops	md	992–1199 pixels
Large for large desktops	lg	1200+ pixels

Photoshop artboards are a special type of layer group that make it easier to manage content for multiple display sizes within a single Photoshop file.

In this exercise, you are going to define an artboard to contain the existing project layout, which was designed for large display sizes. In a later exercise, you will duplicate and modify the existing layout elements to create the required files for extra-small displays.

1. **With metro-site.psd open, choose the Artboard tool (nested under the Move tool).**

   If you don't see the Artboard tool, call the Essentials workspace in the Workspace switcher. The Artboard tool is not available in the built-in 3D workspace, which you used to create the 3D text in the previous stage of this project.

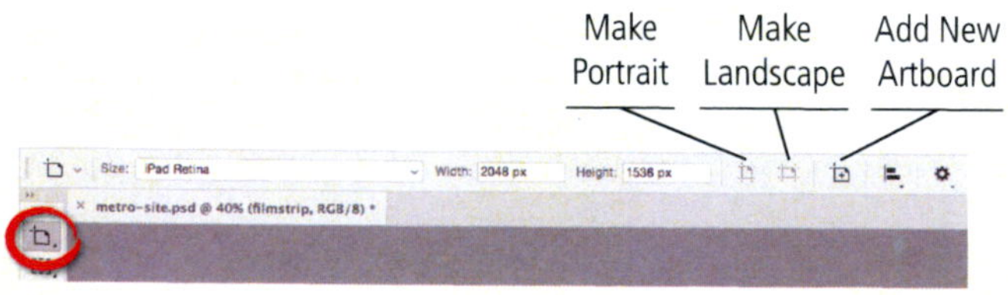

2. **Select the Background layer in the Layers panel. Open the Layers panel Options menu and choose Artboard from Layers.**

   This command creates a new artboard with the boundaries at the outer edges of the selected layer(s). Using the Background layer, your new artboard will be the same size as the canvas for this site layout — which means it will also encompass all the other layers in the file.

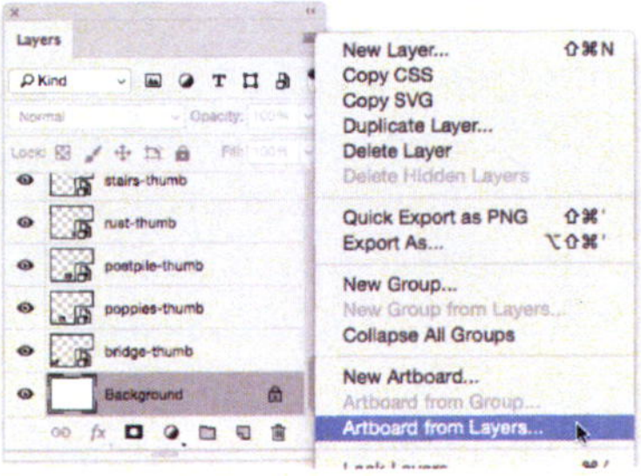

3. **In the resulting dialog box, type LG Display in the Name field and choose iPad Retina in the Set Artboard to Preset menu. Click OK to return to the canvas.**

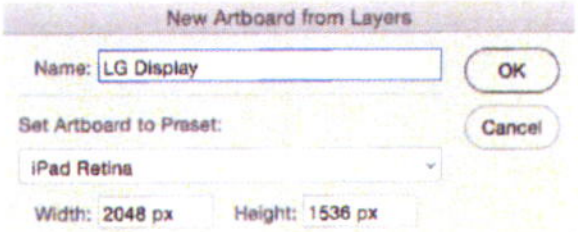

4. **Review the Layers panel.**

   Artboards contain all the layers with content that appears at least partially within the artboard bounds. When you define a new artboard, the locked Background layer is automatically converted to a solid-color fill layer named "Layer 0."

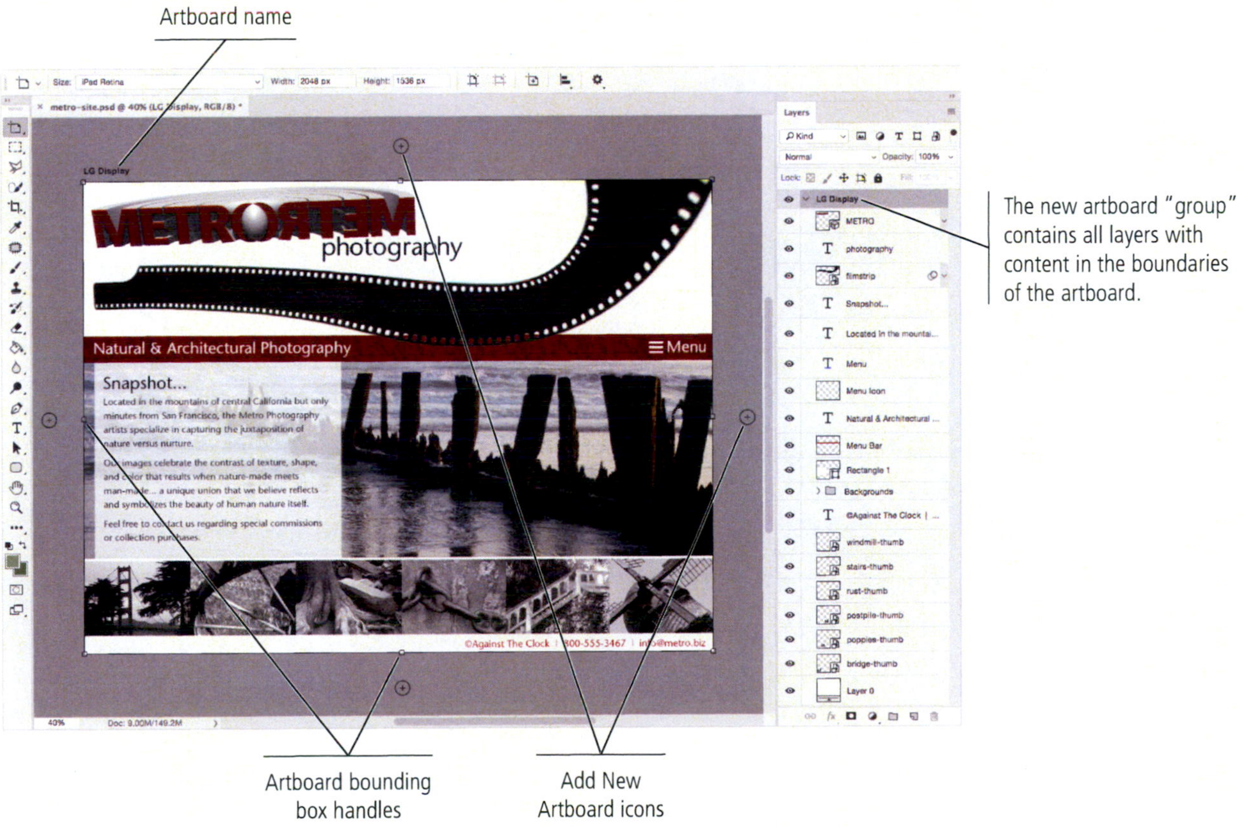

5. **Save the file, then continue to the next exercise.**

Generate Image Assets from Layers

Adobe Generator is a Photoshop plug-in that makes it very easy to create the required web-ready assets from layers in any Photoshop file. Any transformations applied to layer content are processed and become a permanent part of the generated asset.

Three image formats are primarily used for digital delivery:

- **JPEG** (Joint Photographic Experts Group), which supports 24-bit color, is used primarily for continuous-tone images with subtle changes in color, such as photographs or other images that are created in Adobe Photoshop. The JPEG format incorporates **lossy compression**, which means that pixels are thrown away in order to reduce file size; when areas of flat color are highly compressed, speckles of other colors (called artifacts) often appear, which negatively impacts the quality of the design.
- **GIF** (Graphics Interchange Format), which supports only 8-bit color and basic on-or-off transparency, is best used for graphics with areas of solid color, such as logos or other basic illustrations. The GIF format uses **lossless compression** to reduce file size while ensuring that no information is lost during the compression.
- **PNG** (Portable Network Graphics), which supports 8- and 24-bit color, as well as a special 32-bit format allowing support for various degrees of transparency, can be used for both illustrations and continuous-tone images. The PNG format uses lossless compression to create smaller file size without losing image data.

> *Note:*
>
> ***Bit depth** refers to how many bits define the color value of a particular pixel. A **bit** is a unit of information that is either on or off (represented as 1 and 0, respectively). One bit has two states or colors, eight bits have 256 possible colors (2×2×2×2×2×2×2×2=256), and 24 bits have 16,777,216 (2^{24}) possible colors.*
>
> *In an RGB photograph, three color channels define how much of each primary color (red, green, and blue) makes up each pixel. Each channel requires 8 bits, resulting in a total of 24 bits for each pixel ("true color").*

1. **With `metro-site.psd` open, open the Plug-Ins pane of the Preferences dialog box.**
2. **Make sure the Enable Generator option is checked (active), then click OK.**

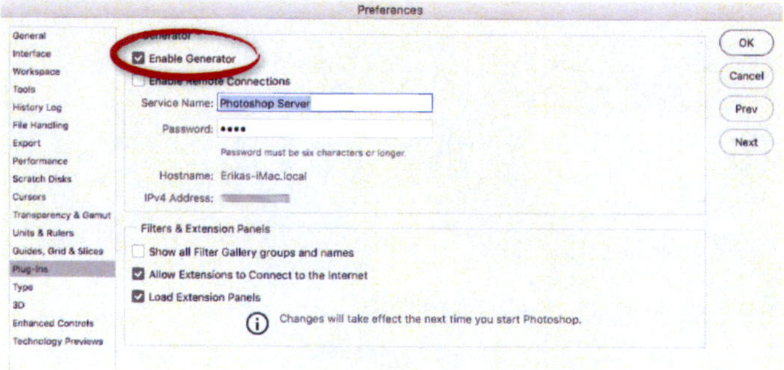

3. **Open the Generate submenu in the File menu and make sure the Image Assets option is checked (active).**

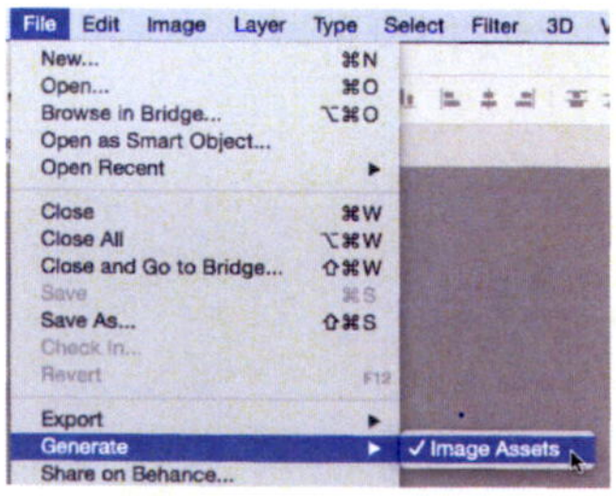

> *Note:*
>
> *To disable image asset generation for the active file, deselect File>Generate>Image Assets.*
>
> *To disable image asset generation for all Photoshop files, uncheck the Enable Generator option in the Plug-Ins pane of the Preferences dialog box.*

4. **In the Layers panel, select both the METRO and photography layers. Click the Create a New Group button at the bottom of the Layers panel.**

   You want the two layers to function together as a single logo in the web page, so you are grouping them together.

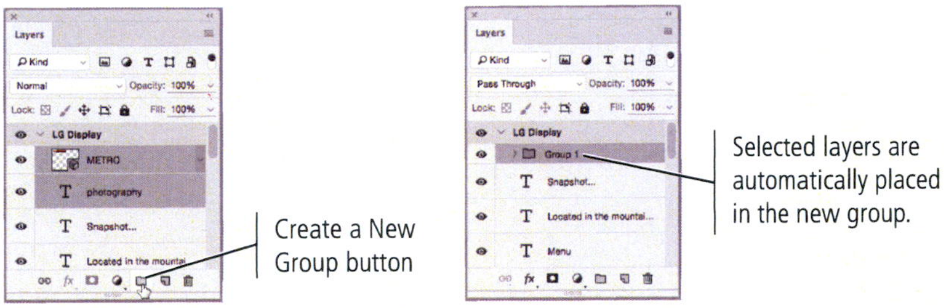

5. **Double-click the new layer group name to select it. Type `logotype-lg.png` as the new name, then press Return/Enter.**

   Renaming a layer group is the same process as renaming a layer.

   You are using the "lg" designation to differentiate this file from the one you will create for extra-small displays in a later exercise.

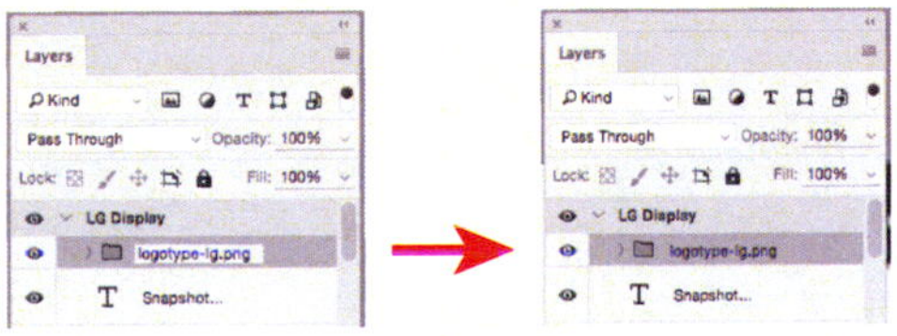

6. **On your desktop, open the WIP>Metro folder.**

   Adobe Generator creates new web assets as soon as you define a layer name that includes an appropriate extension (.jpg, .gif, or .png). A new folder — metro-site-assets — has been added. The logotype-lg.png file, which was generated as soon as you defined the layer group name, exists inside that folder.

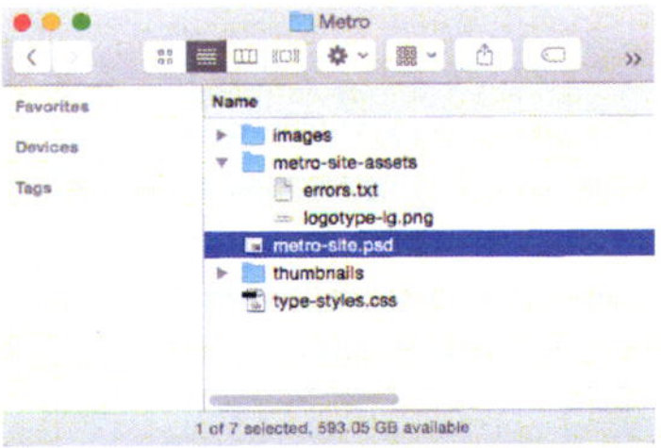

7. **In Photoshop, double-click the filmstrip layer name to highlight it. Type `filmstrip-lg.png` as the new layer name, then press Return/Enter.**

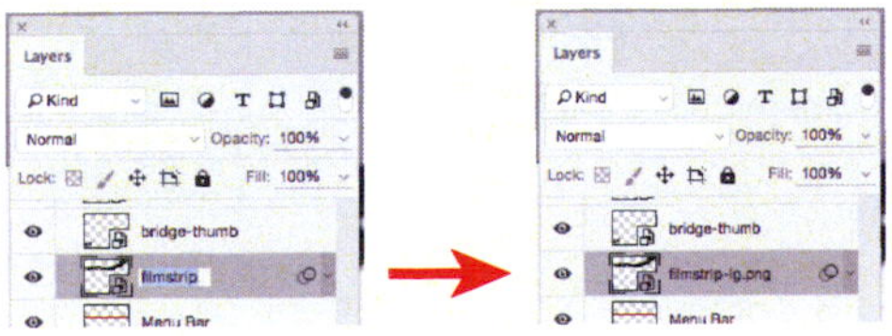

> ***Note:***
>
> *At the time of this writing, original layer order is not maintained when you create a new artboard. Because of this bug in the software, your filmstrip layer might be at a different location in the layer order.*

8. **Repeat Step 7 for the following layers:**

Layer	Rename as:
Menu Icon	menu-icon-lg.gif
Menu Bar	menu-bar-lg.jpg
Backgrounds>pilings	pilings-bkg-lg.jpg
Backgrounds>waves	waves-bkg-lg.jpg
Backgrounds>fountain	fountain-bkg-lg.jpg
Backgrounds>arches	arches-bkg-lg.jpg
windmill-thumb	windmill-thumb.jpg
stairs-thumb	stairs-thumb.jpg
rust-thumb	rust-thumb.jpg
postpile-thumb	postpile-thumb.jpg
poppies-thumb	poppies-thumb.jpg
bridge-thumb	bridge-thumb.jpg

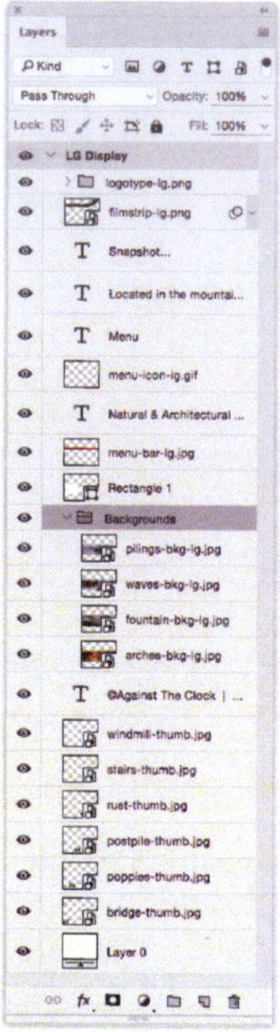

PHOTOSHOP FOUNDATIONS

More about Using Adobe Generator

As you saw in this exercise, **Generator** creates web assets as soon as you define an appropriate file extension for a specific layer (or layer group).

You can also generate multiple files from a single layer by separating asset names with a comma in the Layers panel. For example, the layer name:

menu-bar.jpg, menu-bar.png

creates two separate files in the metro-site-assets folder.

Creating Asset Subfolders

If you want to create subfolders inside the main assets folder, simply include the subfolder name and a forward slash in the modified layer name. For example:

thumbnails/bridge_small.jpg

Changing Asset Quality Settings

You can use complex layer/layer group names to define different compression, quality, and size options in the generated assets. By default:

- JPG assets are generated at 90% quality by default.
- PNG assets are generated as 32-bit images by default.
- GIF assets are generated with basic alpha transparency.

While renaming layers or layer groups in preparation for asset generation, you can customize quality and size.

For JPEG files, you can define a different quality setting by appending a number to the end of the layer name, such as filename.jpg(1-10) or filename.jpg(1-100%). For example:

menu-bar.jpg50%

creates a JPEG file with medium image quality.

For PNG files, you can change the output quality by appending the number 8, 24, or 32 to the layer name. For example:

filmstrip.png24

creates a 24-bit PNG file instead of the default 32-bit file.

Changing Asset Size Settings

You can also use layer names to define a specific size for the generated assets. Simply add the desired output size — relative or specific — as a prefix to the asset name. (Remember to add a space character between the prefix and the asset name.) For example:

200% menu-bar.jpg

10in x 2in logotype.png

50 x 25 menu-icon.gif

If you specify the size in pixels, you can omit the unit; other units must be included in the layer name prefix.

9. **On your desktop, review the contents of the metro-site-assets folder.**

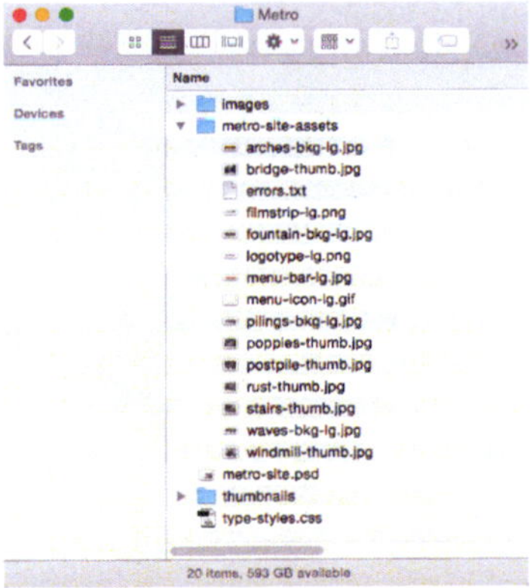

10. **In Photoshop, save metro-site.psd and then continue to the next exercise.**

Copy CSS for Text and Shape Layers

You do not need to be a web programmer to design a site in Photoshop. However, to take best advantage of some of the tools that are available for moving your work into a functional HTML page, you should understand at least the basics of HTML:

- An HTML page contains code that defines the **elements** that make up a page.
- Individual page elements are defined with **tags**. For example, a <div> tag identifies a division or area of the page, and a <p> tag identifies a paragraph of text. Available tags are defined by the version of HTML being used; you can't simply make up tags.
- Specific elements can be identified with user-defined classes, which helps to differentiate them from other same-type elements. For example:

```
<div class="feature-image">
<div class="text-area">
```

- Cascading Style Sheets (CSS) are used to define the properties of HTML elements. CSS files define **selectors**, which contain **property:value pairs** to control the appearance of specific elements in an HTML page. For example:

```
header {
    width: 780px;
    height: 75px;
}
```

- Two types of CSS selectors are relevant to site design in Photoshop:
  - **Tag selectors** define the appearance of HTML tags. These selectors simply use the tag name as the selector name; for example, the **div** selector defines the appearance of all **<div>** tags.
  - **Class selectors** define the appearance of any tag that is identified with the defined class. These selector names always begin with a period; for example, the **.text-area** selector would apply to any element that has the **class="text-area"** attribute.

In this exercise, you will use Photoshop to create CSS classes, which the web designer can apply to various page elements so that your design choices are maintained in the final HTML page.

1. **With metro-site.psd open in Photoshop, change the Snapshot type layer name to h1-lg.**

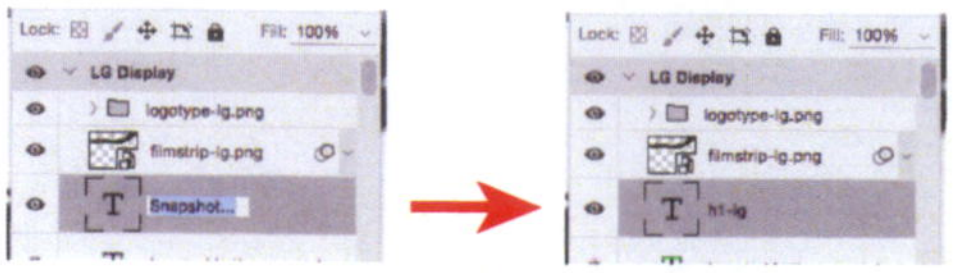

2. **Control/right-click the h1-lg type layer and choose Copy CSS from the contextual menu.**

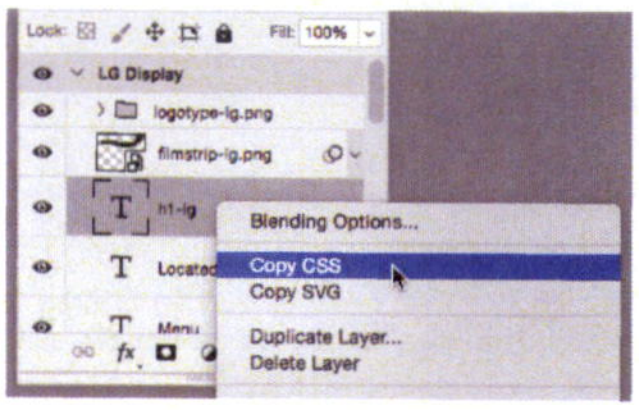

3. **Using any text-editing application, open the file type-styles.css from the WIP>Metro folder.**

We use TextEdit on a Macintosh in our screen shots, but you can use any text editor to complete the following steps.

4. **Place the insertion point on the first empty line at the end of the file, then press Command/Control-V to paste the CSS that was copied in Step 2.**

All CSS copied from Photoshop is created as a class. The selector name, beginning with a period, is taken from the relevant Photoshop layer.

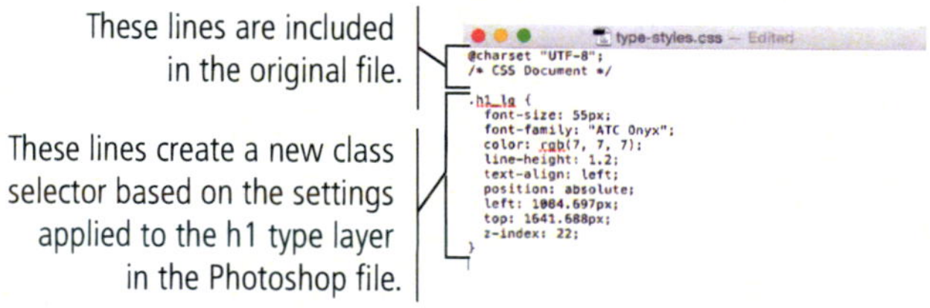
These lines are included in the original file.
These lines create a new class selector based on the settings applied to the h1 type layer in the Photoshop file.

5. **Repeat Steps 1–4 to rename the remaining type layers in the Photoshop file and create the required CSS for each.**

Layer	Rename as:
Located in ...	body-copy-lg
Menu	menu-lg
Natural & ...	subhead-lg
©Against the ...	footer-lg

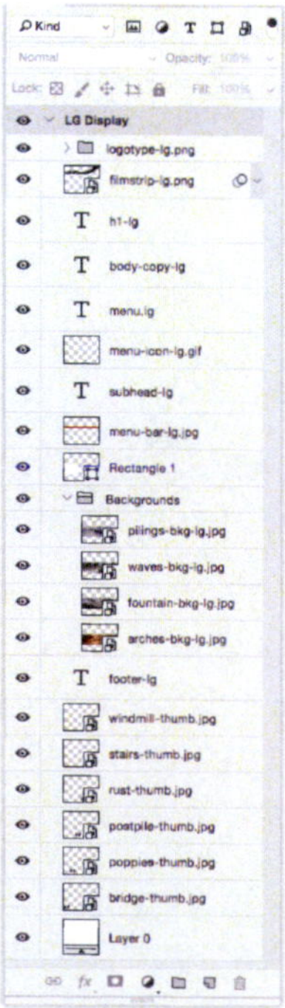

6. **In the Layers panel, rename the Rectangle 1 shape layer as main-content-lg.**

   Although this is not a type layer, you want to communicate the area's transparency to the web designer. Photoshop can generate CSS for any layer that is not a smart object.

7. **Control/right-click the main-content-lg shape layer and choose Copy CSS from the contextual menu.**

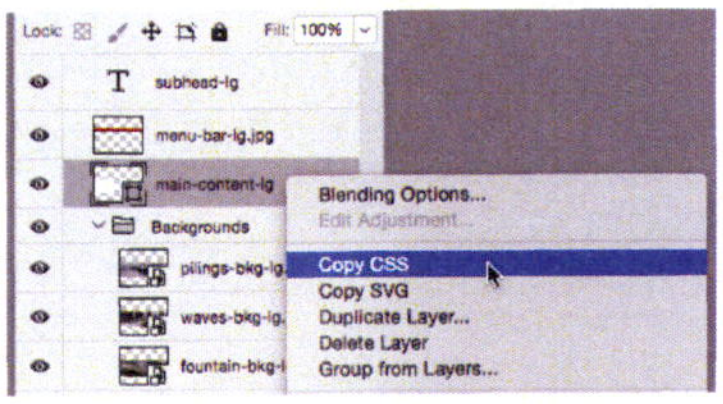

8. **Paste the copied CSS into the type-styles.css file.**

9. **In the .main-content-lg selector, select and delete all but the background-color and opacity lines.**

Select and delete all but the background-color and opacity properties.

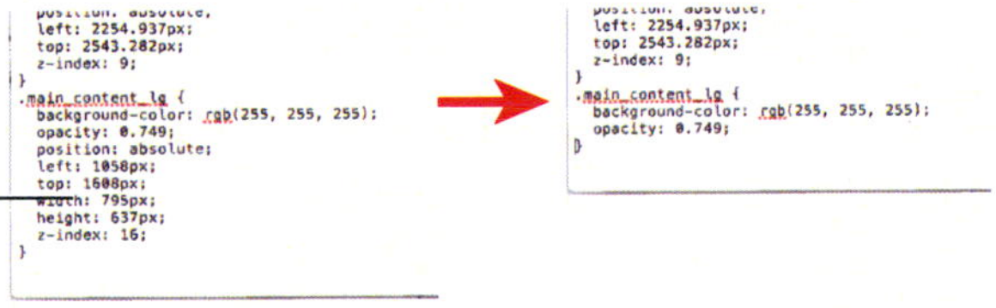

10. **Save type-styles.css, then close it.**

11. **In Photoshop, collapse the LG Display artboard.**

12. **Save the file, then continue to the next exercise.**

Creating Image Slices

PHOTOSHOP FOUNDATIONS

Although the **Slice tool** was intended to cut apart pieces of a web page comp for reassembly in a web design application, it can be used for any situation in which you need to cut up a single image into multiple bits.

In addition to creating image assets from layers and layer groups, you can also create image slices; all visible layers in the slice area are included in the resulting images.

Photoshop offers a number of options for creating slices in your artwork:

- Manually draw a slice area with the Slice tool.
- When the Slice tool is active, click Slices from Guides in the Options bar to automatically slice the file based on existing ruler guides.
- When the Slice Select tool is active and a specific slice is selected in the file, click Divide in the Options bar to divide the slice horizontally or vertically into a specific number of equal-size slices.
- Create a new slice based on specific layer content by selecting one or more layers in the Layers panel, then choosing Layer>New Layer Based Slice

Once slices are created, you can double-click select a specific slice with the Slice Selection tool to edit its settings. In the resulting dialog box:

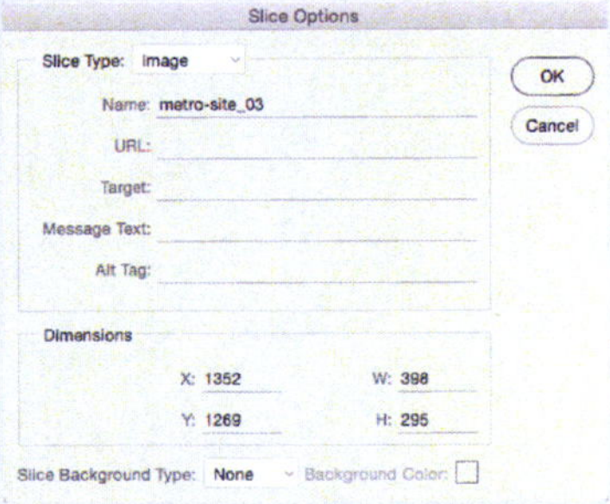

- Name is the file name of the image that is created from the slice.
- URL is the file that opens if a user clicks the slice.
- Target is the location where the URL opens when a user clicks the slice.
- Message Text appears in the browser's status bar.
- Alt Tag appears if image display is disabled.

(URL, Target, and Message are better handled in a web design application such as Adobe Dreamweaver.)

Dimensions fields are automatically filled with the size of the selected slice. You can also change the slice background type and color if the slice contains areas of transparency.

Copy and Edit Artboard Sizes

As we explained earlier, a Photoshop artboard is basically a way of organizing and managing layers so you can create more than one layout in the same Photoshop file. In this exercise, you are going to create a second artboard to create the files you need for extra-small (<768 pixels wide) displays such as smart phones.

1. **With metro-site.psd open, make sure the LG Display artboard is selected in the Layers panel and then activate the Artboard tool in the Tools panel.**

2. **Option/Alt-click the Add New Artboard icon to the right of the existing artboard.**

   When the Artboard tool is active, the Add New Artboard icons appear on all four sides of the active artboard. Clicking one of these icons adds a new blank artboard adjacent to the existing one (the new artboard appears on the same side as the icon you click).

   If you Option/Alt-click one of the icons, the new artboard is a duplicate of the existing one, including all the layers that existed on the previous artboard.

3. **In the Layers panel, expand the LG Display copy artboard.**

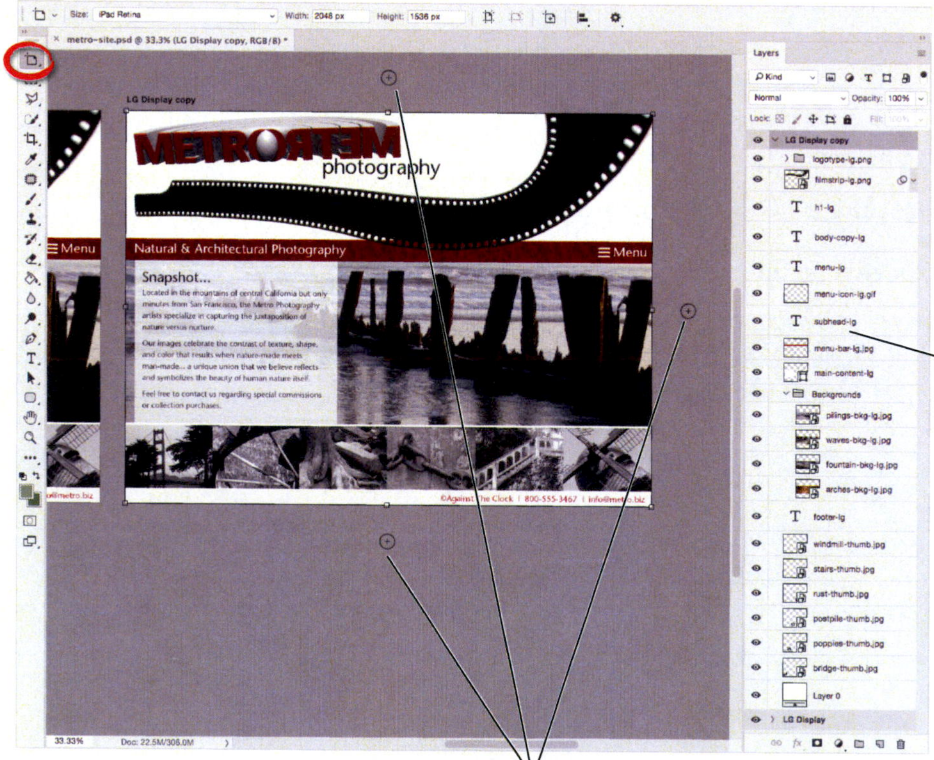

Layers on the original artboard are duplicated in the new artboard.
The new artboard has Add New Artboard icons on the three remaining available sides.

4. **In the Layers panel, change the name of the LG Display copy artboard to XS Display.**

   Renaming artboards uses the same process as renaming layers and layer groups — double-click the existing name in the Layers panel, then type the new name.

5. **With the XS Display artboard active, choose iPhone 6 in the Options bar Size menu. Click the Make Portrait button if necessary.**

When you change the size of an artboard, any layers that no longer have content within the bounds of the artboard are automatically moved outside the artboard group in the Layers panel.

Make Portrait

Make Landscape

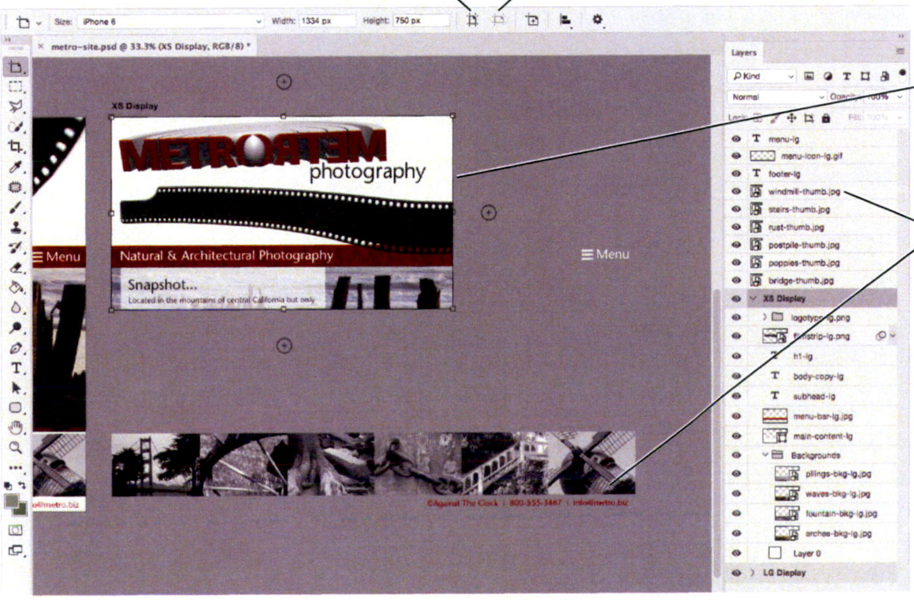

The new artboard size is reflected in the document window.

Layers that don't touch the artboard are moved out of the group in the Layers panel.

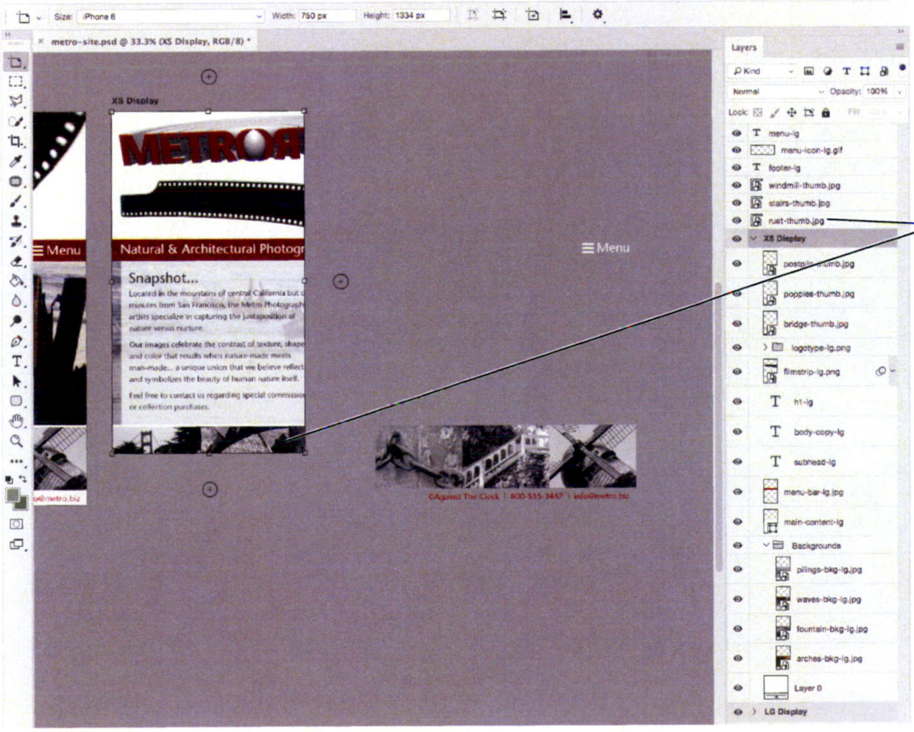

Changes to the artboard size can affect which layers are part of the artboard group.

6. **In the Layers panel, click the menu-lg layer to select it. Press Command/Control, then click the following layer names to add them to the active selection:**

windmill-thumb.jpg	**poppies-thumb.jpg**
stairs-thumb.jpg	**bridge-thumb.jpg**
rust-thumb.jpg	**filmstrip-lg.png**
postpile-thumb.jpg	

7. **With all eight layers selected, click the panel's Delete button; click Yes to confirm the deletion.**

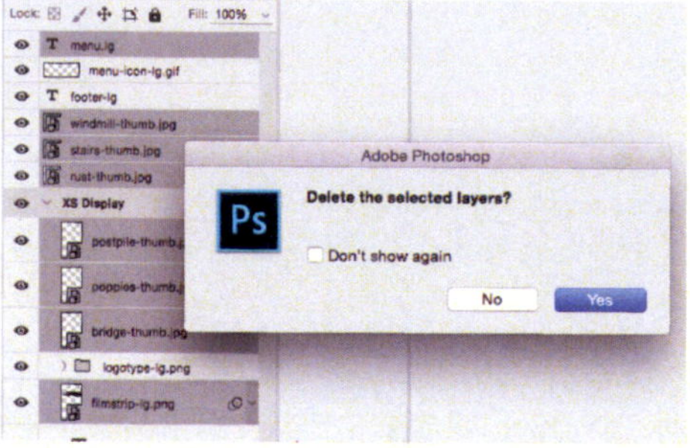

On an extra-small display size, most sites would not include the type of thumbnail images that you see in the large display layout. Because space is at a premium on extra-small displays, you are also deleting the purely decorative filmstrip and the identifier word "Menu."

8. **Save the file and continue to the next exercise.**

Adjust Image Content for Alternate Display Sizes

1. **With `metro-site.psd` open, activate the Move tool in the Tools panel. Turn off the Auto Select option in the Options bar.**

2. **In the Layers panel, change the name of the logotype-lg.png layer group to `logotype-xs.png`.**

   You are going to resize this layer group to fit the smaller display size. If you don't define a separate name for the resized group, Photoshop will not generate a new version of the logotype image. The original logotype-lg.png file is maintained, and it is not overwritten with the resized version.

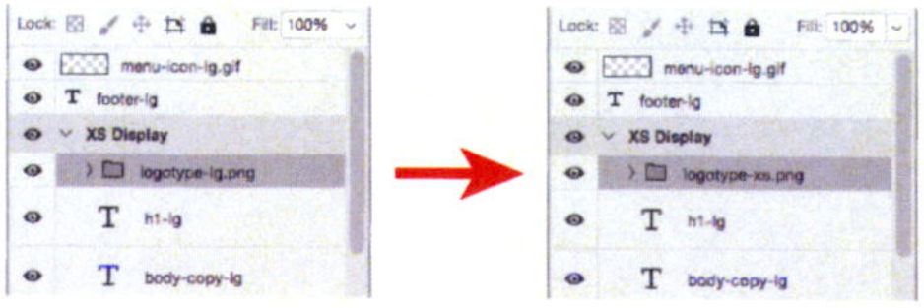

3. **In the Layers panel, expand the logotype-xs.png layer group.**

4. **Control/right-click the Metro 3D layer and choose Convert to Smart Object in the contextual menu.**

   You need to transform the entire layer group. Transforming a 3D layer as you would a regular layer, however, requires the 3D layer to first be converted to a Smart Object.

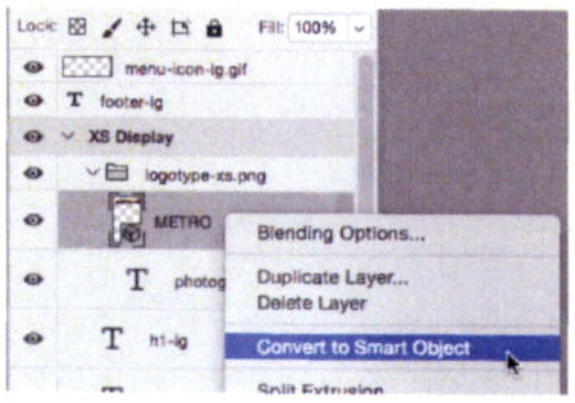

5. **Collapse the logotype-xs.png layer group in the Layers panel.**

6. **Select the logotype-xs.png layer group in the Layers panel, then press Command/Control-T to enter Free Transform mode for the layer group.**

7. **Shift-click and drag the bottom-right bounding box handle until the entire logotype fits in the artboard bounds.**

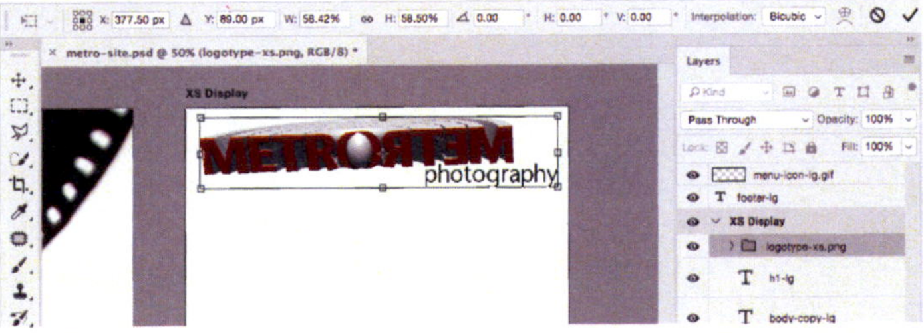

8. **Press Return/Enter to finalize the transformation.**

9. **Choose the menu-bar-lg.jpg layer, then move it up until only a small amount of white space appears below the logotype.**

   Because you did not transform this layer, you do not need to generate a separate file for this image in an extra-small display.

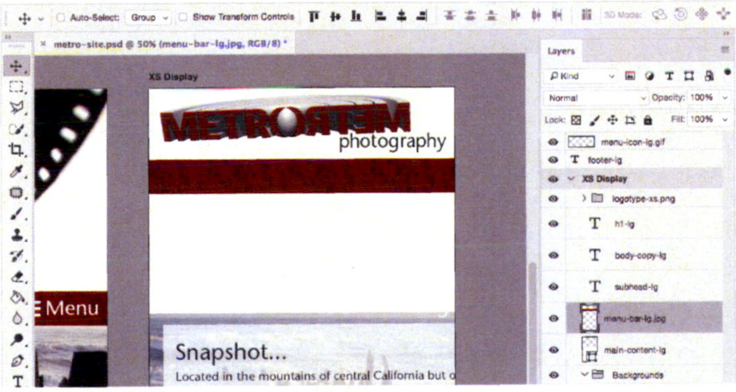

10. **Select the menu-icon-lg.gif layer, then click and drag until the icon artwork appears in the right side of the menu bar area.**

    Because the Auto Select option is not active, you do not have to carefully click the narrow bars of the icon to move this layer's content.

    As soon as you move the layer content within the artboard bounds, the menu-icon-lg.gif layer is moved into the XS Display artboard in the Layers panel.

    Again, you do not need a separate file for this icon so you do not need to change the layer name.

Note:

After moving the layer, you might need to toggle the moved layer's visibility off and back on for it to be visible on the artboard.

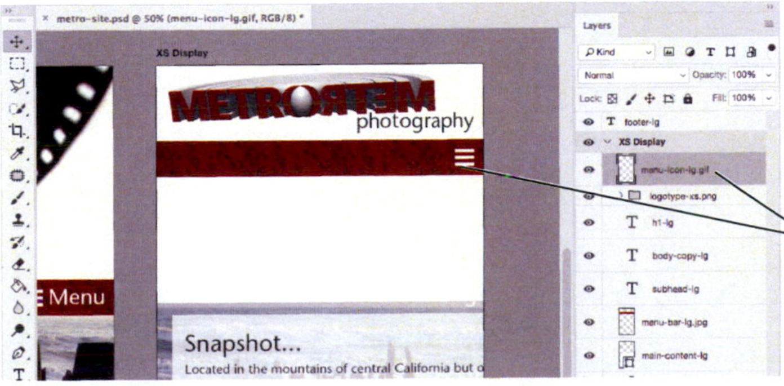

When the layer content is moved into the artboard boundaries, the layer is moved into the artboard group.

11. **In the Layers panel, select the Backgrounds layer group. Press Command/Control-T to enter Free Transform mode for the entire group.**

    By transforming the entire group, you transform all layers in the group at one time.

12. **Enlarge the group, anchoring the bottom-left corner, until the images fill the white space below the menu bar.**

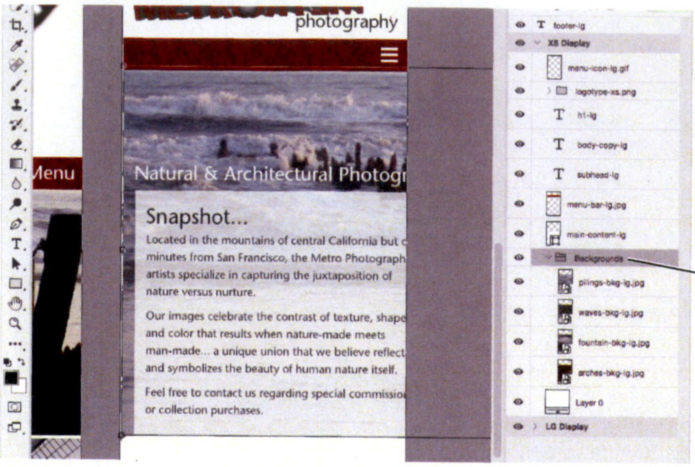

By selecting the group, you can transform all layers in the group at one time.

13. **Press Return/Enter to finalize the transformation.**

14. **In the Layers panel, change the "lg" in each background layer name to `xs`.**

    When Photoshop generates an image based on layer content, the resulting image is cropped at the artboard edges. The background images generated in this step will have significantly different dimensions than the large-size background images generated earlier.

15. **Save the file and continue to the next exercise.**

Generate Type CSS for Alternate Display Sizes

1. **With `metro-site.psd` open, select the subhead-lg layer in the XS Display artboard group.**

2. **Using the Move tool, click and drag until the layer text appears in the menu bar area (as shown after Step 3).**

   As you can see, the type size for the large display does not fit within the available space in the extra-small display. You need to change the type size, then generate additional CSS for the smaller display size.

3. **Activate the Horizontal Type tool, then click to place the insertion point in the layer.**

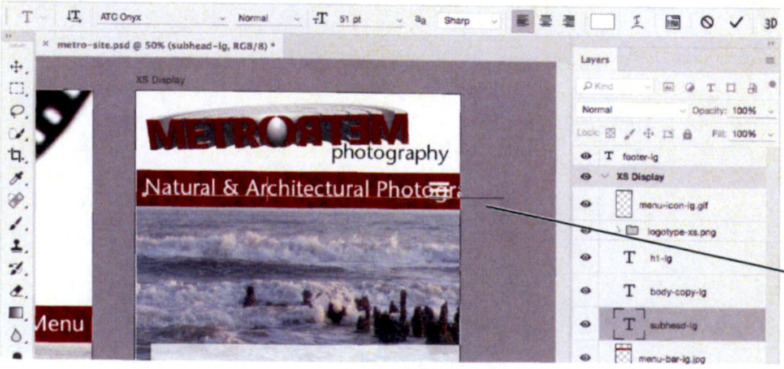

When the insertion point is placed, you can see the entire type path.

4. **Triple-click the active type layer to select all text on that line.**

   When the insertion point is placed in a type layer, you can also press Command/Control-A to select all type on that layer.

5. **Press Command/Control-Shift-< repeatedly to reduce the type size, until the entire heading fits inside the artboard boundaries.**

   This keyboard shortcut reduces the type size by one point. You can press Command/Control-Shift-> to increase the type size by one point.

   If you use the Transform controls to reduce type size on a type layer, the CSS generated by Photoshop does not recognize the transformed type size. For the type size to change in the CSS, you have to manually reduce the type size when the actual type is highlighted.

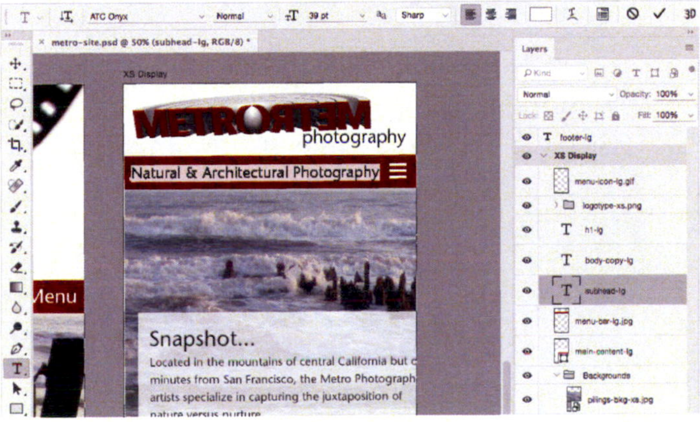

metro-site.psd @ 50% (subhead-lg, RGB/8) *
XS Display
photography
Natural & Architectural Photography
Snapshot...
Layers
footer-lg
XS Display
menu-icon-lg.gif
logotype-xs.png
h1-lg
body-copy-lg
subhead-lg
menu-bar-lg.jpg
main-content-lg
Backgrounds
pilings-bkg-xs.jpg

6. **In the Layers panel, change the subhead-lg layer name to subhead-xs.**

7. **Control/right-click the subhead-xs layer and choose Copy CSS in the contextual menu.**

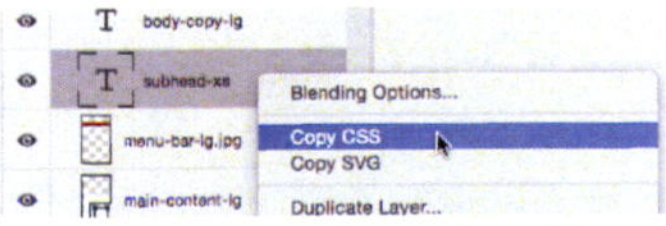

body-copy-lg
subhead-xs
menu-bar-lg.jpg
main-content-lg
Blending Options...
Copy CSS
Copy SVG
Duplicate Layer...

8. **Open type-styles.css (from your WIP>Metro folder) in a text-editing application.**

9. **Place the insertion point at the end of the existing copy and press Command/Control-V to paste the CSS from Step 7.**

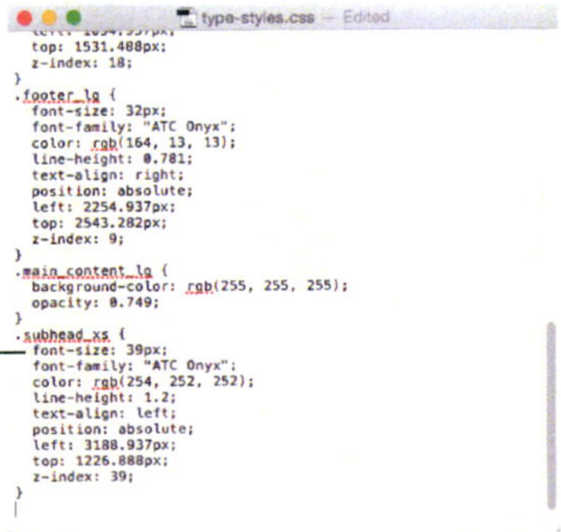

type-styles.css — Edited
top: 1531.488px;
z-index: 18;
}
.footer_lg {
font-size: 32px;
font-family: "ATC Onyx";
color: rgb(164, 13, 13);
line-height: 0.781;
text-align: right;
position: absolute;
left: 2254.937px;
top: 2543.282px;
z-index: 9;
}
.main_content_lg {
background-color: rgb(255, 255, 255);
opacity: 0.749;
}
.subhead_xs {
font-size: 39px;
font-family: "ATC Onyx";
color: rgb(254, 252, 252);
line-height: 1.2;
text-align: left;
position: absolute;
left: 3188.937px;
top: 1226.888px;
z-index: 39;
}

The CSS for the extra-small display size includes the smaller type size.

10. **Return to Photoshop. In the Layers panel, select the h1-lg, body-copy-lg, and main-content-lg layers.**

11. **Using the Move tool, drag the selected layer content left until it snaps to the artboard edge.**

    Because you selected all three layers, their positions relative to one another remains the same when you move the three layers at one time.

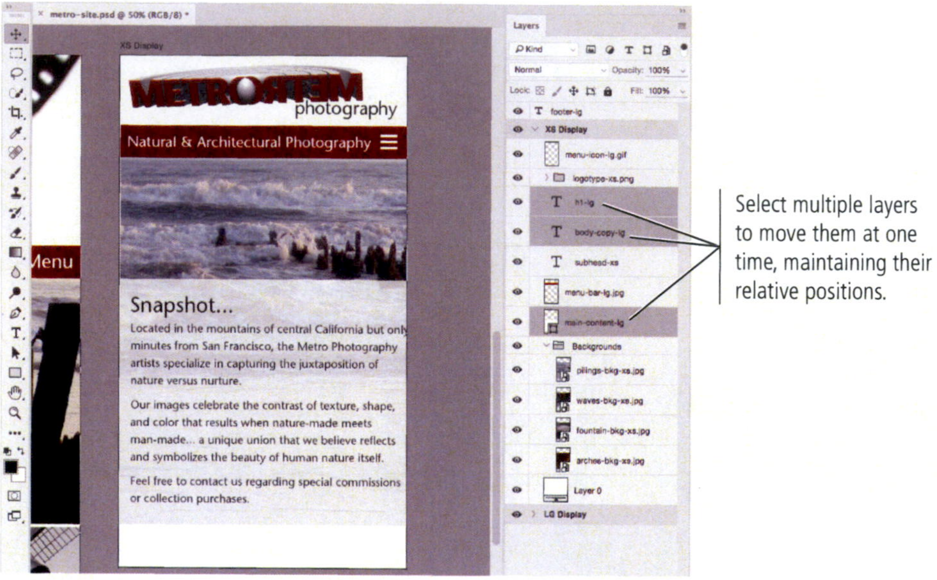

12. **Using the Horizontal Type tool, click to place the insertion point in the body copy text ("Located in the...").**

    Because this is an area-type object, you have to place the insertion point to access the area handles.

13. **Drag the right-center handle until the right edge of the area is approximately 1/8″ inside the artboard edge.**

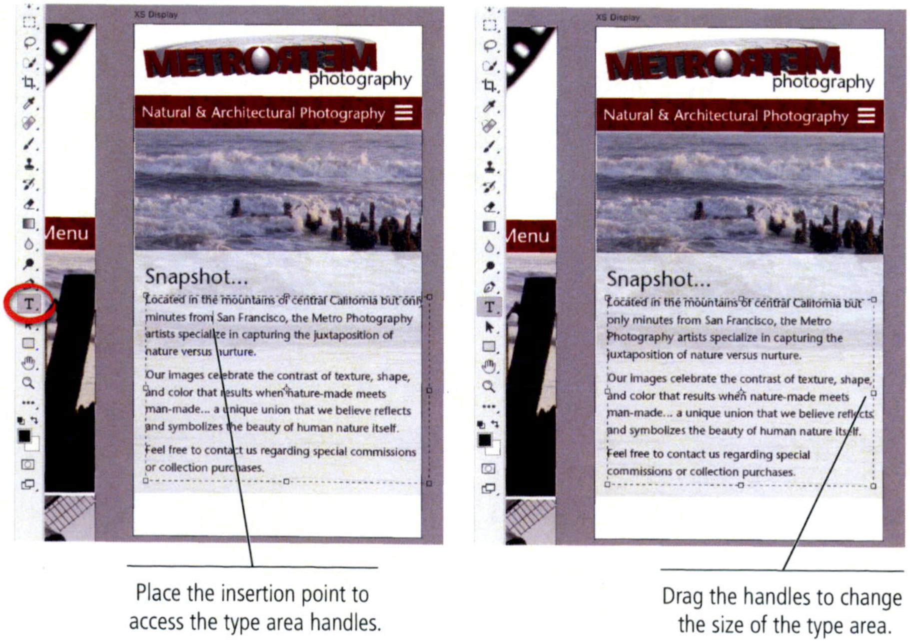

14. **Click the body-copy-lg layer name to select the layer.**

This step also deactivates the type area handles.

15. **Using the Character panel, define a 24 pt font size with 36 pt leading.**

When the layer is selected and the insertion point is not placed, changing type settings affects all text on the selected layer.

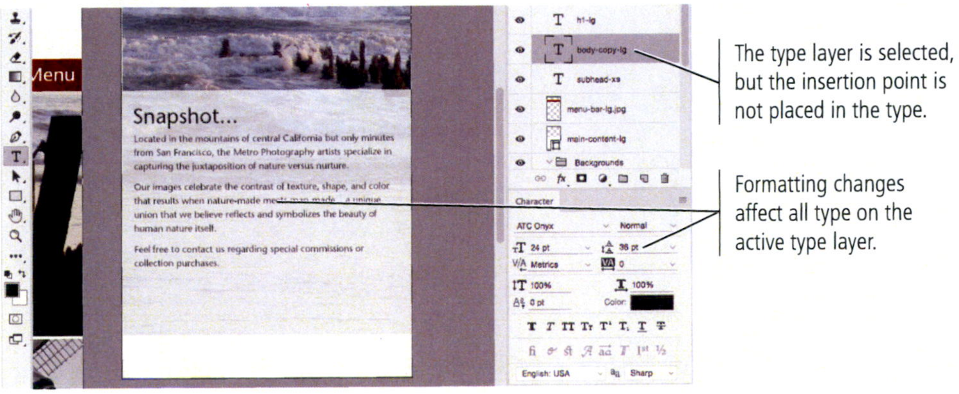

Snapshot...
The type layer is selected, but the insertion point is not placed in the type.
Formatting changes affect all type on the active type layer.

16. **In the Layers panel, change the body-copy-lg layer name to body-copy-xs.**

17. **Control/right-click the body-copy-xs layer and choose Copy CSS in the contextual menu.**

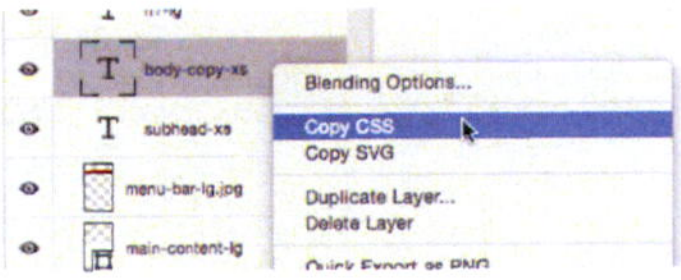

18. **If necessary, open type-styles.css (from your WIP>Metro folder) in a text-editing application.**

19. **Place the insertion point at the end of the existing copy and press Command/Control-V to paste the CSS from Step 12.**

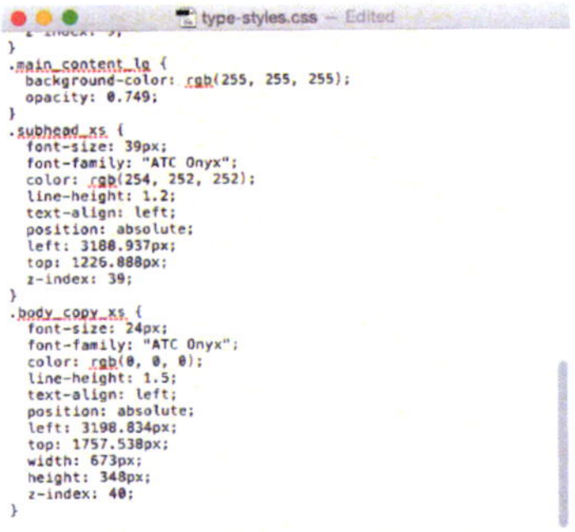

20. Repeat Steps 14–19 to change the type on the h1-lg layer to **44 pt** with **Auto** leading. Change the layer name to **h1-xs**, then copy and paste the layer's CSS into the `type-styles.css` file.

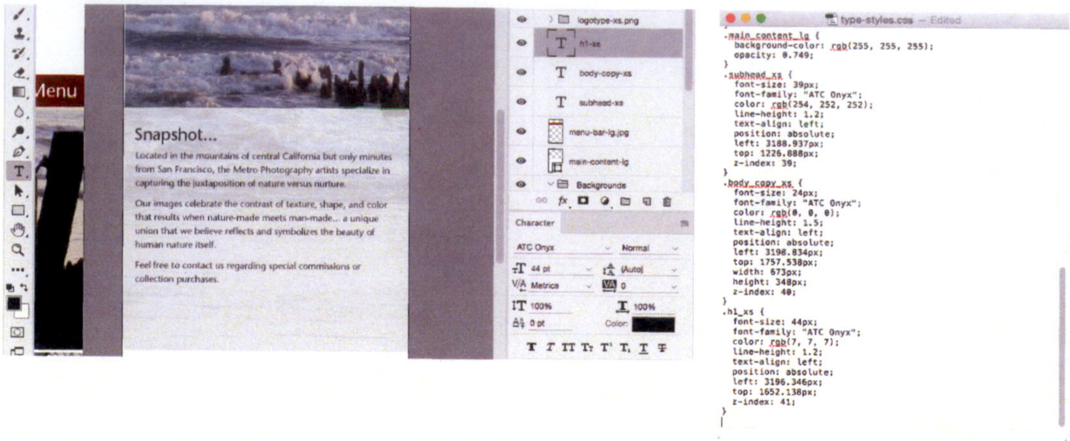
type-styles.css — Edited
.main_content_lg {
background-color: rgb(255, 255, 255);
opacity: 0.749;
}
.subhead_xs {
font-size: 39px;
font-family: "ATC Onyx";
color: rgb(254, 252, 252);
line-height: 1.2;
text-align: left;
position: absolute;
left: 3188.937px;
top: 1226.888px;
z-index: 39;
}
.body_copy_xs {
font-size: 24px;
font-family: "ATC Onyx";
color: rgb(0, 0, 0);
line-height: 1.5;
text-align: left;
position: absolute;
left: 3198.834px;
top: 1757.538px;
width: 673px;
height: 348px;
z-index: 40;
}
.h1_xs {
font-size: 44px;
font-family: "ATC Onyx";
color: rgb(7, 7, 7);
line-height: 1.2;
text-align: left;
position: absolute;
left: 3196.346px;
top: 1652.138px;
z-index: 41;
}

21. Using the basic process you learned in this exercise, make the following changes for the footer text:

- Change the text on the footer-lg type layer to 22 pt with centered paragraph alignment.
- Position the layer so the text is centered in the white space at the bottom of the artboard.
- Change the layer name to **footer-xs**, copy the CSS for that layer, and paste it into the `text-styles.css` file.

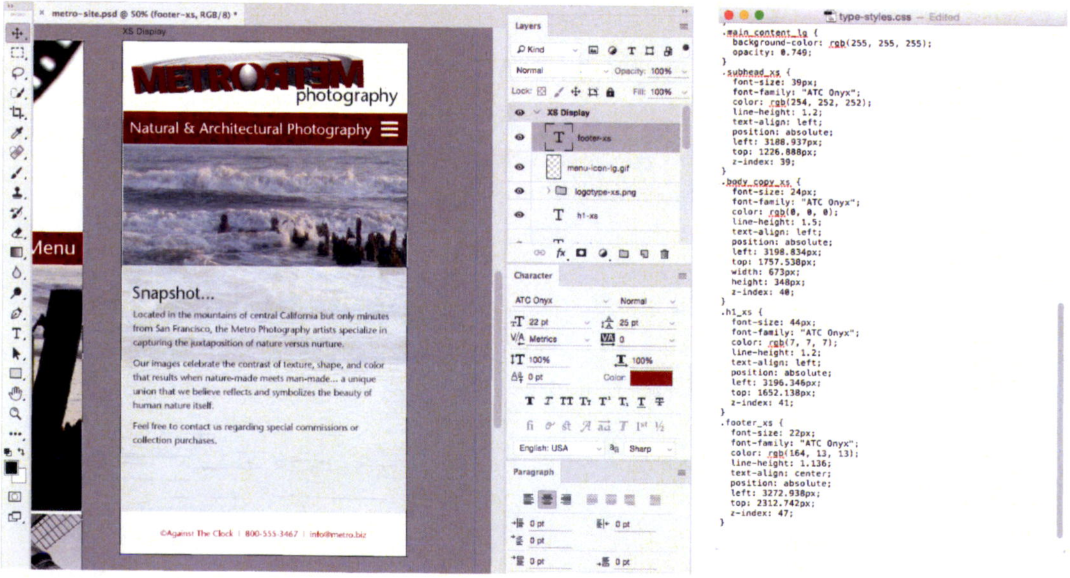
type-styles.css — Edited
.main_content_lg {
background-color: rgb(255, 255, 255);
opacity: 0.749;
}
.subhead_xs {
font-size: 39px;
font-family: "ATC Onyx";
color: rgb(254, 252, 252);
line-height: 1.2;
text-align: left;
position: absolute;
left: 3188.937px;
top: 1226.888px;
z-index: 39;
}
.body_copy_xs {
font-size: 24px;
font-family: "ATC Onyx";
color: rgb(0, 0, 0);
line-height: 1.5;
text-align: left;
position: absolute;
left: 3198.834px;
top: 1757.538px;
width: 673px;
height: 348px;
z-index: 40;
}
.h1_xs {
font-size: 44px;
font-family: "ATC Onyx";
color: rgb(7, 7, 7);
line-height: 1.2;
text-align: left;
position: absolute;
left: 3196.346px;
top: 1652.138px;
z-index: 41;
}
.footer_xs {
font-size: 22px;
font-family: "ATC Onyx";
color: rgb(164, 13, 13);
line-height: 1.136;
text-align: center;
position: absolute;
left: 3272.938px;
top: 2312.742px;
z-index: 47;
}

22. Save and close `text-styles.css`.

23. Save and close `metro-site.psd`.

Project Review

fill in the blank

1. The _______________ command can be used to run an action on all files in a specific folder without user intervention.

2. Align options are available in the _______________ when multiple layers are selected in the Layers panel.

3. True or False: You can edit the text in a type layer that has been converted to 3D. _______________

4. The _______________ tool can be used to create more than one canvas in a single Photoshop file.

5. The _______________ image format allows lossy compression and does not support transparency; it is best used for photos.

6. The _______________ format supports only 8-bit color; it is best used for artwork or graphics with large areas of solid color.

7. The _______________ format supports both continuous-tone color and degrees of transparency.

8. _______________ are used to define the properties of HTML elements.

9. CSS files define _______________, which contain property:value pairs to control the appearance of specific elements in an HTML page.

10. All CSS copied from Photoshop is created as a _______________. The selector name, beginning with a period, is taken from the relevant Photoshop layer.

short answer

1. Briefly explain how actions can be used to improve workflow.

2. Briefly explain three file formats that are used for images on the web.

3. Briefly explain the concept of CSS in relation to web design.

Portfolio Builder Project

Use what you learned in this project to complete the following freeform exercise.
Carefully read the art director and client comments, then create your own design to meet the needs of the project.
Use the space below to sketch ideas; when finished, write a brief explanation of your reasoning behind your final design.

art director comments

Every professional designer needs a portfolio of their work. If you have completed the projects in this book, you should now have a number of different examples to show off your skills using Photoshop.

The projects in this book were specifically designed to include a broad range of *types* of projects; your portfolio should use the same principle.

Using the following suggestions, gather your best work and create printed and digital versions of your portfolio.

client comments

- ❑ Include as many different types of work as possible — book covers, image retouching, art projects, etc.
- ❑ Print clean copies of each finished piece that you want to include.
- ❑ For correction or compositing jobs, include the "before" image as part of the sample.
- ❑ For each example in your portfolio, write a brief (one or two paragraphs) synopsis of the project. Explain the purpose of the piece, as well as your role in the creative and production process.
- ❑ Design an web page interface with thumbnails of your work.
- ❑ Create a portable version of your digital portfolio so you can present your work even when an Internet connection is not available — you never know when you might meet a potential employer.

project justification

Project Summary

The graphic design workflow typically revolves around extremely short turnaround times, which means that any possible automation will only be a benefit. Photoshop actions can be useful whenever you need to apply the same sets of options to more than one or two images. Every click you save will allow you to do other work, meet tight deadlines, and satisfy your clients. In the case of running a batch on multiple images, you are completely freed to work on other projects, be in other places, or even (technically) "work" while you're gone for the evening.

Although many developers use dedicated web design software like Adobe Dreamweaver to build sophisticated websites, the images for those sites have to come from somewhere. It is very common for a designer to build the "look and feel" of a site in Photoshop, then generate the pieces so the developer can more easily reassemble them in the web design application. As you saw by completing this project, Photoshop can even be used to create cascading style sheets (CSS) to communicate the type and object formatting that you define in Photoshop.

Create a 3D extrusion from a type layer
Use puppet warping to distort a layer
Use artboards to create multiple versions in one file
Define an action to resize images
Run a batch to resize and rename multiple images
Generate web assets based on layers and layer groups
Create CSS from type and shape layers
photography
Natural & Architectural Photography
Menu
Snapshot...

Index

Symbols

A

B

C

Index

G

H

I

J

K

L

M

N

O

P

Index

Q

R

S

Index

T

Index

U

V

W

X

Y

Z